Andreas Bübl

STUDIO

Lighting Setups for Portrait Photography

Studio: Lighting Setups for Portrait Photography

Andreas Bübl

ISBN: 978-1-68198-961-7
1st Edition (1st printing, August 2023)
© 2023 Andreas Bübl
All images © Andres Bübl

Rocky Nook Inc.
1010 B Street, Suite 350
San Rafael, CA 94901
USA

www.rockynook.com
Distributed in the UK and Europe by Publishers Group UK
Distributed in the U.S. and all other territories by Publishers Group West

Library of Congress Control Number: 2022945150

Project editor: Maggie Yates
Project manager: Lisa Brazieal
Marketing coordinator: Katie Walker
Copyeditor: Maggie Yates
Layout: Danielle Foster
Cover design: Aren Straiger

Dear Reader,

Has a friend ever asked you to take their picture for a job application? Or to photograph their kids for the grandparents' refridgerator? You're keen to get started at home or in a rented studio, but your last shoot was a while ago. How did all that stuff work with light metering, using light shapers, and setting the flash output? And what's the best way to set up your lights anyway? If your models are getting a little restless while you think about it all, wouldn't it be great if you could just look up the ideal lighting setup in a book?

Well, now you can! In this book, Andreas Bübl uses words and pictures to demonstrate lighting setups for a huge range of portrait situations. He uses in-studio "making of" photos and comprehensive lighting diagrams to show you how to set up your lights and the effects they produce. He also includes sample studio shots that are sure to inspire you on your next shoot, and you can even pick your favorite setup with your model right there while you work. It doesn't matter whether you are shooting a job application photo, a traditional portrait, a beauty shot, or a family photo—you are sure to find a setup that works for every situation. If you are looking to brush up your basic knowledge of studio photography, this book will help you, too. The *Studio Photography Basics* chapter starting on page 2 provides a great summary of everything you need to know.

We are sure that this book will become your trusted companion in the studio. For this second edition, Andreas Bübl has added new ideas in nearly all the chapters, and introduces lots of great ideas for using accessories, backgrounds, and lighting effects creatively. With a total of 116 setups, you are sure to find one that works for you.

I'd love to hear from you if you want to get in touch but for now, have fun using this book, setting up your lights, and clicking away!

Juliane Neumann
Editor, Rheinwerk Fotografie

juliane.neumann@rheinwerk-verlag.de
www.rheinwerk-verlag.de

Rheinwerk Verlag • Rheinwerkallee 4 • 53227 Bonn

Contents

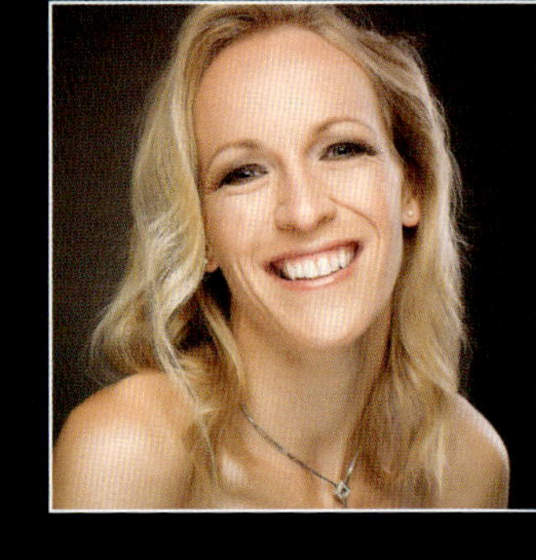

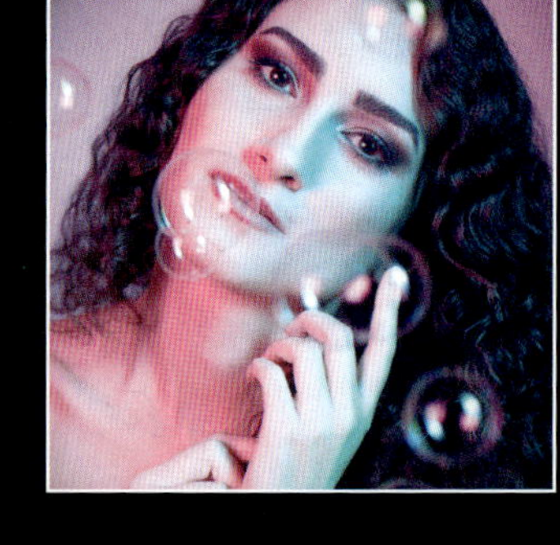

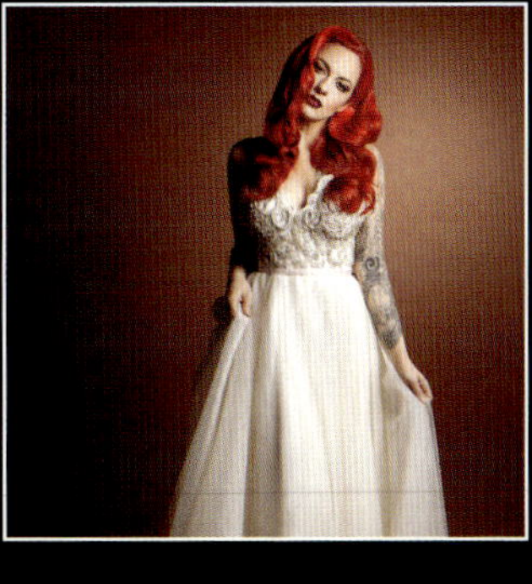

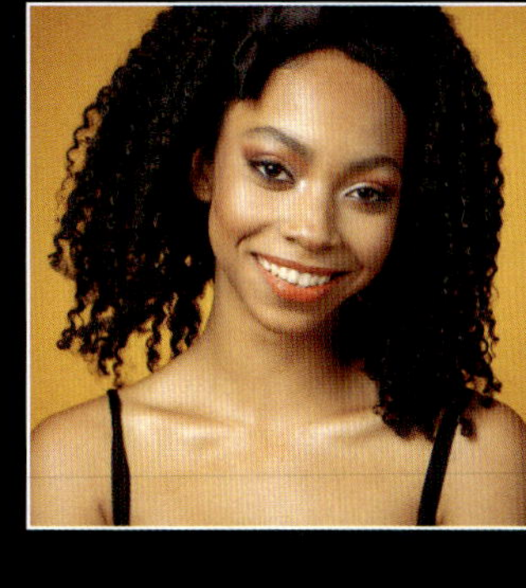

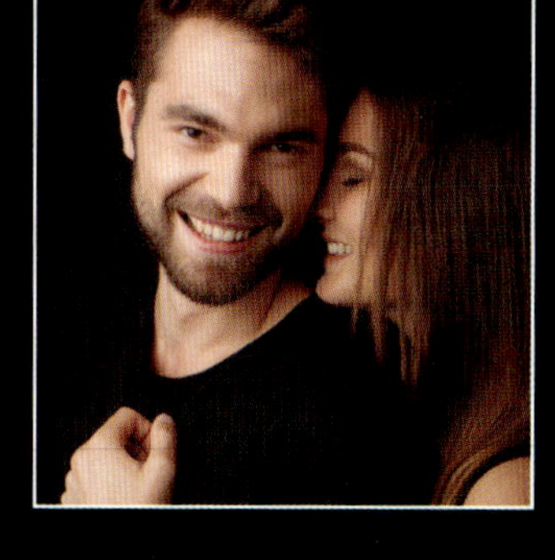

Glamour, Fashion, and Lifestyle 123

Character Portraits 175

Couples and Groups 217

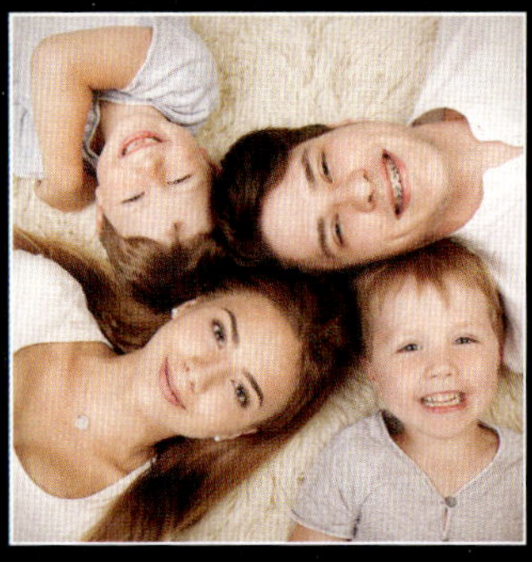

Kids and Families 245

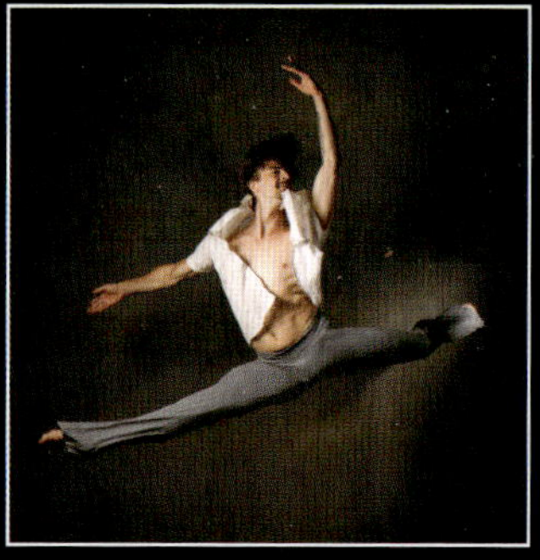

Movement and Action 261

A Kind of Foreword

"What are you doing there?"

"I'm writing a book."

"A book? What kind of book?"

"About photography."

"Aren't there already loads of books like that?"

"There are indeed many books about photography."

"So why are you writing another one?"

"Because this one is going to be different."

"So what's different about it?"

"It's going to be a reference guide."

"Whose preference?"

"No, not preference, reference! Switch off the blender when I'm talking to you!"

"OK, now I can hear you better. What did you say?"

"My book is going to be a reference guide. That's what makes it different."

"OK, so it's going to be a reference guide. What can I look up in it?"

"How to shoot portraits of kids, for example."

"But surely you can do that without a book?"

"Of course you can, but that would be like when you bake a cake …"

"Don't you like my cakes, Andreas?"

The moment has now arrived when the alarm bells probably start ringing for anyone who lives with a partner. And those bells are not just a soft Christmas tinkle, but a real cathedral-style clang!

"Your cakes are always delicious and I love it when you bake!"

"So what's with my baking and your book?"

"You bake cakes intuitively—some flour, a couple of eggs, a slosh of milk, some butter, maybe a little sugar … it's just that sometimes they work out less fluffy, but they're always delicious!"

"My cakes are like you: sometimes they just sit there and don't do much."

"You mean you bake Andreas cake?"

"Exactly."

Luckily, the best wife in the world is always good for a joke and the situation didn't get too out of hand.

"But back to the book. If you were to use a cookbook when you bake cakes, the probability of them always turning out fluffy would be much greater."

"OK."

"It's the same with my book. I'm going to put everything photographers need to know on a two-page spread so they can make perfect pictures faster and more easily."

" I get it. You're writing a cookbook for photographers."

"Exactly. A cookbook for photographers with lots of photos."

"Do I appear in your book?"

When the best wife in the world asks a question like that, there can only be one answer. Otherwise, the book you are now reading would never have been finished. My serious look added weight to the obvious answer:

"Of course, darling, you're going to be in my book too."

A smile flitted across the best wife in the world's face.

"Food's ready. Why don't you take a break before you get back to work on our book."

Beautiful smells wafted their way into my office, and my stomach began to rumble. I can work on my book again later …

Credits

In all photography—and especially portrait photography—there is always an entire team behind every successful image, and the same is true for this book.

▶ Firstly, I want to thank my family. I love you all!

▶ I also want to thank my studio team, including all the models, stylists, and assistants who worked on these images.

▶ And of course, thanks go to my publisher who supported me all the way while I worked on this book.

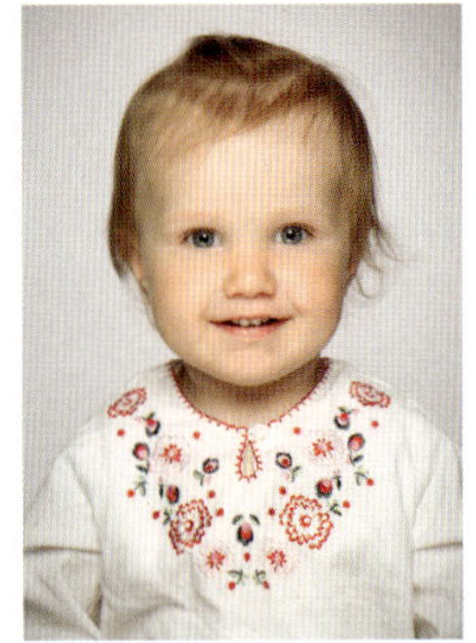

Angelina Maria "Mascha" Bübl
My youngest daughter

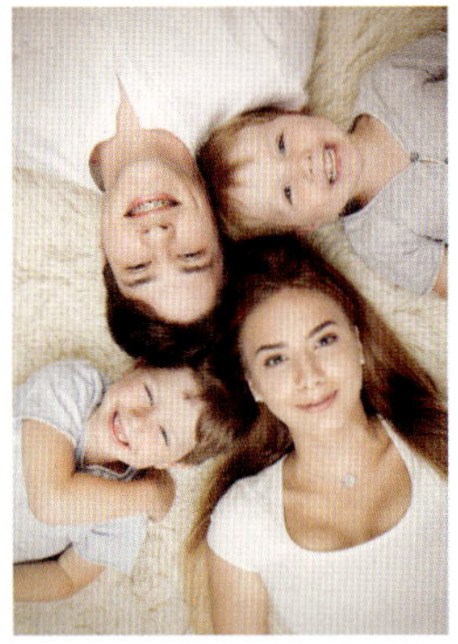

Larissa, Benjamin, Rafael, and Mark Bübl, *my kids*

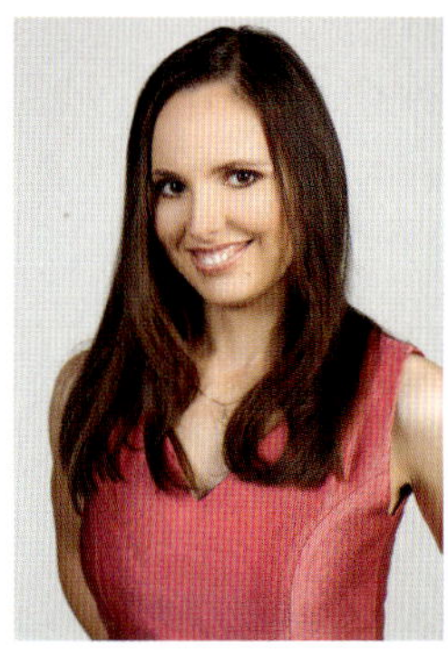

Tanja Bübl Kravchenko
The best wife in the world

Melissa Aksoy
Model

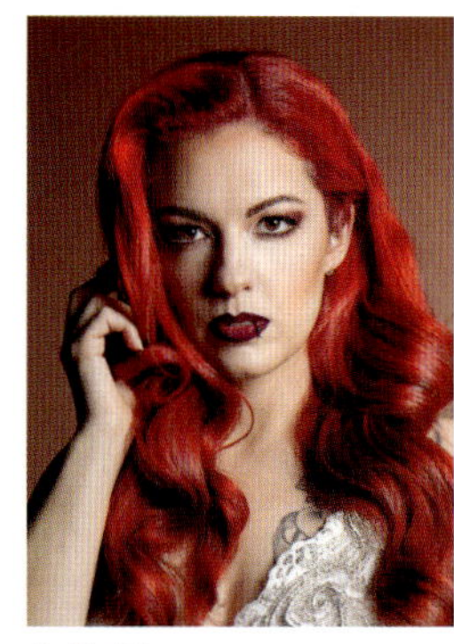

Bella Bianca
Model

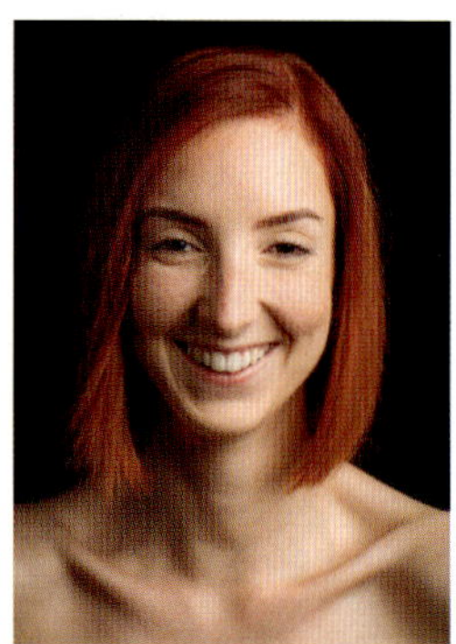

Kristina Cavajda
Model

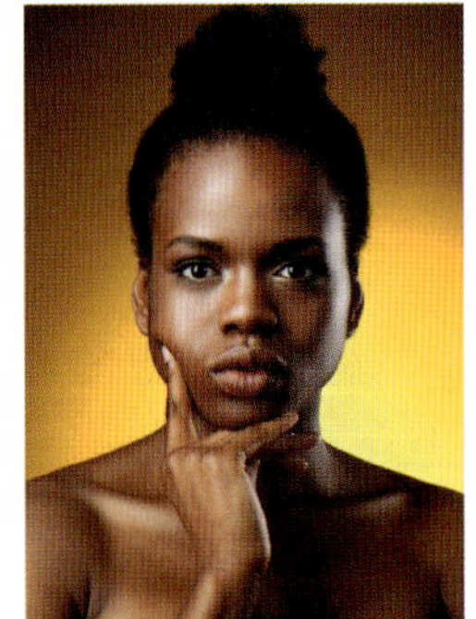

Deborah Dikebo
Model

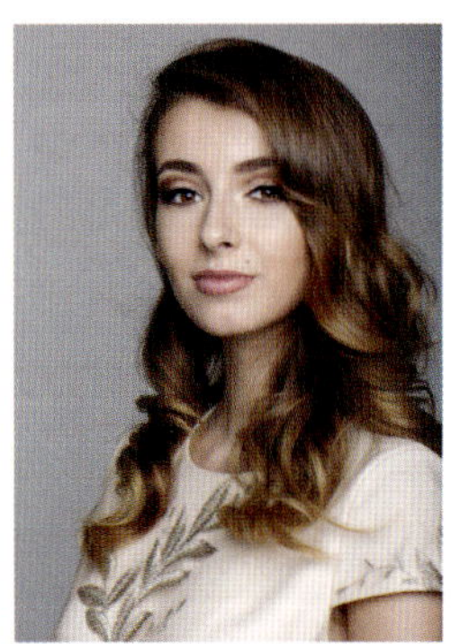

Jessica "Jazz" Egger
Model

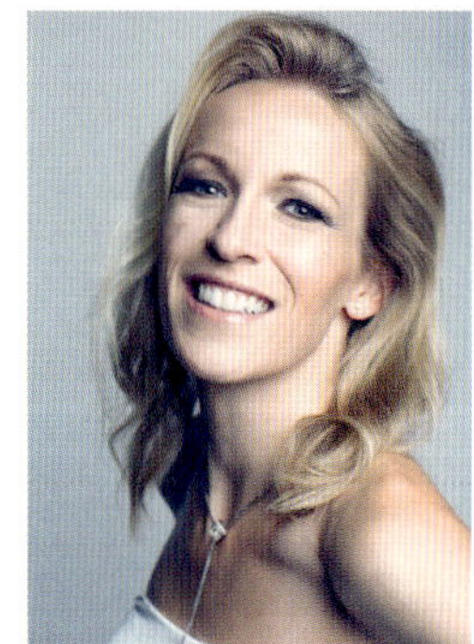

Martina Ehrlich
Model

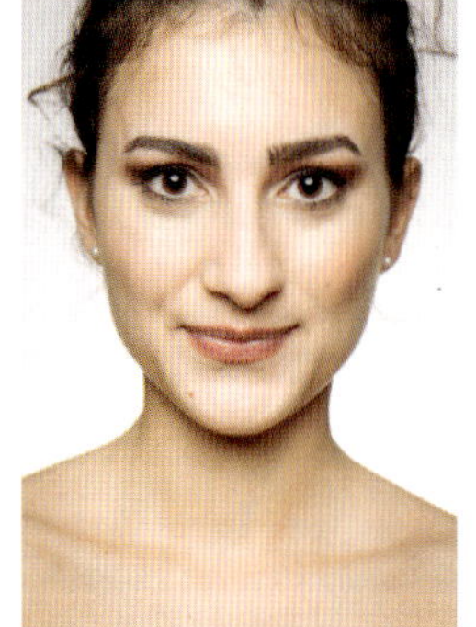

Anika Embacher
Model

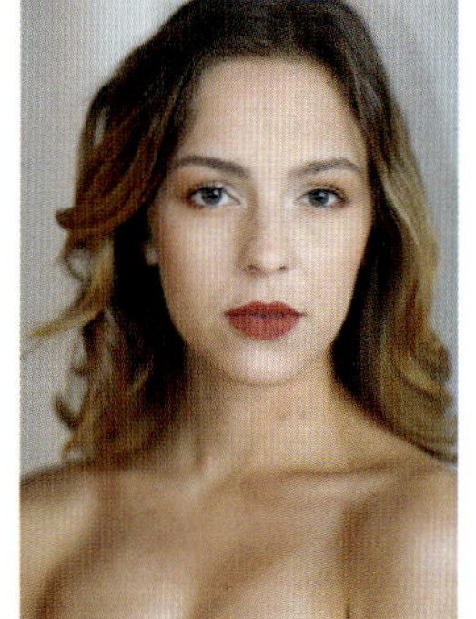

Lisa Enzminger
Model

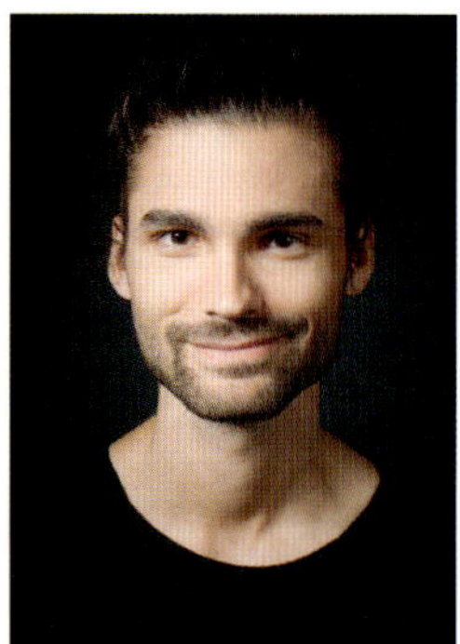

Andreas Grünauer
Model

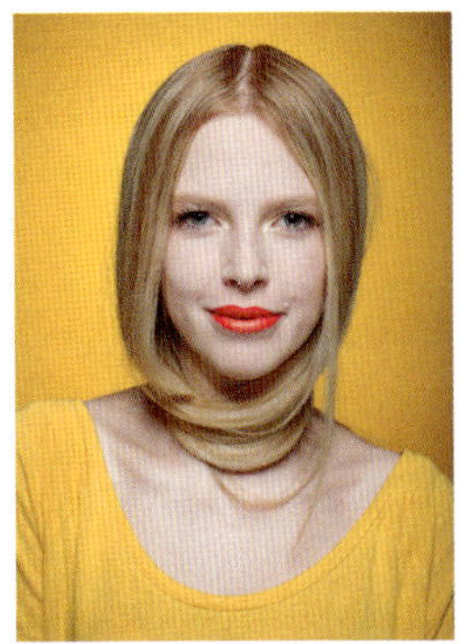

Victoria "Viki" Gunner

Model

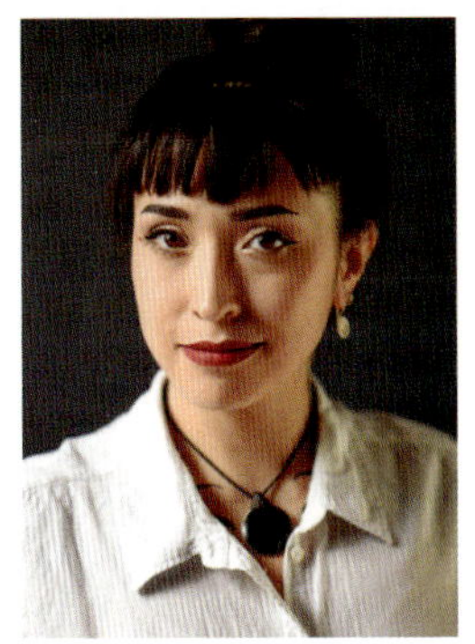

Miyu Haydn

Makeup artist, www.miyu.at

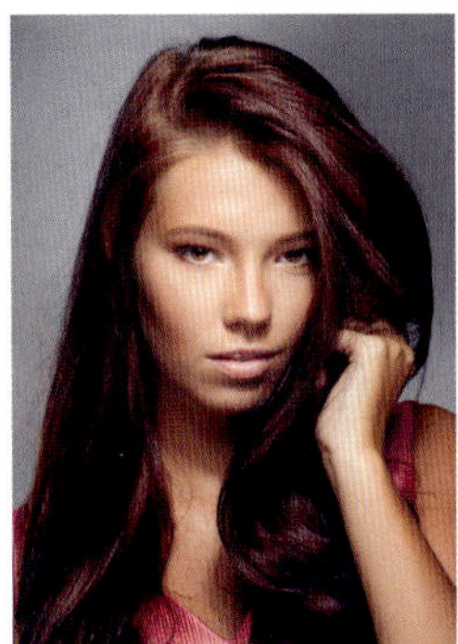

Isabel Jelinek

Model

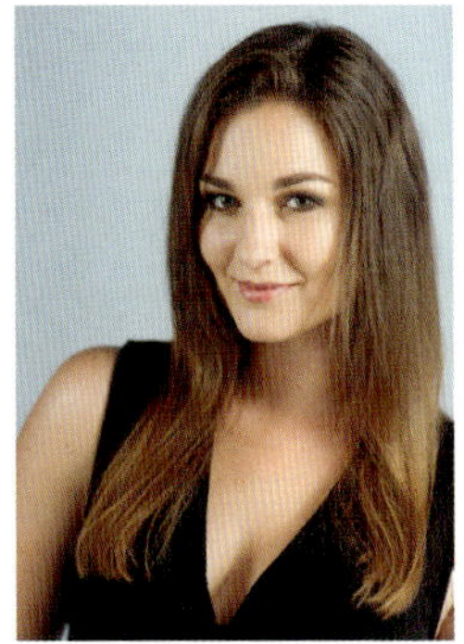

Manon Krulis

Model

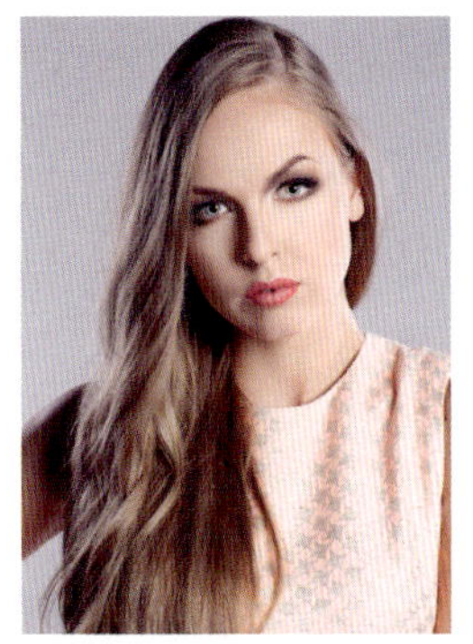

Angelina Lorich

Model

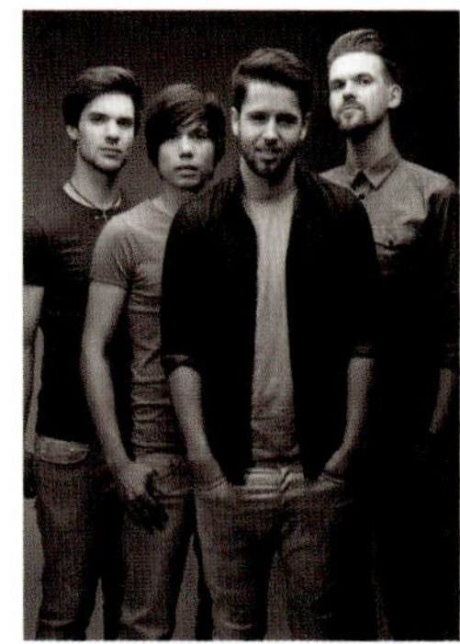

nature band

Musicians

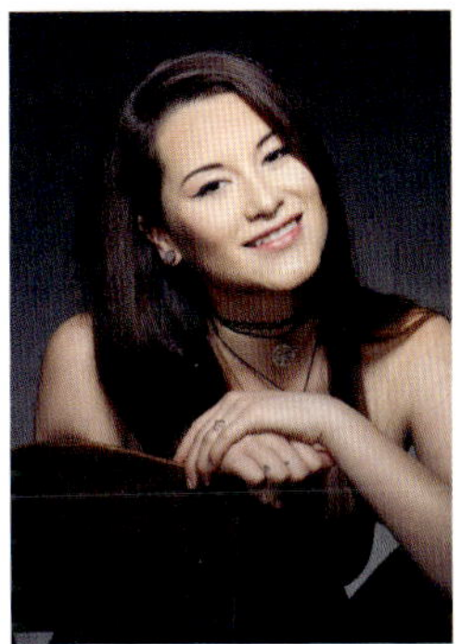

Sonja Plöchl

Model

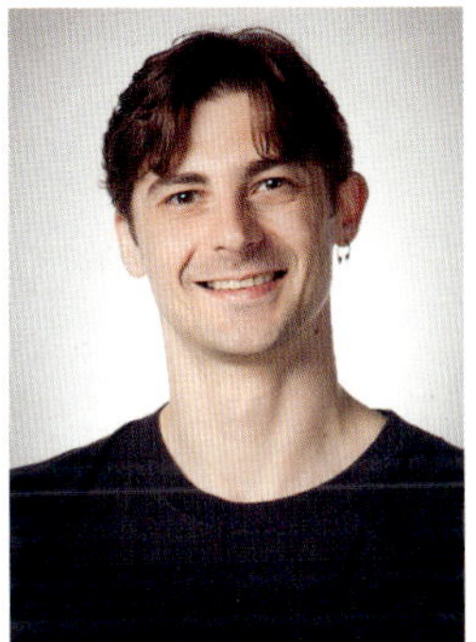

Vladimir Shishov

Soloist at the Vienna State Opera

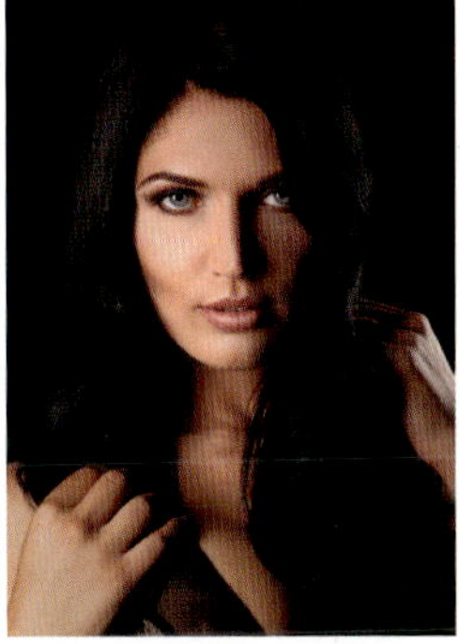

Nicolette "Nicole" Sol

Model

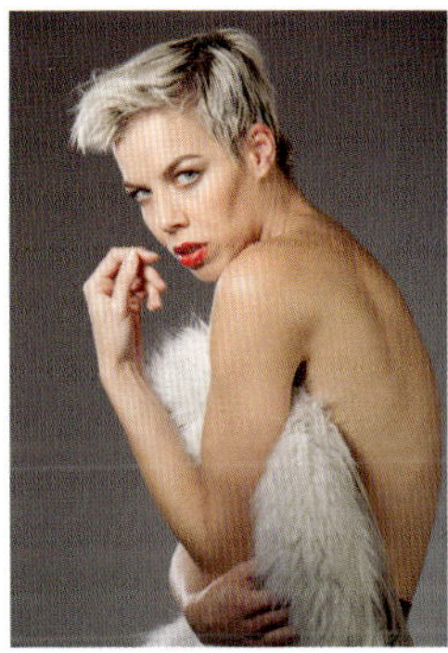

Denisa Strakova

Model

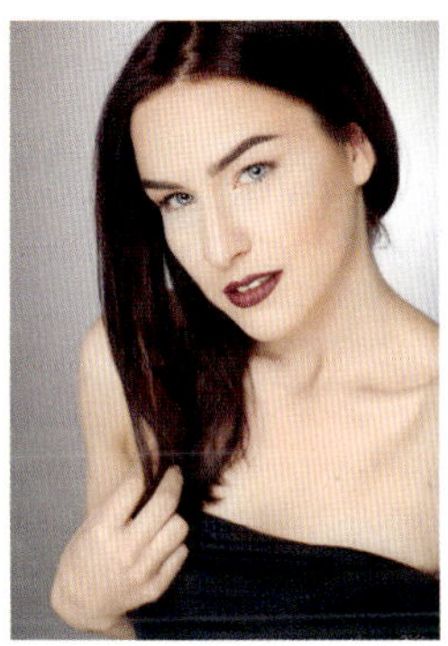

Nicole Stuparek

Makeup artist, www.powderandbrush.at

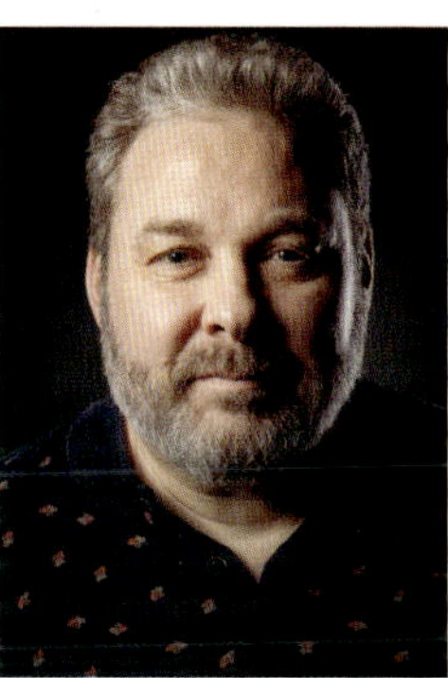

Roland Suschitz

Model

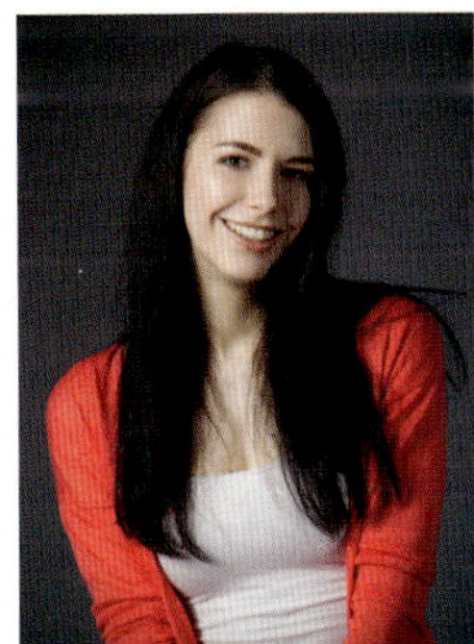

Elisa Valentina

Model

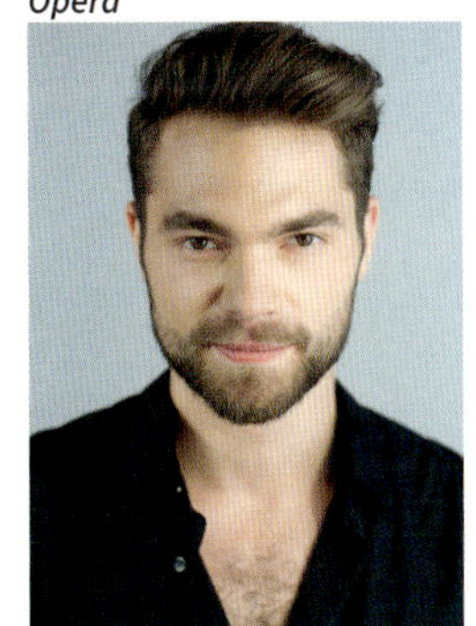

Rafael Werluschnig

Model

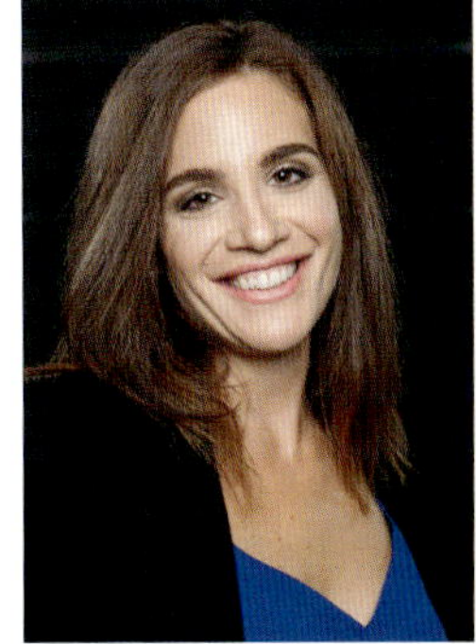

Miriam Woldrich

Model

How to Use This Book

The lighting setups themselves start in the *Classic Studio Portraits* chapter on page 29. Each setup is illustrated clearly and concisely in a two-page spread. The illustration below shows you which information is located where on each page.

Setup Diagrams

The diagrams complement the "making of" photos. They detail the light shapers and other accessories such as reflectors, flags, and diffusers used in the setup. Flash output settings are given in the form of an aperture (f-stop) value, and you can use a handheld light meter to check the settings on the flash heads and adjust them if necessary. For more details, see the *Studio Light Metering* section on page 24.

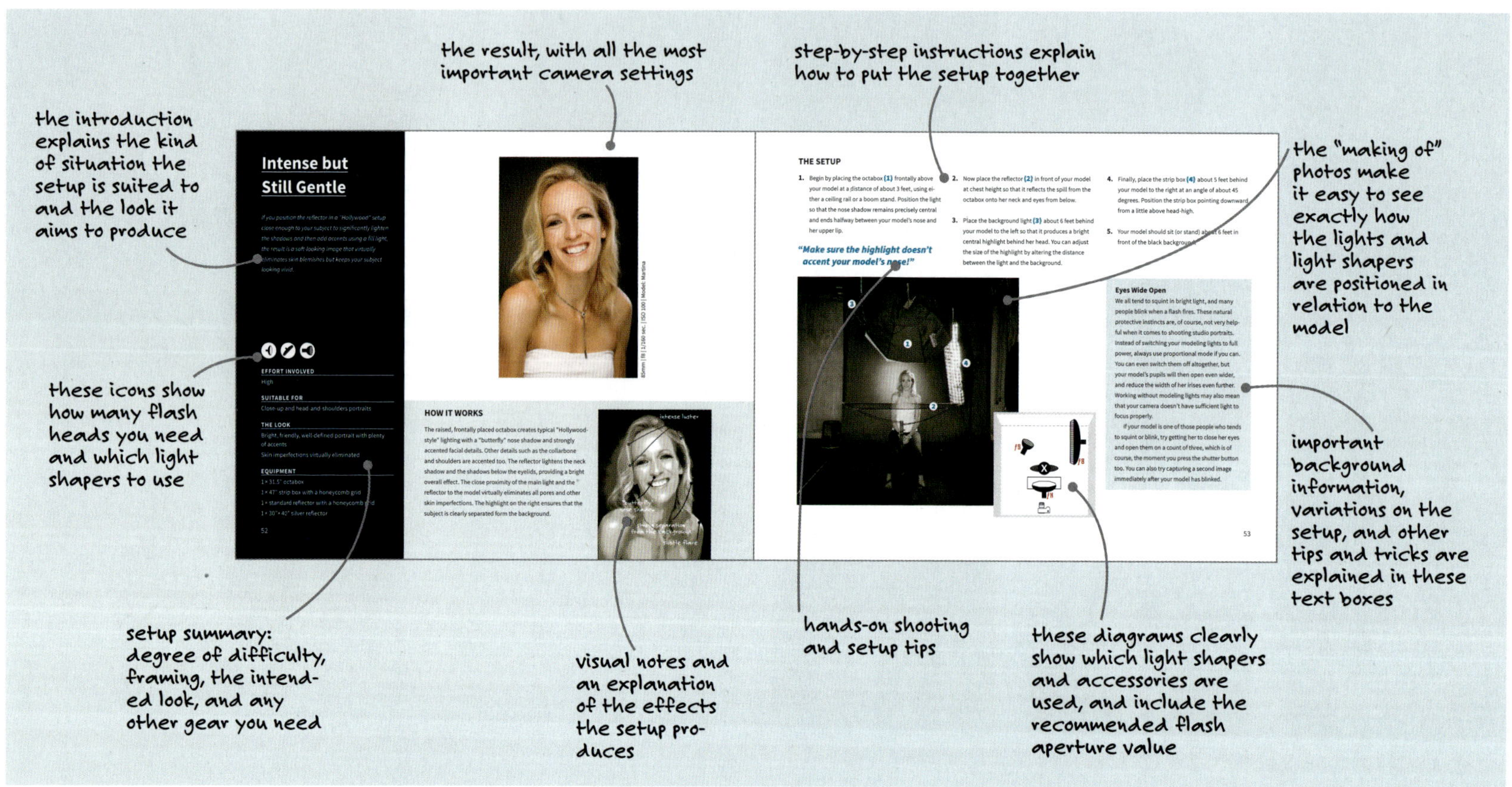

The color of the aperture value tells you how high the flash needs to be placed:

▸ **Red:** above head height
▸ **Yellow:** centrally around head height
▸ **Green:** floor level or slightly higher

A typical lighting setup uses three different light sources:

▸ A *main light*
▸ A *fill light* (also called a *side light*)
▸ *An accent light* (either a *background light* or a *hair light*)

As the name suggests, the *main light* is the major light source for your image and is usually placed to one side of the subject. The *fill light* (or a reflector) brightens the shadows produced on the side of the model that faces away from the main light. An *accent* or *effect light* can be used, among other things, to accent the background or to light your model laterally from behind, thus producing a halo (or "rim light") effect that accents the subject against the background.

As you work through the book, you will see that this standard setup can be used and varied in a multitude of ways. You can of course vary the number of lights you use to achieve the effect you are looking for. It doesn't matter if you use one, three, or five different lights—there are no limits!

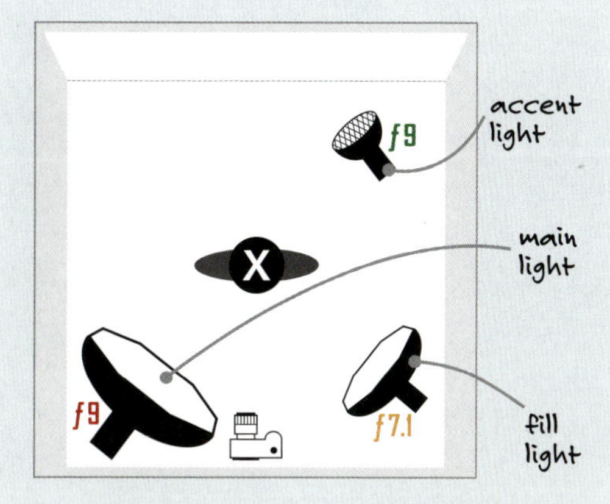

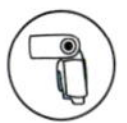 On-camera flash

 Construction site lamp

 Beauty dish

 Beauty dish with a diffuser

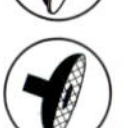 Beauty dish with a honeycomb grid

 Standard reflector

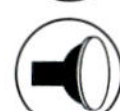 Standard reflector with a diffuser

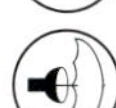 Standard reflector with a translucent umbrella

 Standard reflector with barn doors

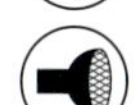 Standard reflector with a honeycomb grid

 Standard reflector with barndoors and a honeycomb grid

 Small octabox

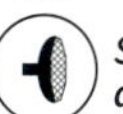 Small octabox with a honeycomb grid

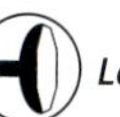 Large octabox

 Large octabox with a honeycomb grid

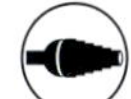 Snoot

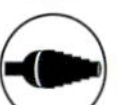 Snoot with a honeycomb grid

 Softbox

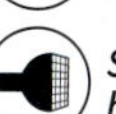 Softbox with a honeycomb grid

 Strip box

 Strip box with a honeycomb grid

Framing

You will usually decide how best to frame your model while you shoot. The closer you are, the more important your model's facial expression will be. We will be using the following framing styles in the course of the book to show the type of framing each setup is designed for.

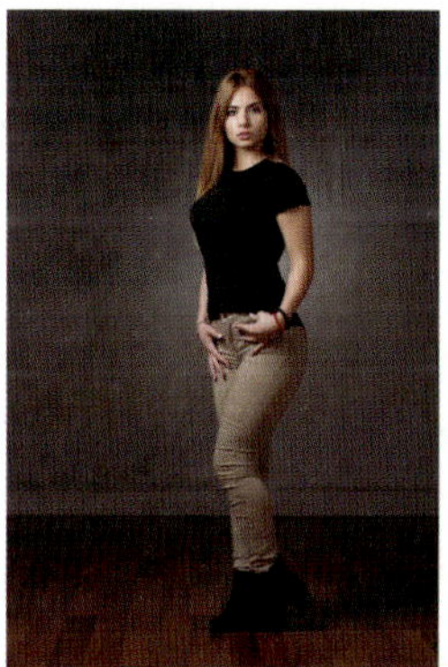

Full length:
Shows the model from head to toe.

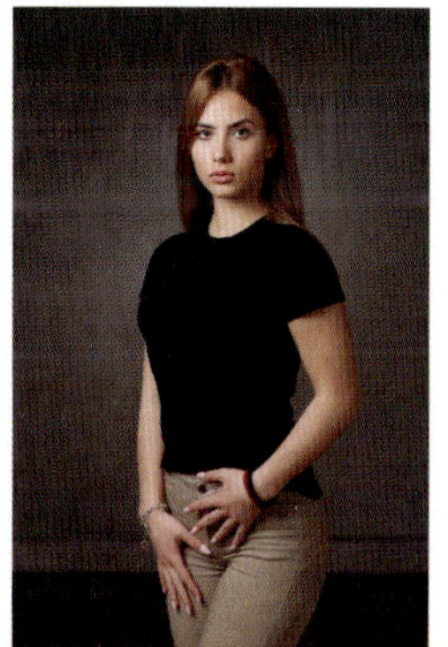

Three-quarter length:
Shows the model from head to hip.

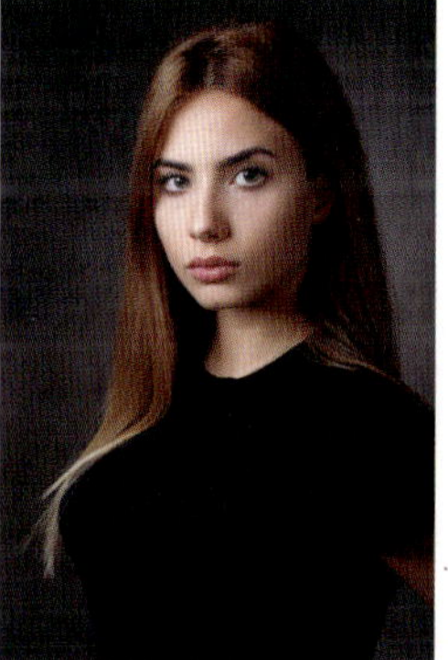

Head and shoulders:
Shows the model's head, shoulders, and, sometimes, the torso too.

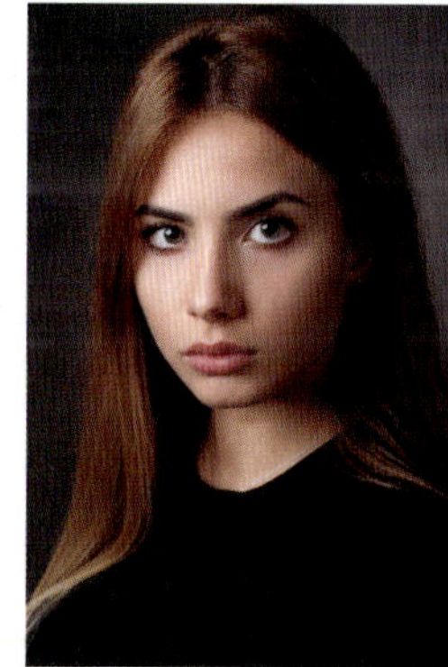

Close-up/Headshot:
Face only.

Studio Photography Basics

Light in a Studio Setting

The word photography means to "paint with light," and this definition is especially true in studio situations. When you are shooting outdoors, you are largely dependent on the available ambient light, but in a studio, you can control the light you use precisely according to your needs. You can use one or more light sources, you can decide how bright you want them to be, and you can influence your results by altering and refining the position of your lights. Shadows play a significant role too, as they are what gives the two-dimensional image on your camera's sensor a three-dimensional feel. A perfectly lit portrait depends on the right combination of light *and* shade.

A successful studio lighting setup depends on four aspects of light—the direction it comes from, its brightness, the type of light, and its color.

Light Shapers

You can't completely control the effects of your lights by adjusting their brightness or their positions. Using light shapers, you can influence how and where the light is diffused and illuminate your subject more evenly.

The Light Shapers section that starts on page 8 introduces the most common types of light shapers and the effects they produce.

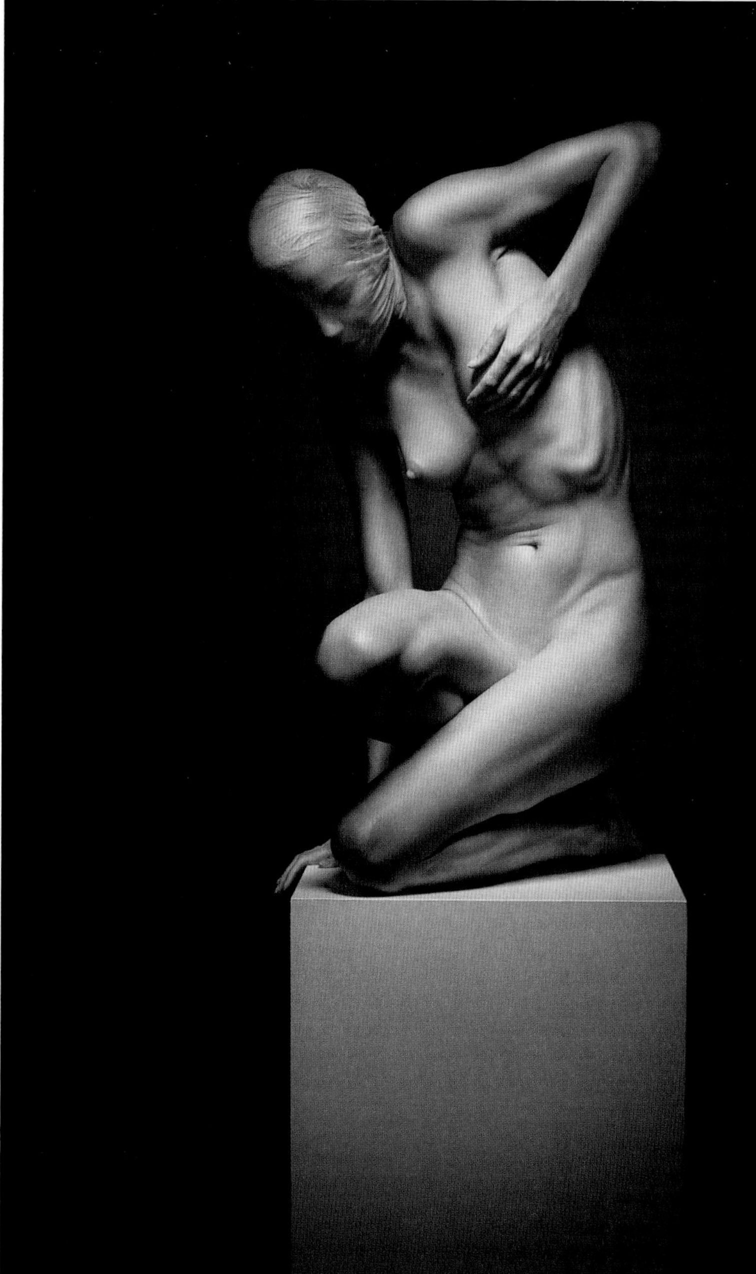

"Nude Art" makes a model look like a sculpture made of stone.
The setup:
A high, frontal beauty dish,
a reflector to lighten the shadows,
and a background light.
85mm | f7.1 | 1/160 sec. | ISO 100 |
Model: Denisa

The Direction of Light

Usually, everything good comes from on high. When light comes from diagonally above it produces a familiar feeling. This is because this is the direction light comes from in nature. A face with a shadow beneath or to the side of its nose, a neck shadow, and moderate eyelid shadows are a familiar sight. Even if the light comes from directly overhead, this is a situation that we are familiar with from standing in the midday sun. In this case, the subject's eye shadows will be deep, the nose shadow will be long, and the neck shadow goes on forever. This kind of light is never particularly flattering if you don't get your model to pose appropriately.

Other common types of light used in photography are backlight or lateral light (i.e., light that comes from the side). The direction light comes from produces highly specific effects, and you must always bear these in mind when setting up a shot. Backlight reduces contrast and produces softer, dreamy-looking images, whereas lateral light produces tension and drama.

The intensity of the light plays a role too and, in a studio, you can alter it at will by adjusting your flash output.

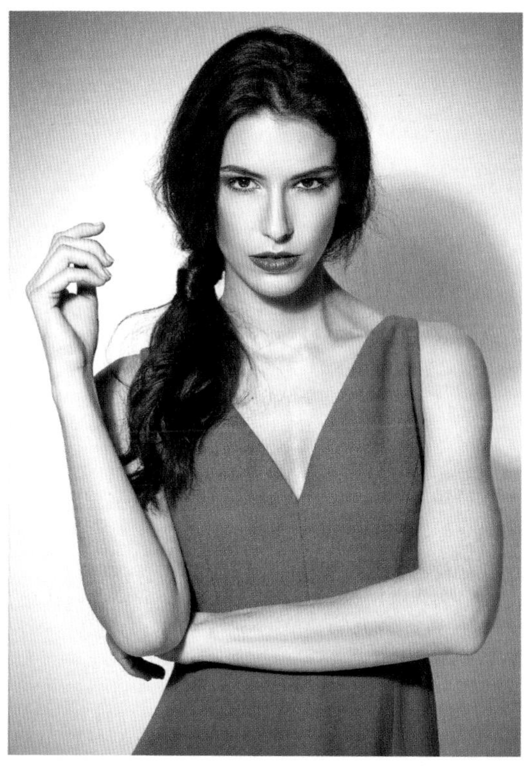

Here, I used a beauty dish positioned diagonally above the subject. The shadows are clearly visible, but the position of the flash head produces a natural look that works well with this particular pose and the model's facial expression.

100mm | f8 | 1/160 sec. | ISO 100 | Model: Elisa

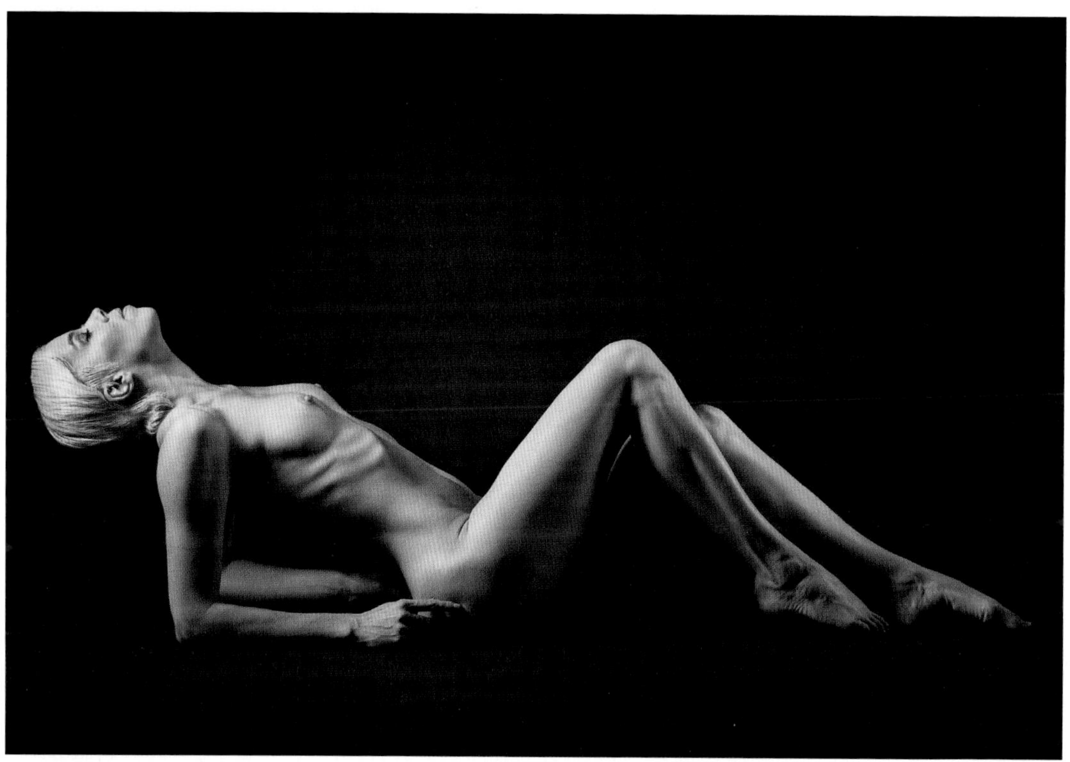

For a portrait captured from in front it isn't usually a good idea to use light that comes exclusively from above. However, this example shows an exception to this rule. I used two overhead strip boxes to accent the curves of the model's body. Because she is almost lying down, the shadows this setup produces have a familiar, natural look.

70mm | f7.1 | 1/160 sec. | ISO 100 | Model: Denisa

Brightness

The brightness of the light you use is a physical quantity that strongly influences the resulting image. Brightness is measured in *candelas*, which describe the luminous intensity of light as perceived by the human eye. However, photography concentrates on the lit subject or surface, so in this context we will be dealing with the intensity (i.e., the level) of illumination, *which is measured in lux using a light meter*. For a constant light source such as a lamp or daylight, you can use your camera's built-in light meter, but once we begin using off-camera flash, you really need to use a handheld light meter to help set up your camera and lights manually. For more details, see the *Studio Light Metering* section on page 24.

To adjust the illumination intensity in a studio, you can adjust the output setting on your flash head and/ or change the distance between your light source and the subject. Note that luminance is reduced by the square of the subject distance. This means that if you double the distance between a light and your subject, the amount of light reaching the subject will be reduced by two f-stops.

Differences in brightness provide you with lots of compositional options. Bright light allows you to use a smaller aperture and increase your depth of field—for example, to keep your model and the background in focus. Or you can reduce the exposure time to freeze movement in dynamic situations. In a studio setting, the shortest exposure time is usually limited to 1/160 or 1/200 sec. This is due to the *flash sync speed* used by most studio flash heads. If you use an exposure time that is shorter than the flash sync speed, you will end up with ugly black stripes in your images, or even completely black exposures. For more details on flash sync speeds, see the *Calculating Exposure Settings* section on page 26. The complete opposite is true of weaker light. In this case, you have to use a much larger aperture to ensure that enough light reaches the camera's sensor. However, this automatically reduces the depth of field in your image, making it necessary to increase the exposure time accordingly (but only so far as to avoid producing camera shake). As you will be working mostly without a tripod, the rule is to make sure that the exposure time you use isn't longer than the reciprocal of the (35mm equivalent) focal length of your lens. In other words, if you are using a 50mm lens on a full-frame

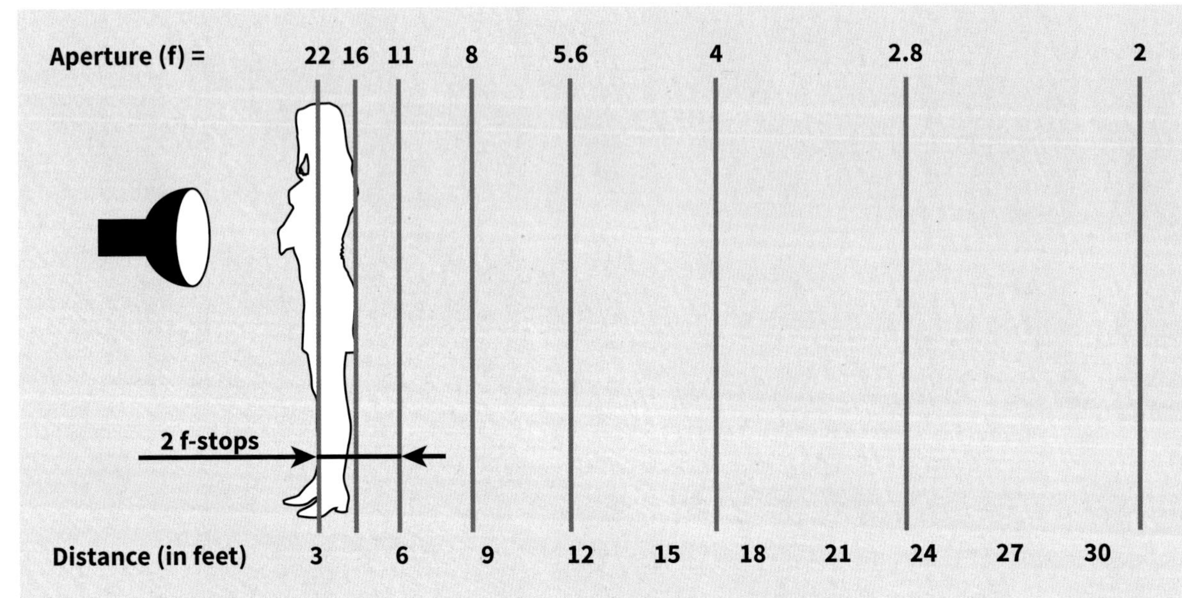

The relationship between subject distance and the brightness of light.

camera, the exposure time shouldn't be longer than 1/50 sec. if you are using a camera with a crop-format sensor, the equivalent focal length increases by the crop factor involved. The formula thus changes to *1/ focal length × crop factor*. For example, if you are using a Nikon DX-series camera with a crop factor of 1.5 and a 50mm lens, the longest exposure time you should use will be 1/75 sec. Because humans cannot remain completely still, you are likely to end up producing motion blur in your portraits if you use exposure times that are too long. For studio work I recommend that you use an exposure time of 1/125 sec. or less.

The output setting you use for your flash head will have a direct effect on the aperture setting you can use and therefore also on the depth of field in the final image.

Manufacturer	Sensor Type	Crop Factor
Canon, Nikon, etc.	FX/Full Frame	1
Nikon, Sony, Fuji	DX/APS-C	1.5
Canon	APS-C	1.6
Panasonic, Olympus	Micro Four Thirds	2

Crop factors for various camera makes and models

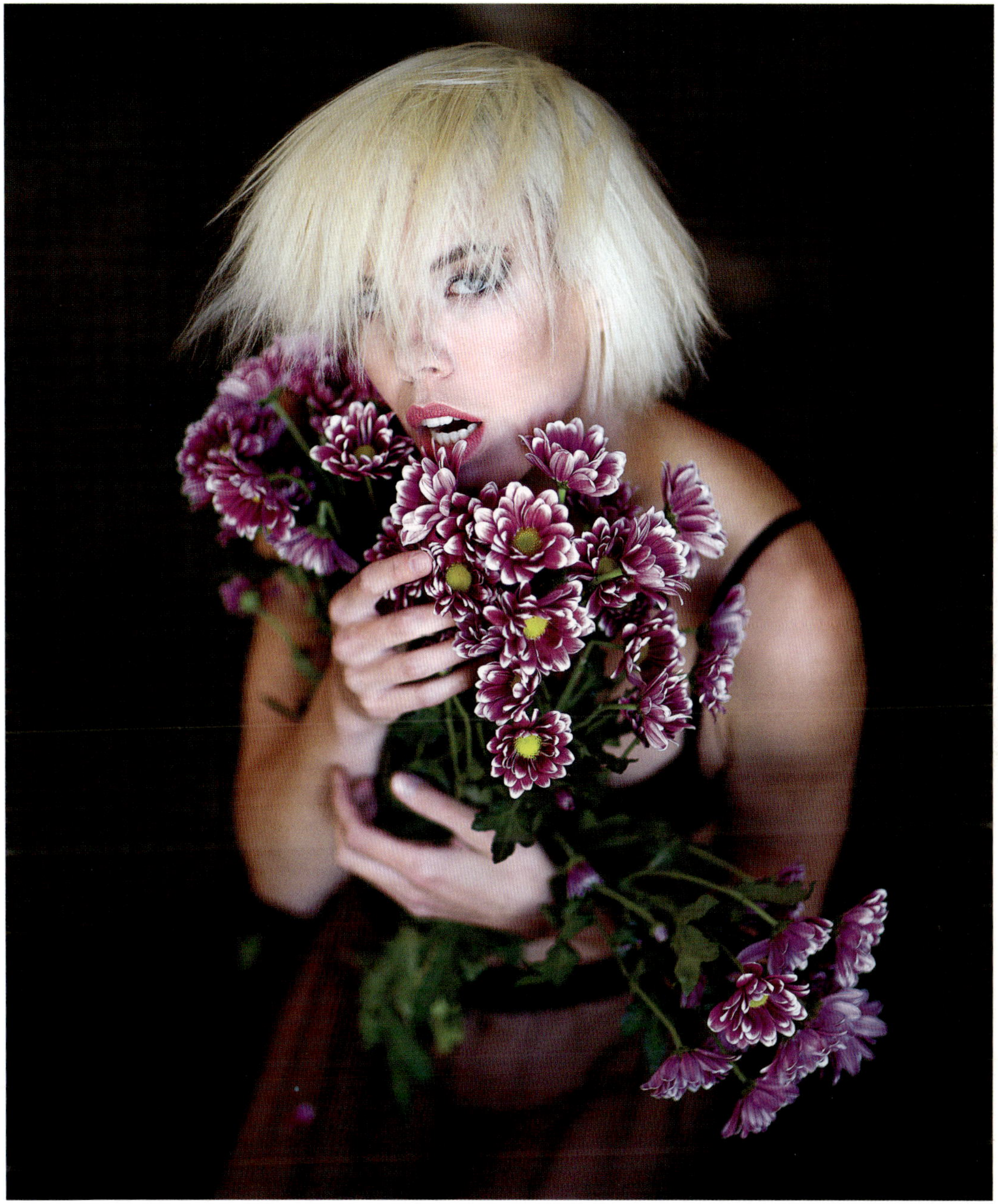

Shallow depth of field in weak light.

85mm | f1.4 | 1/200 sec. | ISO 100 | Model: Denisa

Types of Light

Depending on the size of your light source and the distance to your subject, you will end up with either "hard" light with clear, well-defined shadows or "soft" light with smoother shadows. These differences contribute to the overall "hard" or "soft" look in a portrait.

The larger your light source, the softer the light it emits, and the more diffuse the subject and its shadow appear. The opposite is also true, and the smaller your light source, the harder the light it emits. A hard light source produces crisp shadows and more contrast in the surface it illuminates. Along with its size, the distance between your light source and the subject plays a major role in determining the nature of the shadows in the final image. The farther the light source is from the subject, the harder the shadows it produces.

You can lighten shadows using additional light sources or through the targeted use of reflections. It makes a big difference to the overall effect if the shadows are really dark or only faintly visible.

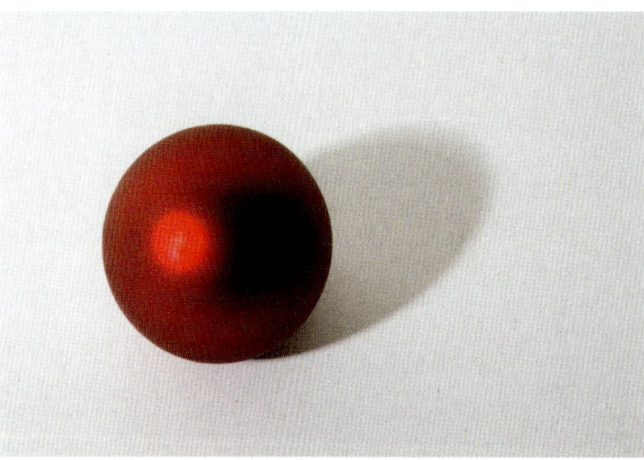
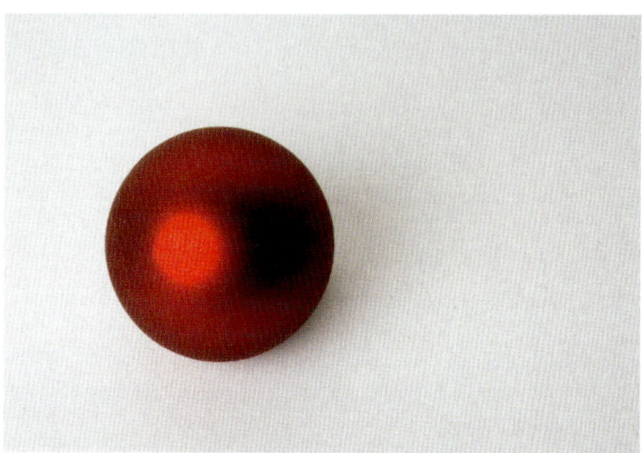

Left: Hard light in a shot of a Christmas tree ornament lit using a standard reflector 6 feet away from the subject.
Right: Soft light in a shot of the same subject lit using a softbox at a distance of 18 inches.

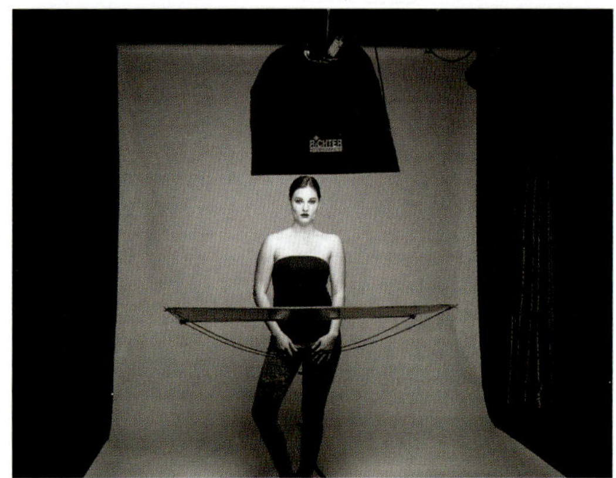

The studio setup showing the reflector used to brighten the shadows.

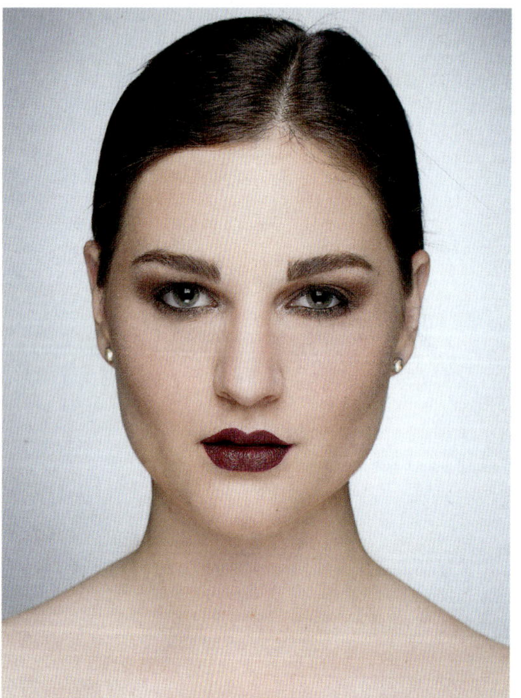
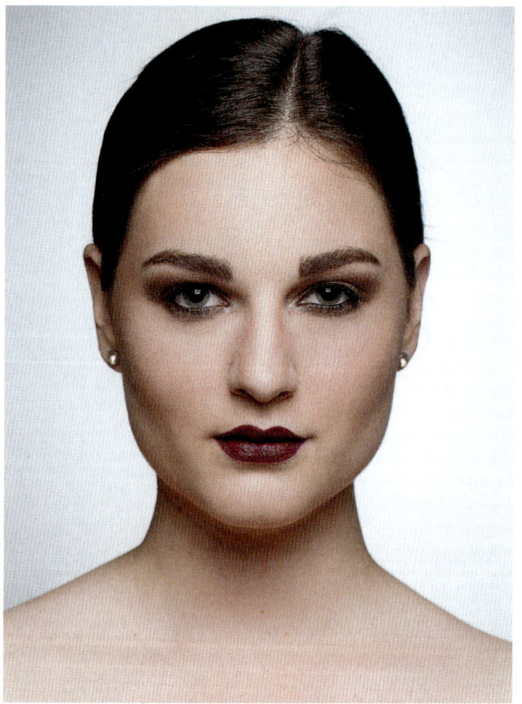

The shot on the left shows the effect of lightening the shadows. The shot on the right uses the same basic setup but without the extra reflector. In this case, the shadows are much darker and produce a much harder overall effect.

100mm | f8 | 1/160 sec. | ISO 100 | Model: Manon

The Color of Light

If you shoot using a red light source instead of a green one, the difference is pretty obvious. You can use colored foils attached to your flash to achieve deliberate, specific color effects.

However, even apparently neutral light sources also have a color that "tints" white objects. A normal light bulb emits warm, yellowy light, whereas flash tubes emit cooler, blue-tinged light. In order to ensure that white tones really are white and other colors are depicted correctly in your finished image, you need to make the appropriate white balance setting either in your camera before you shoot or later during post-processing.

The color temperature of light is measured in units called *Kelvin* (K) that are based on the change in color of an ideal black body with increasing temperature. Put simply, it is like when you heat a piece of iron in a forge and the glowing metal changes color from red to yellow as it heats up.

You can set the white balance in your camera depending on the type of light source you use. Instead of using the camera's built-in settings, you can also set white balance manually using a standardized 18% gray card as a reference.

If you don't use an appropriate white balance setting, your images will have unwanted color casts. If you shoot your images in RAW format, you can correct color casts later during post-processing—for example, using *Adobe Lightroom*. The advantage of the RAW format is that your image file really is "raw" as captured by the camera's sensor, giving you virtually unlimited processing options. If you capture your images using the JPEG format, it is virtually impossible to correct white balance later on. This is just one of many reasons I recommend that you always shoot in RAW mode.

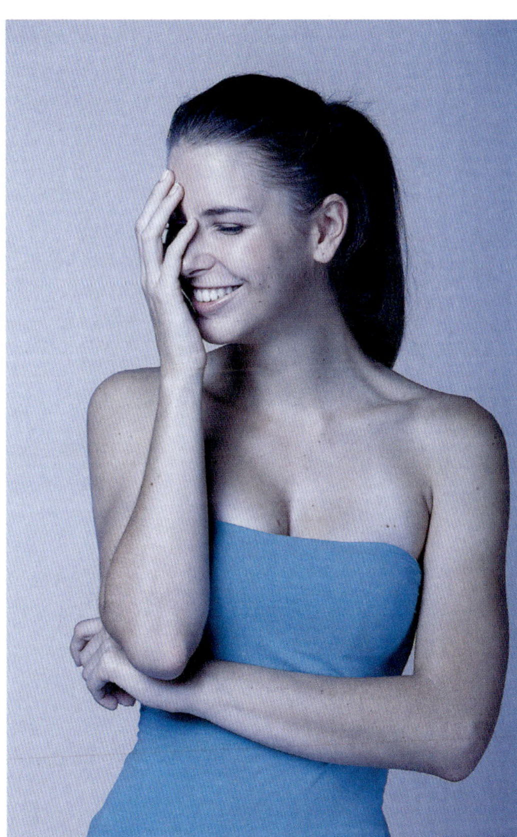

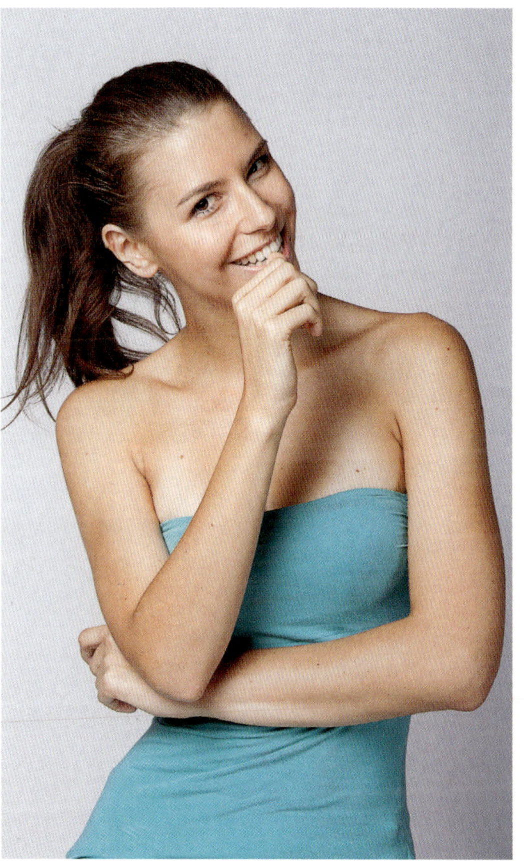

The shot on the left was made using an incorrect white balance setting of 2,800 K (for incandescent light), whereas the one on the right was shot using the correct setting of 5,100 K (flash).

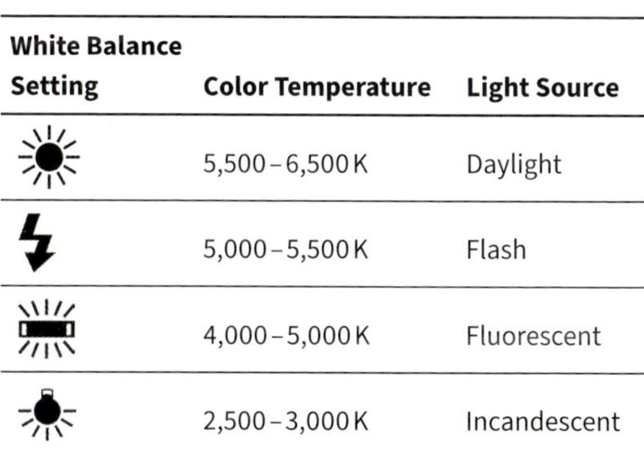

White Balance Setting	Color Temperature	Light Source
☀	5,500 – 6,500 K	Daylight
⚡	5,000 – 5,500 K	Flash
▭	4,000 – 5,000 K	Fluorescent
💡	2,500 – 3,000 K	Incandescent

Camera white balance settings for studio light sources.

Light Shapers

When you work in a studio, you have the benefit of many different types of light shapers that you can use to model the light according to your needs. You can decide whether to use hard or soft light, whether you want your lights to illuminate large areas or smaller, targeted zones, and whether you want it to come from a specific direction. This section provides an overview of the most common types of light shapers and the effects they produce.

Translucent Umbrella

A translucent umbrella looks like a regular umbrella and usually has a diameter of about 3 feet. It produces soft, non-directional light that covers large areas.

Parabolic Reflector

A parabolic reflector looks like a regular umbrella too (these types of reflectors are often referred to simply as umbrellas), but is not translucent and has an additional silver or gold reflective layer on the inside. As the name suggests, an umbrella reflector reflects the light from your flash and also reduces its output somewhat. The light an umbrella produces is non-directional and covers large areas.

Standard Reflector

This is a conical reflector with a white or silver coating on the inside that concentrates the flash light to produce hard, highly directional light with medium spread.

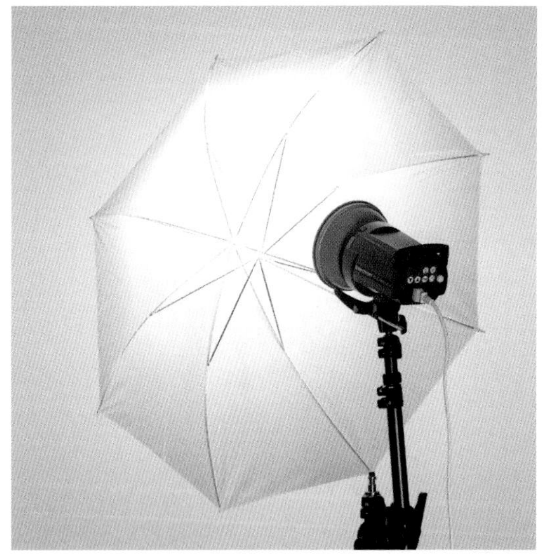

The greater the distance between a translucent umbrella and the flash head, the softer the resulting light will be.

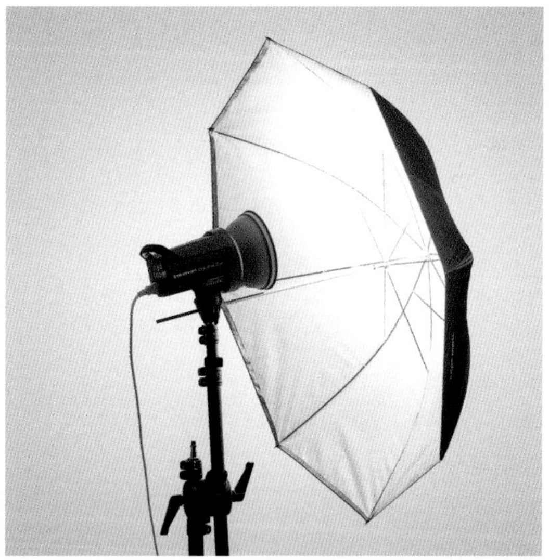

*The indirect, reflected light produced by a flash head and an **umbrella** is soft and has no hard shadows.*

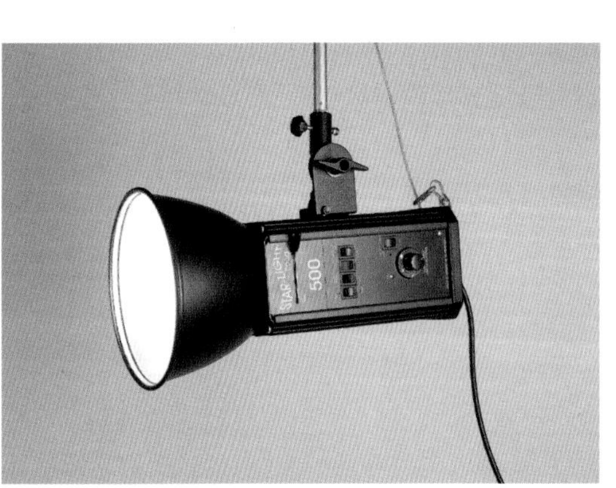

*The diameter of a **standard reflector** determines the spread of the beam it produces.*

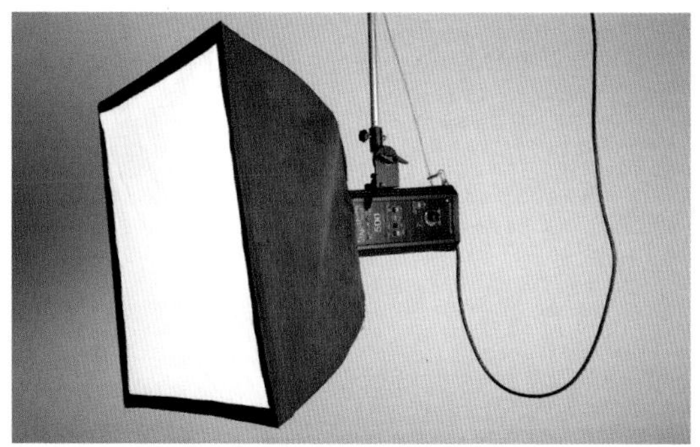

*A square **softbox** is great for soft shadows. It produces square reflections in eyes that look looks like window light.*

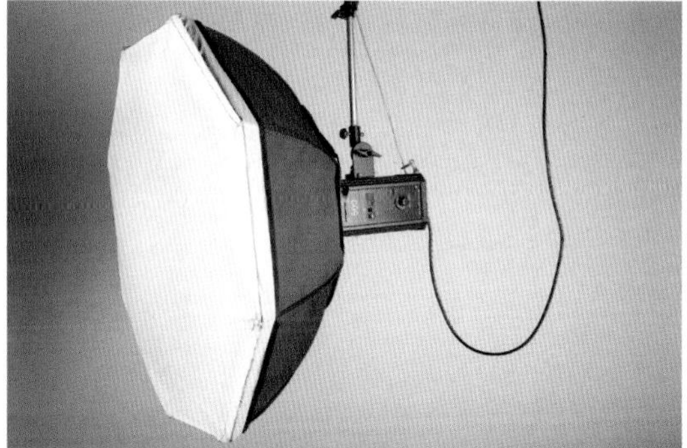

*An **octabox** is ideal for soft shadows. It creates rounder-looking reflections (called "catchlights") in your subject's eyes.*

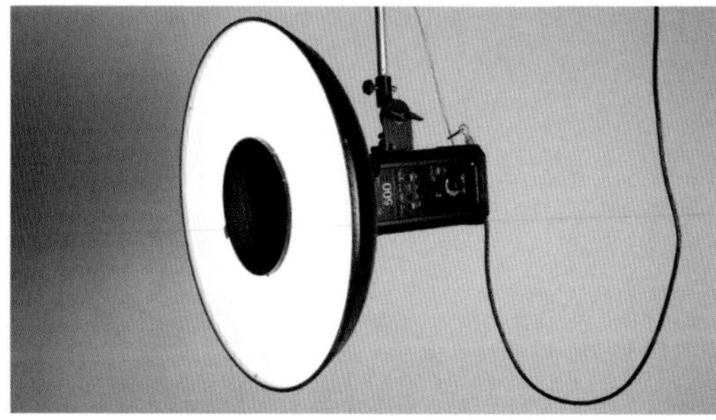

*A **beauty dish** produces uniform light with a crisp edge that is especially suitable for beauty and glamour-style portraits.*

Softbox

Light from a softbox is reflected multiple times from its inner surfaces and is emitted from a large surface. A softbox produces soft, even light that covers large areas. Softboxes come in various shapes and sizes that you can use to light large and small surfaces.

Octabox

This is a common abbreviation for "octagonal softbox." An octabox produces reflections with a much rounder look than those from a square softbox. Diameters of up to 10 feet produce very soft but controllable light. Internal diffusers are available that make the light from an octabox even softer.

Strip Box

A strip box is a special kind of softbox. It is long and thin and ideal for use as an accent light or for producing rim light effects. Light from a strip box is soft, too.

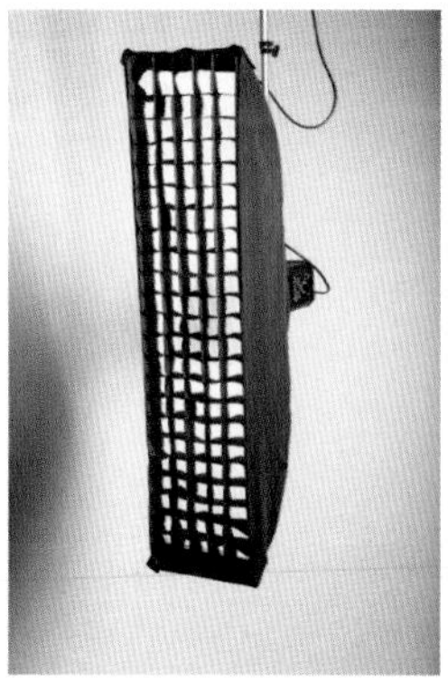

*A **strip box** is great for lighting smaller, clearly delineated areas within the frame.*

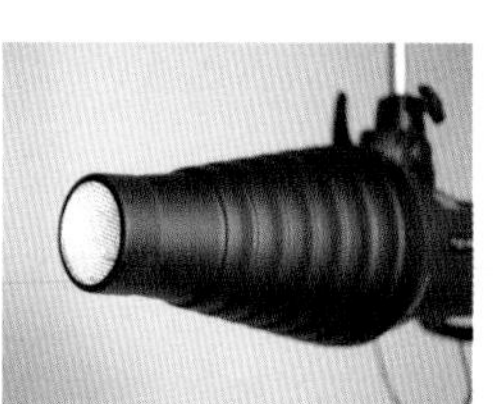

*A **snoot** enables you to set highly targeted highlights.*

Beauty Dish

Like an umbrella, the light from a beauty dish is reflected indirectly by the dish. Its special design produces light with a crisp core and shadows that become softer toward the edges of the light beam. This effect is ideal for accenting hair and makeup.

Snoot

A snoot narrows the light beam from the flash and concentrates it in a small circular patch. The effect is highly directional and quite hard, and is ideal for setting a hair light or other highlights.

Honeycomb Grid

Most studio light shapers can be fitted with additional honeycomb grids. A grid further limits the spread of the light beam but doesn't alter its basic hardness. However, it does reduce the overall brightness of the light.

Barndoors

Barndoors are a popular accessory for use with a standard reflector. The four separate leaves can be swung independently into the light beam to finely control which areas of your subject are lit.

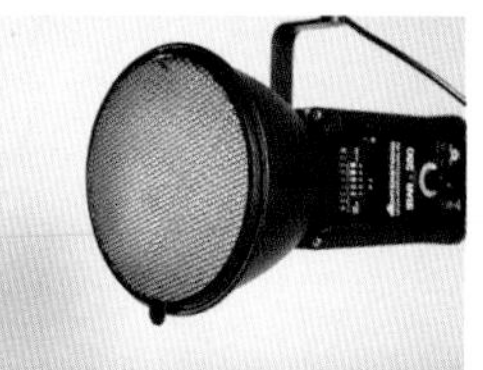

*A **honeycomb grid** (here attached to a standard reflector) limits the spread of light and prevents unwanted spill light.*

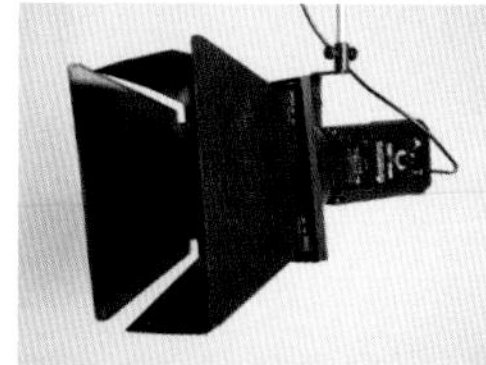

***Barndoors** are used to shape the light beam from a standard reflector and prevent unwanted spill light.*

Light Shaper Effects

The photos here illustrate the effects produced by the various types of light shapers described on the previous page. The flash was positioned identically (frontal and slightly raised) for all of these images. We had to adjust the flash output slightly depending on the type of light shaper we used. To illustrate the effect of light spill, I used a standard reflector with a honeycomb grid to project a beam of light onto the background. I used the same settings to develop all of these images.

1. **24" Softbox:** Soft shadows and good overall illumination. Square catchlights in the model's eyes.

2. **Beauty Dish:** Somewhat harder light with more contrast. The typical double shadow is clearly visible on the model's neck, and the overall focus is on her face. Circular catchlights.

3. **9" Standard Reflector with a Honeycomb Grid:** Hard light with a very narrow beam. The fall-off in brightness on our model's torso is clearly visible. Small, circular catchlights.

4. **9" Standard Reflector:** Hard light and more spill light than the in the shot made using a grid. The model's torso and the background are much brighter. Small, circular catchlights.

5. **31.5" Octabox:** Soft shadows and even overall lighting, like the softbox shot. The larger size of the octabox makes the shadows slightly softer and the spill light lightens the background. Large, rounded catchlights.

6. **5.5" Standard Reflector:** Very hard light and good overall illumination. The shadows are harder than those in the shot made using the 9" reflector. Again, spill light brightens the background a little. Small, circular catchlights

7. **47" Strip box (vertical):** Soft light and very soft, well lit horizontal shadows thanks to its length. The background is brightened by light spill and the light that hits it directly above the model's head. Long, narrow catchlights.

8. **47" Octabox:** Very soft light and good overall illumination. This very large octabox makes the shadows even softer than those produced by the 31.5" version, and the background is brightened even more by light spill. Large, rounded catchlights.

9. **36" Translucent Umbrella:** Soft light and a lot of spill, which contributes to the good overall illumination of the model and the light background. Circular catchlights.

10. **36" Umbrella Reflector:** Soft light and good overall illumination. The light is easier to control than that produced by the translucent umbrella, and there is less spill as a result. Circular catchlights.

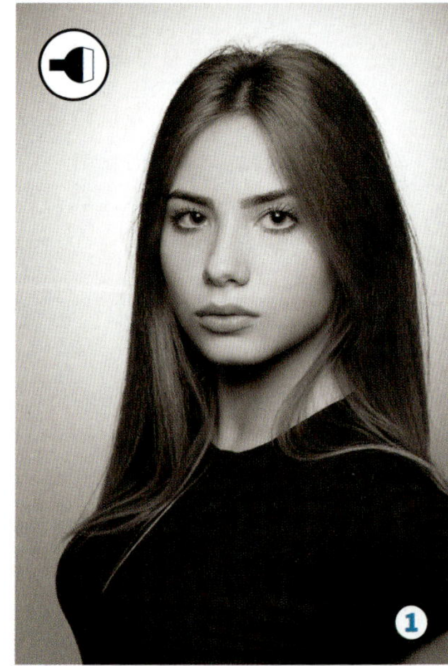

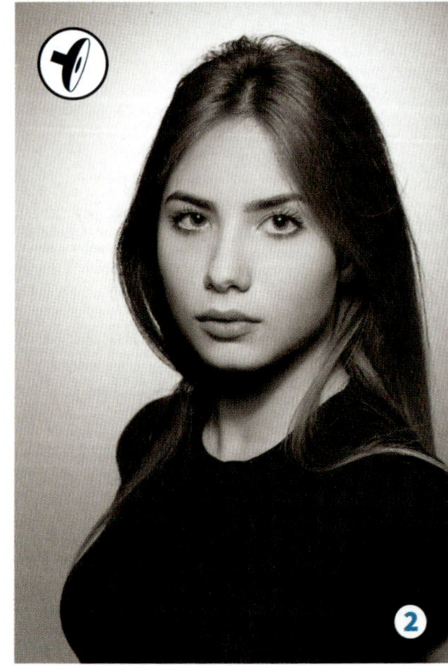

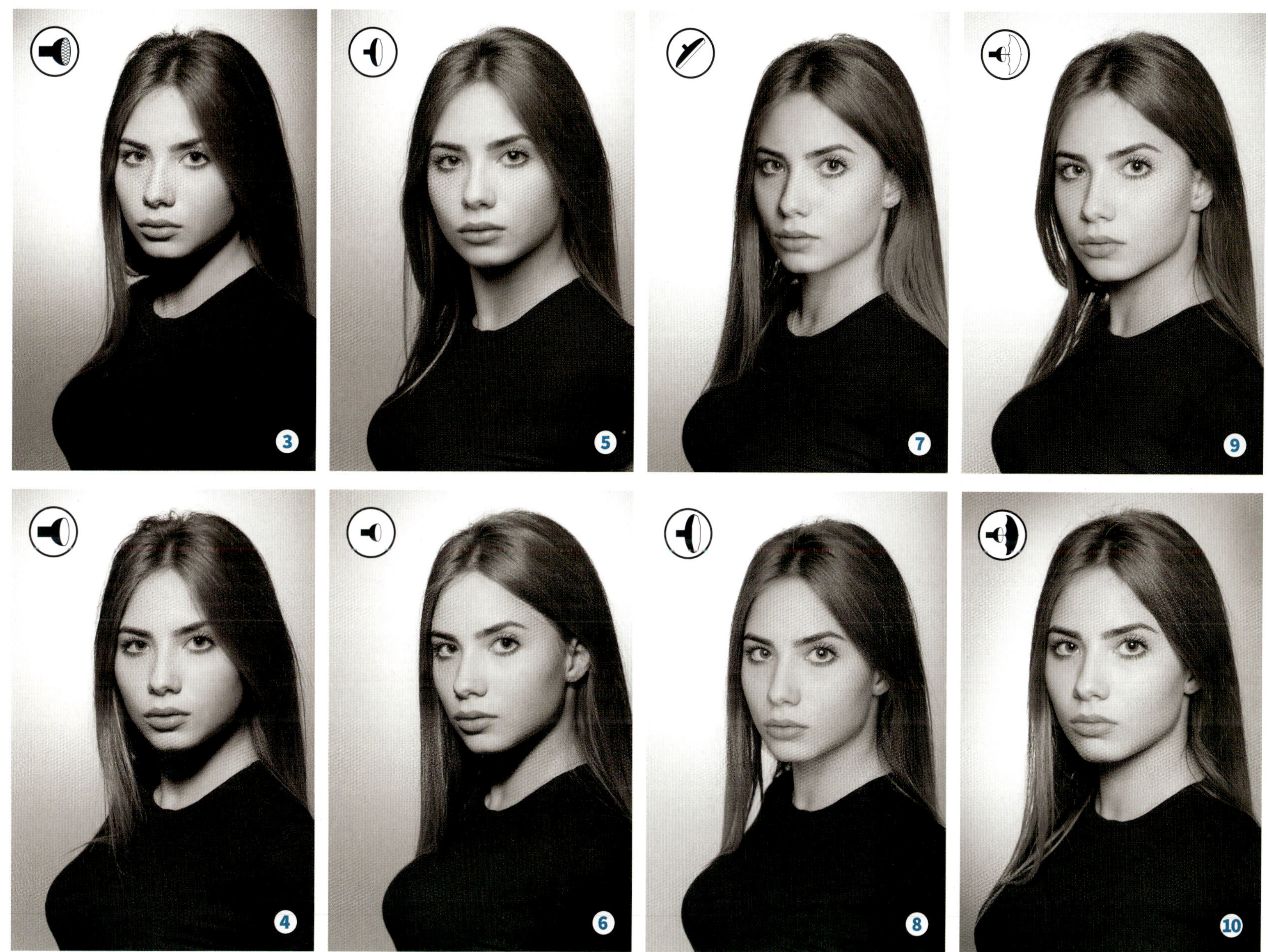

85mm | f7.1 | 1/160 sec. | ISO 100 | Model: Larissa

Reflectors, Diffusers, and Flags

Alongside the light shapers described on the previous pages, there are various accessories you can use to help modify your lighting. The most common of these are reflectors, diffusers, and flags.

Reflectors

Reflectors are used to lighten shadows or as an additional source of light. They are available in a range of shapes and sizes and with different colored surfaces.

The cheapest and simplest reflector you can use is a sheet of Styrofoam. A small, 3-foot square sheet is great for three-quarter length and close-up portraits, and you can use larger sheets for full-length portraits. Styrofoam produces nice soft shadows and brightens shadows in a pleasing, natural-looking way.

A typical silver-surfaced reflector lightens shadows more markedly than Styrofoam. Light reflected from a silver reflector has the same degree of hardness (or softness) and retains the same color temperature as the source.

The closer you place a reflector to your model, the lighter the resulting shadows will be. Different reflector surfaces produce different results. For example, a gold-covered reflector produces much warmer reflections, while a "zebra" reflector (covered with alternating gold and silver stripes) makes the reflected light only slightly warmer. A white reflector produces soft reflections in the same color as the source.

In the studio, reflectors are best used mounted on a purpose-built stand, and most have a built-in swivel mount.

You can purchase separate ball-joint holders to help you position collapsible reflectors and Styrofoam sheets.

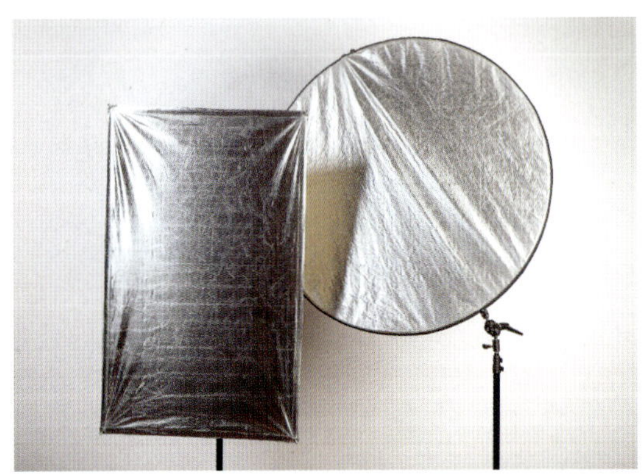

Rectangular and circular portrait photography reflectors. Both of these reflectors have silver surfaces and are mounted on adjustable stands.

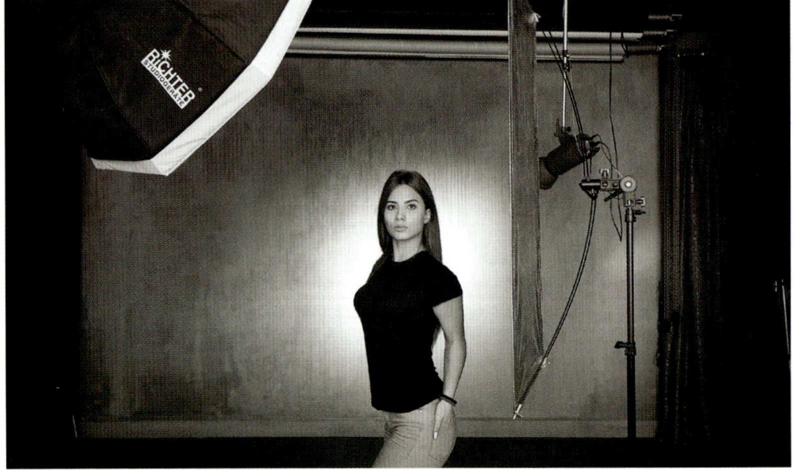

The lighting setup for our reflector comparison series (see the photos on the next page).

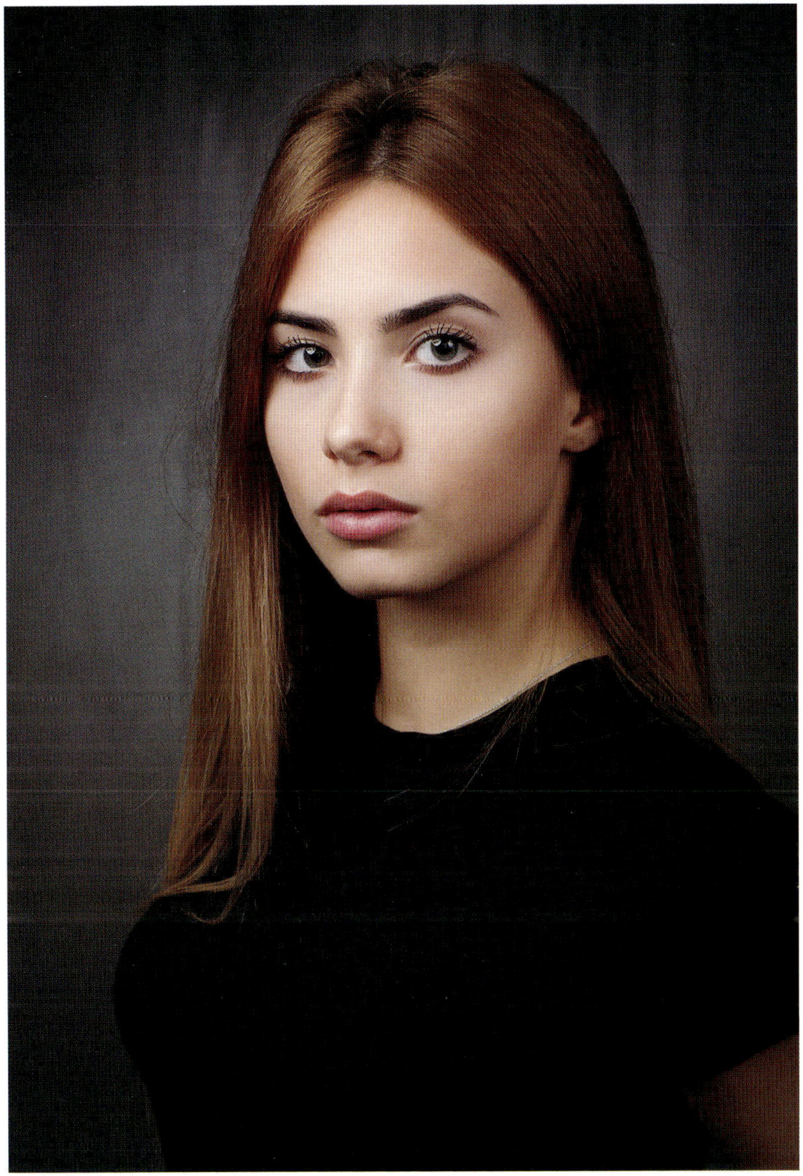

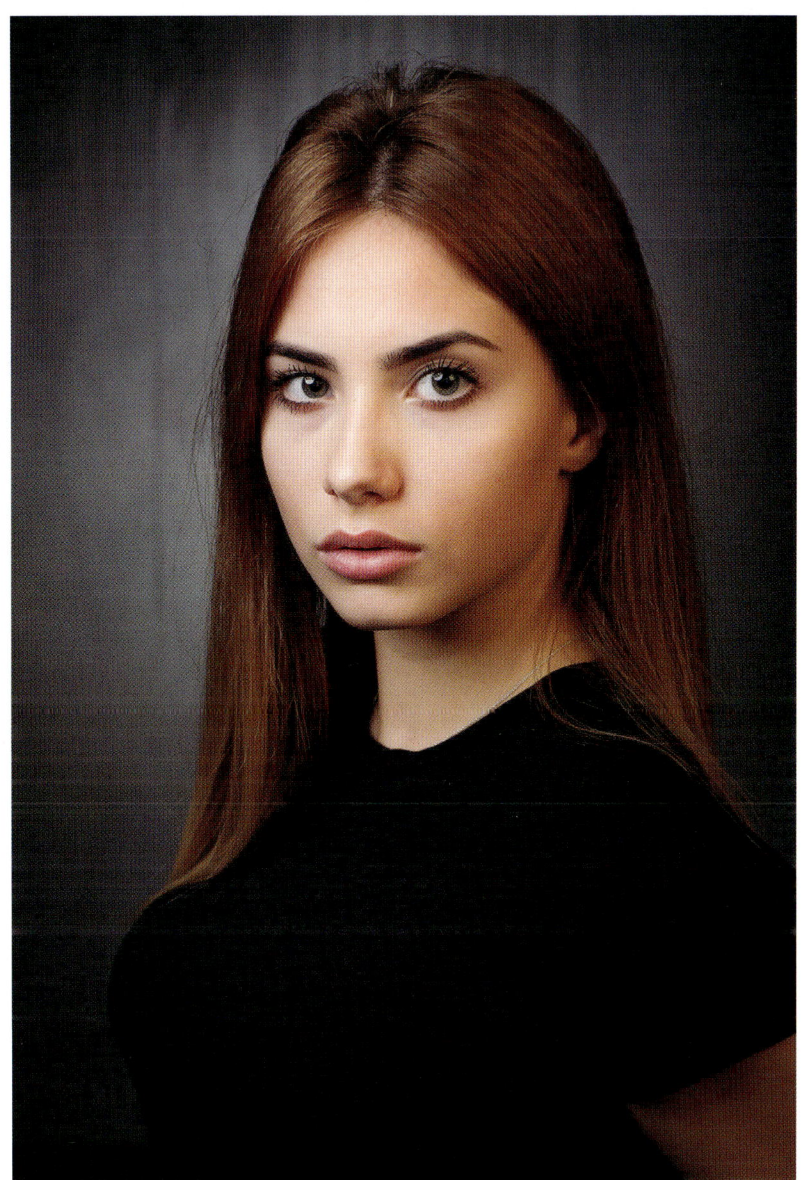

Shot using an octabox on the left and a silver reflector to brighten the right-hand side. The shadows are the same color as the main light.

85mm | f9 | 1/160 sec. | ISO 100 | Model: Larissa

Shot using an octabox on the left and a gold reflector to brighten the right-hand side. In this case, the shadows are warmer than the main light.

85mm | f9 | 1/160 sec. | ISO 100 | Model: Larissa

Diffusers

Soft, softer, softest. This is probably the best way to describe the effects produced by diffusers. Diffusers are the go-to accessory for softening light, but they weaken the light that reaches the subject much more than reflectors do. Instead of using commercially produced diffusers with built-in frames and clamps, you can use curtain material or any kind of thin cloth as an improvised diffuser.
If you take this route, be sure to use white material in order to avoid unwanted color shifts.

Placing a diffuser between the light source and the subject produces a soft lighting effect similar to sunlight on a cloudy day. The degree of softness in the shadows depends on the degree of translucency of the diffuser. The more densely woven the material, the softer the resulting light will be. The light shaper you use and the distance between it and the diffuser will also influence the brightness and the softness of the resulting light.

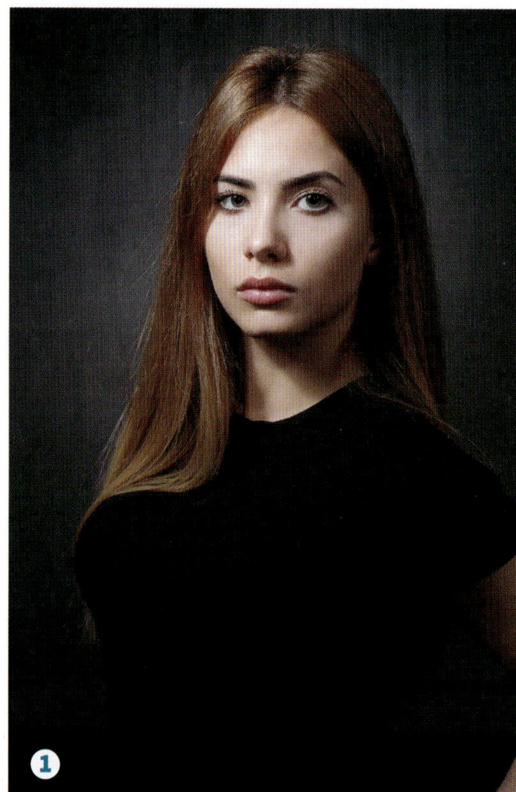

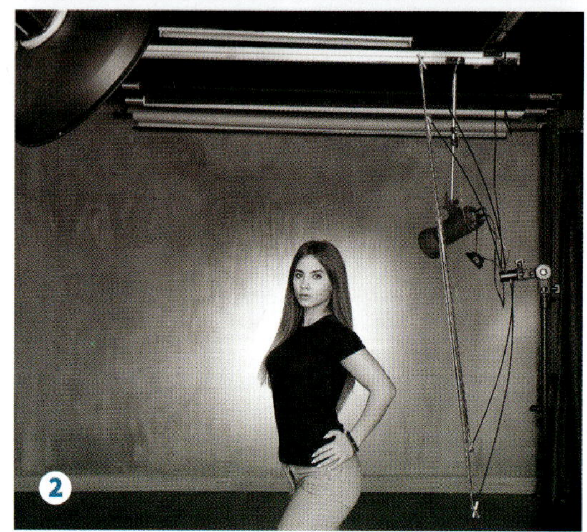

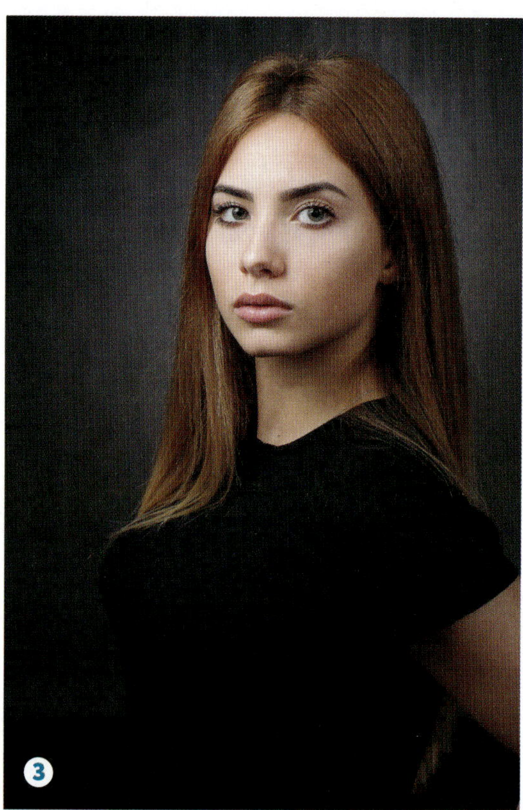

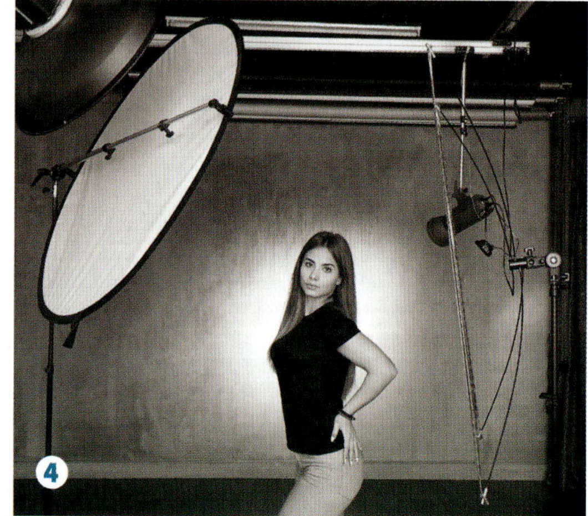

1 *Portrait shot using a beauty dish, a background light, and a reflector. The beauty dish was placed about 3 feet from the subject.*

85mm | f10 | 1/160 sec. | ISO 100 | Model: Larissa

2 *The beauty dish setup.*

3 *Portrait shot using a beauty dish, a background light, and a reflector. This time I placed a diffuser about 12 inches in front of the beauty dish and increased the flash output to keep the model well lit. The beauty dish was placed about 3 feet from the subject.*

85mm | f10 | 1/160 sec. | ISO 100 | Model: Larissa

4 *The beauty dish/diffuser setup.*

A large light shaper such as a softbox produces soft, diffuse light anyway, so adding a diffuser makes the effect even softer. The further your light source is from the diffuser, the larger the area it illuminates and the softer the resulting light will be. The farther you place your light source from the subject, the less bright it will become.

Flags

It is sometimes necessary to dampen reflected light in order to strengthen the shadows in your subject. This is where so-called flags come into play. You can use any dark surface as a flag, whether it is the black reverse of a reflector or any dark, non-reflective fabric such as polyester cotton. You can easily attach dark fabric to an existing Styrofoam reflector. Flags are usually placed the same way as reflectors, but have the opposite effect of darkening rather than lightening shadows.

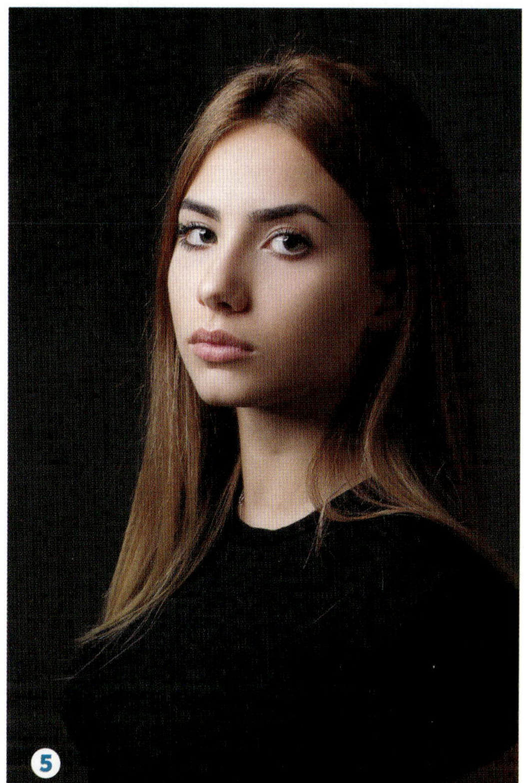

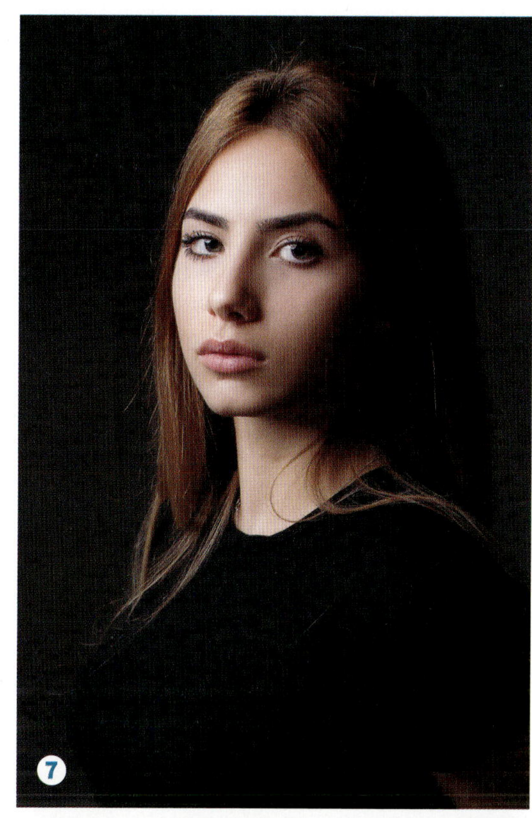

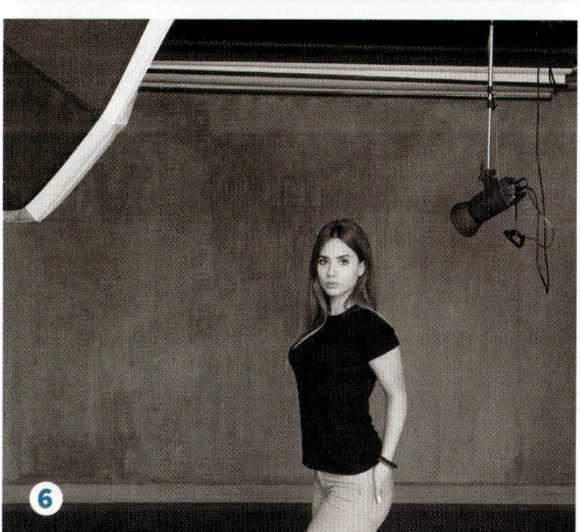

5 *Portrait shot using an octabox. The shadows are still well lit.*
   85mm | f10 | 1/160 sec. | ISO 100 | Model: Larissa

6 *The octabox setup.*

7 *Portrait shot using an octabox and a flag covered with black cotton polyester. Here, the shadows are much darker.*
   85mm | f10 | 1/160 sec. | ISO 100 | Model: Larissa

8 *The octabox/flag setup.*

In a Rental Studio

Into the studio, prepare your background, make your camera settings, set up your lights, and off you go! This is how easy it should be to work in a studio, but to get your workflow running smoothly, you need to get familiar with the studio and all its equipment.

Studio Space

The owner of a rental studio will usually show you around and give you an overview of the available gear. Most studios have a shooting space and various other areas such as a kitchen, bathroom, makeup room, lounge, and meeting room.

In a portrait photography situation, there are at least two people involved, namely you and your model.

Other shoots will require several models, and a makeup artist is often involved too. Before you begin you should talk through the planned shoot with everyone involved. Your model may need to change clothes, and a makeup artist will probably need to handle your model's hair and makeup. You can start work on your setup while your model is getting ready.

Flash Systems

Rental studios use flash systems from various manufacturers. Cheaper models differ from more expensive ones in one or more of the following ways:

- ▶ The number of flashes in a single sequence
- ▶ Consistency in the color of the light they produce
- ▶ Maximum/minimum flash duration
- ▶ Build quality
- ▶ Additional features

If you are planning a project with special requirements—for example, with lots of movement—you should make sure in advance that the studio you book has the right equipment with the necessary technical specifications.

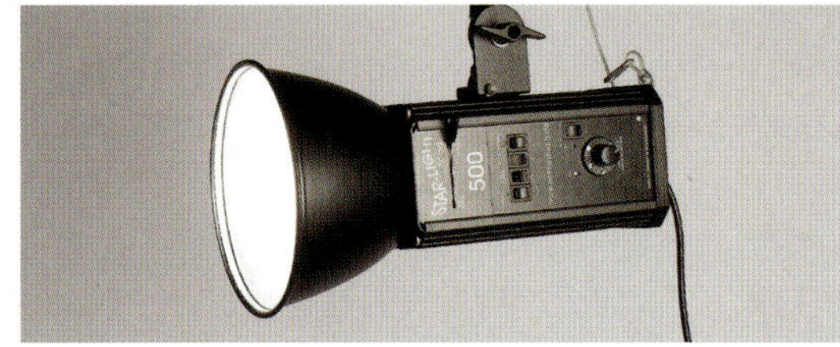

A compact flash head with a circular standard reflector

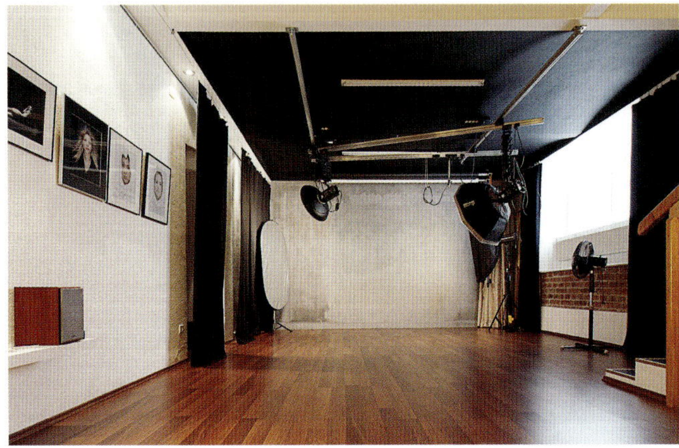
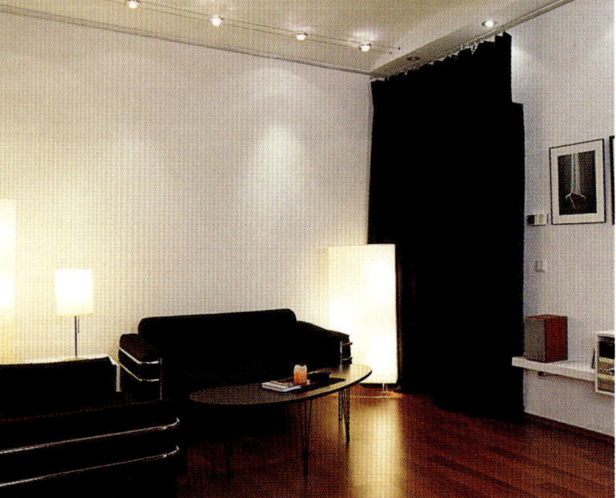
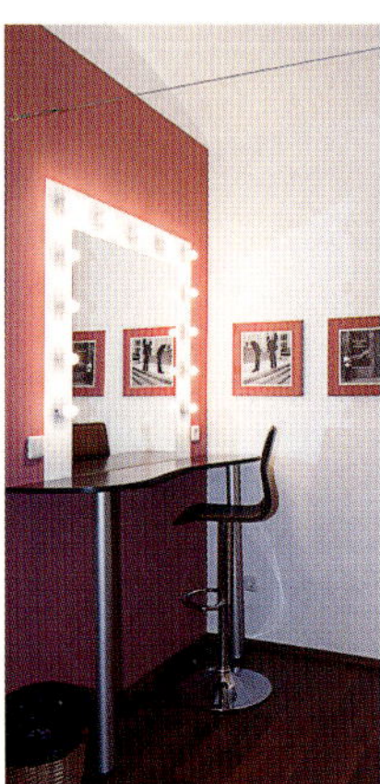
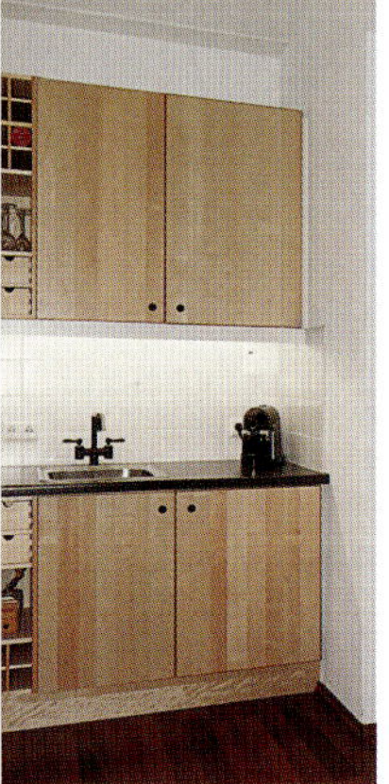

Elements of a typical rental studio (from left to right): shooting space, lounge, makeup area, kitchen

Attaching Light Shapers

The first hurdle you need to take when using studio flash is mounting and unmounting light shapers. Mounting systems vary from manufacturer to manufacturer.

The bayonet systems built in to Bowens, Multiblitz, and Elinchrom flash heads use either a button **(1)** or a slider **(2)** to unlock the bayonet. Once you have unlocked the bayonet, you have to rotate the reflector to remove it and, when you attach a different light shaper, you have to rotate it back to the original position to lock it in place. Some systems lock automatically, while others require you to move a slider or press a button manually.

Some systems (Hensel or Richter, for example) use a locking lever **(3)** on the flash head to affix light shapers. To remove a light shaper, you have to hold it tight while you move the lever. To attach a light shaper, you first have to move the lever to the unlocked position, attach your accessory and then re-lock the lever.

Note that light shapers can get quite hot during a session, so you should let them cool down before you remove them or swap them out.

Setting Up a Flash Head

The basic settings you can make on a flash head are similar, even if they come from different manufacturers.

4 Output: Usually adjusted by rotating a knob or pressing the arrow buttons.

5 Output display: The current setting is shown either by the position of the rotating knob or in a digital display.

6 Modeling lamp mode: This enables you to decide whether the modeling lamp works at full output or proportionally to the current flash output setting. You can of course turn the modeling lamp off completely.

7 Ready signal: This is where you turn the flash ready "beep" signal on or off.

8 Test button: Push this to fire a test flash.

9 Photocell switch: If you aren't using a radio transmitter to synchronize your flash heads, you can switch to photocell operation to trigger additional flash heads when your main flash fires.

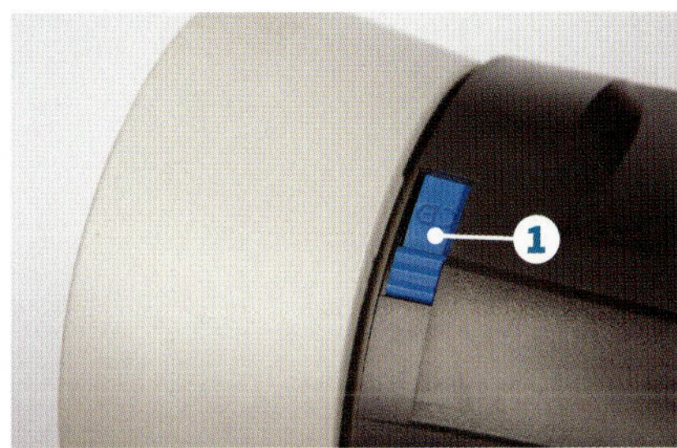

The Elinchrom bayonet locking mechanism

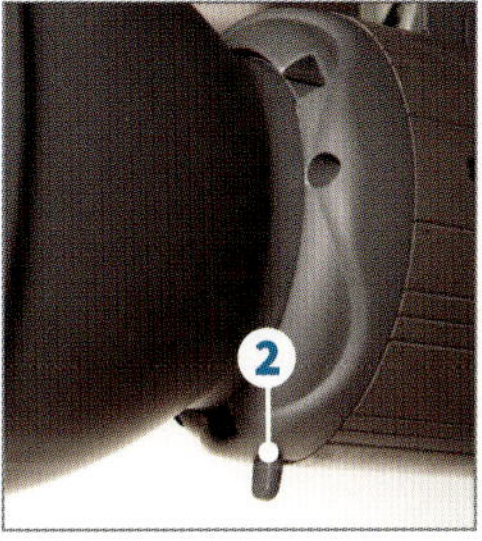

The Bowens bayonet

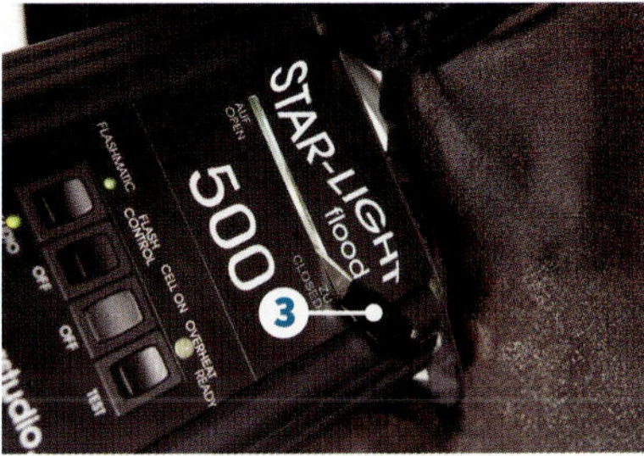

The locking lever on a Richter flash head

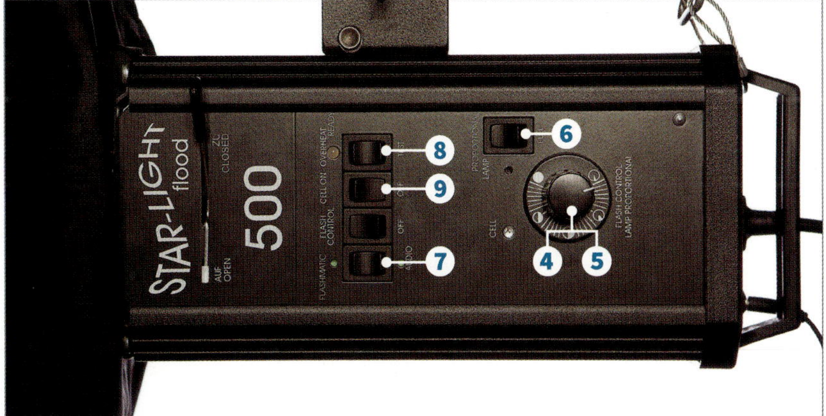

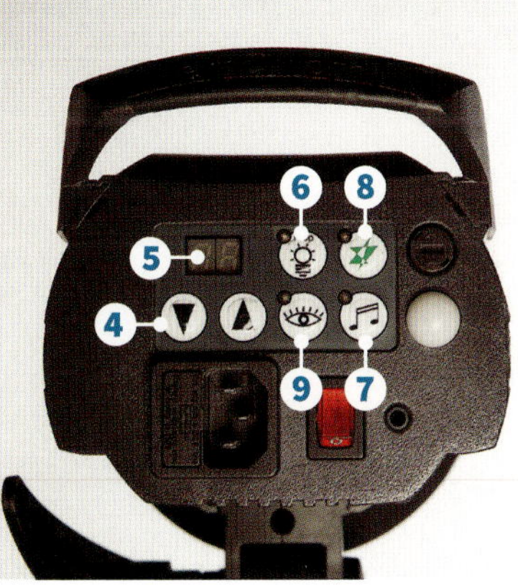

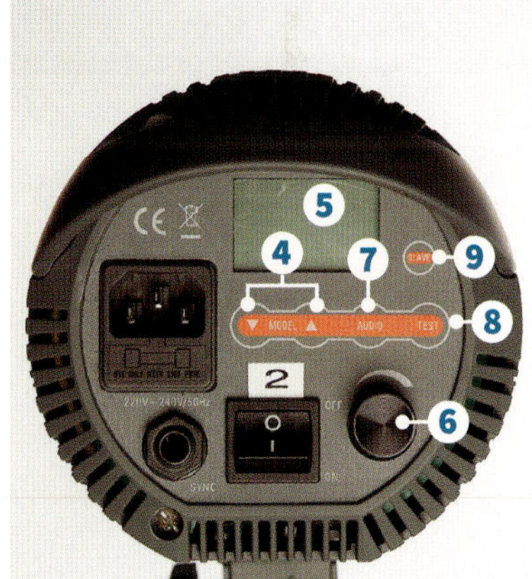

Flash heads from various manufacturers (from left to right): Richter, Elinchrom, and Walimex

Mounting Flash Heads

Flash heads are usually mounted either on a three-legged stand or using an overhead rail system. A ceiling rail makes it easier to position your flash and eliminates all those pesky cables and stands that otherwise clutter up the studio floor and present a multitude of trip hazards. The downside of a fixed ceiling rail is reduced studio height and a more limited area of operation.

Stands are available in a wide range of models and sizes, and are usually spring- or air-cushioned. To safely support your flash head, you need to select a stand that is not too tall and that has sufficiently wide leg spread.

Cushioned light stands brake the movement of the flash head when you lower it, which helps to avoid damage caused by sudden movements while you adjust your gear.

Stands with boom arms are used to position flash heads centrally but without the stand itself getting in the way.

Flash heads are mounted on a stand or an overhead pantograph using a spigot, which is fixed in place using one or two screws on the holder built in to the flash head. Flash heads mounted on an overhead rail system should always be secured using a safety cable in order to avoid accidents should a flash mount work loose for any reason.

As well as attaching it physically to its stand you also need to provide a flash head with power. In other words, you have to plug it in. If the model you are using doesn't have a built-in wireless trigger, you need to plug in an external trigger too. A wireless trigger serves to fire the flash automatically when you press the shutter-release button on the camera.

If you mount your flash heads on stands, make sure the cables lie flat on the floor and don't cause any trip hazards.

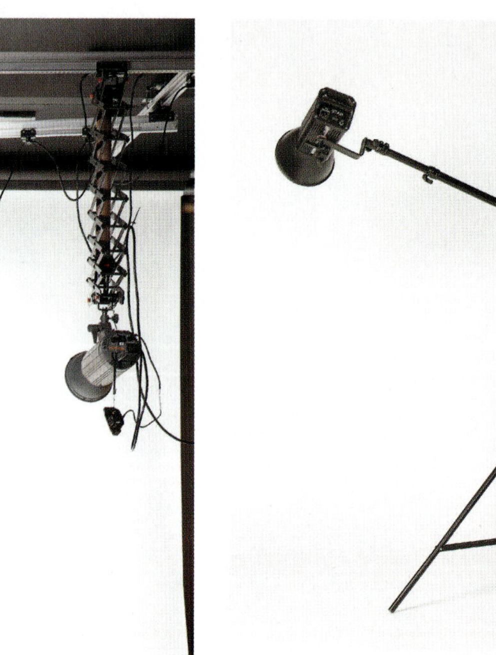

Using a ceiling rail system like the one shown here, you can adjust the height of your flash heads simply by moving them up or down by hand.

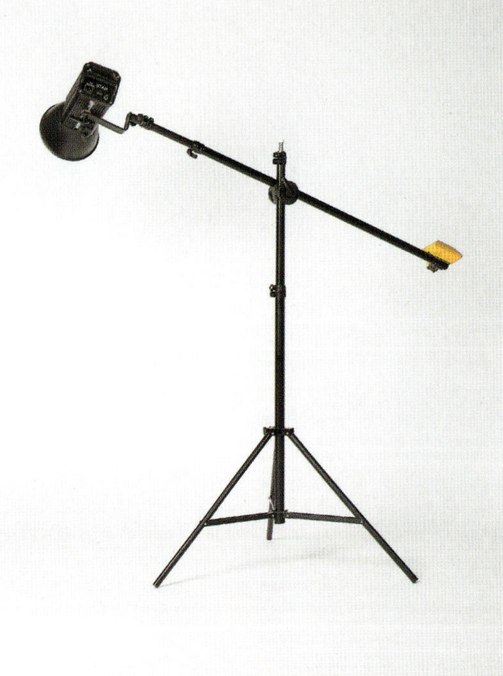

A boom stand with a compact flash head mounted on it. You can adjust the angle of the boom and, in the case of this telescopic model, its length too.

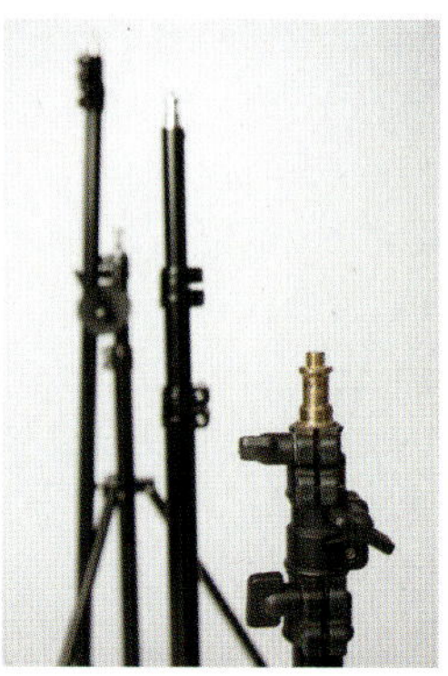

A spigot attached to a light stand

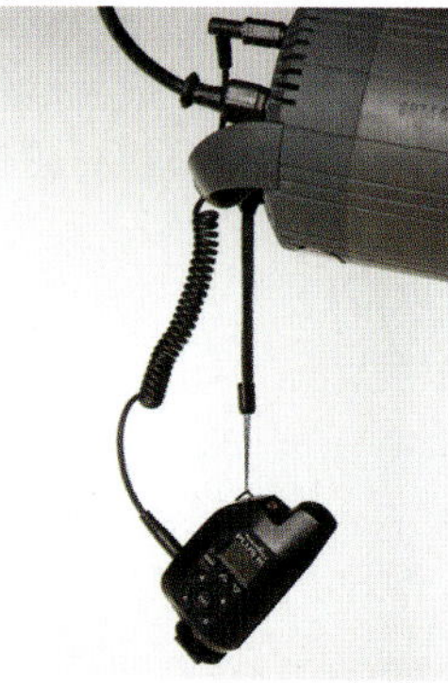

A wireless receiver attached to a flash head

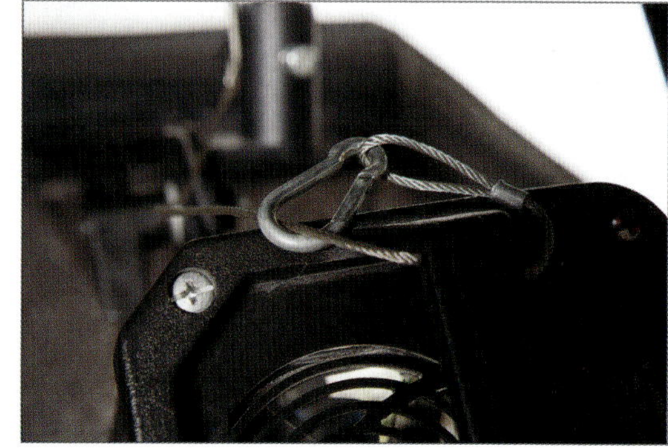

A safety cable used with a ceiling rail system

Infinity Coves and Other Backgrounds

A photo is built up of multiple layers, and the rearmost of these is the background. In the studio, you have multiple background options at your disposal. Every rental studio will have some kind of background system consisting of various colored background rolls made of paper or cloth that can be raised or lowered using chains attached to the rollers.

In theory, you only need to lower the background as far as the floor for a three-quarter-length portrait. However, the first few feet of a background are usually covered in footprints and other marks from previous users, so I recommend that you roll it out further to cover the floor too. This way, the angle between the studio wall and floor will be covered by a smooth transition known as an infinity cove. A good rule of thumb is to cover 10–15 feet of floor with the background material, although this will of course vary depending on the size of the studio and the scene you are shooting. Make sure that no people or gear weigh the background down while you roll it out.

A studio should provide at least black and white backgrounds. Depending on how you set up your lights, you can use a white background to produce background

colors that range from white to dark gray. A black background can be used to produce colors ranging between gray and black. You can alter the background color by placing colored gels over your background flash, too.

Background Brightness

For the photo sequence shown below I used a one-light setup. This consisted of a softbox placed directly in front of and slightly above the model at a distance of about 3 feet. I used a silver reflector below the model's

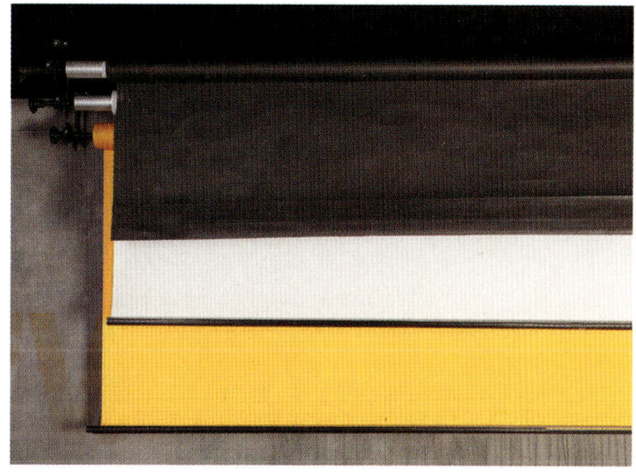

A basic studio background usually consists of rolls of paper in various colors

face to lighten the shadows (this setup is like the *Marlene Dietrich* setup described on page 86, but without the background light). In the image on the far left, the distance between the model and the background was about 10 feet. The brightness of the background depends on the relationship of the distances between the light source, the model, and the background. In the first image, this proportion was 1:3, and produced a dark gray background. I could have produced the same effect by reducing the flash output, placing the flash

A smooth transition between the wall and the floor produces an "infinity cove"

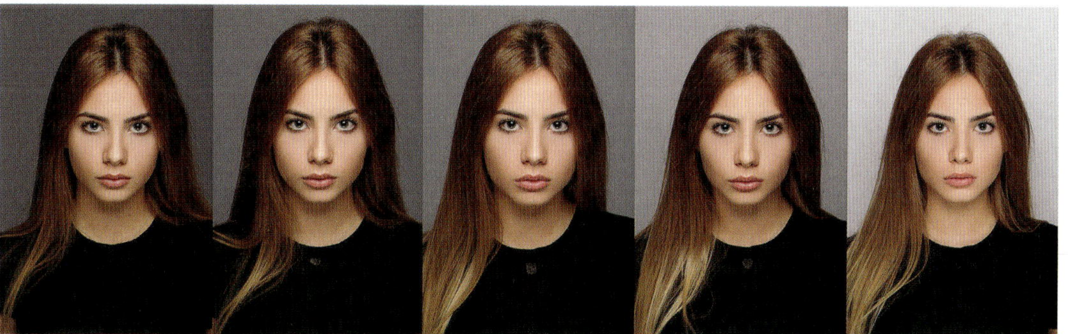

A sequence of images in which the distance between the model and the white background was reduced from shot to shot.

about 20 inches from the model and reducing the distance between her and the background to about 5 feet (i.e., the relationship between the distances remains at 1:3). However, the light illuminating the model's face would have been much softer due to the reduced distance between her and the softbox. For simplicity's sake, we won't consider the effect of this change on the illuminated surface itself. For each of the subsequent shots, the model took a step farther back and I moved the softbox and the reflector to match. The relationship between the distances changed with each step. In the center image, the model stood about 4½ feet from the background and the distance between the softbox and the model was about 3 feet, thus reducing the overall relationship to 1:1.5 and producing a mid-gray background. In the right-hand image, the model stood about 1½ feet in front of the white background, producing a light gray effect. As you can see, it is simple to control the brightness of a white background by altering the distance between it and your model.

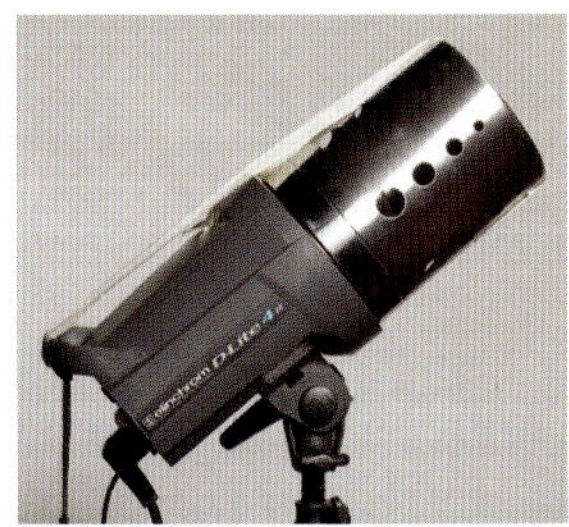

I produced this background texture by attaching a cutlery drainer to the flash.

The cutlery drainer happened to have the same diameter as the flash head, making it simple to tape it in place and use it as an improvised light shaper.

Background brightness also depends on any spill produced by the light shapers you use and on whether the light they produce actually reaches the background.

Another way to alter background brightness is by using a separate flash to illuminate it. This enables you to use shaped light beams and colored gels, or even to project patterns onto the background.

Background Texture

You can make a single-tone background more interesting by using light shapers to produce patterns and textures. You can produce gradients using various standard light shapers such as a standard reflector, a beauty dish, or barndoors. For example, you can use barndoors to create a square highlight or a subtle stripe in the background. Regular aluminum foil is a great tool for producing light textures, and all you have to do is crumple, fold, cut, or tear it and attach the result to a snoot. You can even use ordinary household utensils to create textures and patterns. A cutlery drainer (see below), a sieve, or a dish with cutouts make great impromptu

lighting accessories. The important thing to remember is that anything you attach to a studio flash has to be heat-resistant. Check regularly that your light shapers aren't overheating to avoid the risk of melting or even causing a fire.

Textiles and Other Materials

Using textiles is another great way to bring variety to your backgrounds. If you place curtain material in front of your flash and bounce the light it produces off of a white paper background, the effect is very similar to the soft backlight you get from a window.

Colored and textured textiles are ideal as backgrounds, and you can experiment with other materials too, especially when you are shooting close-ups. Try using gift wrap, wallpaper, or a survival blanket. If you use reflective material, you should position your flash so that the light isn't reflected directly off the background—otherwise you may end up with overbearing or glaring accents. In this kind of situation, it is usually best to place the flash to one side.

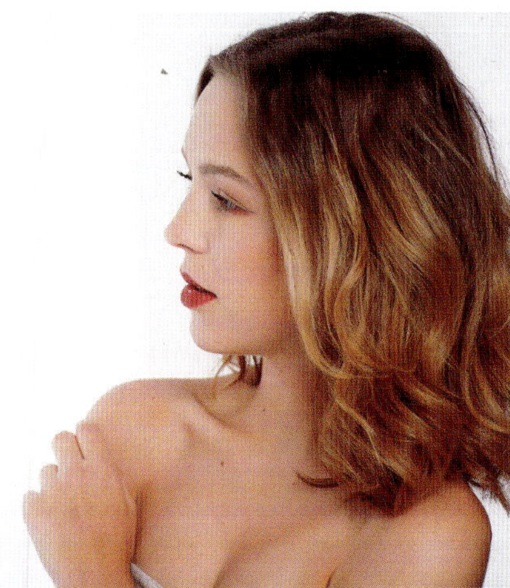

Background effect produced using a curtain and backlight.

Continuous Light vs. Flash

Studio photographers generally stick to using flash, but you can use continuous light or daylight, too.

Daylight

Some studios have windows that enable you to use daylight as a light source for your images. Direct sunlight through a window produces hard light, while a cloudy sky or indirect sunlight produces a softer effect. When I work in a daylight studio, I usually need only a minimal amount of additional gear to create perfectly lit portraits.

However, continuous light doesn't just refer to daylight. Construction site lamps and neon tubes emit continuous light, too. If you want to use these kinds of light sources there are some important differences between them and flash that you need to know about.

Brightness

The biggest difference between continuous light and flash is its brightness. Thanks to recent developments in LED technology, continuous lights are getting brighter all the time, but they still don't compare with the brightness produced by studio flash.

Dimmer light sources have their upsides and their downsides. For example, it is not easy to shoot with flash and a wide open aperture, especially if your flash is too bright or cannot be finely regulated. In such cases, you will have to use specialized accessories such as an ND (neutral density) filter, a diffuser, high-speed flash, or techniques such as bounce flash.

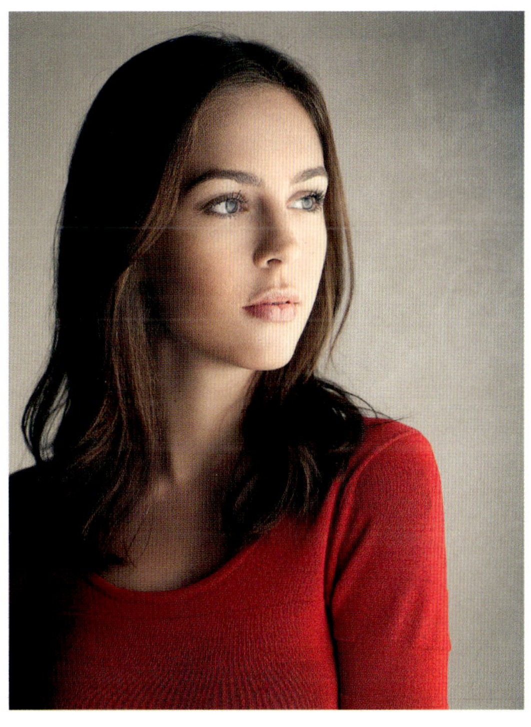

A studio portrait captured using natural light
85mm | f5 | 1/160 sec. | ISO 100 | Model: Lisa

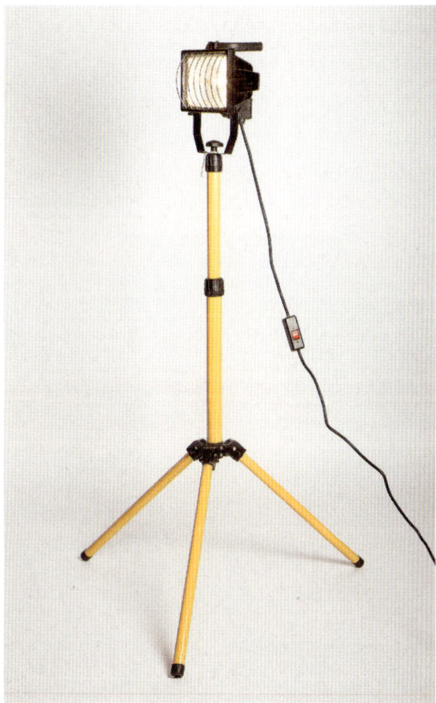

A construction site lamp is a continuous light source

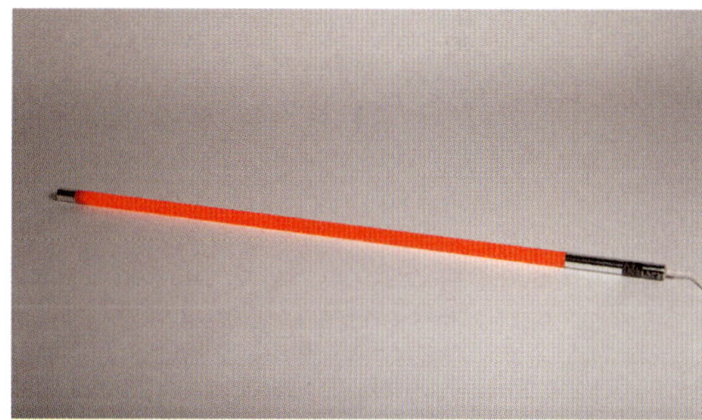

Thanks to the additional flash light, the light produced by this neon tube is hardly visible.

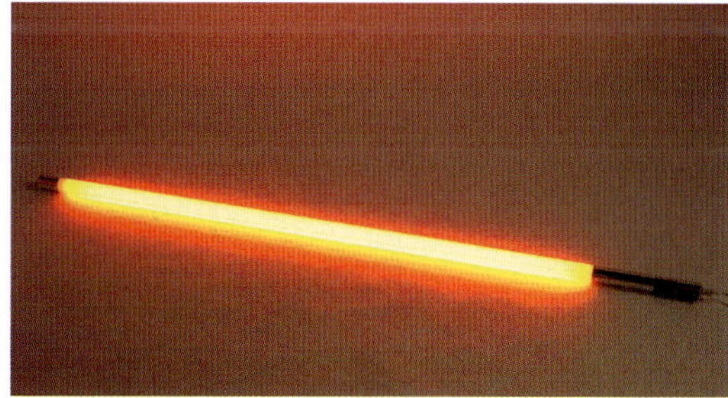

The light from the neon tube is much more effective without additional flash and when captured using a long exposure time of 2.5 sec. at ISO 200.

Shots that require a small aperture or large illuminated surfaces are often difficult to achieve using continuous light. In such cases, you can dial up the light sensitivity in you camera (i.e., the ISO value), although this always comes at the expense of increased noise in the resulting images. How much noise an ISO increase produces depends on the individual camera model you are using.

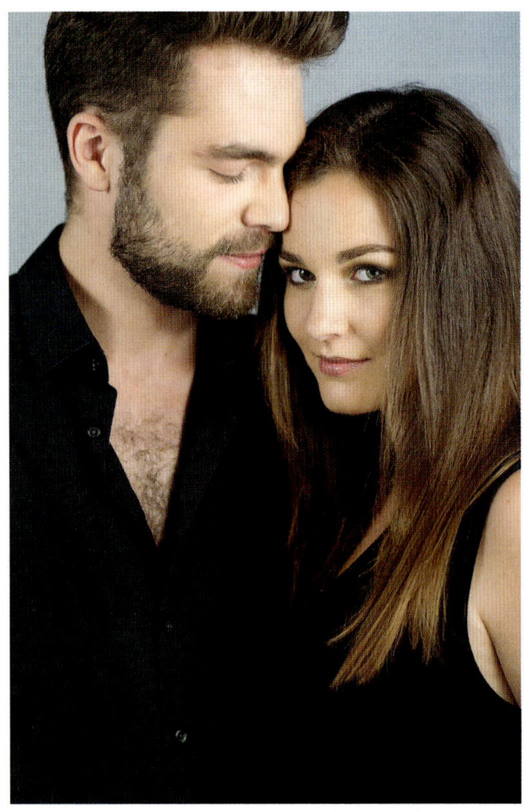

A portrait lit using an LED construction site lamp.

85 mm | f2.8 | 1/160 sec. | ISO 800 | Models: Manon and Rafael

Modeling Light

When you use continuous light, you can see how the light and shadows in your image are going to look before you shoot. In this case, the modeling light and the shooting light are the same thing. In contrast, if you are using flash that doesn't have a separate modeling light (such as an on-camera flash unit), you can't see in advance how your shot is going to turn out, and you have to use a trial-and-error approach to get the result you are looking for. Most studio flash heads have a separate modeling lamp that enables you to visualize your lighting before you shoot.

However, things get more complicated when you use multiple flash heads, as many modeling lights can't be regulated to match the flash output you set, thus making it difficult to get a reliable impression of your lighting effects. Problems can also occur if the modeling light is too weak or the modeling lights from different manufacturers have different strengths. If the modeling light is too weak, you won't be able to adequately judge the contrast between light and shadow in your image, and any ambient light will compound the problem.

The Effect of Ambient Light

Because flash is much brighter than ambient light, any ambient light in the studio won't have much of an effect on your final image. However, if you are shooting using a wide aperture or a long exposure time, or if you are aiming for high-contrast results, you will need to reduce the amount of ambient light as far as possible. It is always a good idea to attenuate any strong ambient light sources (such as direct sunlight), anyway. In contrast to when you use flash, every additional light source makes a difference to the overall look of an image shot using continuous light. Such situations can lead to unwanted mixed-light or multiple-shadow effects.

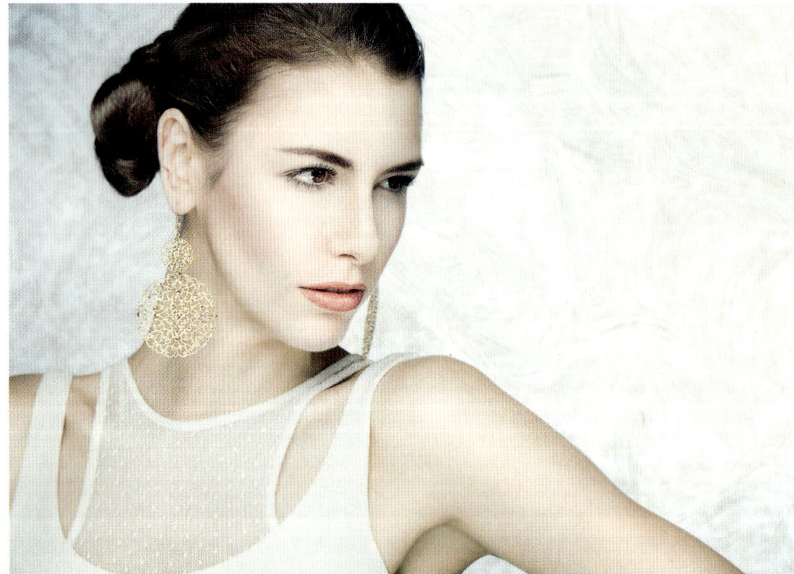

A portrait lit using a softbox and a silver reflector to lighten the shadows.

100 mm | f6.3 | 1/160 sec. | ISO 100 | Model: Elisa

Sequential Shooting

When shooting sequences of shots, the maximum number of shots you can capture depends on the recycle time of your flash. The recycle time increases with the output you set. Recycle times can be as long as two seconds for cheaper models. If you are shooting using continuous light, your sequential shooting speed will be limited only by your camera's capabilities.

Basic Gear

Now that you've gotten to know all those flash heads, light shapers, backgrounds, and other good things, you may be asking yourself if you really need so much gear to capture perfectly lit portraits. Let me assure you: Especially when you are starting out, you don't need to roll out a complete studio full of equipment to capture simple, natural-looking portraits. In fact, all you really need is a single flash head, some kind of light shaper, and a reflector. To start off, I recommend you use a standard reflector with a honeycomb grid, a softbox, and a translucent umbrella.

Minimum Studio Setup

- ▶ 1 flash head (standard reflector with a honeycomb grid)
- ▶ 1 softbox
- ▶ 1 translucent umbrella
- ▶ 1 light stand
- ▶ 1 silver reflector (approx. 30" × 40")
- ▶ 1 reflector holder

Once you have learned how to capture great results with a basic setup, you can start using additional flash heads. Using a second flash, you can add accents or light the background separately. A reflector should be part of your basic kit, whether for lightening shadows or as a second source of light. You need light shapers to provide different lighting moods, so ideally you will have a softbox, a standard reflector with a honeycomb grid, a beauty dish, and perhaps also reflective and translucent umbrellas, too. Other bits and pieces such as light stands, wireless triggers, and reflector holders round out a good setup.

A Basic Set of Studio Gear

- ▶ 2 flash heads (a standard reflector with a honeycomb grid and an additional reflector or translucent umbrella)
- ▶ 1 softbox
- ▶ 1 beauty dish
- ▶ 2 light stands
- ▶ 1 silver reflector (approx. 30" × 40")

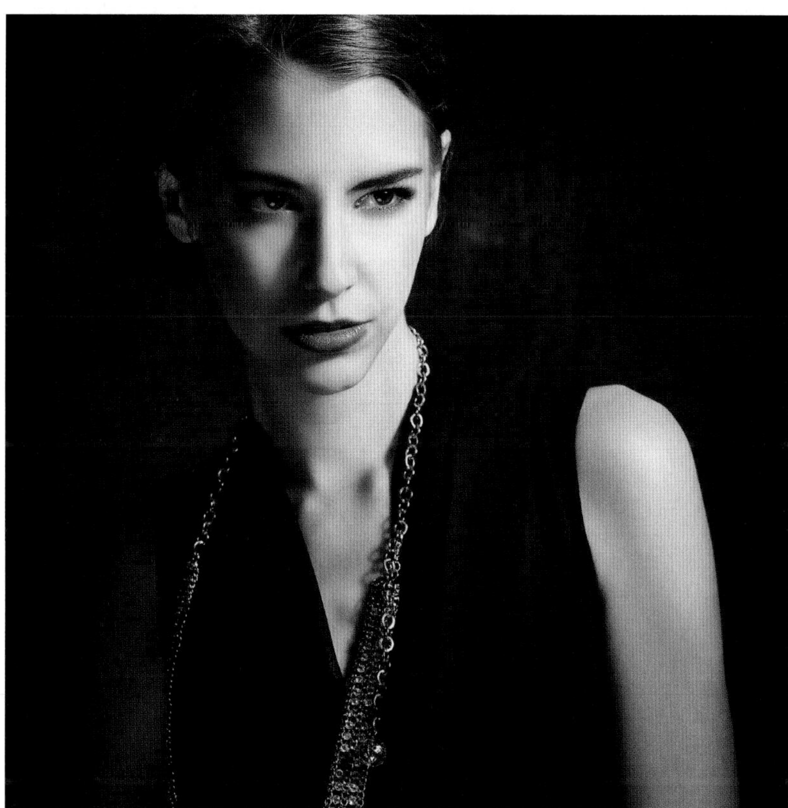

A portrait captured using a beauty dish and a fill light.

70mm | f8 | 1/160 sec. | ISO 100 | Model: Elisa

Studio Light Metering

Even though most of today's cameras have a built-in light meter and automatic (or semi-automatic) program modes that deliver respectable results, working in a studio still requires a different approach. In the studio, you will be shooting in manual mode, and the light that you need to meter isn't actually present at the appropriate moment (i.e., before you press the shutter button and the flash fires). In other words, you need to give the camera a helping hand. To make the appropriate flash settings to capture correctly lit images in the studio you need to use a handheld light meter.

When using a handheld light meter, you begin by selecting the ISO value that you have set in your camera **(1)**. You can then set the exposure time (once again, as set in the camera) **(2)**. To start a light measurement, press the measuring button **(3)**. The light meter will then use your other settings to calculate the appropriate working aperture **(4)**.

There are two basic approaches to calculating a working aperture, either by metering the light emitted by the flash or the light reflected by the subject. This book concentrates on the former method, which uses a white diffusing hemisphere **(5)** to measure the incident light at an angle of around 180 degrees. If you want to meter the light reflected by the subject, you need to shift the hemisphere to the side to reveal the lens beneath. Most handheld light meters are multi-purpose and, alongside flash exposures, enable you to meter in various other modes too—for example, for continuous light.

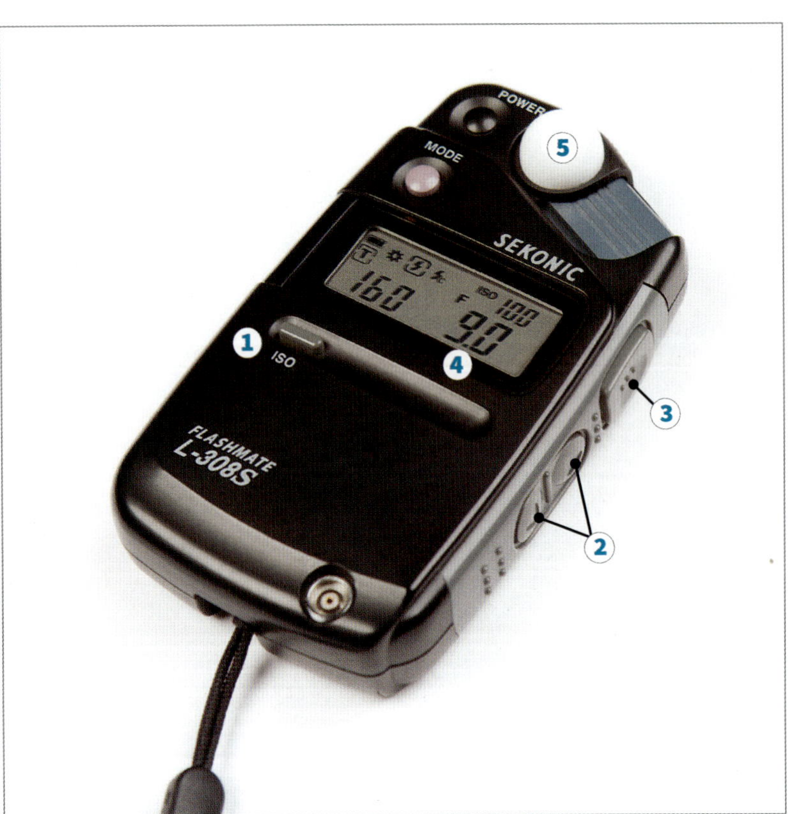

A handheld light meter

ISO and Exposure Time Values

Studio exposure times are usually somewhere between 1/125 and 1/250 sec. To prevent unwanted image noise, it is best to set your studio ISO value as low as possible. ISO 100 is always a good place to start.

Light Metering

Once you have prepared your background and set up your flash heads and any light shapers you want to use, it is time to make the exposure settings in your camera and your flash heads. To begin, set your camera to M (manual) mode and select the aperture, exposure time, and ISO values listed in each setup in the book. Set white balance to **Flash** mode. You then need to mount your flash trigger on your camera's hot shoe and switch it on. Now flick the power switch on your flash head and, if necessary, its wireless receiver.

If you don't want to follow the instructions in the individual setups, see the *Calculating Exposure Settings* section on the next page for details on how to make settings for your particular situation.

For shots that use a single light source, place the configured light meter where you want to meter the brightness of the incoming flash light—for example, at around head height close to your subject. Point the white hemisphere at your flash, press the measuring button on the light meter and then press the *Test* button on your camera's flash trigger. The flash will fire and the light meter will display the appropriate working aperture. If the aperture setting the light meter displays is not the one you want, you will need to adjust your flash output and try again.

If you are using multiple light sources, you can either switch on the individual flash heads separately and meter them one at a time, or simply cover the flash head(s) you aren't metering. This way, you can produce various effects—for example, a highlight that is deliberately dimmer than your main light.

Metering for the Background

When you are metering for your background, you should switch all your light sources on, as they all have an effect on background brightness. To meter for the background, hold the light meter close to your background and point its diffuser toward the camera before pressing the measuring button and firing a test flash.

If you don't end up with the aperture value you are looking for, you can either adjust the output on your background flash and/or alter the distance between your model and the background.

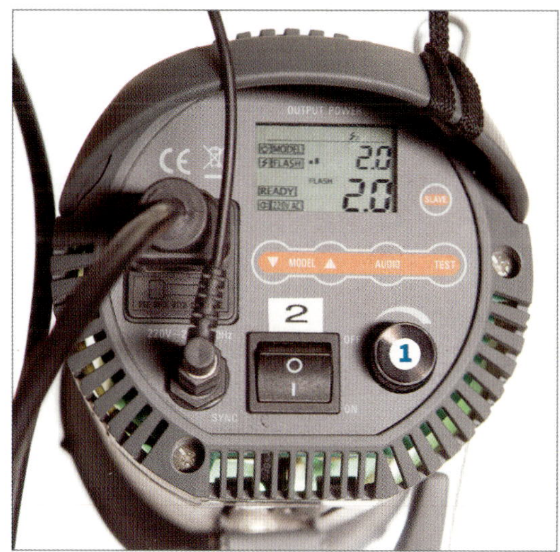

Setting flash output using a rotating dial. **(1)**

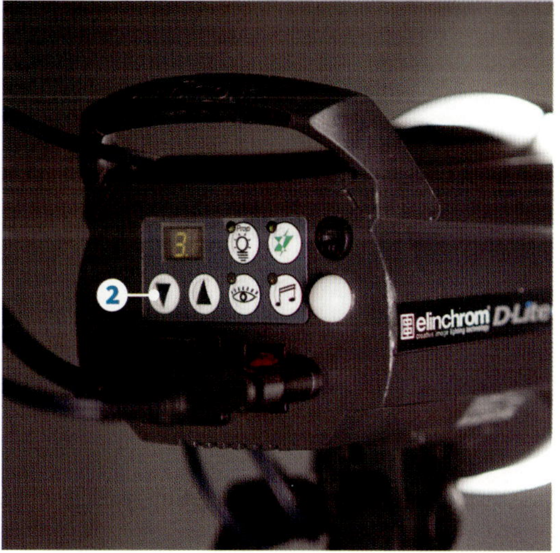

Setting flash output using up/down buttons. **(2)**

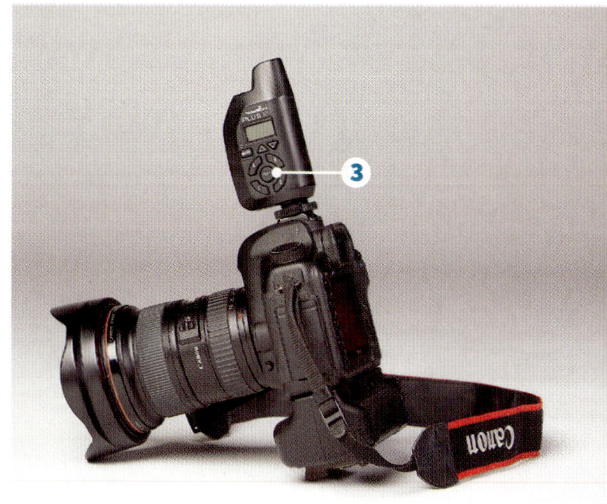

*An SLR camera with a wireless trigger mounted on its hot shoe. The **Test** button **(3)** is clearly visible.*

Calculating Exposure Settings

Because working in a studio enables you to set up consistent, unchanging lighting conditions, the actual exposure settings begin with the camera.

1. Setting the ISO Value

A studio flash system will usually provide more than enough light so, in oder to avoid producing image noise, you should set your camera's ISO to the lowest available value.

2. Setting the Exposure Time

If you are not shooting a high-speed sequence or making a long exposure, the exposure time you use will depend on the flash sync speed of the flash system you are using. This is the shortest exposure time at which the camera and the flash system can effectively synchronize, and is limited by the period of time during which the travel of the camera's shutter curtains leaves the image sensor completely uncovered. If you select an exposure time that is too short, you will end up with a black stripe at the edge of your image that increases in size every time you further reduce the exposure time. If you continue to reduce the exposure time, at some point the resulting image will turn out completely black.

The flash sync speed for most SLR (single-lens reflex) cameras is between 1/125 and 1/250 sec. To stay on the

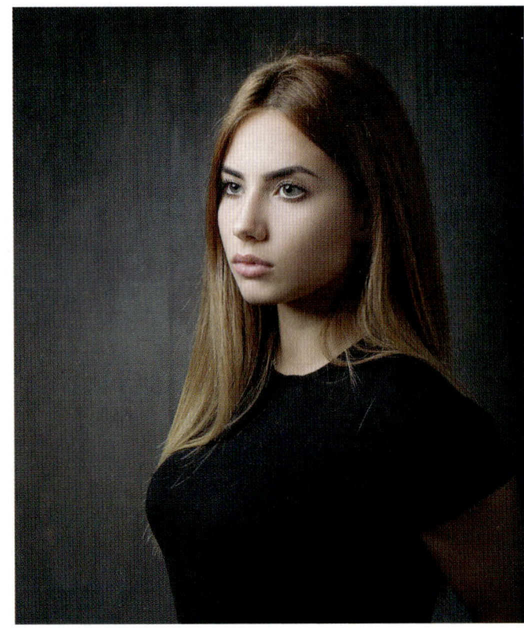

Flash sync speed 1/160 sec., exposure time set to 1/200 sec. The result is a dark, narrow stripe on the right.

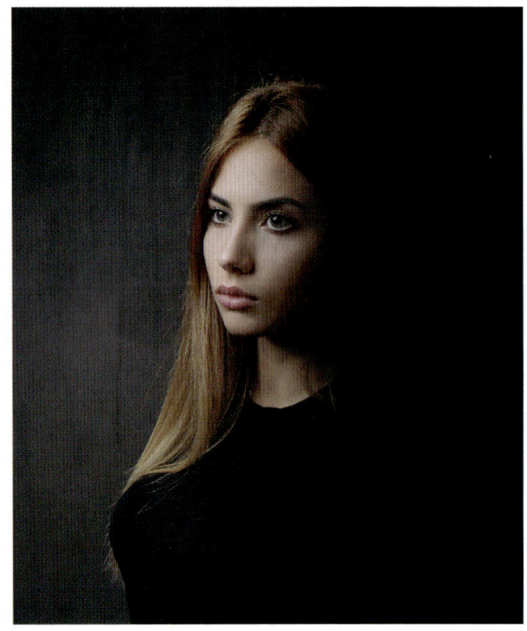

Flash sync speed 1/160 sec., exposure time set to 1/320 sec. The result is a major dark stripe on the right.

Flash sync speed 1/160 sec., exposure time set to 1/500 sec. The result is a broad, dark block on the right and an image that is almost completely black.

safe side, select either 1/125 sec. or the value specified by your camera's manufacturer.

If you are using a flash system designed for high-speed shooting, you can use shorter exposure times. This is because the flash sync speed is no longer the critical factor. Today's high-speed systems allow exposure times of 1/8000 sec. or even shorter. The actual values you can use will be listed in the flash system's user manual.

3. Selecting the Aperture

The aperture you set depends largely on the overall effect you are looking for in your image. If you want shallow depth of field, select a wide aperture.

The widest available aperture depends on the lens you are using, but will usually be somewhere between f1.2 and f4. For the increased depth of field that is usual in fashion shoots, you should select an aperture between f8 and f13.

4. Setting Flash Output

Once you have made all the required settings in your camera, the only setting left is the flash output.

You can either use a light meter to determine which values to use for each flash head (see pages 24–25 for more details on how) or you can make test shots and use the results you can see on the camera monitor to tweak your flash settings accordingly.

For example, if you have set your camera to f8, 1/60 sec., and ISO 100, you should set the main light to a value that gives you an aperture value of f8 when metered close to your model's face. Oriented around this value, you can then set up your other flashes according to your own specific needs. For example, If you want the background to appear 1 f-stop darker, set the aperture to f5.6.

If you take the test shot route, make sure that your camera's monitor is set up to match the results you view on your computer. If the camera monitor setting is too dark, you will end up with images that appear too bright when you view them on your computer.

The camera's histogram display is usually a reliable tool for judging the distribution of bright and dark tones within the frame and is a great aid to setting exposure values in tricky situations.

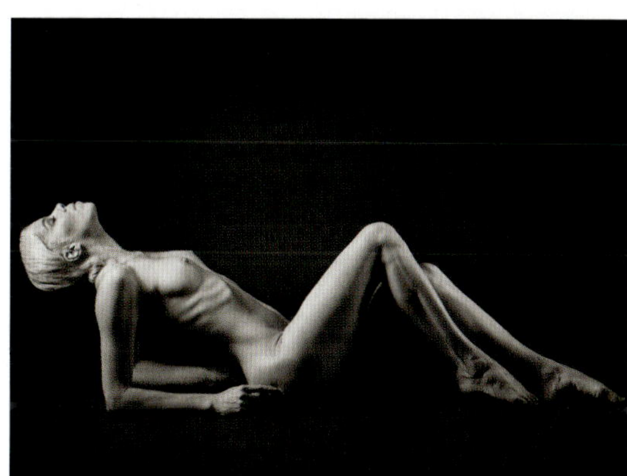

An image made up of mostly dark tones. The histogram shows a corresponding bunching of tonal values toward the left.

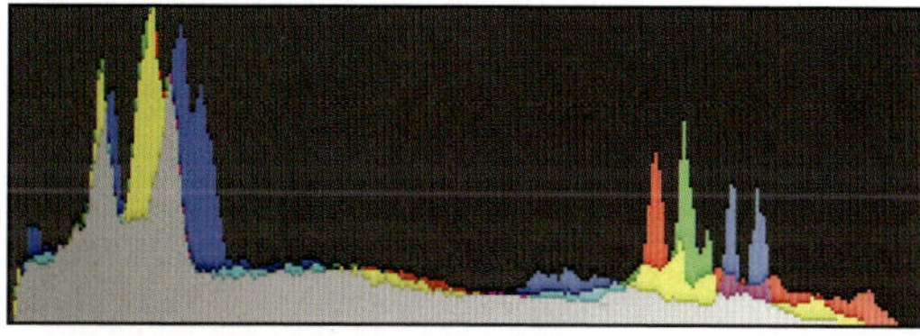

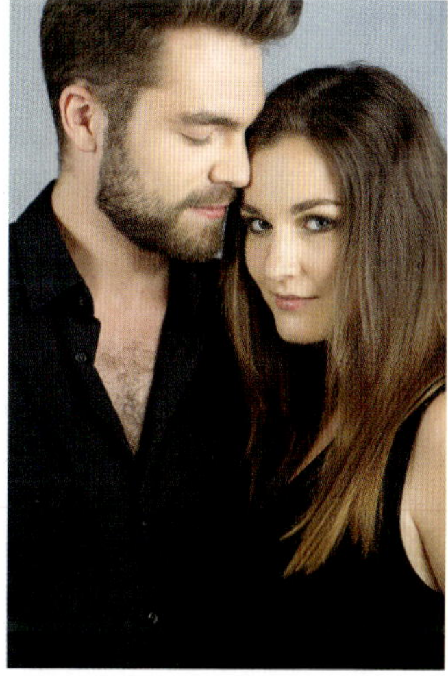

Balanced distribution of tonal values. The histogram registers values across the entire spectrum from left to right. The dark clothes produce the peaks at the dark end of the spectrum, while the light background and the models' skin produce the peaks at the light end.

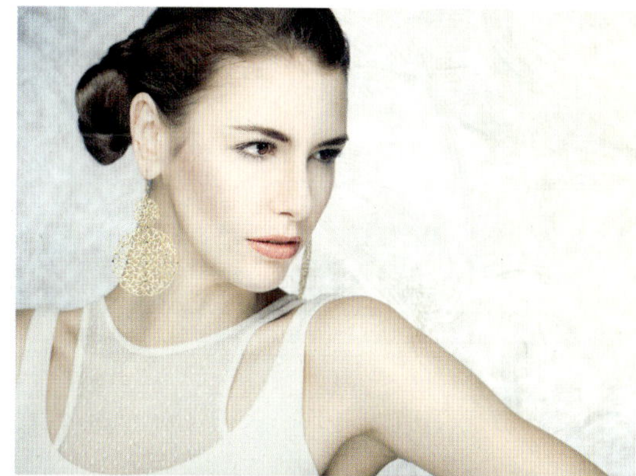

An image made up of mostly bright tonal values. The histogram shows a corresponding bunching of values toward the right.

Classic
Studio Portraits

Classic Studio Portraits

In the early days of photography, portraits was one of the most important genres. The trick in portrait photography is to produce an image that is as attractive as possible. It doesn't matter whether you are taking photos for a job application, a distinctive character portrait, or a beauty shot—the most important factors in a successful image are the emotions and the mood conveyed by the person it shows. Perfect lighting, ideal camera settings, and a clever camera angle won't help you at all if your model is tired, in a bad mood, or just plain tense. It is essential to establish a rapport right from the first handshake. Take time to chat with your model, build up trust, and create a relaxed atmosphere. While you are getting to know your model, you can get an idea of their particular skills and perhaps any issues that will limit your choice of poses, lighting setups, and camera angles.

The Best Side

Unless you are planning a head-on shot, one side of your model's face will receive more exposure than the other. As most humans don't have completely symmetrical faces, you should select your model's "best side" for your shoot. The easiest way to find out which side this is, is to ask the person concerned. Most people know which is their better side or how to hide their own perceived imperfections.

Pay attention to asymmetries. If one of your model's eyes is noticeably smaller than the other, you can compensate by making sure that this side faces the camera. This way, the larger eye is farther away from the camera and thus appears slightly smaller.

Some people have an asymmetrical hairline or lips, hair that falls asymmetrically, or an asymmetrical nose. If, for example, your model has an asymmetrical nose, the "best" side will be the one the nose points toward, and you should make sure that your main light comes from that side too.

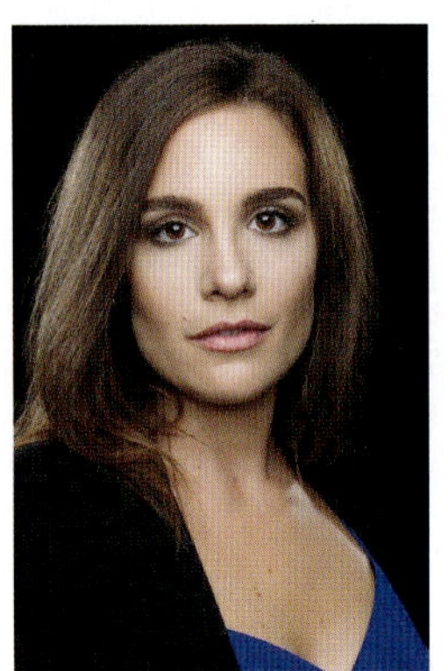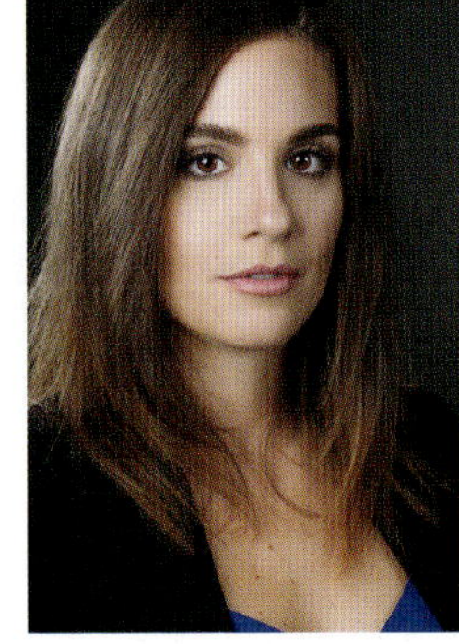

In the head-on shot on the left, you can clearly see that the model's right eye (on the left in the image) is slightly smaller than her left eye. In the right-hand image, this effect is balanced out by the model turning her head slightly to the left.

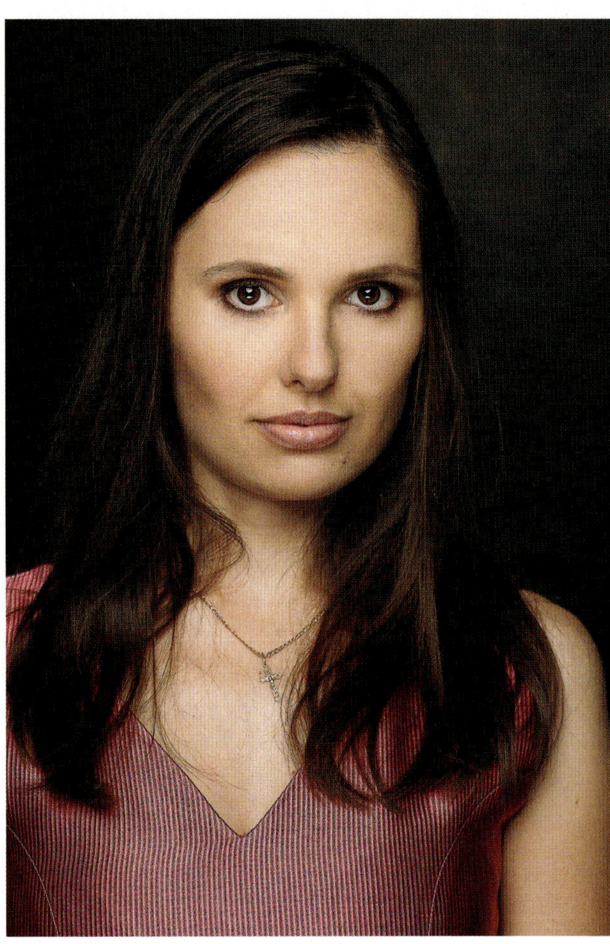

A classic studio portrait captured using a softbox and a reflector.

85mm | f8 | 1/160 sec. | ISO 100 | Model: Tanja

Narrow and Broad Lighting

The way you position your lights can help to mask unwanted details. We'll start by looking at short ("narrow") and long ("broad") lighting. Broad lighting illuminates the side of the subject's face that faces toward the camera, which makes the face appear broader. Narrow lighting illuminates the side of the face that faces away from the camera, leaving the side facing the camera in shadow and making it appear narrower. If you want to make someone's face appear slimmer than it really is, narrow lighting is the way to go.

Sculpting with Shadows

Shadows are a photographer's principle modeling aid. Lateral light accentuates vertical details, while light placed above the subject makes horizontal details appear more distinctive. For example, a light placed above and to the front of your model will accentuate their facial expression and accent the contours of their cheekbones.

Reducing shadows can conceal unwanted details too. For example, the soft, flat light produced by an octabox placed directly in front of your model (either as a main light or a fill light) can help to disguise creases or other skin imperfections.

Choice of Lens

Your choice of lens is another important factor in the look of the resulting image. The distortion produced by a wide-angle lens can quickly turn a small nose into one that appears much larger. If you want your model's nose to appear smaller than it really is, you need to use a short telephoto lens (i.e., 85mm and up for a full-frame camera). Conversely, you can make a small nose appear larger by selecting a lens with a focal length that is equal to or shorter than standard (i.e., 50mm or less).

Camera Position

Altering the camera position is another way to change the appearance of a face. Details that are closer to the camera always appear larger than those that are farther away. You can use this optical effect to disguise potential anatomical imperfections. Long noses appear shorter if captured from a low camera position, just as a short nose appears longer if photographed from above. You can increase this effect by asking your model to tip their head up or down.

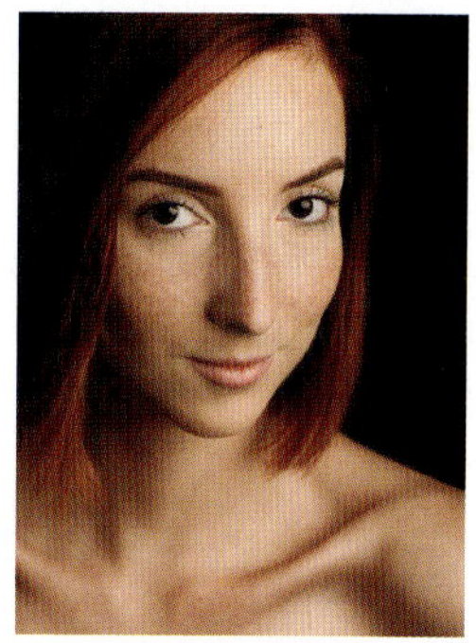
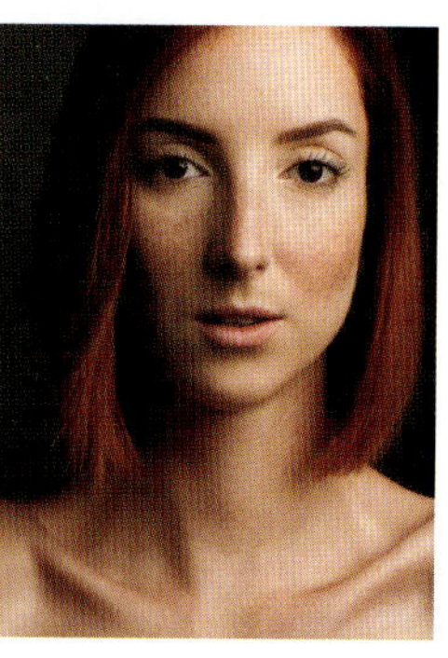

The effect of altering the camera position. The image on the left was captured from a raised position, making the model's nose appear longer. The image on the right was captured head-on, making the model's nose appear shorter.

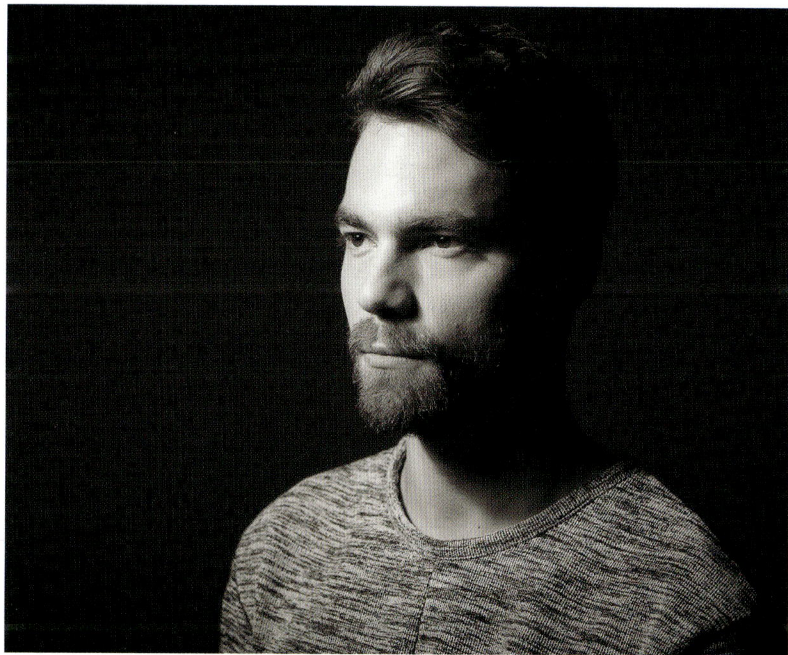

In this example of narrow lighting, the side of the model's face that faces away from the camera is illuminated.

Two Flashes for Most Situations

A two-flash setup is ideal if you want to capture a classic portrait—for example for a job application. The simplest variation on this theme involves using an octabox as your main light and a translucent umbrella as a fill light. This setup is guaranteed to give you a well-lit image but provides plenty of options for manipulating light and shadow within the frame.

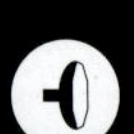 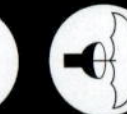

EFFORT INVOLVED

Low

SUITABLE FOR

All kinds of portraits

THE LOOK

Classic, natural-looking portrait

Well-lit shadows

Accented face

EQUIPMENT

1× 31.5" octabox

1× translucent umbrella

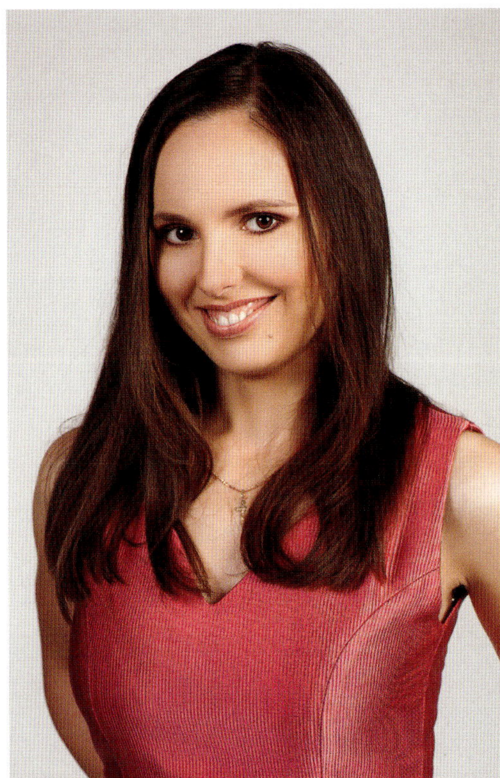

85mm | f8 | 1/160 sec. | ISO 100 | Model: Tanja

HOW IT WORKS

Marlene Dietrich knew that high, frontal light produces a flattering effect, and she often deliberately tilted her face toward the light to make the most of this effect. This setup is also known as Marlene Dietrich lighting. The setup accentuates the eyes, cheekbones, and shape of the face. The upper eyelid shadows and the lighter tone in the lower portion of the eyes underscores the shine of the eyes. The neck shadow is relatively broad and, with the hair, forms a frame around the face. The reflector ensures that the eye, nose, and neck shadows aren't too dark to produce a subtle overall feel.

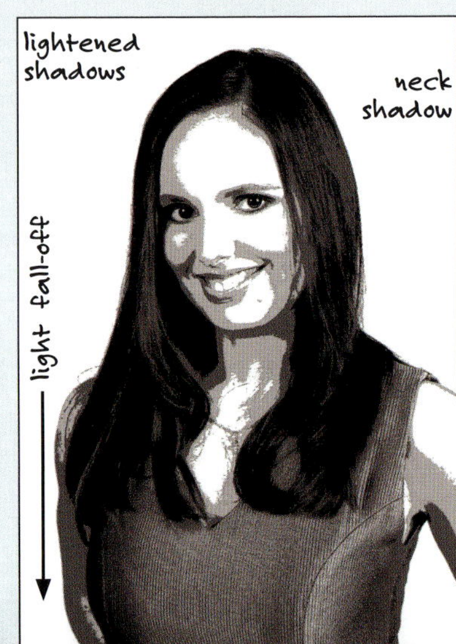

THE SETUP

1. Place the octabox main light **(1)** about 5 feet to the front right of your model at an angle of about 30 degrees. Set it up so that the nose shadow doesn't touch your model's upper lip and the neck shadow is clearly visible.

2. Place the translucent umbrella **(2)** on the left to mirror the position of the main light at the same distance form your model.

The V-shaped "clamshell" setup is clearly visible. The model is standing about 5 feet from the white paper background. The broad, soft beam produced by the translucent umbrella also provides plenty of spill, giving the background an even, light gray tone.

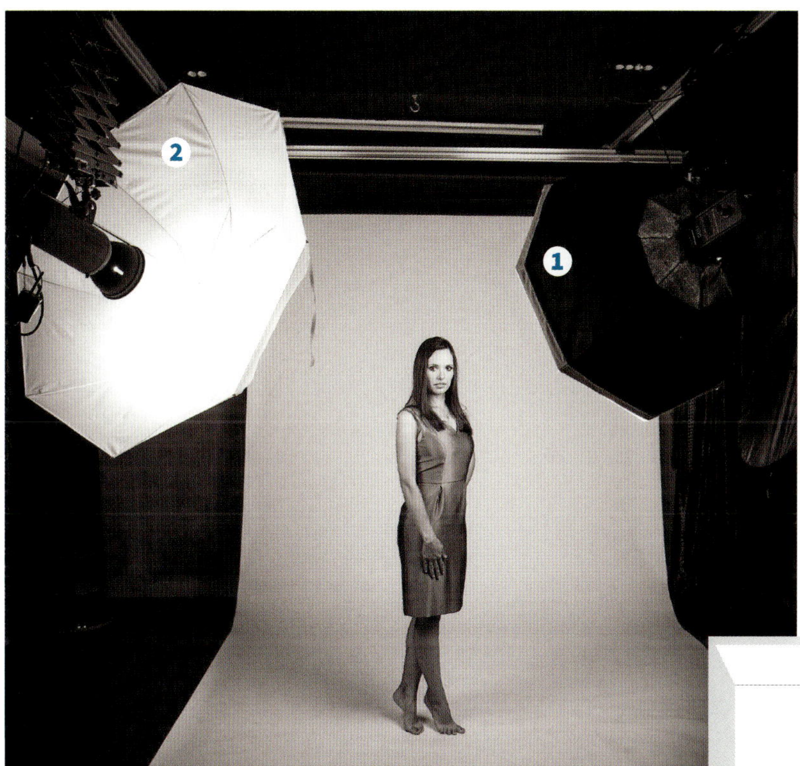

> *"Pay close attention to the facial shadows and always bear your model's best side in mind."*

Variations

An octabox as a main light and a translucent umbrella as a fill light make it easy to change the pose from 45 degrees to the left through head-on to 45 degrees to the right. If your model faces the octabox, the result is broad lighting, whereas the effect is more like a classic portrait if she faces directly toward the camera (see the image below). If she faces the fill light, the result is a narrow lighting effect. Remember though, that not every head posture works for every model.

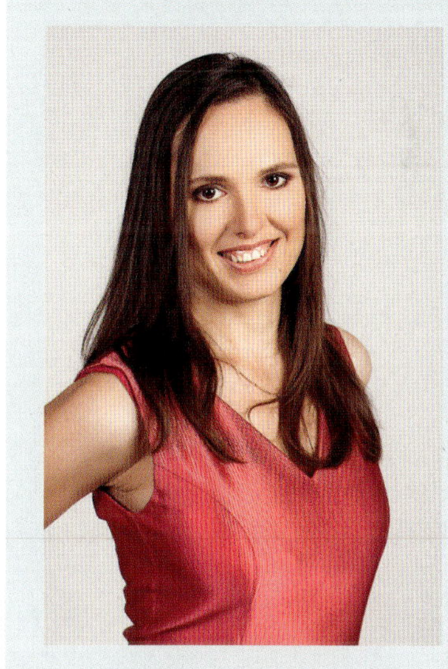

Extreme Soft Light

Soft light flatters the facial features, reduces pores and creases, and produces soft shadows. The main objective of this classic portrait setup, captured using a small octabox, is to draw attention to the model's radiant expression. Additionally, the octabox produces pleasing, round catchlights in her eyes.

EFFORT INVOLVED

Low

SUITABLE FOR

Close-up to three-quarter-length portraits

THE LOOK

Soft portrait with reduced contrast
Skin pores and creases hardly visible

EQUIPMENT

1 × 31.5" octabox

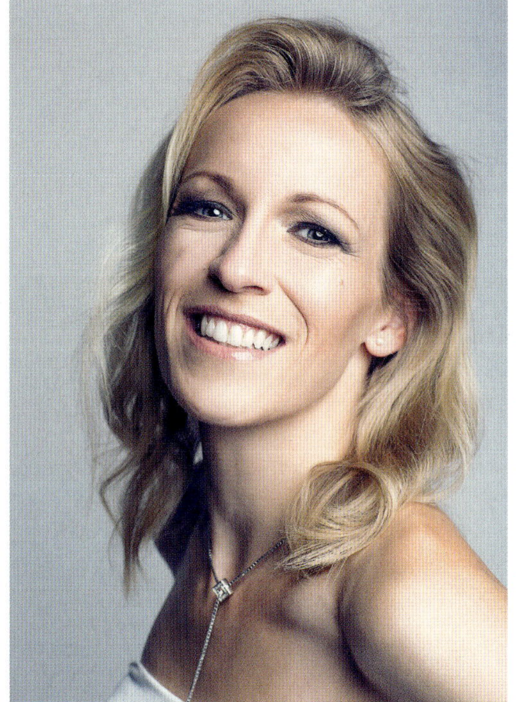

85mm | f7.1 | 1/160 sec. | ISO 100 | Model: Martina

HOW IT WORKS

The classic position of the octabox produces natural-looking light. Soft light softens the edges of the shadows for a friendly look. The round catchlights in the subject's eyes are another particularly pleasing feature. The octabox produces sufficient light to make the eyes really glow, and the diagonal, downward-pointing shadows add texture to the face. The offset position of the main flash produces a light-to-dark gradient in the background that is directly opposed to the light illuminating the subject. The background is lighter on the left than the right, whereas the subject is more brightly lit on the right than on the left. This helps to distinguish the subject clearly from the background.

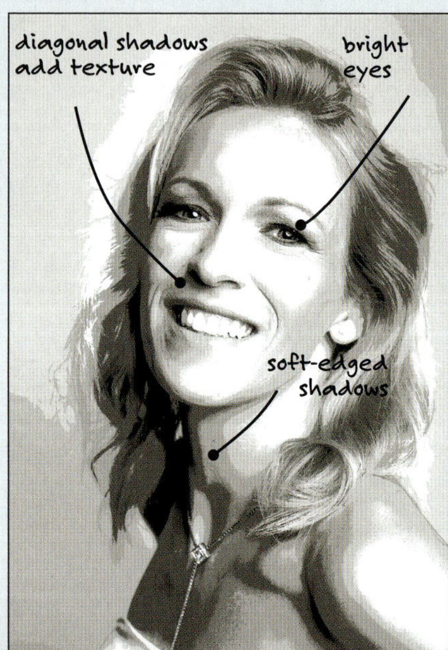

THE SETUP

1. Position your model about 3 feet from the white paper background.

2. Place the small octabox **(1)** about 3 feet to the front right of your model in a raised position and at an angle of about 30 degrees.

3. Adjust the height of the octabox so that the neck shadow is clearly visible and the nose shadow doesn't quite touch your model's upper lip.

4. Pay attention to the light gradient in the background. You can alter how it looks by rotating the the flash head toward or away from the background. Remember to keep an eye on how this alters the lighting on your model's face while you work.

Don't forget that you can alter the brightness of the background by altering the distance between it and your model. If you do take this route, be sure to keep the distance between the octabox and your model the same.

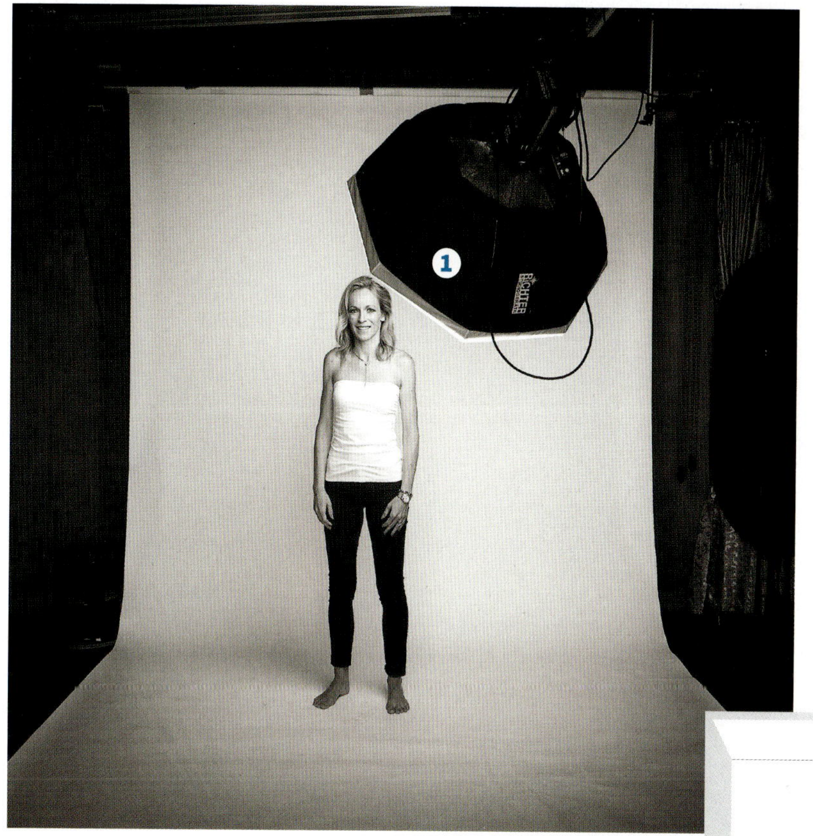

Octaboxes: Sizes and Subject Distance

How does the soft light produced by an octabox change when you alter the subject distance or the size of the light source? Quite simply, the larger an octabox is and the closer you place it to your model, the softer the resulting light will be. The breadth of the light an octabox emits is also reduced the closer you place it to your subject. If you want to illuminate a full-length portrait using soft light, you need to use a very large octabox in order to illuminate the model's entire body while keeping the light at an appropriate distance.

"The closer an octabox is to the subject, the softer the resulting light will be. This reduces the visibility of skin pores and creases."

Lighter Shadows on the Fly

If you want to keep your effort to a minimum but still retain control over the differences in light and dark from side to side in your shot, you can always use a reflector instead of a second light. In this setup, the main light is a large octabox and we used a 30"×40" reflector to lighten the shadows. This kind of reflector is large enough for use in full-length portraits too.

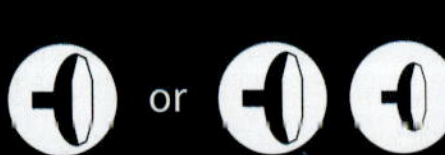

EFFORT INVOLVED

Low

SUITABLE FOR

All kinds of portraits

THE LOOK

Classic soft portrait with plenty of options for controlling light and shadow

EQUIPMENT

1× 47" octabox

1× 30"×40" silver reflector, or 1× 31.5" octabox

36

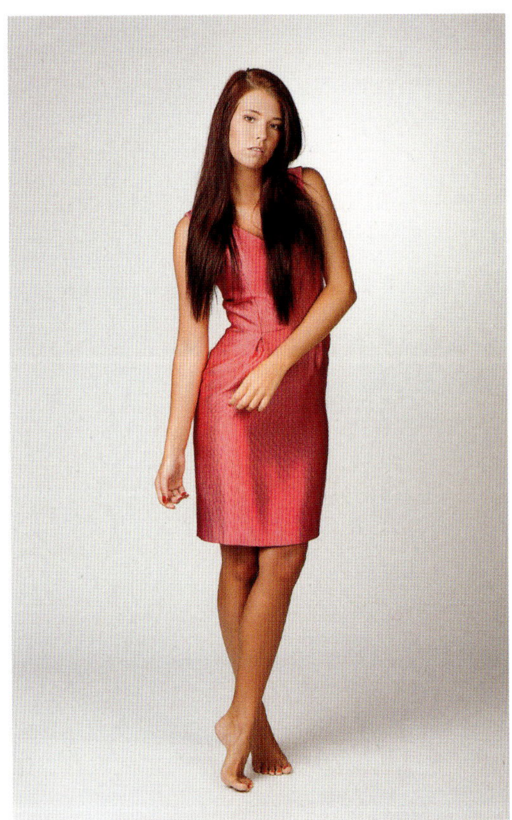

35mm | f8 | 1/160 sec. | ISO 100 | Model: Isabel

HOW IT WORKS

Because this setup is based on a single flash, the subject casts a diagonal shadow on the floor that reaches almost to the background. The raised position of the octabox produces soft nose and chin shadows that are lightened by the reflector. This lightening reduces overall vividness but helps to create a softer overall look. Skin pores and creases are softened too. You can alter the degree of lightening in the shadows by adjusting the distance between the reflector and your model.

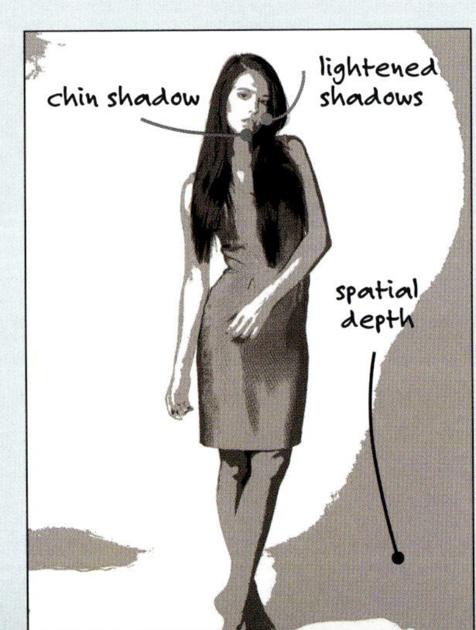

THE SETUP

1. Place the 47" octabox **(1)** about 5 feet from your model in a raised position and at an angle of about 20 degrees. Adjust its height so that the nose shadow and the shadow your model casts on the floor are clearly visible.

> *"Position your main light so that your model's legs are sufficiently well lit, too."*

2. Set up the reflector **(2)** at front right about 3 feet from your model and adjust it so that it reflects the spill light from the octabox onto your model from above. This helps to define the shadow-side contours in her face and body.

3. To create a light gray background, position your model about 6 feet in front of the white background.

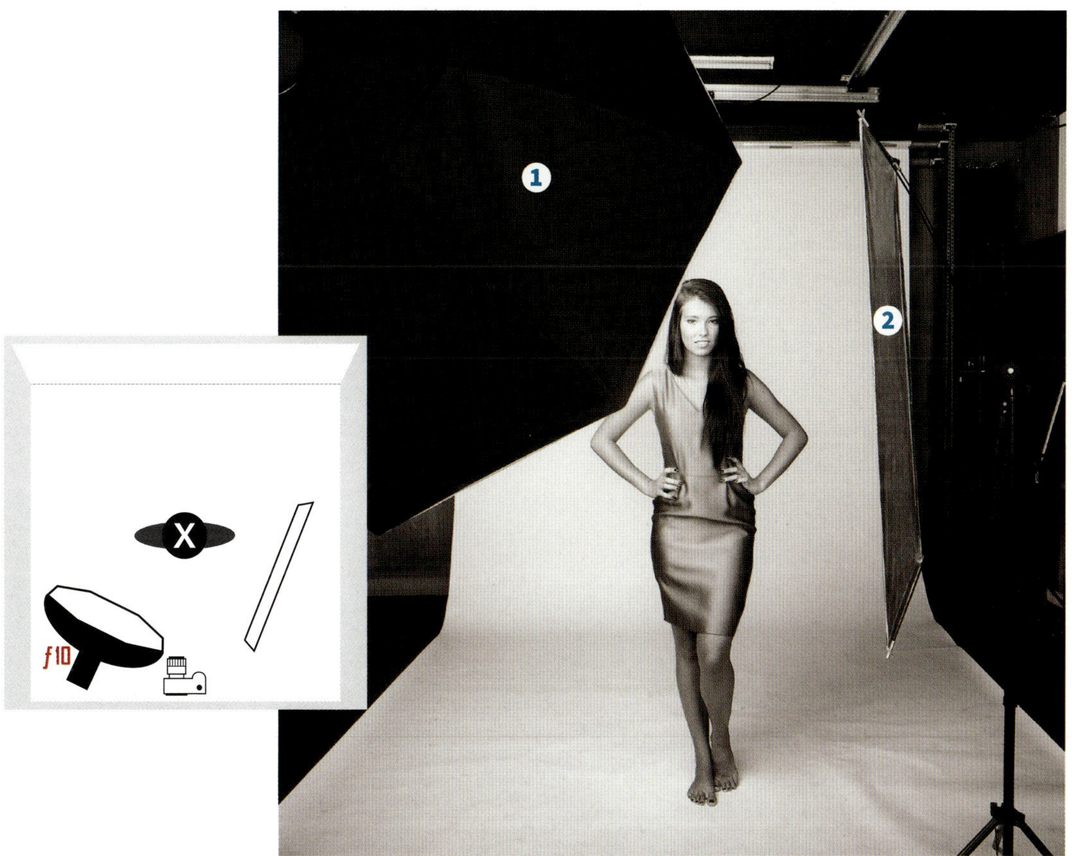

Focus on the Face

This setup concentrates on the model's face. It uses a classic setup with an octabox and a reflector but, to place more emphasis on the subject's face, an additional flash with a standard reflector and a honeycomb grid is used to produce an obvious vignette in the background.

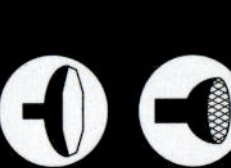

EFFORT INVOLVED

Medium

SUITABLE FOR

All kinds of portraits

THE LOOK

Classic portrait with strong accent on the subject's face and emphasis on her cheekbones as well as the overall pose

EQUIPMENT

1× 47" octabox

1× 30"×40" silver reflector

1× standard reflector with a honeycomb grid

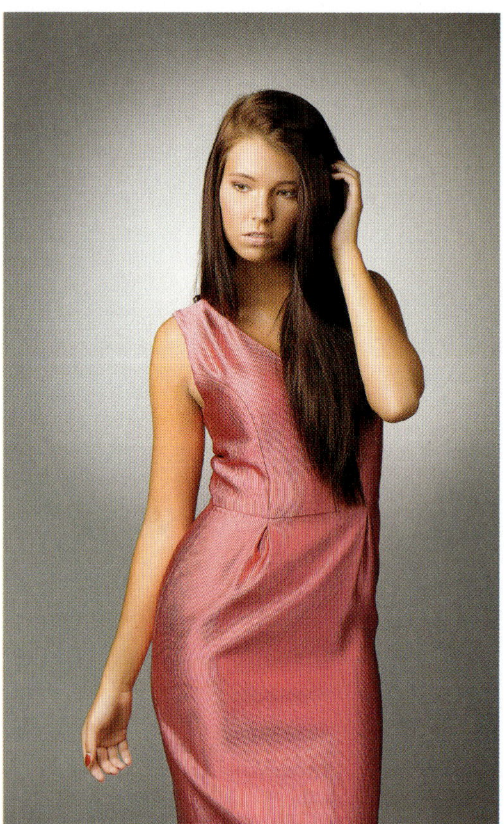

85mm | f8 | 1/160 sec. | ISO 100 | Model: Isabel

HOW IT WORKS

The large octabox is placed diagonally in front of the subject, producing soft shadows on the neck and cheek. The cheek line on the shadow side is well defined and helps to give the face a pleasing overall look. The nose shadow underscores the line formed by the nose and the eyebrow. The light side of the face is lit softly and brightly, producing a delicate look. The lateral main light produces a bright reflection in the subject's dress that accentuates the basic S-shaped pose. The background light draws the viewer's attention to the model's face.

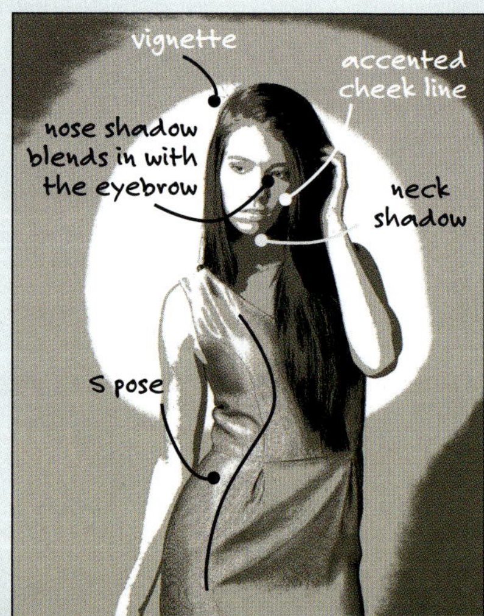

THE SETUP

1. Place the large octabox **(1)** at front left about 5 feet from your model and at an angle of about 30 degrees.

2. Position the octabox slightly above head height so that your model's nose shadow points diagonally downward.

3. Place the reflector **(2)** about 3 feet from your model so that the shadows are slightly lightened. Make sure the reflector is positioned straight enough to reflect light downward.

4. Your model should stand about 8 feet from the white background. This produces a dark gray background that you can manipulate in the next step.

5. The background light is a standard reflector with a honeycomb grid **(3)** mounted on a light stand and placed to the left behind your model. Position it to illuminate the background between your model's head and waist. The distance you choose will depend on the type of flash you use and its beam angle.

Concentrate on the background while you shoot and use a camera position that keeps the background spot effect directly behind your model.

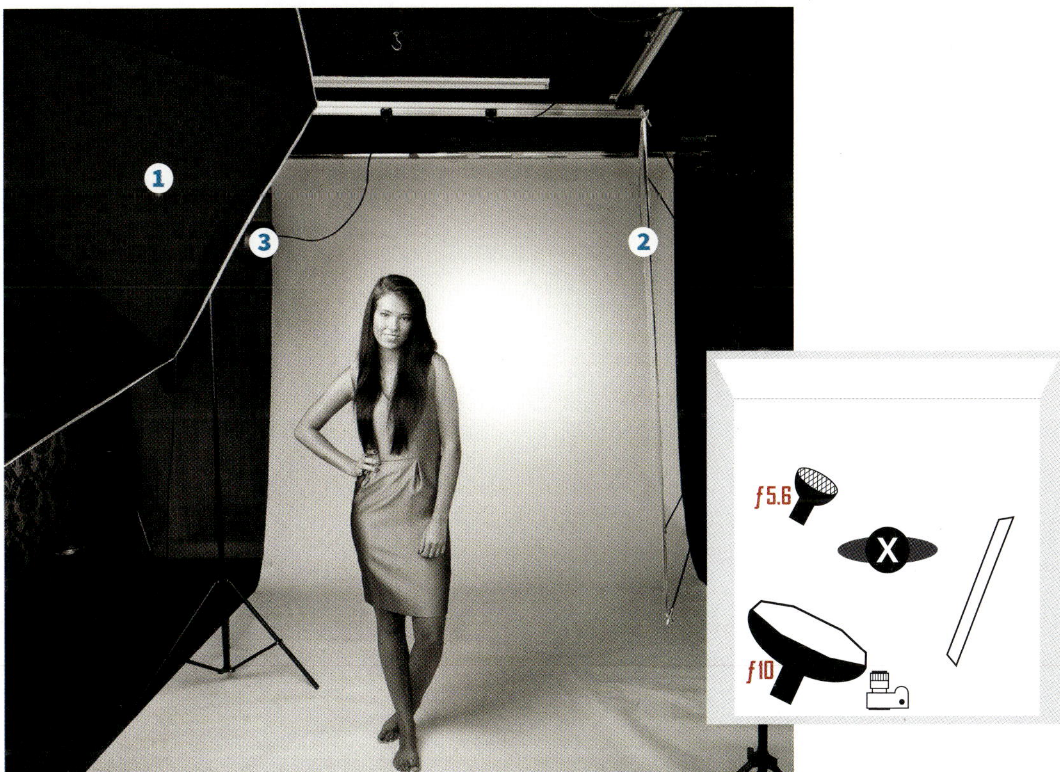

Setting Up the Background Light

To get a pronounced vignette effect, you need to make sure the background isn't lit too brightly by the main light. Start with a distance between the main light and the background that produces the gray tone you want at the edges of the frame. If this distance is too short, the background will be too bright and the contrast with the effect of the background light too weak (possibly even undetectable). Now set up the background light so that the pool of light it forms is directly behind your model. You can then vary the diameter of the accent light by altering the distance between the flash and the background. Don't forget that you will need to adjust flash output to match any changes you make to its position.

"Vary the height of the background spot to give yourself more height options for your camera position."

Use A Fill Light to Produce Accents

If you want to accent your subject's hair or outline, the best approach is to set a fill light and use a dark background. This increases the overall contrast and underscores the rim light effect produced by your fill lights. This example uses a large octabox to accent the subject's gentle facial expression and another octabox to lighten the shadows.

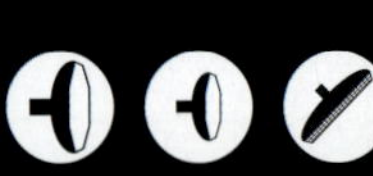

EFFORT INVOLVED

Medium

SUITABLE FOR

Close-up to three-quarter-length portraits

THE LOOK

Intimate portrait with a dark background
Fill light accents the hair and adds gloss

EQUIPMENT

1× 47" octabox
1× 31.5" octabox
1× 47" strip box with a honeycomb grid

40

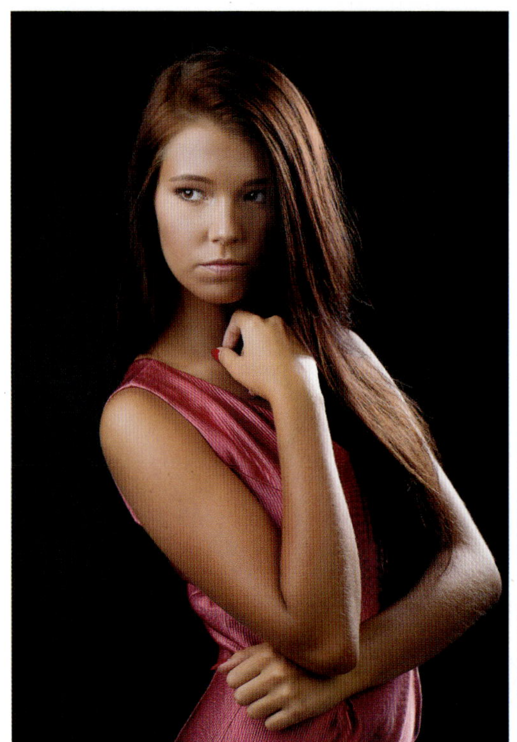

85mm | f7.1 | 1/160 sec. | ISO 100 | Model: Isabel

HOW IT WORKS

The octabox positioned diagonally in front of the subject produces clear light and shadow sides to the face, although the fill light lightens the shadow side sufficiently to keep the facial expression discernible. The soft, bright light makes the light side of the face appear softer. The slightly raised main light creates a nicely three-dimensional feel with a clear neck shadow. The overall look is clearly feminine. The highlight on the right-hand side adds gloss to the hair and the light/dark/light effect produced by the light side of the face, the dark side of the face, and the hair light ensures that the viewer's attention zooms in on the subject's face.

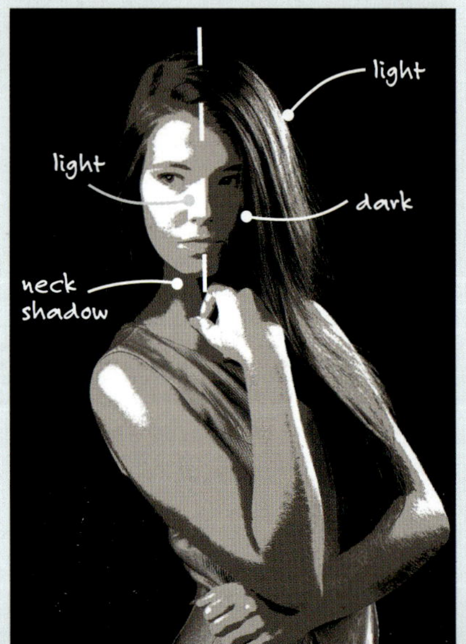

THE SETUP

1. Place the 47" octabox main light **(1)** about 5 feet to the front left of your model at an angle of about 45 degrees.

2. Position the main light above head height so that it produces a clear neck shadow and a nose shadow that points diagonally downward.

3. Now place the smaller octabox **(2)** to the right, at the same distance and angle as the main light. Position this light above head height, too.

4. Position the gridded 47" strip box **(3)** about 6 feet behind your model to the right and angled slightly downward to produce the desired hair light.

5. To give yourself enough space to maneuver the strip box, position your model about 8 feet in front of the black background.

"The octabox produces nice round catchlights in the model's eyes."

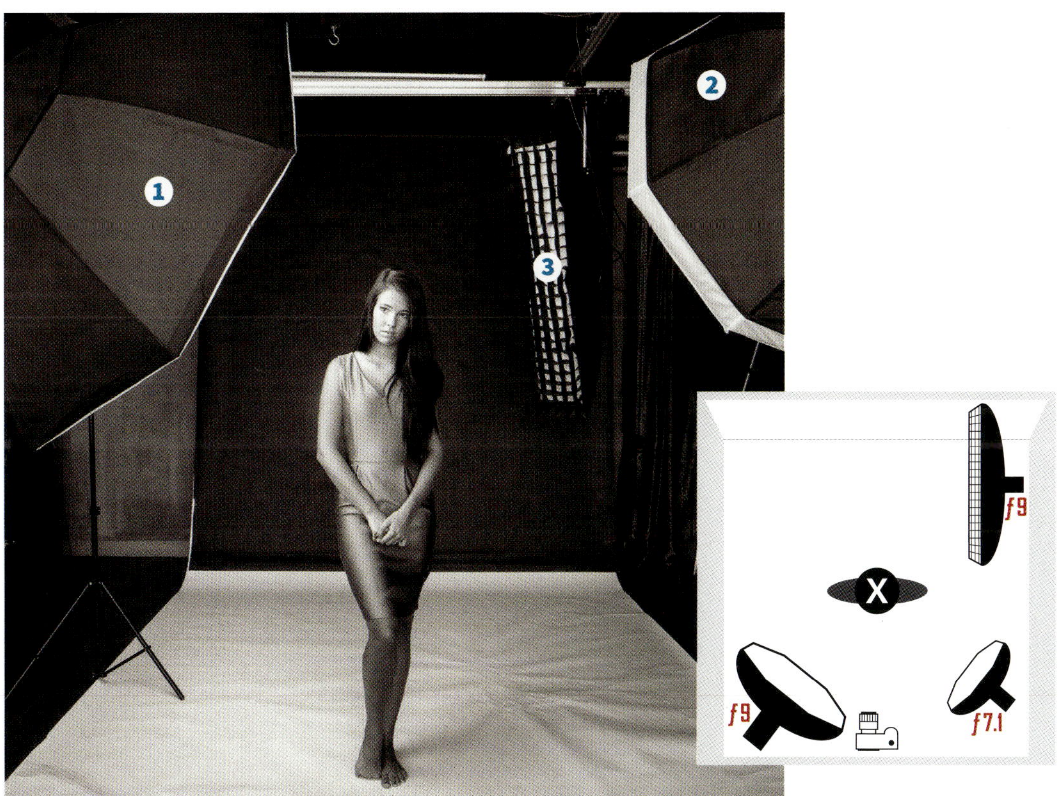

Quick Tip for Male Portraits

This setup works for male subjects too, but it works better if you reduce the brightness of the fill light by about 1 f-stop. This produces more contrast and a slightly harder feel to the image. Of course the pose and facial expression in a male portrait needs to be harder and perhaps more edgy than the one of the more dainty female model shown here. The setup on page 66 shows how to produce this kind of effect using slightly different light shapers.

Variations

If your model turns her face toward the fill light, you can use it to accent her facial contours. Here, you need to pay attention to the effect of the highlight on the bridge of your model's nose, which should form a clear line and not just illuminate the tip of her nose.

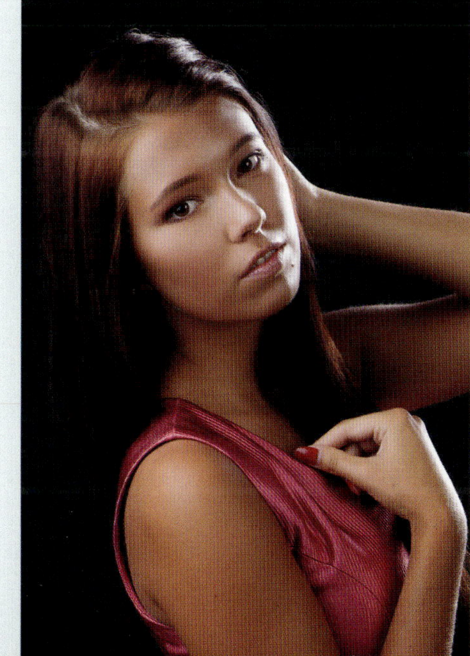

Colored Hair Light

You can use this setup for various types of portraits. For instance, you can keep your model's face in sharp focus while defocusing her shoulders to draw attention to her face. Or you can add a colored hair light to create an interesting accent. You can of course use a white hair light instead. This is a versatile setup, and the high camera position prevents a double chin from spoiling the shot.

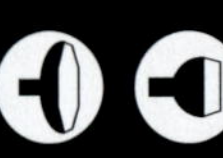

EFFORT INVOLVED

Medium

SUITABLE FOR

Close-up and medium-length portraits

THE LOOK

Classic intense portrait shot

Soft shadows

Accentuates the face

Prevents double chins

Brown-toned smokey eyes and nude lips

EQUIPMENT

1 × 35" octabox

1 × 24" softbox with a colored gel

1 × 30"× 40" silver reflector

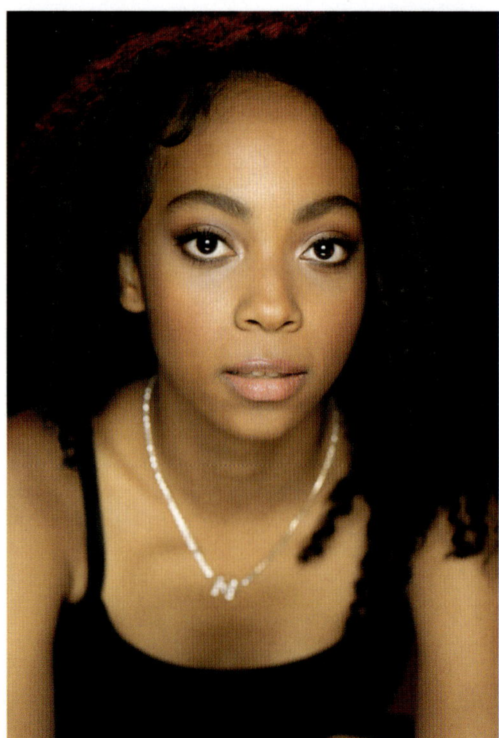

85mm | f2.8 | 1/125 sec. | ISO 100 | Model: Melissa

HOW IT WORKS

This classic, frontally lit portrait setup reduces shadows and produces a fairly flat, two-dimensional look. A raised camera position and a wide aperture setting defocuses the subject's neck and shoulders and draws extra attention to the face. The distribution of light within the frame underscores this effect. The broad, soft main light is flattering and can almost completely mask any skin blemishes. The nose shadow is weak and the frontal lighting makes for bright, glowing eyes. The close proximity of the reflector lightens the shadows from below and produces a second reflection in the subject's eyes that you can retouch later if you want.

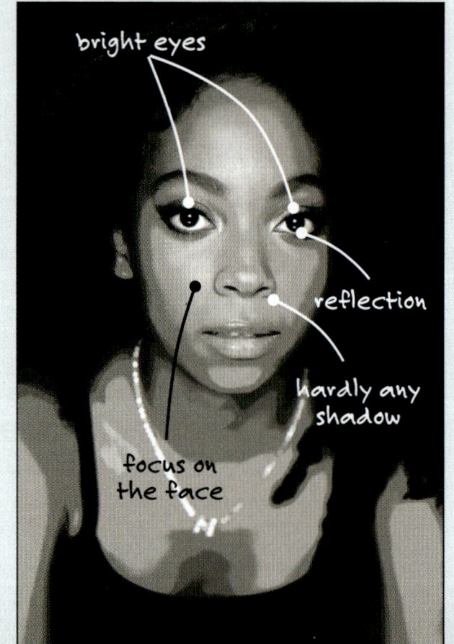

THE SETUP

If you want to shoot using a raised camera position, you have two options depending on the amount of space available in the studio. If space is limited, you can get your model to kneel and rest her elbows on a stool, as shown in the image below. This enables you to freely position the octabox and to shoot from a standing position. If the studio you are using has high ceilings, you can save your model the trouble of kneeling and you can shoot from above using a stool or a small ladder.

1. Place the softbox with the colored gel **(1)** behind and slightly above your model's head at a distance of about 3 feet.

2. Place the main octabox **(2)** directly in front of your model at a height that makes the nose shadow virtually invisible when she looks up at the camera. The distance between the main light and your model should be about 5 feet.

3. Place the reflector **(3)** in front of your model so that it slightly lightens the shadow under her chin. The background is less important when you are shooting from above. In the photo on the left, you can see the black flag that I placed behind the subject to prevent reflections from the floor spoiling the overall effect.

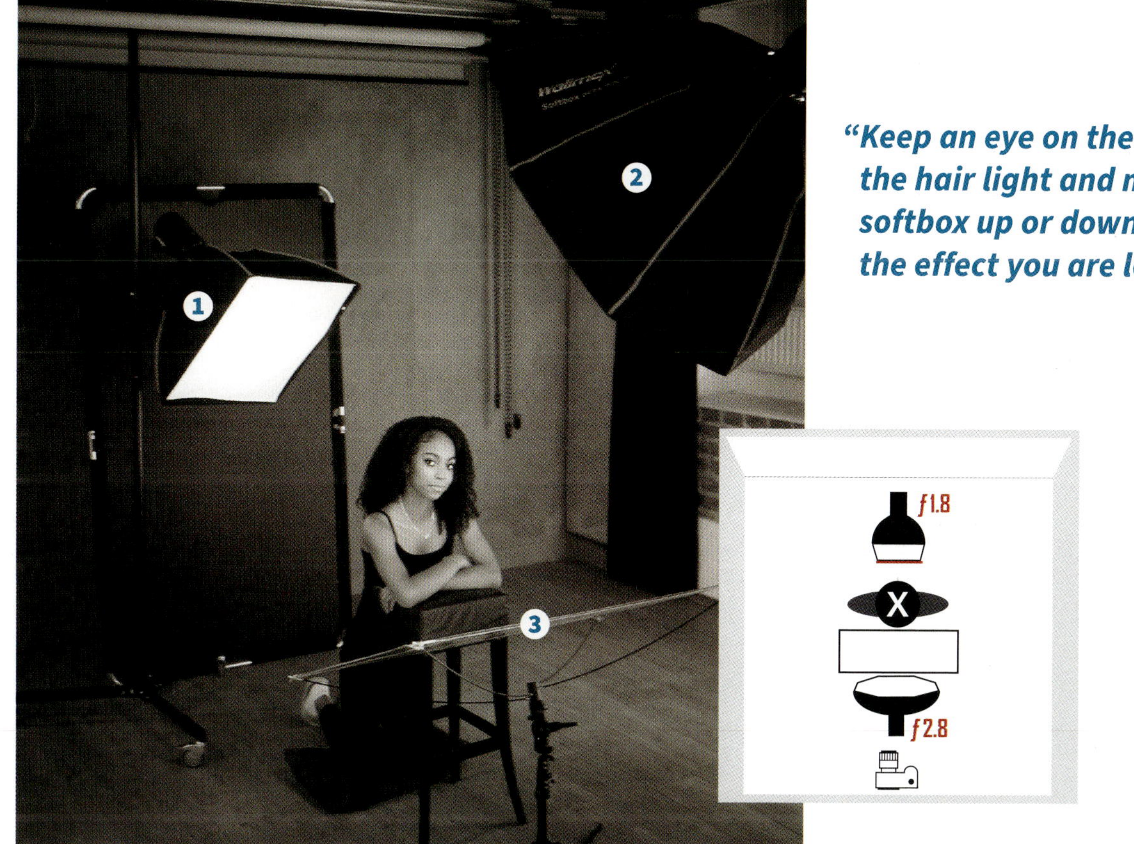

"Keep an eye on the effect of the hair light and move the rear softbox up or down to create the effect you are looking for."

Overhead Light

This is a slightly unconventional one-light setup. It produces an intense gradient between the top of the model's head and her torso, and accentuates the eyes. This setup is especially good for close-ups and three-quarter-length shots, or any situation in which you want to emphasize the subject's eyes. Its simplicity makes it great for beginners or for situations where you have a limited amount of equipment to choose from.

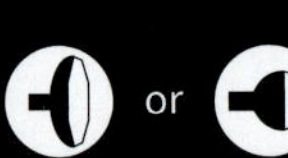 or

EFFORT INVOLVED

Low

SUITABLE FOR

Close-ups

THE LOOK

Intense, classic portrait

Soft shadows

Focus on the eyes

Brown-toned smokey eyes and nude lips

EQUIPMENT

1 × 35" octabox or 24" softbox

1 × 43" circular silver reflector

85mm | f1.8 | 1/125 sec. | ISO 100 | Model: Melissa

HOW IT WORKS

The raised position of the main light produces a strong accent on the upper portion of the subject's face. Here, eyes and nose form the brightest areas of the image, and the viewer's attention is inescapably steered toward the eyes. The low reflector nicely lightens the lower portion of the frame. The soft light from the octabox reduces the effects of skin imperfections. The raised main light produces a broad neck shadow that creates a clear visual break between the face and torso. Using a single main light in a high position creates a relatively weak reflection in the subject's eyes that gives the expression a slightly feisty feel.

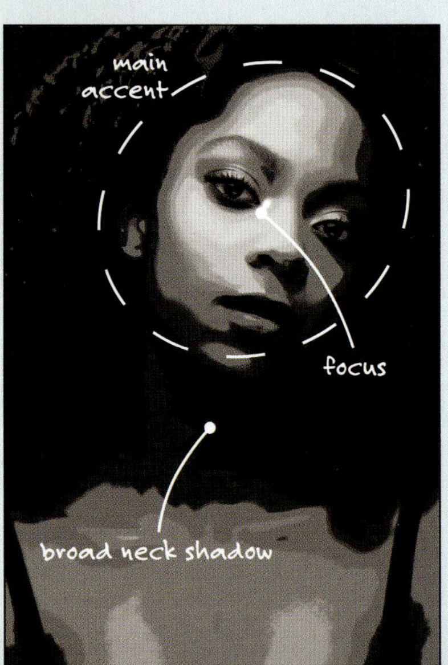

THE SETUP

1. Place the octabox **(1)** above your model to illuminate her face at a slight angle. The image below illustrates perfectly what I mean. The distance between the octabox and your model should be between 12 and 20 inches.

2. Now place the reflector **(2)** abot 20 inches from your model's face so that it lightens the neck shadow. Your model should be standing about 5 feet in front of a white or colored background. This distance makes the color of the background clearly visible in the resulting image.

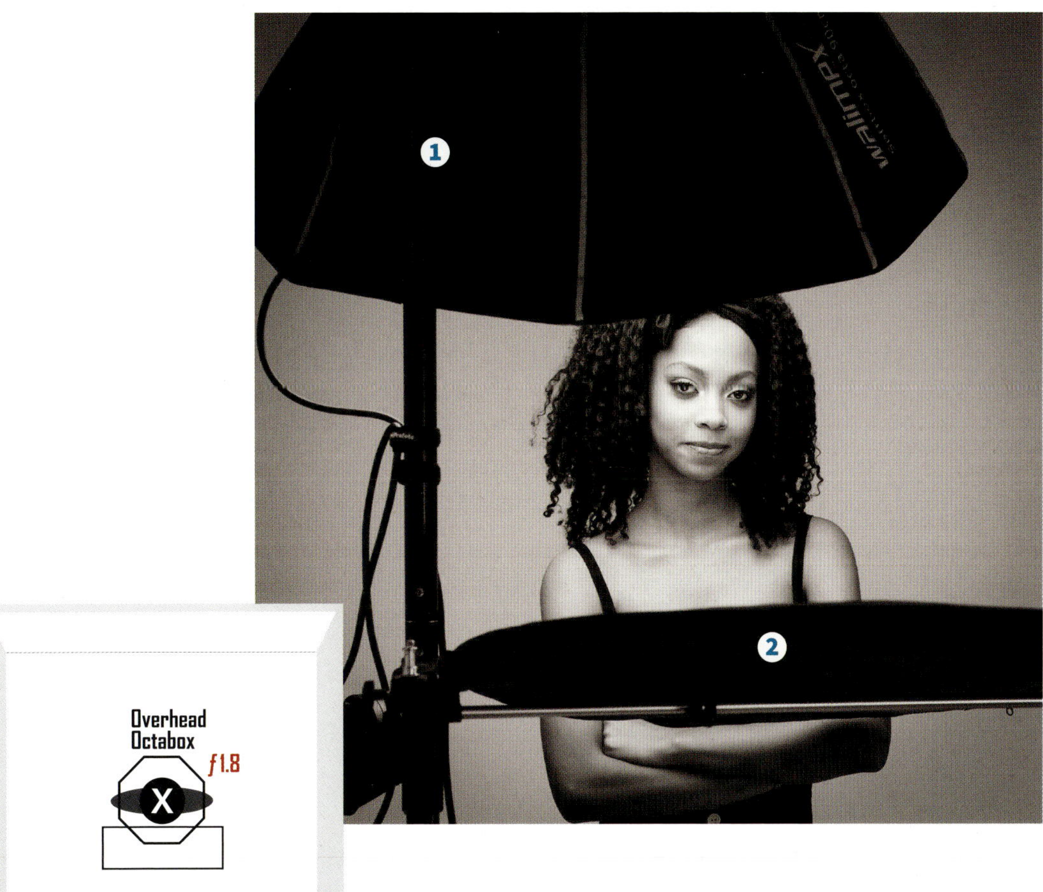

"For a tight setup like this, you need to shoot from close below the octabox/softbox in order to avoid producing a 'frog's-eye view' effect."

Variations

The tight lighting setup limits your framing options. However, you can still experiment with landscape-format shots. This approach produces a calmer overall effect and it is always a good idea to include a couple of shots like this in any sequence you shoot.

Classic Hollywood Lighting

The "Hollywood" setup—also known as the "butterfly" setup due to the shape of the nose shadow it produces—is a classic portrait setup. The standard variant of this setup uses no reflector at all, but the version shown here uses a single reflector placed directly below the model's face. This setup is great for accenting eyes, facial features, and cheekbones.

EFFORT INVOLVED

Low

SUITABLE FOR

Close-ups and three-quarter-length portraits

THE LOOK

A soft overall look that accentuates the cheekbones
Bright eyes

EQUIPMENT

1 × 31.5" octabox
1 × 30"×40" silver reflector

46

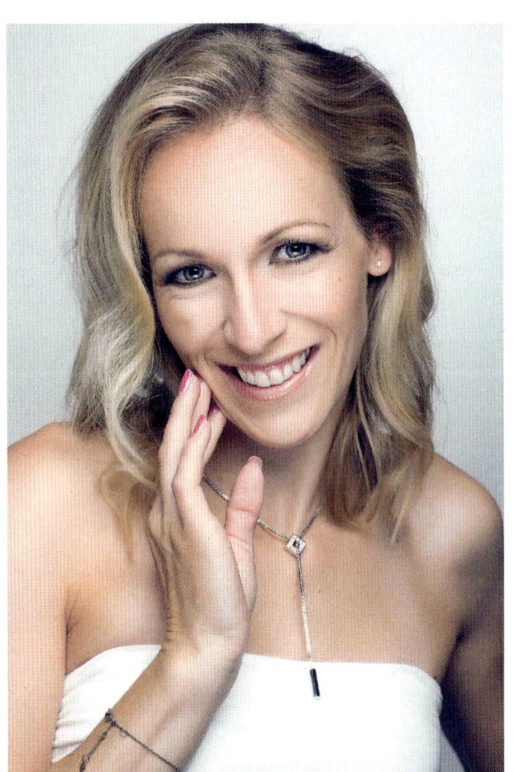

85mm | f8 | 1/160 sec. | ISO 100 | Model: Martina

HOW IT WORKS

This setup accentuates the eyes and the cheekbones and thus the overall shape of the subject's face. The upper eyelid shadows and the lighter tone in the lower portion of the eyes underscores the shine of the eyes. The neck shadow is relatively broad and, together with the hair, forms a frame around the face. The reflector ensures that the eye, nose, and neck shadows aren't too dark to produce a subtle overall feel.

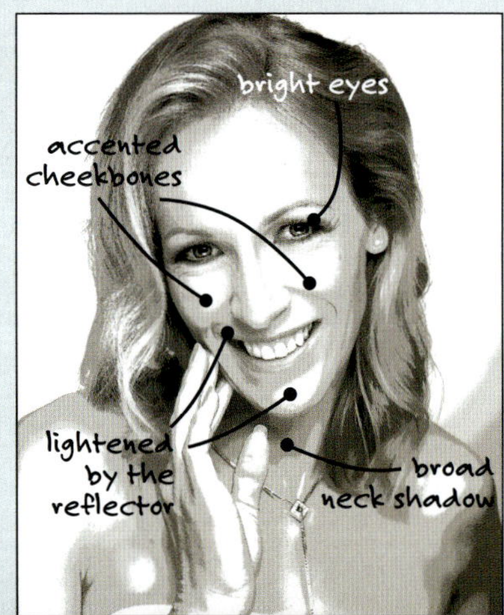

THE SETUP

1. Mount the octabox **(1)** on a ceiling rail or a boom stand about 3 feet above your model at an angle of 45 degrees. Position it to create a nose shadow that ends just above her upper lip.

2. Place a low stand directly in front of your model at chest height and mount the reflector **(2)** in a position that lightens the neck and nose shadows. You can adjust the degree of lightening by altering the angle of the reflector.

3. The distance between your model and the background should be between 5 and 6 feet.

"This setup is ideal for seated poses."

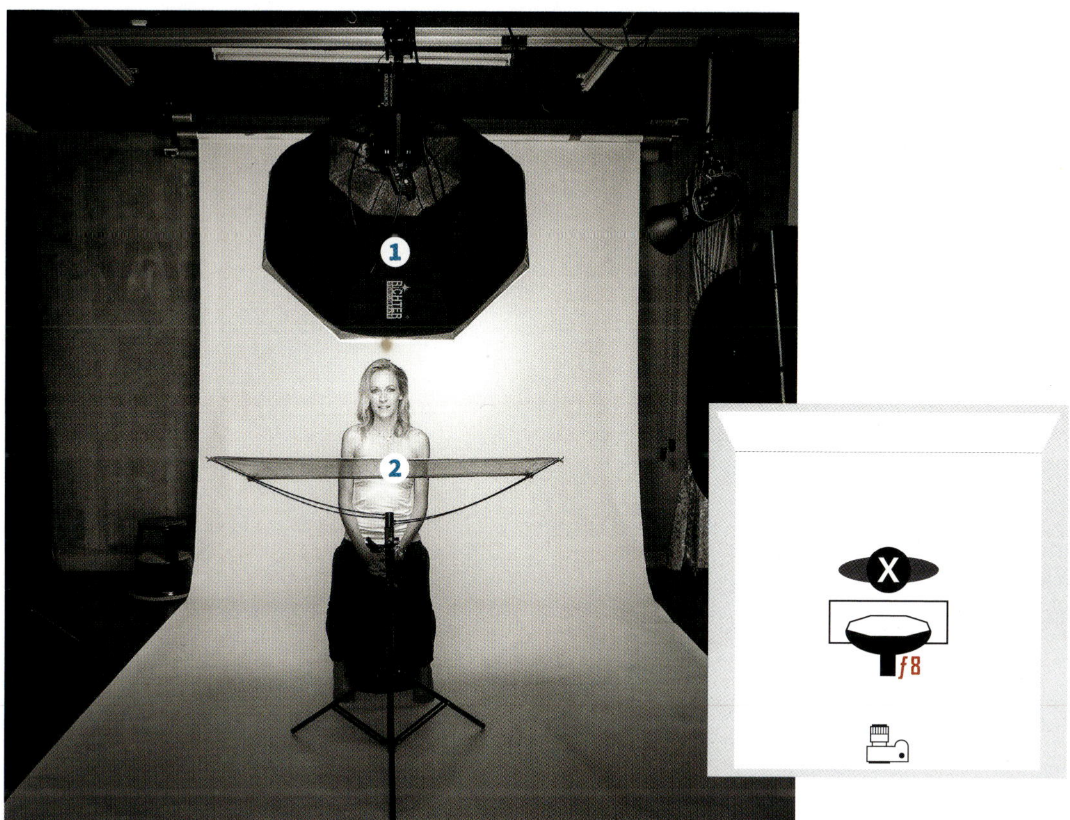

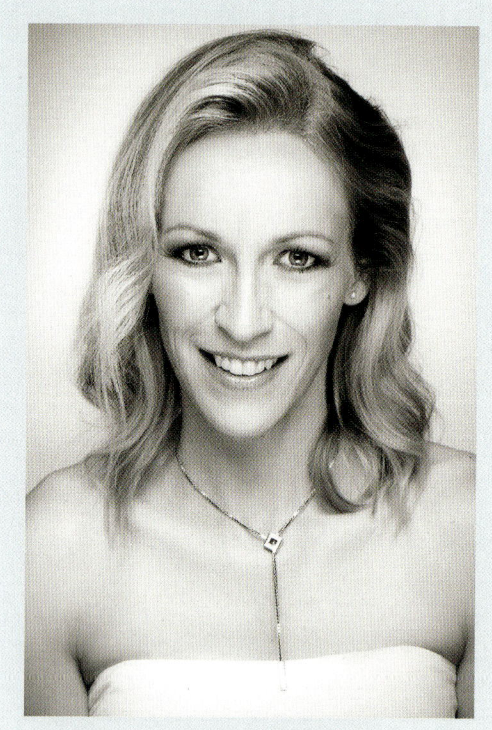

A Black-and-White Classic

Because the model isn't looking straight into the camera, the examples on the opposite page don't show the typical "butterfly" shape in the nose shadow. If you want to create the classic Marlene Dietrich look, you need to get your model to look dead ahead. This centers the shadow and the gradient it produces. The classic look this setup produces is ideal for images developed in black and white.

Soft-Style Hollywood Lighting

This is a variation on the classic "Hollywood" lighting theme shown on the previous page. Instead of a reflector, this variant uses a horizontally placed strip box to lighten the shadows. This softens the lateral shadows and the shadow on the bridge of the subject's nose.

EFFORT INVOLVED

Medium

SUITABLE FOR

Close-up or head-and-shoulders portraits

THE LOOK

Soft overall look with extra-soft "Hollywood" accents

Gently accented facial contours

EQUIPMENT

1× 24" softbox

1× 47" strip box with a honeycomb grid

1× standard reflector with a honeycomb grid

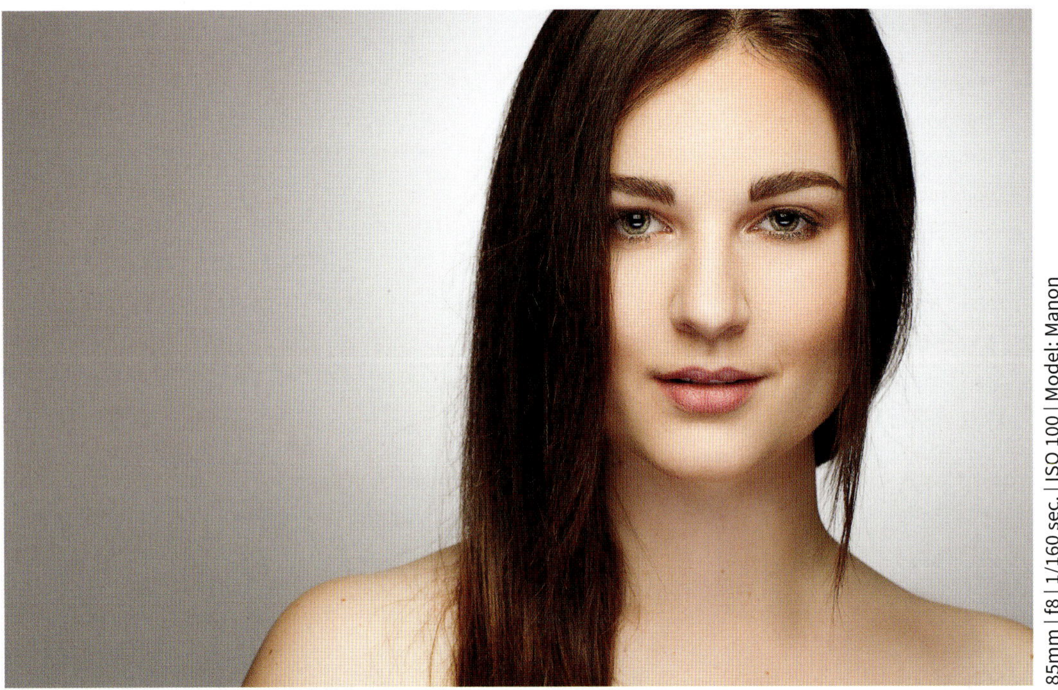

85mm | f8 | 1/160 sec. | ISO 100 | Model: Manon

HOW IT WORKS

This strip box-based version of the "Hollywood" setup produces a softer overall look than the classic version. It gently accents the subject's facial contours and cheekbones without overdoing things. The eyes and lips are also accented by the raised, frontal light source. The neck shadow is soft but nevertheless sufficiently distinct to provide a visual break between the subject's head and shoulders. The strip box gives the eyes a soft glow and keeps the background shadows relatively light. The background light draws the viewer's attention to the subject's face and produces a vignette effect toward the edges of the frame.

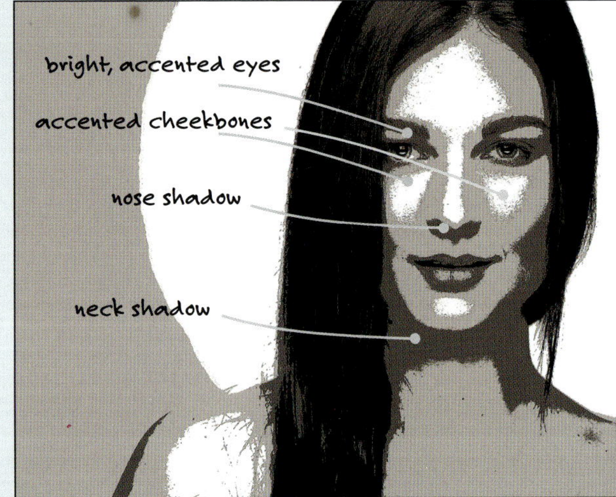

THE SETUP

1. Mount the octabox **(1)** above your model at an angle of 45 degrees using either a ceiling rail or a boom stand. Position the light about 3 feet from your subject so that it creates a nose shadow that ends precisely halfway between the tip of her nose and her upper lip.

2. Mount the strip box **(2)** horizontally on a low stand at about belly height and position it to illuminate your model's face. Here too, the distance between light and model should be about 3 feet.

3. Place a standard reflector with a honeycomb grid **(3)** behind your model to produce a pool of light directly behind her head.

4. Your model should stand 5 to 6 feet from the white background.

You can adjust the intensity of the shadows produced by the strip box by altering its output. Lighter shadows produce a softer overall effect while darker shadows produce a harder-looking image. The choice is yours and you can use whichever settings work best with your model.

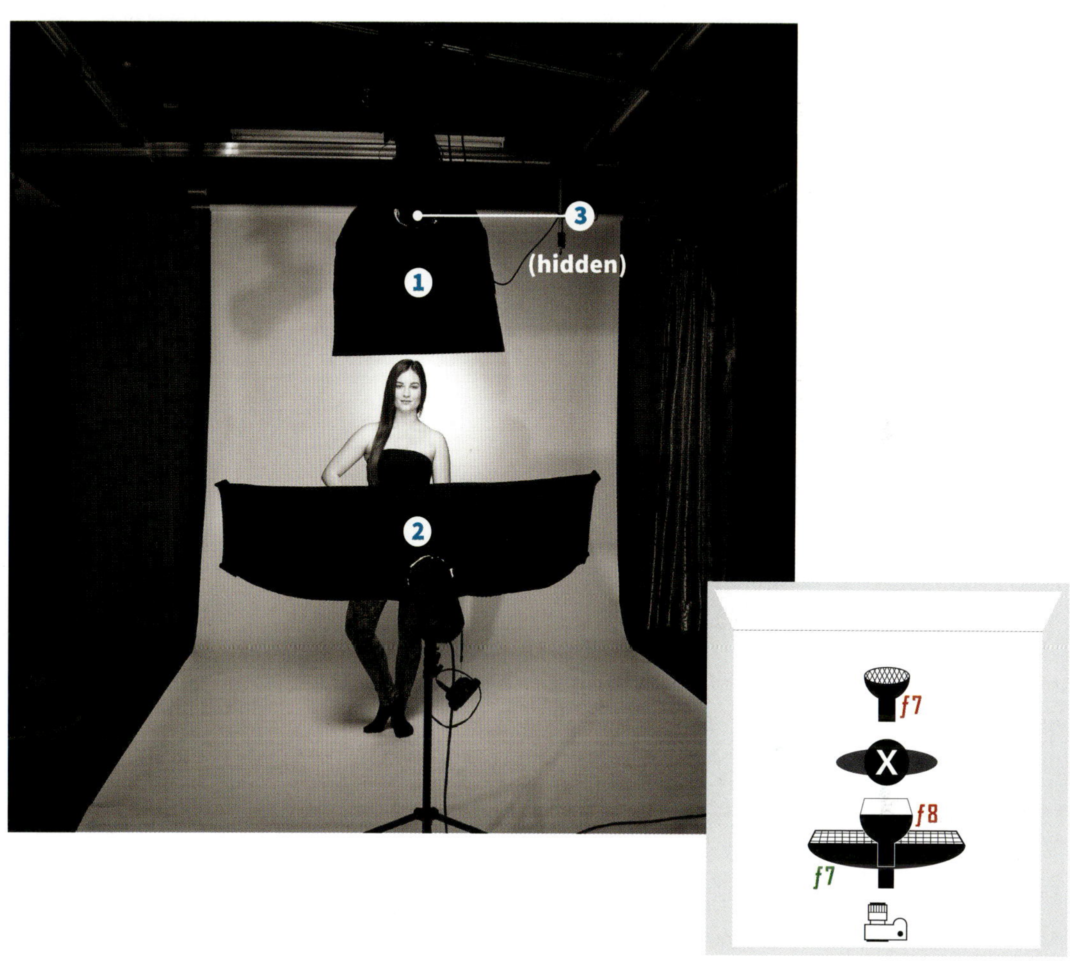

"Let your model's hair hang over her face to make it appear narrower."

Cropping Close-Ups

In close-up shots, you will often have to crop your model's face at the editing stage. A slight crop of a subject's hair, ears, or chin often looks unintentional, so it is usually better to go for broke and use a more adventurous crop—for example, between your model's hairline and the crown of her head, or even in the middle of her forehead. This approach gives a portrait a more intense and immediate look.

Lots of Contrast Against a Dark Background

Dark backgrounds often risk swamping the subject. However, the right lighting setup keeps the background dark while adding vividness to the subject's face. This setup even accents the subject's shadow-side hair.

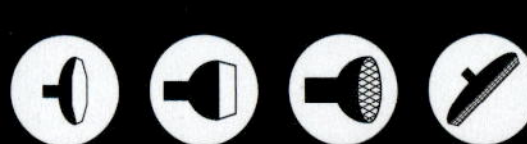

EFFORT INVOLVED

High

SUITABLE FOR

All kinds of portraits

THE LOOK

High-contrast portrait with soft shadows
Image has depth and vividness

EQUIPMENT

1× 31.5" octabox
1× 24" softbox
1× standard reflector with a honeycomb grid
1× 47" strip box with a honeycomb grid

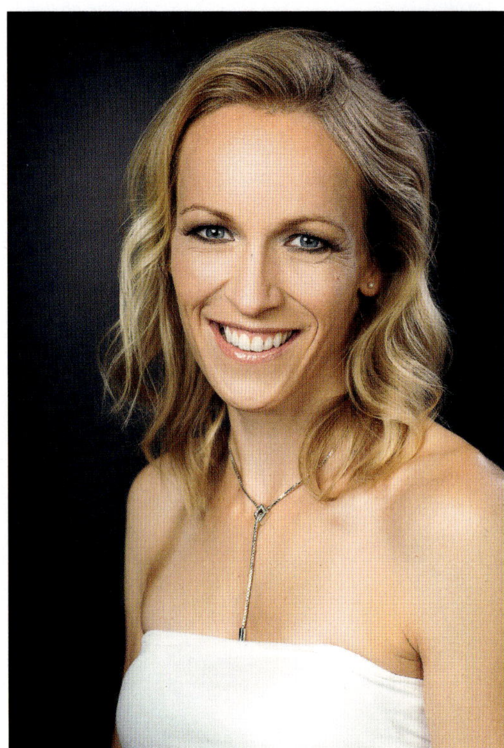

HOW IT WORKS

The octabox produces a soft main light that frames the face and reduces the effect of skin pores and creases. Using a softbox as a fill light increases this effect. The main light's raised, lateral position produces noticeable shadows on the neck, the cheek, and the nose, thus creating the necessary overall vividness. A spotlight in the background adds depth to the image, while the highlight on the right provides additional accents and subtly illuminates the shadow side. This combination of four separate lights uses the clearly lit hair to frame the subject's face and grab the viewer's attention.

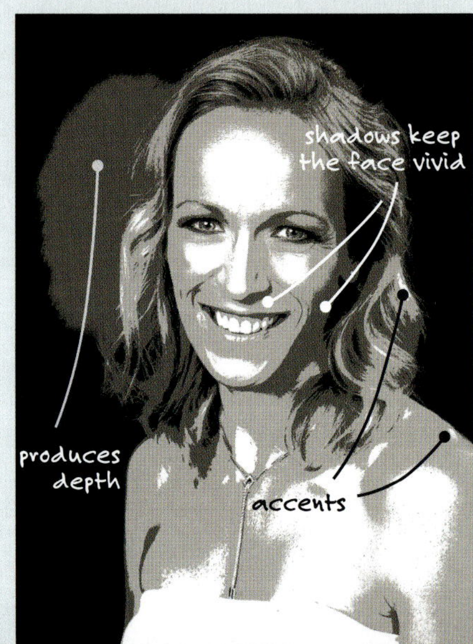

THE SETUP

1. Place the octabox **(1)** in a raised position about 5 feet from your model at about 45 degrees to the left. Set the flash output to produce noticeable neck and nose shadows, but make sure the nose shadow doesn't actually reach your model's upper lip.

2. Place the softbox fill light **(2)** about 3 feet to the right of your model at an angle of about 45 degrees with its center at around eye level.

3. Place the strip box **(3)** diagonally behind your model at about 45 degrees and at a distance of about 3 feet. Set the light so that the highlight it produces illuminates your model's hair without directing additional spill light to her face.

4. Place the standard reflector **(4)** for the background to the left of your model in a raised position to produce a pool of light behind her head that is more obvious on the lit side of her face.

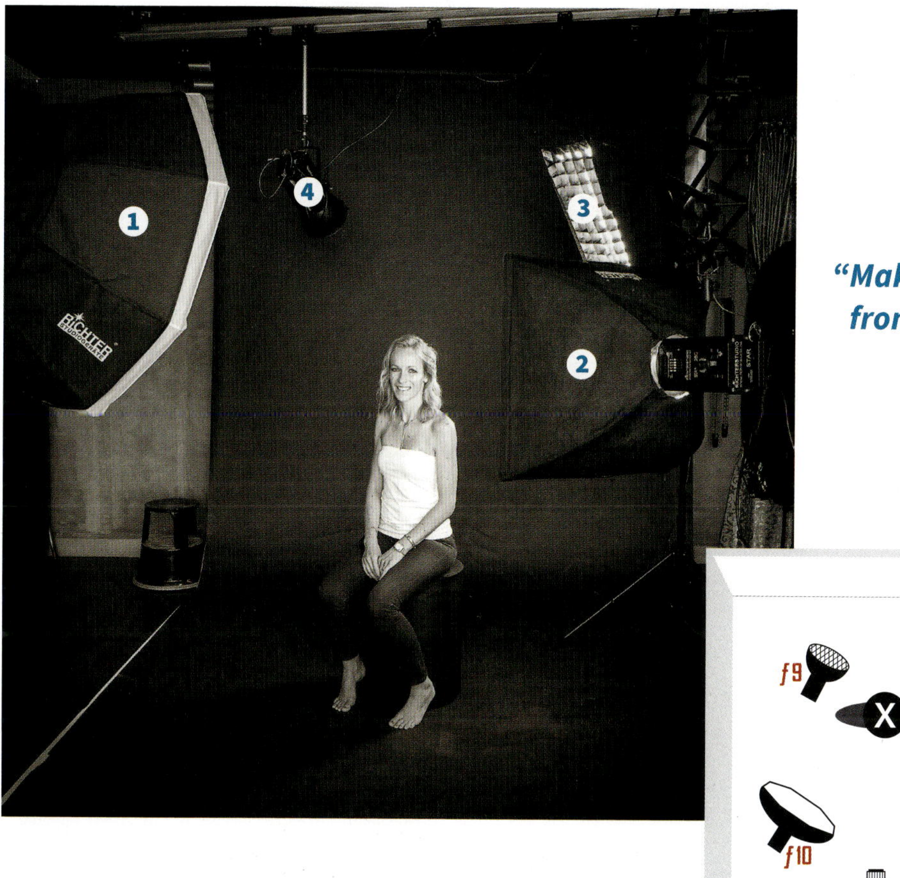

"Make sure the accent light provides an even glow from the top of your model's head to her upper arm."

Positioning the Fill Light

The primary purpose of a fill light is to lighten shadows, and this is most effective when you place your fill light close to the camera axis. This makes a ring flash the ideal fill light, as the shadows it produces are cast directly behind the subject, leaving only the shadows produced by the main light visible in the final image. If you don't have a ring light, it helps to place the fill light to the side and slightly raised. Even though this doesn't lighten all the main light's shadows, it still adds vividness to the resulting images. When using a lateral fill light, make sure that it doesn't produce any unwanted crossover shadows.

Intense but Still Gentle

If you position the reflector in a "Hollywood" setup close enough to your subject to significantly lighten the shadows and then add accents using a fill light, the result is a soft-looking image that virtually eliminates skin blemishes but keeps your subject looking vivid.

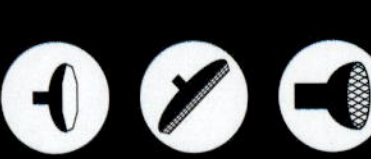

EFFORT INVOLVED

High

SUITABLE FOR

Close-up and head-and-shoulders portraits

THE LOOK

Bright, friendly, well-defined portrait with plenty of accents

Skin imperfections virtually eliminated

EQUIPMENT

1× 31.5" octabox

1× 47" strip box with a honeycomb grid

1× standard reflector with a honeycomb grid

1× 30"×40" silver reflector

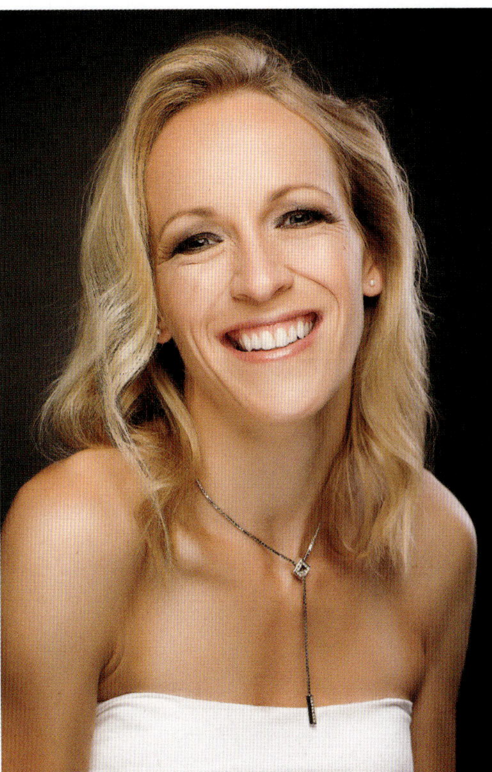

85mm | f8 | 1/160 sec. | ISO 100 | Model: Martina

HOW IT WORKS

The raised, frontally placed octabox creates typical "Hollywood-style" lighting with a "butterfly" nose shadow and strongly accented facial details. Other details such as the collarbone and shoulders are accented too. The reflector lightens the neck shadow and the shadows below the eyelids, providing a bright overall effect. The close proximity of the main light and the reflector to the model virtually eliminates all pores and other skin imperfections. The highlight on the right ensures that the subject is clearly separated form the background.

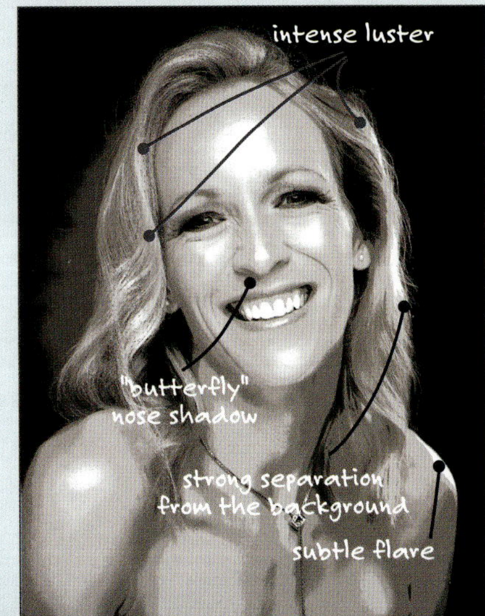

THE SETUP

1. Begin by placing the octabox **(1)** frontally above your model at a distance of about 3 feet, using either a ceiling rail or a boom stand. Position the light so that the nose shadow remains precisely central and ends halfway between your model's nose and her upper lip.

"Make sure the highlight doesn't accent your model's nose!"

2. Now place the reflector **(2)** in front of your model at chest height so that it reflects the spill from the octabox onto her neck and eyes from below.

3. Place the background light **(3)** about 6 feet behind your model to the left so that it produces a bright central highlight behind her head. You can adjust the size of the highlight by altering the distance between the light and the background.

4. Finally, place the strip box **(4)** about 5 feet behind your model to the right at an angle of about 45 degrees. Position the strip box pointing downward from a little above head-high.

5. Your model should sit (or stand) about 6 feet in front of the black background.

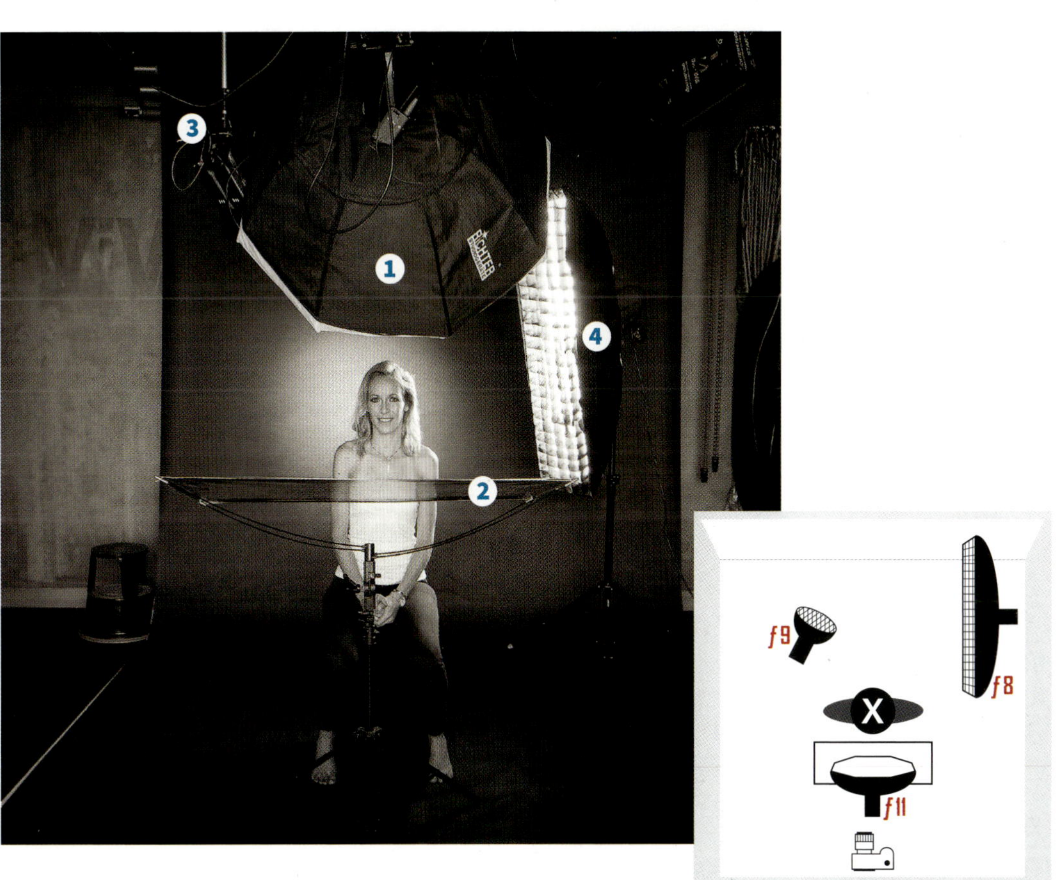

Eyes Wide Open

We all tend to squint in bright light, and many people blink when a flash fires. These natural protective instincts are, of course, not very helpful when it comes to shooting studio portraits. Instead of switching your modeling lights to full power, always use proportional mode if you can. You can even switch them off altogether, but your model's pupils will then open even wider, and reduce the width of her irises even further. Working without modeling lights may also mean that your camera doesn't have sufficient light to focus properly.

If your model is one of those people who tends to squint or blink, try getting her to close her eyes and open them on a count of three, which is of course, the moment you press the shutter button too. You can also try capturing a second image immediately after your model has blinked.

Minimalistic but Effective

This is a great setup for producing intense but appealing portraits using a minimum of gear. The combination of a dark background and dark clothing ensures that the main accent is on the subject's face. This is a classic setup that has been used by many famous photographers over the years and is still often used to portray film stars.

EFFORT INVOLVED

Low

SUITABLE FOR

Close-up or head-and-shoulders portraits

THE LOOK

Classic intense portrait

Distinct shadows

Strongly accented face

Brown-toned smokey eyes and nude lips

EQUIPMENT

1 × 20" beauty dish with a diffuser

1 × 30" × 40" silver reflector

85mm | f2.8 | 1/125 sec. | ISO 100 | Model: Melissa

HOW IT WORKS

The diagonally placed main light produces a highly three-dimensional image. The hard light from the beauty dish is softened by the diffuser, thus reducing the effects of pores and other skin imperfections. The raised main light produces diagonal nose and neck shadows. The close proximity of the light shaper to the subject creates obvious light fall-off toward the torso, which helps to accent the face. The shadow side is very dark, but the reflector nevertheless highlights the details and texture in the darker portions of the image. The single light source produces a highly pleasing reflection in the eyes that really livens up the result.

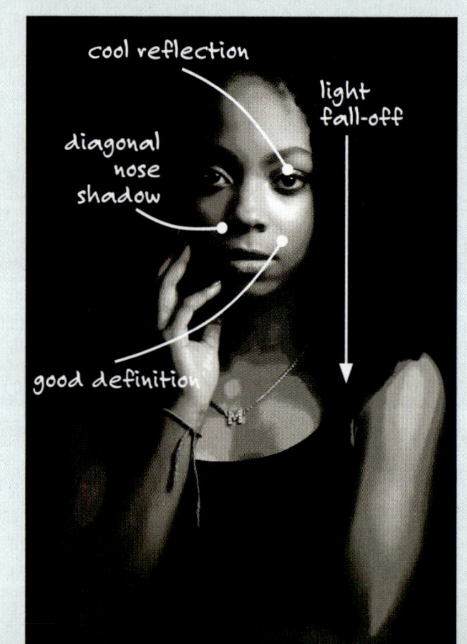

THE SETUP

1. Place the beauty dish **(1)** in a raised position 3 feet to the right at about 45 degrees to your model. Set up the light to produce a clear neck shadow and a diagonal nose shadow that points toward her cheek.

2. Now place the reflector **(2)** about 3 feet to the left of your model with its center at head height. Use the reflector to gently lighten the shadows in her face.

3. Get you model to stand about 5 feet from the black background. As you can see, I used a flag in the background. You can of course use a black cloth, a polyester sheet, or anything else black that you have lying around for your background.

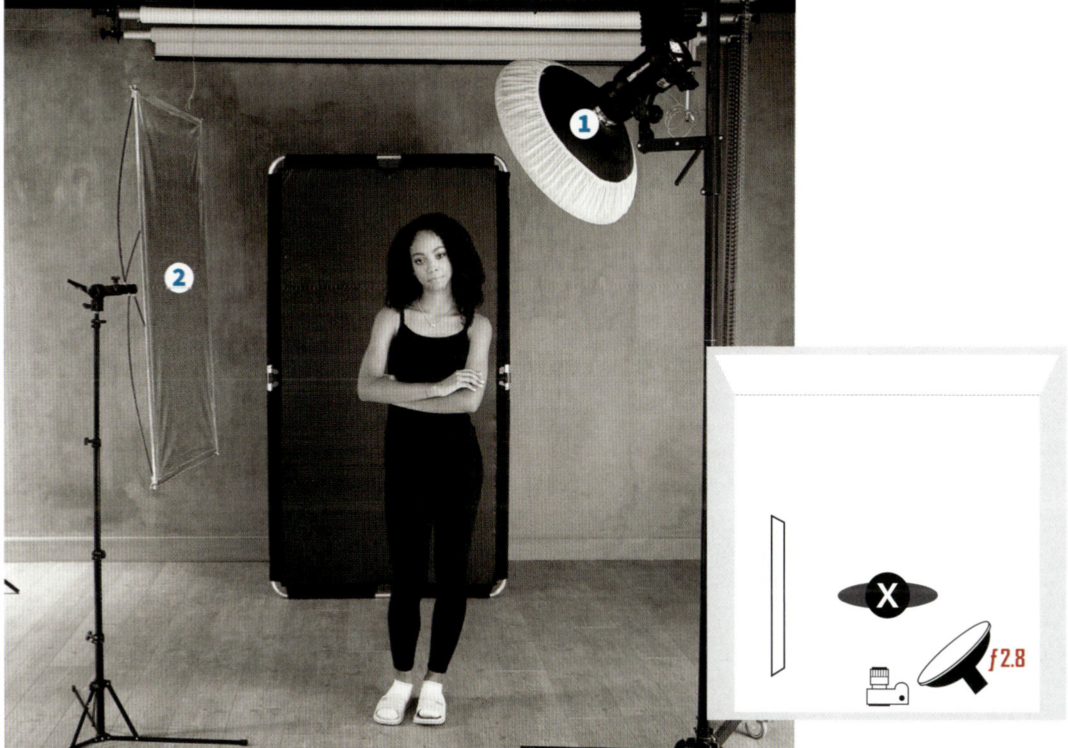

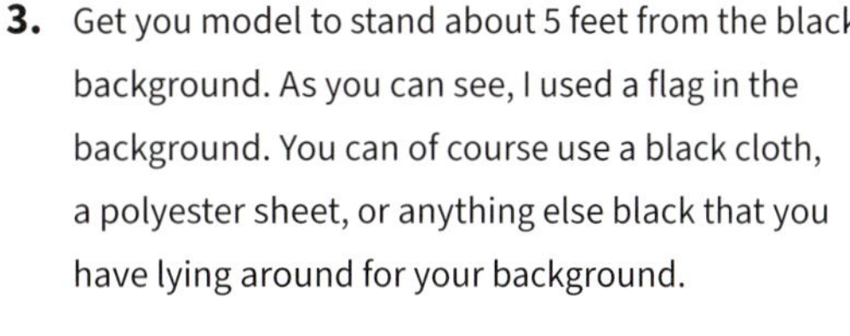

Variations

The joy of one-light setups like this one is that it is simple to produce variations on your basic look. For example, placing the beauty dish further away from your model will reduce the light fall-off effect between her face and her torso. Try different positions and see how you like the effects they produce. In the image below I placed the beauty dish head-on and moved it back. To compensate, I opened the aperture up to f1.2 to produce a softer overall effect.

If you like this kind of portrait, try converting your images to black and white. This is really effective because the model's skin is the brightest part of the image and the lighting setup strongly accents her face. Hollywood, here we come!

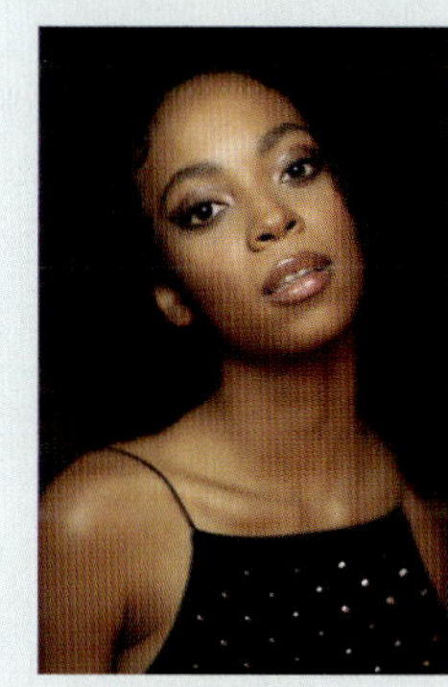

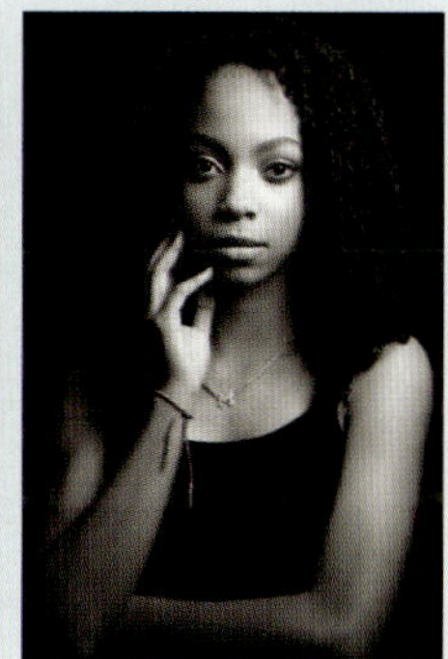

"Pay attention to the brightness fall-off toward your model's torso. The closer your main light is to the subject, the more intense this effect will be."

A Chair as a Styling Aid

An overhead main light and a strong fall-off effect toward the model's body create a powerful effect, and the chair adds form to the image. Your model can lean on it or sit down and use her legs to create all sorts of shapes to make the image more interesting and dynamic.

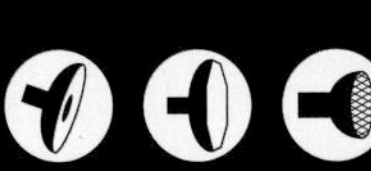

EFFORT INVOLVED

High

SUITABLE FOR

Full-length shots

THE LOOK

A powerful look with strong shadows
An intense pose with lots of geometric lines and angles

EQUIPMENT

1× beauty dish
1× 47" octabox
1× standard reflector with a honeycomb grid
1× reflector, silbern (110 cm×70 cm)

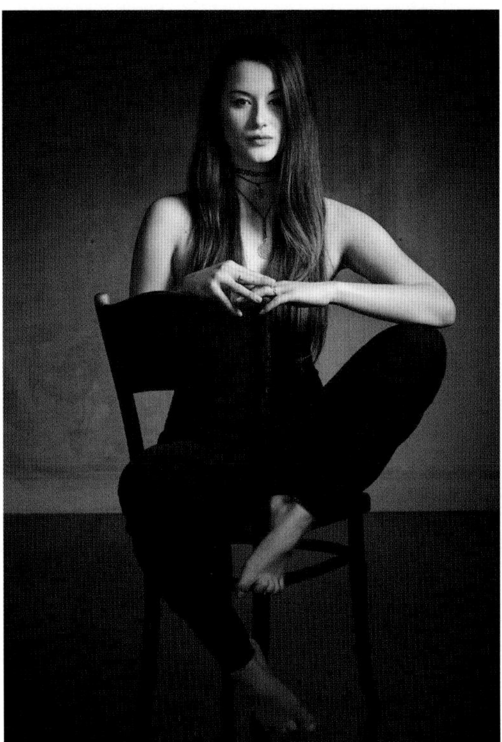

HOW IT WORKS

The very high position of the main light creates strong brightness fall-off toward the subject's body that shifts focus to the face and shoulders. There is an obvious darker side to the face that automatically accents the brighter side. The shadows are lightened by the octabox and the reflector, and provide sufficient light to keep plenty of details discernible, while the background highlight surrounding the subject's torso creates sufficient contrast to make her entire body part of the composition. The mass of details, the clever styling, and the model's intense gaze produce an image that keeps you looking and coming back for more.

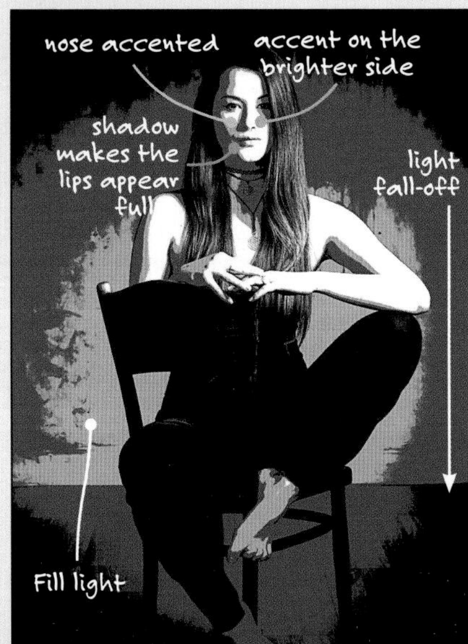

THE SETUP

1. Position your model and the chair about 10 feet in front of a dark background.

2. Place the beauty dish **(1)** about 3 feet to the right of your model at an angle of about 30 degrees. It should point directly at your model's face from a height of about 8 feet.

3. Place the octabox fill light **(2)** about 10 feet away and slightly to the right of your model but close to your shooting position. The low position of the octabox compared to that of the main light lightens the shadows in the lower portion of your model's body.

4. Place the gridded standard reflector **(3)** for the background light to the right about 3 feet from your model to provide a pool of light in the background behind her torso.

5. Place the reflector **(4)** to the left about 5 feet from your model so that it reflects the spill from the octabox and subtly lightens her left-hand side.

"This pose creates a lot of shapes that all steer the viewer's gaze toward the model's face."

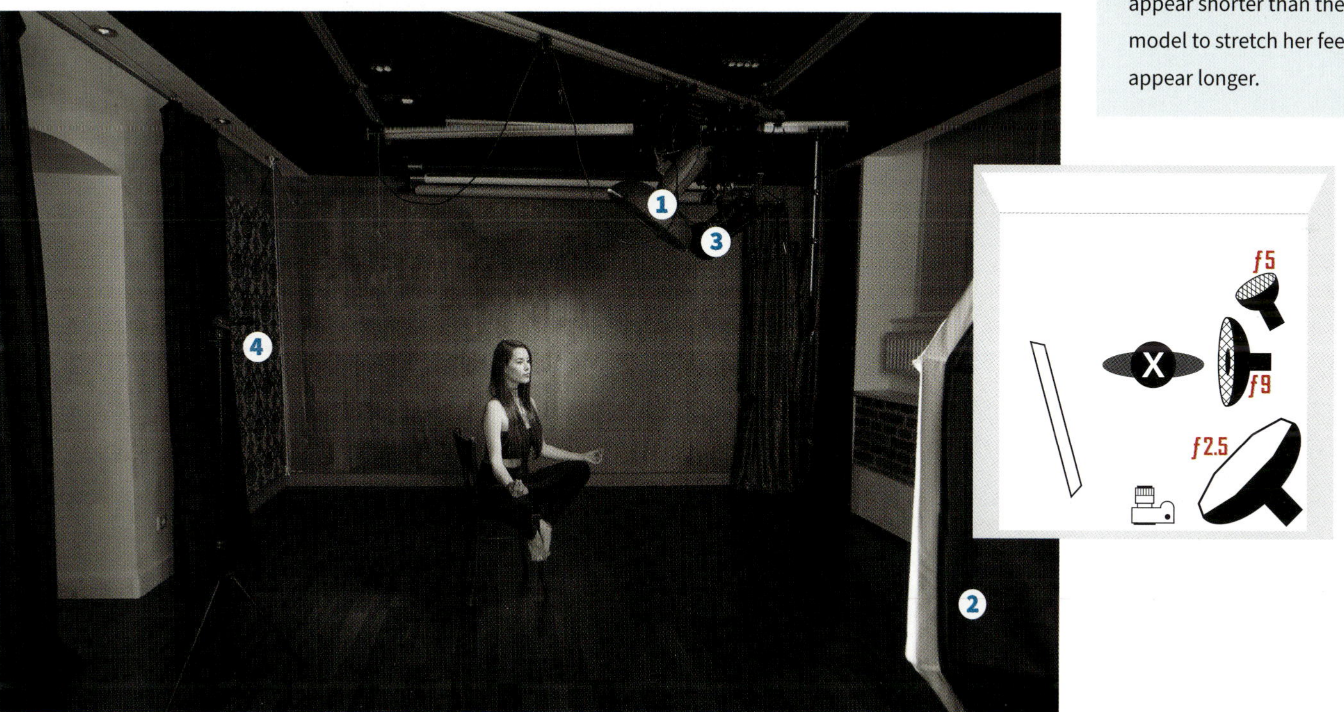

Accented Full-Length Portrait

You can use a strip box to light full-length portraits from quite close. This produces less background light and gives you more options for setting your background light. This enables you to place more emphasis on your subject's upper body and thus produce a natural-looking image with plenty of posing options.

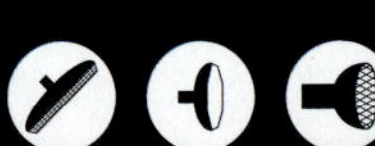

EFFORT INVOLVED

Medium

SUITABLE FOR

Full-length portraits

THE LOOK

Natural-looking full-length pose that places special emphasis on the model's torso

Friendly, positive look

EQUIPMENT

1× 47" strip box with a honeycomb grid

1× 31.5" octabox

1× standard reflector with a honeycomb grid

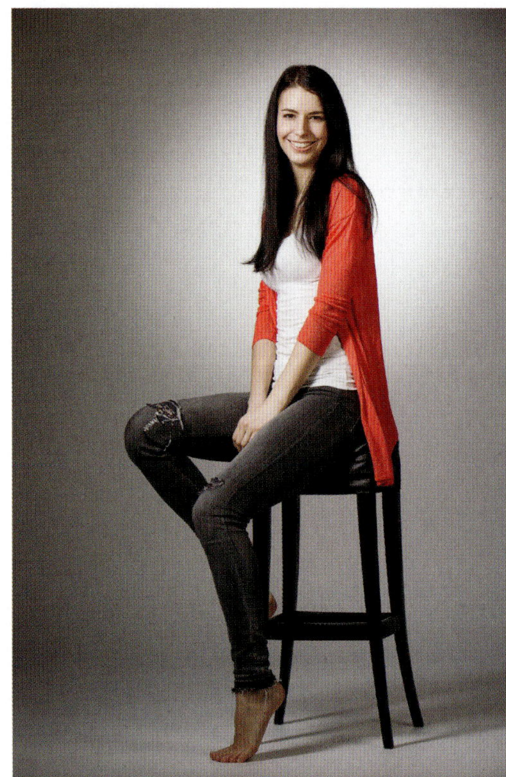

100mm | f8 | 1/160 sec. | ISO 100 | Model: Elisa

HOW IT WORKS

The strip box produces even lighting from the subject's head down to around the knees without any significant fall-off. The diagonal position of the main light creates obvious shadows and a pleasing three-dimensional look. The background highlight emphasizes the subject's upper body and, together with the floor highlight created by the strip box, produces a pleasing vignette from top to bottom of the frame. The image has plenty of contrast that separates the subject nicely from the background and produces plenty of detail. The lightened shadows convey a friendly, positive feel.

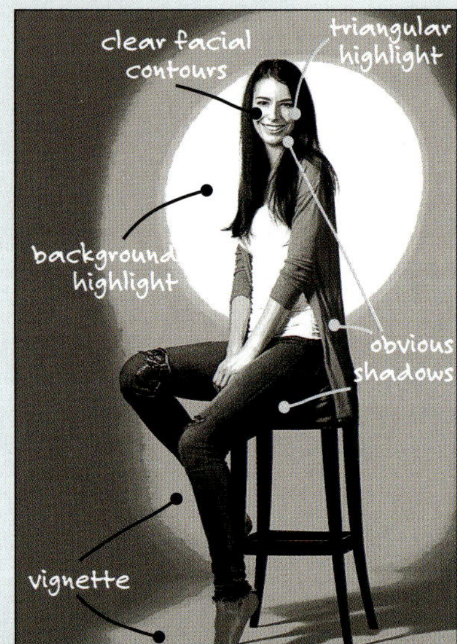

THE SETUP

1. Place the strip box **(1)** about 5 feet to the left of your model at an angle of about 45 degrees. Position it to form a triangular highlight on the shadow side of her face, and to evenly illuminate her entire body down to about knee level.

2. Place the fill octabox **(2)** slightly above head height about 6 feet to the right and in front of your model at an angle of about 45 degrees.

3. Place the standard reflector for the background **(3)** slightly behind and about 3 feet away from your model. Position it so that the pool of light it produces hits the backdrop at about chest height.

4. Your model should sit about 6 feet from the background on a bar stool.

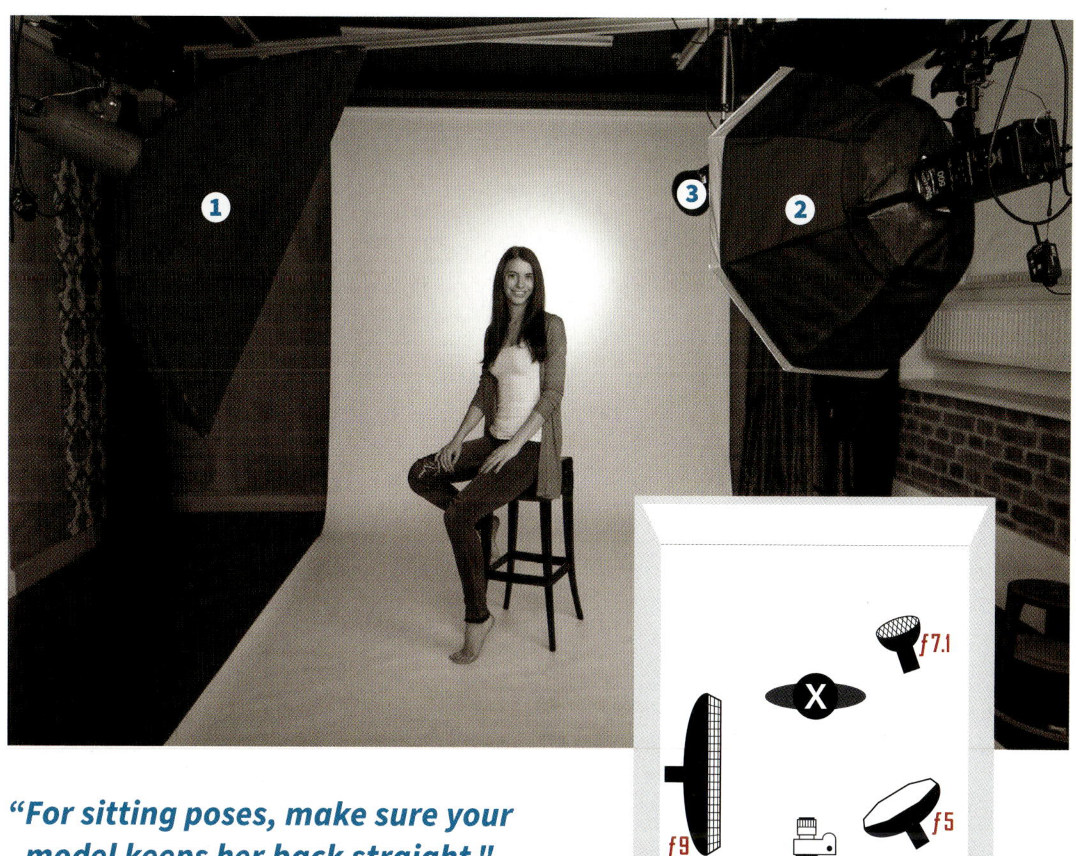

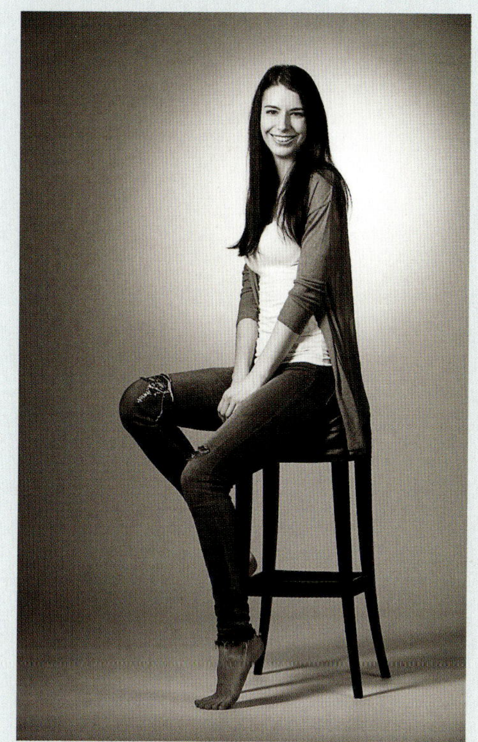

Variation in Black and White

Because this setup provides plenty of shadow detail, it is well suited to conversion to black and white. The textures in the model's clothes are still clearly visible, even in the shadows, and the image has plenty of fairly dark and light areas. The black-and-white version—which of course provides no color contrast—shows a broad and attractive distribution of grayscale tones.

Classic Business Portrait

Business portraits are classics too, and the subject is always keen to look their best. In a business context, we are usually aiming for a self-confident look. This is a typical three-point octabox/fill light/background light setup. A low shooting position underscores the confident look.

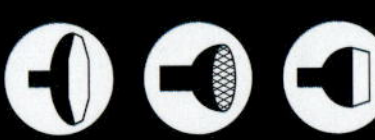

EFFORT INVOLVED

High

SUITABLE FOR

Three-quarter length or head-and-shoulders portraits

THE LOOK

Portrait with clear lines and strong emphasis on the subject's character

Styling radiates self-condfidence

EQUIPMENT

1× 47" octabox

1× standard reflector with a honeycomb grid

1× 24" softbox

1× reflector, silbern (110 cm × 70 cm)

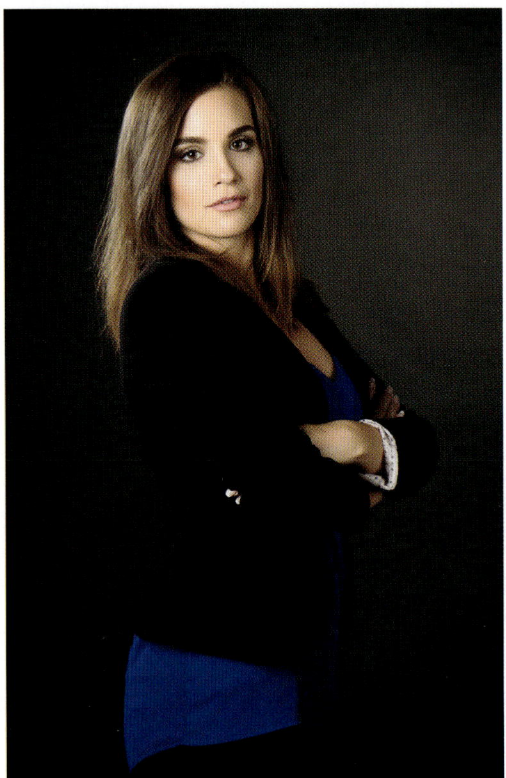

85mm | f9 | 1/160 sec. | ISO 100 | Model: Miriam

HOW IT WORKS

The even light from the slightly raised octabox creates a narrow neck shadow that visually separates the subject's head and torso without appearing too heavy-handed. The facial contours, too, are accentuated by a raised main light. The highlight from left rear accentuates the shape of the entire head, which immediately captures the viewer's attention. The background light at top right separates the relatively dark hair on the shadow side from the dark background. The low shooting position and the pose emphasize the confident overall look.

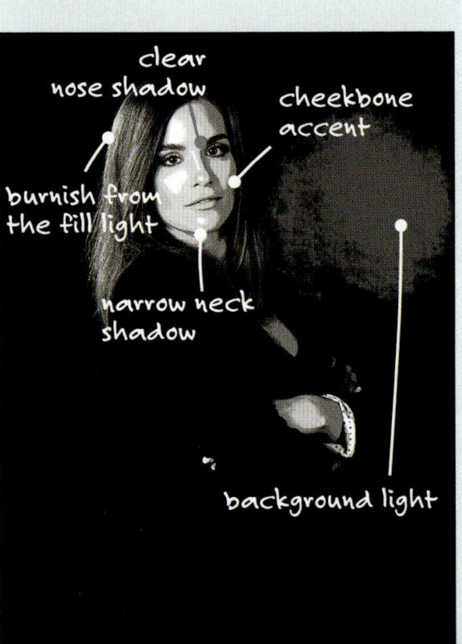

THE SETUP

1. Place the octabox **(1)** in a raised position about 3 feet from your model and at an angle of about 45 degrees. Fine-tune its position to provide a narrow neck shadow.

2. Place the reflector **(2)** about 3 feet to the right and at 90 degrees to your model. Make sure it evenly lightens the shadows at head and thigh level.

3. Place the gridded standard reflector **(3)** at a height of about 8 feet to the left rear of your model at a distance of about 6 feet and at an angle of about 45 degrees. The highlight it produces should lighten your model's hair and back.

4. Place a softbox **(4)** on the right about two feet from the background to provide the background accent.

5. Position your model about 6 feet from the black background.

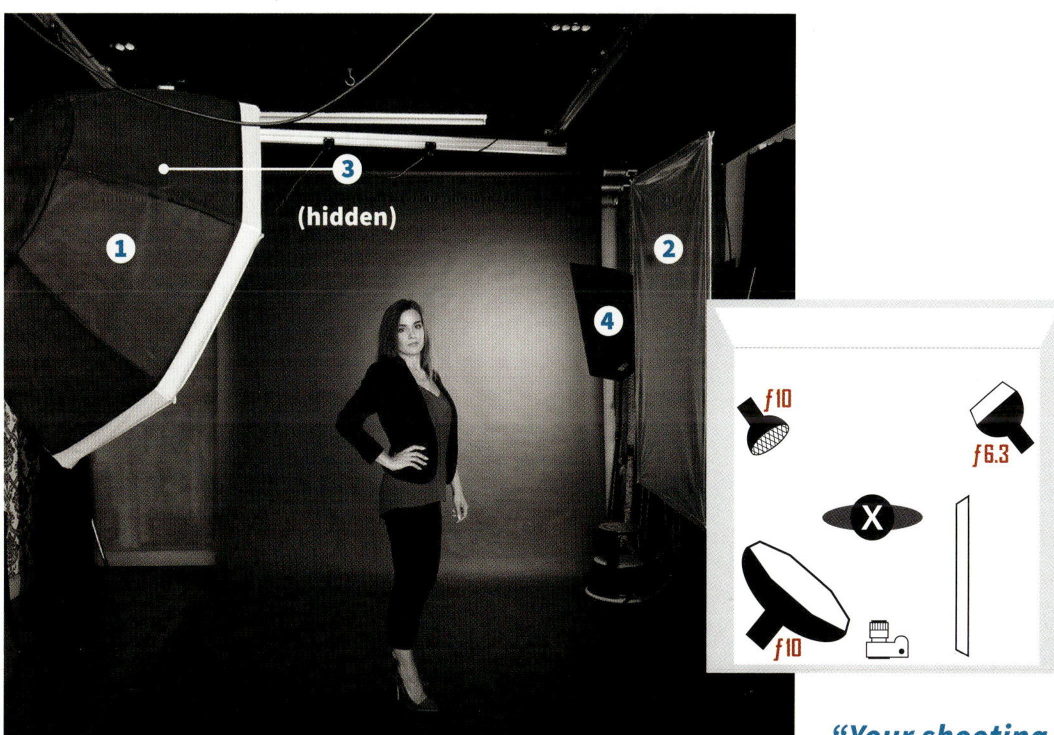

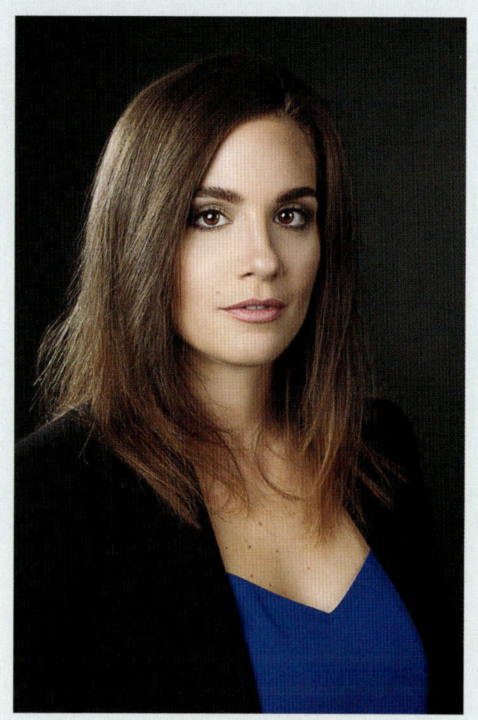

Framing and Shooting Position

This setup is ideal for three-quarter-length and head-and-shoulders portraits. When shooting this kind of portrait, note the effect your shooting position has on the results. If you shoot at eye level, your subject will appear on the same level with you and the image will lose some of the self-confident feel that shooting from below creates. Shooting at eye level is more suitable for photos of colleagues or for job applications.

"Your shooting position always has an effect on the look and feel of a portrait."

Quick and Easy Full-Length Portrait

If you are in a hurry and you need a well-lit and friendly looking portrait, this is the setup for you! All you need is a strip box for the main light and a reflector to lighten the shadows. This simple setup gives you full control over the background and foreground while giving you plenty of options for creating well-defined portraits, whether for business, for a job application, or simply for fun.

EFFORT INVOLVED

Low

SUITABLE FOR

Full-length shots

THE LOOK

A simple full-length setup that involves minimal effort

Even lighting with a "Rembrandt" accent

EQUIPMENT

1 × 47" strip box with a honeycomb grid

1 × 30"× 40" silver reflector

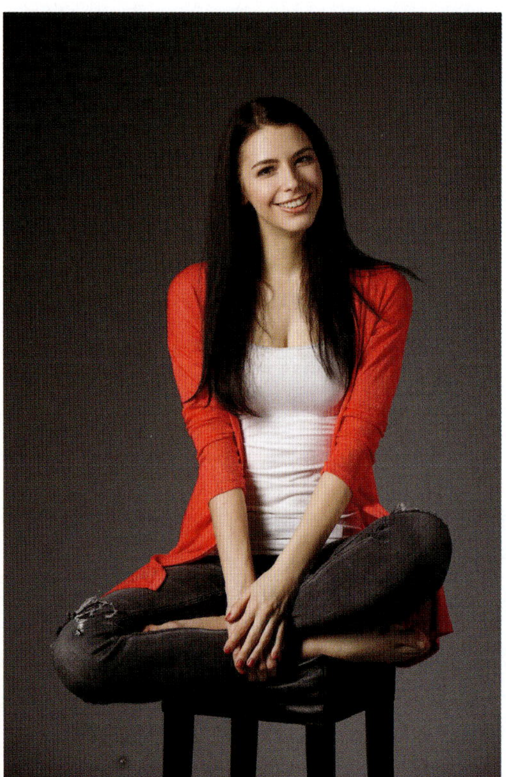

120mm | f8 | 1/160 sec. | ISO 100 | Model: Elisa

HOW IT WORKS

Using just one light that illuminates the subject from diagonally above produces a highly natural look that accents horizontal and vertical details. The tilt of the subject's head creates a triangle of light beneath her eye on the shadow side. This technique, known as "Rembrandt" lighting, places special emphasis on the subject's eyes and mouth and produces a pleasing, balanced look. The subtle vignette directs attention to the subject, who is nicely separated from the background. The reflector lightens the shadows, providing even lighting on the shadow side without too much contrast.

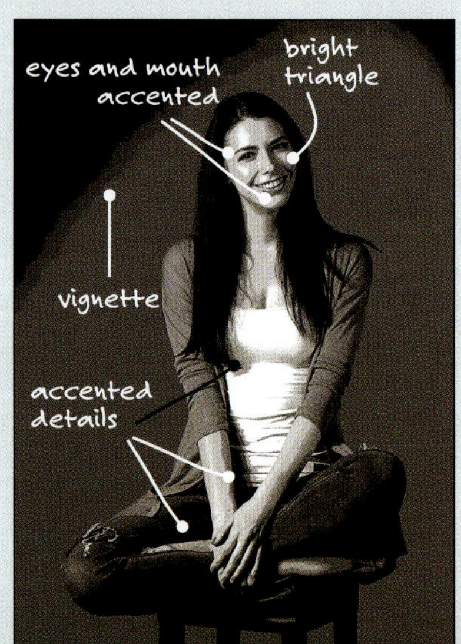

THE SETUP

1. Place the strip box **(1)** to the left about 5 feet from your model at an angle of about 45 degrees. Position the light so that it forms a triangle of light under your model's eye on the shadow side and evenly lights her body from her head to around knee height.

2. Place the reflector **(2)** to the right about 3 feet from your model at 90 degrees and slightly above head height. Position it to lighten all the shadows between face and knee height.

3. Place your model on a bar stool about 6 feet from a white background. This subject distance creates a medium-gray background.

"Place the strip box at a distance that evenly lights your model from top to bottom. Pay attention to the background lighting, too."

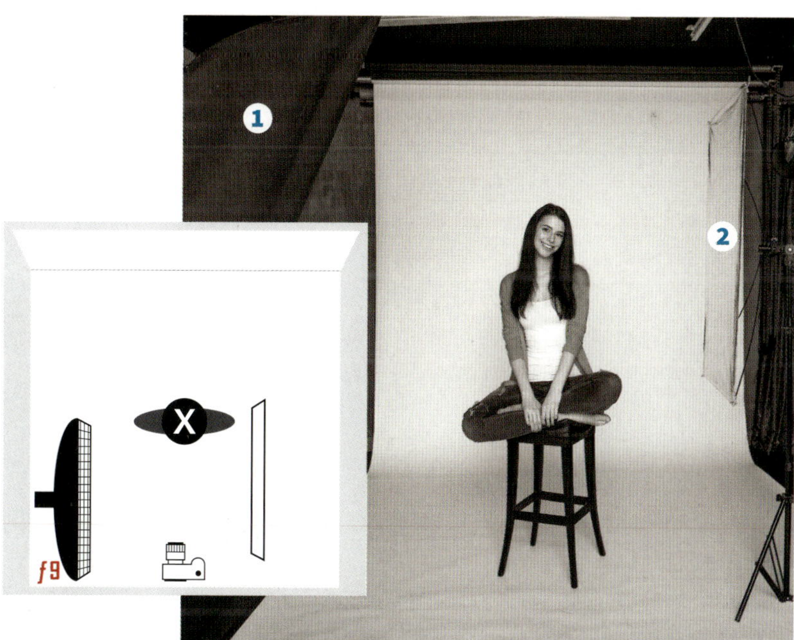

"Rembrandt" Lighting

As the name suggests, this portrait lighting technique stems from the work of the Dutch master painter Rembrandt van Rijn, who used the so-called triangle technique in many of his portraits. This setup uses this approach to create portraits in which only one side of the model's face is clearly lit. The other side disappears almost completely in shadow and is only vaguely discernible. The result is a portrait with a dark, somber feel. This lighting technique is still extremely popular.

The basic Rembrandt setup uses just one light shaper but nevertheless produces dramatic, punchy images. To get the right effect, the main light has to be positioned above the model's head and tilted diagonally. It is easiest to set up if you get your model to position their head before you position the light. An angle of 45 degrees usually does the trick. You can then fine-tune the position of your light to produce the triangle effect. You may have to alter the height of your light too.

Practically speaking, you can use just about any kind of light shaper to produce this effect. Your choice will depend on how soft or hard you want your results to look.

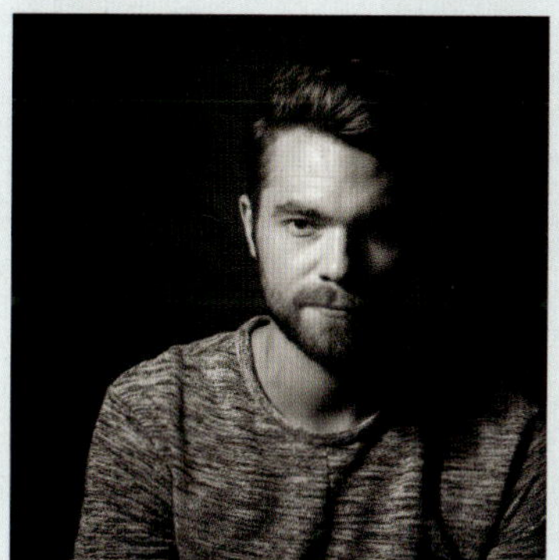

The typical Rembrandt look with a "closed" triangle of light.

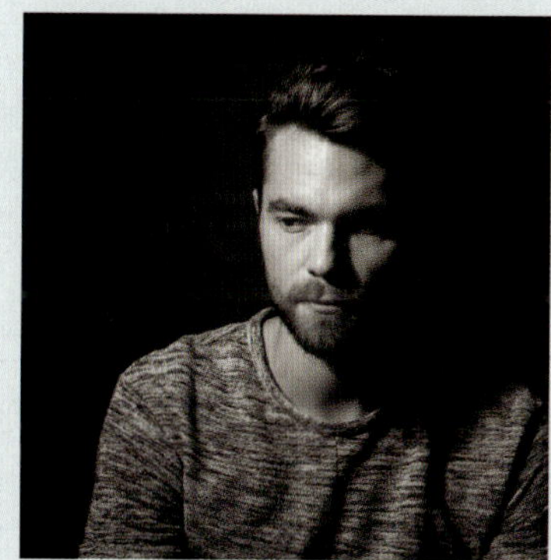

A slight movement of the model's head "opens" the triangle and spoils the classic Rembrandt look.

High-Contrast Business Portrait

All you need to produce this kind of high-contrast business portrait are two accent lights and a large octabox. The focus of this shot is completely on the subject's face, and the lack of fill and background lights produce a strong, highly three-dimensional image.

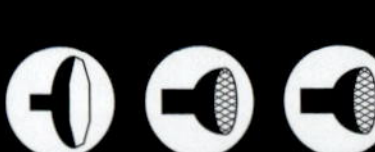

EFFORT INVOLVED

Medium

SUITABLE FOR

Close-up and three-quarter-length portraits

THE LOOK

A strong, high-contrast portrait

Eye-level shooting position

Reduced skin blemishes

EQUIPMENT

1 × 47" octabox

2 × standard reflectors with honeycomb grids

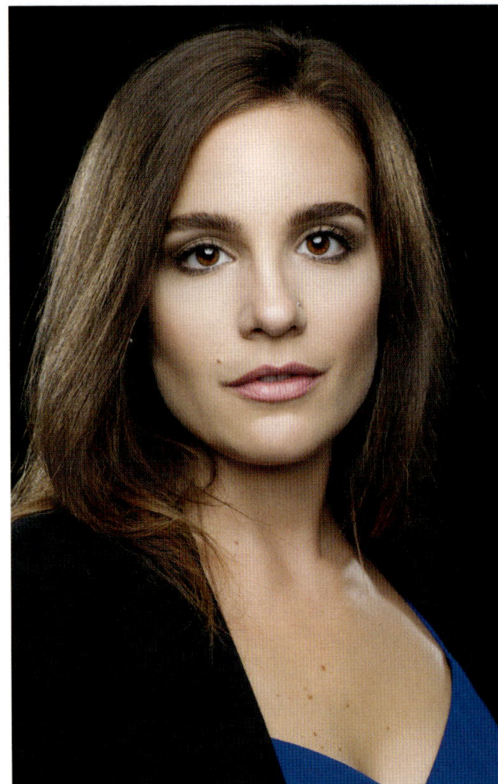

85mm | f9 | 1/160 sec. | ISO 100 | Model: Miriam

HOW IT WORKS

The twin fill lights produce strong separation between subject and background, and glossy-looking hair. The raised, frontal main light accents the cheekbones and contours in the subject's face. The shadow makes the lips appear fuller and underscores the shape of the mouth. The neck shadow produces clear visual separation between the head and body. The medium-high position of the main light means that sufficient light reaches the subject's eyelids, giving the eyes an intense glow. Strong contrast and well-defined shadows give this image a highly three-dimensional look.

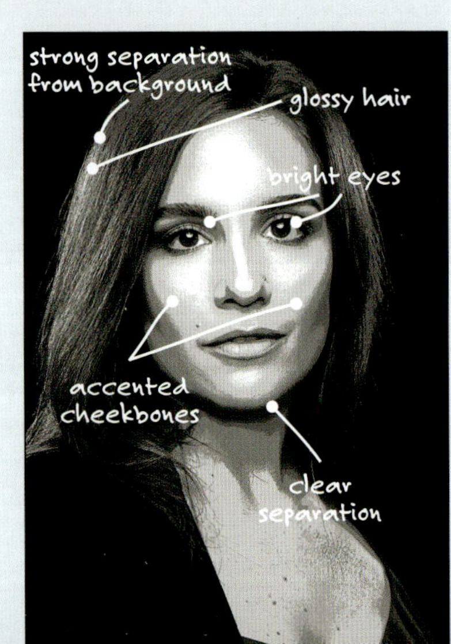

THE SETUP

1. Place the octabox **(1)** about 3 feet from your model in a raised frontal position so that it produces a small shadow beneath her nose.

2. Now place the two standard reflectors **(2)** and **(3)** to the left and right behind your model, both about 6 feet away at an angle of about 45 degrees. Position both lights about 8 inches higher than your model's head to produce highlights on her hair and shoulders, but not in her face.

3. Place your model about 5 feet in front of the black background.

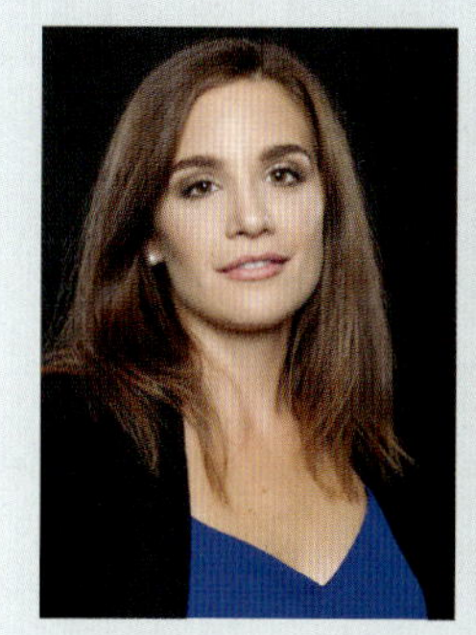
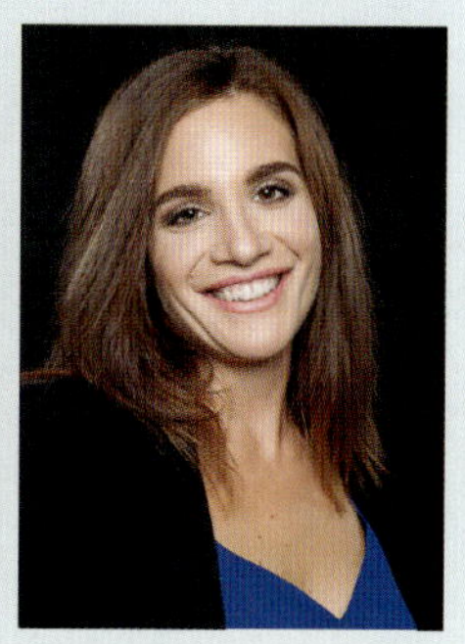

Fitness for Purpose

Business portraits use different facial expressions for different purposes. For example, if a portrait is to be used on a company website, the subject may want to greet customers with a smile. Portraits captured for a job application should show a smile too, albeit one that is perhaps a little more discreet.

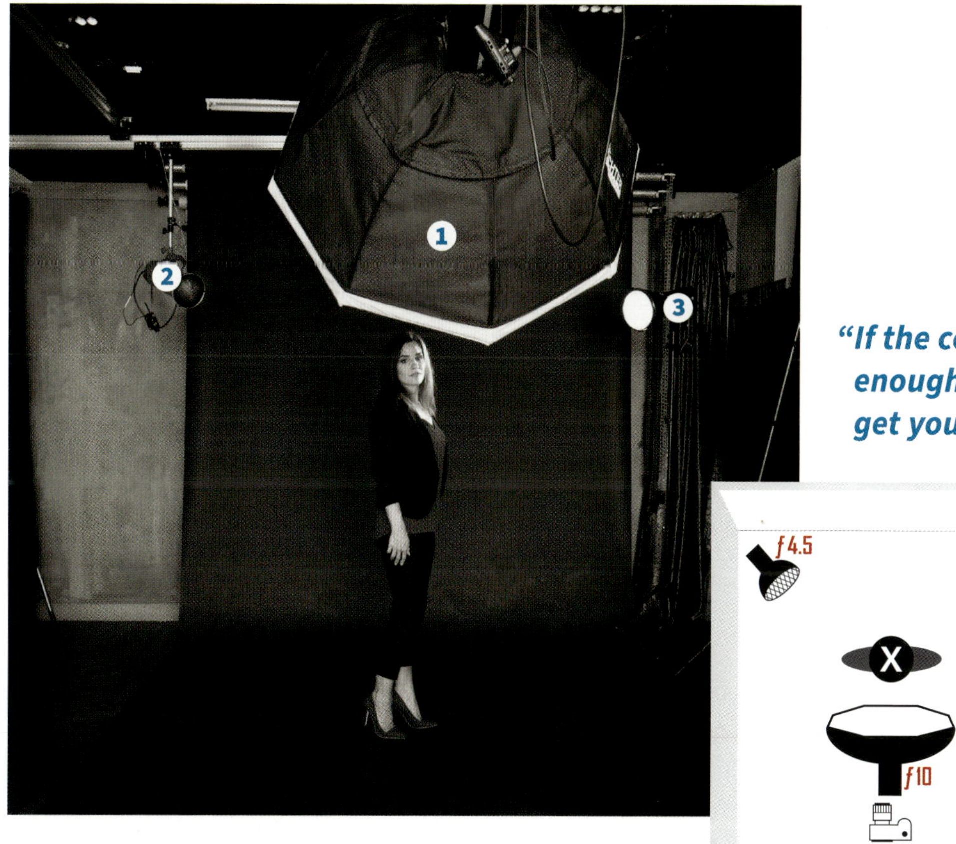

"If the ceiling in the space you are using isn't high enough to accommodate the setup, you can always get your model to sit for this pose."

Business Portrait in Black and White

If you want to develop a business portrait in black and white, you need to pay close attention to the overall contrast in your image while you shoot. You should aim for a finely graded monochrome image with a broad range of grayscale tones. This setup hinges on high-contrast facial lighting. The model's outline is accented by the fill and background lights.

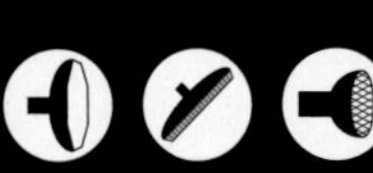

EFFORT INVOLVED

Medium

SUITABLE FOR

Three-quarter length and head-and-shoulder portraits

THE LOOK

Black-and-white portrait with strong contrast
Emphasis on the face
Subtle outline accents

EQUIPMENT

1 × 47" octabox
1 × 47" strip box with a honeycomb grid
1 × normal reflector with a honeycomb grid

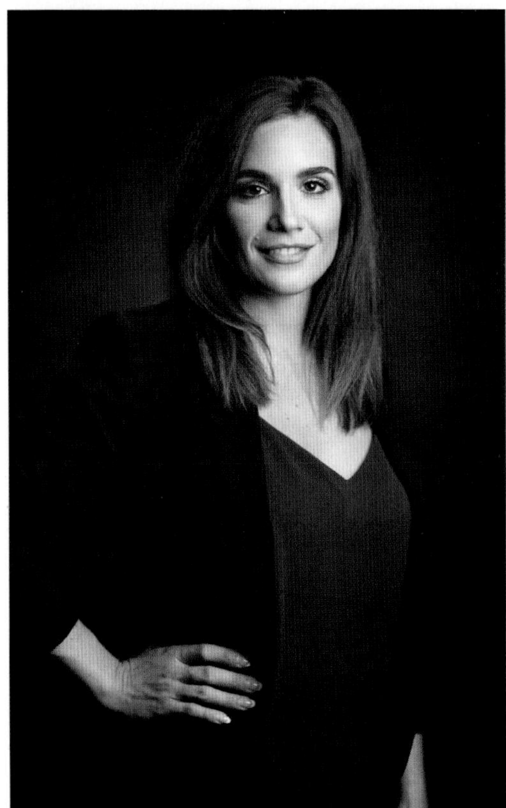

85mm | f8 | 1/160 sec. | ISO 100 | Model: Miriam

HOW IT WORKS

The strong contrast automatically steers the viewer's gaze toward the subject's face. The lateral main light accentuates the facial contours and emphasizes the cheekbone on the shadow side. The low position of the main light produces light fall-off toward the subject's midriff, making the subject's body less significant and keeping the viewer's focus on the face. The fill light gives subtle substance to the body contours on the shadow side. The background light forms a vignette that provides additional gray tones in the final monochrome image.

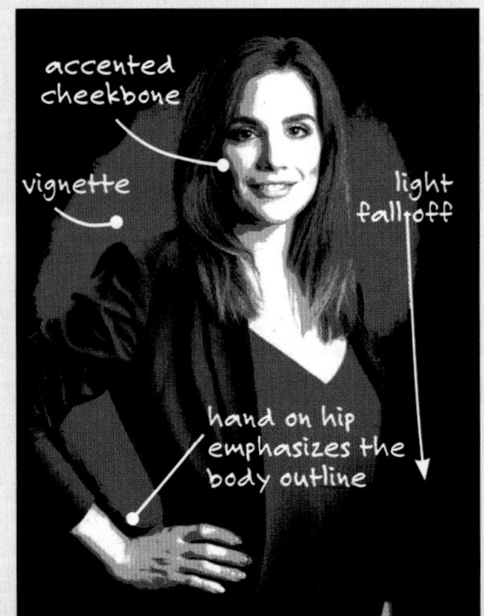

THE SETUP

1. Place the large octabox **(1)** about 3 feet to the right of your model at about 45 degrees. Set it to a height that produces a slight shadow beneath your model's right nostril.

2. Place the strip box **(2)** at left rear about 5 feet from your model. The center of the strip box should be positioned just over head hight so that it gently lights her head and shoulder.

3. Place the gridded standard reflector for the background **(3)** about 5 feet to the right of your model. Position it at head height at an angle that produces a pool of light in the center of the backdrop.

4. You model should stand about 6 feet away from the black background.

5. You can adjust the size of the background light by altering its distance from the background. If you move the background light, remember to adjust its flash output accordingly.

"To avoid diverting attention from the subject's face in black-and-white portraits, get your model to wear clothes with a narrow range of gray tones."

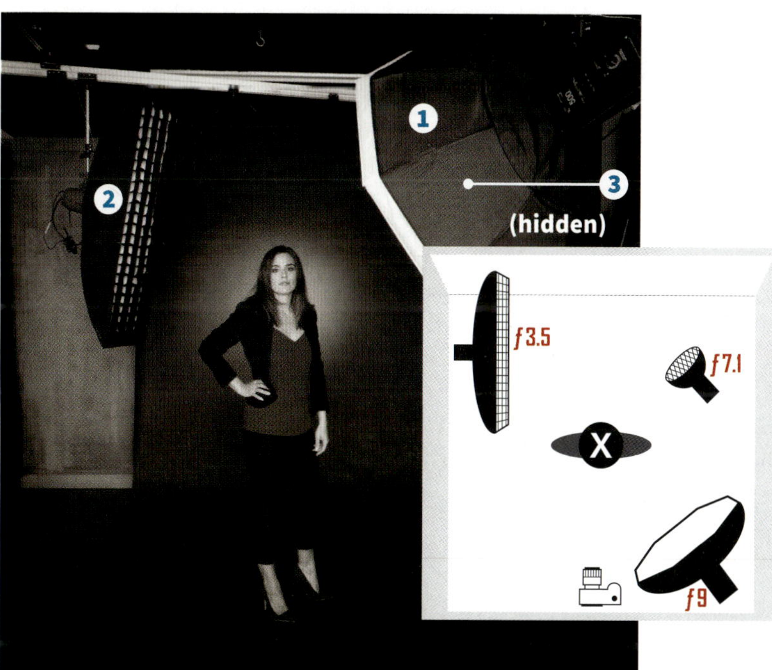

Black-and-White Conversion

An image needs to encompass a broad range of grayscale tones and shouldn't use color as part of the composition if you want to effectively convert it to black and white (using Lightroom, for example). In Lightroom's Develop module, pressing the V key converts the image you are viewing to grayscale. You can then immediately see whether you need to tweak the tonal values in your image or whether they work in black and white as they are.

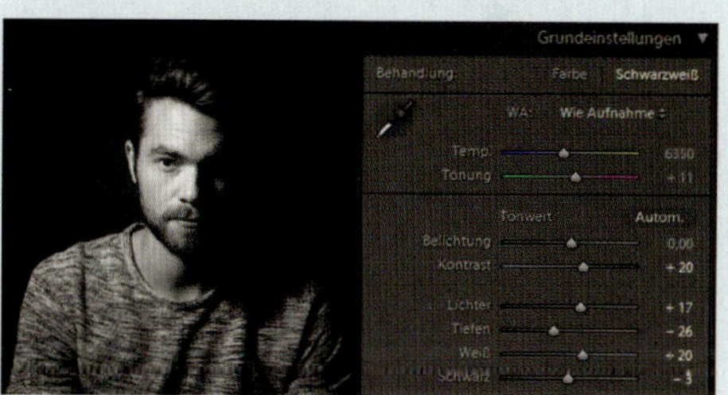

If you are happy with the overall look of your black-and-white image, you can then fine-tune exposure, contrast, highlights, shadows, and the white and black points to taste. I generally increase the contrast (+20) and highlight (+15) settings, and darken the shadows (-20). I also raise the white point by between +5 and +20. These values are only meant as a rough guide, and you should always experiment with values that suit your personal preferences and the particular image you are working on. In Lightroom's Black & White panel, you can use the color sliders to adjust the brightness of the individual grayscale tones.

Modern Business Portrait

Modern business portraits use strong accents to create bold images. This setup draws a clear and compelling line between the light and shadow sides of the subject's face. The subject's facial expression plays a significant role in the overall effect, too.

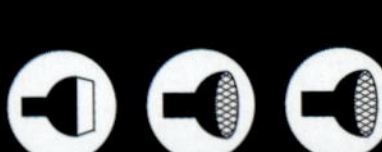

EFFORT INVOLVED

High

SUITABLE FOR

Head-and-shoulders portraits

THE LOOK

Strong, heavily accented business portrait
Clearly differentiated light and shadow sides

EQUIPMENT

1 × 24" softbox
2 × standard reflectors with honeycomb grids
1 × 30" × 40" silver reflector

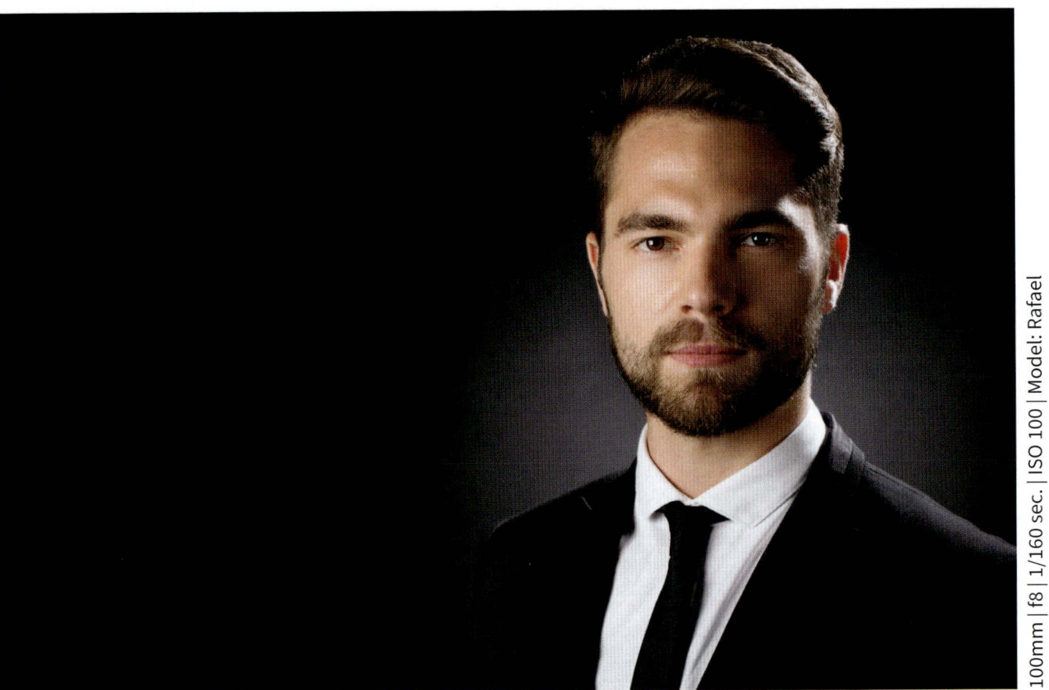

100mm | f8 | 1/160 sec. | ISO 100 | Model: Rafael

HOW IT WORKS

The narrow background spot beam nicely separates the subject from the background. The highlight on the right shapes the face, gives the hair a glossy sheen, and accentuates the shoulder line. The main light makes the right-hand side of the subject's face virtually shadow-free, which immediately attracts the viewer's attention. The position of the main light also creates a strong shadow on the left-hand side of the face while still retaining detail in the left eye. There are catchlights in both eyes. The strong contrast between the two sides of the face draws the viewer in and makes them swing their gaze from side to side.

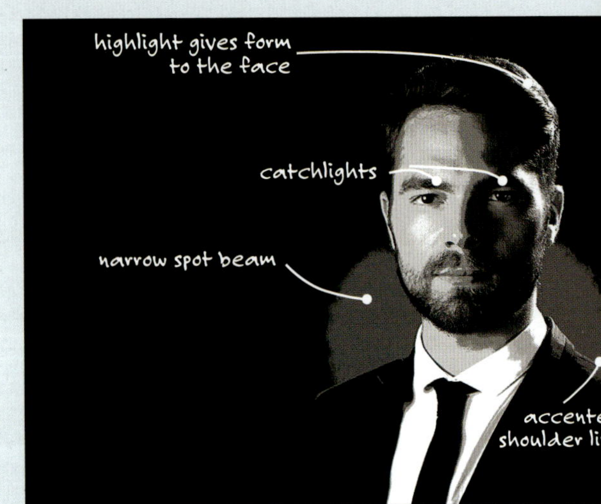

THE SETUP

1. Place the main softbox **(1)** about 3 feet to the left of your model slightly above head height and at an angle of about 60 degrees. Make sure that it produces reflections (so-called catchlights) in both of your model's eyes.

2. Place a silver reflector **(2)** about 3 feet to the right and slightly lower than the main light.

3. Place the gridded standard reflector **(3)** at right rear at a height of about 8 feet and 6 feet away from your model. Position it so that it produces a clear accent from the top of his head to the end of his shoulder.

4. Place the background standard reflector with its grid **(4)** directly behind your model at a height of about 5 feet. The resulting pool of light should be at neck height and shouldn't reach further up than the center of your model's head.

5. Your model should stand about 10 feet from the black background.

"The reflections in the subject's eyes are what brings a portrait to life. Without them, the eyes appear dull and hollow."

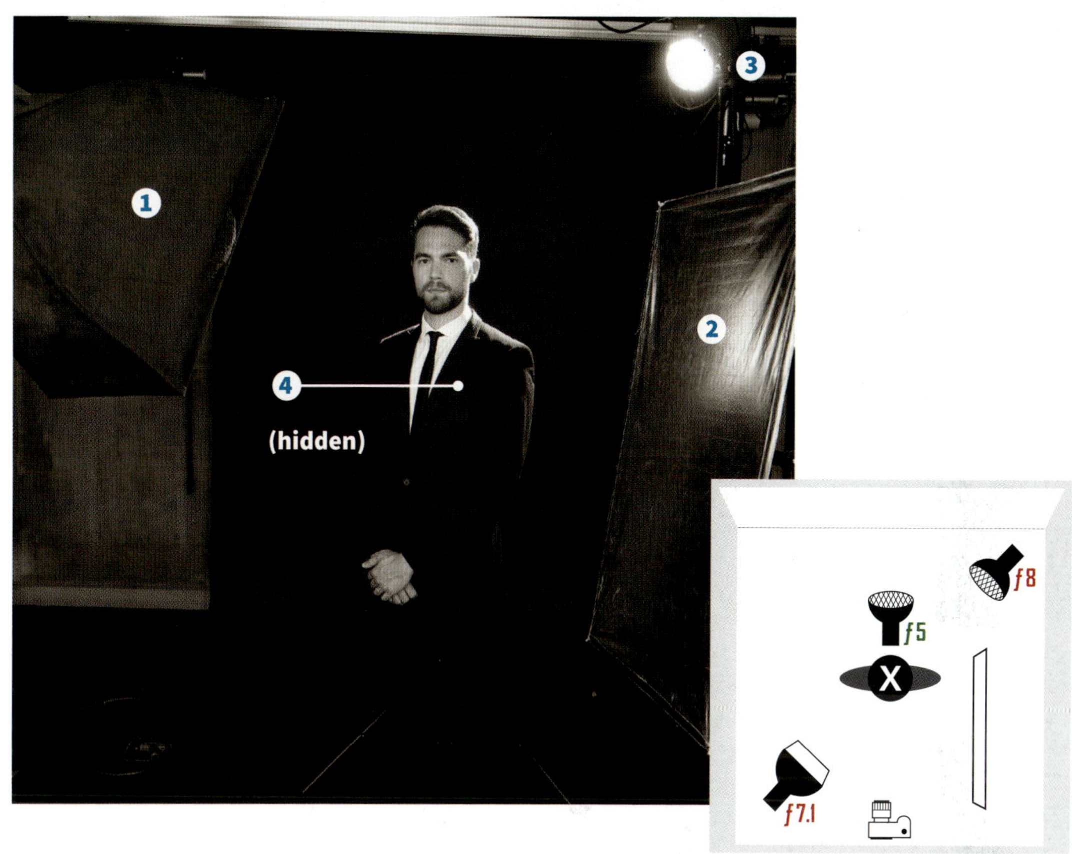

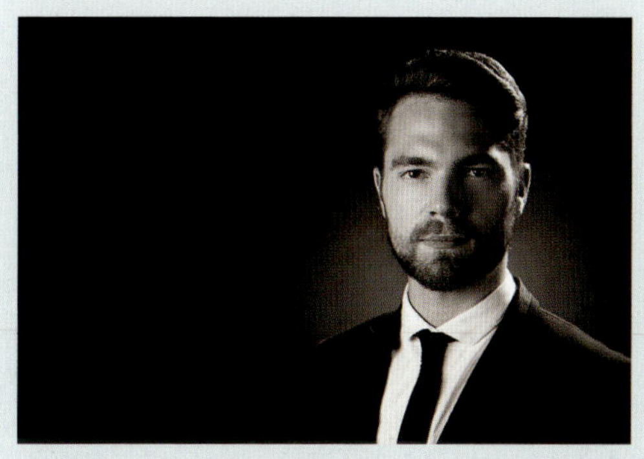

Variations

This high-contrast setup is great for shooting color or black-and-white images. When converting to black and white, make sure that your image contains deep black and (almost) pure white tones. This ensures that the monochrome variant looks really punchy.

Using On-Camera Flash

You won't always have access to a full set of studio gear, so don't be afraid to use an on-camera (or "system") flash instead. System flash is fine for shooting classic, well-lit portraits. The dark gray walls and black ceiling in my studio make bounce flash impossible, so for this shot I used on-camera flash as my only light source to produce this edgy, punchy-looking portrait.

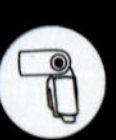

EFFORT INVOLVED

Low

SUITABLE FOR

Close-up and three-quarter-length portraits

THE LOOK

Punchy portrait with hard shadows

EQUIPMENT

1× on-camera system flash

1× curtain

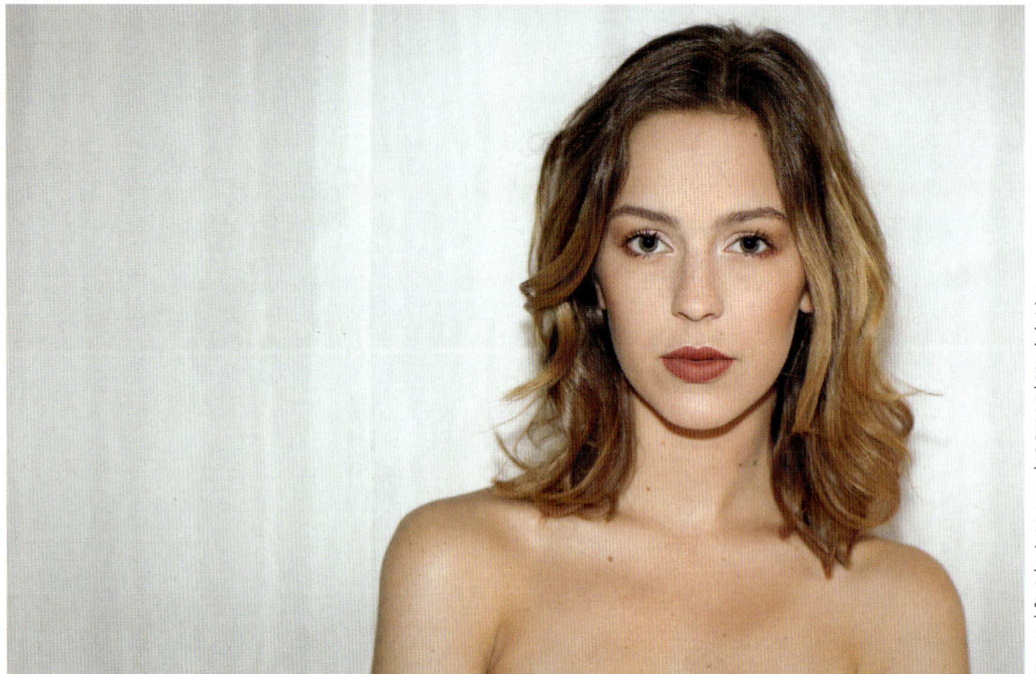

85mm | f2.8 | 1/125 sec. | ISO 200 | Model: Lisa

HOW IT WORKS

When shooting in landscape mode, the on-camera flash above the camera produces frontal light from a slightly raised position. This very hard light produces a strong neck shadow that provides clear delineation between the subject's head and body. Facial contours are generally well defined. Because the flash is very close to the lens axis, it illuminates the eyes directly, giving them a strong, high-contrast look. The curtain material backdrop reduces the strength of the background shadows, and its texture provides a slightly softer look that contrasts nicely with the hard-edged portrait.

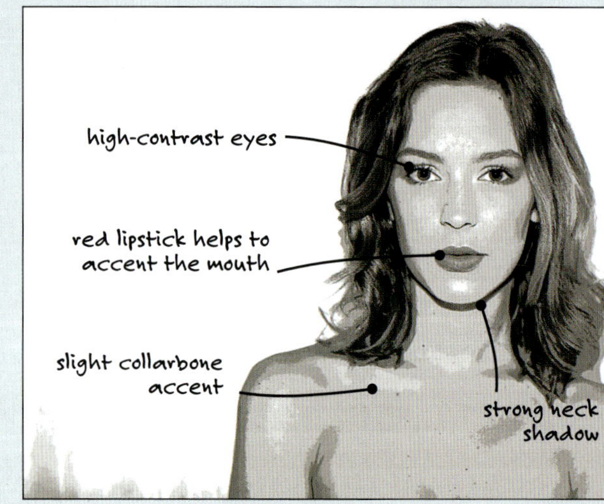

THE SETUP

1. Mount your system flash **(1)** on your camera and set it to TTL (through-the-lens) mode. Because the subject is relatively bright, you will need to set flash compensation to +1 f-stop. If you want to illuminate your model from above, you will have to shoot in landscape format.

2. Get your model to stand directly in front of the textile backdrop **(2)**.

3. Take a slightly diagonal shooting position. This creates a slight fall-off effect on the left-hand side of the backdrop.

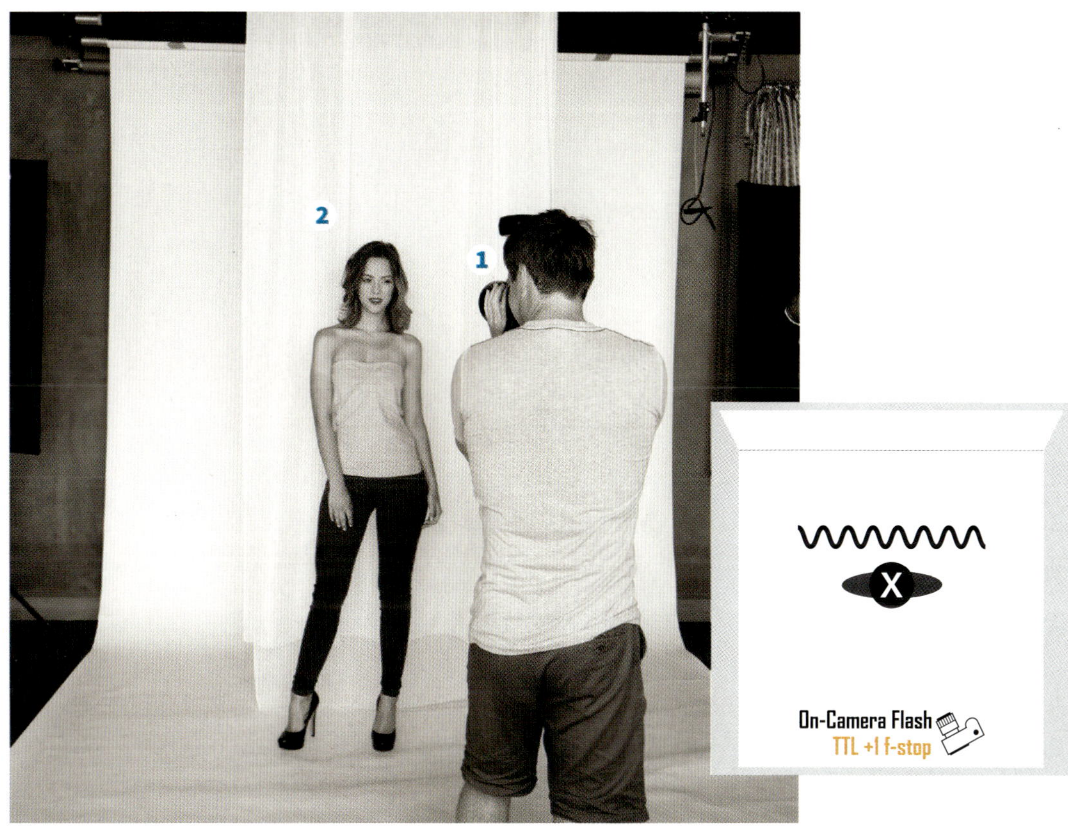

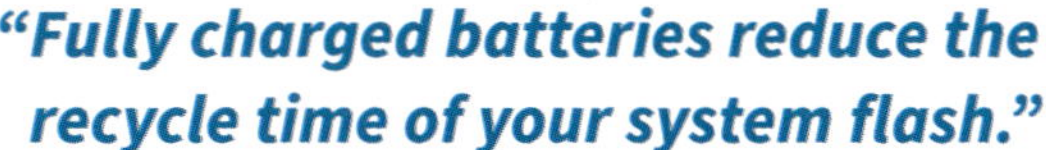

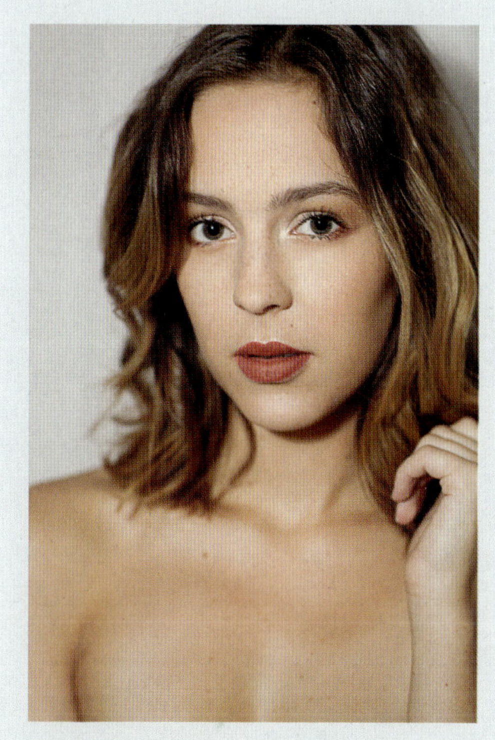

Portrait Format

If you shoot using on-camera flash in portrait format, the flash is located to the side of the lens axis and produces unnatural-looking lateral light. To compensate for this, get your model to turn her head slightly toward the flash. This simple trick makes the light appear more frontal and eliminates any unwanted lateral nose shadows. Shoot at eye level to produce the desired neck shadow.

"Fully charged batteries reduce the recycle time of your system flash."

On-Camera Flash II

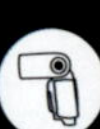

To create a gentle-looking portrait using on-camera flash, you can use a silver reflector to bounce the light from the flash. The reflector serves as the light source, keeping the light in the resulting image soft but targeted.

EFFORT INVOLVED

Medium

SUITABLE FOR

Close-up, head-and-shoulders, and three-quarter-length portraits

THE LOOK

Delicate, sensuous portrait with soft shadows
Daylight look (without daylight)
Shallow depth of field

EQUIPMENT

1× system flash
1× 30"×40" silver reflector
1× Vorhang

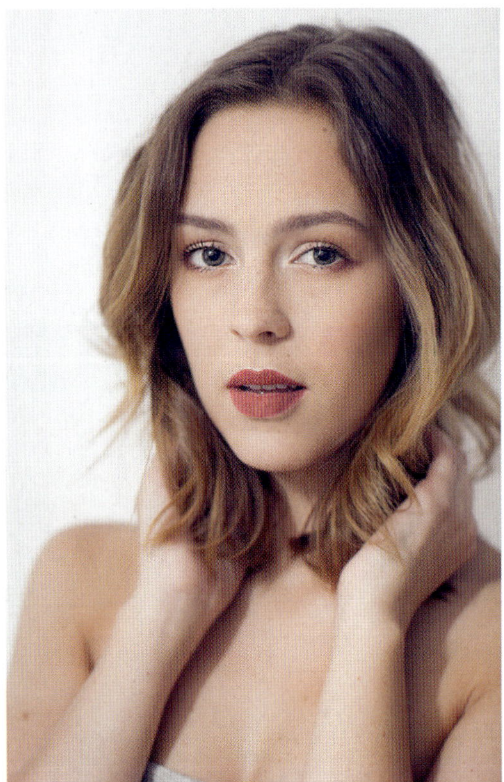

85mm | f2.8 | 1/125 sec. | ISO 100 | Model: Lisa

HOW IT WORKS

The reflector placed above and to the left of the camera produces soft, natural-looking light. The slight turn of the model's head produces a narrow highlight and the soft cheek shadow is further lightened by the flash. The slight shadows on the eyelids give the eyes a slightly more intense look. The lips are accented by the shadow beneath the lower lip, and the twin shadows produced by the reflector and the flash are clearly visible to the right of the arms. This effect is similar to the one produced by a beauty dish, and gives the image a gentle overall feel.

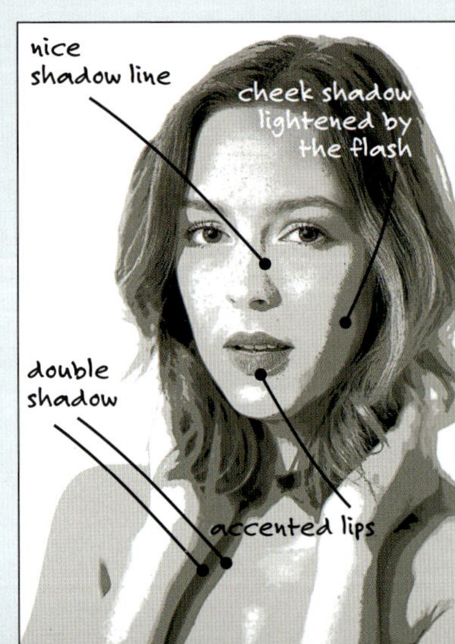

THE SETUP

1. Position your model about 20 inches in front of a white fabric backdrop **(1)** or a white wall.

2. Place the silver reflector **(2)** about 3 feet to the left of your shooting position at a height of about 7 feet. Angle the reflector so that the light is reflected toward your model from above. Most system flash units don't have a separate modeling light, so you will most likely have to make test shots to check the effects of your setup.

3. Rotate the head of your flash **(3)** so that it points at the reflector. Set it to TTL mode and set flash compensation to +1 f-stop.

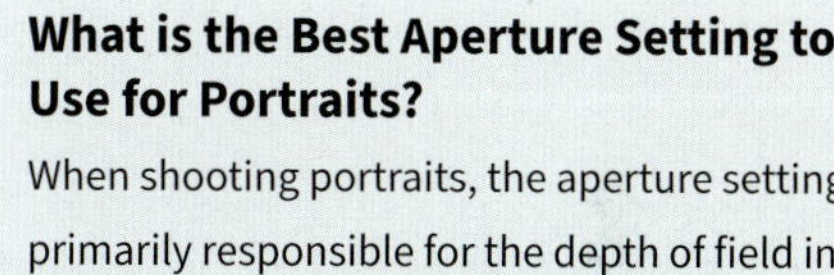

"Because the reflector serves as the light source, you can use a gold reflector instead of a silver one to produce a warmer overall look."

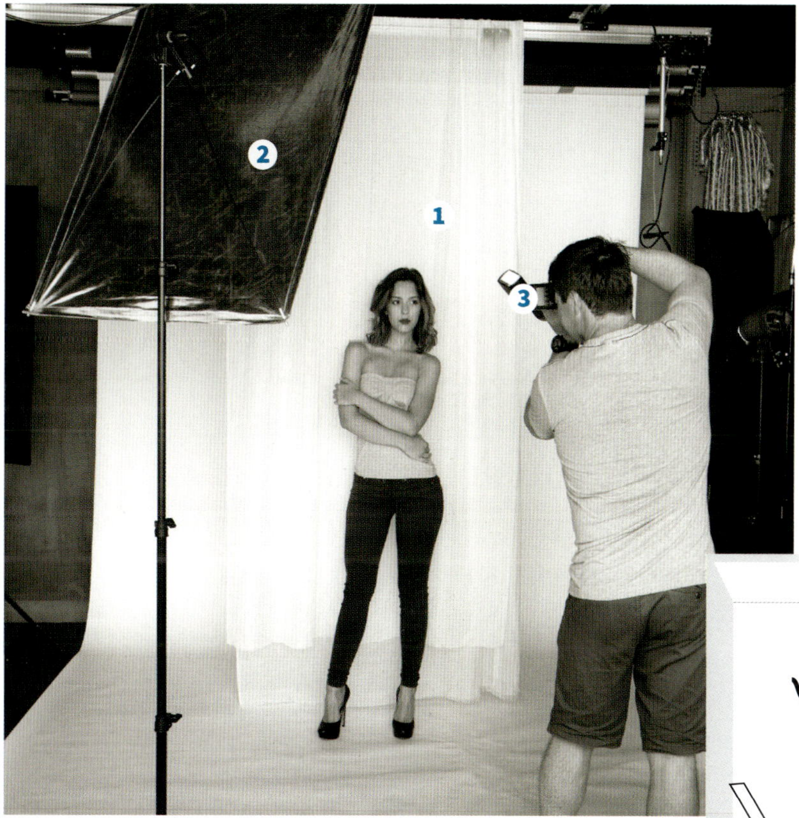

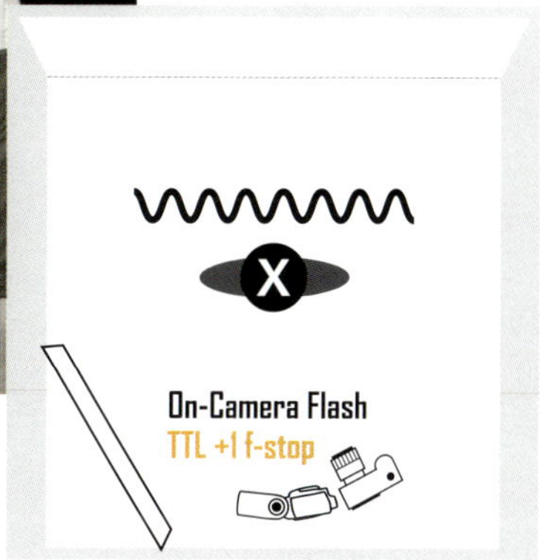

What is the Best Aperture Setting to Use for Portraits?

When shooting portraits, the aperture setting is primarily responsible for the depth of field in the final image. When you are working in a studio, you can control your lighting very precisely and adjust your working aperture accordingly. If you use a wide aperture like I did for the shot shown opposite, the result is very shallow depth of field. This focuses attention on the model's eyes and her face, and the lack of focus elsewhere within the frame gives the entire image a softer feel. When you are working with a wide aperture, you have to make sure that you focus on precisely the right part of your subject. For most shots, we recommend that you use a medium aperture setting between f5.6 and f11. This produces more depth of field than a wide aperture and the result will look slightly harder, but you will have more scope when it comes to focusing, especially if your model moves while you shoot. For catalog and product shots, you need to keep as much of the subject in focus as possible, so you should use an aperture of f11 or smaller.

Window Light

Most studios have a window to the world outside. If the weather is bright enough, you can use daylight to shoot relatively simple, natural-looking portraits. If the available light is too bright, all you need is a curtain to tone things down and produce wonderful soft-look images. In contrast to flash light, when you are shooting in daylight, you have to position the model and the camera to suit the light source.

74

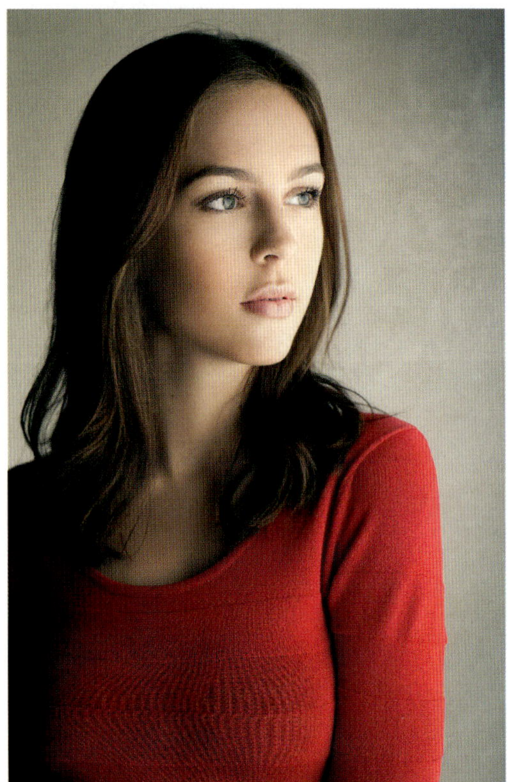

85mm | f5 | 1/160 sec. | ISO 100 | Model: Lisa

HOW IT WORKS

The very soft lateral light produces a short lighting effect with very soft shadows that makes the subject's head appear narrower and thus more accentuated. The large window opening ensures that the subject is evenly lit with well-defined vertical details. The large reflections in the eyes provide a lively look that is simultaneously natural and mellow. The very soft shadows gently frame the face and accentuate its contours. The reflections within the room softly lighten the shadows, which contributes to the gentle, intimate feel of the image.

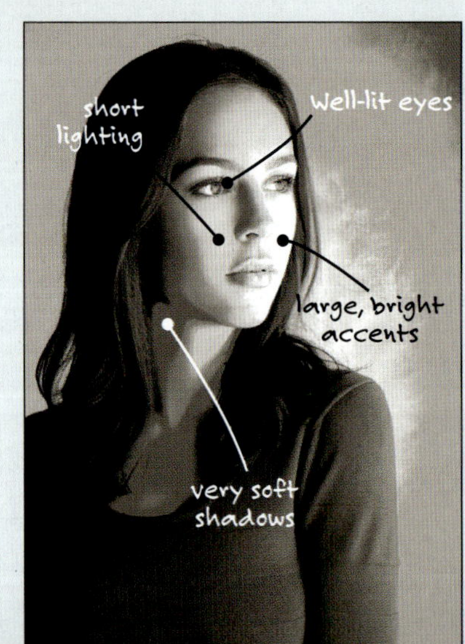

For this setup you don't have to set up the lights your-self, but you do have to position your model, the back-drop, and the camera to suit the available daylight.

As in the Construction Site Lamp setup on page 78, I used a lighting model to set up the camera before Lisa got dressed and made up for the shot.

1. If there are no clouds, no curtain, or the window glass isn't frosted, you can make the light appro-priately diffuse by hanging a curtain between the window and your model, or by placing a diffuser in front of the window.

"Begin by setting your aperture and exposure time and then adjust the ISO setting to fine-tune the exposure."

2. To ensure that the light in the image comes from above, position your model 3 to 6 feet from the window.

3. Get your model to turn her head toward the window to produce a slightly oblique short lighting effect. Make sure the cheek shadow accentuates your model's cheek contours.

Stronger Shadows

If you reproduce this setup in a small, bright room, you will notice that the shadows aren't as strong as those shown here. This is because light-colored walls produce a lot of reflections and random, bounced light. If you want more intense shadows, you can use a flag as described on page 15.

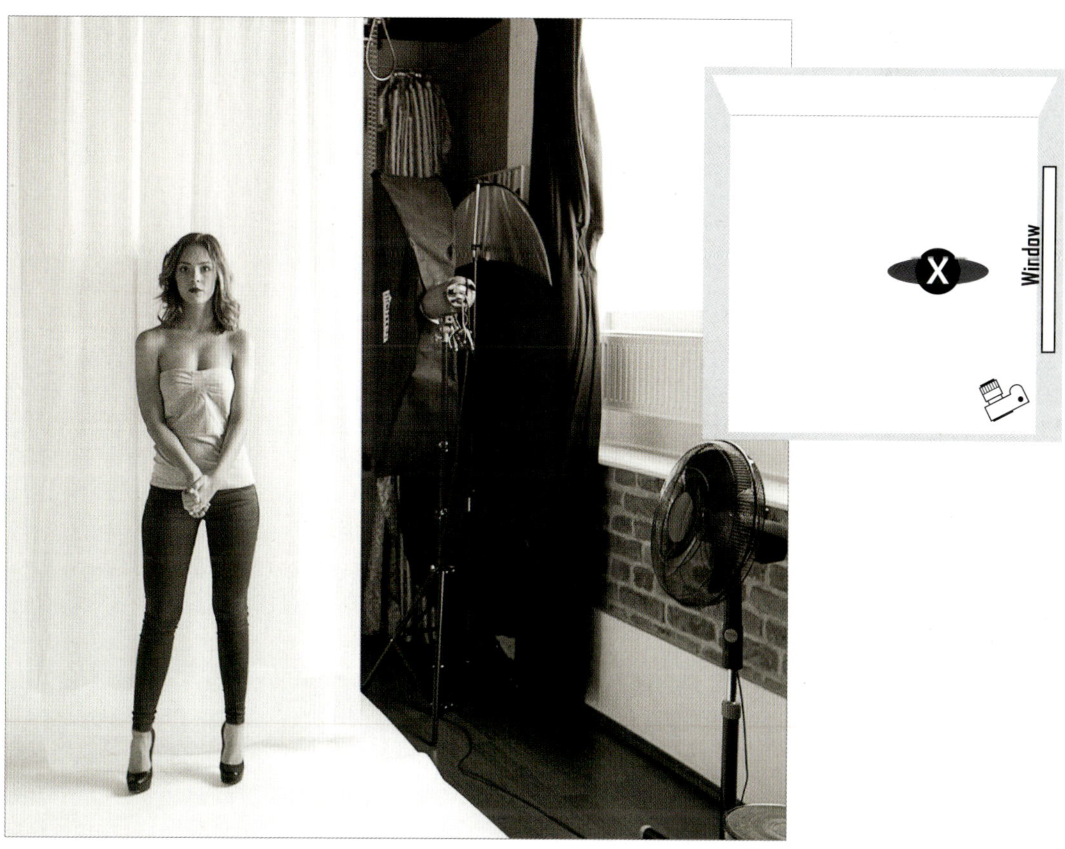

On-Camera Flash III

If your studio space has a window, you can shoot daylight portraits. You can add on-camera flash to produce extra accents in your daylight shots. A large window provides soft main light, while the on-camera flash serves as a fill light. In this shot, I used a curtain backdrop to create a more intimate, private feel.

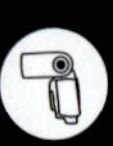

EFFORT INVOLVED

Medium

SUITABLE FOR

Close-up to three-quarter-length portraits

THE LOOK

Delicate, sensual portrait with soft shadows

Natural daylight look

Accented body contours

EQUIPMENT

1× on-camera flash

1× large window

1× curtain

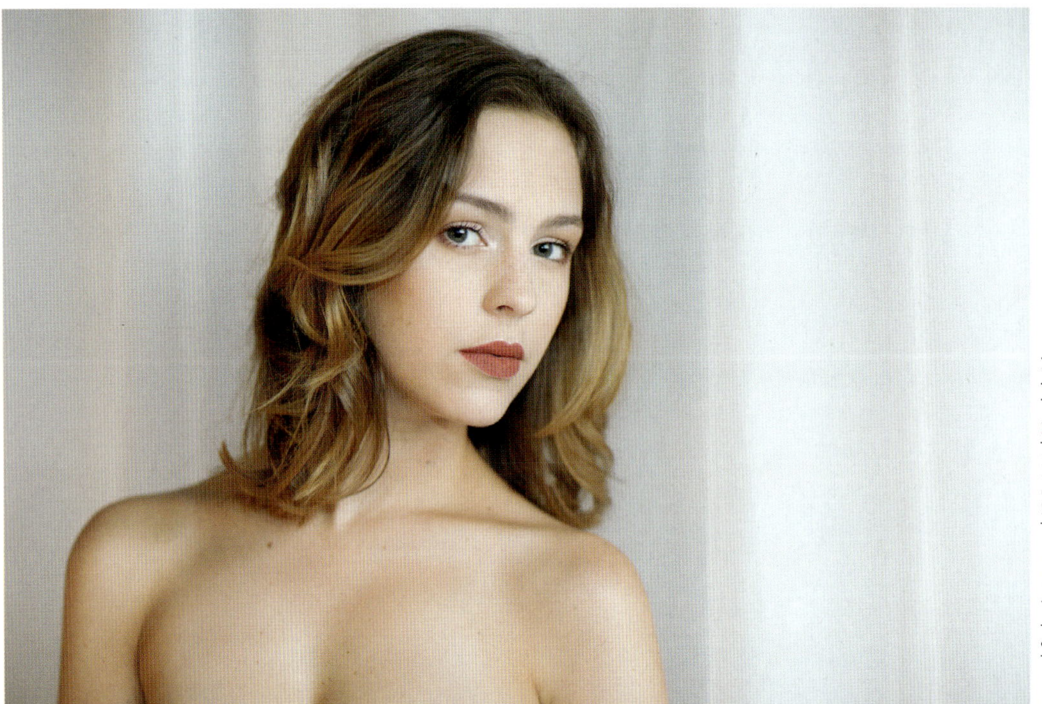

85mm | f2 | 1/125 sec. | ISO 800 | Model: Lisa

HOW IT WORKS

The lateral main light produces well-defined contours in the subject's upper body and underscores her feminine shape. Facing slightly toward the window produces a short light effect with a soft shadow on the cheek, while the neck shadow visually separates the subject's head from the rest of her body. The soft shadows produce a sweet and subtle overall look. The texture in the backdrop adds depth and provides a slight diversion, and the light fall-off toward the left adds depth, too. The flash lightens the shadows and softens the overall impression.

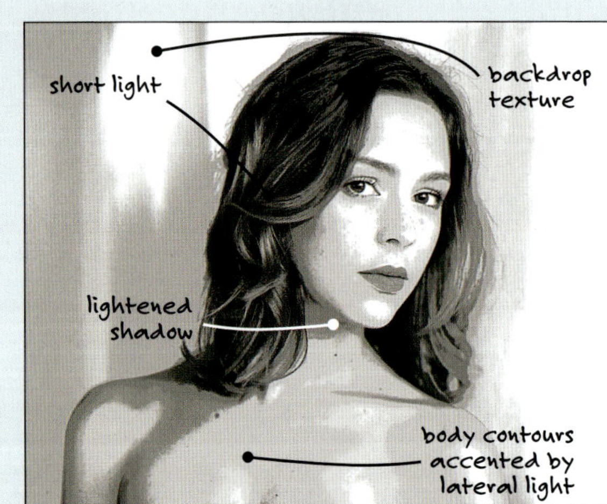

THE SETUP

Instead of setting up your lights to suit your model, this setup requires you to position your model, the backdrop, and the camera to suit the available window light.

1. If there is no curtain or the window glass isn't frosted, place a curtain in front of your model (or a diffuser in front of the window) to soften the light.

2. Place your model 3 to 6 feet from the window so that the light comes from slightly above and accents her body contours.

3. Get your model to turn her head toward the window so that the light reaching her face is almost head-on. The cheek shadow should accent the cheek contour.

4. Place a lightly folded curtain **(1)** behind your model at 90 degrees to the window.

5. Mount the system flash **(2)** on your camera and set it to TTL mode with -2 stops of flash exposure compensation.

"Make sure the flash only lightens the shadows and doesn't dominate the main (window) light."

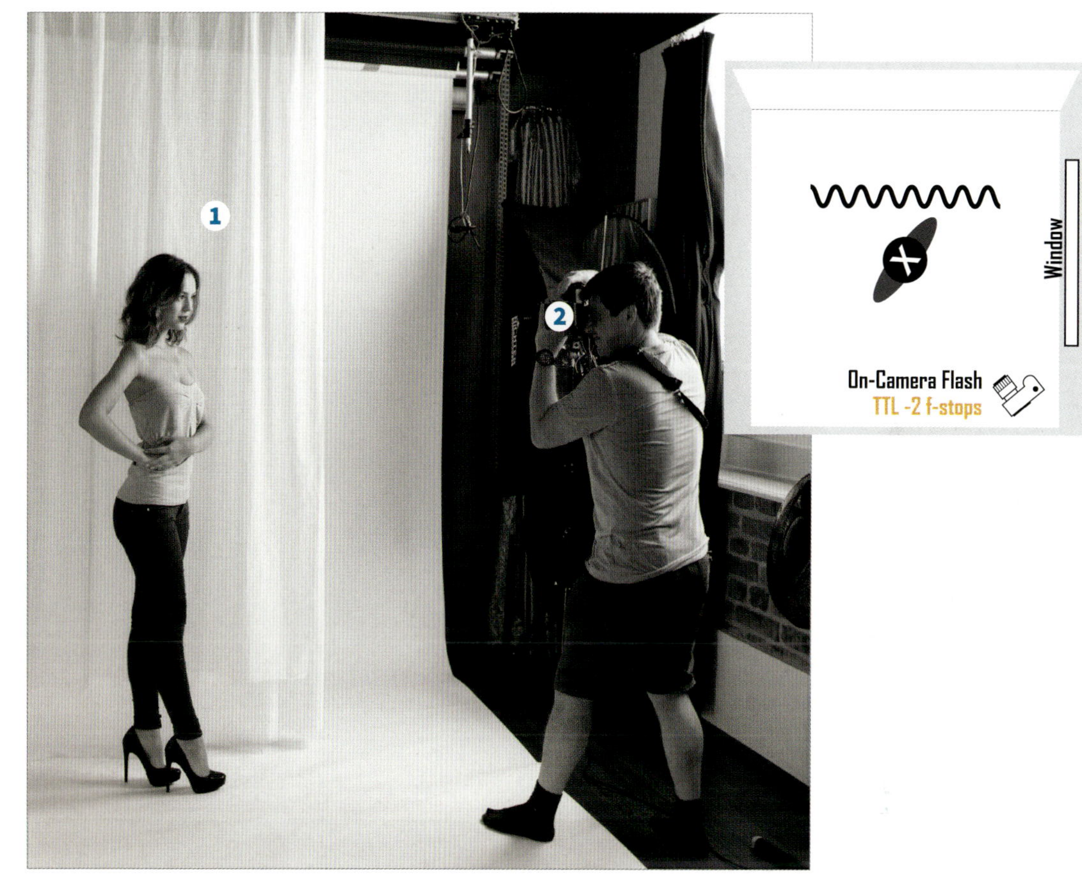

TTL Flash and Flash Exposure Compensation

TTL (through-the-lens) flash mode calculates the required flash output using the amount of light that reaches the sensor through the lens. The camera also uses the metering mode you set (spot or center-weighted, for example) to fine-tune flash output and produce a correctly exposed image. The flash exposure compensation setting enables you to adjust flash output to suit your personal preferences and/or the situation at hand. If, for example, you want to use your flash as a fill light to lighten the shadows, you can reduce its output by dialing in a negative compensation value of -1 or -2 f-stops.

Construction Site Lamp

A simple construction site lamp from a hardware store makes a great studio light for capturing silky-smooth portraits. Progress in LED technology has produced lamps that are extremely bright but that don't get as hot as incandescent lamps. This means you can shoot pleasing, well-lit portraits with a natural look, even if your studio doesn't provide real daylight.

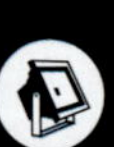

EFFORT INVOLVED

Low

SUITABLE FOR

Close-up to three-quarter-length portraits

THE LOOK

Evenly lit portrait with accentuated eyes
Natural daylight look

EQUIPMENT

1× 500W LED construction site lamp
1× 30"×40" silver reflector

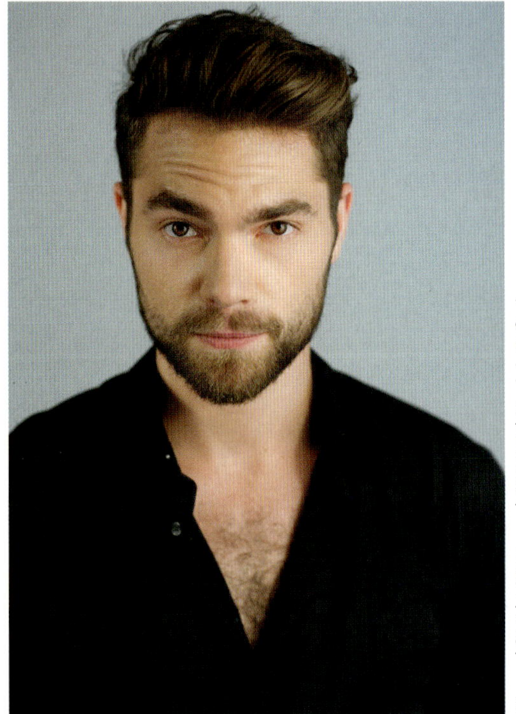

85mm | f2.8 | 1/160 sec. | ISO 800 | Model: Rafael

HOW IT WORKS

The light from the lamp shines through a curtain and is therefore especially soft. It produces virtually no shadows on the light side of the face, making it appear completely free of blemishes. The raised reflector means the shadow side of the face is only slightly darker and produces clear facial contours. Because the curtain distributes the light very evenly, there is virtually no light fall-off toward the subject's chest, thus underscoring the daylight look. This setup emphasizes the subject's eyes, while the nasal contour is reduced by the faint shadows. This cheap and simple setup is great for shooting strong but natural-looking portraits.

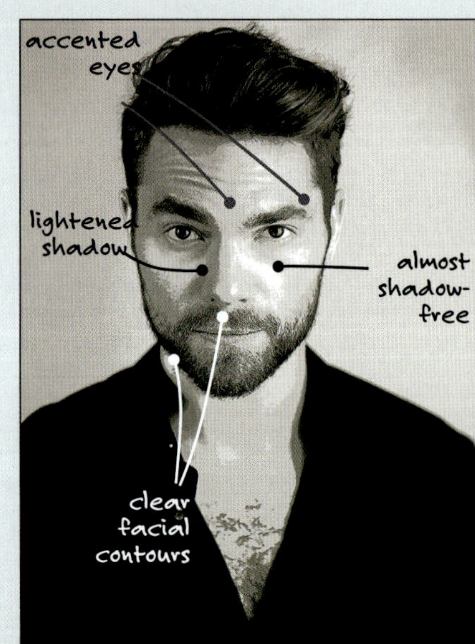

THE SETUP

For this "making of" shot, Manon stepped in for Rafael, who was busy getting made up for the shoot. This doesn't change the setup and, if you are in a hurry, using a lighting model can keep things moving along.

1. Place a regular construction site lamp **(1)** about 5 feet from your model at an angle of about 45 degrees. Set it up at a height of about 6 feet and point it at your model's face.

2. Place a double-layered white curtain **(2)** between your model and the lamp at a distance of about 2 feet. Fix it to a mobile backdrop stand or a boom stand.

3. Position your model about 5 feet from the white background.

4. Place the reflector **(3)** about 30 inches to the left of your model at 90 degrees. Make sure the reflector is set up vertically.

5. The camera settings of f2.8 and ISO 800 reflect the relatively weak light provided by the construction site lamp.

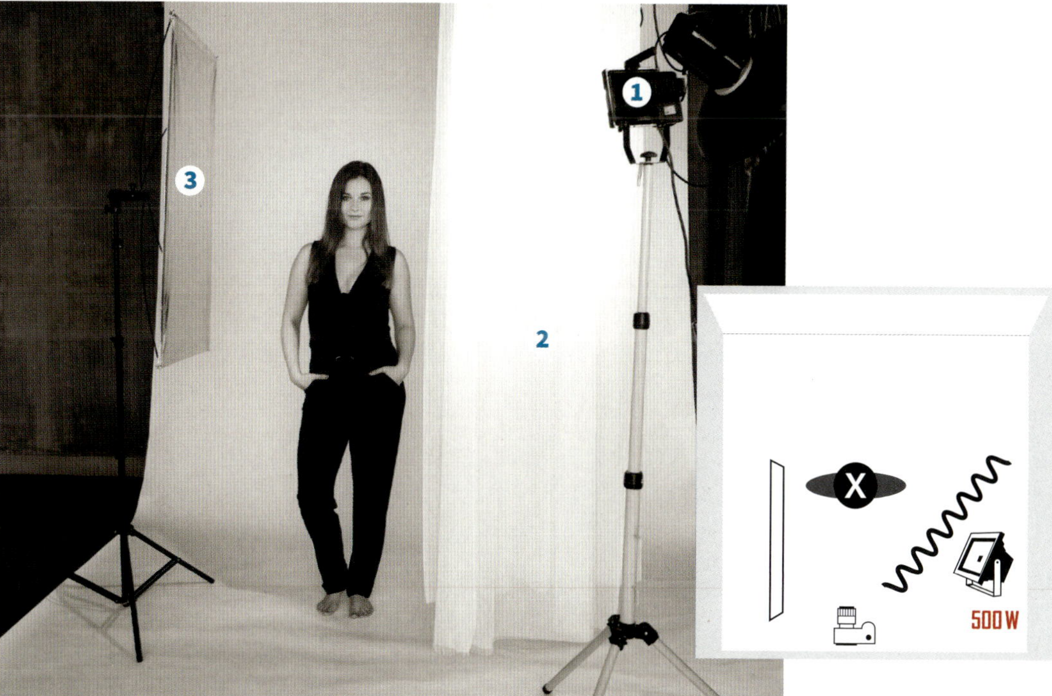

Using Fabric as a Diffuser

Curtain material is great for softening the light in your photos. To avoid unintentionally altering the colors in your images, be sure to use white, translucent fabric. The softness of the light depends on the thickness of the material you use. Linen or cotton will produce much softer light than a thin polyester curtain. Using multiple layers of fabric will also soften the light. Remember that fabric swallows a lot of light output, so you will need to adjust your flash output, the aperture setting, the exposure time, the ISO setting, or the distance between your model and your light accordingly.

As an alternative to using colored gels on your light, you can use colored fabric to play with the colors in your images, too.

"Using a lighting model allows you to save time setting up your lights while the actual model prepares for the shoot."

Beauty Portraits

Beauty Portraits

The old aphorism states that "beauty is in the eye of the beholder." As a photographer, you can use flattering lighting effects to directly influence the perceived beauty of your subject.

Beauty portraits use colors, accessories, and often intense makeup to emphasize a person's visual appeal. Such images are highly stylized and you can enhance the scene using lighting effects to place accents, create a specific mood, and to hide blemishes.

A beauty portrait isn't designed to portray a person's look, character, or personal attributes. It is much more about working hard with your model to capture an idealized facial expression—often aloof, or cool, or perhaps even a little arrogant. This is the challenge of beauty portraiture. Perfect results require excellent styling, an ideal lighting setup, and great teamwork from the model, the makeup artist, and the photographer.

Setting highlights to accentuate facial and body details is a lot of fun and helps to produce really punchy images.

Beauty lighting setups range from a simple neon tube to complex four-flash setups, and each has its own set of options for accentuating, exaggerating, or reducing the effects of specific features.

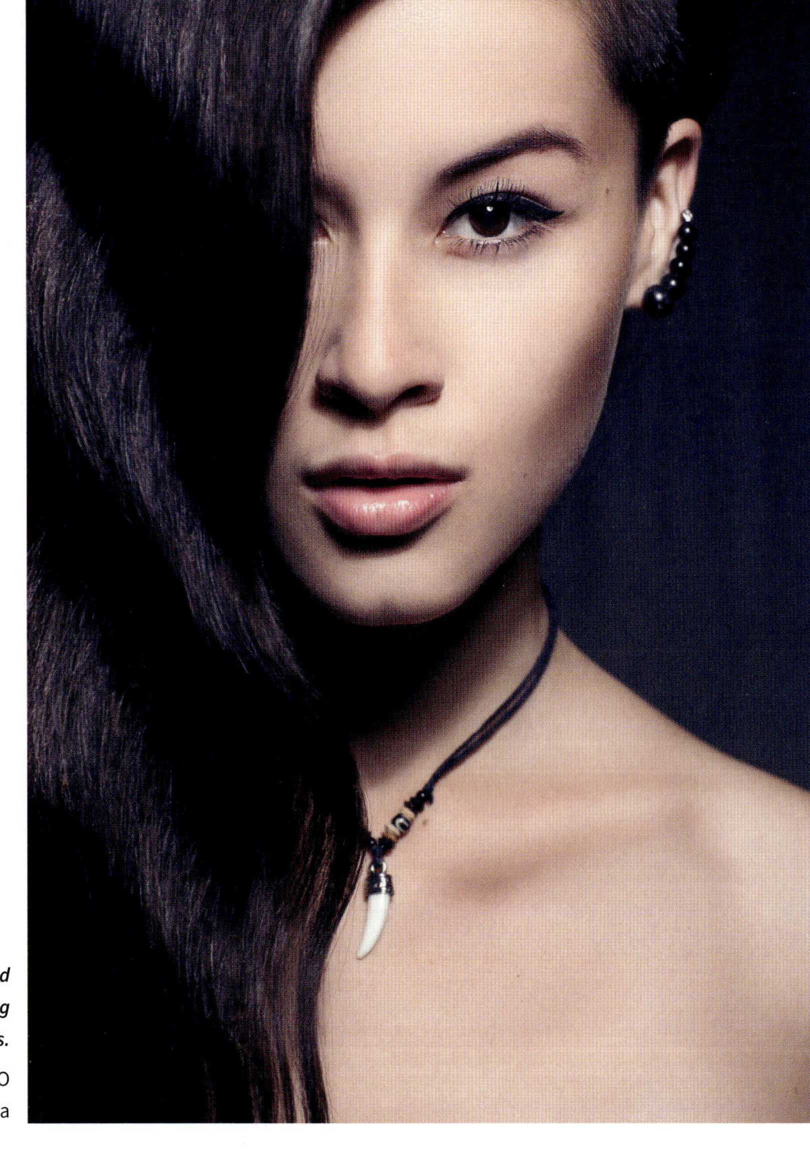

A beauty portrait finished using high-end retouching techniques.

85mm | f8 | 1/160 sec. | ISO 100 | Model: Sonja

Beauty shots are used primarily in magazines and for advertising purposes, but amateur photographers and models can have a lot of fun trying out this kind of work too, and you can find plenty of excellent beauty shots in amateur online portfolios. Most beauty shots end up being retouched to some degree, and computer-based beauty retouching ranges from simple removal of skin blemishes to complex, high-end post-processing that can take several hours. If you are starting out in beauty photography, you will need to familiarize yourself with various retouching techniques. Most of the images in this chapter are retouched, and I spent an average of 30–45 minutes on each.

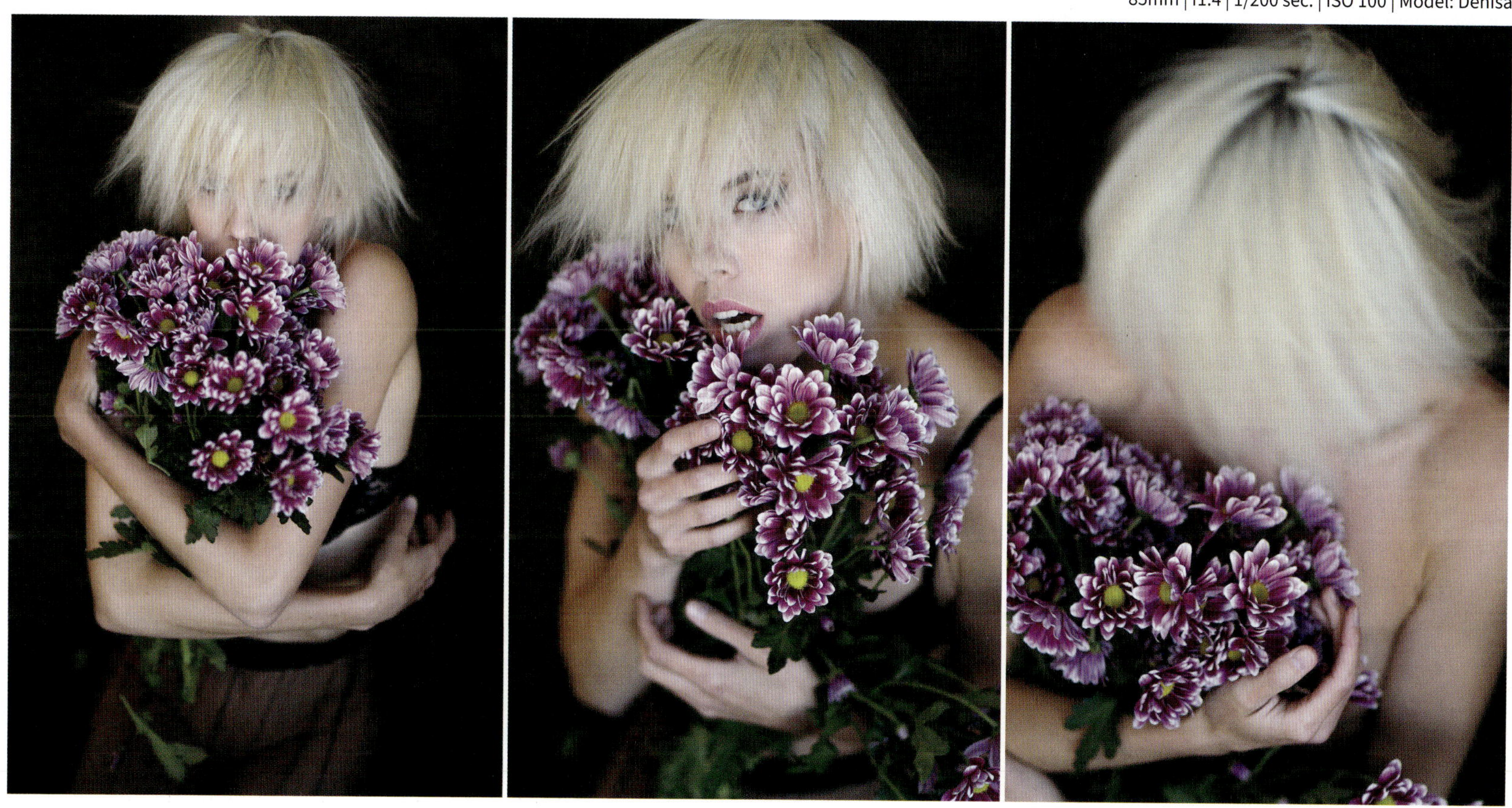

A sequence of experimental beauty shots, captured using a wide aperture while the model performed various movements.

85mm | f1.4 | 1/200 sec. | ISO 100 | Model: Denisa

Highlighting Accessories

A simple two-flash setup is ideal for putting accessories such as necklaces or hair ornaments center stage. The softbox produces soft shadows, while the translucent umbrella helps to further soften them to taste, providing a balanced overall look.

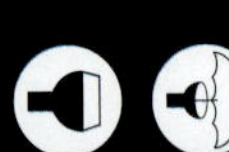

EFFORT INVOLVED

Low

SUITABLE FOR

Close-up to three-quarter-length portraits

THE LOOK

Soft, balanced beauty portrait
Eyes emphasized using dark eye-shadow
Focus on the pearl necklace

EQUIPMENT

1× 24" softbox
1× 36" translucent umbrella

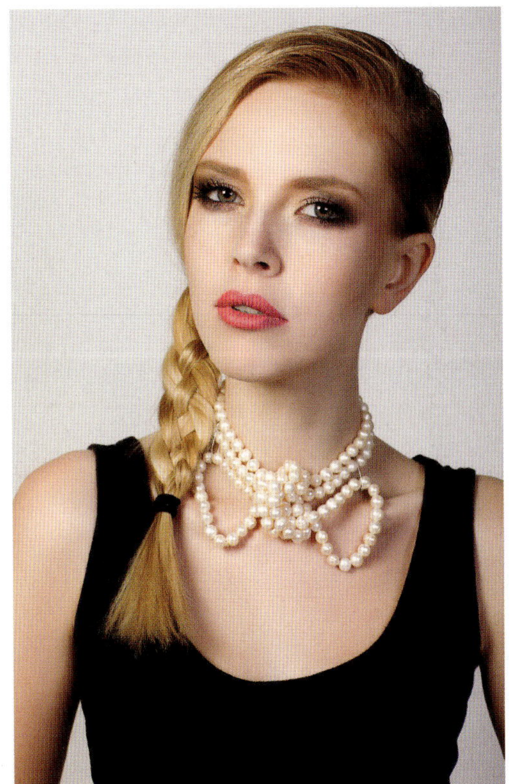

85mm | f8 | 1/160 sec. | ISO 100 | Model: Viki

HOW IT WORKS

The diagonal position of the softbox produces a soft main light, and the rotation of the subject's head creates a short light effect and a broad shadow on the left-hand side of the face. This makes the face appear narrower and automatically draws the viewer's attention to the well-lit side. The darkly made-up eyes have a powerful effect, underscored by the gleam of the catchlights. The pearl necklace is well-lit, too, and forms a second focal point. The twin flashes produce highlights on every pearl, which underscores their luster. The light gray background is subtle and accents the classy feel of the image.

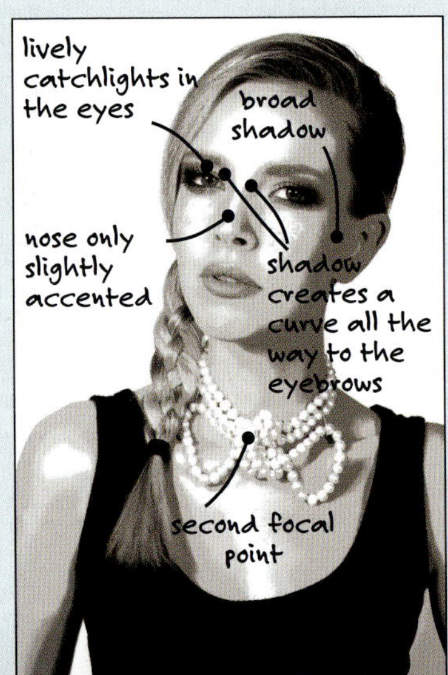

THE SETUP

1. Place the softbox **(1)** about 3 feet to the left of your model in a slightly raised position and at an angle of about 45 degrees. Position it to produce a slight nose shadow and a narrow chin shadow.

2. Now position the fill light **(2)** with the translucent umbrella also slightly raised at about 45 degrees to the right. The fill light should be about 5 feet from your model.

The V shape formed by the lights is clearly visible in the photo below. The model is standing about 3 feet from the white background. The soft, highly diffuse light produced by the translucent umbrella provides plenty of spill that gives the background an evenly-lit, light-gray tone.

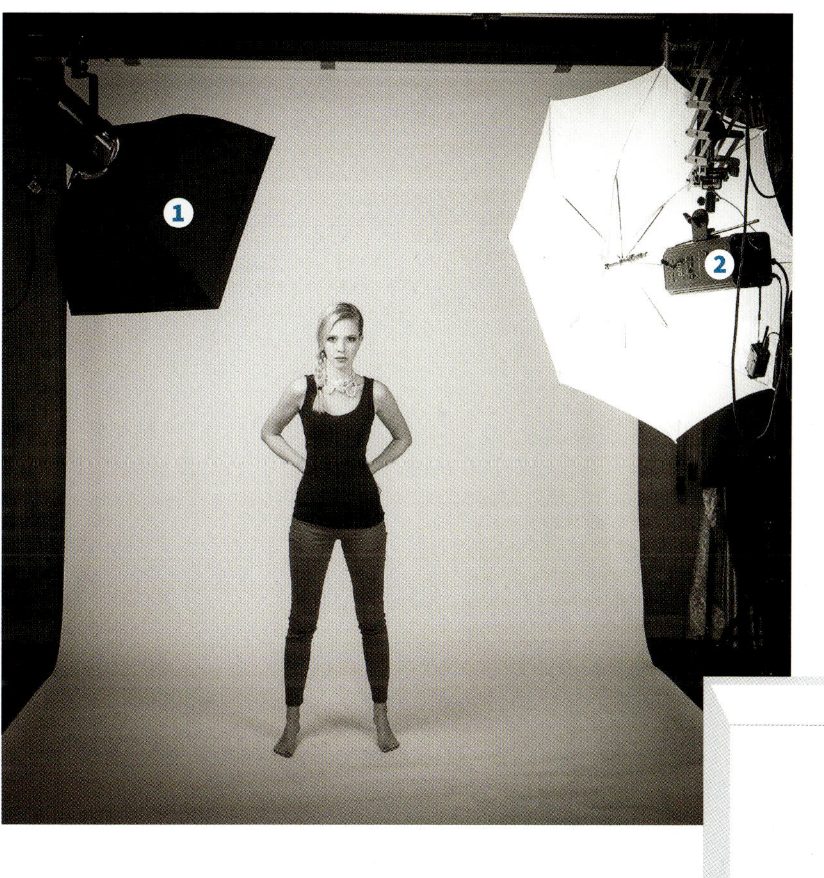

"Make sure your model rotates her head to produce a short light effect."

The Classic Two-Light Setup

This V-shaped "clamshell" setup is a classic portrait setup, whereby one light serves as a main light and the other as a fill light that lightens the shadows. It is quick to set up and you can easily control the amount of shadow you produce, from really dark to virtually invisible (when both lights have the same output setting). These settings also alter the depth of the image, from highly three-dimensional to quite flat-looking. But take care—this setup can easily produce unwanted crossover shadows.

Marlene Dietrich Style

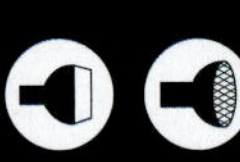

EFFORT INVOLVED

Medium

SUITABLE FOR

Close-up to three-quarter-length portraits

THE LOOK

Intense beauty portrait
Strongly accented facial contours
Androgynous look, accented by the tied-back hair

EQUIPMENT

1 × 24" softbox
1 × standard reflector with a honeycomb grid
1 × 30"× 40" silver reflector

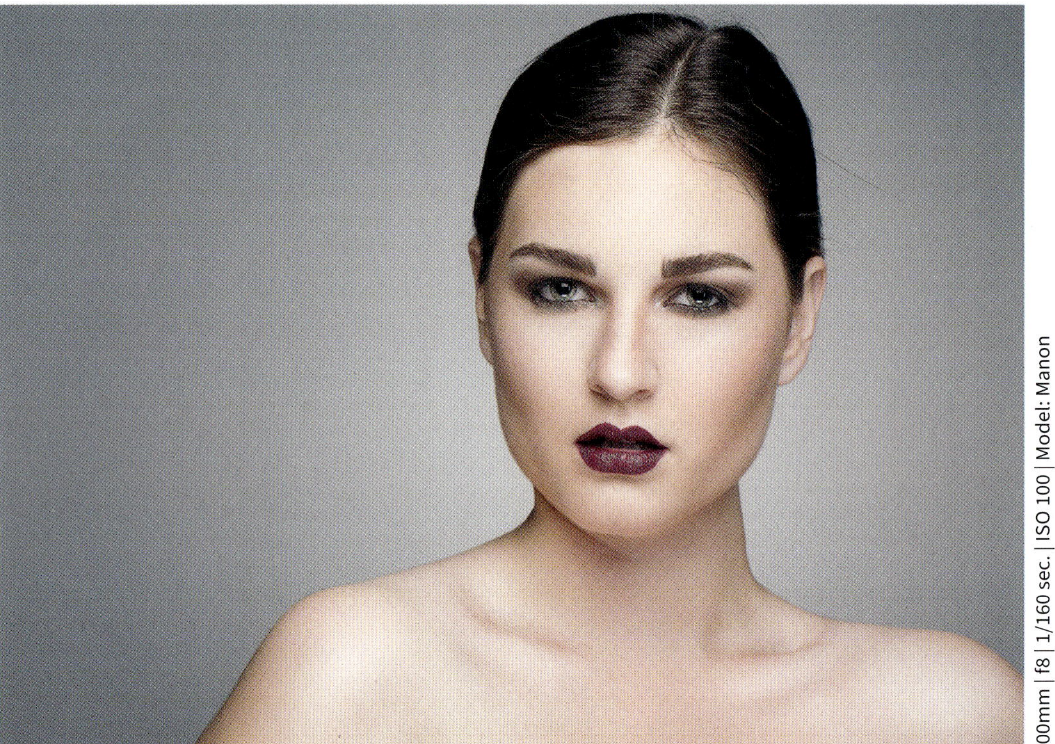

100mm | f8 | 1/160 sec. | ISO 100 | Model: Manon

HOW IT WORKS

The strongly accented facial contours and the dark cheekbone shadows give this image a hard, almost masculine look. The high, frontal lighting emphasizes the lips and eyes. The reflector produces a soft chin shadow that provides visual separation between the face and shoulders. The reflector brightens the eyes, and the shadows beneath the eyelids intensify the subject's expression. The background light forms a vignette that helps to frame and accentuate the face. This lighting produces a highly three-dimensional look that makes the subject stand out against the background.

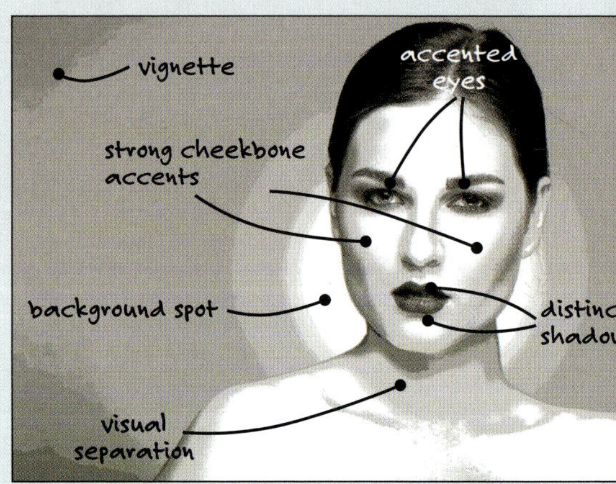

THE SETUP

1. Using a ceiling rail or a boom stand, place the soft-box **(1)** about 3 feet from your model in a raised frontal position and pointing down at an angle of about 45 degrees. Position the light to form a shadow beneath your model's nose that ends halfway between her nose and upper lip.

2. Mount the reflector **(2)** directly in front of your model on a low stand at waist height. Position it to lighten the neck and nose shadows.

3. Place the background reflector **(3)** directly above your model at a height of about 8 feet. Position it at an angle that produces a spot effect on the backdrop behind your model's head at about nose level.

4. Position your model between 5 and 6 feet from the white background. You can alter the degree of shadow lightening in your model's face by adjusting the angle of the reflector.

"The slightly open mouth adds an erotic touch."

Styling and Facial Expression

The overall feel of a beauty shot depends strongly on your model's facial expression and the styling you apply. You need to plan the look of a shot in advance and discuss it with your model and your makeup artist before you start in on the shoot. This way, you can be sure that you have all the right outfits, accessories, and makeup on hand. Clarify what you expect from your model and your makeup artist before you set up your lights, and support your model during the shoot with feedback on her pose and her expression. A continuous dialog of pointers, and perhaps jokes and anecdotes too, will help to buoy up the mood and make the shoot a success.

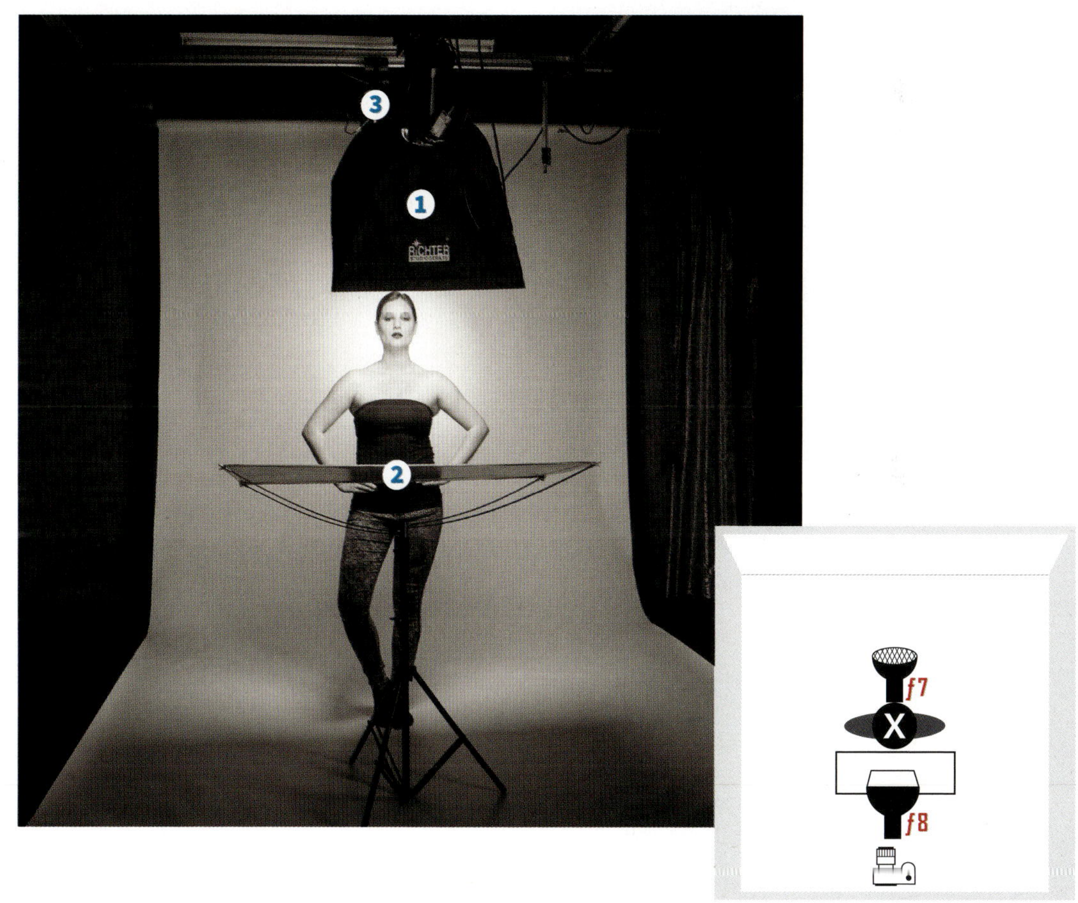

Punchy Contrast from a Beauty Dish

A beauty dish simultaneously produces strong contrast and even, overall lighting, but you will need additional gear if you want to exert more control over where the viewer looks. This setup deliberately makes the face the brightest part of the frame. The strong background vignette further accentuates the face and gives the composition a clear center.

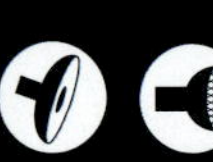

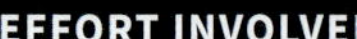

EFFORT INVOLVED

Medium

SUITABLE FOR

Close-up to three-quarter-length portraits

THE LOOK

Focus on the face

Subtle, almost vulnerable look but with punchy, high-contrast lighting

EQUIPMENT

1× beauty dish

1× standard reflector with a honeycomb grid

1× 30" ×40" silver reflector

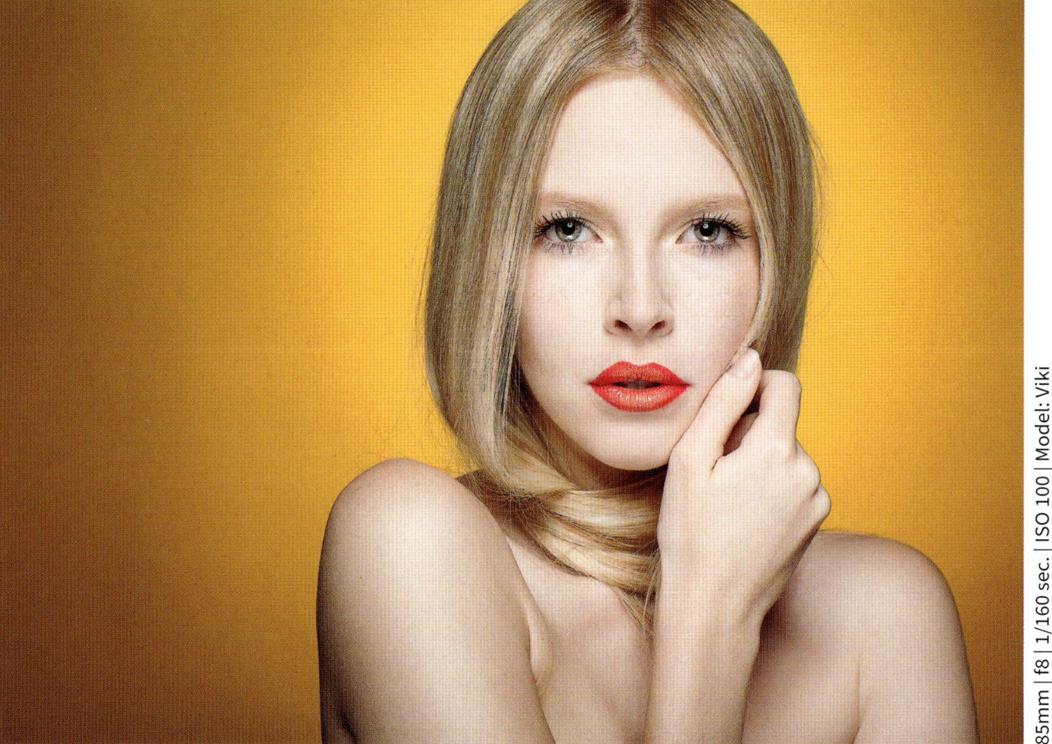

85mm | f8 | 1/160 sec. | ISO 100 | Model: Viki

HOW IT WORKS

The background vignette coupled with the bright facial lighting focuses attention on the subject's face with the main emphasis on the eyes. There are distinct shadows beneath the subject's eyelids, but the reflector compensates for these by lightening the rest of the eye area. The nose and cheekbone shadows are subtle and contribute to the soft overall feel. The neck shadow and the hair frame the subject's face. The clear light fall-off makes the upper body significantly darker than the face, leaving just the highlights on the shoulders and collarbone as accents.

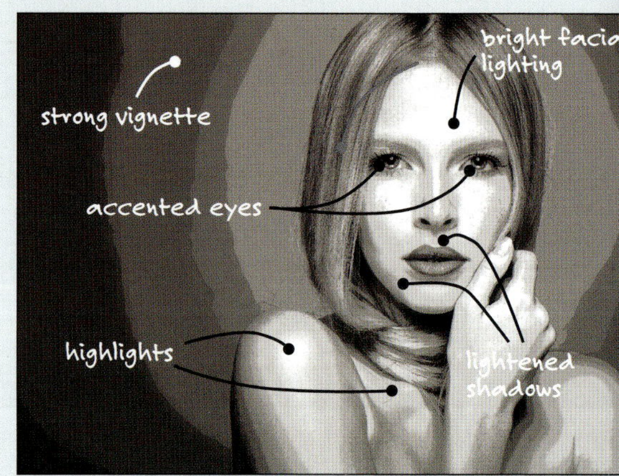

THE SETUP

1. Mount the beauty dish **(1)** on a ceiling rail or a boom stand and place it frontally above your model at a distance of about 3 feet and at an angle of about 30 degrees. Adjust it to create a relatively broad neck shadow.

2. Mount the reflector **(2)** at chest height in front of your model so that it lightens the nose and eye shadows.

3. Place the background reflector **(3)** centrally behind your model at a height of about 8 feet using either a ceiling rail or boom stand. Position it to produce a pool of light directly behind your model's head.

4. Your model should be standing between 5 and 6 feet from the yellow background.

Working with Contrast

The setup is carried by the punchy light from the beauty dish, the colored background, and the strong vignette effect. In comparison, the model appears almost vulnerable. This impression is underscored by her gentle expression, her hunched shoulders, and the way her hand touches her cheek. Feel free to play with this kind of contrast between visual elements, and work with your model to produce the look you are aiming for.

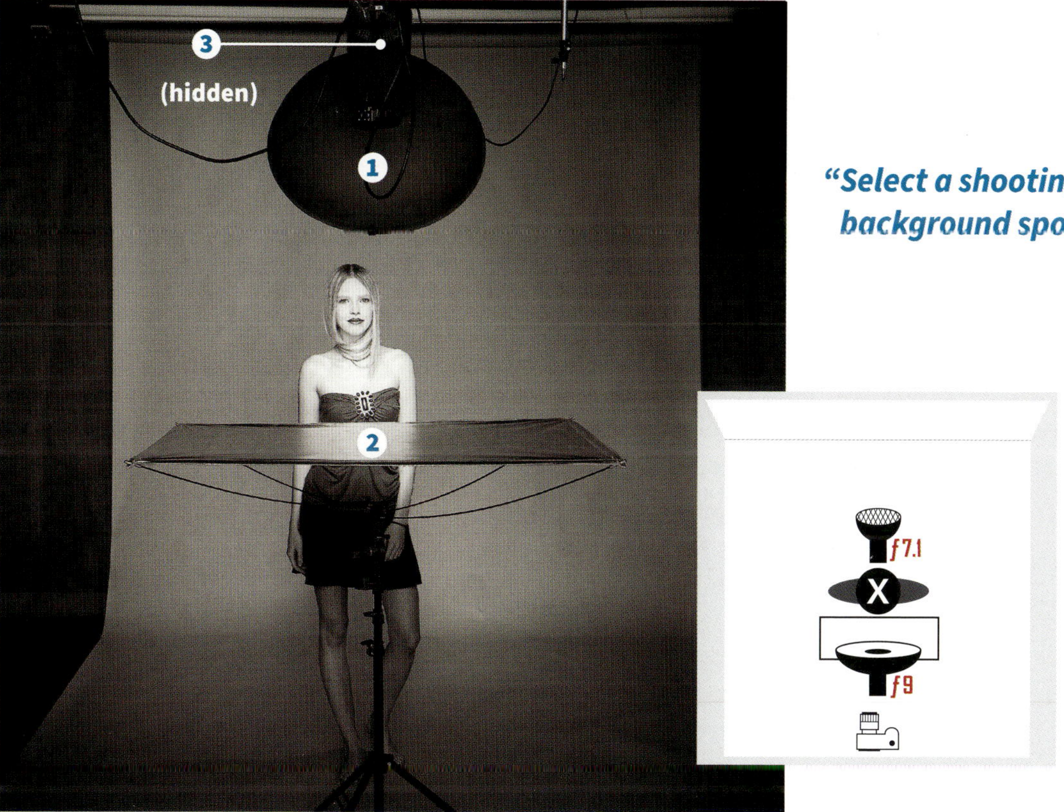

"Select a shooting position that places the background spot directly behind your model's head."

Strong Accents from Four Flashes

Multiple highlights provide extra accents that invite the viewer to explore the image. In this shot, the hair and shoulder highlights separate the subject from the background and emphaisze distinct areas within the frame. The classic "Hollywood" base setup provides plenty of contrast and ensures that the subject's face remains center stage.

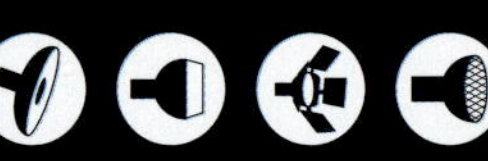

EFFORT INVOLVED

High

SUITABLE FOR

Close-up to three-quarter-length portraits

THE LOOK

Brightly lit face

Background vignette

Hair and shoulder highlights

EQUIPMENT

1× beauty dish

1× 24" softbox

1× standard reflector with barndoors

1× standard reflector with a honeycomb grid

1× 30"×40" silver reflector

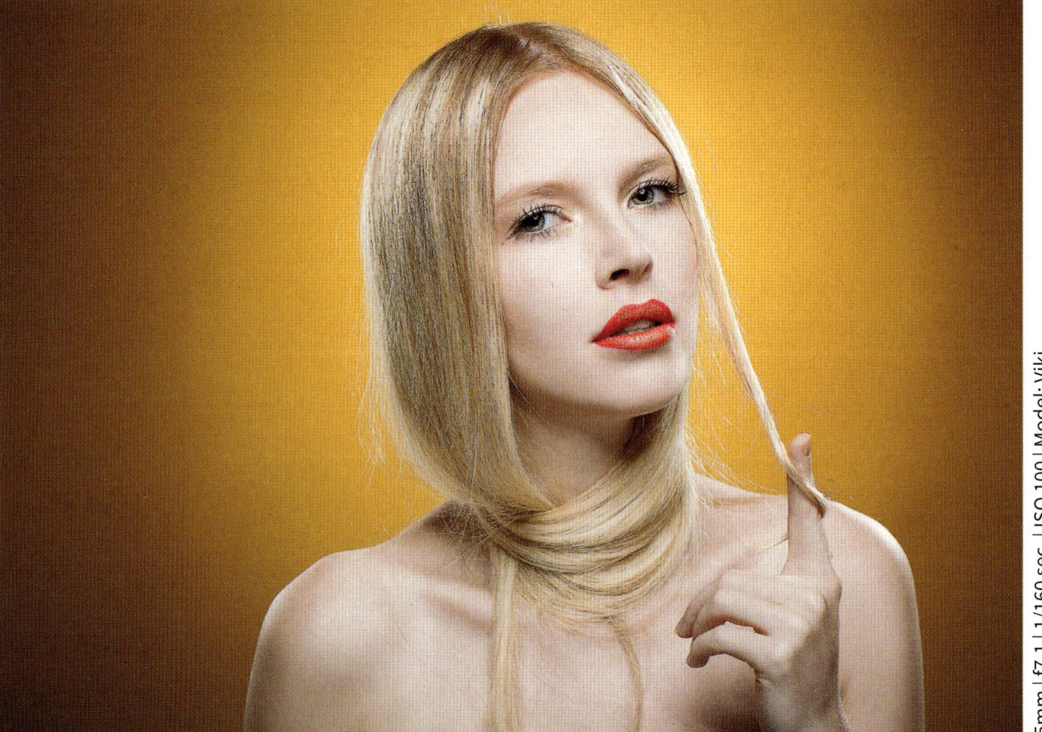

85mm | f7.1 | 1/160 sec. | ISO 100 | Model: Viki

HOW IT WORKS

The use of four separate lights and a yellow background produces a striking, splashy image. The background vignette and the bright facial light completely focus the viewer's attention on the subject's face. The highlights produce halo effects on both sides, although the one on the right produced by the barndoors is harder than the one on the left. It lights the lock of hair on the right and accents the right cheek and the shoulders. The sparkling lips appear fuller thanks to the shadow beneath, and the neck shadow frames the face from below.

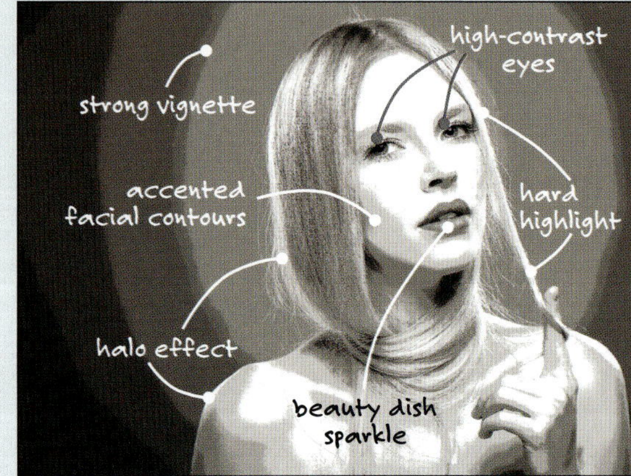

THE SETUP

1. Mount the beauty dish **(1)** on a ceiling rail or a boom stand and place it frontally above your model at a distance of about 3 feet and at an angle of 45 degrees. Adjust it to create a clear neck shadow and a slight nose shadow when your model raises her head.

2. Mount the reflector **(2)** at chest height in front of your model so that it lightens the nose and eye shadows.

3. Place the background reflector **(3)** centrally behind your model at a height of about 8 feet using either a ceiling rail or boom stand. Position it to produce a pool of light directly behind your model's head.

4. Place the softbox **(4)** at head height about 5 feet behind your model on the left. Angle it at about 45 degrees so that it creates halo-style highlights on your model's hair and shoulders.

5. Place the standard reflector with the barndoors **(5)** about 6 feet away to the right above head hight and angled at about 30 degrees. Close the barndoors almost completely to create a narrow highlight that illuminates your model's left shoulder.

6. Get your model to stand about 8 feet from the yellow background.

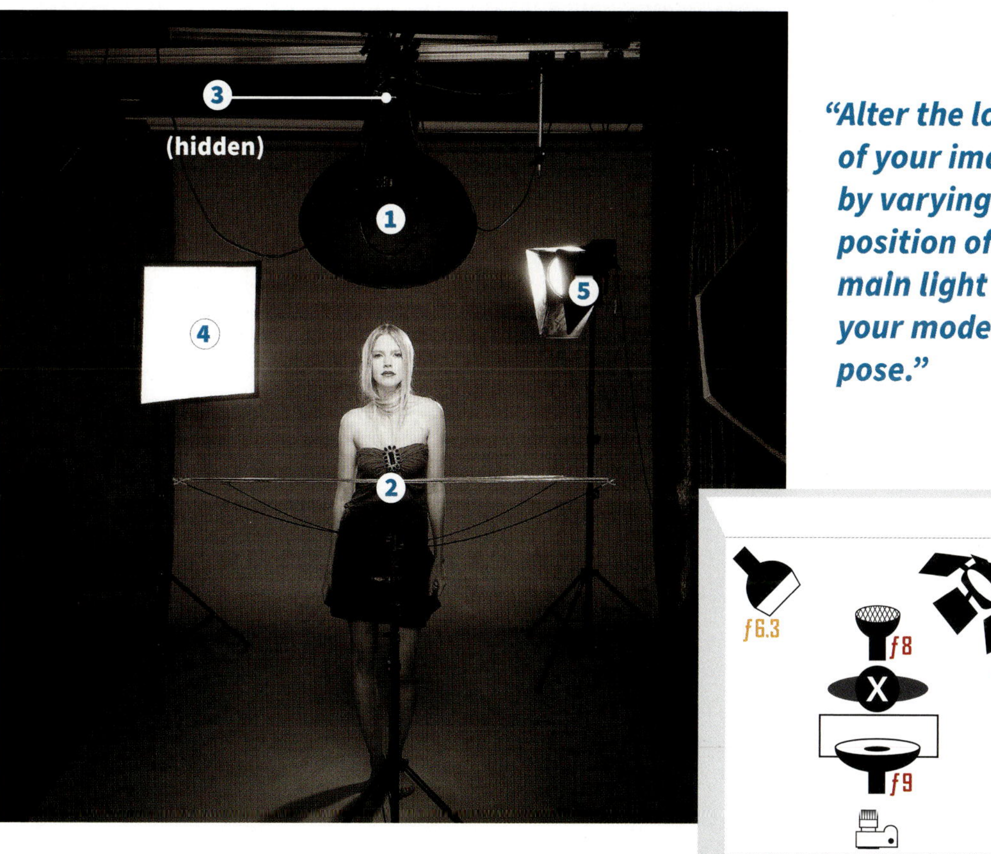

> *"Alter the look of your image by varying the position of the main light and your model's pose."*

Softer Reflections

An alternative look using the same basic setup involves switching to portrait format, moving the beauty dish to the left, adjusting the reflector accordingly, and getting your model to turn her head slightly to the left. The tighter framing reduces the vignette effect, and the right-hand side of her face (from your point of view) and the lock of hair are now in shadow and are less bright as a result. The result is more balanced and focuses less strongly on the face alone. The right-hand highlight now lights only the top of my model's head and her shoulder.

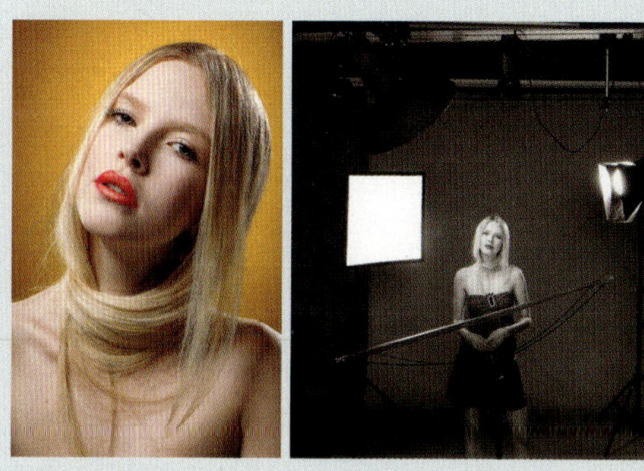

Subtle Accents for Long Hair

If your model has long hair, you can use it as a prominent styling element, either theatrically or—as shown here—as part of a mellow composition. Alongside the model's hair, the leading role is played by a strip box that provides the highlights, and an octabox that provides soft shadows and an evenly lit background.

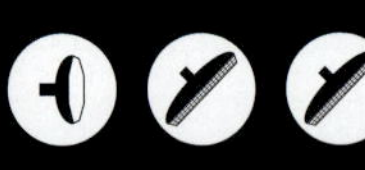

EFFORT INVOLVED

High

SUITABLE FOR

All kinds of portraits

THE LOOK

Powdery portrait with soft shadows

Emphasis on the subject's hair

EQUIPMENT

1× 31.5" octabox

2× 47" strip boxes with honeycomb grids

1× 30"×40" silver reflector

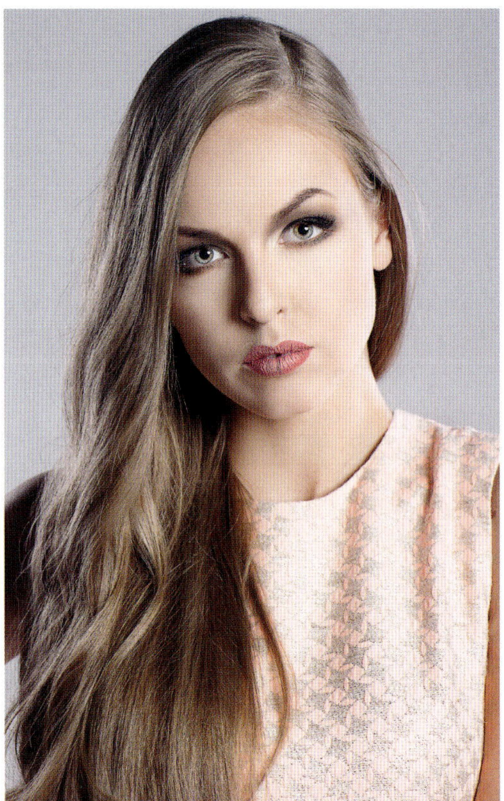

85mm | f8 | 1/160 sec. | ISO 100 | Model: Angelina

HOW IT WORKS

The octabox main light produces soft shadows that flatter the subject's face. Because it is positioned to the side, it produces clear cheek and nose shadows on the left. The subject's light-colored eyes are well lit and you can even make out the fine nuances in the irises. The eyes are additionally accented by the shadows beneath the upper eyelids and the clear catchlights. The right fill light provides a highlight that also gives extra glow to the cheek and neck. The main light makes the hair look silky and the left fill light adds a subtle reflection.

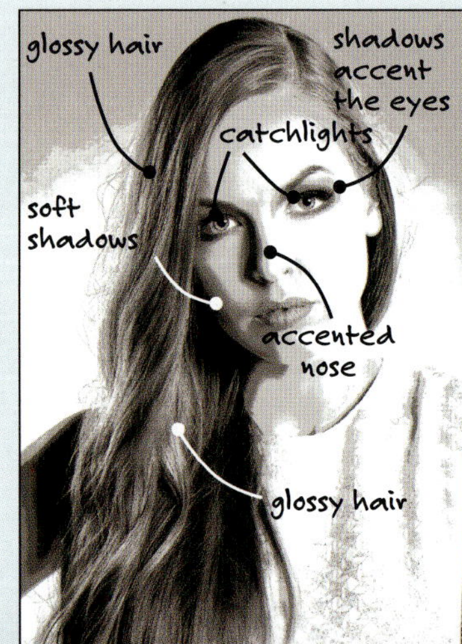

THE SETUP

1. Place the octabox **(1)** about 6 feet to the right of your model in a slightly raised position and at an angle of about 45 Degrees. Position it to produce a visible shadow under the tip of her nose.

2. Mount the reflector **(2)** on a stand above head height about 5 feet from your model, and position it to lighten the nose shadow.

3. Place the strip box **(3)** about 5 feet behind your model to the left and at an angle of about 45 degrees at around head height. Position it so that it produces a distinct highlight on her hair and shoulder.

4. Place the second strip box **(4)** about 5 feet away to the right at head height and likewise at an angle of 45 degrees. Set it up so that the highlight it produces lights your model's cheek but doesn't reach the tip of her nose.

5. Get your model to stand about 6 feet in front of the white background.

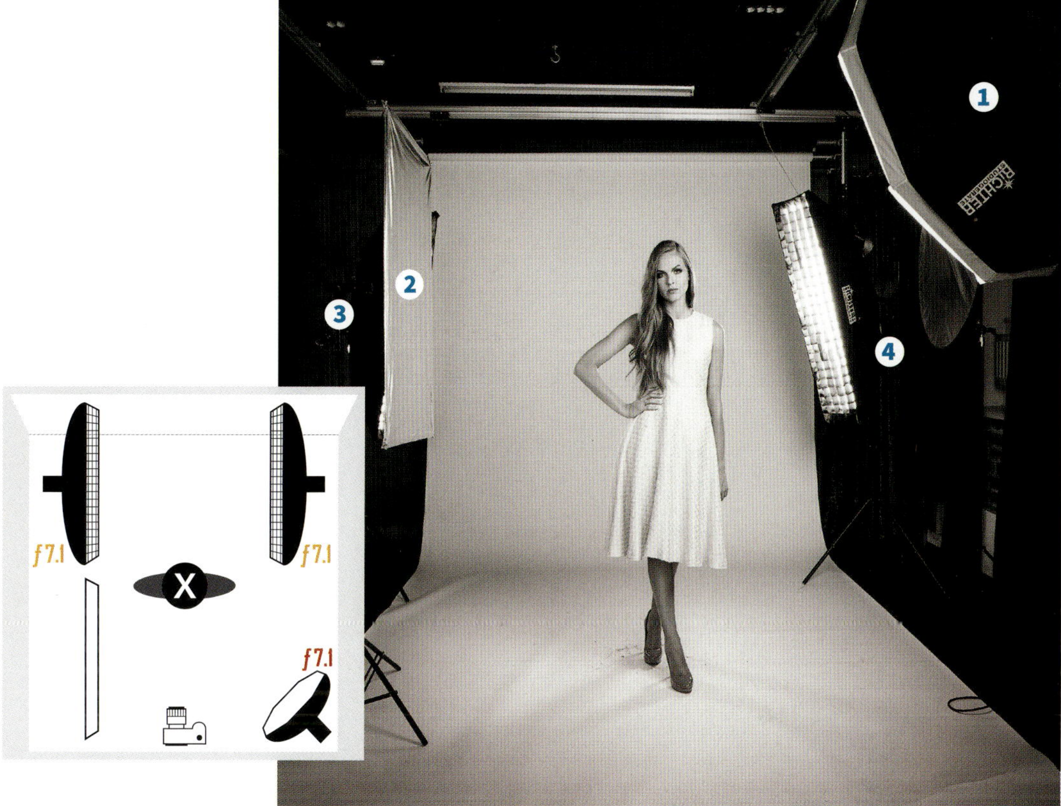

Well-Groomed Hair

If you are using your model's hair as a prominent feature in a shot, you have to make sure that it looks the part. It is always a good idea to have a hair straightener on hand to deal with flyaway hair. Hair spray should be part of your standard kit too (or gel for short hair).

"If your model wears her own street shoes for a shoot, you should clean them thoroughly before you begin to avoid marking the backdrop (unlike in the photo above!)."

Selective Facial Accents

The extremely hard light makes this high-contrast portrait particularly striking. As a neat side effect, the reflected light from the twin flashes also provides a nice highlight in the background. This three-light setup is fairly complex, but the results are worth the extra effort, whether you are shooting for an advert, for your portfolio, or for the model's sedcard.

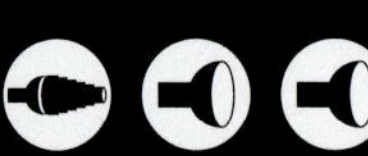

EFFORT INVOLVED

Medium

SUITABLE FOR

Close-up to three-quarter-length portraits

THE LOOK

Striking portrait with prominent facial accents
Conspicuous shadows
Bold eye makeup, matte lips
Cheek glow

EQUIPMENT

1 × snoot or spot with a gobo
2 × standard reflector

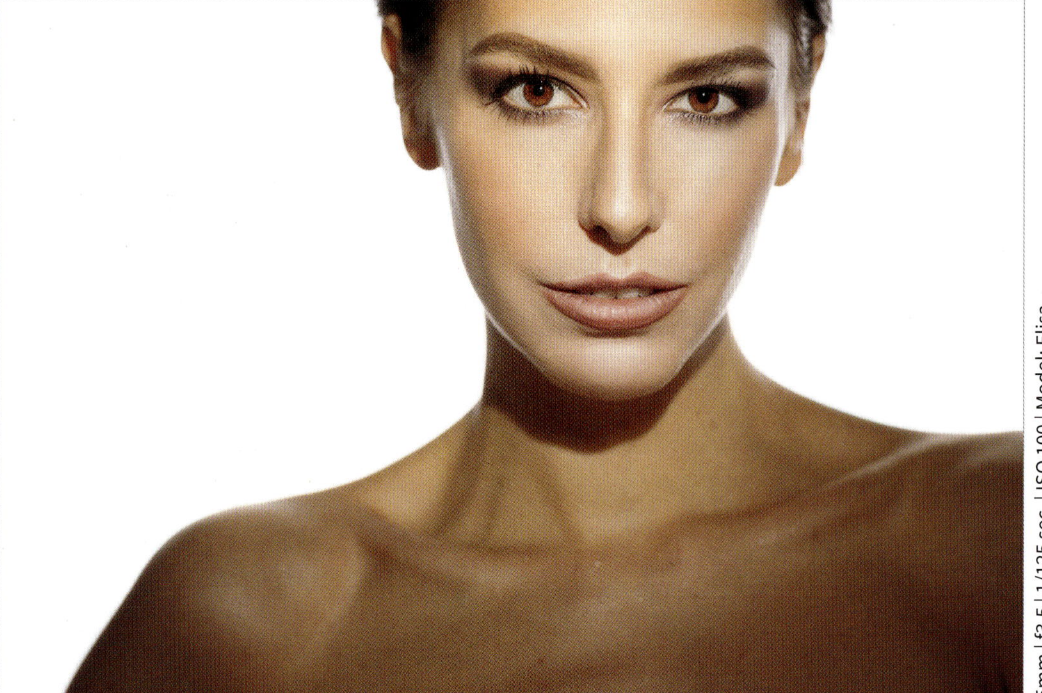

85mm | f3.5 | 1/125 sec. | ISO 100 | Model: Elisa

HOW IT WORKS

The extreme lighting gives this image extremely high contrast, making it pretty unforgiving when it comes to showing pores. The slightly raised main light creates a central nose shadow and a clear neck shadow. The gobo on the spot produces highly targeted light on the subject's face, giving the image a highly three-dimensional, sculpted look. The single, narrow-beam main light produces very small reflections in the subject's eyes and helps to emphasize the color of the irises.

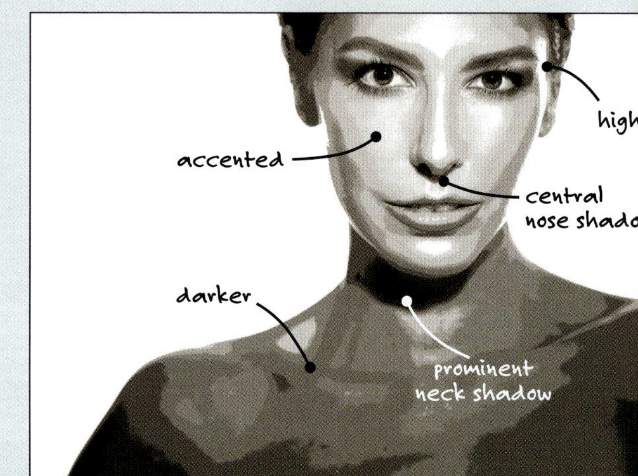

THE SETUP

1. Place the gobo spot **(1)** in front of your model in a slightly raised position and set it up so that it illuminates just your model's face. You can alter the distance between the spot and your model depending on the size of the hole in the gobo. In this case it was about 3 feet.

2. Now place the two standard reflectors **(2)** to the right and left of your model so that they point toward the background at an angle of about 45 degrees.

3. Select the distances between your model and the background, and between your model and the reflectors, so that fill lights highlight your model too. For this shot, my model stood about 18 inches from the background and the reflectors were positioned about 3 feet to the right and left.

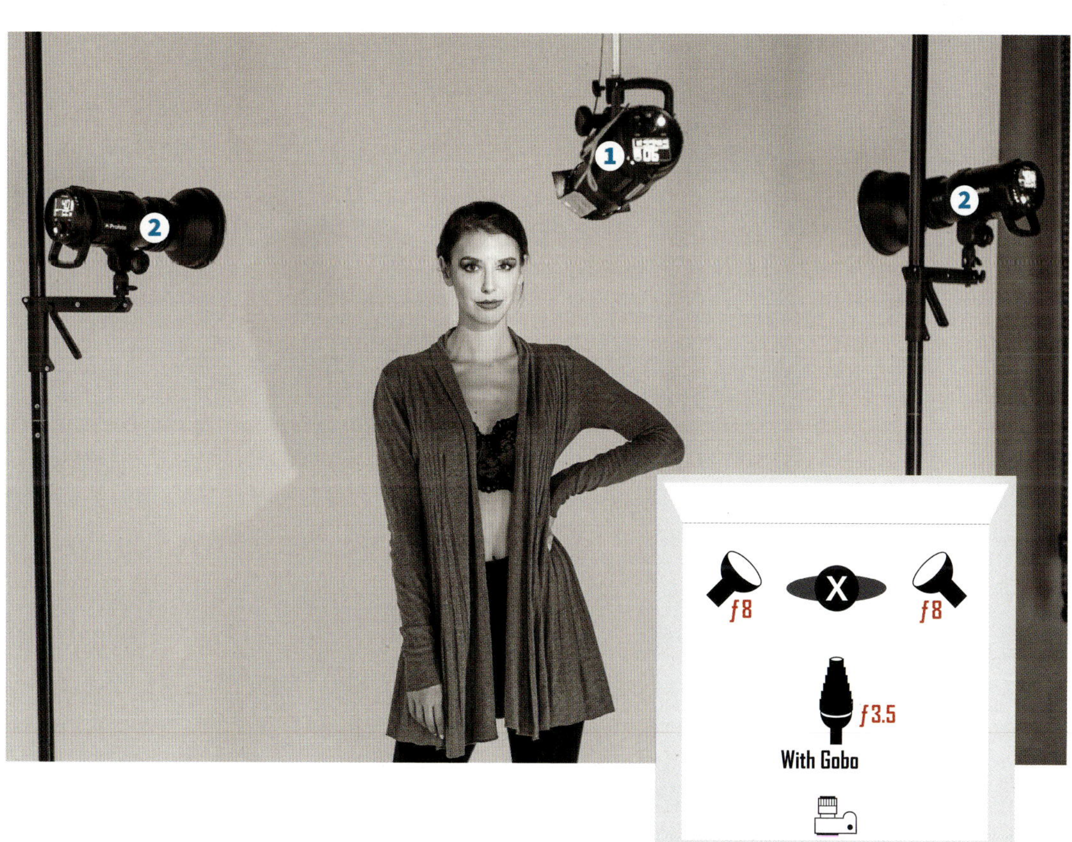

Cardboard Gobo

A simple piece of card with a hole in the shape of your choice is all you need to turn a spot lamp into a narrow, sculpted spotlight source. A circular spot source is easier to set up in a portrait shot.

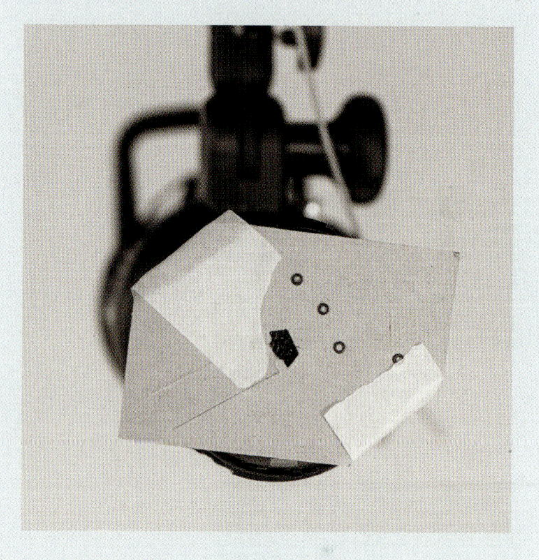

"When light hits a reflective surface, the angle of incidence is the same as the angle of reflection (think of a pool ball bouncing off the cushion on a pool table). That's exactly what happens to the light here when it hits the white background."

How to Produce a Cool Look

This cool look is based on tightly tied-back hair, bold makeup, and a highly specific facial expression/head posture. The lighting setup produces highlights on the cheeks and shoulders, and gives the chin and shoulders a sculpted look.

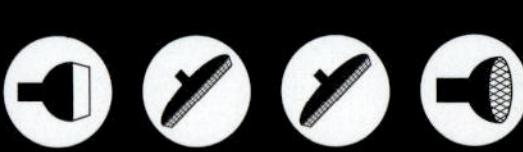

EFFORT INVOLVED

High

SUITABLE FOR

Close-up to three-quarter-length portraits

THE LOOK

Cool portrait with bright accents

Slightly raised chin gives the subject a distanced look

EQUIPMENT

1× 24" softbox

2× 47" strip boxes with honeycomb grids

1× standard reflector with a honeycomb grid

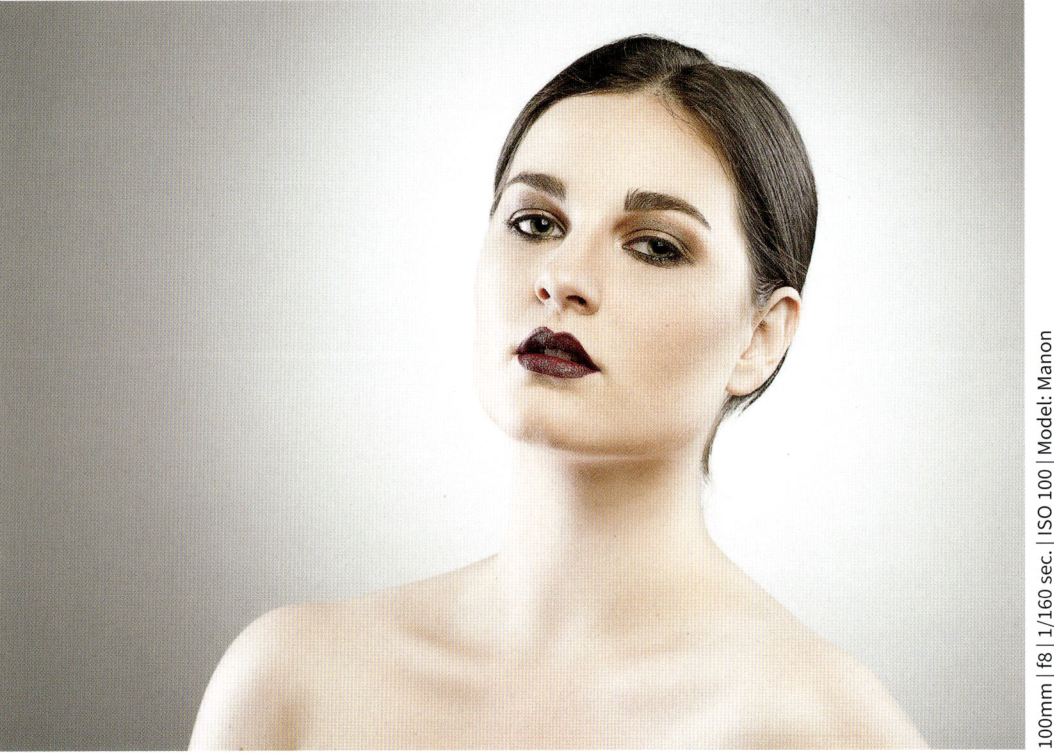

HOW IT WORKS

The closely positioned softbox gives the facial lighting a very soft touch, while its raised position produces a pronounced neck shadow that visually separates the head from the shoulders. The shadows contribute to the sculptural look of the image. The twin lateral effect lights produce highlights at the temples, cheeks, neck, and shoulders. Slight overexposure in the neck makes it appear slimmer, and the reflection under the chin emphasizes the facial contours. The gradient in the background helps to focus attention on the subject's face.

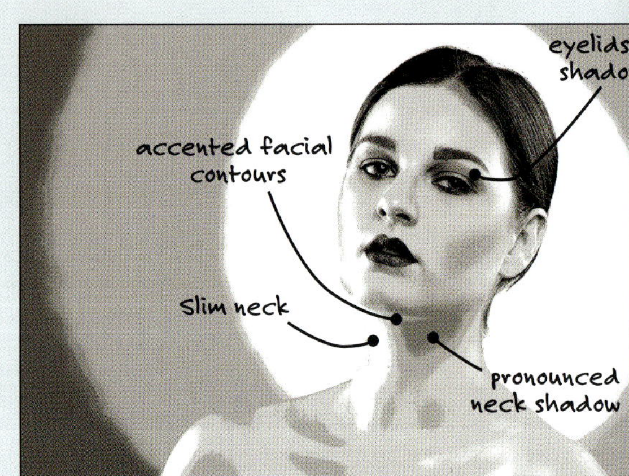

THE SETUP

1. Mount the softbox **(1)** frontally on a ceiling rail or a boom stand at a distance of about 3 feet and an angle of about 45 degrees so that the light reaching your model comes from above.

2. Place the strip boxes **(2)** to the left and right behind your model at about chin height so that the line of her chin is highlighted.

3. Place the gridded background reflector **(3)** above your model so that it brightens the background behind her head.

4. The distance between your model and the white background should be about 5 feet. This produces a background gradient from white to medium gray.

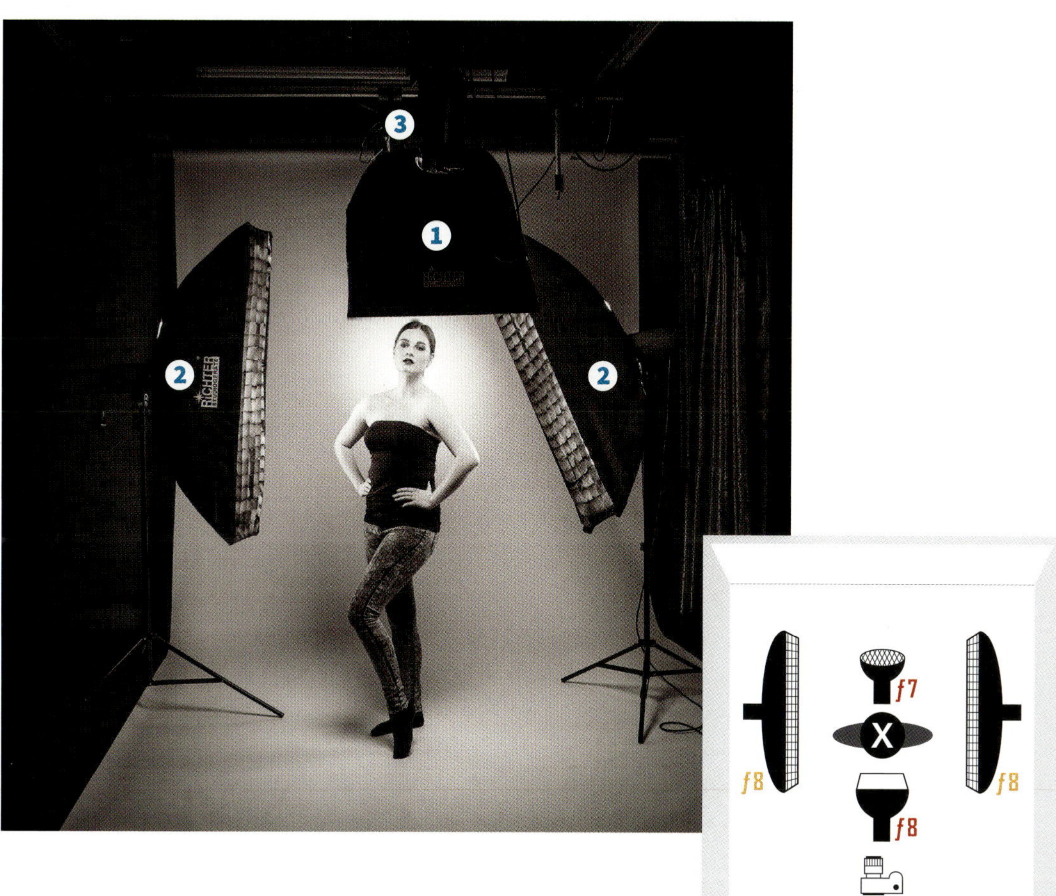

Variations

You can create variations on the highlights and reflections by getting your model to rotate her head or her torso, or by changing her head posture. In the image shown here, she tilted her head slightly downward, making the chin shadow disappear and producing an additional narrow reflection along the line of her cheekbone. The combined effect of these changes makes her neck appear shorter and the overall look much warmer.

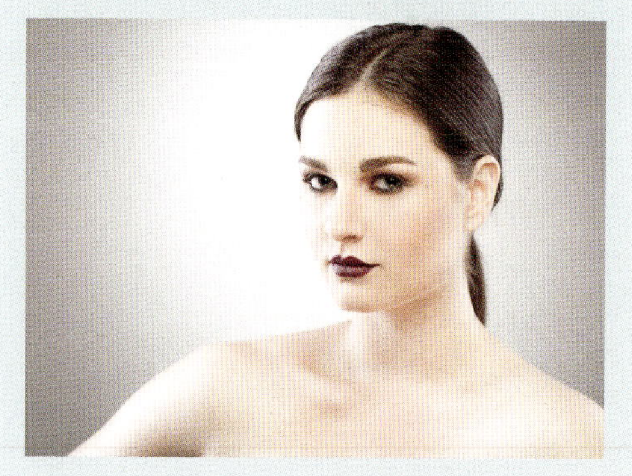

A Flokati Rug as a Separator

Reducing the composition to show just one half of the subject's face focuses the viewer's attention on a single eye. This simple, one-light setup produces an unusual portrait that shines thanks to its simplicity and the feeling of depth it creates. This type of image is great for advertising situations, for your portfolio, or simply as an eye-catcher. You can use other things as a separator too, such as other types of rugs, a wool blanket, or bubble wrap.

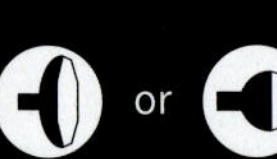 or

EFFORT INVOLVED

Low

SUITABLE FOR

Close-up to three-quarter-length portraits

THE LOOK

Unusual, contemporary portrait

Well-lit shadows

Accented facial features

Brown-toned smokey eyes and intense, dark red lipstick

Loose hair

EQUIPMENT

1 × 24" (or 31.5") octabox

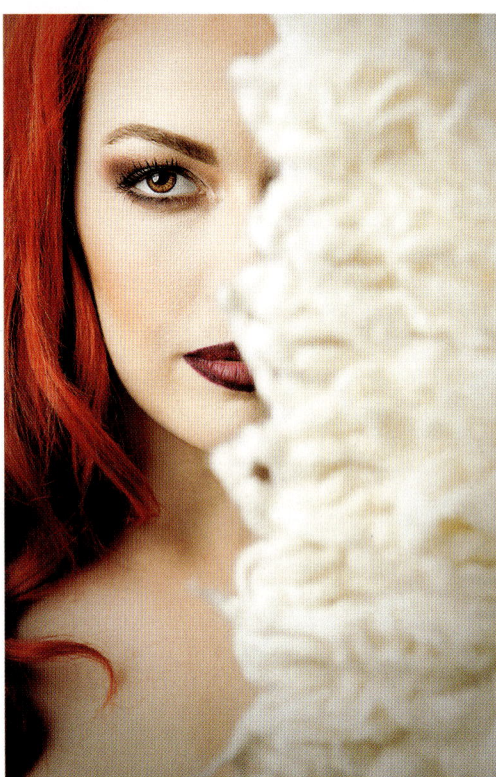

62mm | f4 | 1/125 sec. | ISO 100 | Model: Bianca

HOW IT WORKS

This setup eliminates nearly all the shadows and the result is correspondingly two-dimensional. The general lack of shadows helps to mask even major skin blemishes. The raised position of the main light produces a slight but noticeable chin shadow that separates the head from the shoulders. The large surface of the light source evenly illuminates the separator in the foreground and the subject's face. The clear reflection of the light source makes the visible eye gleam.

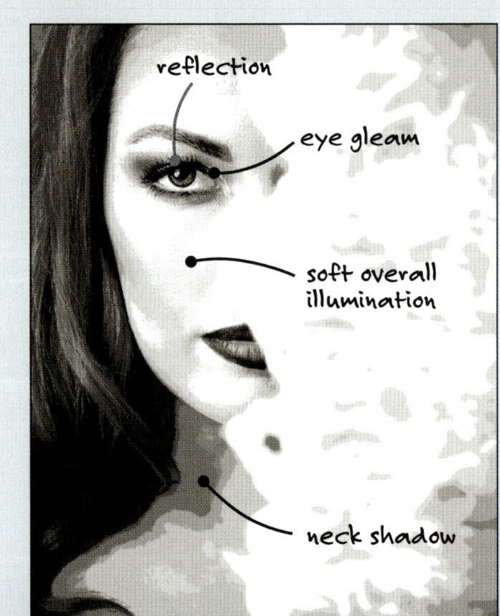

THE SETUP

1. Place the octabox **(1)** about 3 feet to the left of your model at an angle of about 30 degrees. Position it so that the neck shadow is clearly visible and the nose shadow doesn't quite reach your model's upper lip.

2. If you attach your separator **(2)** to a light stand, your model can use her hands to vary its position.

3. Position the separator about 18 inches from your model. If you opt for framing that is broader than the close-up I used, you will need to position your model about 3 feet in front of the background.

4. The softbox produces soft, broad light and plenty of spill, which lights the background (if it is visible at all) very evenly. In this case, the white background has a consistent light-gray tone.

"Make sure you light your model and the foreground evenly."

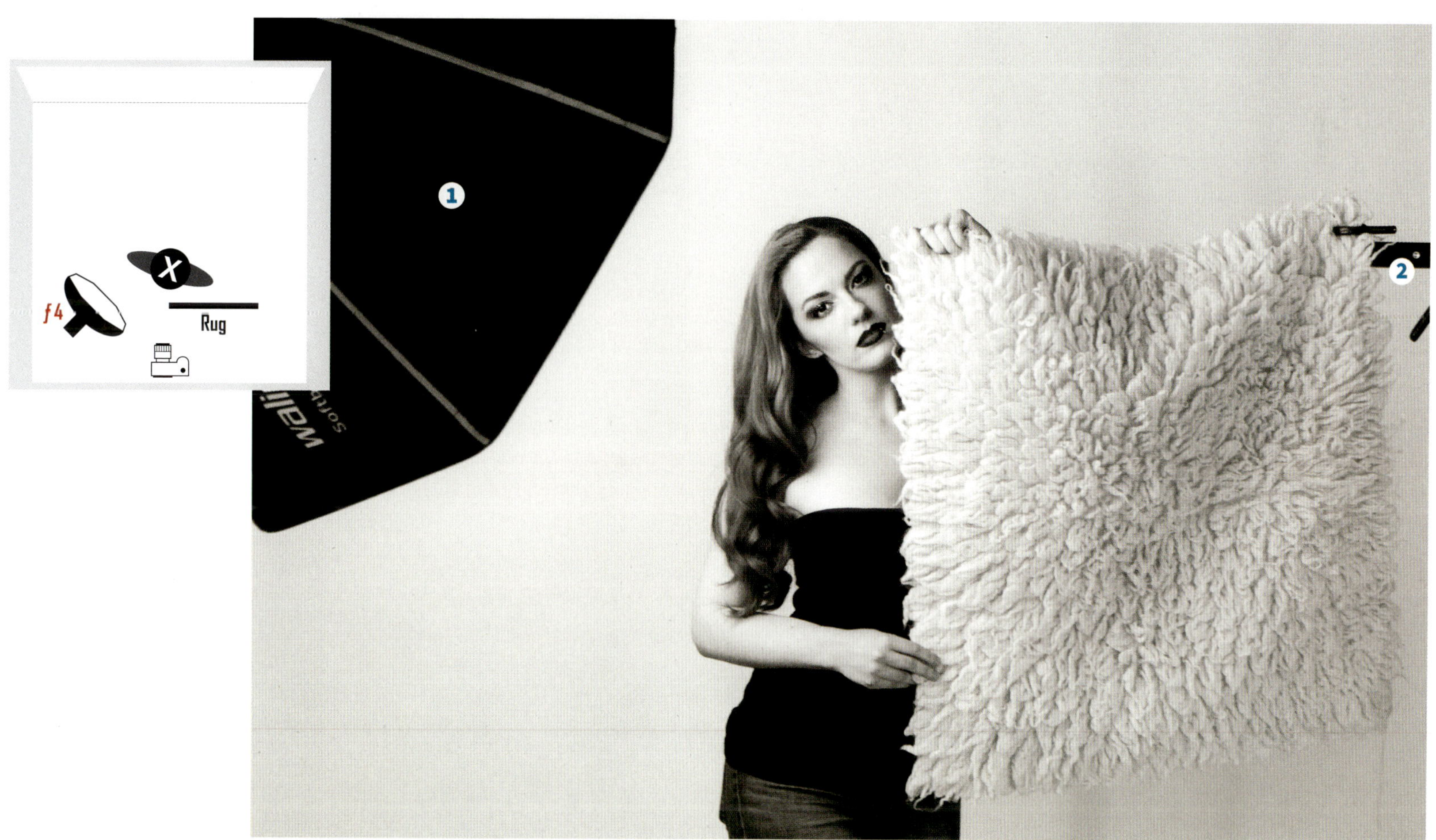

Using Reflected Light

Reflected light can be really useful in beauty portraits, too. This setup uses just one light and a reflector that produces soft, even light in the subject's face. The beauty dish produces a wonderful highlight on the subject's hair and neck.

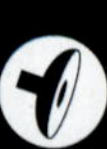

EFFORT INVOLVED

Low

SUITABLE FOR

Close-up to three-quarter-length portraits

THE LOOK

Simple beauty portrait with clear facial highlights

Natural makeup, tied-back hair

Strapless top

EQUIPMENT

1× beauty dish

1× 30"×40" silver reflector

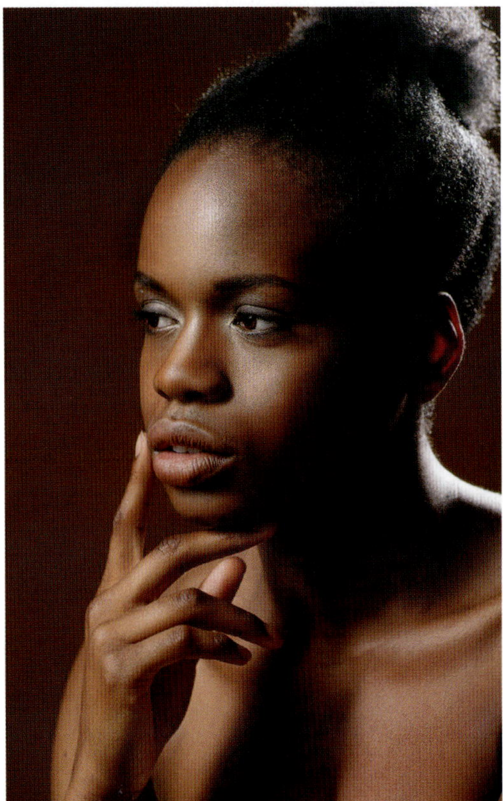

85mm | f6.3 | 1/160 sec. | ISO 100 | Model: Deborah

HOW IT WORKS

The surface of the reflector produces even lighting in the subject's face and upper body. The diagonally raised position of the reflector and the head rotation produce a narrow highlight that keeps the face and body looking slim. The highlights on the forehead, cheek, nose, and lips produce nicely three-dimensional contours. The position of the head produces a strong neck shadow that provides clear visual separation between the head and shoulders. The yellow background is lit softly by spill light that helps to emphasize the facial contours.

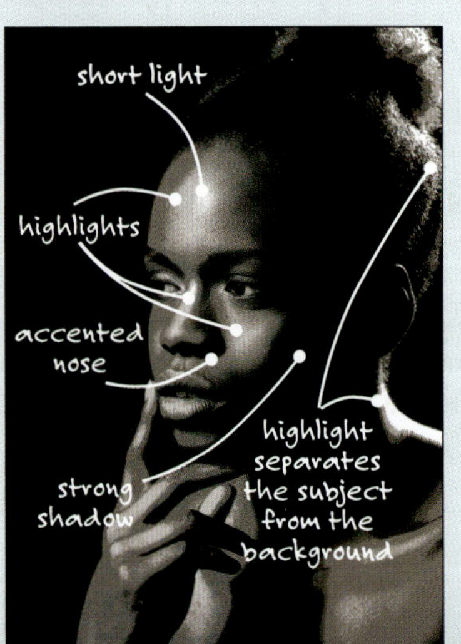

THE SETUP

1. Begin by placing the beauty dish **(1)** about 3 feet behind your model in a raised position and at an angle of about 45 degrees. Position it so that the focal point of the light shines over your model's head but also produces a clear highlight on her hair and neck. The highlight shouldn't reach farther than your model's lower jaw.

2. Now place the silver reflector **(2)** about 30 inches to the left of your model in a raised position. The reflector should reflect the main light onto your model from above so that a slight shadow forms beneath her nose. Meter the brightness of the reflected light as if it were a conventional light source. You can alter the brightness of the reflected light by adjusting the distance between the reflector and your model.

3. The distance between your model and the yellow background should be about 6 feet. Make sure that sufficient spill reaches the background. If the background is too dark, reduce the distance between your model and the background. Conversely, if the background is too bright, move your model farther away from it.

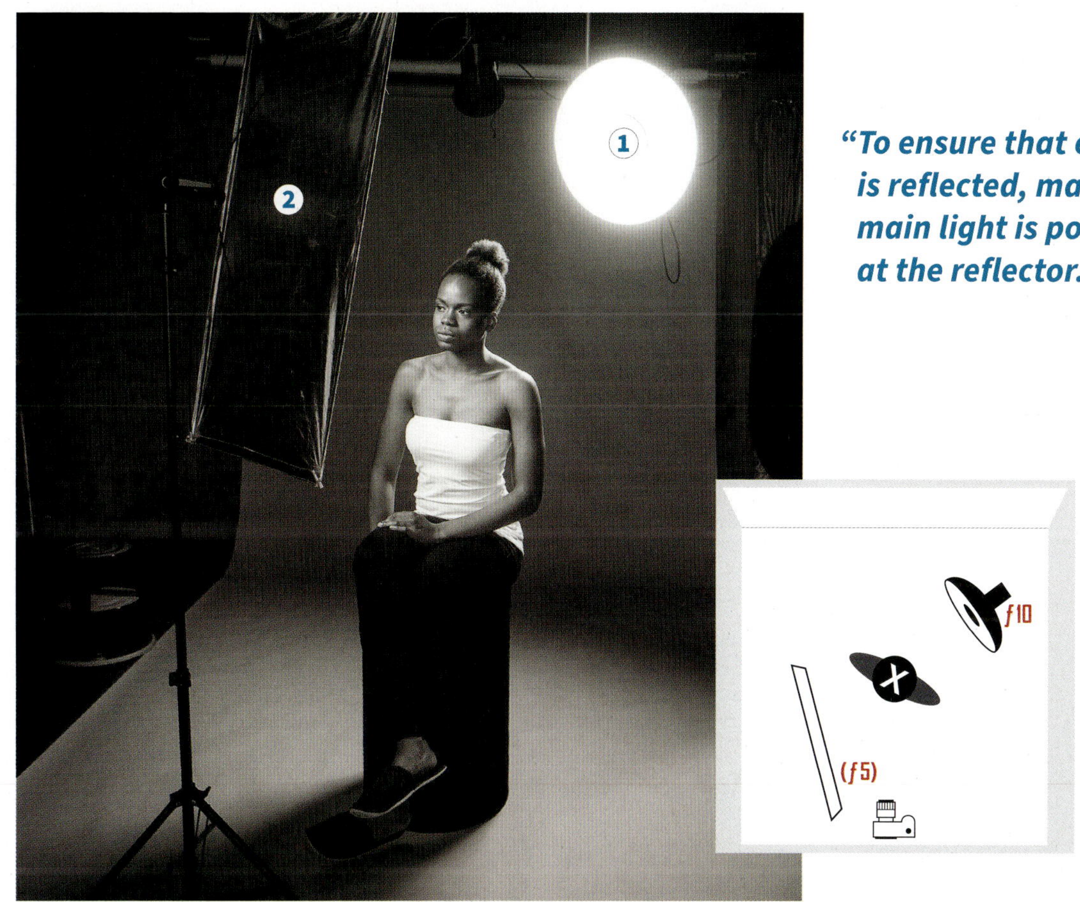

"To ensure that enough light is reflected, make sure the main light is pointed directly at the reflector."

"Hero" Lighting for Eye-Catching Portraits

This classic portrait setup uses two lights set up opposite one another. This produces wonderful, dramatic highlights that are really effective in many kinds of beauty portraits.

EFFORT INVOLVED

Medium

SUITABLE FOR

All kinds of portraits

THE LOOK

Striking beauty portrait that focuses strongly on the subject's presence

Facial highlights

Natural makeup, tied-back hair

Strapless top

EQUIPMENT

2 × 47" strip boxes

1 × standard reflector with a honeycomb grid

1 × 30" × 40" silver reflector

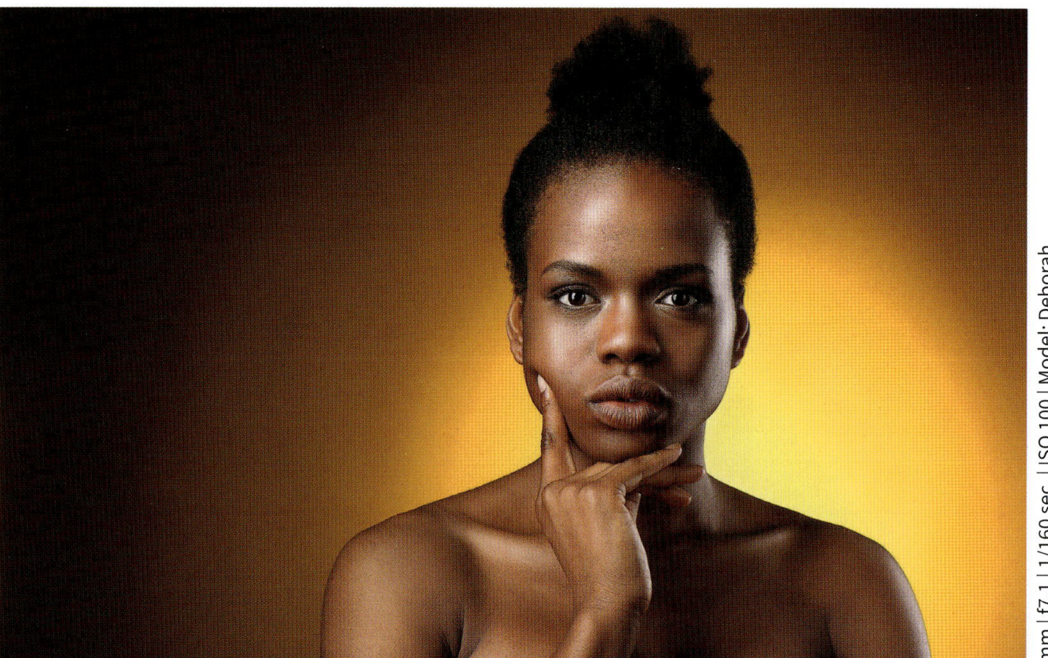

HOW IT WORKS

The twin strip boxes placed opposite one another produce a bold light/dark/light effect in the subject's face and body. Combining a yellow backdrop with the subject's dark skin tone produces a balanced image with a kind of sunset effect in the background. The spot aimed at the backdrop enhances this effect. The raised, lateral position of the main light produces shadows that give the subject depth and substance. The eyes and lips are accented, and the body contours come nicely to the fore. The fill light on the left emphasizes the line of the cheekbone and sets accents on the neck and upper arm.

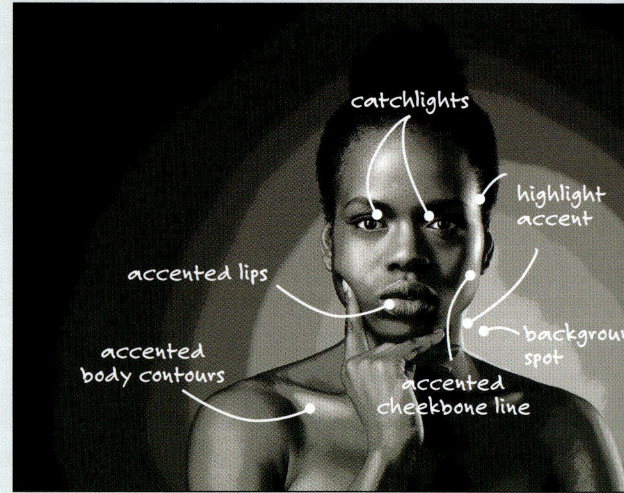

THE SETUP

1. Place the main strip box **(1)** about 3 feet in front of your model to the left at an angle of about 45 degrees. Position it a little higher up to produce a triangle of light on the shadow side and a nose shadow that points diagonally downward.

2. Place the accent strip box **(2)** about 5 feet behind your model to the right at an angle of about 45 degrees. Position the center of the light around head height and point it slightly downward. It should produce accents on your model's cheek, neck, and upper arm.

3. Position the silver reflector **(3)** high but close to your model (about 18 inches) on her left. Use the reflector to slightly lighten the shadow side of your model's face and body.

4. Mount the gridded background spot **(4)** centrally behind your model on a ceiling rail or a boom stand at a height of about 8 feet. Position it so that the pool of light it forms is focused at shoulder height and ends at around forehead level.

5. To produce the desired vignette effect with clear fall-off toward the edges of the frame, your model needs to stand about 8 feet in front of the yellow backdrop.

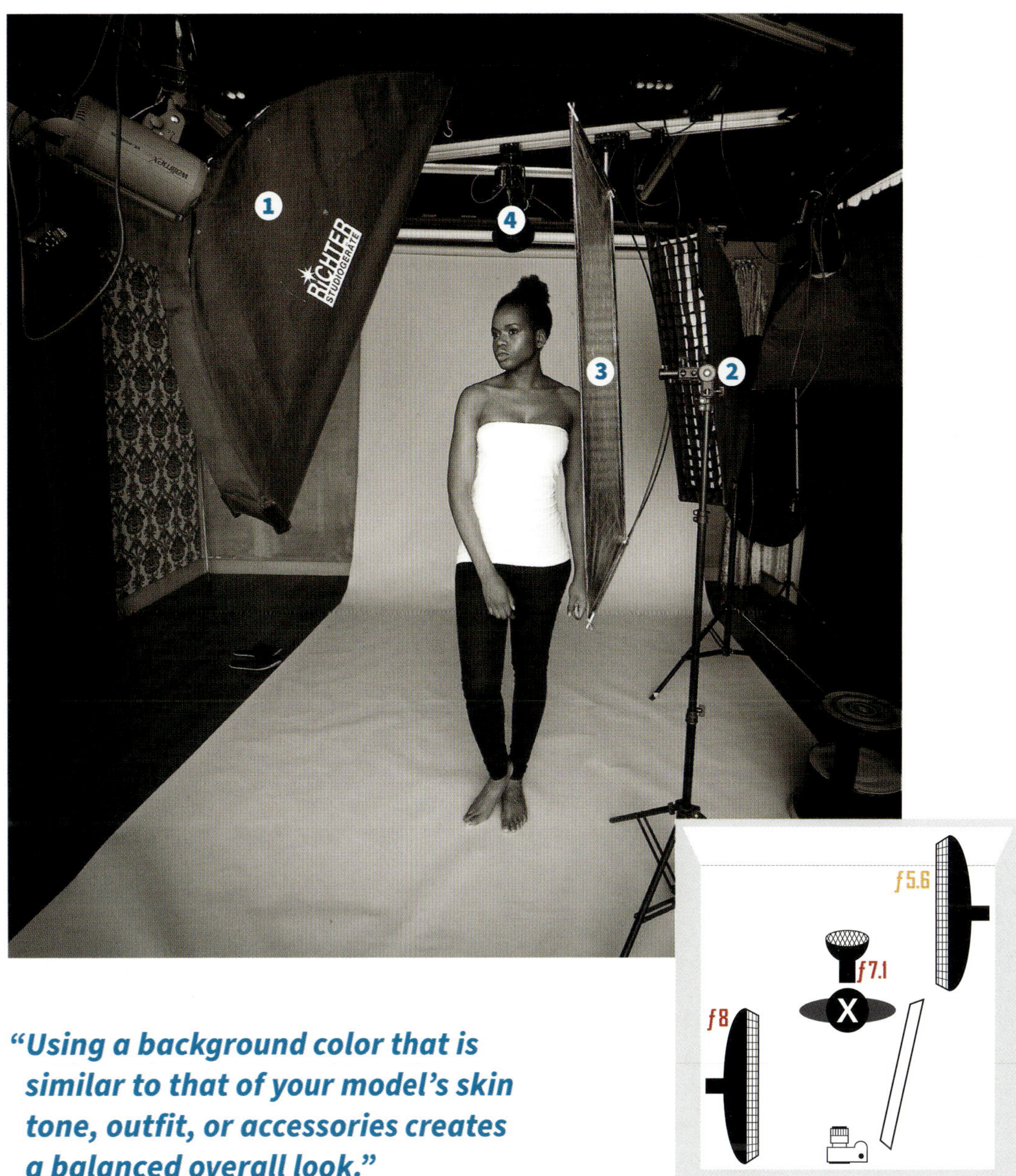

"Using a background color that is similar to that of your model's skin tone, outfit, or accessories creates a balanced overall look."

Soft Backlight

Many beauty shoots require a soft look. This setup produces a diffuse mood with a feel that is similar to the daylight look produced when the subject stands in front of a window. This setup, with its bright, even lighting, is ideal for advertising makeup.

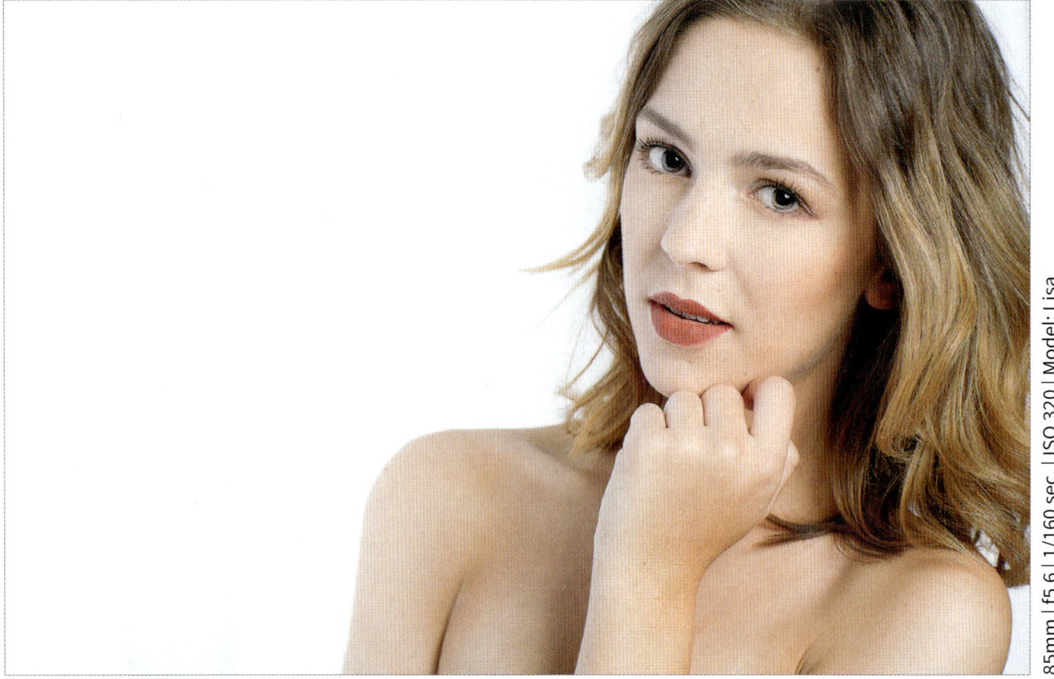

85mm | f5.6 | 1/160 sec. | ISO 320 | Model: Lisa

EFFORT INVOLVED

Medium

SUITABLE FOR

Close-up to three-quarter-length portraits

THE LOOK

Bright beauty portrait with a soft overall feel
Natural makeup and accented lips

EQUIPMENT

2 × 47" strip boxes
1 × 31.5" octabox

HOW IT WORKS

The light from the strip boxes is softened by the curtain material, producing soft shadows and contours. The raised octabox main light produces just enough shadow to keep the portrait from drifting into soft focus. The bright backlight produces soft highlights on the subject's cheek, shoulder, and arm, as well as very subtle highlights on the nose and lips. The overall effect is nicely balanced and looks a lot like a daylight shot taken near a window. The curtain material in the background provides texture (a white wall would be too sterile). There is nothing in this image that distracts from the subject's face.

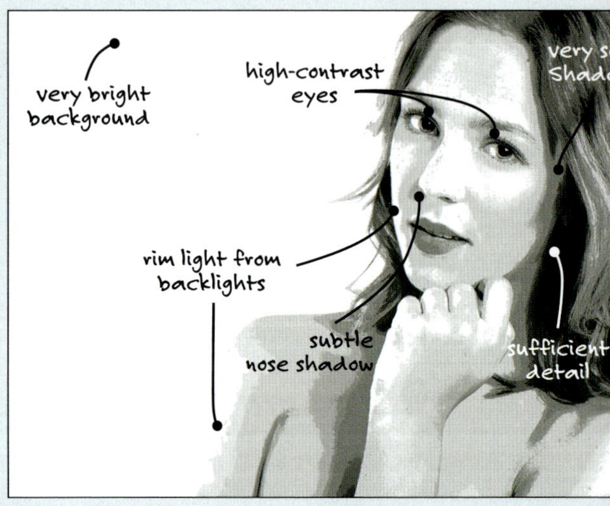

THE SETUP

1. Begin by placing a double-layered white curtain **(1)** about 3 feet in front of a white background.

2. Place the strip boxes **(2)** about 10 feet apart to the right and left of the curtain at head height, and point them slightly downward toward the backdrop.

3. Place the octabox **(3)** about 6 feet from your model in a raised position at front left, and at an angle of about 45 degrees. Position it to produce a nose shadow that points diagonally downward.

4. Position your model about 8 to 10 inches from the curtain.

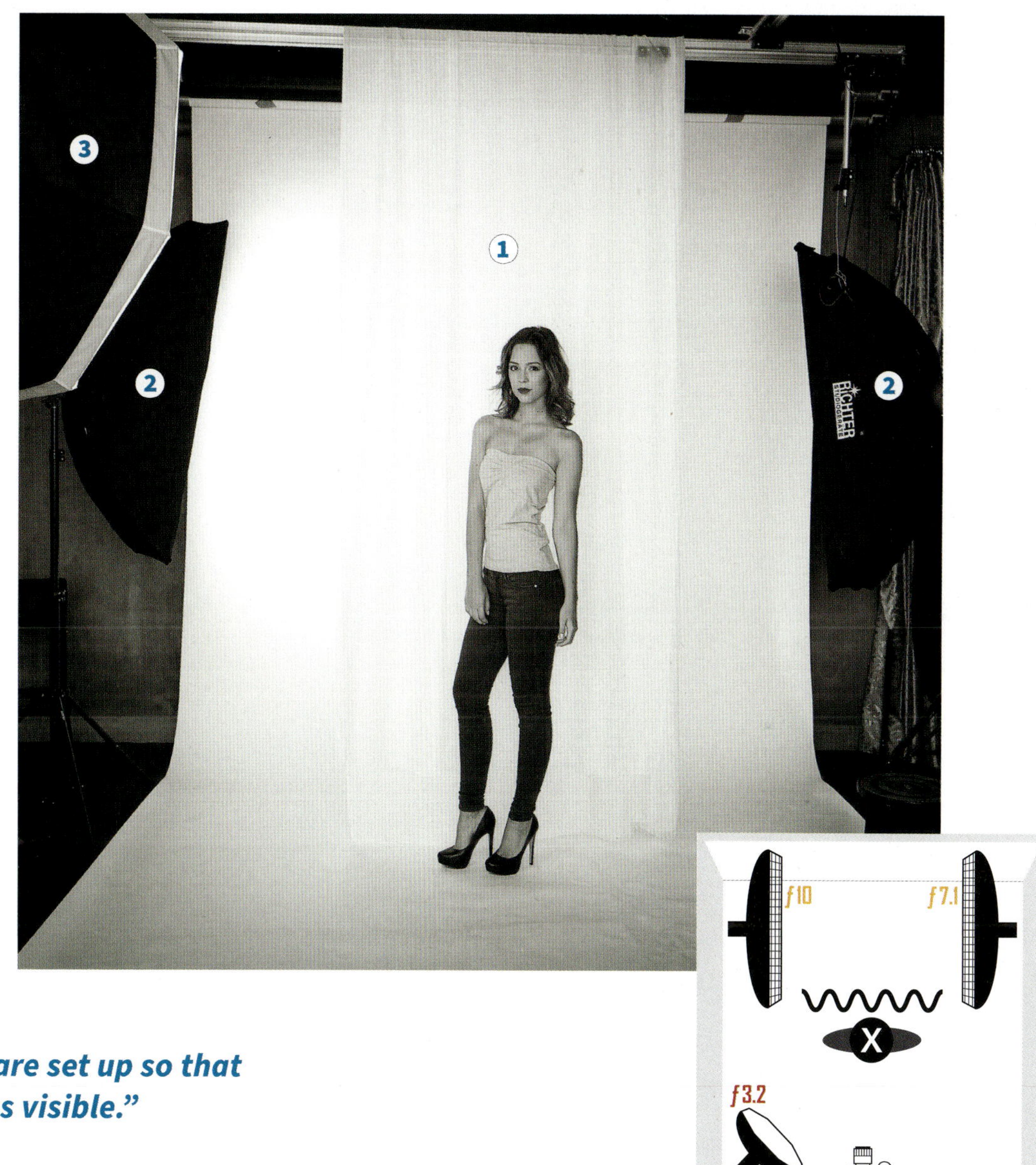

"Make sure your background lights are set up so that the texture in the backdrop remains visible."

Neon Beauty Light

You can shoot great beauty portraits using just a fluorescent tube from a DIY store. The only other ingredients are a white wall, a reflector, and, of course, an enchanting model. The light is relatively broad and therefore quite soft, and helps to mask pores and skin creases (and may even save you some retouching later on). In the case of the image shown here, I developed it using Lightroom but performed no other post-processing.

EFFORT INVOLVED

Low

SUITABLE FOR

Close-up to three-quarter-length portraits

THE LOOK

Simple beauty portrait with soft lighting and gentle contours

Natural makeup that matches the subject's outfit

EQUIPMENT

1× 36W fluorescent tube

1× 30"×40" silver reflector

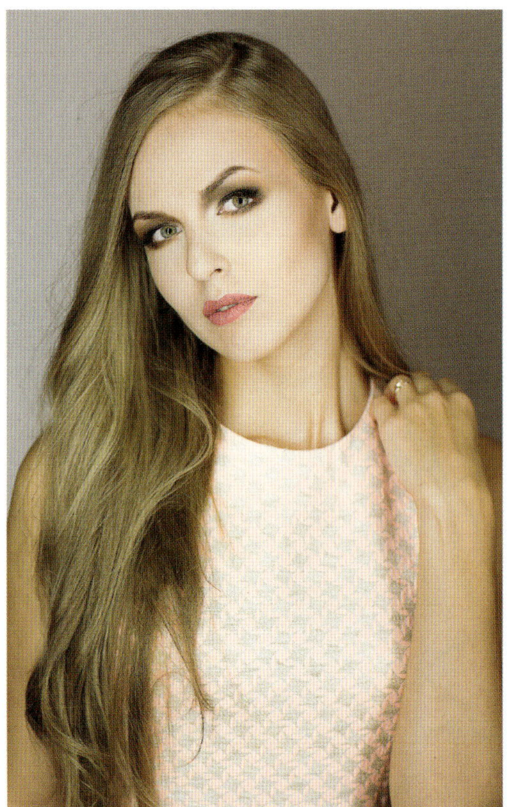

85mm | f2.8 | 1/100 sec. | ISO 800 | Model: Angelina

HOW IT WORKS

The raised position of the fluorescent tube means that the light comes from above and creates a subtle neck shadow that separates the subject's head from her body. The narrow tube lights the subject's face and the center of her body, and the obvious light fall-off toward both sides of the frame accents the face. Horizontal shadows accent the nose, cheek, jaw, and neck. Vertical shadows produce soft contours (on the lips, for example). The neon tube also creates thin catchlights. There is a clear light-to-dark gradient from left to right.

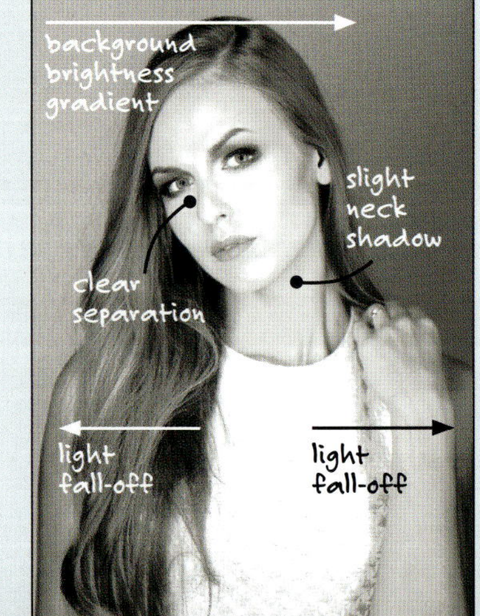

THE SETUP

1. Mount the fluorescent tube **(1)** vertically on a telescopic stand and position it high up about 18 inches to the left of your model at an angle of about 45 degrees. Position the tube so that its lower third is at head height.

2. Place the silver reflector **(2)** about 18 inches to the right of your model at an angle of about 45 degrees. Position it to lighten the shadow side of your model's face.

3. Place your model 2 to 3 feet in front of the white background.

When you are shooting in continuous light, you need to pay attention to the ISO setting in addition to the usual exposure time and aperture settings. I wanted to use a wide aperture for this shot, so I used an aperture setting of f2.8. Because Angelina is very good at standing still and because I have a steady hand, I chose an exposure time of 1/100 sec., which is slightly longer than the 1/125 sec. recommended in the *Calculating Exposure Settings* section on page 26. Once I had my basic settings, I set the corresponding ISO value for a correct exposure.

> *"Pay attention to the color of the light your neon tube produces and set your camera's white balance accordingly."*

White Balance in Continuous Light

If you use continuous light in a studio, you need to adjust your white balance setting accordingly. The safest approach is to use a manual white balance setting and to shoot in RAW format. This way, it is relatively easy to correct color casts or other anomalies. For more details, see the section The Color of Light on page 7.

If you can, use 865 daylight bulbs/tubes. The figure 8 stands for color rendering index 80, which means the tube produces reliably colored light. The 65 designation stands for a color temperature of 6500K (i.e., daylight). If you use this type of lamp, you can either use a manual white balance setting of 6500 or use the Daylight preset.

Bright Light, Mellow Tones

High-key setups are popular in beauty photography situations, largely because the extreme lightened shadows provide a flawless complexion. For this shot, I wanted to create a cool look that accented the subject's super-silky hair. The result is predestined for magazine or advertising use.

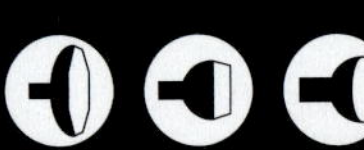

EFFORT INVOLVED

Medium

SUITABLE FOR

Close-up to three-quarter-length portraits

THE LOOK

A radiant portrait with a perfect complexion
Natural makeup with delicate colors
Reflections in the subject's accessories

EQUIPMENT

1× 47" octabox
1× 24" softbox
1× standard reflector

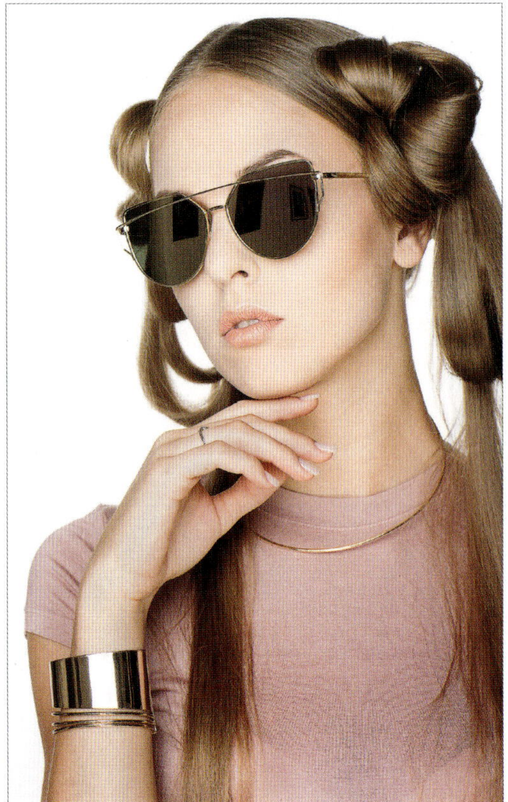

85mm | f8 | 1/160 sec. | ISO 100 | Model: Angelina

HOW IT WORKS

The soft light from the raised, frontal octabox produces very soft shadows that make the face appear very smooth. The visible chin shadow is brightened by the softbox but still helps to frame the face. The soft lighting accentuates the delicate colors, which provide a nice contrast to the cool-looking accessories and the reflections they produce. Because the octbaox and the softbox provide light from above and below, the subject's hair has an especially silky look. The bright, even background light doesn't distract from the subject.

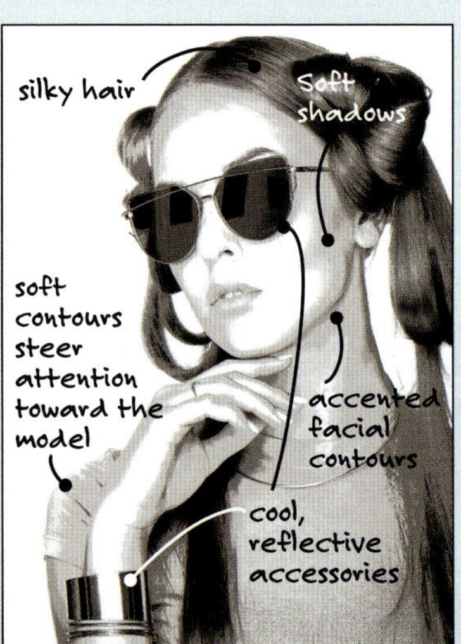

THE SETUP

1. Place the large octabox **(1)** about 3 feet from your model in a slightly raised position and at an angle of about 15 degrees. Position it to produce a subtle neck shadow.

2. Place the softbox fill light **(2)** on the floor 3 to 5 feet from your model. The shape of the softbox angles the light upward but, if the angle isn't steep enough, use a low stand to raise it up a little.

3. Mount the background reflector **(3)** centrally behind your model on a ceiling rail or a boom stand at a height of about 8 feet.

4. Place your model about 3 feet in front of the white background.

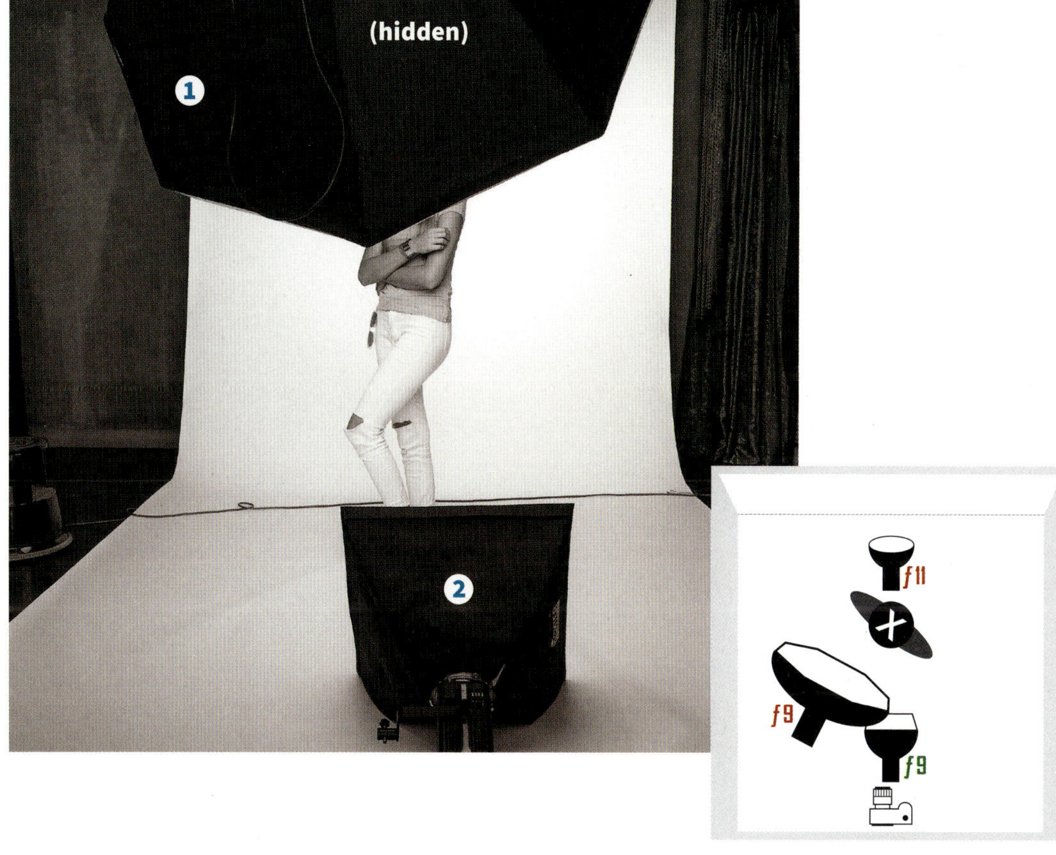

"Pay close attention to what gets reflected. You don't want to see yourself or your studio gear in the finished image!"

Reflections in Eyeglass Lenses

Watch out for unwanted effects when photographing reflective surfaces. A slight adjustment of the tilt or angle or your model's head is all it takes to remove or alter the kind of reflection you get (see the image opposite). Strong reflections have their place in beauty shots too, as the example below shows.

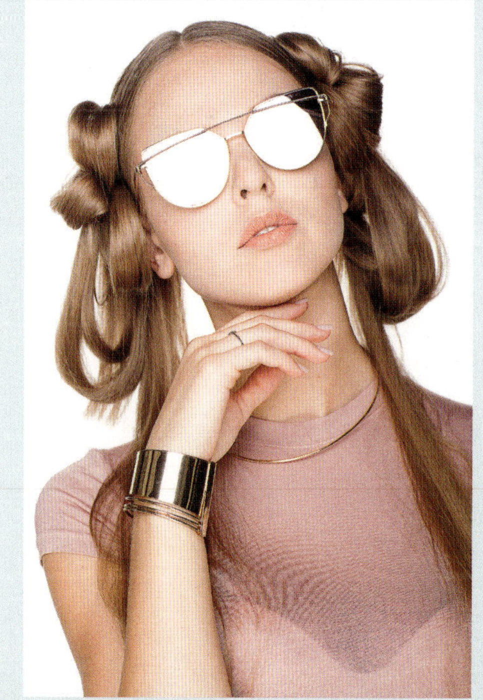

High-Key Portait with Color Accents

This popular high-key setup uses a large octabox to produce intense backlight. The result features many delicate highlights in the subject's shoulders, hair, and back. The light shining through the flower petals adds to the overall appeal of the image.

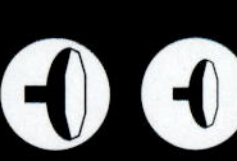

EFFORT INVOLVED

Medium

SUITABLE FOR

Close-up to three-quarter-length portraits

THE LOOK

High-key beauty portrait with strong backlight and lots of highlights

Strong masking of skin imperfections

Makeup and flowers match the model's hair

EQUIPMENT

1× 47" octabox

1× 31.5" octabox

1× 30"×40" silver reflector

2× Styrofoam fill reflectors

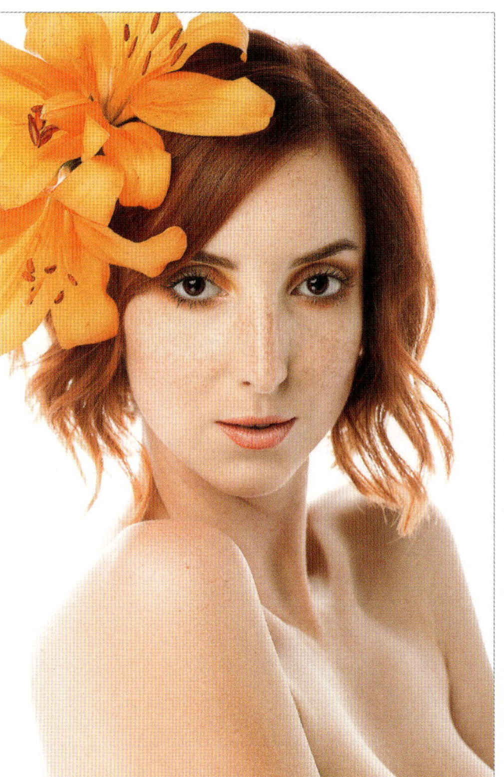

100mm | f8 | 1/160 sec. | ISO 100 | Model: Kristina

HOW IT WORKS

The raised octabox produces soft shadow accents beneath the eyebrows and lips. Together with the delicate nose and cheek shadows, these provide a good three-dimensional feel. The large octabox in the background produces highlights in the subject's back, shoulders, and hair, which contribute to the feeling of air-iness and the accenting of the body contours. The bright orange flower petals complement the subject's hair and makeup and balance the colors nicely. The silver reflector and the Styrofoam sheets gently lighten the remaining shadows.

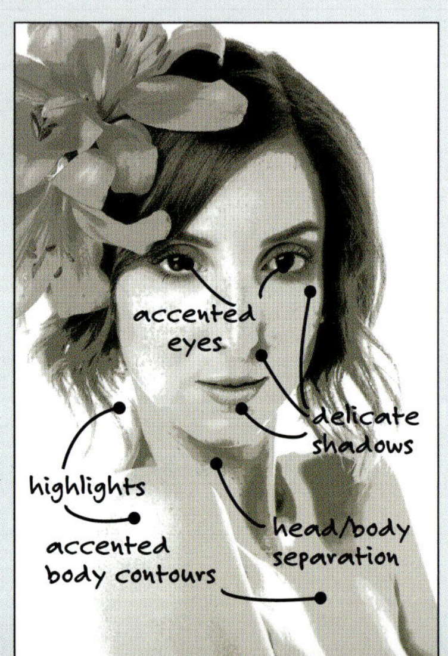

THE SETUP

1. Place the large octabox **(1)** behind your model and point it directly toward the camera with its center at neck height.

2. Place the two fill reflectors **(2)** about 3 feet apart on the left and right of the octabox at a distance of about 20 inches.

3. Now place the smaller octabox **(3)** in a raised position to the left at an angle of about 45 degrees. Position it about 3 feet from your model so that it produces a nose shadow that points diagonally downward and ends about halfway between the tip of your model's nose and her upper lip.

4. Place the silver reflector **(4)** about 20 inches from your model at belly height and at an angle that lightens the shadows in her face.

5. Place your model in the center of the setup between the two fill reflectors.

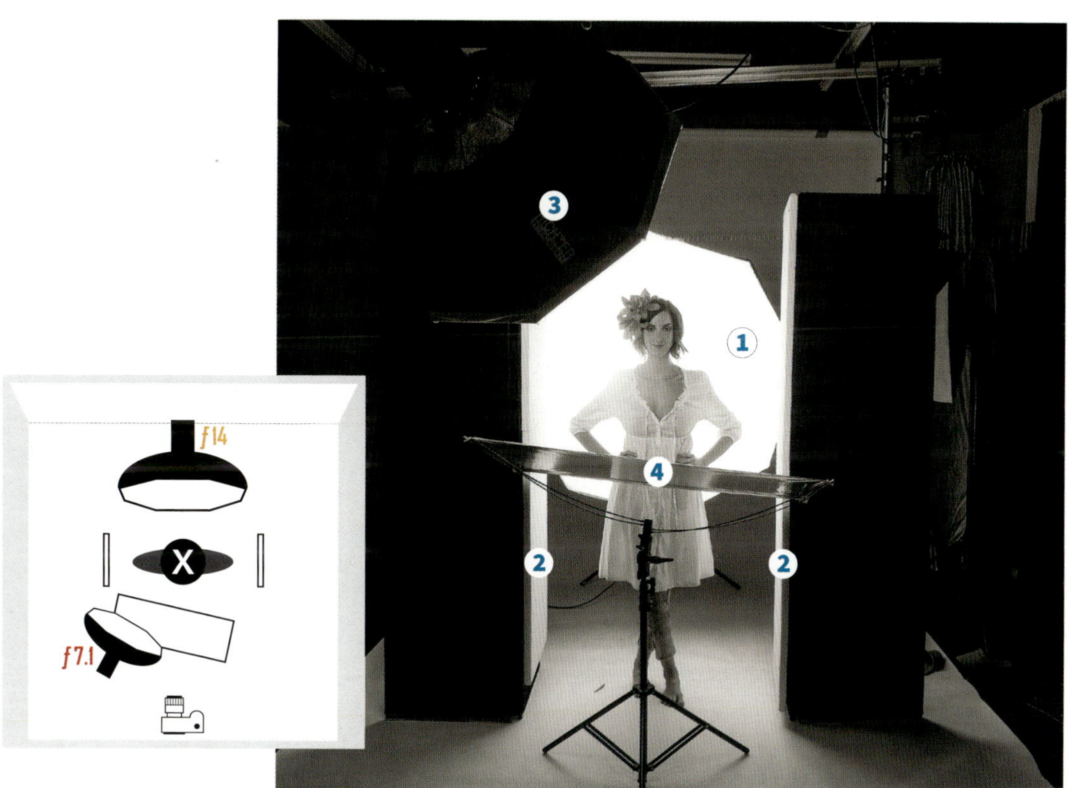

Variations

If your model turns her body away from the camera, her slightly hunched shoulders form a line that points toward her head. This also masks her body contours and focuses the viewer's attention more directly on her face.

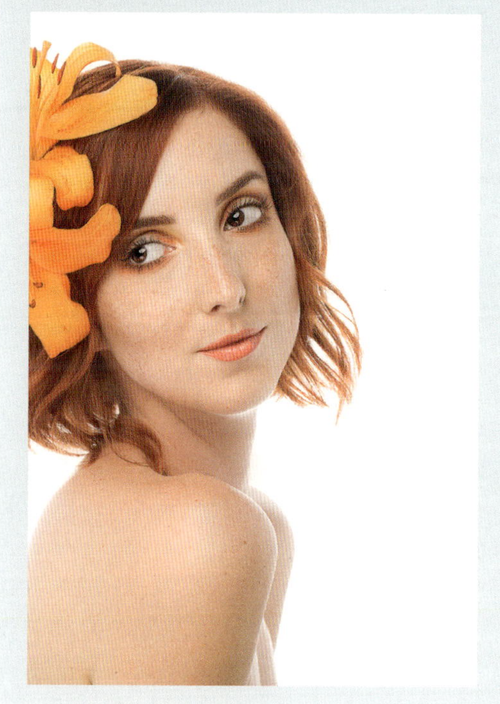

Beauty Portrait with Rembrandt-Lighting

This classic setup is named after the 17th century Dutch painter Rembrandt van Rijn, who often painted portraits using this particular mood lighting. In a photographic studio, it is a simple one-light setup that is great for producing beauty portraits with a classic look. The black-and-white conversion underscores the classic feel of the image.

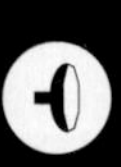

EFFORT INVOLVED

Low

SUITABLE FOR

Close-up to three-quarter-length portraits

THE LOOK

Timeless Rembrandt portrait lighting
Glamorous makeup, smokey eyes, and dark lips
Tied-back hair and strapless top

EQUIPMENT

1 × 31.5" octabox

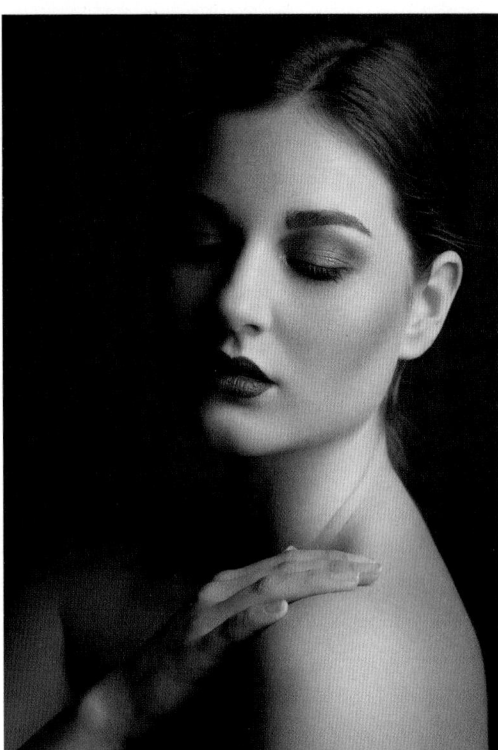

100mm | f8 | 1/160 sec. | ISO 100 | Model: Manon

HOW IT WORKS

The very high, lateral position of the main light produces intense shadows and a highly three-dimensional look. The lighter side of the subject's face is accented, with clearly defined contours. There is an obvious diagonal that reaches from the soft, glossy hair to the lower arm and that divides the image into lighter and darker sides. The shadow side of the face is lit by the classic Rembrandt triangle and provides subtle details that are just visible. The lowered eyes and the hand on the shoulder give the image a calm feel. Finally, the black-and-white conversion produces a truly timeless beauty portrait.

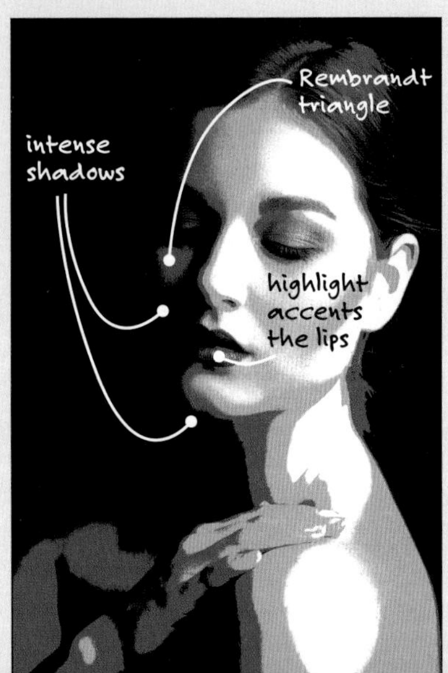

THE SETUP

1. Begin by positioning your model about 20 inches in front of a black background.

2. Mount the octabox **(1)** high up about 3 feet to the right of your model and at an angle of about 45 degrees. At this stage, your model should position her head as you want it in the final image and then remain completely still. Now position the light to produce the Rembrandt triangle on the shadow side of your model's face. The nose shadow should point diagonally downward and blend in with the cheek shadow.

Rembrandt Lighting Requires Precision!

Even the tiniest movements can spoil the Rembrandt effect, either because the triangle of light disappears, becomes too small, or simply falls apart and forms a separate nose shadow. This is why it is essential for your model to hold her position while you set up your light.

Once you have everything set up, it is actually a good idea to get your model to make minimal head movements between shots and, once she has moved an inch or so from her original position, to move her head back again and try incremental movements in the opposite direction. This way, you can experiment with different-sized Rembrandt triangles and you can be sure of capturing the perfect look for your model and your own personal preferences.

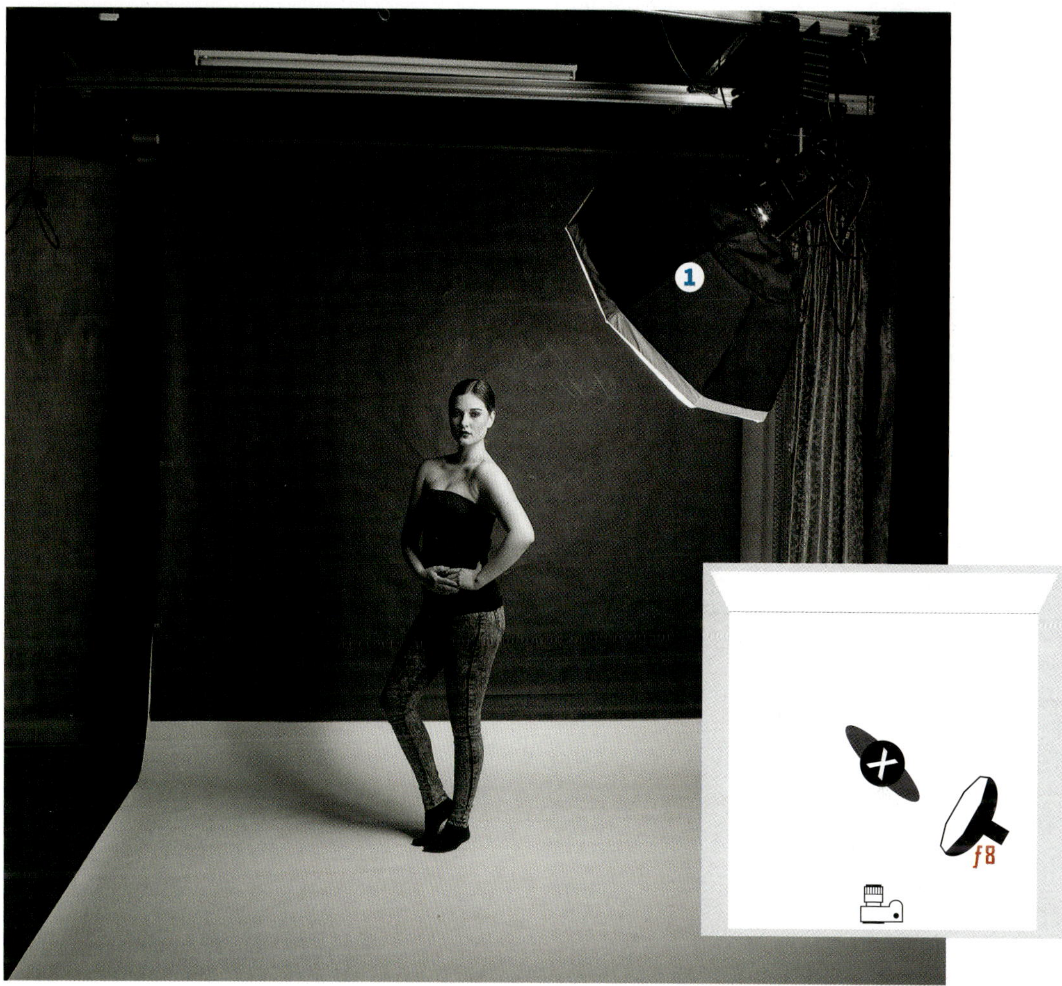

"If you want your image to have a classic look, you need to apply the golden ratio, balanced design, or any other combination of tried-and-trusted compositional rules."

Playing with Light and Shadow

Beauty portraits can be experimental too! This setup shows how to use simple tools to produce an interesting light/shadow contrast. The result is a striking image that is worthy of a slot on a magazine cover.

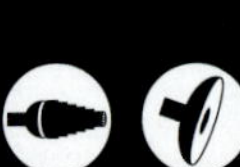

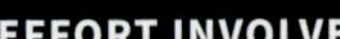

EFFORT INVOLVED

Medium

SUITABLE FOR

Close-up to three-quarter-length portraits

THE LOOK

Sophisticated light/shadow effect
Unobtrusive makeup but distinctive eyeliner

EQUIPMENT

1× snoot with a honeycomb grid

1× beauty dish

1× 12" square card gobo with slits

2× flags

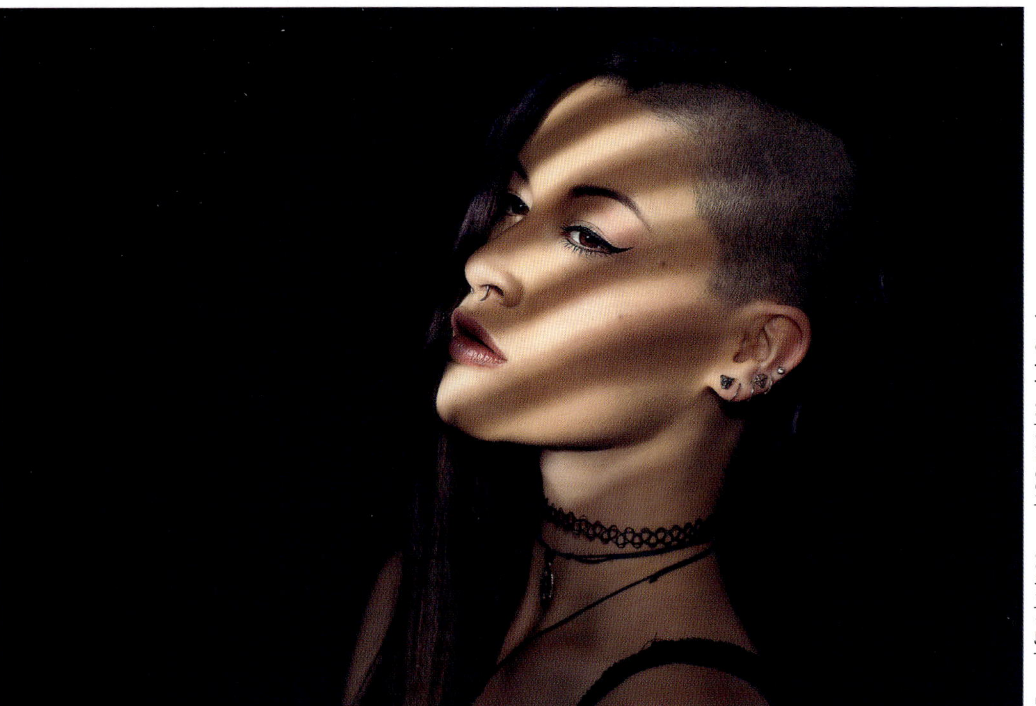

HOW IT WORKS

The position of the subject's head means the face is actually frontally lit and a hard shadow produces a clear line of separation between the face and the weakly lit body. The diagonal streaks of light accent the shape of the face and provide a clear focal point for the viewer. Catchlights in both eyes produce a lively look. The eyes, nose, and mouth are brightly lit, providing accents for the most important facial features. The body is just distinguishable against the not-quite-black background. I desaturated the image during post-processing to give it an almost monochrome feel that accentuates the unusual look.

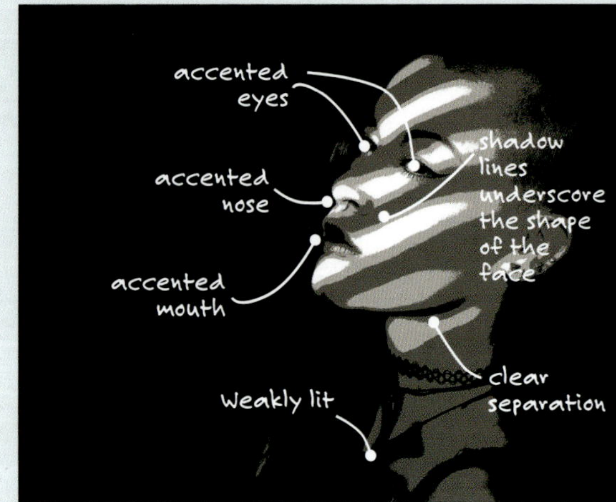

THE SETUP

1. Position your model about 3 feet from the black background.

2. Place the snooted light **(1)** about 12 feet to the front left of your model in a slightly raised position at an angle of about 45 degrees. Position it to light your model's face and to produce a slight nose shadow.

3. Mount the slit cardboard gobo **(2)** on a stand between the snooted light and your model (about 15 inches from her face). Vary the height and angle of the gobo until you are satisfied with the shadow pattern it produces.

4. Use two flags **(3)** to dampen any spill light that reaches your model's body beneath the shadow produced by the gobo. You can use reflectors here too, or any other opaque material.

5. Finally, place the beauty dish **(4)** in a central, raised position about 6 feet from your model.

Keep a careful eye on the shadow patterns while you shoot and get your model to try out different head postures to produce different light and shadow effects—for example, in and around her eyes.

"The narrower the gobo light source and the farther it is from the gobo, the sharper and more intense the shadow effect will be."

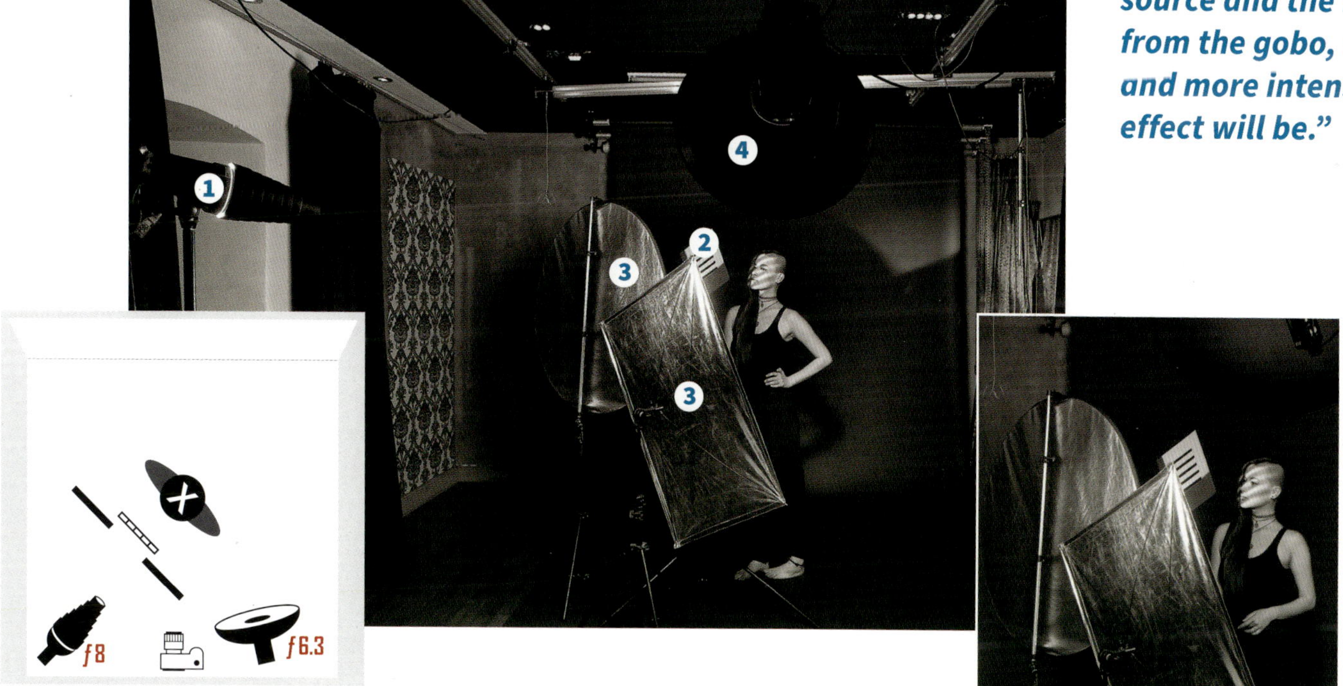

This detail clearly shows the cardboard gobo and the effect of the flags on the shadows beneath it.

Two-Color Background

Color accents are great for accenting and framing specific areas in an image. This type of effect is great for magazine editorials and steers the viewer's attention to exactly the right place within the frame. It is also a great way to experiment with complementary or contrasting colors.

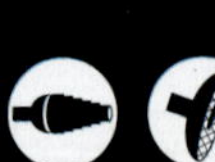
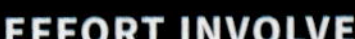

EFFORT INVOLVED

Medium

SUITABLE FOR

Close-up to three-quarter-length portraits

THE LOOK

Two-color background grabs the viewer's attention
Natural look with accented eyes and glossy lips

EQUIPMENT

1× snoot with a colored gel
1× beauty dish with a honeycomb grid
1× 30"×40" silver reflector

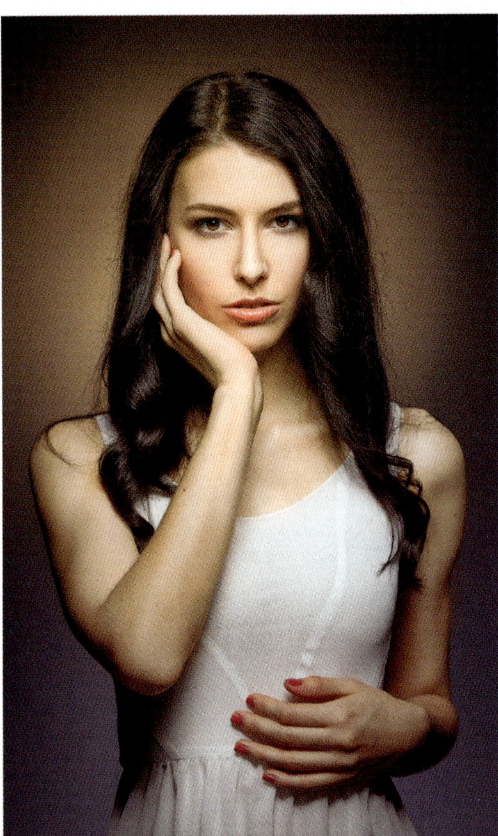

115mm | f10 | 1/160 sec. | ISO 100 | Model: Elisa

HOW IT WORKS

This setup is almost identical to the previous one. The clear light fall-off from top to bottom produces additional focus on the face, and the bright accent behind the head intensifies this effect. The two-color background is an interesting additional feature that I intensified by increasing the blue channel value in the shadows during post-processing. The vignette effect in the corners also helps to concentrate the viewer's attention on the subject.

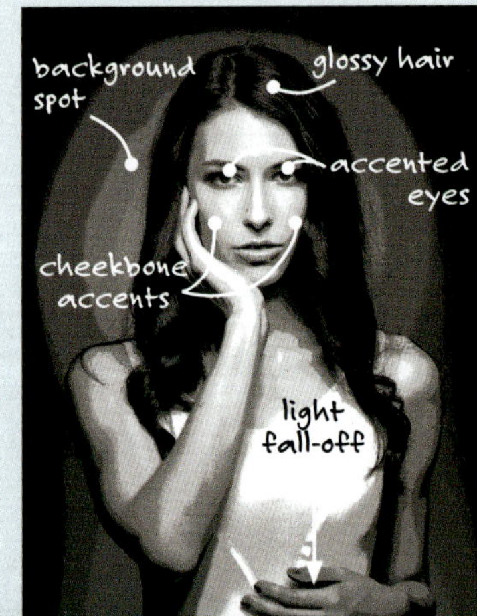

THE SETUP

1. Place the beauty dish **(1)** about 5 feet from your model in a raised, central position. Position it to produce a central nose shadow that ends between your model's nose and upper lip.

2. Mount the silver reflector **(2)** horizontally on a low stand directly in front of your model at about belly height so that it lightens the shadows in her face.

3. Place the snooted spot **(3)** about 3 feet from your model on the right so that its light hits the background at precisely head height. Attach an orange gel to the snoot to produce a brown/orange background tone. You can adjust the size of the spot by altering the distance between the light and the background.

4. Position your model about 6 feet in front of the white background.

"Make sure that the beauty dish produces a vignette effect in the background."

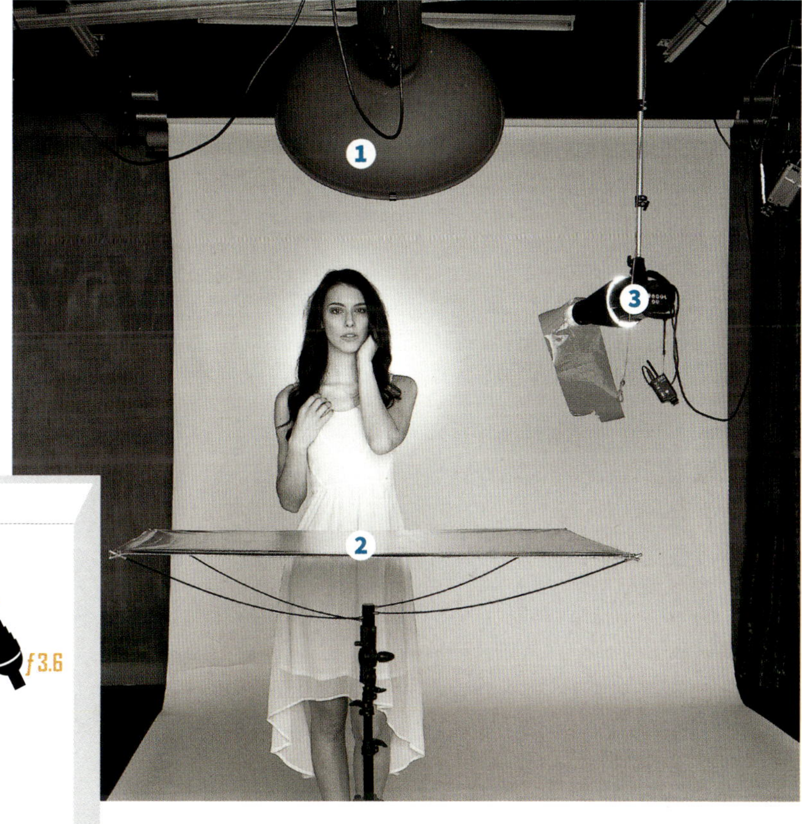

Adjusting the Background Color(s)

Intensifying the blue/magenta background effect requires a bit of post-processing. I began by developing the RAW image file in Lightroom and increasing color temperature to 5700K to intensify the skin tone and enhance the orange tint in the background. I then tweaked a couple of tonal values and did some quick beauty retouching in Photoshop. I enhanced the blue and red tones in the shadows and reduced the reds in the highlights using a Curves adjustment.

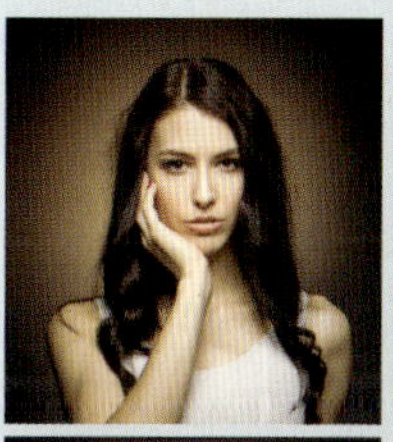
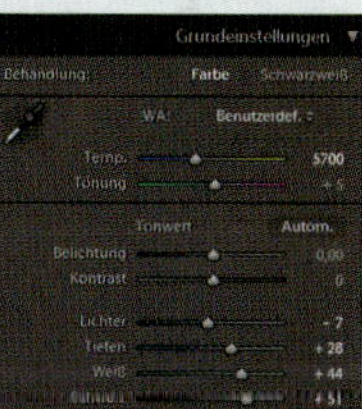
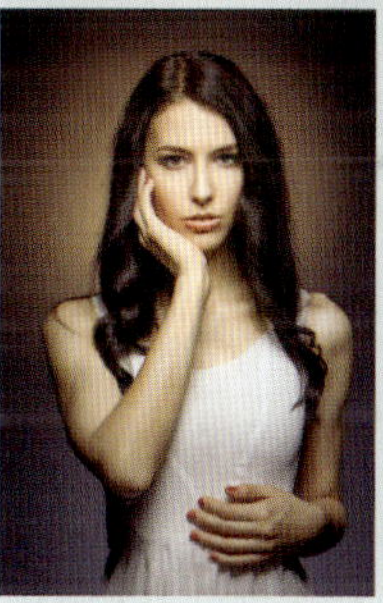
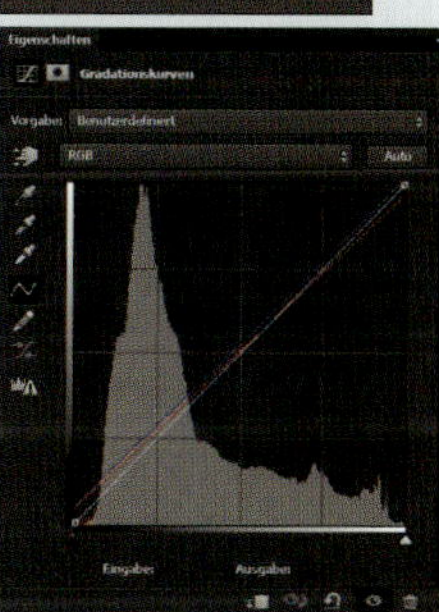

If you don't want to get involved in post-processing, you can simply use a softbox with a magenta-colored gel to light the background. Increase the distance between your model and the background to reduce the amount of background light coming from the beauty dish, then position the extra softbox behind your model and adjust its output to provide a suitable degree of illumination.

Colored
Soap Bubbles

This setup enables you to add color and colored highlights to your image. You can use two identical or two different light shapers. I recommend that you use softboxes, octaboxes, or strip boxes to produce the kind of soft overall effect you can see here. They provide flattering light and produce nice highlights in the soap bubbles. You can use any colors you like, but I like to use colors from opposite sides of the color circle to create a little bit of tension. Delicate tones generally work better in this kind of shot.

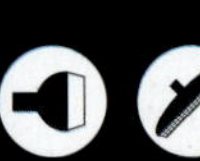 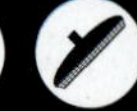

EFFORT INVOLVED
Low

SUITABLE FOR
Close-up to three-quarter-length portraits

THE LOOK
Straightforward, colorful portrait
Well-lit shadows
Smokey eyes, subtle lip styling, accented curly hair
Strapless dress, accented face

EQUIPMENT
1 × 24" softbox with a colored gel
1 × 47" strip box with a honeycomb grid and a colored gel

118

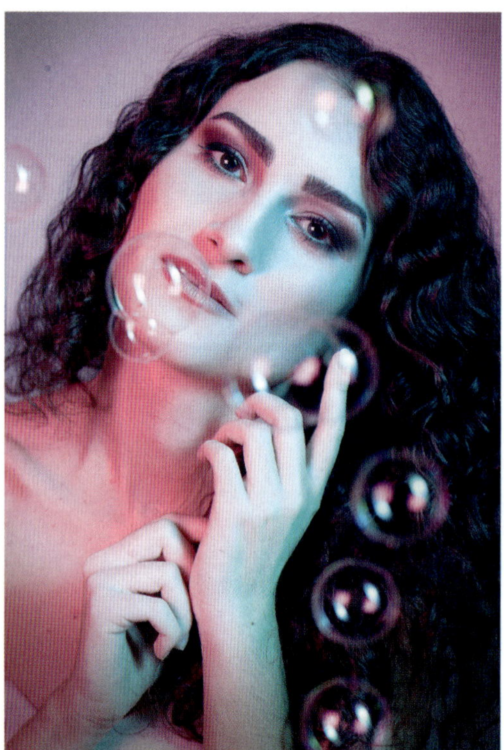

85mm | f4 | 1/125 sec. | ISO 100 | Model: Anika

HOW IT WORKS

The shadows in this setup are well lit and colored thanks to the different-colored lights. The soft overall light flatters the subject and masks skin imperfections. The raised clamshell lighting produces a central neck shadow and accents the cheekbones. The subject's curly hair is also accented by highlights produced by the light coming from the side. A vignette added at the post-processing stage focuses the viewer's attention on the subject's face, and the highlights in the soap bubbles are an additional eye-catcher. The twin light sources produce double catchlights in the eyes.

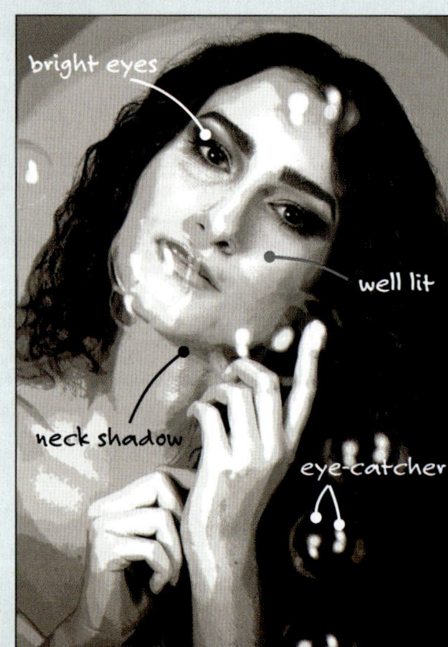

THE SETUP

1. Place the strip box **(1)** about 3 feet from your model in a raised position to the right at an angle of about 45 degrees. Position it to produce a clear neck shadow and so that the nose shadow doesn't quite reach your model's upper lip.

2. Now place the softbox **(2)** about 3 feet away in a similar raised position at about 45 degrees to the left. The V-shaped "clamshell" setup is clearly visible in the photo below.

3. Position your model about 20 inches in front of the white background. Because both lights produce broad, soft light with plenty of spill, the background is lit evenly in the colors of the gels mounted on the lights.

4. Position your bubble-blowing assistant to the right or left behind your flash and as close as possible to your model without actually impinging on the frame.

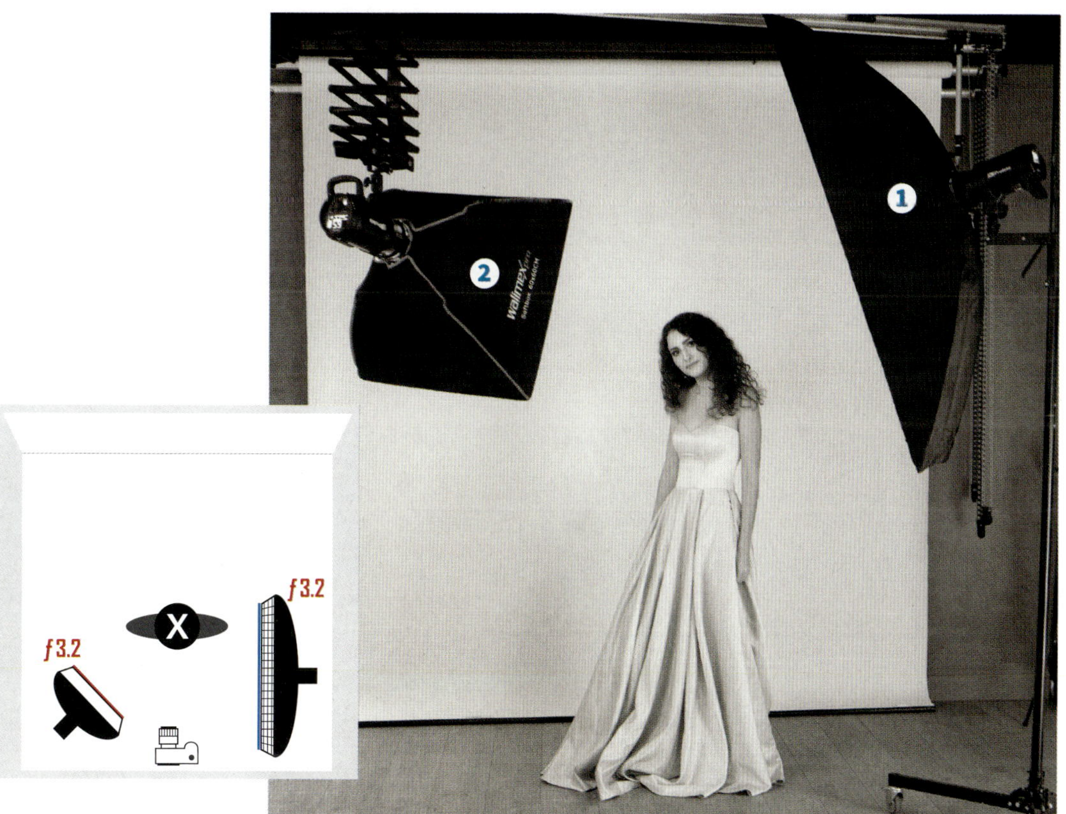

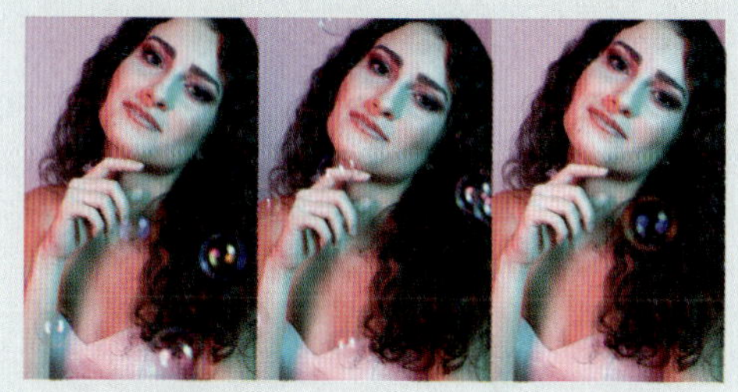

Tips for Creating Perfect Soap Bubbles

You will need an assistant for this shot, and a bit of practice in advance will help things along while you work. Some soap bubble mixtures are better than others, so try out as many as you can. If you blow gently and constantly, you will get more bubbles of a consistent size and shape. Get your assistant to take a deep breath and breathe out gently but steadily through pursed lips while the soap bubbles float past your model. Let your assistant practice making bubbles before your model settles into her pose and you start shooting.

A patient model is a bonus on a shoot like this.

"Keep an eye on the color gradient in the background and move your model back or forward to adjust its brightness."

Complementary-Colored Flash

You've probably already heard about the color circle and complementary colors, and it's exactly this kind of color contrast that this setup is all about. Its aim is to produce exciting, out-of-the-ordinary images. This example uses green and red, but you can just as well use blue and yellow, or even similar colors that produce a more harmonious, balanced look.

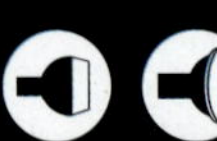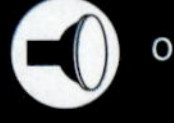 or 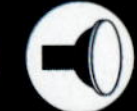

EFFORT INVOLVED

Low

SUITABLE FOR

All kinds of portraits

THE LOOK

Unusual and exciting portrait
Colored shadows
Accented facial contours
Brown-toned smokey eyes and nude lips

EQUIPMENT

1 × 24" softbox (or 31.5" octabox) with a colored gel
1 × 12" standard reflector with a diffuser and a colored gel

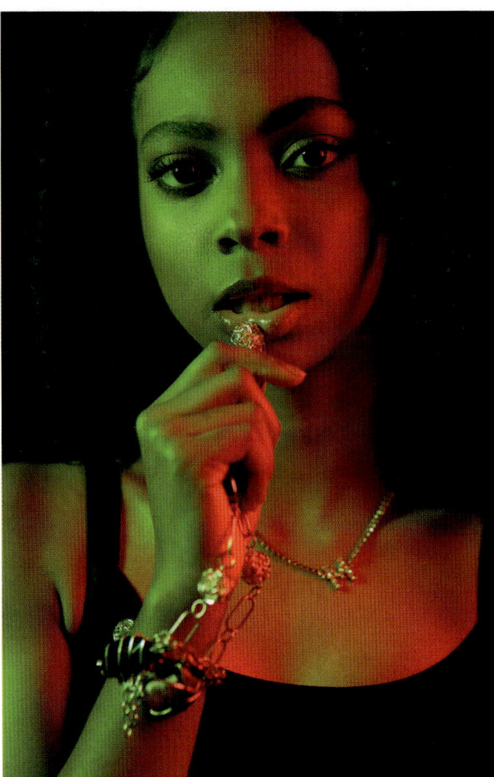

85mm | f2.8 | 1/125 sec. | ISO 100 | Model: Melissa

HOW IT WORKS

The shadows are well lit by the complementary-colored flashes, giving us an exciting and highly three-dimensional image. The clamshell lighting setup accentuates the subject's facial contours, but does tend to emphasize skin imperfections, which you may then have to reduce or remove during post-processing. The slightly raised position of the lights produces a central neck shadow. You can alter the balance of the colors by getting the subject to turn their head. The similar output from both lights produces two distinct catchlights.

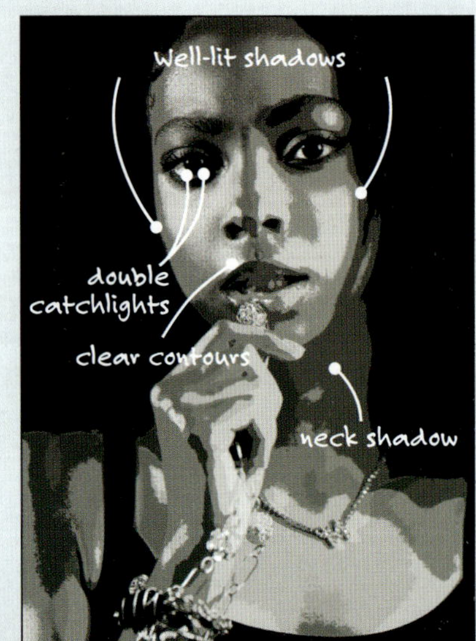

THE SETUP

1. Place the softbox with the red gel **(1)** about 3 feet to the right of your model in a slightly raised position. Position it to light the right-hand side of her face so that her cheek doesn't disappear into the shadow, and make sure it is high enough to produce a neck shadow.

2. Now place the second light **(2)** at a similar height about 5 feet from your model. The "clamshell" position of the lights is clearly visible in the photo below.

3. Your model should stand about 6 feet from the dark background. Because the lights are both quite close to your model and don't produce much spill, the backdrop looks black in the finished image.

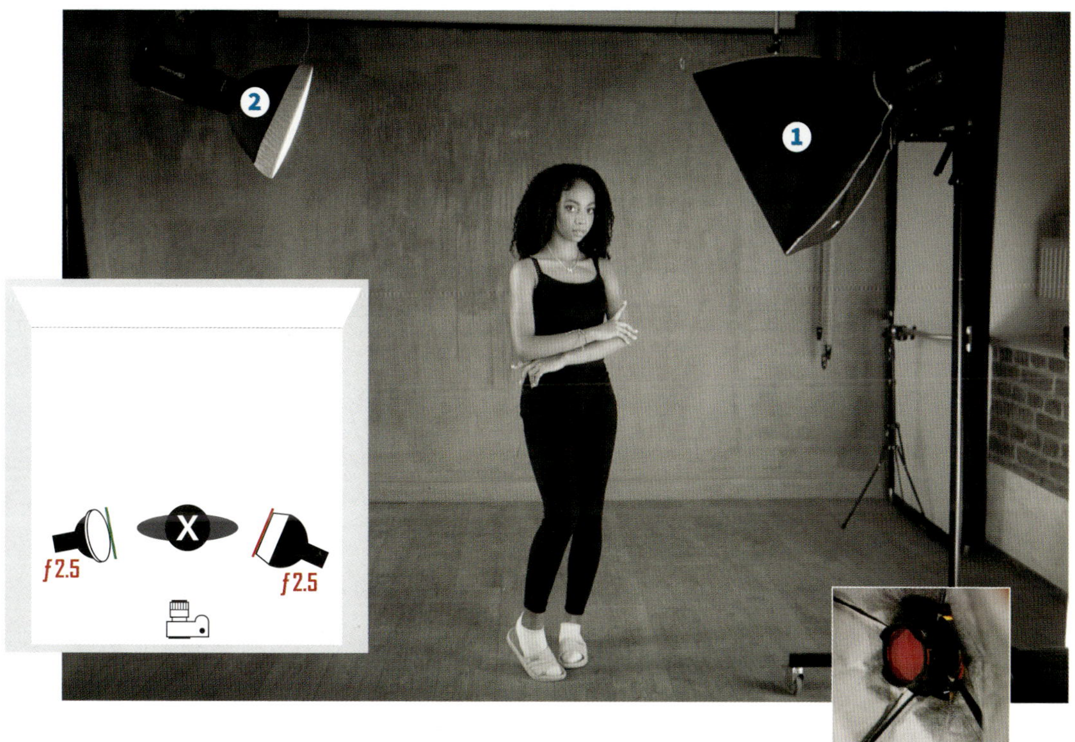

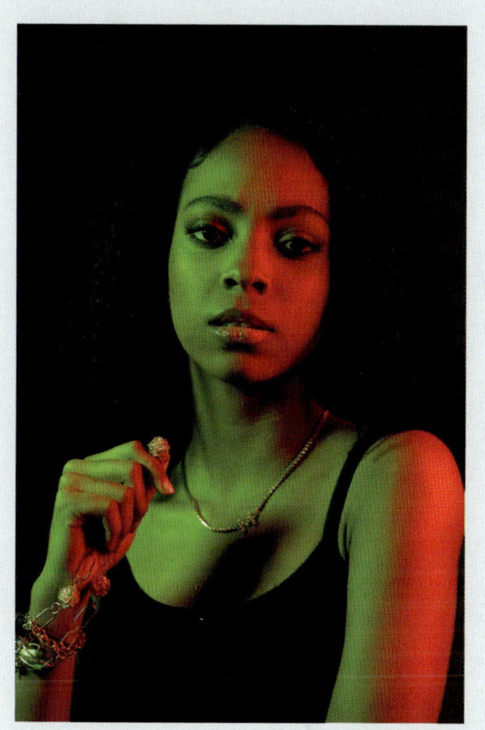

Variations

This setup is great for close-up, head-and-shoulders, and three-quarter-length portraits. If you use strip boxes with colored gels, you can shoot full-length portraits, too. Vary the crop while you shoot, and get your model to turn to the left and right to produce varied color balance and a good selection of images to choose from.

"Keep an eye on the balance between the two colors to the left and right sides of your image and, if necessary, move your lights to achieve the result you are looking for."

Glamour, Fashion, and Lifestyle

Glamour, Fashion, and Lifestyle

The word "glamour" means different things to different people, from vibrant to opulent, or just plain luxurious. It comes originally from the Scottish word glamoury, which means "magical." The term was first used in the 1920s to describe the aura surrounding movie stars, and the first glamour photos were produced to promote the work of Hollywood's greats. In time, the term came into increasingly common use and the boundaries between glamour and other genres began to blur. Nowadays, any highly styled, elegant, or even coolly erotic photos are included in the catch-all term Glamour Photography.

Images with (More Than) a Touch of Glamour

Glamour photography is basically about portraying elegance and luxury, so you need to pay close attention to your model's hair, makeup, and general styling. Glamour photos are characterized by bright lights that emphasize the model's qualities along with the main features of the styling you use. For this kind of shot, you will often need to work with makeup artists and hair stylists to achieve an appropriate look, although you can always intervene and adjust your model's makeup and hair while you shoot. To create the images in this book, I worked with two stylists who combine all of

these skills and always produce fantastic results. I also like to work with designers who can provide high-end clothes that suit the shoot I am working on. The clothes presented in this chapter are all from the designer Yelena Divis.

Glamour shots often require you to style your surroundings, too, whether in the studio or on location. For the purposes of this book, I decided to do without images that involve too much environmental styling, as this is often expensive and is also a highly individual aspect of a shoot. At the end of the day, it is down to you and your creativity to modify the basic setups shown here to suit your own personal preferences and goals.

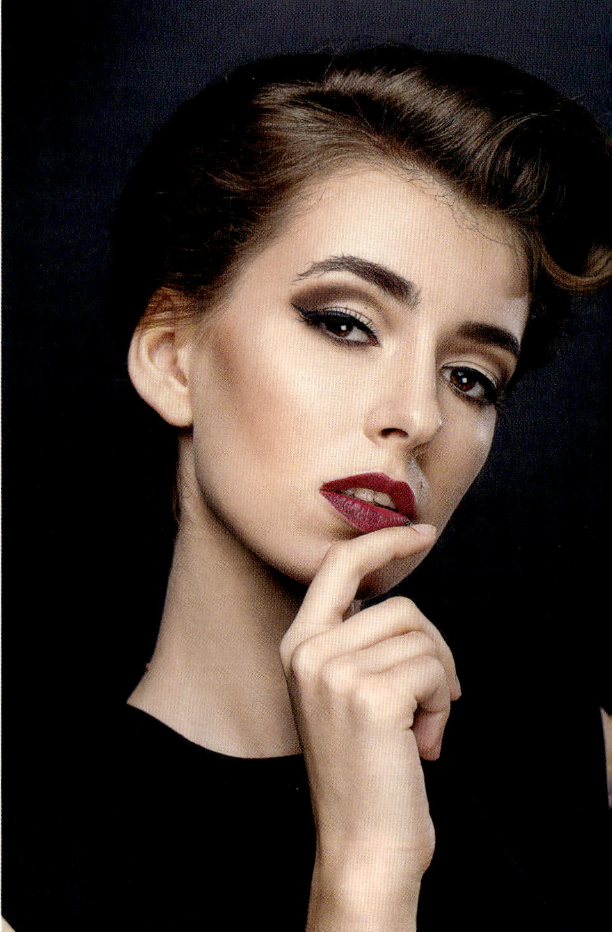

Location fashion shoot for Yelena Divis using available light.

50mm | f2.5 | 1/100 sec. | ISO 100 | Model: Manon

Fashion Is Not Just Fashion

In contrast to the relatively young genre of glamour photography, fashion photography has been around since the end of the 19th century. Although it served originally to simply present clothes, this genre too has developed over the years to become a full-fledged industry with many offshoots and sub-genres that aren't always easy to differentiate from one another. Fashion photography nowadays bridges editorial, fashion portrait, beauty, lifestyle, haute couture, lingerie, commercial, people, catwalk, and catalog images. There is no real fixed idea of what each sub-genre means either, and *Vogue* magazine is sure to have a different idea about what "fashion" means than Wal-Mart. But the one thing that is clear to everyone involved is that it's usually all about clothes, even if there's sometimes an element of lifestyle, product placement, or just pure attitude. The person in the shot is usually just a part of what's going on, and is more or less important to the final result, depending on the situation.

One important difference is whether you are shooting for a client or for your own purposes. If there is a client involved, you are sure to have to fulfill certain demands, and there will be other people involved with the shoot, either in the background or hands-on in the studio. Clients often have their own stylist or editor, and perhaps an art director too, who will be making sure that the client's ideas are put into practice. In such cases, you are providing a service and you will most likely be limited in how much of your own creativity you can

Our hair and makeup artist Nicole created a very glamorous look for this portrait.

100mm | f8 | 1/160 sec. | ISO 100 | Model: Jazz

apply. In contrast, when you are working on your own projects there is no limit to what you can do on a shoot.

Styling is essential in fashion photography, and you will often need to work with a makeup artist and/or a hair stylist. If you are just starting out and you don't feel ready to employ other people, you can either get your model(s) to do their own makeup, or ask stylists who are just starting out if they would like to practice with you and use the results in their portfolio or as a reference. Of course, it helps to convince others if you already have some great images of your own to show!

Contemporary and/or unusual clothes are essential to the success of a fashion shoot. Again, when you are starting out, you can ask your models to bring clothes of their own that suit the concept of the shoot. Later, once you have some successful shoots under your belt, you can ask clothing designers if they would like you to work for them. Or you can ask designer fashion stores to lend you a few pieces for a shoot. Of course, anyone you borrow clothes from will want to see a benefit, such as using the results for advertising or to pep up their social media channels.

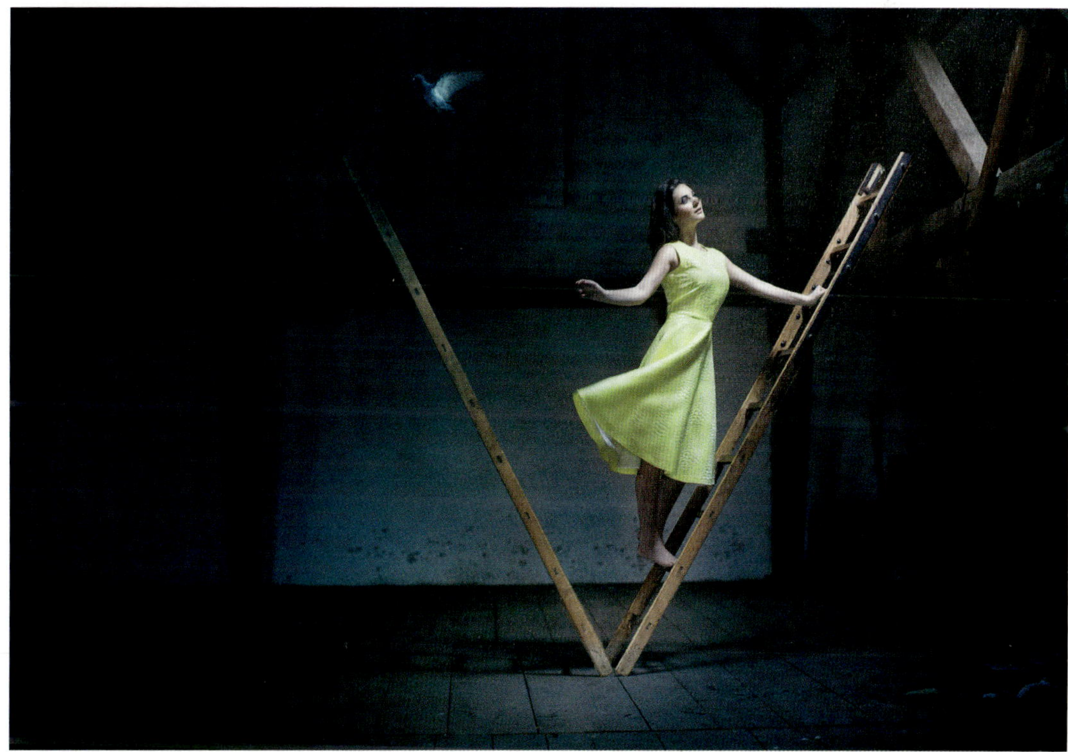

Quick and Easy Glamour Portrait

If you are in a hurry and you only have one light, our old friend "Hollywood" lighting comes to the rescue. Although the concept of "quick" is a relative one when it comes to styling, which can (and should) take a while!

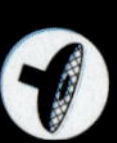

EFFORT INVOLVED

Low

SUITABLE FOR

Close-up to three-quarter-length portraits

THE LOOK

Intense, high-contrast glamour portrait

Dark background, light concentrated on the face and upper body

Bold eye makeup, eyeliner, glossy lips

Shiny, glamorous curly hair

EQUIPMENT

1× beauty dish with a honeycomb grid

85mm | f10 | 1/160 sec. | ISO 100 | Model: Jazz

HOW IT WORKS

The simple combination of a single beauty dish and a black background produces dark shadows and a high-contrast image in which the subject really shines. The high, central position of the light produces highlights on the forehead and cheek, and provide a nicely three-dimensional feel. The subject's generous curls reflect the light with a soft glow. The head rotation produces a subtle broad light effect that nevertheless accents the line of the cheek. The small but clear neck shadow provides good visual separation. The strong fall-off toward the bottom of the frame ensures that the viewer's attention remains on the subject's face and upper body.

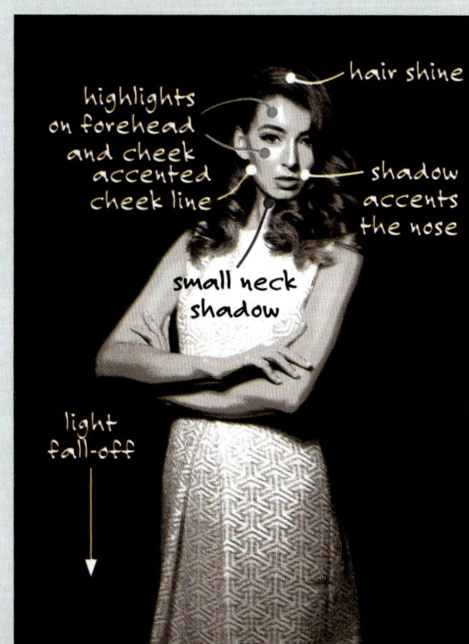

THE SETUP

1. Mount the gridded beauty dish **(1)** on a ceiling rail or a boom stand in a raised, frontal position about 5 feet from your model and pointing down at an angle of about 45 degrees. Position it to form a nose shadow that ends halfway between your model's nose and upper lip, and so that there is a clear light fall-off from around belly height toward the bottom of the frame.

2. Position your model about 18 inches from the black background and make sure her shadow only begins at about shoulder height. This helps to keep her facial contours visible even if she has dark hair.

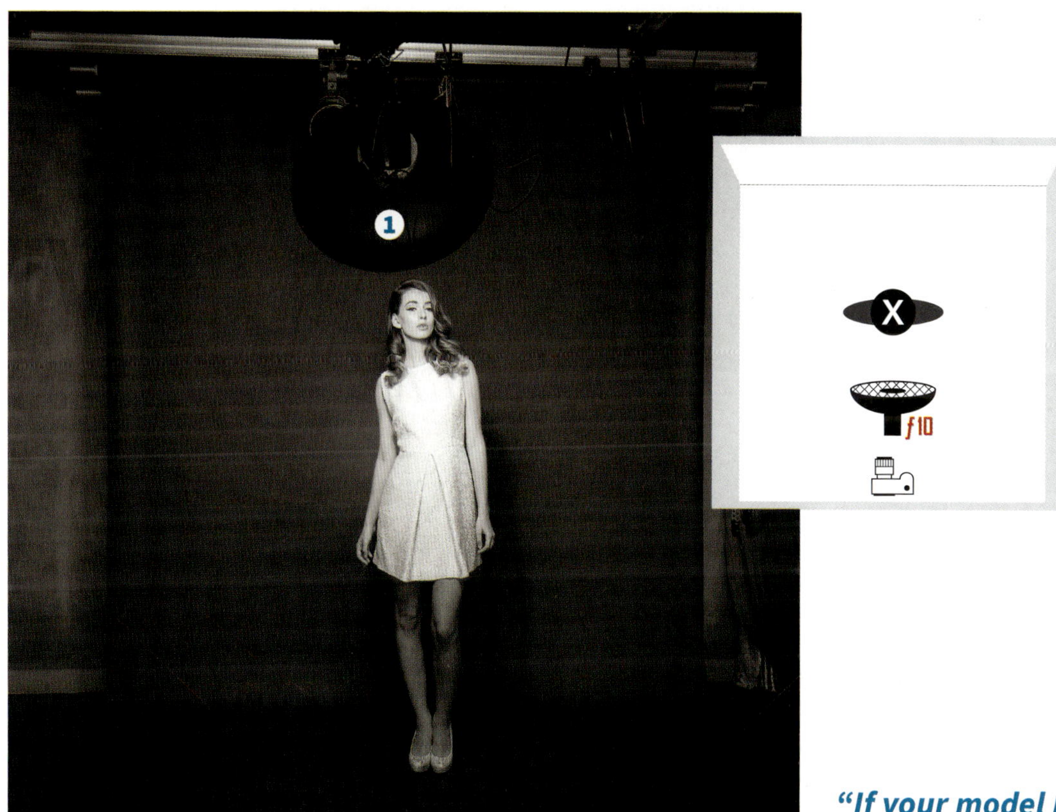

Preparation and Work Time

A glamour shoot begins with an idea or a concept. Once you know what you are aiming for, you need to find a suitable model who is available for the slot you are planning. When you are starting out, you can try online modeling platforms (such as *modelmayhem.com*), or one of the many modeling groups on Facebook or other social media channels. Professional models use agencies. Once you have a model lined up, you need to find one or more people to help you with hair and makeup styling. For a simple shoot, a combined hair/makeup artist will usually suffice. Don't forget to brief everyone in advance about the concept for the shoot. A moodboard made up of your collected photos and sketches is a great way to get everyone up to speed on the look you are aiming for. At the same time, you can organize the outfits and accessories you need. Always ask the people you work with if they have favorite clothes or accessories that they can bring along.

Once you are up and running, you need to reckon with a couple of hours' work for hair and make-up, and you can prepare your lighting setup while your model is getting ready. Once everything is set up, the shoot itself will take another hour or two.

"If your model has light-colored hair, you can get her to move forward to further darken the background and enhance her overall shine."

Classic Glamour Setup

If the styling is good, all you need to produce a radiant, high-contrast glamour portrait is a classic high beauty dish/lateral reflector setup.

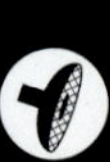

EFFORT INVOLVED

Low

SUITABLE FOR

Close-up to three-quarter-length portraits

THE LOOK

Radiant, high-conrast glamour portrait
Strong eye makeup/eyeliner, glossy lips
Big, shiny, curly hair

EQUIPMENT

1× beauty dish with a honeycomb grid
1× 30"×40" silver reflector

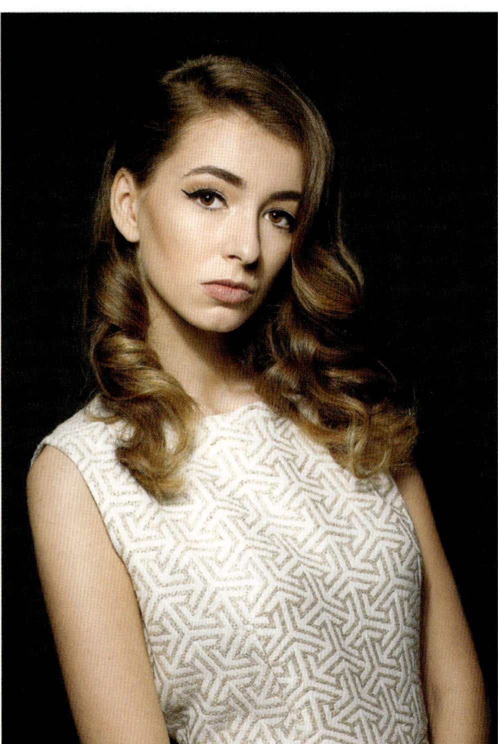

85mm | f10 | 1/160 sec. | ISO 100 | Model: Jazz

HOW IT WORKS

The benefits of the classic diagonally raised main light are particularly obvious in this shot. The high degree of definition in the hair and face make the subject appear to leap out of the frame. The forehead and cheek highlights accentuate the light side of the face and the skilled application of rouge by the makeup artist adds an extra accent to the line of the cheekbone. The curls in the hair have a natural glow and appear nice and full. The neck shadow helps to define the chin and jaw lines, and provides clear separation between the head and body. The dark background adds to the subject's radiance.

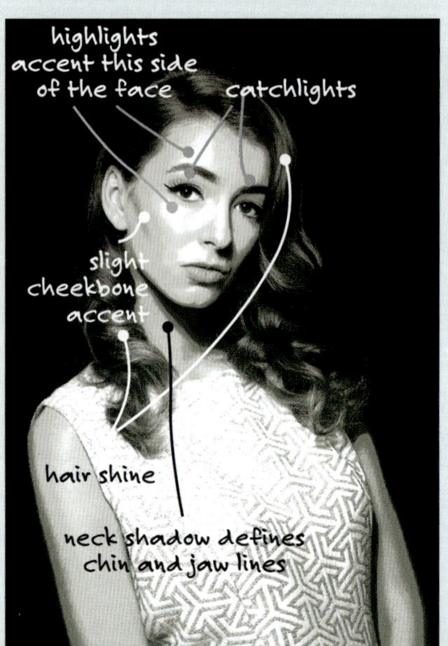

THE SETUP

1. Place the gridded beauty dish **(1)** about 3 feet to the left of your model in a raised position and pointing down at an angle of about 45 degrees. Position it to create a nose shadow that points diagonally downward without reaching your model's upper lip, and to ensure clear light fall-off from about belly height toward the bottom of the frame.

2. Mount the reflector **(2)** on a stand about 3 feet from your model in a slightly raised position, and set it up to lighten the nose shadow.

3. Position your model about 18 inches from the black background.

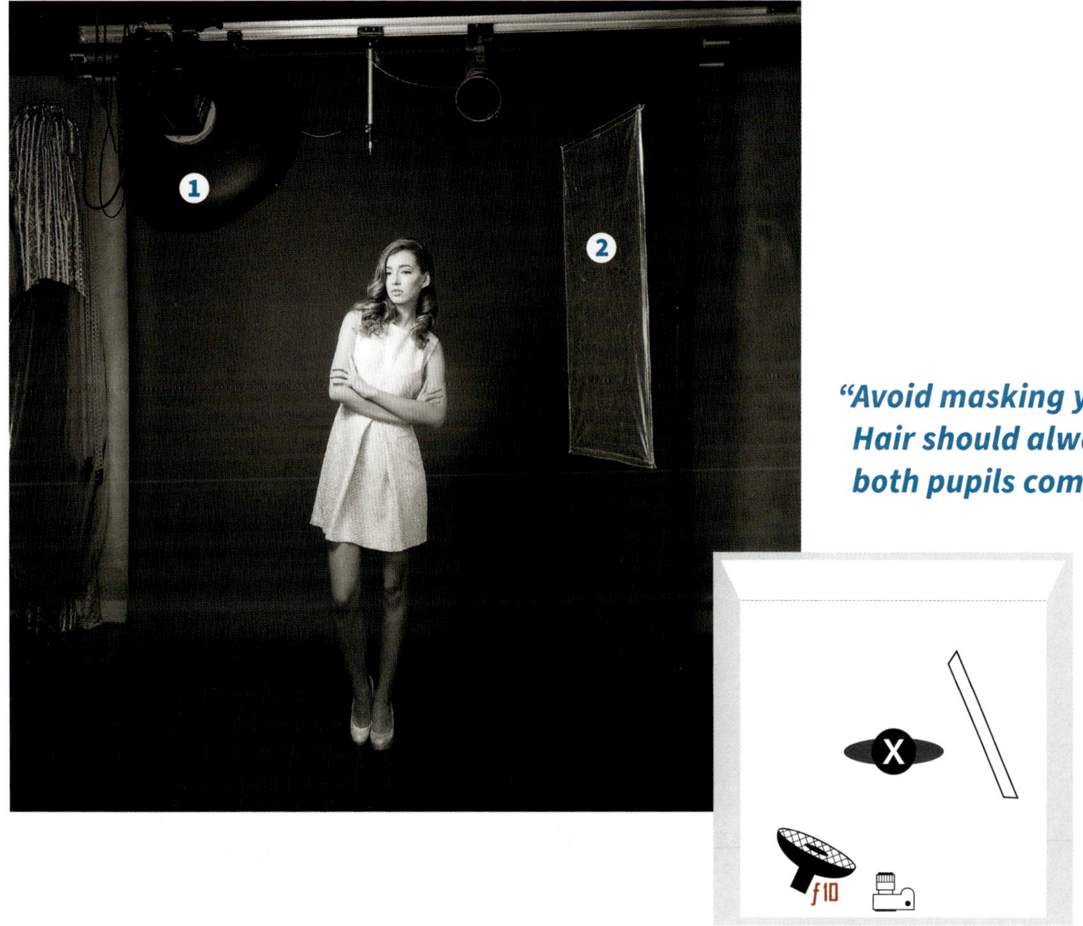

Working with Makeup Artists and Hair Stylists

If you don't have a regular hair stylist or makeup artist, it is a good idea to do a few test shoots with various people. This way, you will quickly find out who you get on well with and who has ideas and techniques that work well with your personal shooting style. Always send your stylist(s) a moodboard or some kind of summary of the concept for the shoot in advance. This way, they can not only get all the necessary props together, they can also contribute their own ideas to the shoot. Once you have found the right stylist, your teamwork will develop and your results will improve all the time.

"Avoid masking your model's pupils. Hair should always be styled to keep both pupils completely visible."

High-Contrast Glamour Portrait

If you want to separate your subject more clearly from the background and add extra accents, you will need to add an accent light to your setup. This is sure to give your shot that certain extra something.

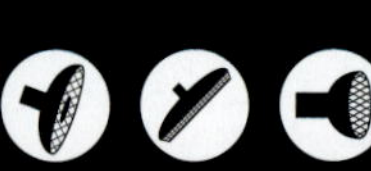

EFFORT INVOLVED

Medium

SUITABLE FOR

Close-up to three-quarter-length portraits

THE LOOK

Highly accented portrait with extra highlights
Bold eye makeup, eyeliner, and glossy lips
Glossy, glamorous, curly hair

EQUIPMENT

1× beauty dish with a honeycomb grid
1× 47" strip box with a honeycomb grid
1× standard reflector with a honeycomb grid
1× 30"×40" silver reflector

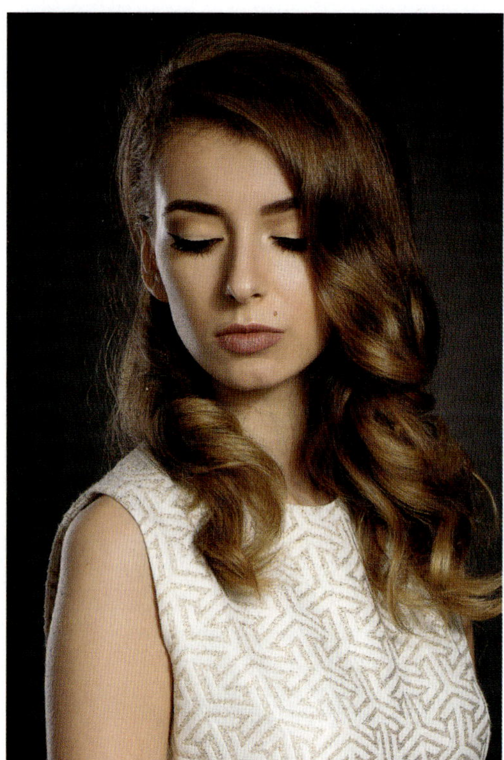

85mm | f10 | 1/160 sec. | ISO 100 | Model: Jazz

HOW IT WORKS

The raised main light accents the facial shape and contours and give the subject a well-defined look. The accent light further emphasizes the shape of the face and, together with the cheek shadow, makes the face appear narrower. The accent light provides a slight rim light effect on the upper arm that subtly accents its contours. The accent light on the left also produces interesting effects in the subject's flyaway hair. The soft neck shadow is sufficiently visible to separate the face from the body. The background vignette and the bright spot behind the subject's head keep the viewer focused on the face.

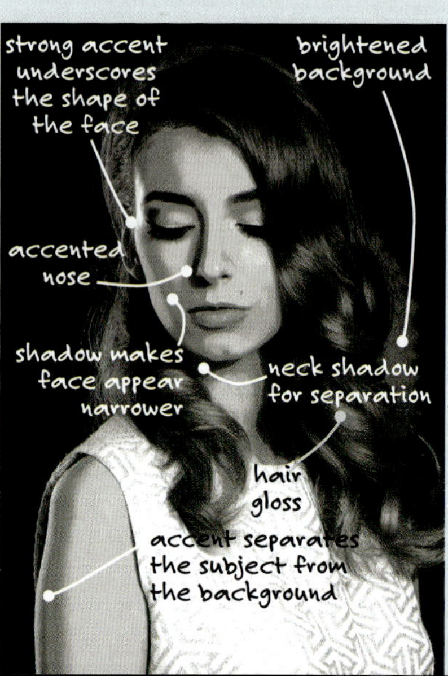

THE SETUP

1. Place the gridded beauty dish **(1)** about 5 feet to the right of your model in a raised position and pointing down at an angle of about 45 degrees. Position it to create a nose shadow that points diagonally downward without reaching your model's upper lip and to ensure clear light fall-off toward the bottom of the frame from about belly height.

2. Mount the reflector **(2)** on a stand about 3 feet to the left of your model in a slightly raised position, and set it up to lighten the nose shadow.

3. Now place the strip box accent light **(3)** to the left rear about 5 feet from your model at an angle of about 45 degrees. Position the center of the light at head height so that the accents it produces reach your model's hair, cheek, neck, and upper arm.

4. For the background spot, mount a gridded standard reflector **(4)** centrally on a ceiling rail or a boom stand behind your model at height of about 8 feet. Set it up to form a spot that has its focus at around shoulder height and that ends at around forehead level.

5. Position your model about 3 feet from the black background.

To achieve the right effect, an accent light has to be positioned very carefully. In the example below, the subject has turned her head too far and the highlight on her cheek disappears as a result. The highlight on her upper arm is also no longer in the frame.

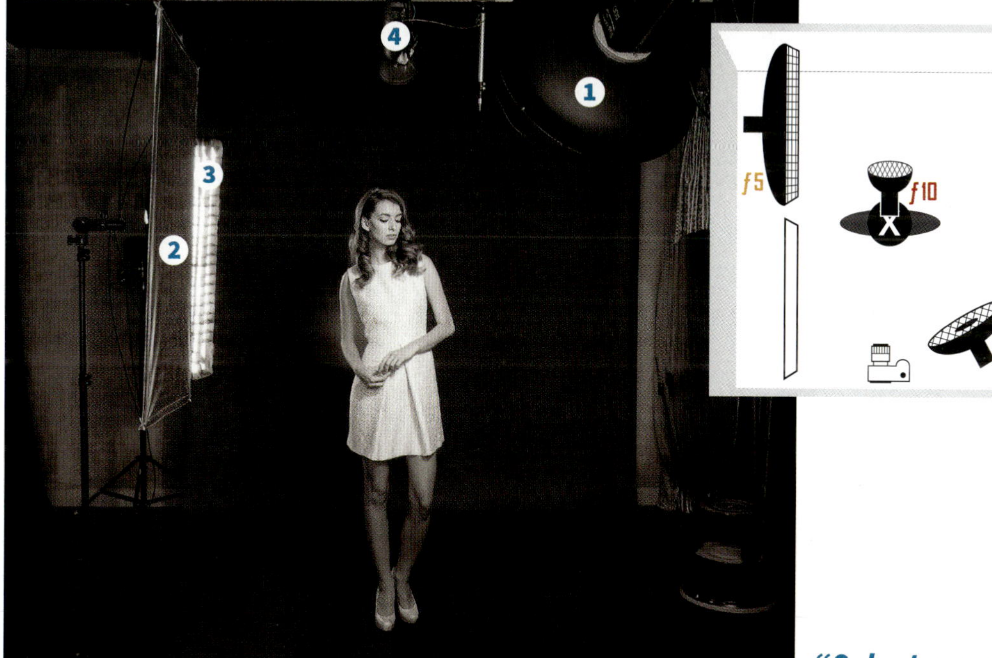

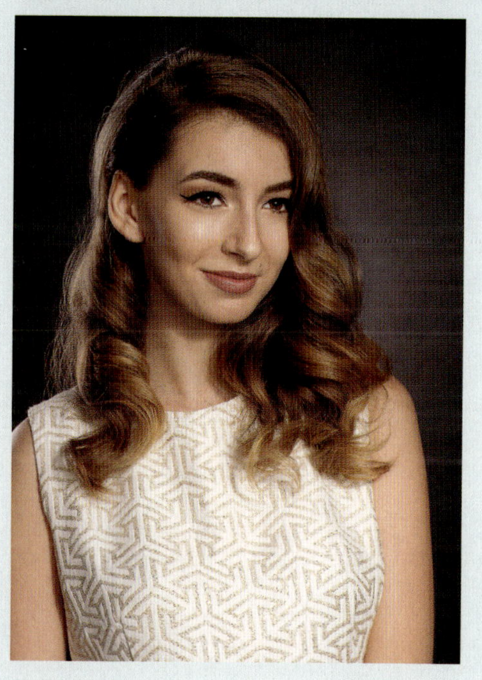

Extra Gloss for Your Model's Hair

This setup uses a hair light to add even more gloss and a rim light effect to the subject's hair. This focuses the viewer's attention strongly on the subject's head, and there are no other distracting accents anywhere else on her body.

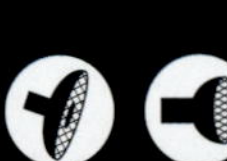 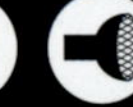

EFFORT INVOLVED

Medium

SUITABLE FOR

Close-up to three-quarter-length portraits

THE LOOK

Glamour portrait with extra accents on the subject's hair

Bold eye makeup, eyeliner, and glossy lips

Glossy, glamorous, curly hair

EQUIPMENT

1× beauty dish with a honeycomb grid

1× standard reflector with a honeycomb grid

1× 30" × 40" silver reflector

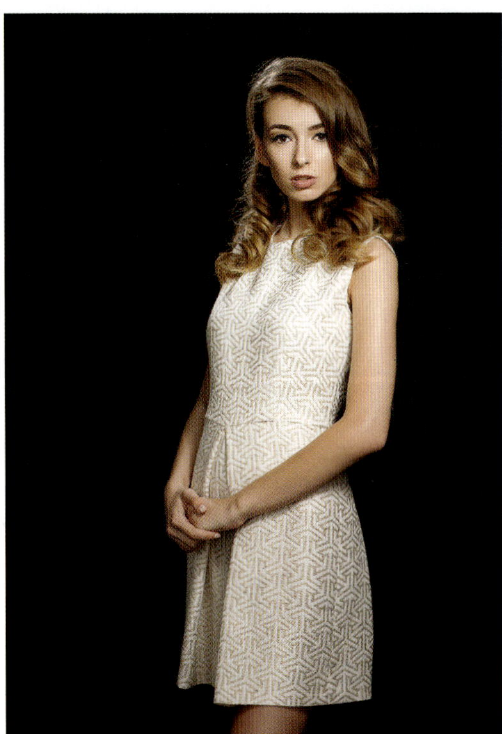

85mm | f10 | 1/160 sec. | ISO 100 | Model: Jazz

HOW IT WORKS

The diagonally positioned beauty dish produces a high-contrast image with natural-looking shadows that are mellowed by the reflector. The overall image is well defined, but with obvious light fall-off toward the subject's legs that also helps to focus attention on the head and upper body. The shadows beneath the nose and the lower lip accentuate the nose and mouth, while the hair light creates a clear halo around the head that nicely separates the subject from the background. The glossy look produced by the beauty dish and the highlight from the hair light provide a clear frame for the face.

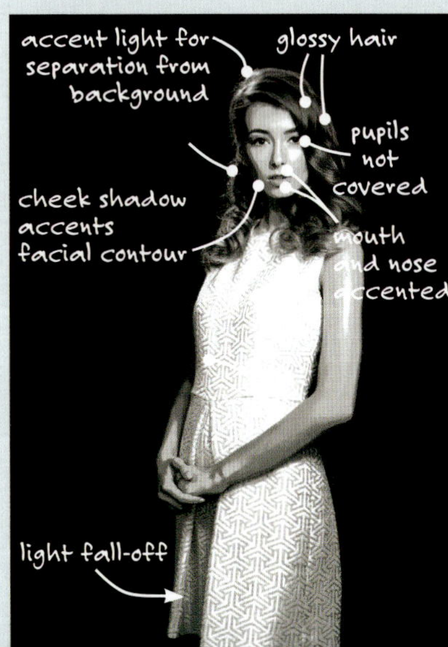

1. Place the gridded beauty dish **(1)** about 5 feet to the right of your model in a raised position and pointing down at an angle of about 45 degrees. Position it to create a nose shadow that points diagonally downward without reaching your model's upper lip and to ensure clear light fall-off toward the bottom of the frame from about belly height.

2. Mount the reflector **(2)** on a stand about 3 feet to the left of your model in a slightly raised position, and set it up to lighten the nose shadow.

3. Mount the gridded hair light **(3)** on a ceiling rail or a boom stand about 5 feet to the left rear of your model at a height of about 8 feet. Position it to light the back of your model's head from above and provide a hair light on the top left of her head.

4. Position your model about 5 feet in front of the black background.

"Take care to position your hair light so that it only lights the top of your model's head, but not her ear, her curls, or her shoulder."

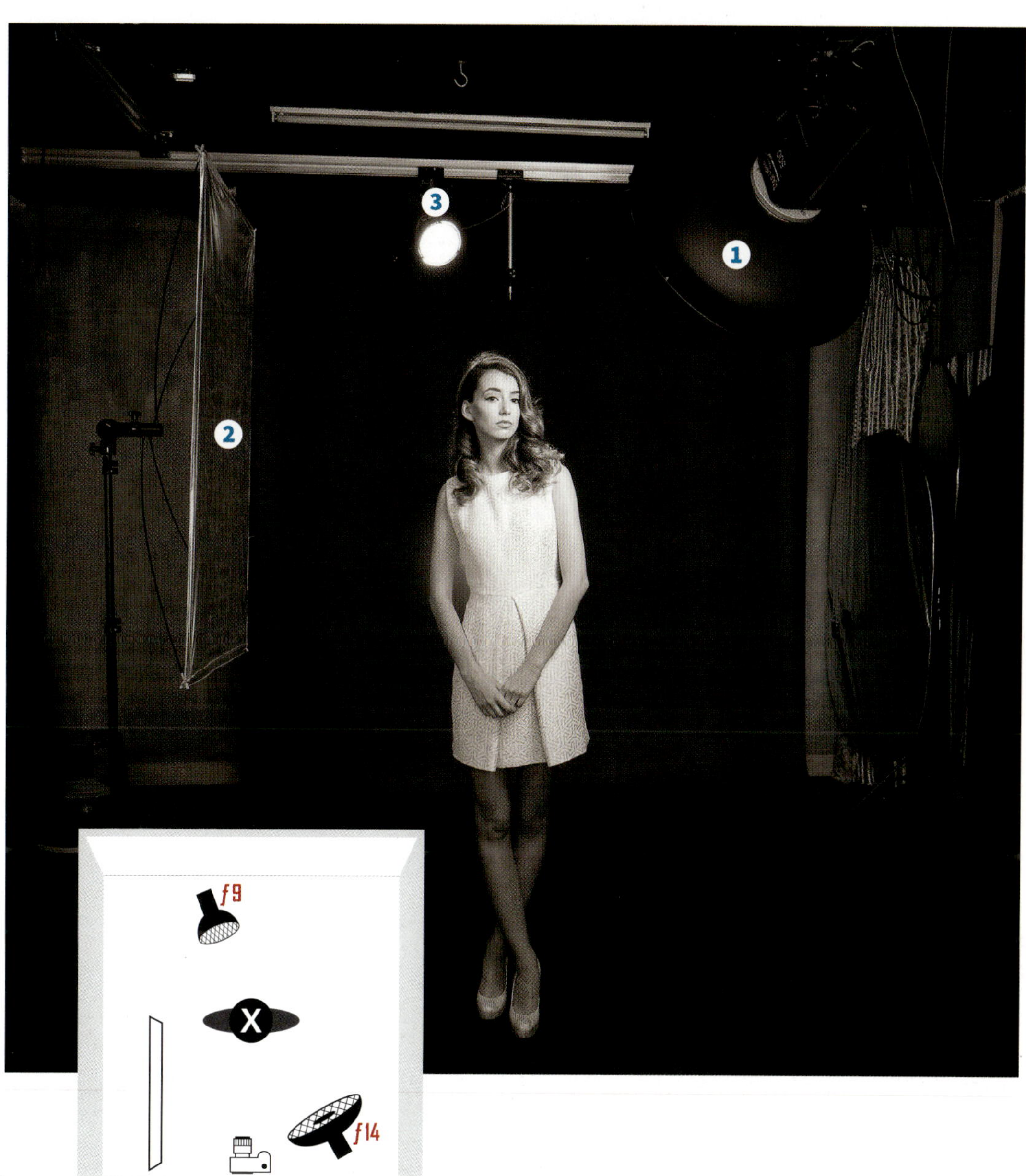

Bokeh Background

Alongside the lights you use to illuminate your model, you can use the background as an important element in your composition, too. This setup shows how to use crumpled aluminum foil to create a colored background bokeh effect that instantly creates a party atmosphere.

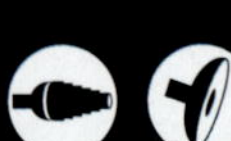
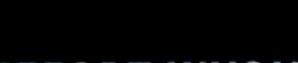

EFFORT INVOLVED

Medium

SUITABLE FOR

Close-up to three-quarter-length portraits

THE LOOK

Warm-toned bokeh-style background
Natural look with glossy lips

EQUIPMENT

1× snoot with a colored gel
1× beauty dish
1× 30" ×40" silver reflector
1× crumpled sheet of aluminum foil

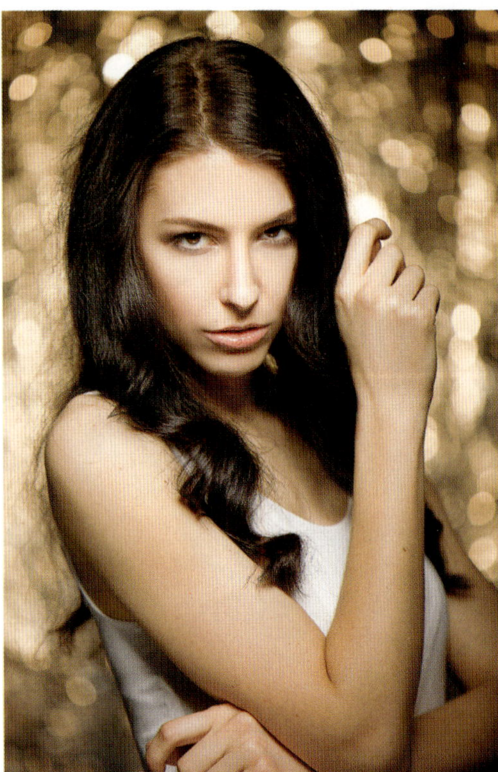

200mm | f2.8 | 1/160 sec. | ISO 100 | Model: Elisa

HOW IT WORKS

This image is carried by the bokeh-style background that frames the subject and forms a kind of makeshift stage. The classic "Hollywood-style" lighting setup uses a high, frontal beauty dish and a silver reflector to accent the subject's facial contours and cheekbones. The lips and eyes are accented too. The neck shadow visually separates the face from the rest of the body and, together with the hair, forms a frame for the face. The reflector brightens the eyes and the shadows beneath the eyebrows intensify the facial expression. The unusual background and the lighting setup produce a well-defined result.

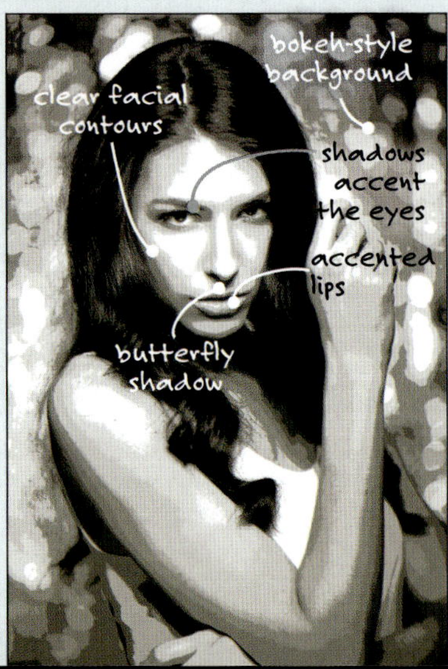

THE SETUP

1. Crumple four or five 6-foot lengths of regular aluminum foil and then flatten them out and hang them from a portable rail **(1)** to form a textured backdrop. Place the backdrop directly in front of your regular background.

2. Position your model about 6 feet in front of the foil backdrop.

3. Place the gridded beauty dish **(2)** about 5 feet in front of your model in a raised position. Position it to create a central nose shadow that ends halfway between the tip of your model's nose and her upper lip.

4. Mount the silver reflector **(3)** on a stand and place it directly in front of your model at around belly height so that it slightly lightens the facial shadows.

5. Place the snooted spot **(4)** about 6 feet to the right of your model and point it directly at the foil backdrop. Attach an orange gel to the snoot to create a warm, golden background effect.

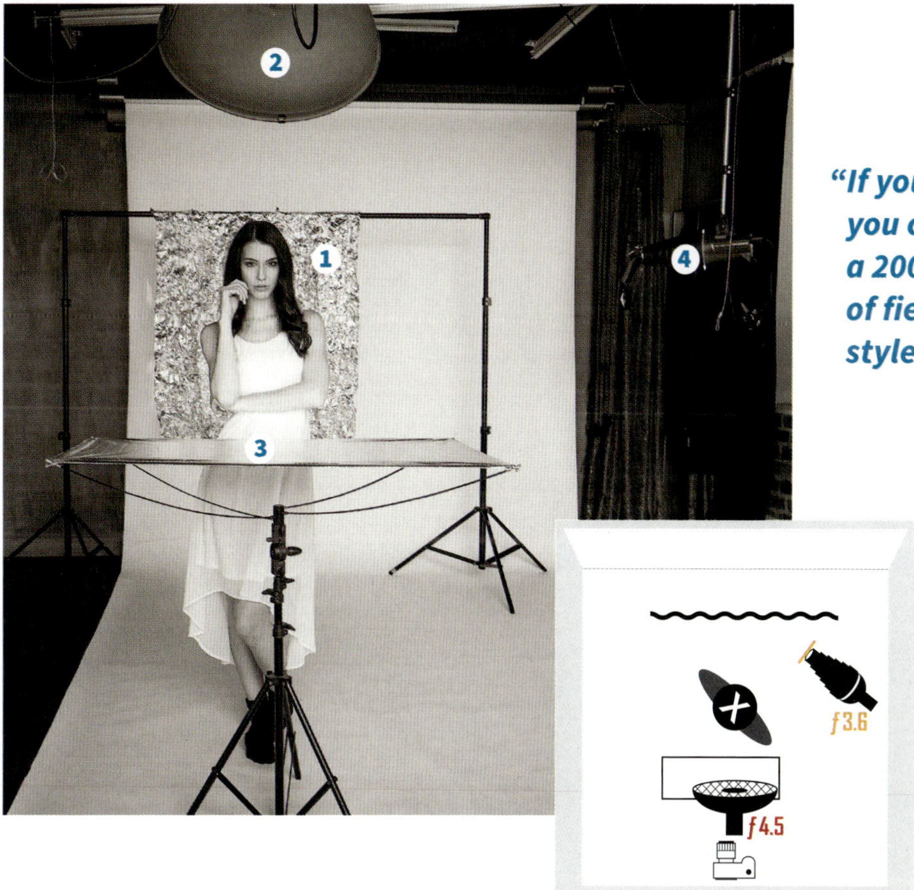

"If your studio is large enough, you can use a long lens (I used a 200mm) to reduce the depth of field and enhance the bokeh-style effect in the background."

A Soft
Bokeh Frame

This is an old trick that wedding photographers often use to create sweet-looking character portraits. The bokeh-style vignette underscores the subject's aura. All you need to create this clever effect is a translucent plastic bag and a free hand!

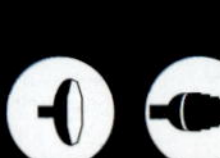

EFFORT INVOLVED

Low

SUITABLE FOR

All kinds of portraits

THE LOOK

Bokeh vignette and soft light create a moody, delicate look

Pink-toned, natural-looking makeup

EQUIPMENT

1× 31.5" octabox

1× snoot

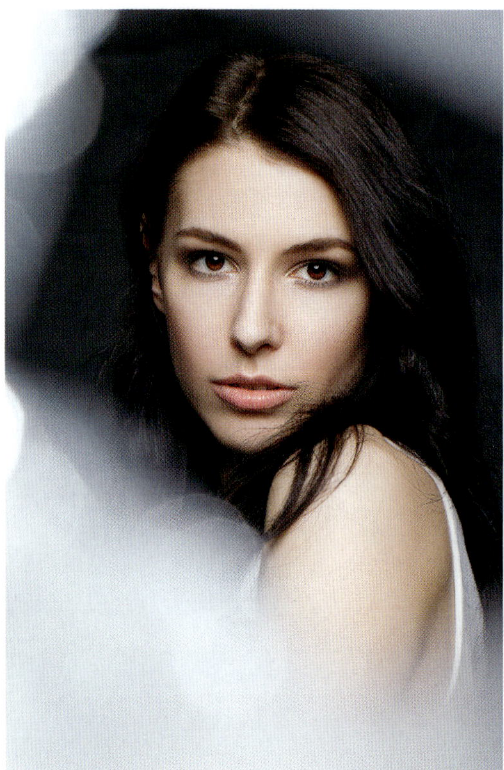

100mm | f8 | 1/160 sec. | ISO 100 | Model: Elisa

HOW IT WORKS

The raised, central octabox produces typical "Hollywood" light with a "butterfly" nose shadow and accented facial contours. The main light emphasizes the eyes, and the shadows beneath the upper eyelids intensify the effect. This setup gives the subject a lot of scope for altering her expression. The spill light and close proximity of the subject make the background appear dark gray, and the subject's hair remains well defined as a result. The soft overall light underscores the gentle facial expression, and the bright bokeh frame adds the finishing touch to the soft, airy look of the image.

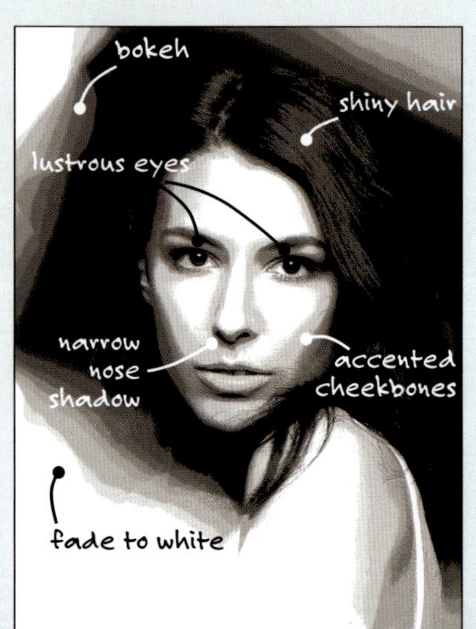

THE SETUP

1. Take a translucent plastic bag or sheet and roll it up to form a crumpled ring with a hole that is slightly narrower than the front element of your lens. This simple accessory is the main prop for this setup.

2. Mount the octabox **(1)** on a ceiling rail or a boom stand high in front of your model at a distance of about 5 feet and at an angle of about 30 degrees. Position it to produce a small shadow beneath your model's nose.

3. Now place a snooted spot **(2)** about 3 feet to the right of your model at head height. Point the snoot directly at your bokeh ring.

4. Position your model about 5 feet from the black background.

5. Vary the size of your bokeh ring or the distance between it and your lens to produce different effects.

Variations

For this version of the shot I used a different crop and my model has adopted a really charming expression.

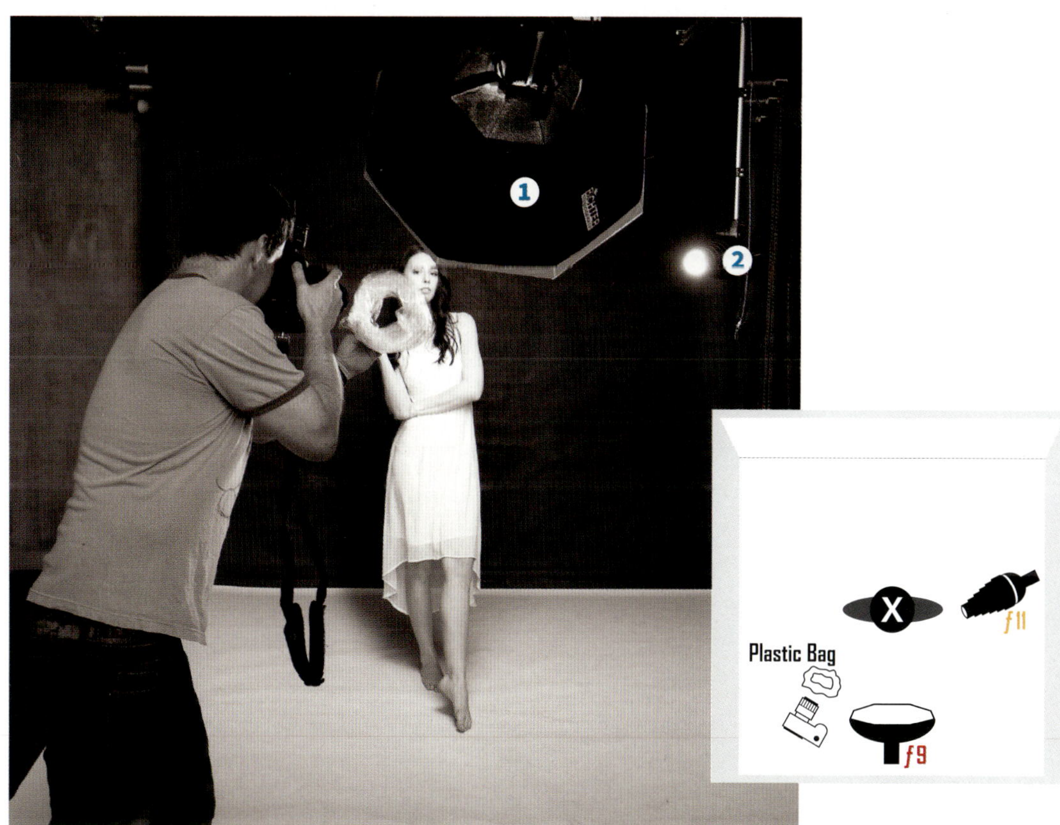

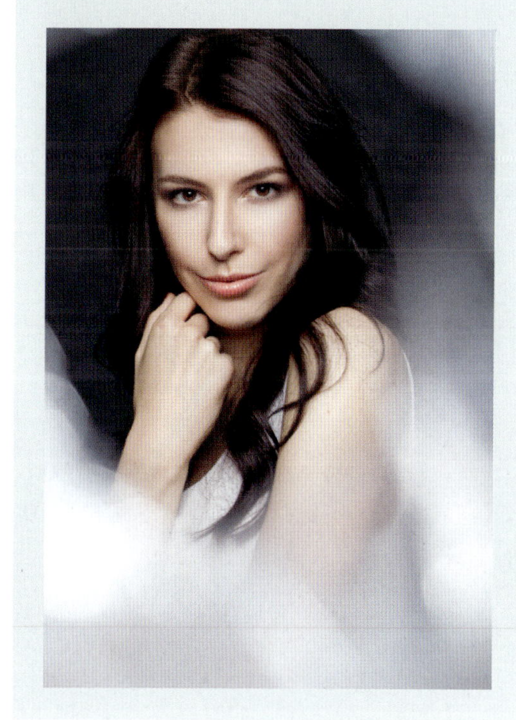

"

Spotlight Accent

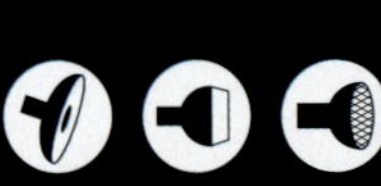

EFFORT INVOLVED

Medium

SUITABLE FOR

Close-ups, head-and-shoulders portraits

THE LOOK

Cool, elegant glamour portrait with a bright spot accent on a dark background

Eyes and lips accented with dark, matte makeup

Classic tied-back hair

EQUIPMENT

1× beauty dish

1× 24" softbox

1× standard reflector with a honeycomb grid

138

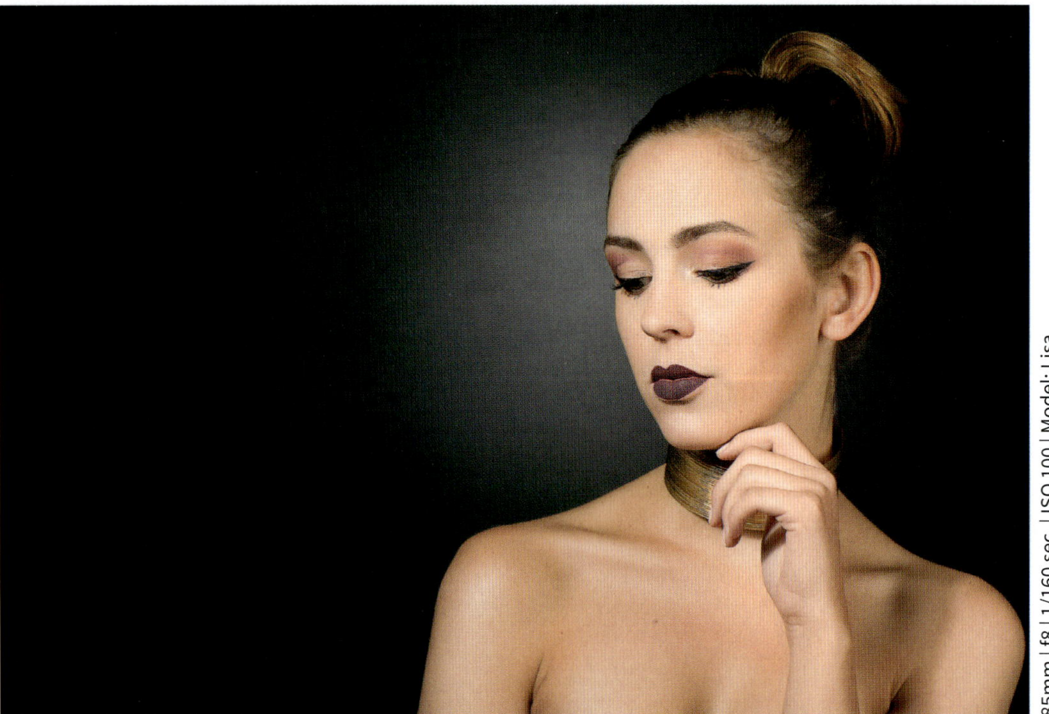

85mm | f8 | 1/160 sec. | ISO 100 | Model: Lisa

HOW IT WORKS

The slightly decentered background spot focuses attention directly on the subject's face. The diagonal position of the beauty dish and the subject's head posture produce very even lighting on the face, and highlight the darker tones in the eyes and lips. The body contours are nicely defined by this light too, providing a tactile-looking image with subdued interplay between light and shadow. There is a subtle shadow between the ear and the subject's hand, and the broad necklace with its subtle highlights provides clear separation between the head and torso.

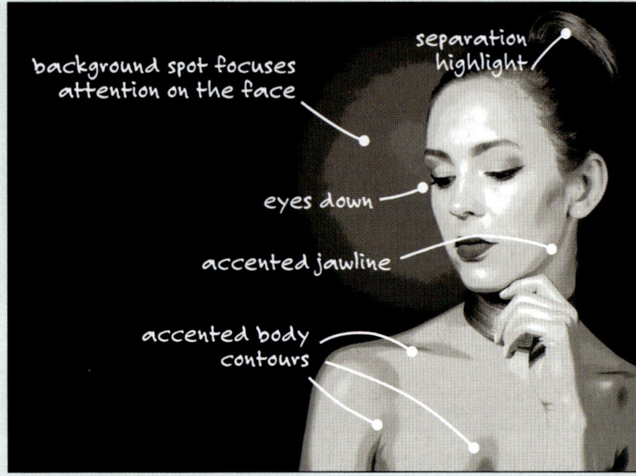

THE SETUP

1. Place the beauty dish **(1)** in a raised position about 3 feet to the left of your model at an angle of about 45 degrees. Position it to produce a slight nose shadow.

2. Now place the softbox **(2)** about 3 feet to the front right of your model at an angle of about 45 degrees. The center of the flash should be at about head height and should point slightly downward.

3. Mount the gridded background spot **(3)** on a low stand directly behind your model at chest height. Set it up so that its focus is behind your model's right eye and the pool of light it produces is the same size as her head.

4. Position your model about 5 feet from the black background so that there is an obvious vignette effect toward the edges of the frame.

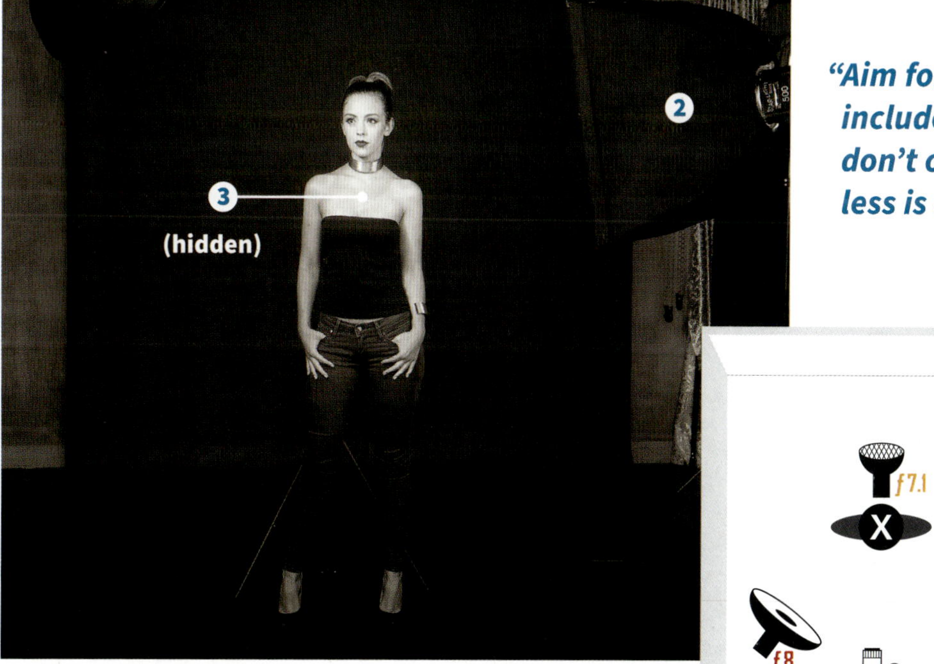

"Aim for a balanced look when you include jewelry in your shots and don't overdo things. Remember: less is often more!"

Creating Contours with Accent Lights

Two softbox accent lights produce strong contours that clearly separate the subject from the background. This effect supports the overall definition in the image and creates a beautiful aura surrounding the subject.

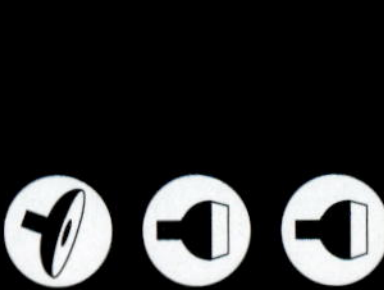

EFFORT INVOLVED

Medium

SUITABLE FOR

Close-up to three-quarter-length portraits

THE LOOK

Glamour portrait with glowing contours
Lips and eyes accented with matte magenta tones
Classic tied-back hair

EQUIPMENT

1× beauty dish
2× 24" softboxes

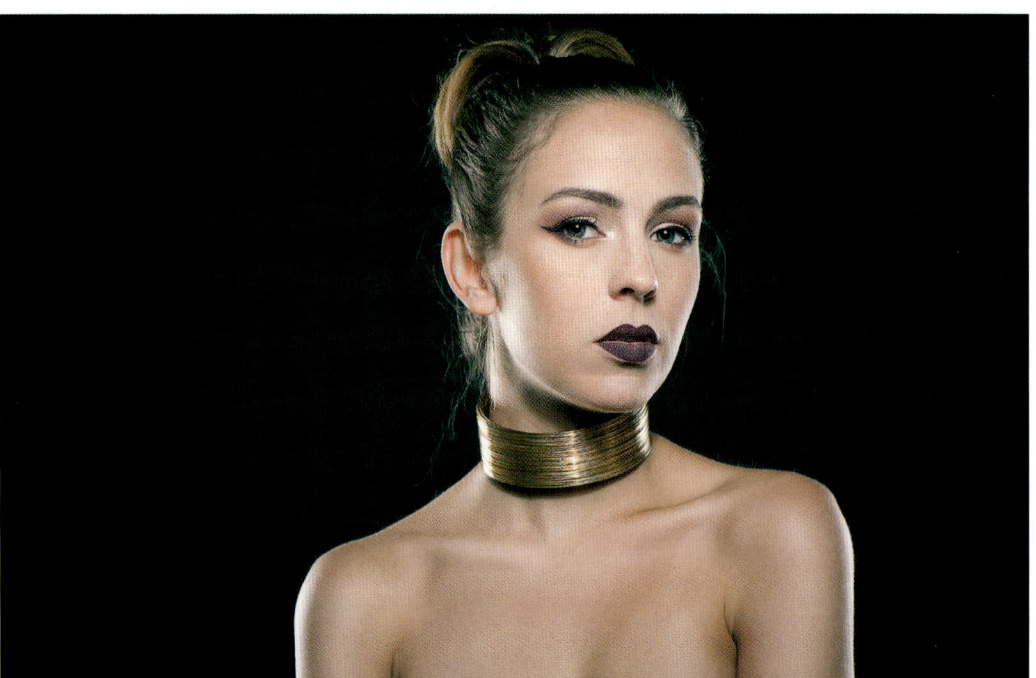

HOW IT WORKS

The twin softbox accent lights to the left and right produce bright highlights and excellent separation between the subject and the dark background. The high, frontal beauty dish gives the eyes a sparkling look, with shadows beneath the upper eyelids and clear catchlights. The lighting setup and the bold makeup demand attention. The shadows on the upper body emphasize its contours and create interesting light/shadow interplay. The three highlights in the dominant neckpiece simultaneously accent the jewelry and provide an obvious neck line.

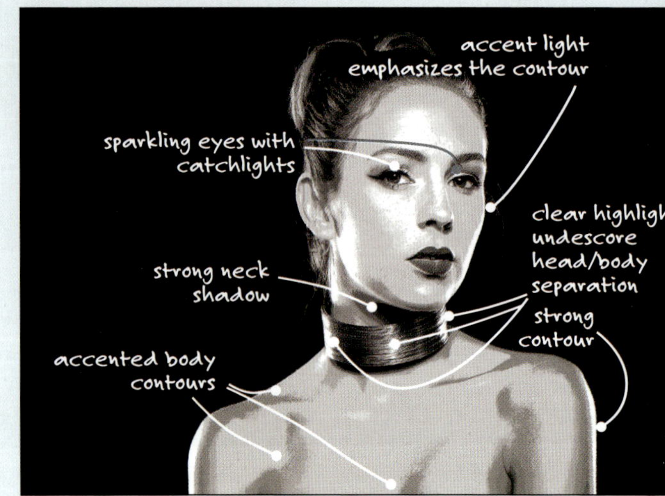

THE SETUP

1. Mount the beauty dish **(1)** on a ceiling rail or a boom stand about 3 feet from your model in a raised, frontal position and at an angle of about 45 degrees. Position it to produce a small shadow beneath your model's nose.

2. Place one of the softboxes **(2)** about 5 feet to the left rear of your model at head height and at about 45 degrees. Position it to produce strong highlights on her cheek and shoulder.

3. Place the second softbox **(3)** to mirror the position of its twin. Position it to produce a clear highlight on your model's cheek but that doesn't reach her nose.

4. Position your model about 5 feet in front of the black background. The softboxes produce quite a lot of spill that slightly brightens the center of the backdrop.

"Rotating the softboxes toward the back or front varies the brightness of the background."

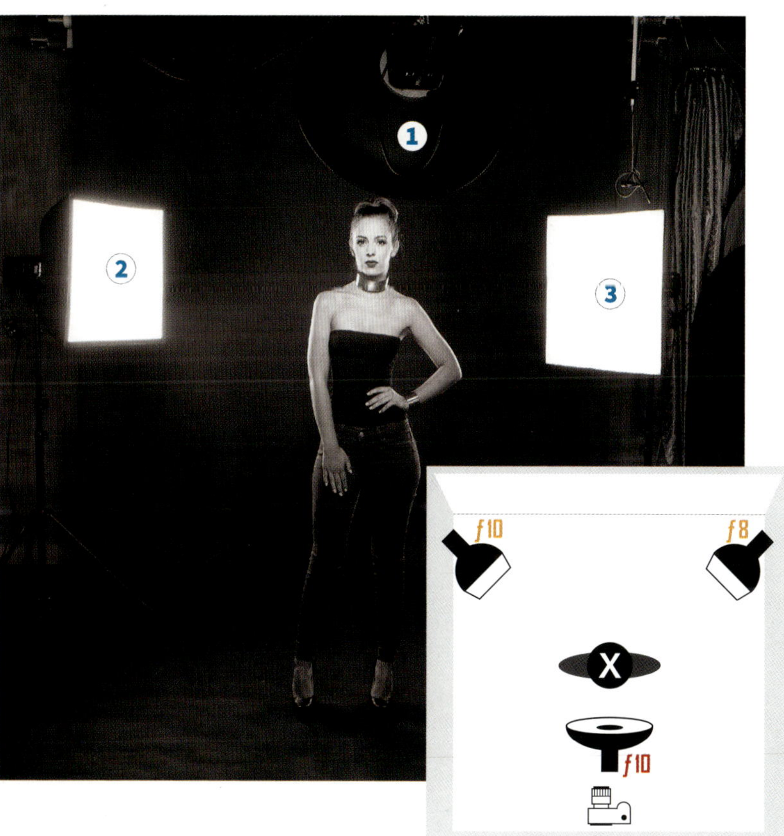

Changing the Color Look During Post-Processing

All photographers have highly personal preferences when it comes to the coloring in their images. Extreme looks quickly trend up and down again, while a little bit of subtle correction is often all you need to give your images a final polish. Today's software offers virtually unlimited options for changing the look of an image, but the easiest way to make a difference is often simply to alter the white balance setting to provide a cooler or warmer overall look. For example, you can use the Lightroom Split Toning panel to tweak the shadows and highlights. Another way to achieve a similar effect is to adjust the blue, red, and green values in the Curves panel.

In this example, I adjusted white balance from 6350K to 5350K to produce a cooler look. I then adjusted the highlights and shadows using the Split Toning panel.

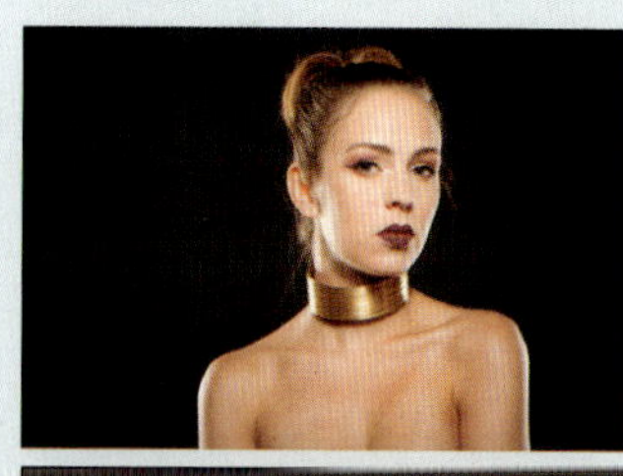
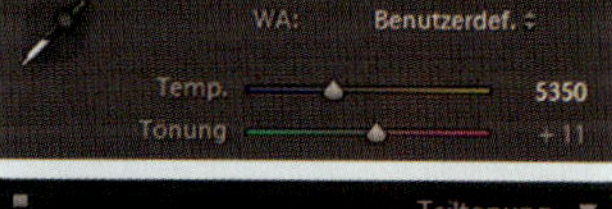

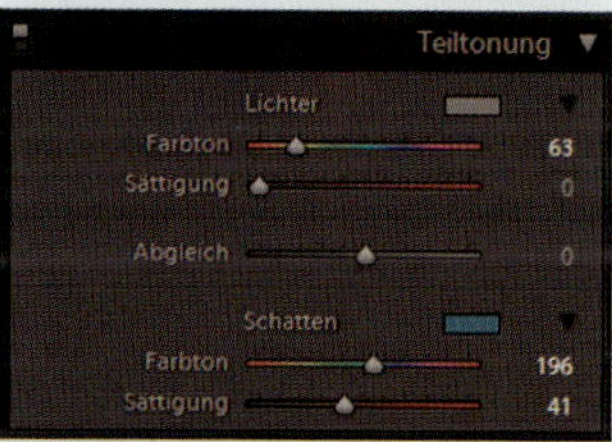
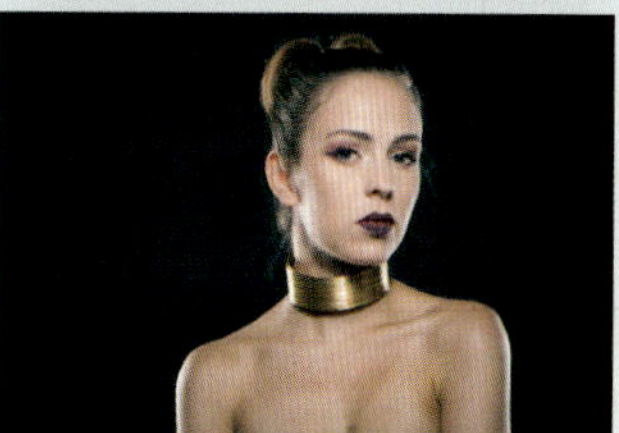

Two-Flash Fashion

With the right background and skilled lighting, you can create wonderful fashion photos using a minimum of gear. Rental studios often have a huge selection of backdrops to choose from, so you can select your background to suit the outfit or, as in this example, to suit the color of the subject's hair. This simple setup is quick to build, and the soft look is not only flattering, it also reduces the effort involved in post-processing.

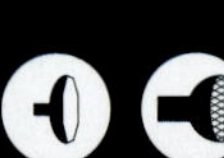

EFFORT INVOLVED

Low

SUITABLE FOR

Close-up to three-quarter-length portraits

THE LOOK

Strong, classic portrait
Deep shadows
Emphasis on the face
Brown-toned smokey eyes, intense dark red lipstick
Big hair with big curls

EQUIPMENT

1 × 31.5" octabox
1 × standard reflector with a honeycomb grid

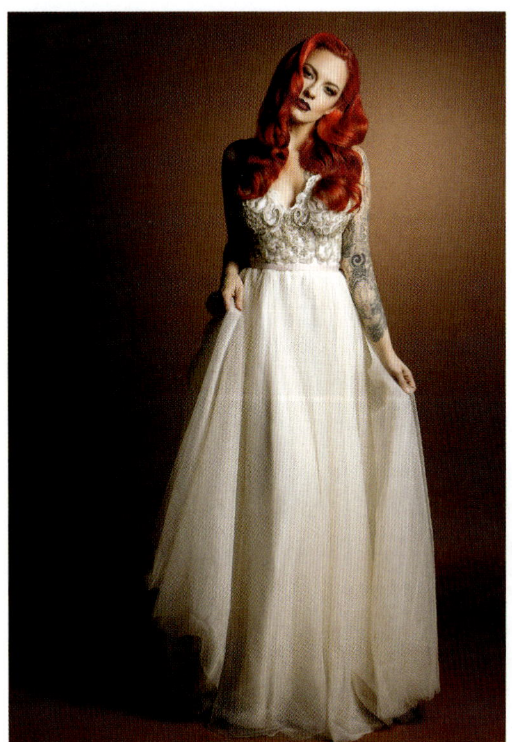

85mm | f4 | 1/125 sec. | ISO 100 | Model: Bianca

HOW IT WORKS

A frontal main light and a single background light produce a classic look, and the close proximity of the octabox emphasizes the subject's upper body. The brightness clearly falls off toward the legs and thus accents the subject's face and the intricate embroidery in the dress. The soft, slightly off-center light with its relatively low position creates even lighting that helps to mask any skin blemishes. The deep shadows give the image plenty of substance and underscore the glossy hair. The background flash lightens the background behind the shoulders.

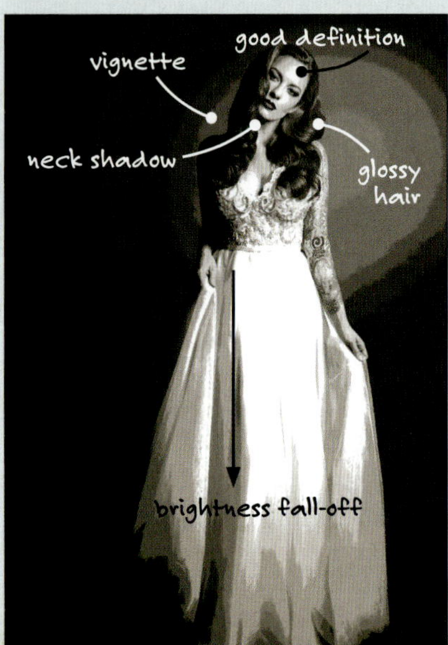

THE SETUP

1. Place the octabox **(1)** in a slightly raised position about 5 feet to the right of your model at an angle of about 45 degrees. Position it to produce a clearly visible neck shadow and a nose shadow that points diagonally downward toward her cheek.

2. Now place the gridded background reflector **(2)** about 3 feet to the right of your model at slightly above head height. Position it to brighten the area behind your model's shoulders.

3. Position your model about 5 feet from the brown backdrop.

Variations

Don't forget to try out different crops and different head postures during a shoot. Make sure you leave plenty of empty space within the frame so that the viewer can follow your model's gaze.

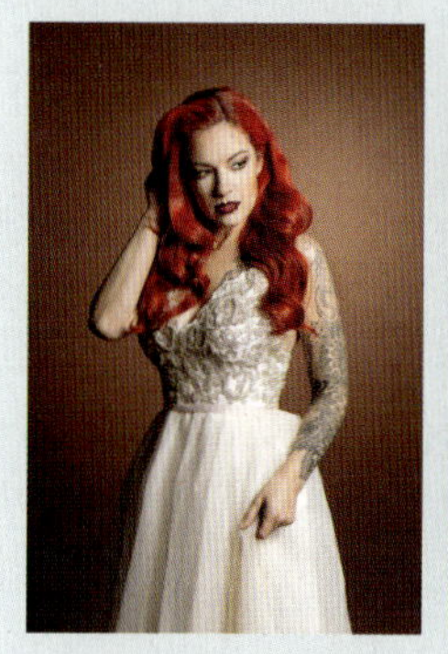
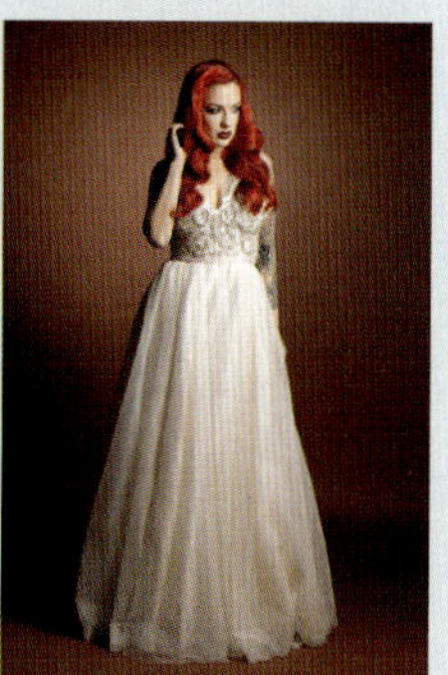

Crop and pose variations

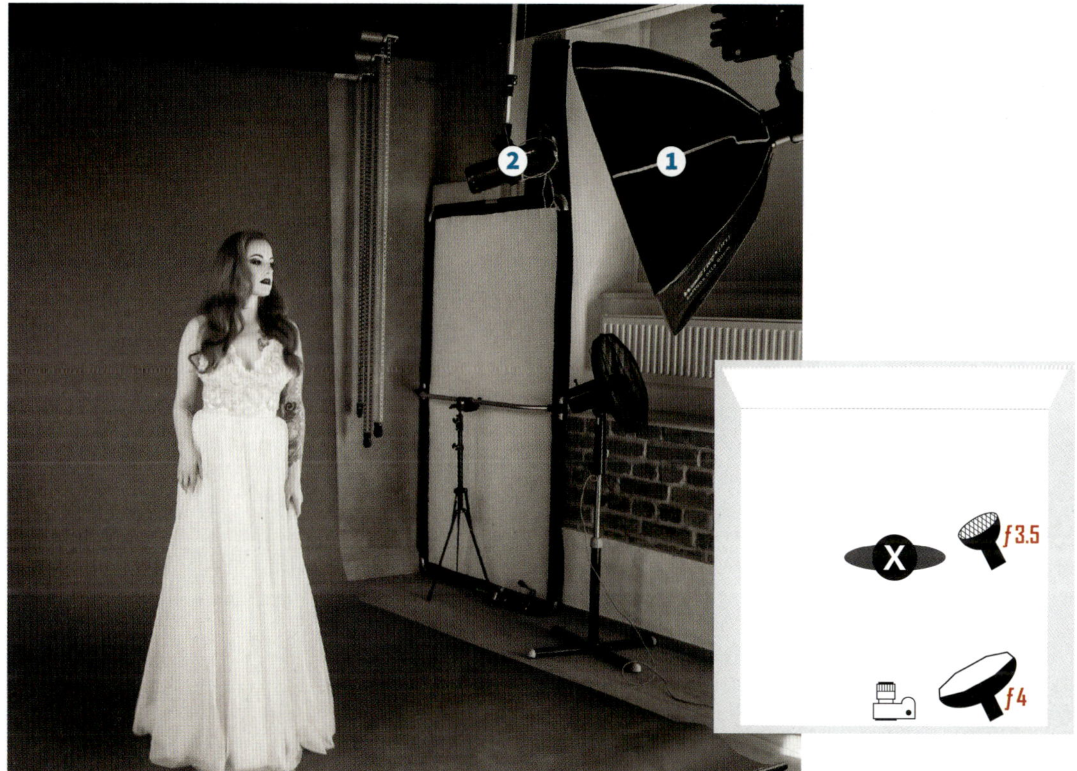

"Keep an eye on the shadows your model casts on the background and, if they are not quite right, move the softbox and/or adjust the distance between your model and the background accordingly."

Games with Colored Lights

Fluorescent tubes are great for producing unusual or experimental glamour shots. These images have a futuristic look, and the different colored lights provide a varied look that you can adjust to accent different parts of your subject.

EFFORT INVOLVED

Low

SUITABLE FOR

Close-up to three-quarter-length portraits

THE LOOK

Experimental, futuristic-looking glamour portrait
Gray-toned smokey eyes and dark lipstick
Reflective jewelry

EQUIPMENT

2 × 36W flourescent tubes (red and blue)

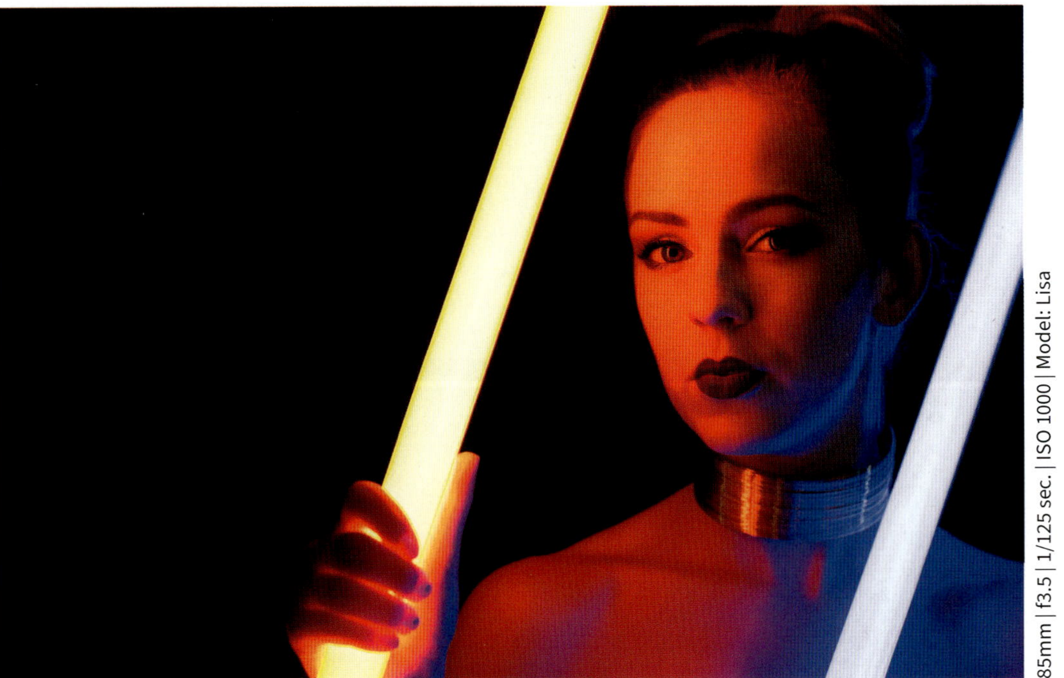

HOW IT WORKS

A fluorescent tube produces a similar sort of light to that of a strip box. The light side of the face is well lit and the right eye accented. The slightly raised position of the light also makes the lips appear fuller. There is just enough light on the shadow side to illuminate half of the left eye and produce a catchlight that keeps the image from looking too bleak. The blue fluorescent tube functions as an accent light that emphasizes the facial contours with a blue rim light and forms a nice curve from ear to chin. The colored reflections on the necklace provide additional highlights.

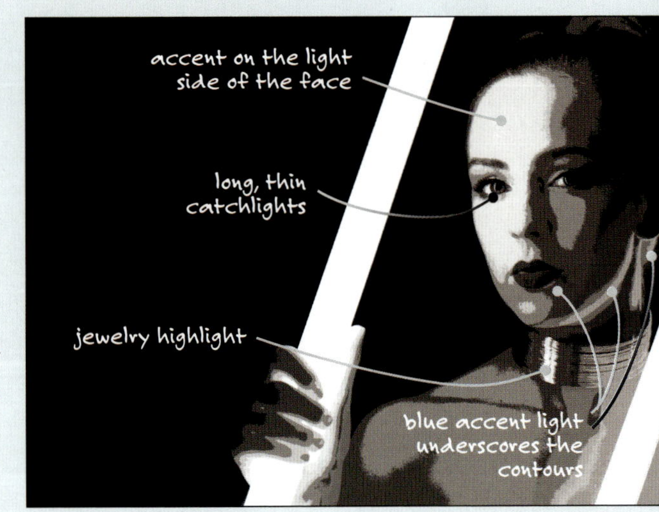

THE SETUP

1. Fluorescent tubes don't give off much light, so you will need to increase your ISO setting accordingly. For this shot, I set it to ISO 1000. You will need a slightly wider aperture than normal (in this case f3.5) and you should increase the exposure time to 1/125 sec. This is still short enough to minimize the risk of camera shake.

2. Position your model about 6 feet from the black background.

3. Get your model to hold the tubes so that the red light comes from the side and diagonally above.

4. The blue tube should be placed quite close to her shoulder so that its light comes from below and to the side.

5. Experiment with different positions to create different effects while you work. The great thing about continuous light is that you can see immediately how changes you make affect the look of the image, so you can fine-tune as you go along.

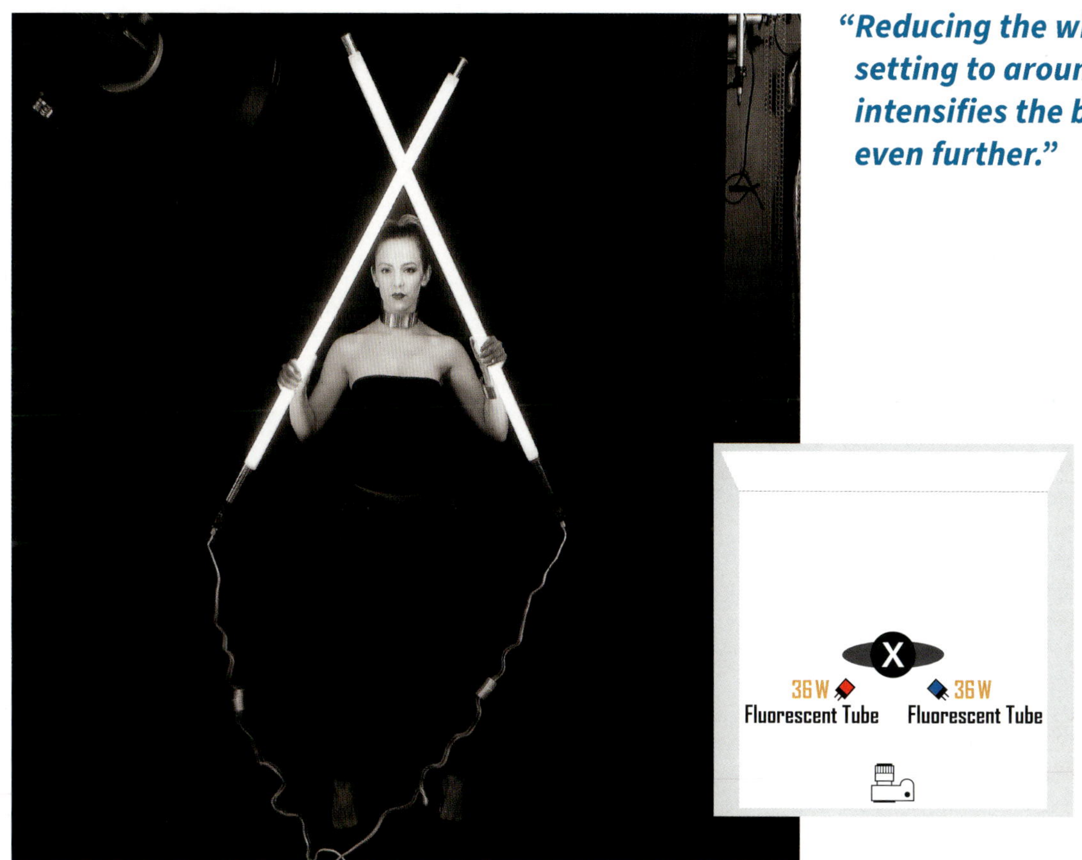

Fast Fashion

If you need to produce a quick portrait on the fly for a catalog or a website, all you really need is one large octabox. The broad, even light is sufficient even for full-length portraits and provides enough light for the background, too.

EFFORT INVOLVED

Low

SUITABLE FOR

All kinds of portraits

THE LOOK

Simple, balanced fashion portrait
Soft lighting with subtle shadows
Strong, brown-toned eye makeup and glossy lips

EQUIPMENT

1 × 47" octabox
if necessary, 1 × 30"×40" silver reflector

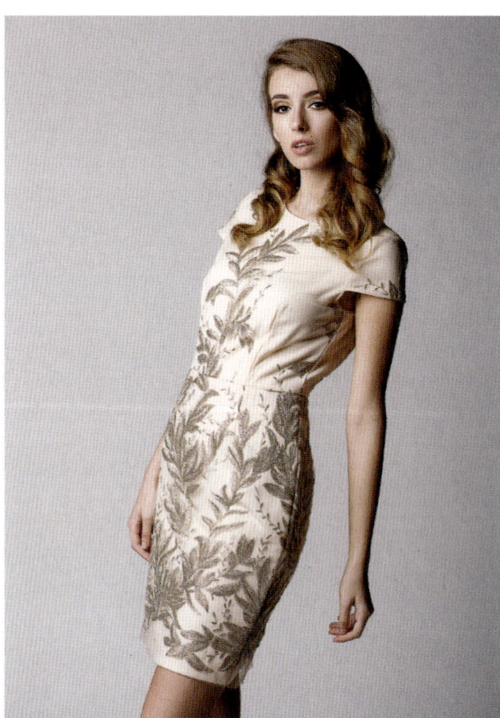

HOW IT WORKS

The high, diagonally placed octabox provides a soft overall light. The relatively large distance between the subject and the light ensures that the subject is evenly lit, with only slight fall-off toward the right. There is also a corresponding left-to-right gradient in the background that reduces the contrast between the subject and the background. The head posture creates a short light effect and the soft nose shadow creates a nice curve toward the eyebrows. The large light source produces a natural-looking gloss in the hair that fits in well with the shimmering sliver embroidery in the dress. The leaning pose fills the frame nicely. The dress is well presented and contrasts nicely with the background.

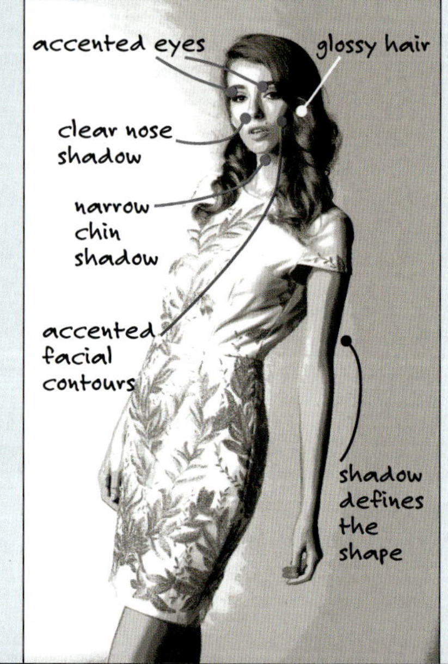

THE SETUP

1. Place the octabox **(1)** about 6 feet to the front left of your model in a slightly raised position and at an angle of about 45 degrees. Position it to form a slight nose shadow and a narrow shadow beneath your model's chin.

2. Position your model about 6 feet in front of the white background.

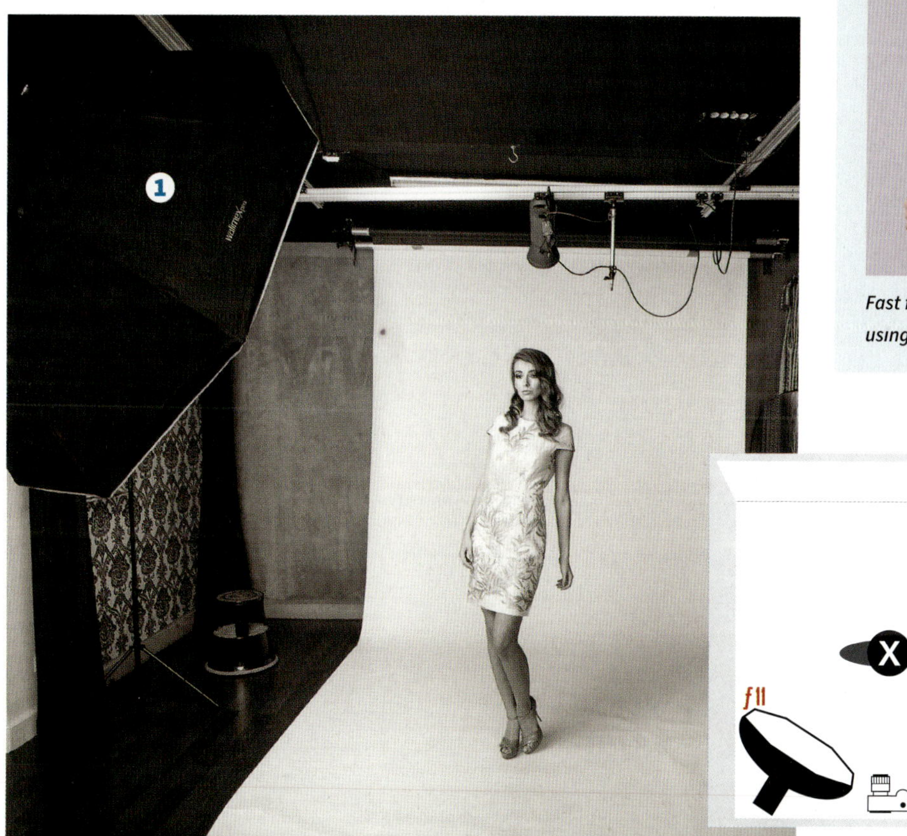

Variation with a Reflector

If you want to lighten your shadows but still keep things simple, all you need to do is set up a silver reflector to the right of your model. This softens the overall effect and illuminates the dress more evenly.

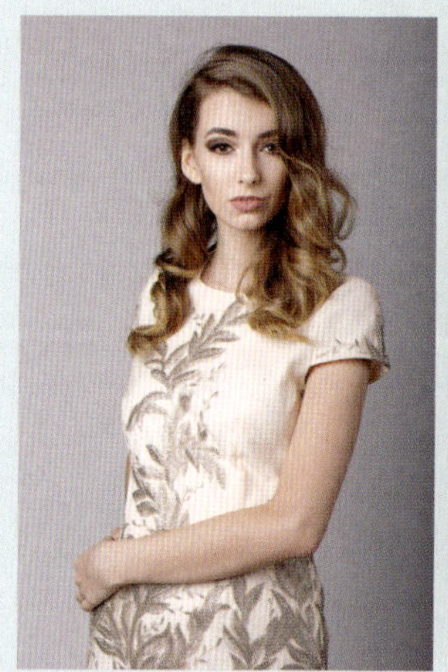

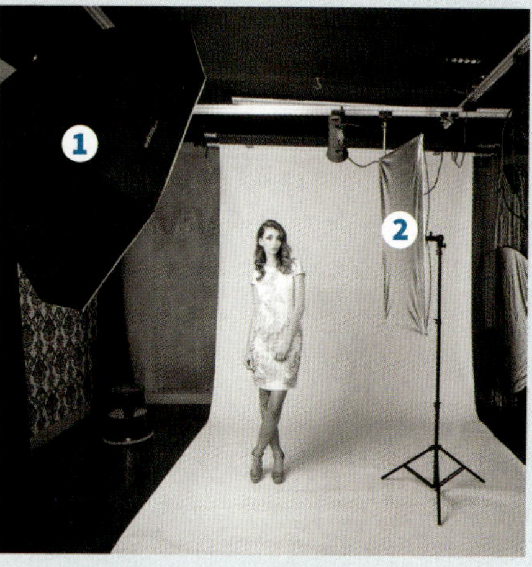

Fast fashion portrait captured using an octabox and a reflector.

The "making of" shot for the variation with a reflector **(2)**.

"Your model's ability to pose as instructed is extremely important on a fashion shoot. Always book an experienced model if you can."

Close-Up Fashion Portrait

If you are shooting clothes, you should always take some detail shots. To ensure that close-ups don't look sterile or boring, you can use a full lighting rig for your close-up shots. Images like this have an aura all their own, and are a great way to frame and present important details.

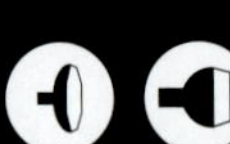

EFFORT INVOLVED

Medium

SUITABLE FOR

Close-ups and head-and-shoulders portraits

THE LOOK

Close-quarters fashion setup for detail shots
Very soft light for glowing skin
Bold, brown-toned eye makeup and glossy lips

EQUIPMENT

1× 31.5" octabox
1× 24" softbox
1× standard reflector with a honeycomb grid

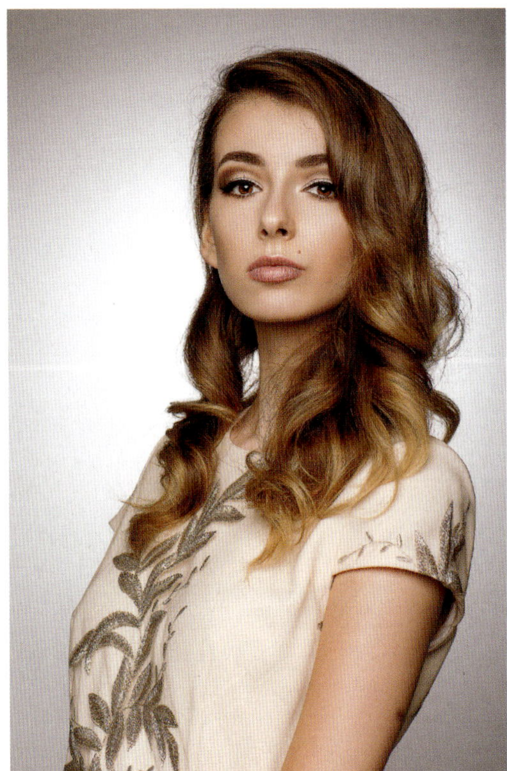

85mm | f9 | 1/160 sec. | ISO 100 | Model: Jazz

HOW IT WORKS

The high, frontal main light gives you plenty of leeway for altering the head and body posture. Your subject can move freely and present all the desired details individually. The clothing is well lit and the softbox lightens all the shadows evenly. The background spot steers the viewer's gaze toward the center of the frame and thus to the subject's face and clothing. The facial contours are accented by the cheek highlight and soft shadows keep the nose and mouth interesting but not dominant. The catchlights keep the overall look lively and the natural-looking hair gloss doesn't distract from the dress.

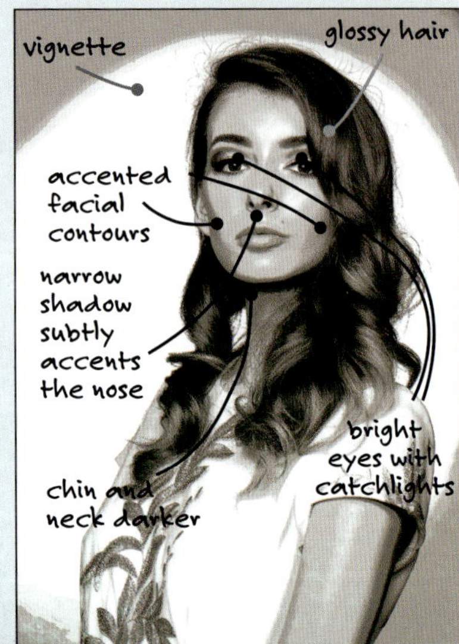

THE SETUP

1. Mount the octabox **(1)** on a ceiling rail or a boom stand and position it to illuminate your model frontally from above at an angle of about 45 degrees. The distance between the light and your model should be about 5 feet. Position it to cast a narrow shadow directly beneath your model's chin.

2. Now mount the softbox fill light **(2)** directly in front of your model on a low stand, or simply put it on the floor.

3. Mount the gridded background spot **(3)** behind your model on a ceiling rail or a boom stand at a height of about 8 feet. Position it to focus at around shoulder height and to create a pool of light that reaches no further than the top of her head.

4. Position your model about 5 feet in front of the white background.

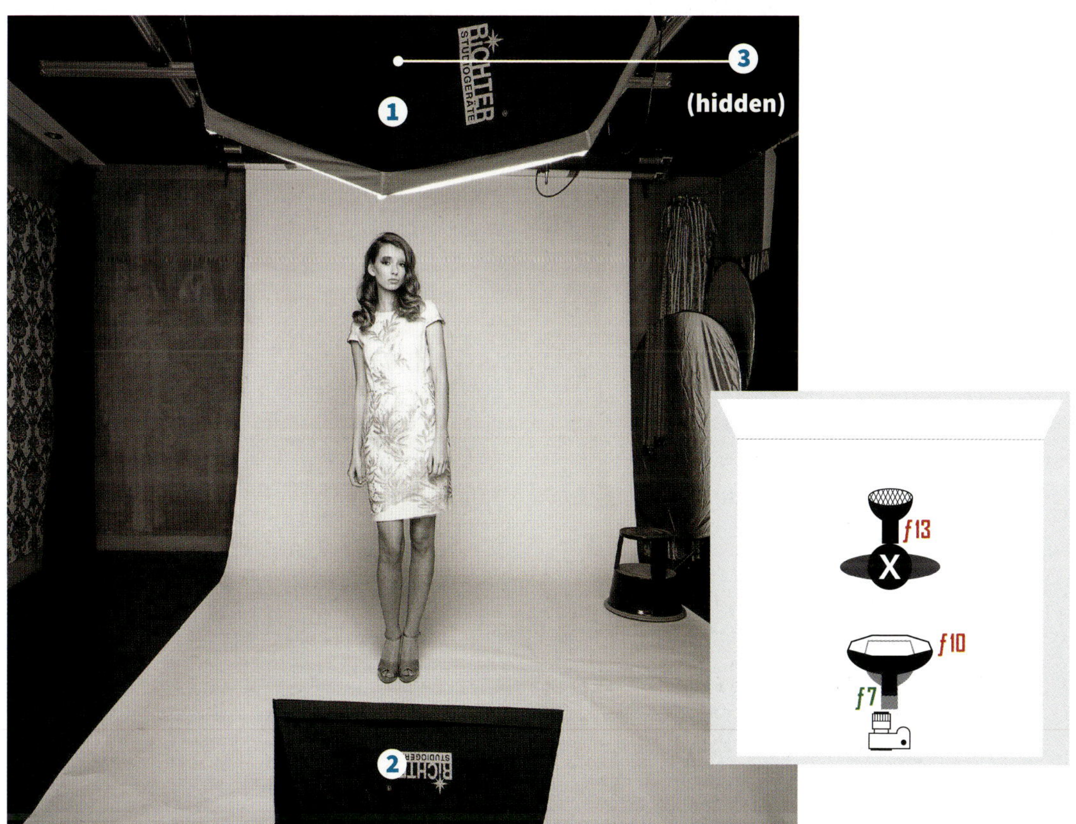

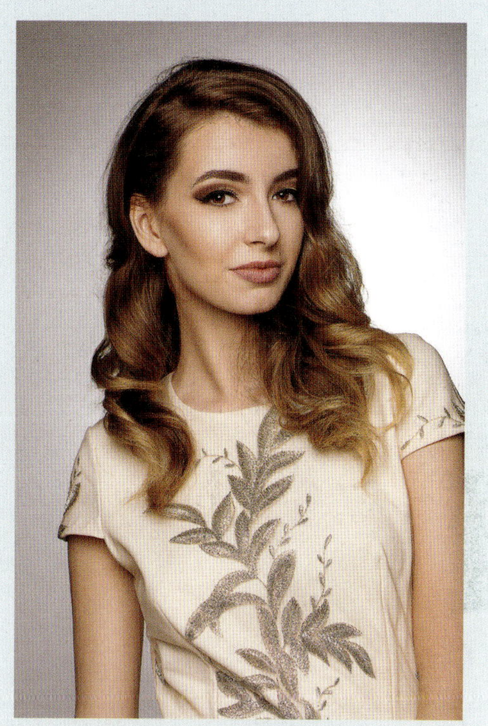

Variation

In this version of the shot, my model rotated her head and body counterclockwise. This creates a broad, frontal lighting effect in her face and gives strong emphasis to the embroidery in the dress.

"Your model's expression is particularly important in close-up shots and must suit the overall look of the image."

Elegant Lifestyle Portrait

*Lifestyle and fashion photography are closely related. This lifestyle shot is based on the "little black dress" look popularized by Audrey Hepburn in **Breakfast at Tiffany's** and radiates classic elegance.*

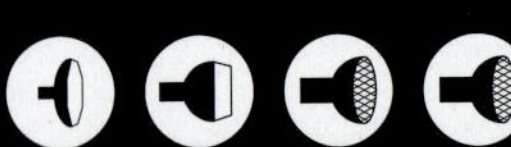

EFFORT INVOLVED

High

SUITABLE FOR

All kinds of portraits

THE LOOK

Elegant lifestyle portrait with a dark background

Glamorous brown-toned makeup, accented lips, updo hair

Black dress

EQUIPMENT

1 × 31.5" octabox

1 × 24" softbox

2 × standard reflectors with honeycomb grids

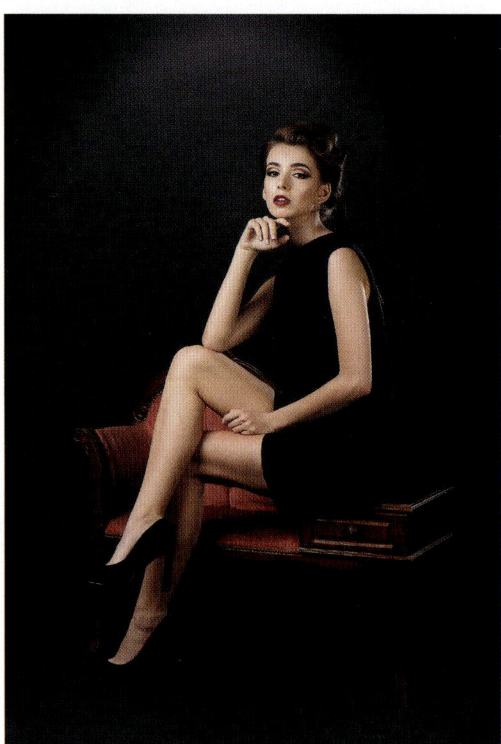

85mm | f8 | 1/160 sec. | ISO 100 | Model: Jazz

HOW IT WORKS

Careful positioning of multiple lights produces a whole raft of accents and highlights. The diagonally positioned octabox produces a soft main light that accents the subject's body contours. The delicate nose shadow and the clear cheek shadow give the face nice definition. The softbox on the right lightens the shadows and produces a smooth overall look. The accent light separates the subject clearly from the dark background and creates subtle rim lights on the dress, the subject, and on the furniture prop. The background light creates a conspicuous vignette with strong fall-off toward the bottom of the frame.

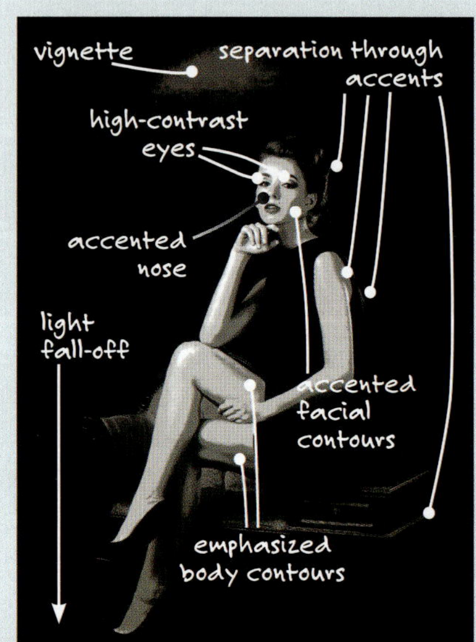

THE SETUP

1. Place the octabox **(1)** about 5 feet to the left of your model in a slightly raised position and at an angle of about 45 degrees. Position it to cast a soft nose shadow and a narrow shadow directly beneath your model's chin.

2. Now place the softbox fill light **(2)** about 5 feet to the right of your model at about belly height and at an angle of about 45 degrees. The V-shaped "clamshell" setup is clearly visible in the photo below.

3. Now place the accent light **(3)** behind your model at an angle of about 45 degrees so that it produces clear accents on her hair, back, and upper arm, and also on the furniture prop.

4. Place the background reflector **(4)** behind your model at a height of about 8 feet and position it so that it brightens the background while keeping the shape of the light beam visible.

5. Position the prop with your seated model about 6 feet in front of the black background.

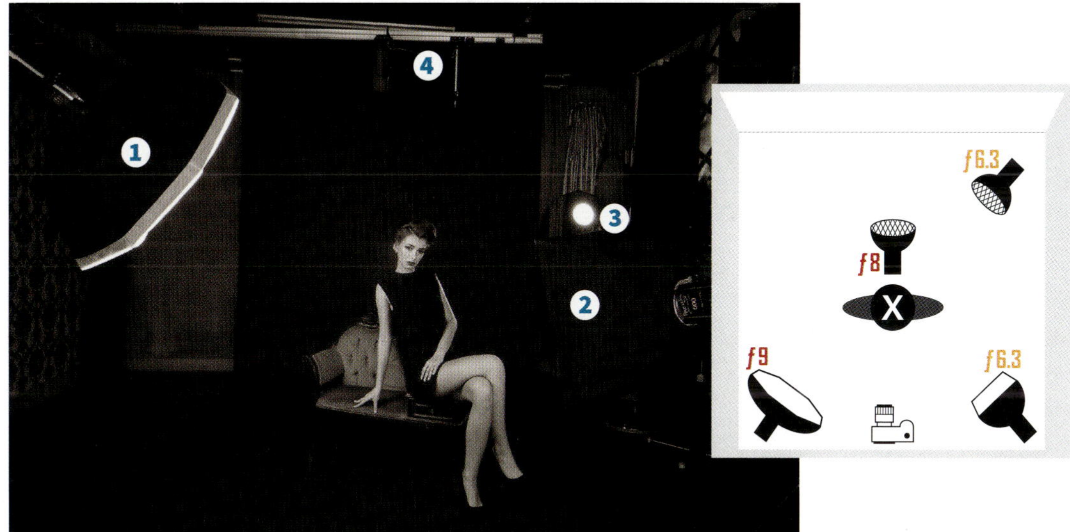

Variation

Capturing some detail shots is always a good idea, and is a great way to create variety when you are shooting a sequence. This setup is suitable for close-ups, too, so get bold and take a step or two closer to your model. Getting your model to change her pose and posture enables you to vary the effects produced by the main and fill lights, from broad to narrow lighting.

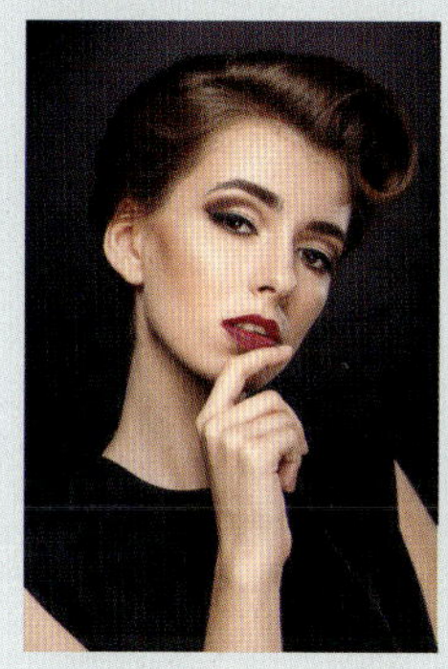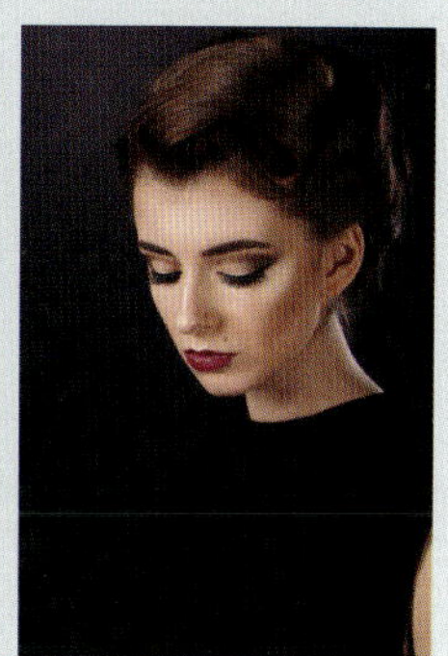

Left: Broad lighting (illuminating the side of the face pointed toward the camera) combined with fill light creates accents on the model's cheek and the bridge of her nose.
Right: Narrow lighting (illuminating mainly the side of the face that points away from the camera) combined with fill light accents the model's neck and the rear portion of her jawline.

> **"When you are shooting dark clothes in front of a dark background, make sure you lighten the background enough to separate it from the clothing on display."**

Fashion To Go

If you are looking for a quick-and-easy setup for capturing modern-looking portraits, this is your go-to solution! A strip box main light and a standard reflector for the fill and background effects are all you need.

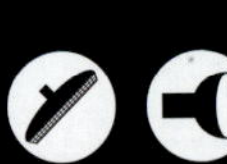
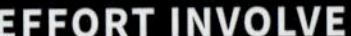

EFFORT INVOLVED

Low

SUITABLE FOR

All kinds of portraits

THE LOOK

Contemporary portrait style that is quick to set up and shoot

Gray-toned smokey eyes, pink lips

EQUIPMENT

1× 47" strip box with a honeycomb grid

1× standard reflector

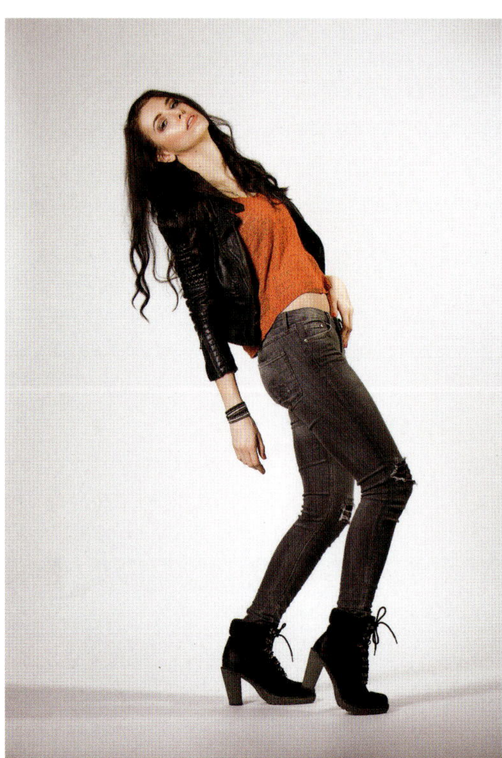

95mm | f7.1 | 1/160 sec. | ISO 100 | Model: Elisa

HOW IT WORKS

The strip box main light enables you to target your light from head to toe. This approach accents the vertical lines and glossy details in the faux-leather jacket. The cheek highlights emphasize the cheekbone contour and the soft but clear neck shadow provides good separation between the subject's head and body. The main and fill lights produce accents on the lips that make them appear fuller. The accent produced by the fill light produces a kind of clamshell effect but lights the subject's front, too. The twin shadows on the floor provide a visual basis that prevents the subject from appearing to float in mid-air.

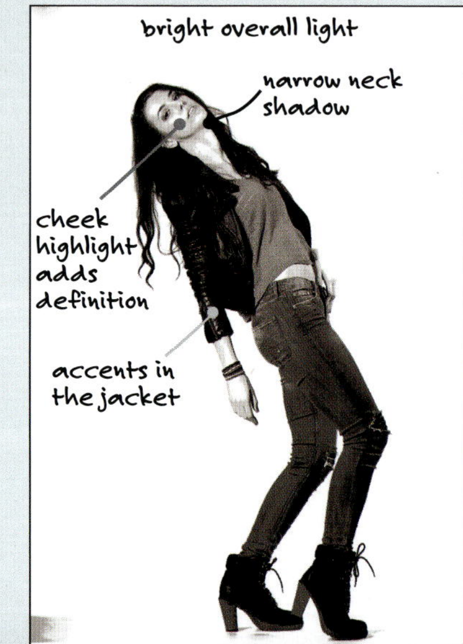

THE SETUP

1. Place the strip box **(1)** about 6 feet to the left of your model at about head height and at an angle of about 45 degrees. Position it to produce a narrow shadow beneath your model's chin.

2. Now place the background reflector **(2)** about 6 feet away from your model to the front and slightly raised. Position it to light your model from the side and to provide sufficient light for the background.

3. Position your model about 3 feet from the white background.

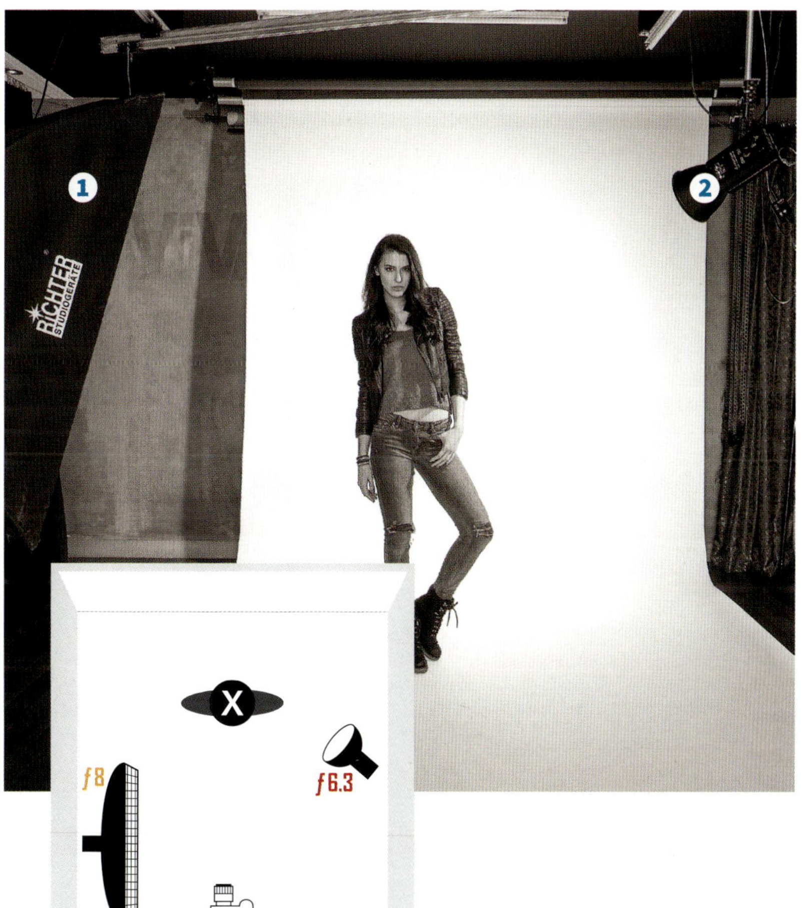

Strong Poses

Modern fashion portraits are characterized by strong, expressive poses that keep the image interesting and make the viewer's eye linger. After all, getting people to look at their images for as long as possible is exactly what advertisers are aiming for.

However, it's simply impossible for your model to hold an athletic pose, so to capture precisely the right moment you need to focus in advance and keep the shutter button pressed halfway while your model is moving into position.

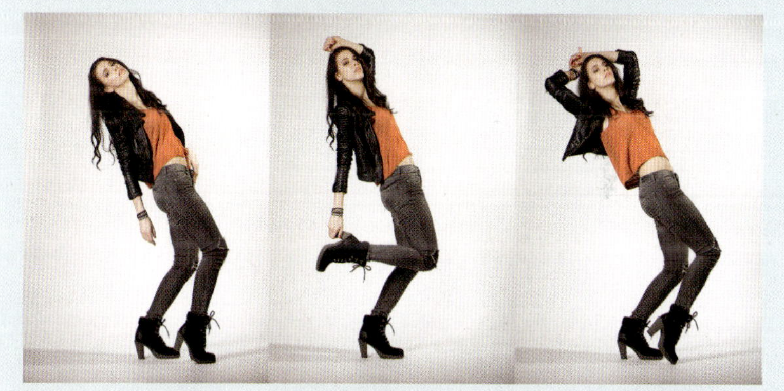

Expressive poses bring the outfit to the fore.

Double Accents

An accent light is great for emphasizing lines and two accent lights are twice as good! In this setup, I used two fill lights to accent the subject's body contours and the line of the dress. A setup like this requires a soft main light, so in this case I used an octabox.

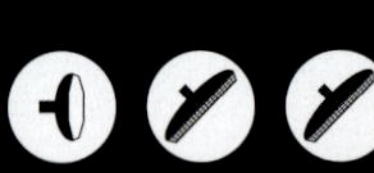

EFFORT INVOLVED

Medium

SUITABLE FOR

All kinds of portraits

THE LOOK

Cool fashion shot that accents vertical lines
Gray-toned eye makeup, matte pink lips

EQUIPMENT

1 × 31.5" octabox
2 × 47" strip boxes with honeycomb grids
1 × 30" × 40" silver reflector

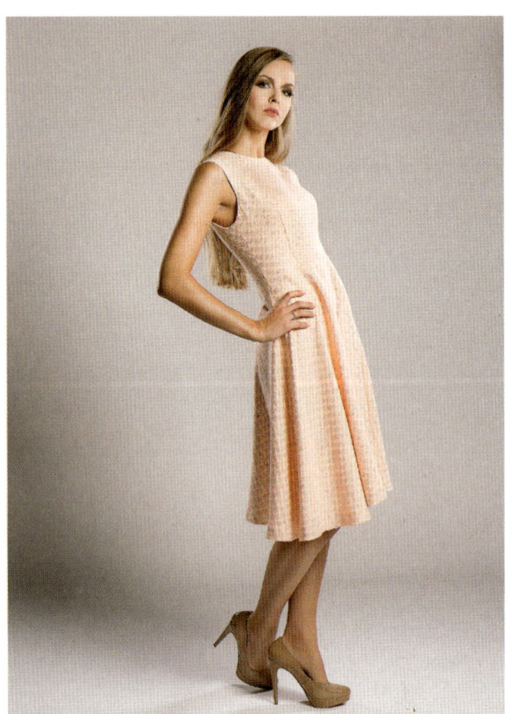

85mm | f8 | 1/160 sec. | ISO 100 | Model: Angelina

HOW IT WORKS

The diagonally positioned main light produces a soft look with natural-looking shadows, while the reflector brightens the shadows enough to produce a balanced overall look. The subject's upper body is well defined and the slight light fall-off toward the legs keeps the viewer's attention in the upper portion of the frame. The fill light on the right produces clear accents on the subject's head and torso, while the left-hand fill light accents the contours in the subject's back and the folds in the dress. There is a slight vignette in the background that helps to focus attention on the subject. The shadows on the floor add depth and provide a counterpoint to the light-colored dress.

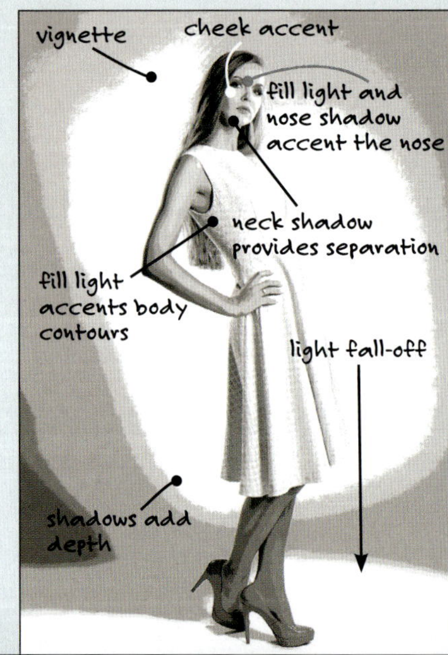

THE SETUP

1. Place the octabox **(1)** about 6 feet to the front right of your model in a raised position and at an angle of about 45 degrees. Position it to produce a slight neck shadow.

2. Mount the reflector **(2)** about 3 feet to the left of your model in a raised position and set it up to lighten the nose shadow.

3. Now place the fill strip box **(3)** about 5 feet to the left behind your model at an angle of about 45 degrees. Position it with its center at about shoulder height so that it produces highlights on your model's hair, back, and upper arm.

4. Place the second strip box **(4)** about 5 feet behind your model to the right at an angle of about 45 degrees. Set it up to produce clear accents on your model's face and upper body.

5. Position your model about 5 feet from the white background.

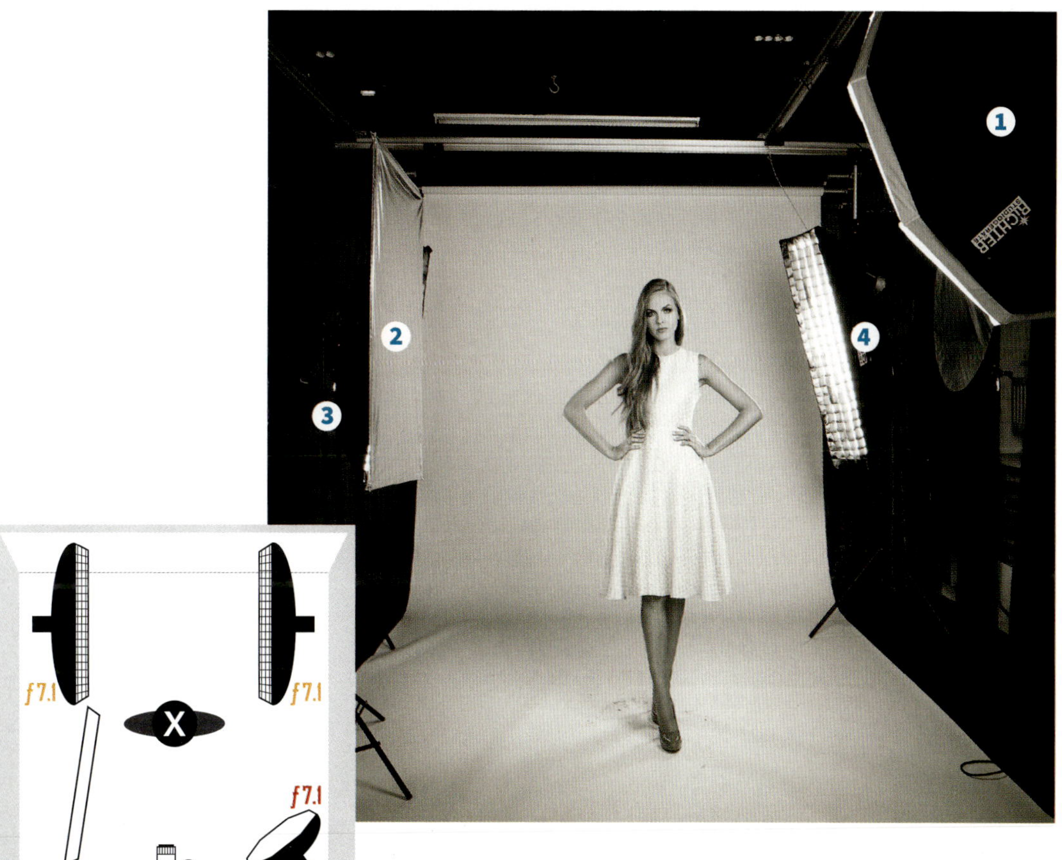

"Folds in clothing are best accented by light from the side."

Accenting Vertical Lines

The fall of the folds in clothing produces vertical lines within the image, and the best way to accent these lines is to produce shadows using light that comes from the side. Lateral light accents body contours, too, and the shadows it produces make arms and legs look slimmer. Always use diagonal or lateral light for shots like this.

Colored Light and Shadow

Light and shade are inseparable, but for this shot, a regular gray shadow was simply too boring. The coral-red designer dress cried out for a color contrast that I decided to place in the shadow behind the subject. Blue is the complementary color to red/orange tones, so it didn't take long to decide which color to use!

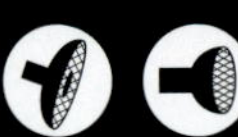

EFFORT INVOLVED

Medium

SUITABLE FOR

Close-up to three-quarter-length portraits

THE LOOK

High-color fashion portrait with strong color contrast

Gray-toned smokey eyes, coral-red lipstick matches the dress

EQUIPMENT

1× beauty dish with a honeycomb grid

1× standard reflector with a honeycomb grid and a colored gel

1× 30" ×40" silver reflector

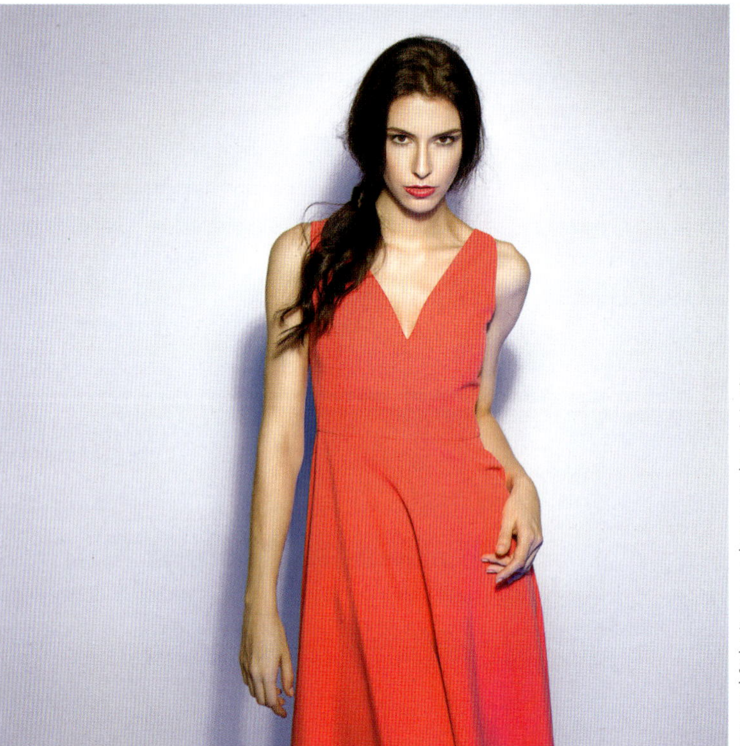

100mm | f8 | 1/160 sec. | ISO 100 | Model: Elisa

HOW IT WORKS

The high, frontally placed beauty dish strongly accents the face and body contours. The cheekbones are especially well defined and add to the facial contours. The dark neck shadow visually separates the head from the rest of the body, and turns both the face and the dress into real eye-catchers. The raised main light produces nice light/shade interplay in the shoulders and collarbones. The star of this setup, is of course, the blue shadow that contrasts beautifully with the red dress. The complementary shadow color accentuates the dress and makes the entire image really interesting.

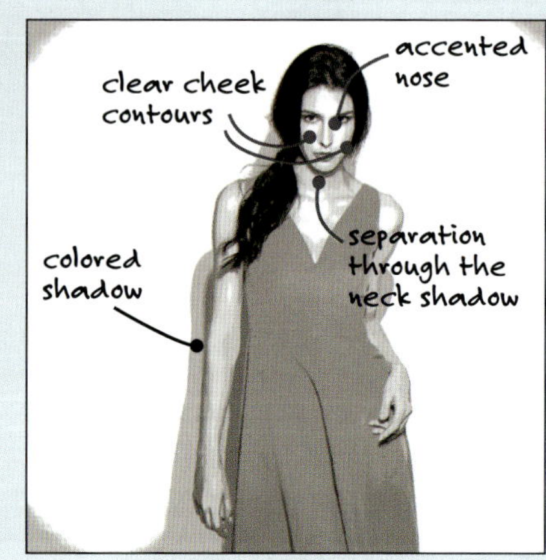

THE SETUP

1. Mount the gridded beauty dish **(1)** on a ceiling rail or a boom stand about 10 feet above and to the front of your model and pointing down at an angle of about 30 degrees. Position it to light your model evenly and to produce a slight shadow beneath her nose.

2. Place your model about 12 inches from the white background.

3. To create the colored shadow, place the gridded standard reflector **(2)** to the right of your model at a distance of about 6 feet and at an angle of about 45 degrees. Point it downward and attach a blue gel to the front of the reflector.

4. Lay a silver reflector **(3)** on the floor in front of the gelled standard reflector and adjust the angle of the flash so that its reflected light forms a shadow on the backdrop.

5. The relatively large distance between the model and the beauty dish produces a harder look with strong shadows that contribute to the overall look of the image. You can adjust the strength of the shadows by altering the distance between your model and the main light.

> *"Alongside the obvious color contrast, the contrast between the classically elegant dress and the model's unkempt hair is a great additional stylistic element."*

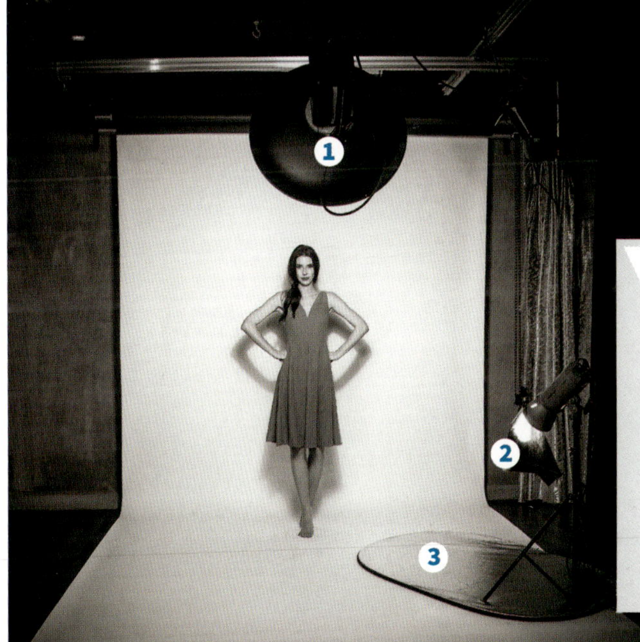

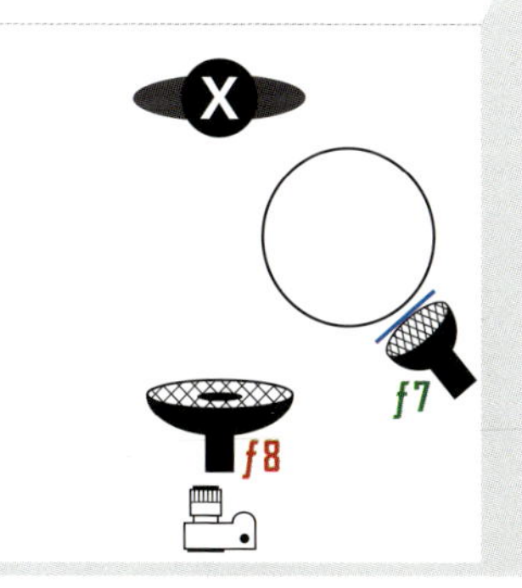

Using Complementary Colors

Complementary colors are a great tool for accenting or intensifying specific tones. A quick look at the color circle will help you find the right complementary color for a single-color dress, but finding the right complement for a multi-color pattern requires a bit more finesse. A dominant color is a good place to start looking for a complementary color, but the trick simply doesn't work if a piece of clothing already has complementary colors in its pattern. The "non-colors" (black, gray, and white) are the exceptions to this rule as they have no complements. For these tones, you can use any color you like for your shadow.

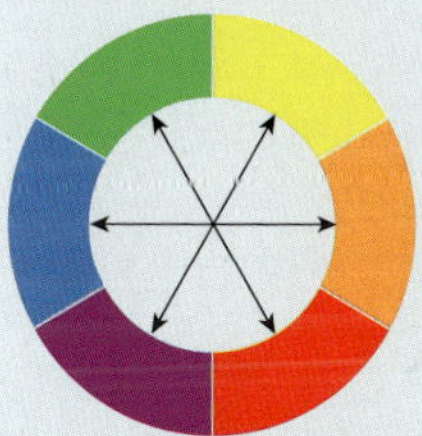

The color circle showing the basic complementary colors.

Shadow Variations

You can alter the position of the shadow behind your model by moving the beauty dish to the left or right, and you can create a variety of looks by getting your model to alter her pose too.

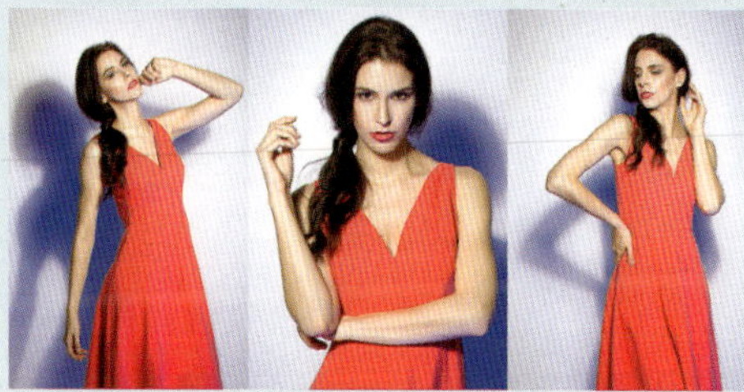

Fashion in Backlight

Backlight has its place in fashion photography, too, and it produces multiple fine highlights that contrast nicely with the flares that backlight creates. The simplest route to a backlit portrait is to light the background way too brightly.

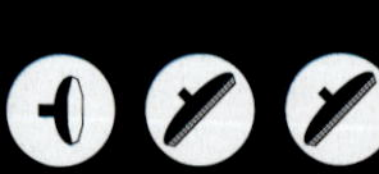

EFFORT INVOLVED

Medium

SUITABLE FOR

All kinds of portraits

THE LOOK

Gentle-looking fashion portrait captured using backlight

Gray-toned smokey eyes and pink lips

EQUIPMENT

1 × 31.5" octabox

2 × 47" strip boxes with honeycomb grids

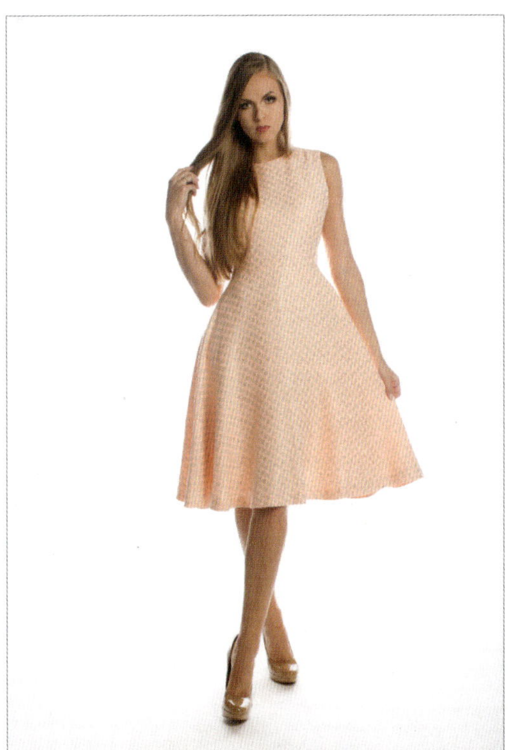

HOW IT WORKS

The obvious eye-catcher in this image is the very bright background that produces multiple highlights and flares to accent the body contours. The background creates the impression that there is a really bright light that the subject is somehow emerging from. The light from the diagonally positioned octabox creates clear shadows that add depth in spite of the soft overall feel. The face retains its contours and the neck shadow provides visual separation between head and torso. The direct backlight reduces overall contrast and underscores the soft, natural-looking feel.

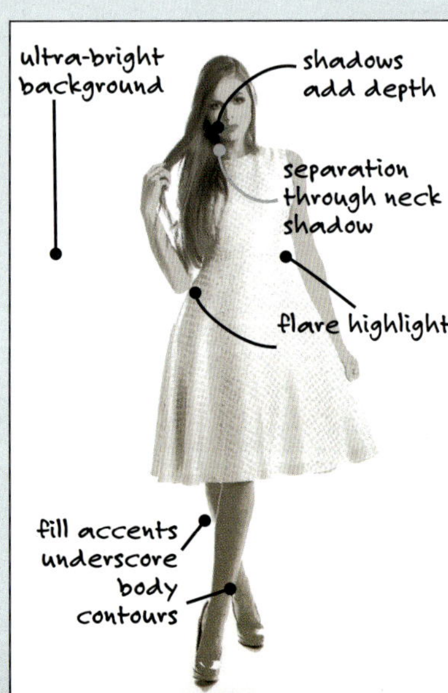

THE SETUP

1. Place the octabox **(1)** in a raised position on the right about 5 feet from your model and at an angle of about 45 degrees. Position it to produce a nose shadow that remains visible beneath the tip of your model's nose.

2. Place the first strip box **(2)** about 5 feet to the left of your model at head height. Position it so that its light hits the background to the left of your model.

3. Place the second strip box **(3)** the same way on the right so that its light hits the background behind your model from the other side.

4. Position your model about 5 feet from the white background.

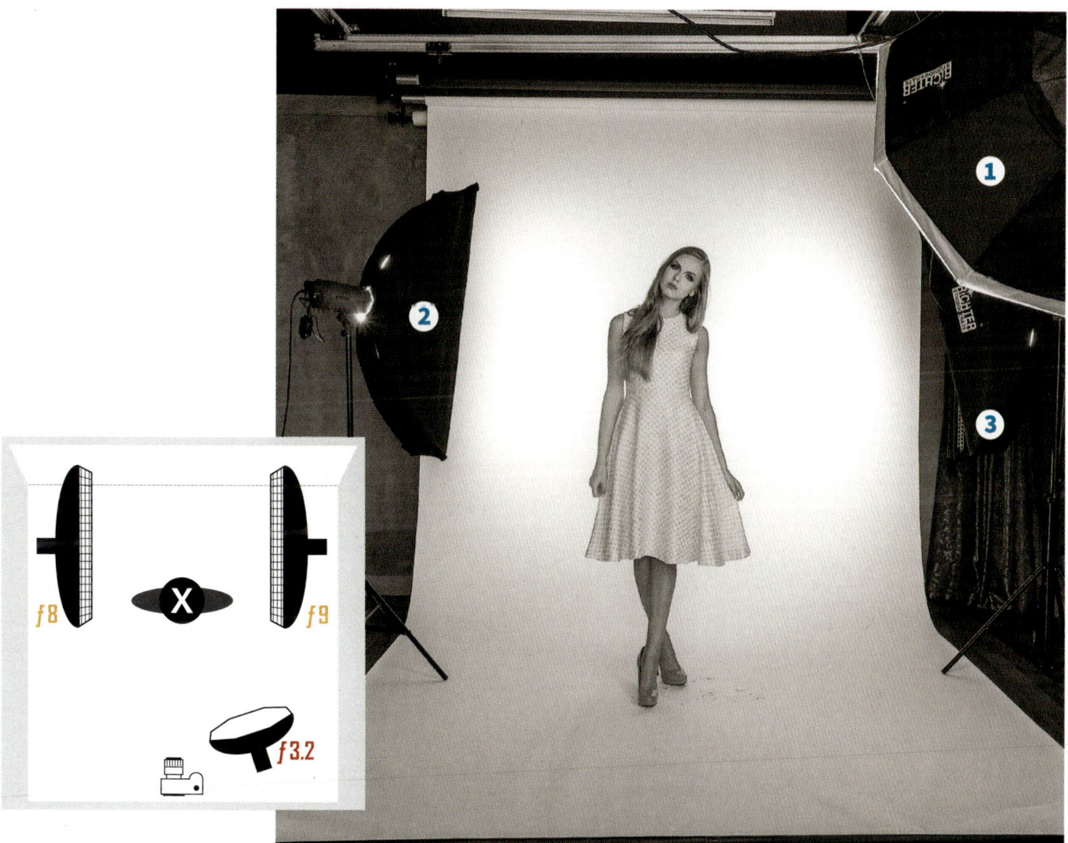

Post-Processing Tip: Floor Cleanup

Studio floors aren't always as clean as you'd like. However, retouching any marks individually is simply too much effort. An easy way to achieve the same effect is to fire up Photoshop and apply the **Blur > Surface Blur** filter to a layer copy of your image using appropriate Radius and Threshold values (in this example I set R34, T34). Then simply add a black layer mask (Alt-click on the mask icon) to mask out the floor. That's all there is to it, and it doesn't take more than a minute.

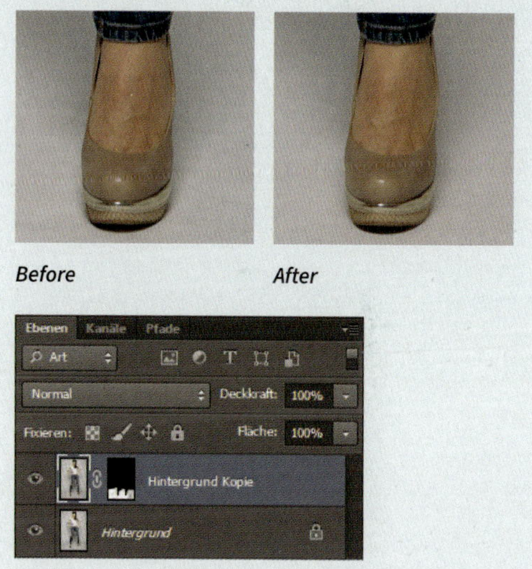

Before   *After*

"Make sure the twin strip boxes illuminate different areas in the background to produce even-looking backlight."

Clamshell Fashion Lighting

The fill lights from behind in this setup create a bright rim light around the subject and add glow to the dress. This kind of setup is popular for magazine or catalog shoots as it separates the clothing clearly from the background. Here, the frontal beauty dish also accents the subject's face and figure. This setup takes a bit of work, but the result is a high-contrast, Vogue-style image to die for.

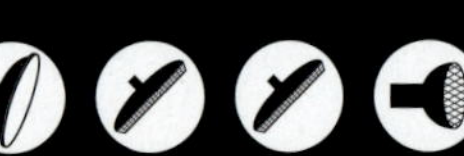

EFFORT INVOLVED

High

SUITABLE FOR

Three-quarter and full-length portraits

THE LOOK

Powerful classic portrait
Strong shadows
Accented face
Brown-toned smoky eyes and matte lips
Highlights on the cheeks
Strong emphasis on the clothing

EQUIPMENT

1 × 20" beauty dish with a diffuser
2 × 47" strip boxes with honeycomb grids
1 × standard reflector with a honeycomb grid

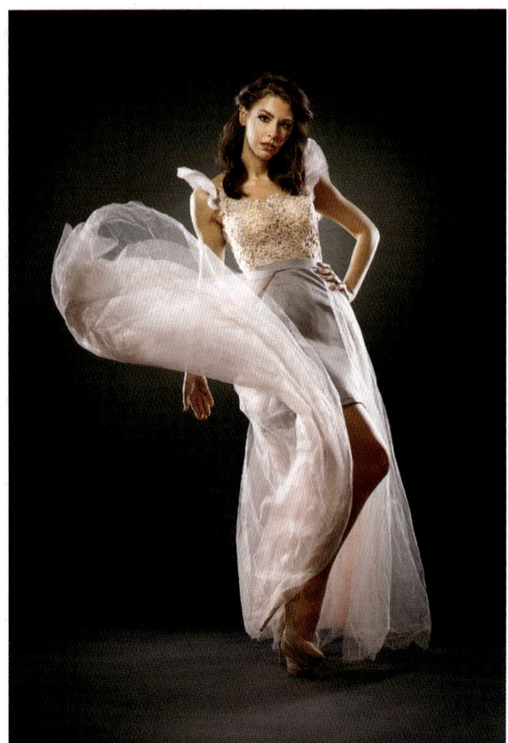

70mm | f2.8 | 1/80 sec. | ISO 100 | Model: Elisa

HOW IT WORKS

The twin fill lights from behind create a clear outline and rim lights on the subject's hair, arms, and dress, while the fill light produces a highlight on the cheek. The classic "beauty dish from front left" setup ensures that the face is well lit. The nose shadow points diagonally toward the cheek, and the neck shadow provides good separation between face and body. The eyes remain bright and the subject's figure is well defined. The backlight that shines through the material of the dress provides an additional highlight. The additional background flash steers the viewer's eye toward the center of the frame. Multiple strong contrasts make this a powerful look.

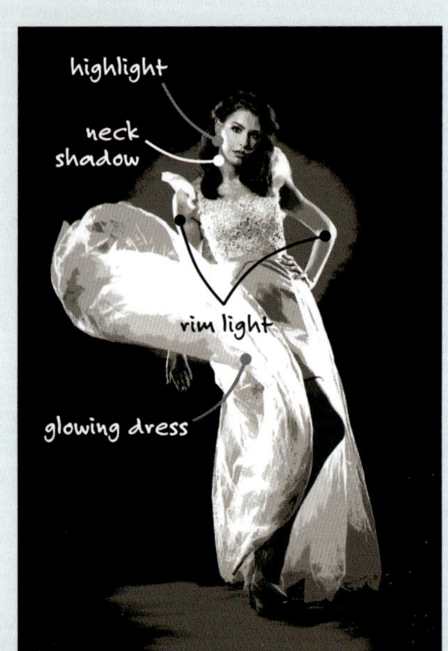

THE SETUP

1. Place the beauty dish **(1)** about 6 feet to the front left of your model in a raised position and at an angle of about 45 degrees. Position it to produce a clear neck shadow and a nose shadow that points diagonally toward your model's cheek.

2. Place the twin strip boxes **(2)** behind your model on the right and left in slightly raised positions at about 45 degrees. Now tip the strip boxes downward so that they illuminate your model from head to toe.

3. Finally, set up the gridded standard reflector **(3)** above head height to the right of your model. Point it downward to focus on a point in the background at around belly height.

Variations

If you are shooting for a catalog or a website, it is always a good idea to capture a wide variety of different crops and poses.

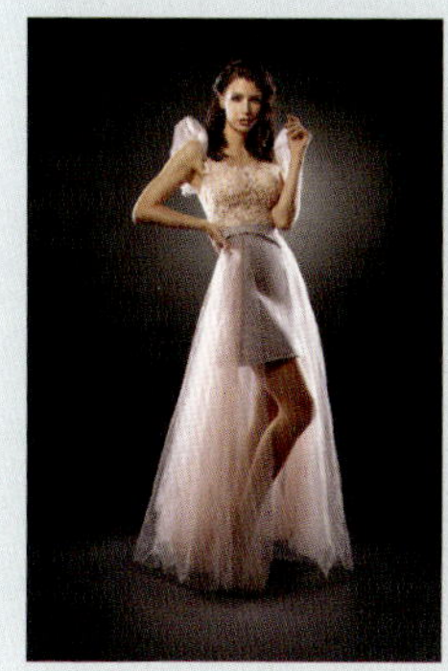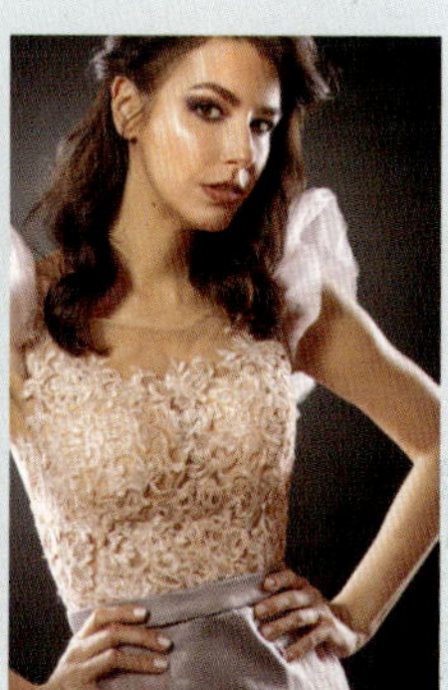

Variations using different crops and poses.

"You can vary the rim light effect by altering the distance between your model and the strip boxes."

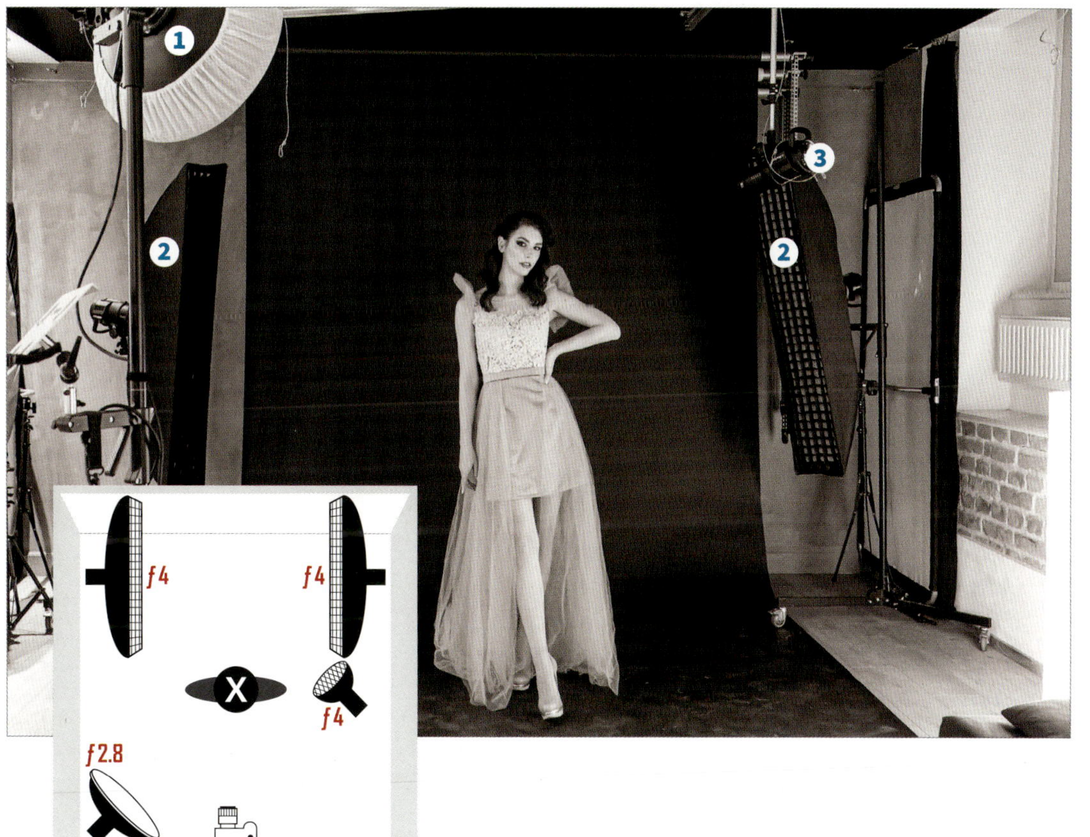

Jill Greenberg-Style Portrait

American photographer Jill Greenberg is well known for her high-contrast, heavily retouched portraits. This style is great for producing punchy fashion portraits. The lighting setup is pretty complex and you can only produce the final look with the help of some fairly intense post-processing.

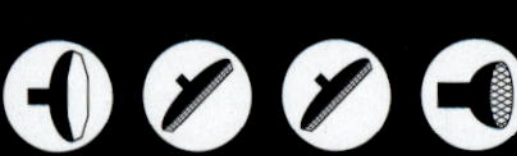

EFFORT INVOLVED

High

SUITABLE FOR

Close-up to three-quarter-length portraits

THE LOOK

Punchy, high-contrast fashion portrait
Natural-looking makeup with soft pink lips

EQUIPMENT

1× 47" octabox
2× 47" strip boxes with honeycomb grids
1× standard reflector with a honeycomb grid
1× 30"×40" silver reflector

162

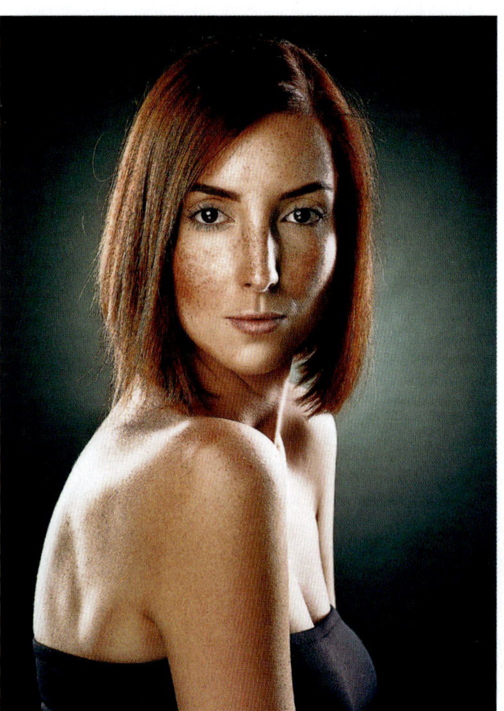

HOW IT WORKS

The diagonally placed octabox produces light and dark sides to the face and clear, downward-pointing shadows. This gives the image a well-defined look and adds sparkle to the eyes. Because the reflector only reduces the shadow on the left, the contrast in the right-hand portion of the image remains strong. The twin fill lights produce intense highlights in the subject's back, shoulders, and chest, and also adds glow to the hair, which clearly frames the face. The right-hand fill light produces additional highlights on the cheek and nose that interrupt the otherwise heavy shadows. The background vignette focuses attention on the subject's face.

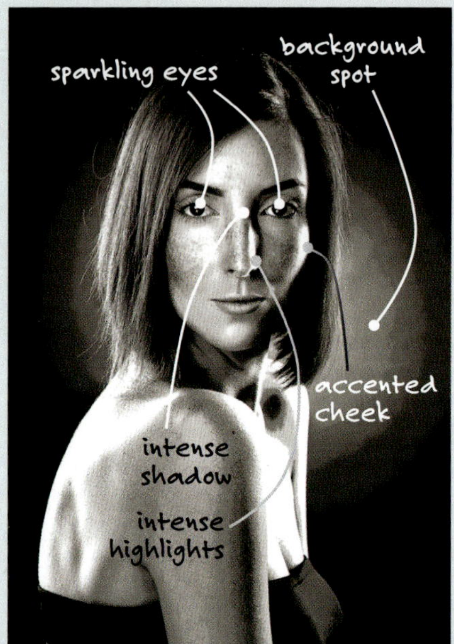

THE SETUP

1. Place the octabox **(1)** about 3 feet from your model in a raised position and at an angle of about 45 degrees. Set it up to produce a narrow neck shadow and shadows that point diagonally downward.

2. Now place one of the strip boxes **(2)** about 5 feet behind your model to the left and slightly above head height at an angle of about 45 degrees. Position it to produce clear highlights on your model's hair and shoulders.

3. Place the other strip box **(3)** about 5 feet to the right behind your model—again slightly above head height and at an angle of about 45 degrees. Position it to produce clear highlights on your model's cheek, nose, and chest.

4. Place the reflector **(4)** horizontally in front of your model at hip level and position it to slightly reduce the shadows on the left.

5. Place the gridded standard reflector **(5)** about 18 inches from the background. Position it slightly above head height so that it produces a pool of light at around neck height.

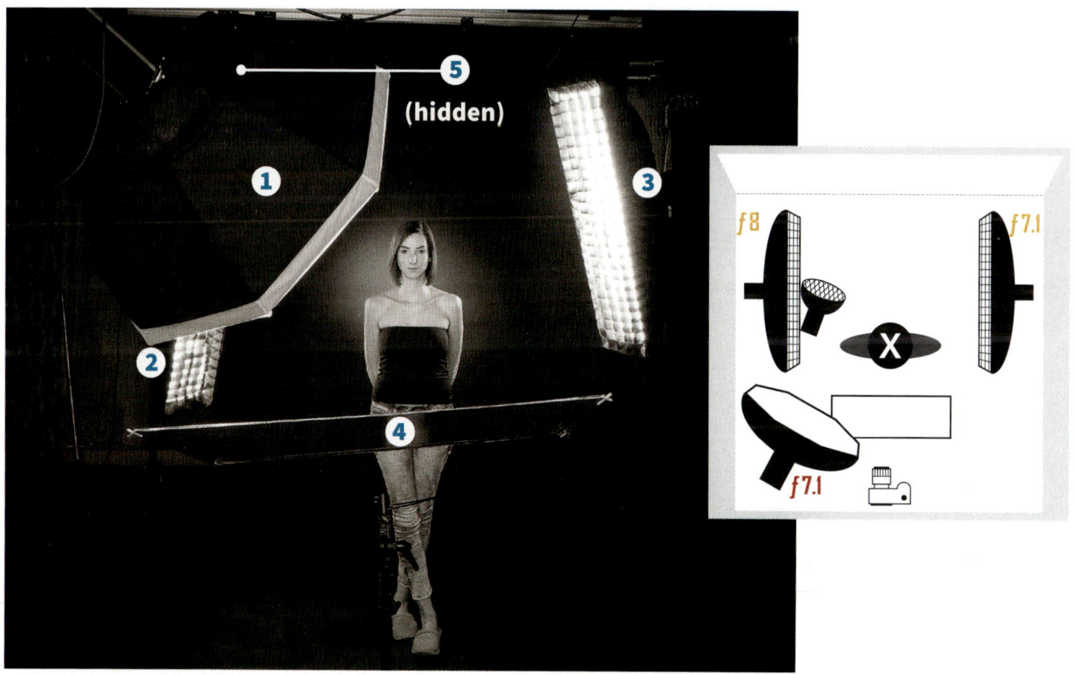

"Your model needs to take on a strong, tight pose to make this style work."

Games with
Colored Gels

I am going to use this setup to introduce you to the world of colored gels. Gels are not only great for toning the light that comes from your flashes and light shapers, you can use them as accessories in their own right too. This way, you can create intense colored details and play with matching or contrasting colors directly within the frame. The gel and the lipstick in this shot are a great example. As always, feel free to experiment and find your own ways to mix and match your colors.

EFFORT INVOLVED

Medium

SUITABLE FOR

Close-up to three-quarter-length portraits

THE LOOK

Unusual, modern portrait

Strong neck shadow

Strongly accented face

Smokey eyes, red lipstick

Tied-back hair

Dark outfit

EQUIPMENT

1 × standard reflector with a honeycomb grid

2 × 47" strip boxes with honeycomb grids

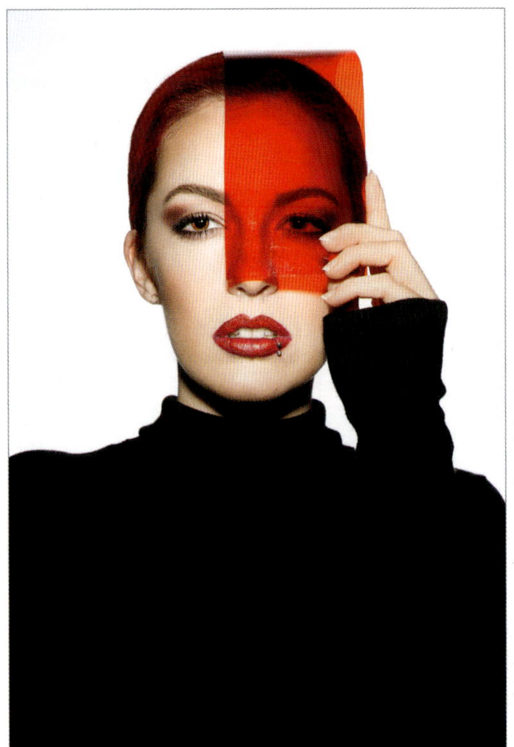

70mm | f8 | 1/125 sec. | ISO 100 | Model: Bianca

HOW IT WORKS

There is clear separation between the face and the bright white background, and the dark top adds a stark light/dark contrast that perfectly balances the top and bottom portions of the frame. The frontal lighting produces even light fall-off from front to back, and provides good overall definition. The hard light gives the eyes sparkle and underscores the red tones in the lips and the gel. The visible cheekbone is clearly accented and, along with the tied-back hair, emphasizes the shape of the subject's face. The subtle highlights in the eyes add a lively touch. This image is carried by clear shapes, strong separation, and, of course, the colored highlights.

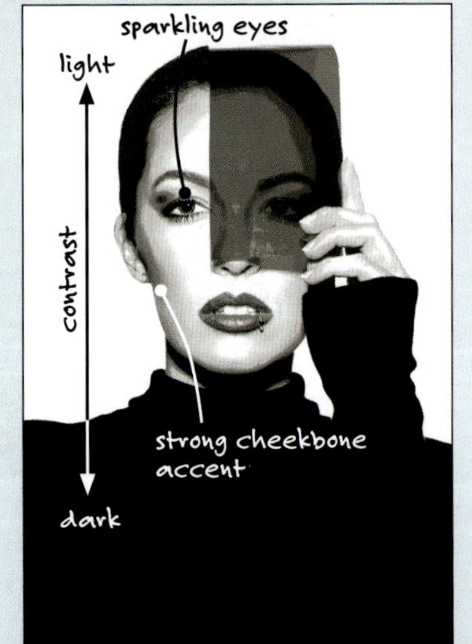

THE SETUP

1. Place the gridded standard reflector **(1)** about 3 feet in front of your model in a slightly raised position. As an alternative, you can use a gridded spot instead. Position the light to produce a distinct neck shadow but no shadow beneath your model's nose.

2. Now place the gridded strip boxes **(2)** about 3 feet to the right and left behind your model, and set them up to evenly light the background.

3. Position your model about 3 feet from the background.

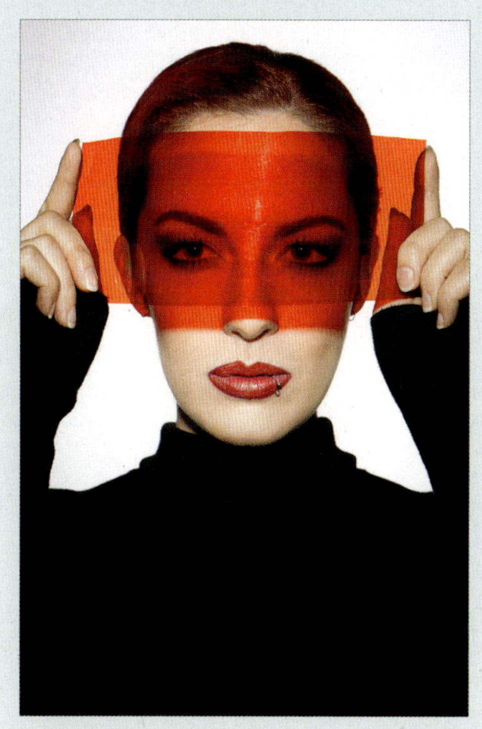

Variations

Depending on the size and shape of your gel, you can vary the way your model uses it during the shoot. Try using circular gels, or long strips, or perhaps a gel with holes cut in it.

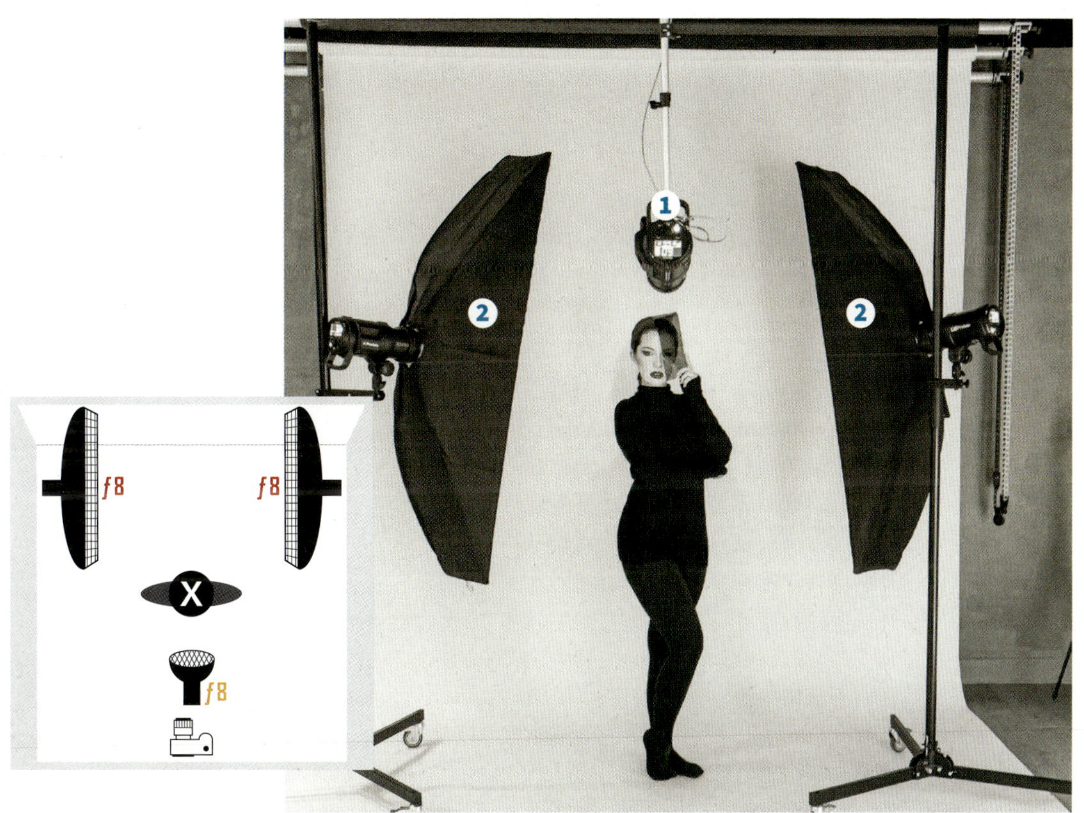

Adjusting White Balance for a Cooler Look

All you need to create a high-contrast fashion shot is a beauty dish for your main light and a standard reflector to light the background. If you then dial your white balance setting down to about 4100K, you can give your photos a cool look with minimum effort.

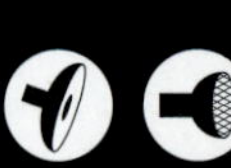
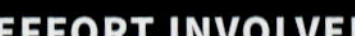

EFFORT INVOLVED

Low

SUITABLE FOR

Close-up to three-quarter-length portraits

THE LOOK

Deliberately cool-looking fashion portrait
Pink-toned natural-looking makeup
Casual outfit and loose hair

EQUIPMENT

1× beauty dish
1× standard reflector with a honeycomb grid

166

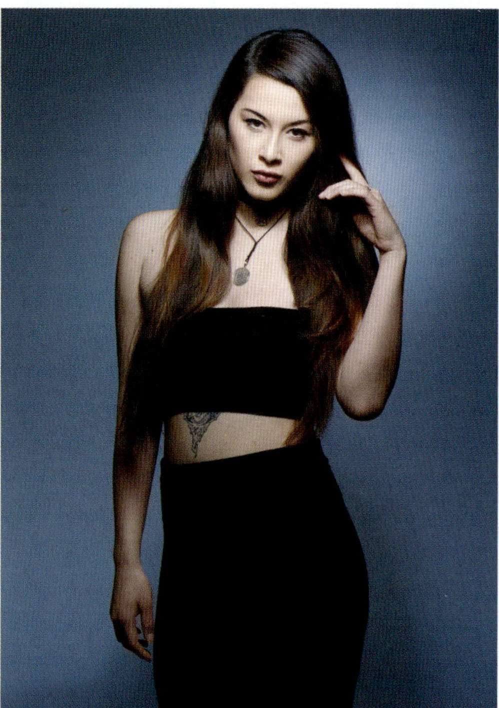

85mm | f13 | 1/160 sec. | ISO 100 | Model: Sonja

HOW IT WORKS

The high, frontal main light strongly accents the facial contours as well as the eyes and lips. The neck shadow is broad and stark. Reflections from the spill light hitting the white background are sufficient to keep the shadows from looking too dark and keep the main details clearly visible. The light fall-off toward the subject's lower body focuses attention on the face and upper body, and this effect is underscored by the background lighting. Overall, the subject is strongly separated from the background. The white balance setting of 4100K makes the colors appear cooler and the gray background appear blue in the final image. All in all, a cool-looking fashion portrait with plenty of contrast.

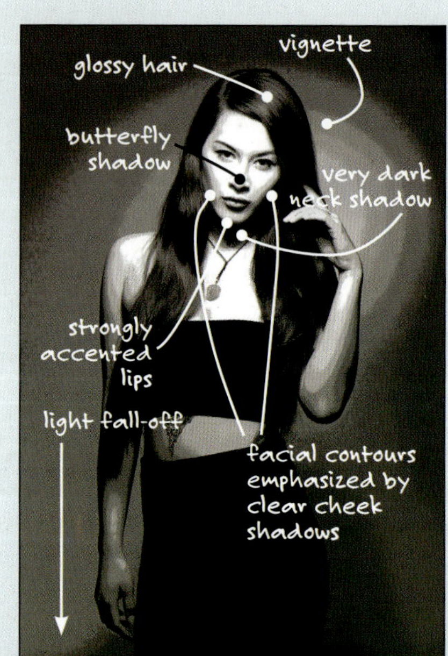

THE SETUP

1. Mount the beauty dish **(1)** on a ceiling rail or a boom stand and place it about 3 feet in front of your model pointing down at an angle of about 45 degrees. Set it up to produce a shadow right beneath your model's nose that ends halfway between her nose and her upper lip (the famous "butterfly" shadow).

2. Place the background reflector **(2)** about 3 feet to the right of your model at a height of about 6 feet. Position it so that its light focuses on a point behind your model's head at around neck level.

3. Position your model about 6 feet from the white background.

4. Set your camera's white balance value to 4100K. If there is no manual option for this setting, use the Fluorescent preset.

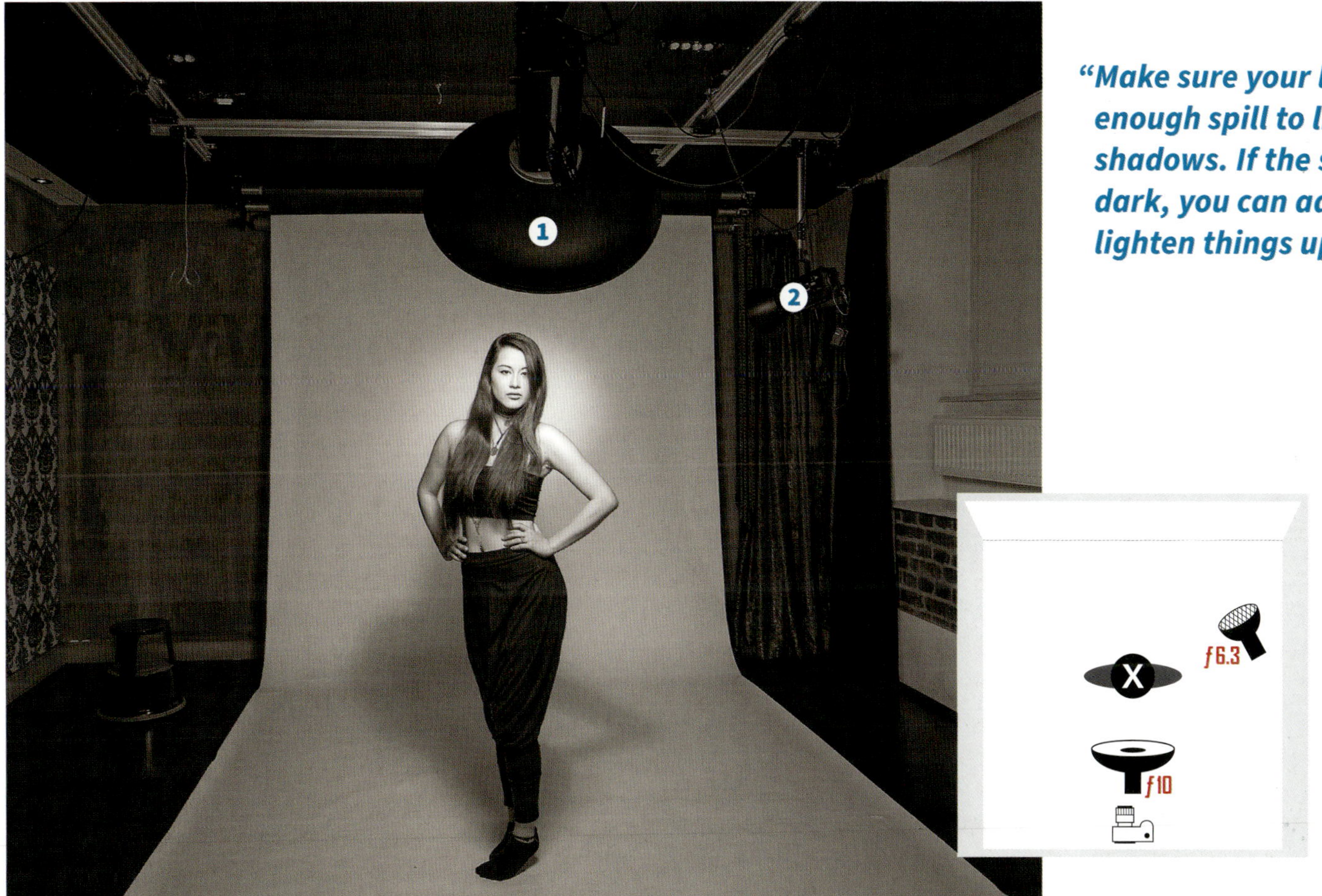

"Make sure your lights produce enough spill to lighten the shadows. If the shadows are too dark, you can add a reflector to lighten things up."

A Radiant Dress

This setup is a great choice for translucent dresses. The backlight produces an eye-catching rim light that frames the skirts and separates the subject beautifully from the background. In spite of its effectiveness, this setup consist of just two lights and is easy to build. It is suitable for magazine and advertising shoots, but also for lavish fashion shots.

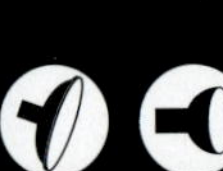
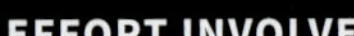

EFFORT INVOLVED

Low

SUITABLE FOR

Three-quarter length and full-length portraits

THE LOOK

Flamboyant fashion portrait

Clear shadows

Accented face

Brown-toned smokey eyes, subtle lip makeup

Emphasis on the clothes

EQUIPMENT

1 × beauty dish with a diffuser

1 × standard reflector

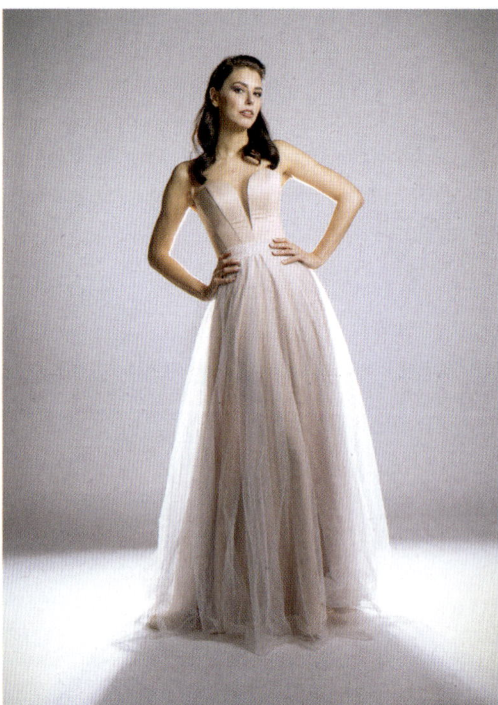

57mm | f5.6 | 1/125 sec. | ISO 100 | Model: Elisa

HOW IT WORKS

The slightly lateral main light produces plenty of definition, and its relatively close proximity to the subject keeps the facial details clear. The hard light form the beauty dish is softened by the diffuser and the raised position of the light produces a diagonal nose shadow. The neck shadow provides clear separation between head and body. The closely positioned light also produces obvious light fall-off toward the subject's torso and thus draws attention to the face, while the rim light on the dress provides an interesting visual counterpoint. The background vignette created by the beauty dish provides an effective frame for the subject.

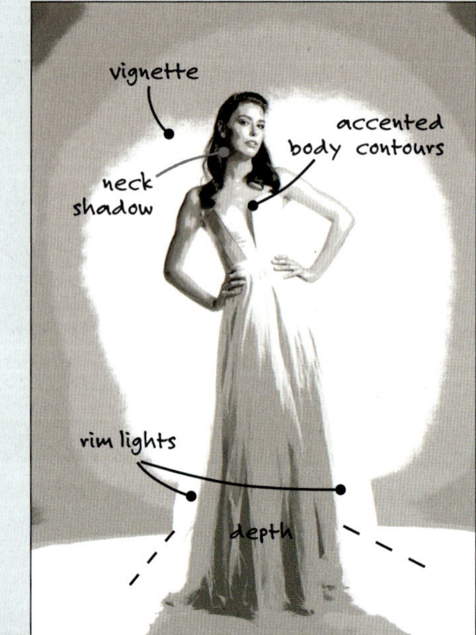

THE SETUP

1. Place the beauty dish **(1)** in a slightly raised position about 5 feet in front of your model to the right at an angle of about 30 degrees. Set it up to produce a clear neck shadow and a nose shadow that points diagonally toward your model's cheek. Don't forget to keep an eye on the background vignette produced by the beauty dish too.

2. Now place the standard reflector **(2)** about 18 inches behind your model at belly height and pointing in her direction. The flash and its stand need to be completely masked by the subject.

3. Position your model about 5 feet from the white background.

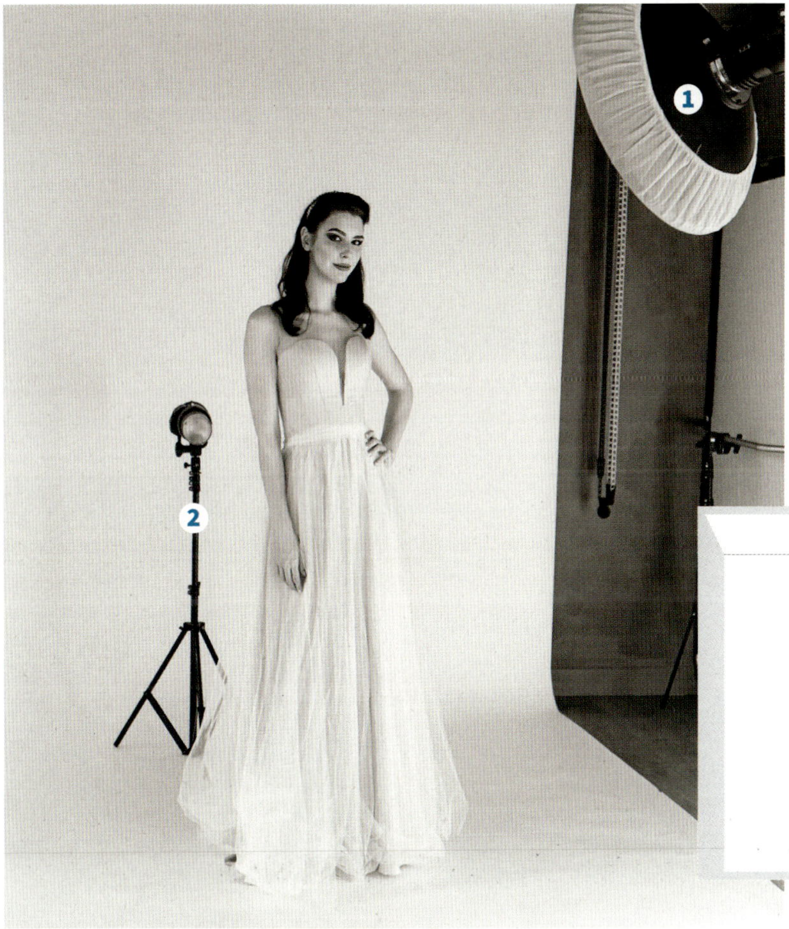

> *"Don't forget that you can adjust background brightness by altering the distances between the main light, the subject, and the backdrop."*

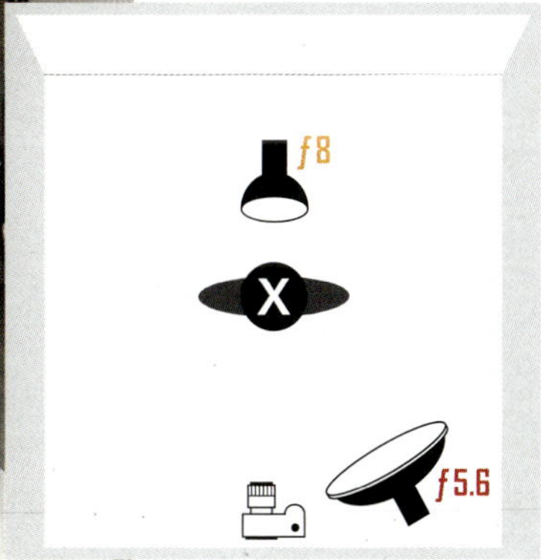

Variations

For a simpler variant of this shot, leave out the backlight (or just switch it off). The result is a classic beauty setup that uses just a single beauty dish.

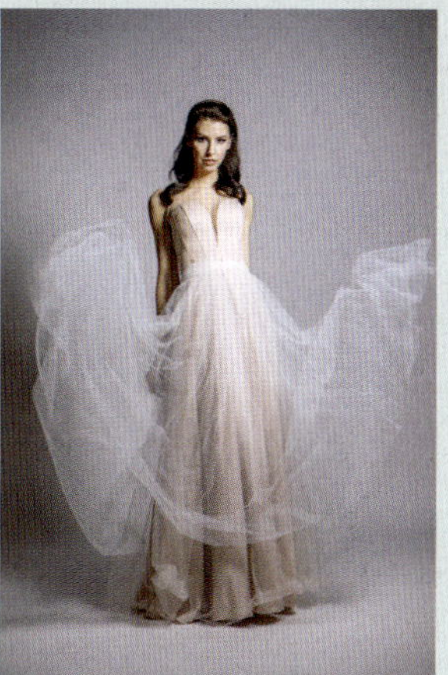

Variation using just a beauty dish but no backlight.

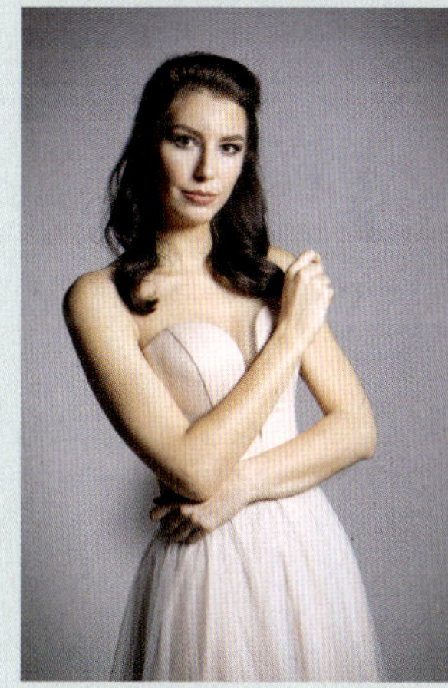

Closer crops are useful in magazine and catalog shoots, and are often essential for web presentations.

Highlights from Fill Lights

A dark-haired subject, dark clothing, and a dark background are the perfect ingredients for playing visual games with body contours. Twin strip-box fill lights provide the necessary accents.

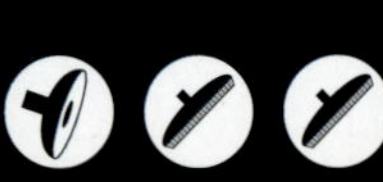

EFFORT INVOLVED

Medium

SUITABLE FOR

All kinds of portraits

THE LOOK

Fashion portrait with strong contours in front of a dark background

Pink-toned, natural-looking makeup and bold eyeliner

Dark outfit

EQUIPMENT

1× beauty dish

2× 47" strip boxes with honeycomb grids

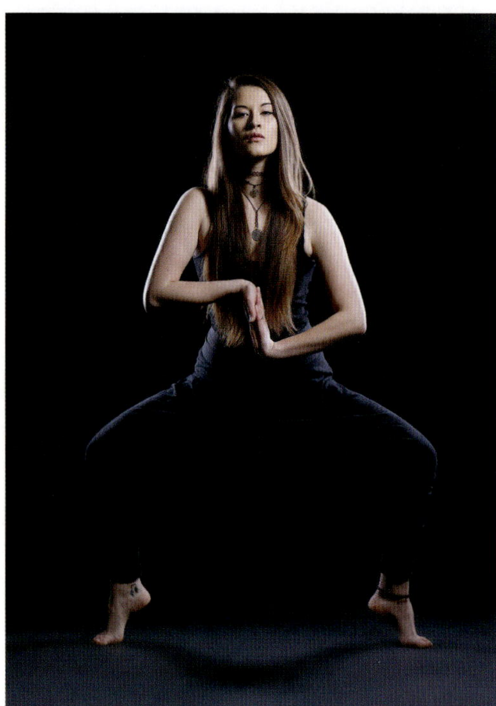

85mm | f5 | 1/160 sec. | ISO 100 | Model: Sonja

HOW IT WORKS

The diagonally placed beauty dish provides plenty of definition, and the diagonal nose shadow that results accents the eyes and the nose. The dark neck shadow and the shadows cast by the hair make the neck appear very slim and draw attention to the subject's face and yoga-posed arms. The head and arms form a triangle that gives the pose an impression of stability in spite of the tip-toe pose. The twin fill lights create visual contours all around the subject and provide good separation from the background. The spill light that lightens the black background to dark gray is an important element that helps to separate the black leggings from the black background.

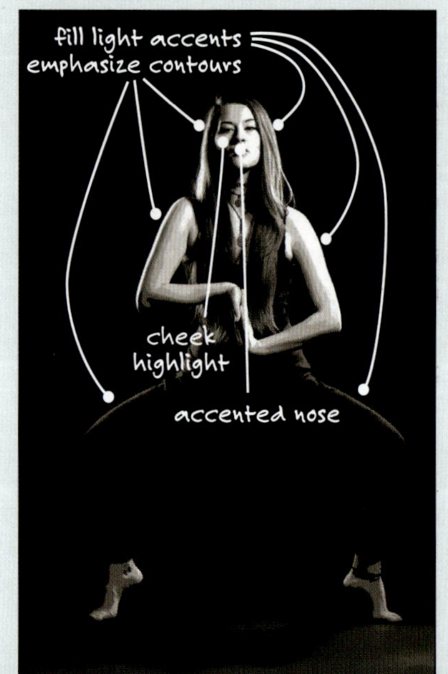

THE SETUP

1. Place the beauty dish **(1)** about 6 feet to front right of your model in a raised position and at an angle of about 45 degrees. Position it to produce a clear nose shadow that points diagonally downward.

2. Now place one of the strip boxes **(2)** about 3 feet to the left of your model at about head height and at an angle of about 45 degrees. Fine-tune its position to produce a rim light from head to toe.

3. Place the other strip box **(3)** on the right and mirror the position of the left-hand light to produce rim highlights from head to toe.

4. Position your model about 6 feet from the black background and make sure that sufficient spill light from the strip boxes reaches the background. If the background is too dark, move your model back. Conversely, if the background is too bright, move your model and your fill lights farther away from it.

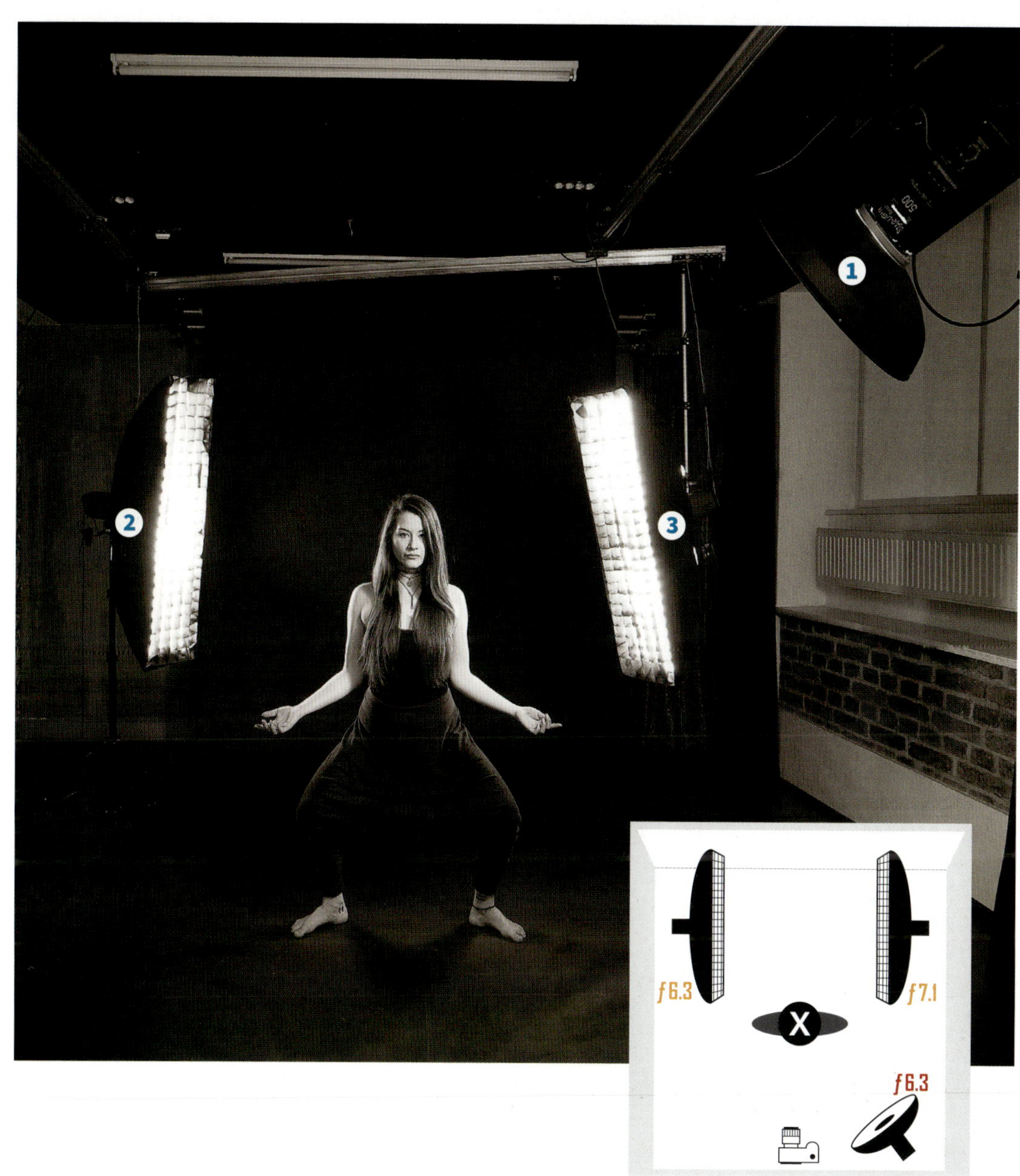

Colored Background

Colored backgrounds are ideal for balancing or contrasting colors. In this shot, the subject's dark hair and the dark dress provide a strong contrast with the yellow background and bring the dress to the fore. The multiple lights enable you to retain complete control over your shadows so you can fine-tune them to suit your particular model, the pose, and the clothes your are picturing. This is a highly variable setup that you can use in a wide variety of situations.

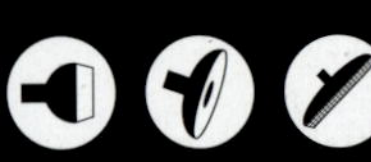

EFFORT INVOLVED

Medium

SUITABLE FOR

All kinds of portraits

THE LOOK

Strong portrait with strong shadows
Accented facial features
Brown-toned smokey eyes and nude lips

EQUIPMENT

1 × 24" softbox
1 × 20" beauty dish
1 × 47" strip box with a honeycomb grid

172

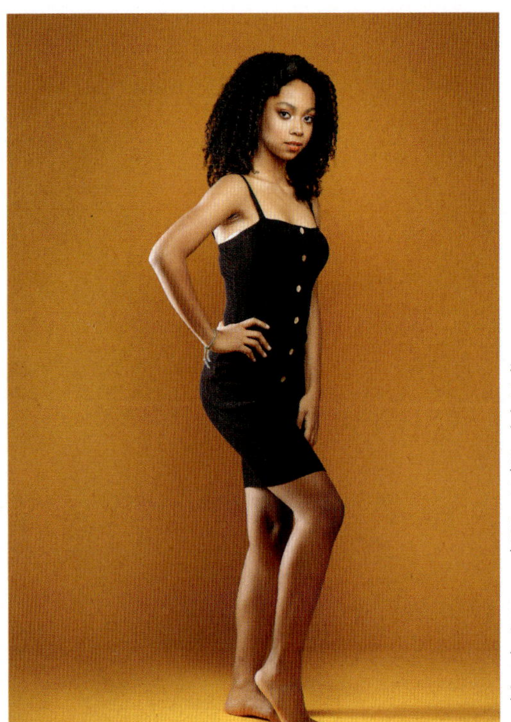

85mm | f6.3 | 1/125 sec. | ISO 100 | Model: Melissa

HOW IT WORKS

The diagonally placed, diffused beauty dish produces a soft look with natural-looking shadows, and the softbox lightens the shadows enough to provide a balanced overall feel. The neck shadow remains clear and separates the head visually from the body. The subtle light fall-off toward the bottom of the frame focuses attention on the upper body. The accent light on the left produces strong highlights on the visible arm and the legs, and helps to define the line of the back. The soft vignette in the background is interrupted by the slight shadow cast by the centrally placed softbox. The shadows in the curve of the background and those cast by the subject provide the necessary feeling of depth.

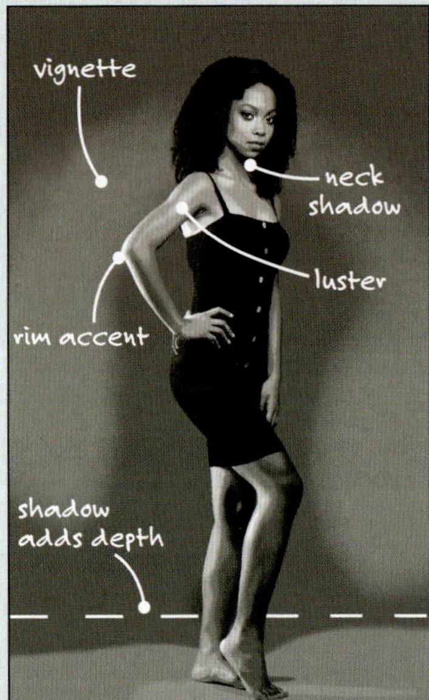

THE SETUP

1. Begin by placing the softbox **(1)** head-on about 5 feet from your model in a slightly raised position. Set it up to create a clear neck shadow.

2. Place the beauty dish fill light **(2)** about 5 feet to the front right of your model in a raised position and at an angle of about 45 degrees. Position it to slightly lighten the shadows on the right.

3. Now place the strip box **(3)** on the left behind your model with its center about 3 feet from her hips. Position it to produce a bright rim light on the left.

4. Your model needs to stand about 5 feet in front of the yellow background.

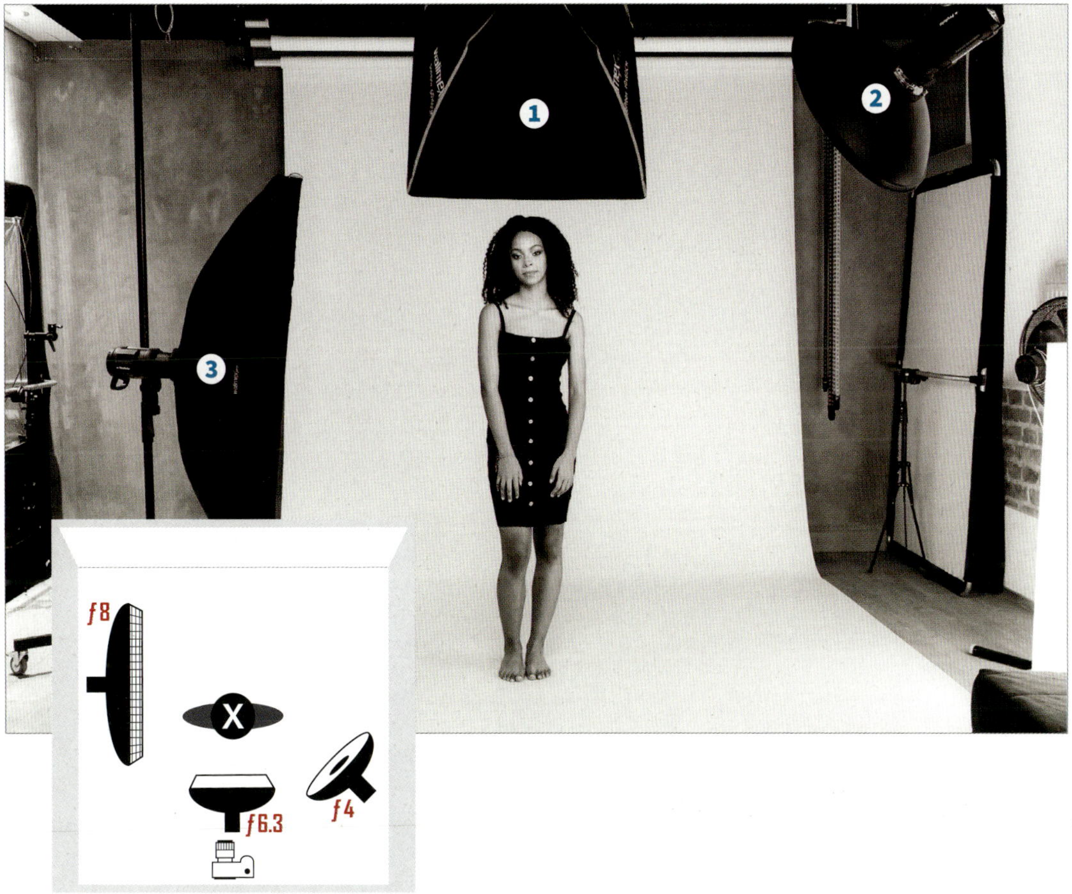

Variation

This setup works for close-up shots too.

173

Character
Portraits

Character Portraits

Character portraits employ skillful composition and lighting. Above all, the subject's expressions and gestures need to capture the essence of the subject in a single photo. This task is just as demanding as a fashion shoot but in a completely different way. You need to build up a rapport with the person you are photographing, either before the shoot or by creating a relaxing atmosphere that brings out the best in your subject while you work. For this kind of work, it is essential to make sure you have enough time to prepare and carry out your planned shoot.

Capturing Personality

A character portrait should show the subject as they are. And that is the first major hurdle—how can a photographer find out who a person really is? People behave differently in different situations, and are often self-conscious or nervous if they have no experience in front of a camera. In other words, they don't show their true selves. Maybe we should approach things this way: a character portrait aims to provide a window to a person's soul but is actually more likely to show how that person prefers to see themselves—or how you see them in your role as a photographer. What I am trying to say is that character portraits are often subjective, and the better you know your subject, the easier it will be to tease out and capture their most important personal attributes.

Humphrey Bogart in *Casablanca* summed up the situation when he said: "Here's looking at you, kid." A person's eyes often say more about them than their body language, which often appears stiff and artificial. If the eyes don't shine, the image looks contrived and the smile forced. This is where real emotions come into play. If you can get your subject to laugh, their whole face lights up. In contrast, if you are looking to capture a serious, thoughtful expression, you need to get your subject into a suitable mood. Try telling a story to distract your subject and get their mind to wander.

Preparation: Styling, Background, and Lights

Character portraits are all about the person being photographed, so clothing, lights, and composition serve to underscore their personality, not distract from it. To retain focus on the subject's face, character portraits are often head-and-shoulders or close-up shots.

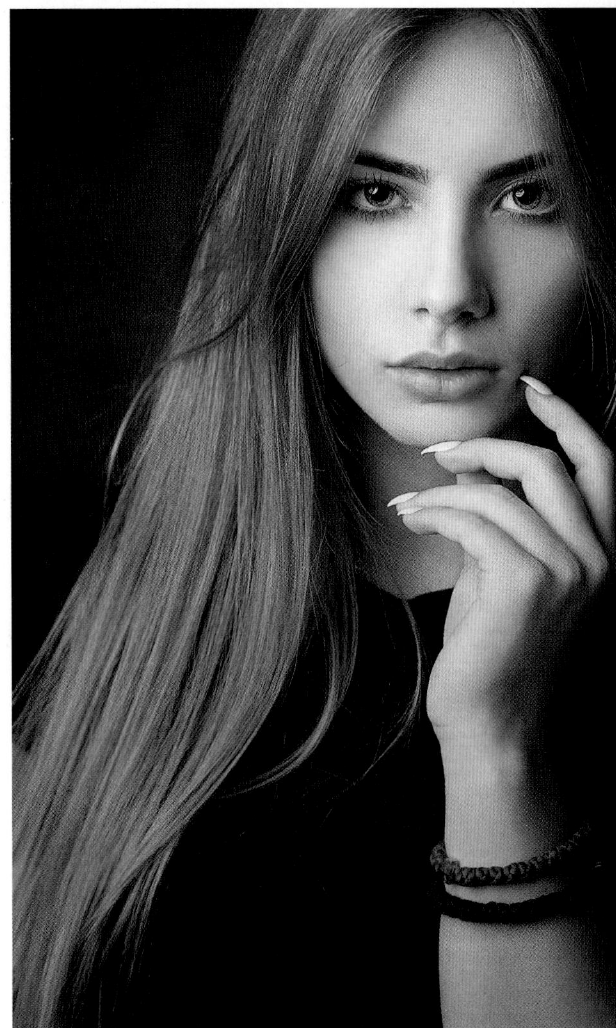

A black-and-white portrait captured using a large octabox, a reflector, and a background light.

85mm | f6.3 | 1/160 sec. | ISO 100 | Model: Larissa

For this kind of shot, your subject should bring their own clothes that they feel comfortable in. Your subject mustn't feel in any way "disguised." Hair and makeup should be in keeping with your subject's regular, every-day style, so you will rarely need a dedicated stylist for this kind of shoot.

You can use the mood created by your lights and the background to adjust the overall look of an image to suit its subject. For example, this could be soft light in front of a bright background for a portrait of a soft-spoken or jolly person, or high-contrast light in front of a dark background for a portrait of a particularly striking face, or to underscore a subject's serious nature. You can decide on the color of your background and the lighting setup on the fly once you have met your subject and checked out what they are wearing.

The example on the right is less of a character por-trait and more of a "characteristic" portrait. I wanted the image to show the muscular subject's passion for dance alongside his personality. A dark background and the hard light from a beauty dish emphasize the discipline and rigor, but also the self-confidence that the subject exudes.

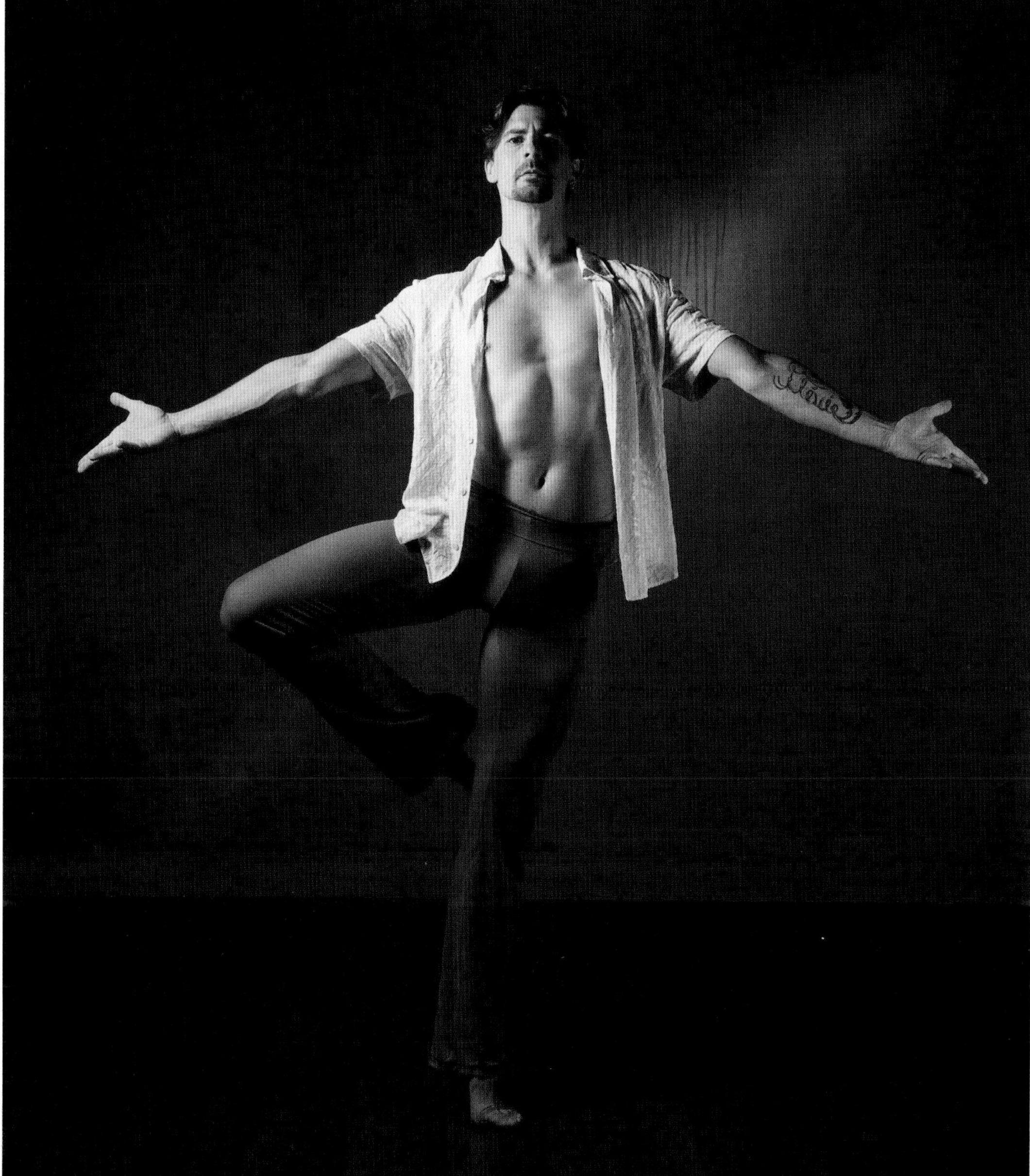

Portrait of a dancer captured using a beauty dish and a stan-dard reflector with barndoors in the background.

55mm | f11 | 1/160 sec. | ISO 100 | Model: Vladimir

Classic Character Portrait

This setup produces a classic "up close and personal" look. I deliberately used a shorter lens to enable me to get physically closer to the subject. The classic one-light beauty dish setup produces a striking character portrait with minimum effort.

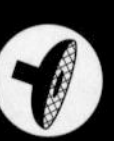

EFFORT INVOLVED

Low

SUITABLE FOR

Close-up and head-and-shoulders portraits

THE LOOK

Striking portrait using high-contrast lighting in front of a dark background

Natural-looking makeup and a dark shirt

EQUIPMENT

1× beauty dish with a honeycomb grid

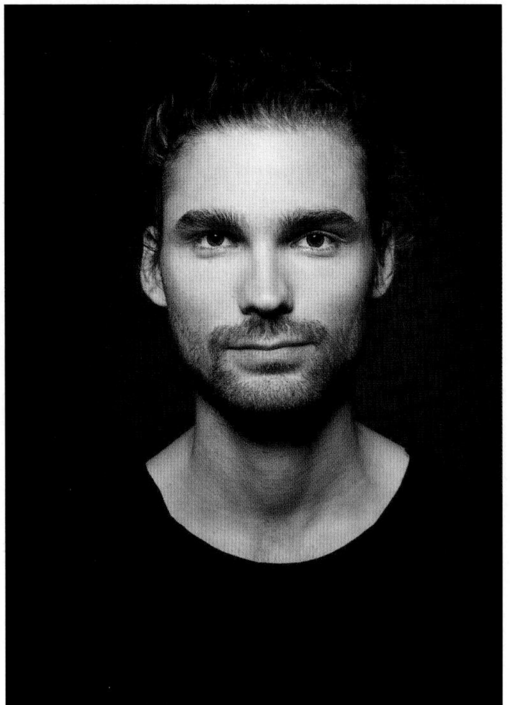

50mm | f8 | 1/160 sec. | ISO 100 | Model: Andreas

HOW IT WORKS

The slightly raised, frontal position of the beauty dish produces clear lighting in the subject's face and light fall-off toward the bottom of the frame. The facial contours are gently accented, while the cheekbones and jawline are clearly defined. The shadows beneath the eyebrows add contrast to the eyes. Along with the strong neck shadow, the hair and the dark background provide a frame for the face. The dark shirt blends almost completely into the background, which helps to draw the viewer's attention to the face. The subject's head contrasts nicely with the central, dark-gray portion of the background and the vignette effect adds depth. The three-dimensional feel is enhanced by the high, frontal lighting and the short lens.

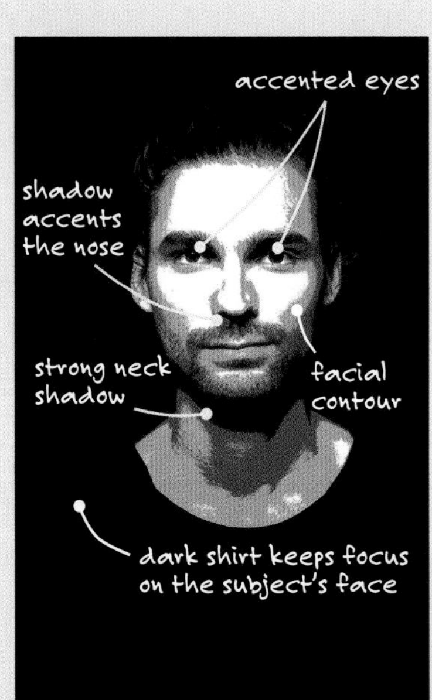

THE SETUP

1. Mount the beauty dish **(1)** on a ceiling rail or a boom stand about 3 feet in front of your subject and pointing down at an angle of about 30 degrees. Position it to form a slight shadow under your subject's nose and to brighten the background directly behind him.

2. Position your model about 3 feet from the black background.

3. Take care with the background lighting. You subject's own shadow should remain invisible behind him and the light should produce a clear vignette effect. You can vary both these effects by altering the distances between your subject and the background and/or your model and the light source.

Less Is More

To help the viewer concentrate on the essentials, you should always leave out any unnecessary details in a shot like this. Character portraits are all about the subject's face, not their clothes, their jewelry, or other accessories.

Such portraits are often more effective if you develop them in black and white. A monochrome image helps the viewer to concentrate on the subject's facial expression, whereas colors can be distracting. However, this isn't a hard-and-fast rule, especially if you want to use color contrast as a compositional tool or to accent a personal attribute such as a subject's red hair.

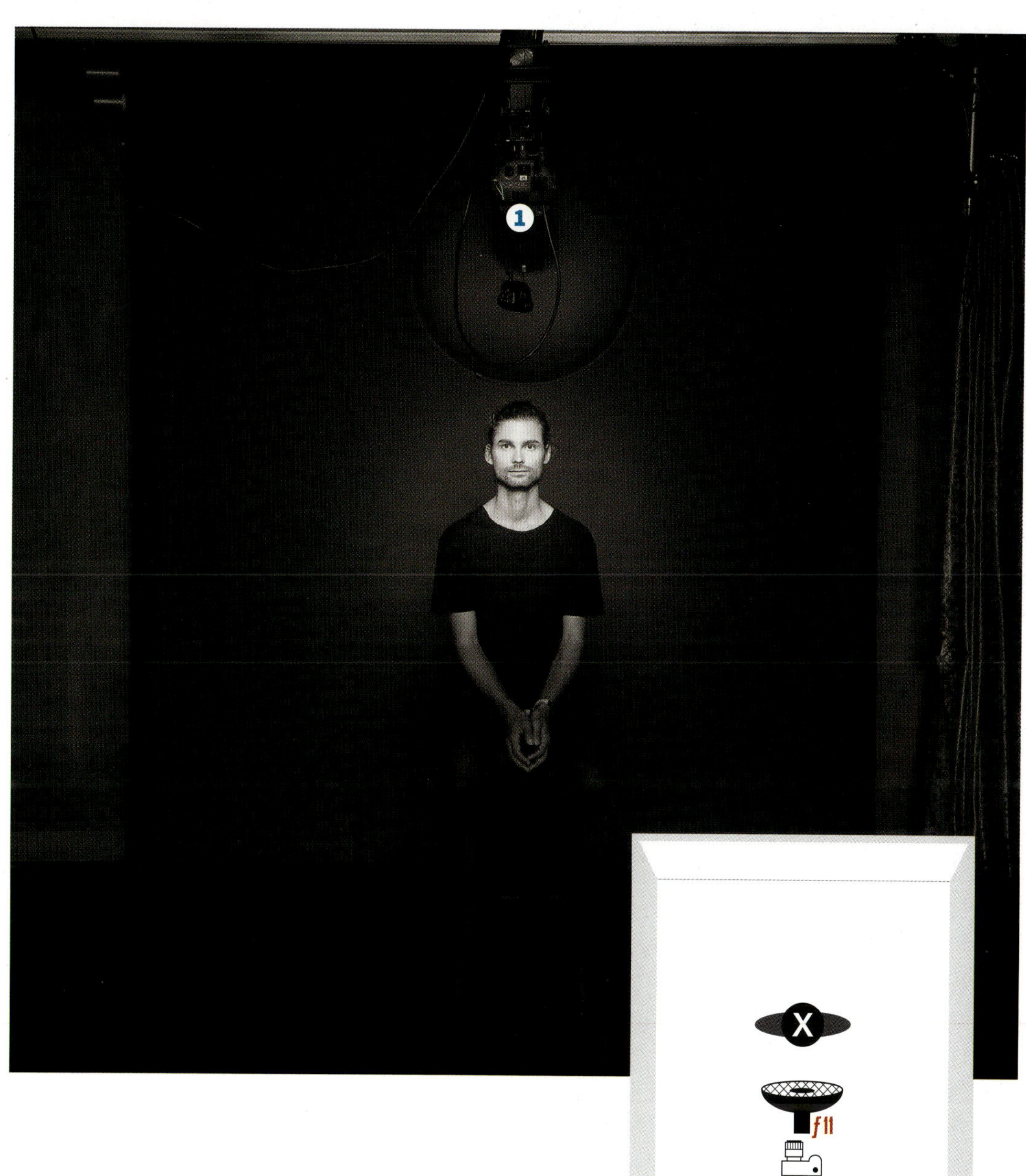

Distinctive Character Portrait

In bygone times, painters often worked with the only available source of light, namely the light that came in through the window. A single, lateral light source is still used today to produce a classic portrait look. This setup accents one side of the face while leaving the other almost completely in shadow. The strong contrast provided by this "split" effect is highly masculine and is thus often used for portraits of men. Adding a soft light shaper helps to reduce the effect of any imperfections in the subject's skin.

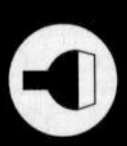

EFFORT INVOLVED

Low

SUITABLE FOR

Close-up to three-quarter-length portraits

THE LOOK

Classic male portrait style
Distinctive shadows
Strong facial accents

EQUIPMENT

1 × 24" softbox
1 × 43" circular silver reflector

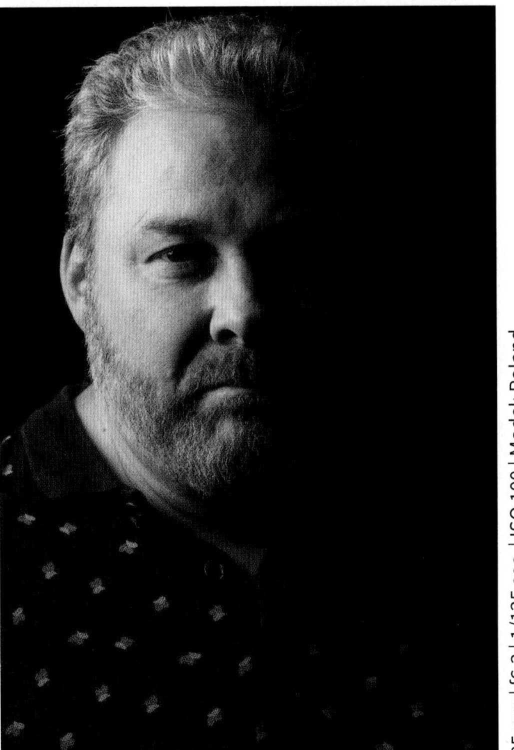

85mm | f6.3 | 1/125 sec. | ISO 100 | Model: Roland

HOW IT WORKS

In this shot, the subject's face is clearly divided into light and dark sides. The raised, lateral position of the softbox produces soft but distinctive shadows that give the image plenty of depth. The light side of the face is accented strongly and the contours are well defined. The dark background on the left is an important element that contrasts with the brightly lit areas and balances the overall composition. The left-hand side of the face is nicely separated from the background, while the right-hand side blends almost completely into the background. The details on the right are only vaguely discernible.

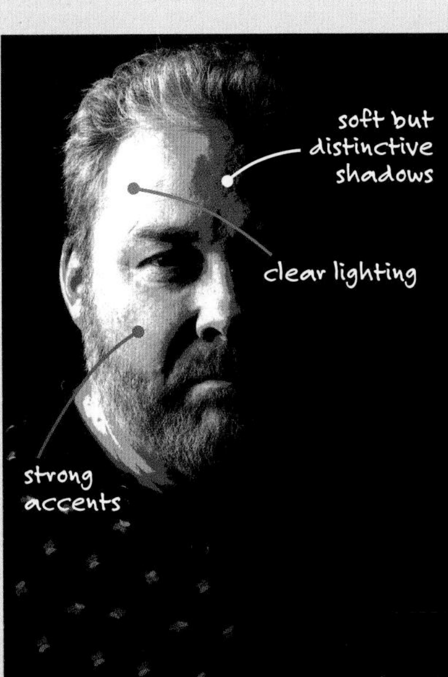

THE SETUP

1. Begin by positioning your model about 5 feet in front of the black background.

2. Place the softbox **(1)** about 3 feet to the left of your model in a slightly raised position. Your subject should pose before you fine-tune the lighting, and needs to stay in position while you make any adjustments. Now move the light as far forward as you can so that the side of your subject's face that faces the light is well lit while no light reaches the cheek on the shadow side.

3. Place the reflector **(2)** about 5 feet to the right of your subject and position it to slightly lighten the shadows on the dark side of his face.

"The slight lightening of the shadows on the dark side ensures that the viewer can just discern the shape of your subject's head and separate it visually from the background."

Gaining Your Subject's Trust

It is essential that the subject of a photo shoot feels comfortable in front of the camera. For character portrait shoots, the general mood in the studio and the chemistry between you and your subject are extremely important. To gain a subject's trust, you need to take time to get to know them and keep talking while you shoot. A person will only reveal their true character in a relaxed and friendly atmosphere.

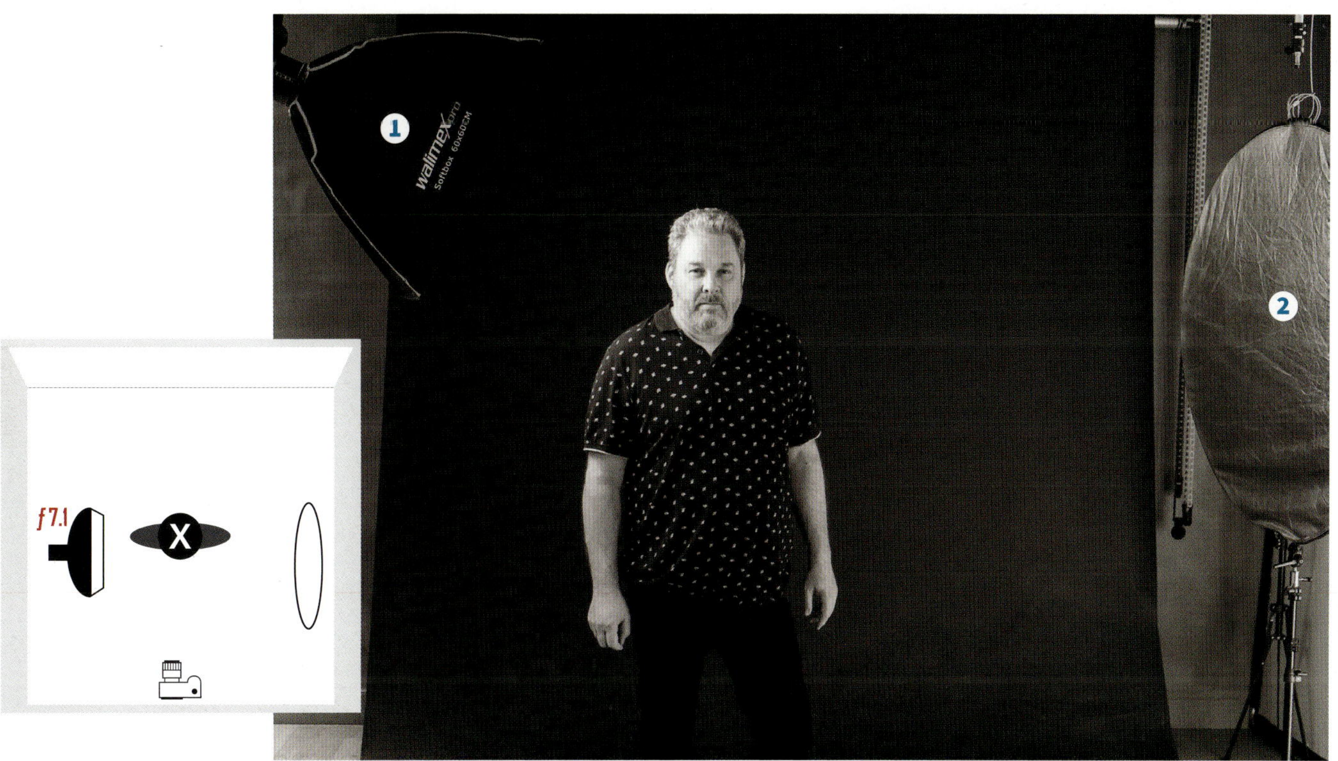

Adding Depth Using Accent Lights

Whether you want to accent tied-back hair, loose hair, or facial contours, accent lights are the key to creating a real eye-catcher. In this shot, I wanted to accent the subject's hair, which is an imporant part of his personality.

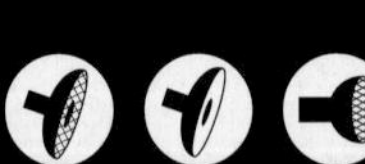

EFFORT INVOLVED

Medium

SUITABLE FOR

Close-up and head-and-shoulders portraits

THE LOOK

Accent lights emphasize contours and add depth
Natural-looking makeup and a dark shirt

EQUIPMENT

1× beauty dish with a honeycomb grid
1× beauty dish
1× standard reflector with a honeycomb grid

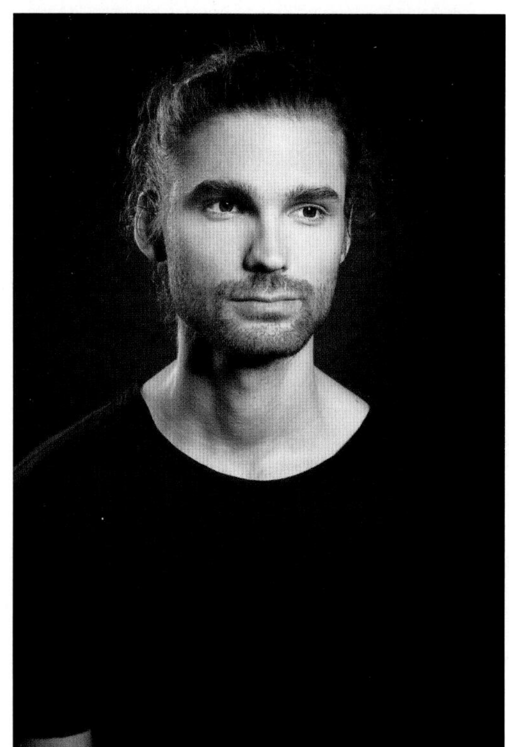

HOW IT WORKS

The raised diagonal position of the main light gives the image depth and brings the subject's facial contours to the fore. The dark shadow under the right eyebrow compensates for the fact that the right eye is slightly higher than the left eye, and the slight nose shadow gives the nose a subtle accent. The accent light emphasizes the facial contours and the tied-back hair. The slight hair gloss and the few loose hairs give the image a natural look. The neck shadow gives definition to the chin and the jawline. The subdued vignette in the background with its center behind the head focuses attention on the face. The way the subject looks past the camera underscores the thoughtful nature of the pose.

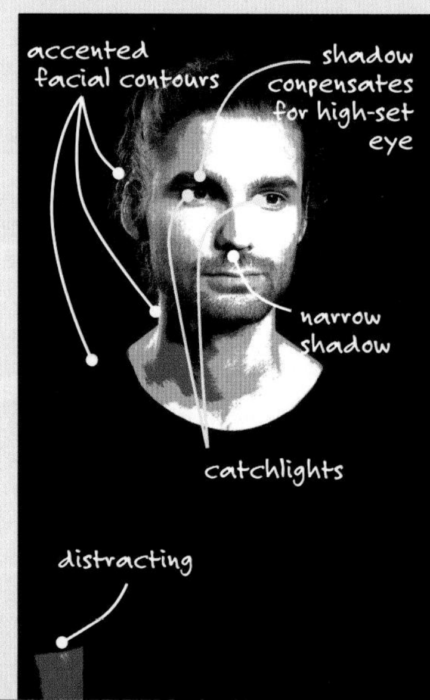

THE SETUP

1. Place the gridded beauty dish **(1)** about 5 feet to the right of your model in a slightly raised position and at an angle of about 45 degrees. Position it so that the nose shadow points diagonally downward but doesn't reach your subject's upper lip. Light fall-off toward the bottom of the frame should set in at about chest height.

2. Now place the accent beauty dish **(2)** about 3 feet to the left behind your subject at an angle of about 30 degrees. Position it so that its center is just above head height. This light should produce accents on your subject's hair, cheek, neck, and shoulder.

3. Mount the gridded background spot **(3)** on a ceiling rail or a boom stand slightly behind your subject at a height of about 8 feet. Position it to focus at around nose level and to create a pool of light that reaches as far as your subject's forehead.

4. Position your subject about 5 feet from the black background.

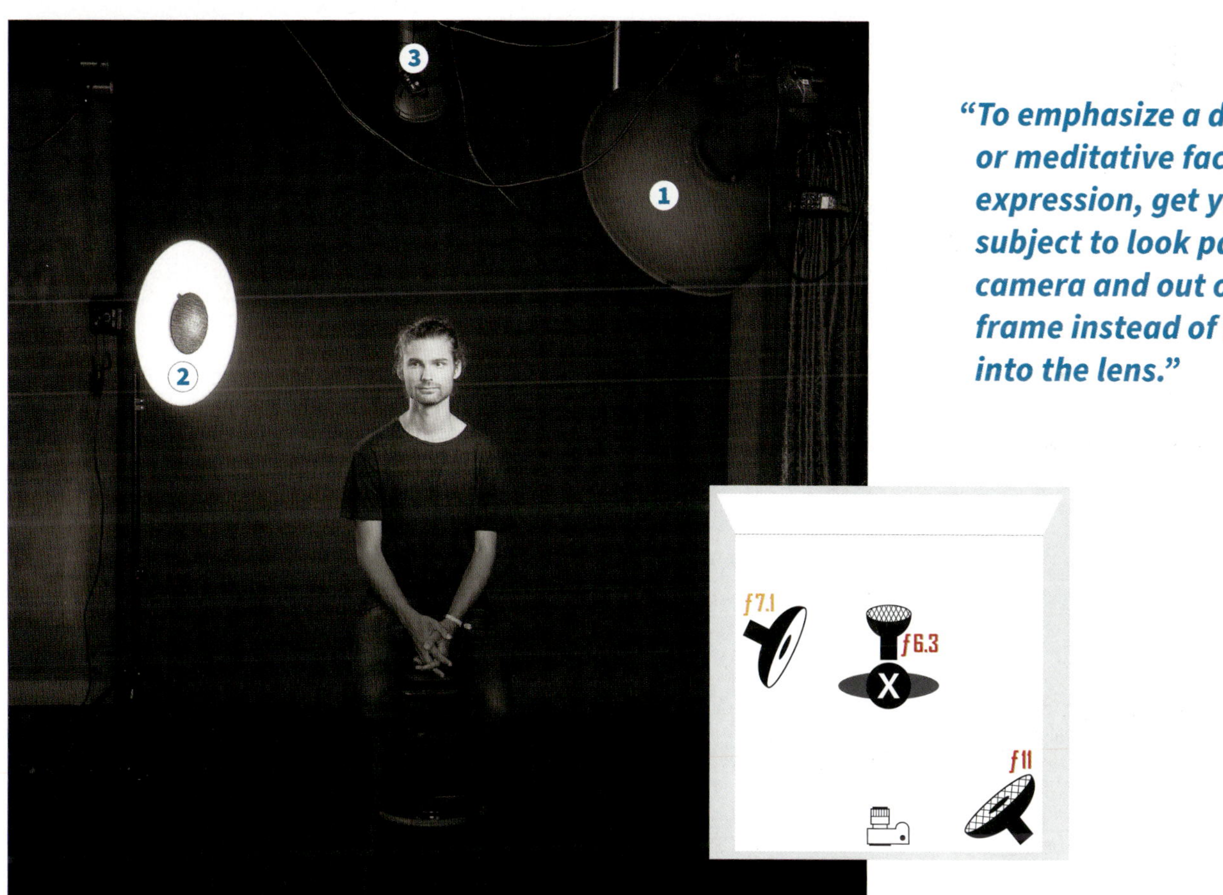

> *"To emphasize a dreamy or meditative facial expression, get your subject to look past the camera and out of the frame instead of directly into the lens."*

Cool Character Portrait

This setup is designed to produce a cool and casual feel. The twin accent lights produce a halo effect and intense shadows around the eyes that give the subject's expression a cooler look. The result is a highly three-dimensional image that portrays an uncompromising face.

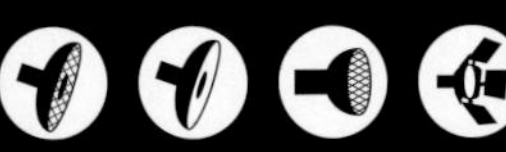

EFFORT INVOLVED

High

SUITABLE FOR

Close-up and head-and-shoulders portraits

THE LOOK

High-contrast portrait with interesting accents and great depth

Natural-looking makeup and a dark shirt

EQUIPMENT

1× beauty dish with a honeycomb grid

1× beauty dish

1× standard reflector with a honeycomb grid

1× standard reflector with barndoors

1× 30" × 40" silver reflector

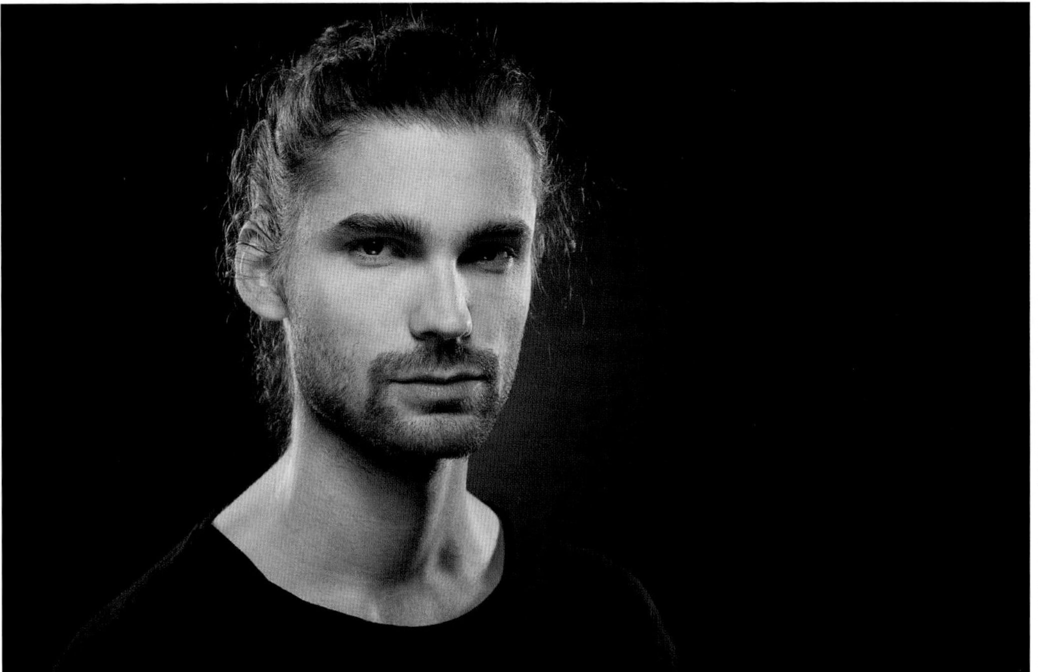

50mm | f8 | 1/160 sec. | ISO 100 | Model: Andreas

HOW IT WORKS

The beauty dish produces intense light with fall-off toward the upper body, and its raised position creates a distinct neck shadow that visually separates the head from the body. The shadows around the eyelids, nose, and upper lip provide good definition in the face. The lateral accent lights produce highlights that help to define the subject against the background. The additional background flash produces a slight gradient that focuses attention on the face. The rim light on the shoulder ensures that the subject's body contours don't completely blend in with the background.

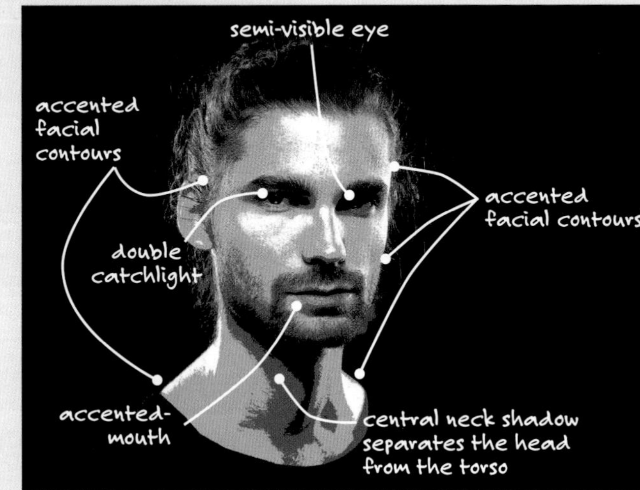

THE SETUP

1. Mount the beauty dish **(1)** on a ceiling rail or a boom stand and place it centrally about 3 feet from your subject and pointing downward at an angle of about 45 degrees. Position it to form a nose shadow that ends halfway between the tip of your subject's nose and his upper lip.

2. Mount the reflector **(2)** on a low stand directly in front of your subject at chest height and position it to slightly lighten the neck and nose shadows.

3. Now place the beauty dish **(3)** about 3 feet to the left at around head height and at an angle of about 30 degrees. Set it up to produce a rim accent that reaches from your subject's head to his shoulder.

4. Place the standard reflector with the barndoors **(4)** about 3 feet to the right of your subject at head height and at an angle of about 30 degrees. Set it up to produce a rim accent that reaches from your subject's head to his shoulder.

5. Mount the background reflector **(5)** directly above your subject on a ceiling rail or a boom stand at a height of about 8 feet. Position it to project a pool of light behind your subject's head with its center at nose level.

6. Position your subject about 6 feet from the black background.

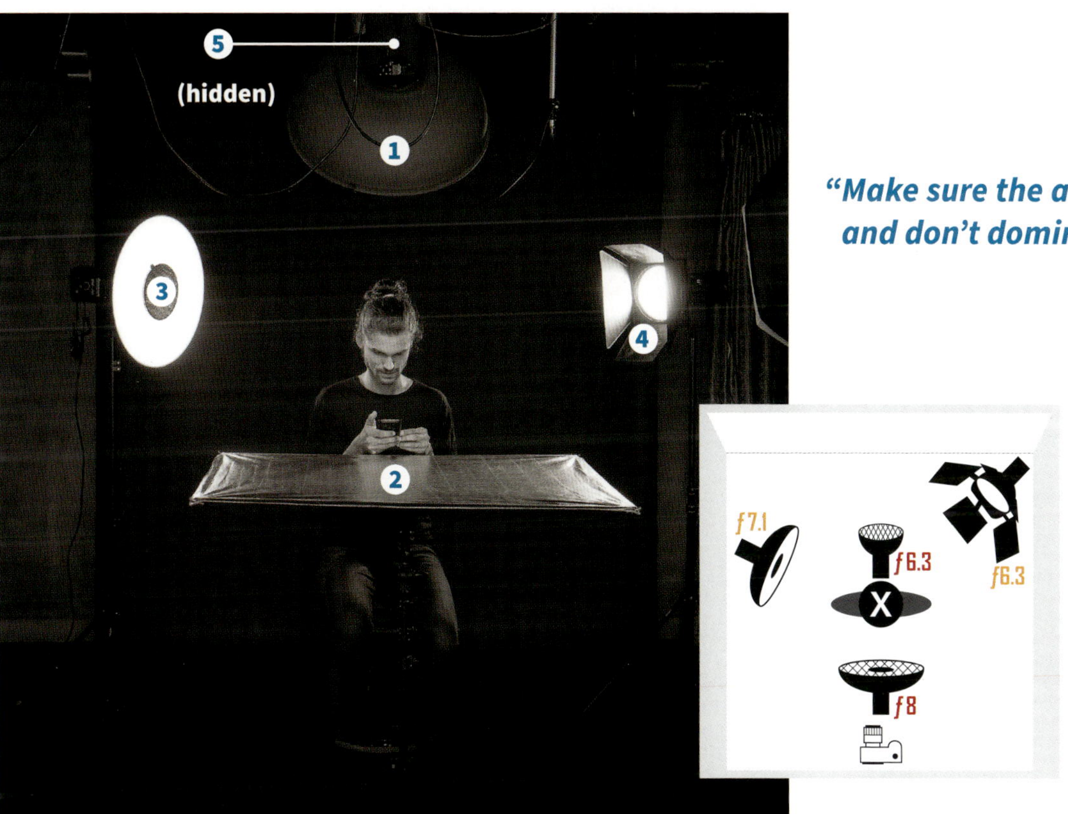

"Make sure the accent lights only provide accents and don't dominate the scene."

How Accent Lights Work

If you want to produce subtle accents, place the accent flash heads behind your subject to produce narrow rim lights, and make sure you select a suitable flash output setting. The accents shouldn't be the first thing to attract the viewer's attention.

Composing with Empty Space

A portrait subject doesn't always have to be in the center of the frame. Try shooting a profile portrait and leaving some space in the direction of your subject's gaze. This simple setup gives you plenty of options for teasing the best out of your subject. The primary focus of this shot is on the subject's face and the high-contrast presentation of the facial expression. This is a great setup for capturing a few quick shots between other jobs.

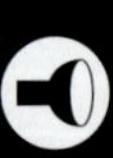

EFFORT INVOLVED

Low

SUITABLE FOR

Close-up to three-quarter-length portraits

THE LOOK

High-contrast portrait
Strong shadows
Accented face
Brown-toned smokey eyes and nude lips

EQUIPMENT

1 × standard reflector

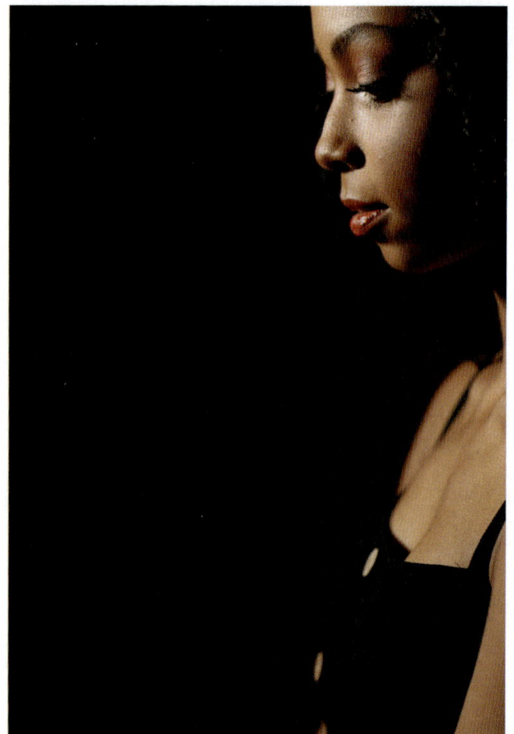

85mm | f3.5 | 1/125 sec. | ISO 100 | Model: Melissa

HOW IT WORKS

The lateral, slightly raised light source and the profile pose produce an image with a heavily accented facial expression. The strong shadows create a nice feeling of depth. The standard reflector provides hard light and strong shadows that leave any skin blemishes in full view. The subject is clearly separated from the very dark background and the facial contours are clearly defined without becoming obtrusive. The bright highlights on the bridge of the nose, the forehead, the cheeks, and the lower lip give the image an air of intimacy, and the tight crop contributes to this effect.

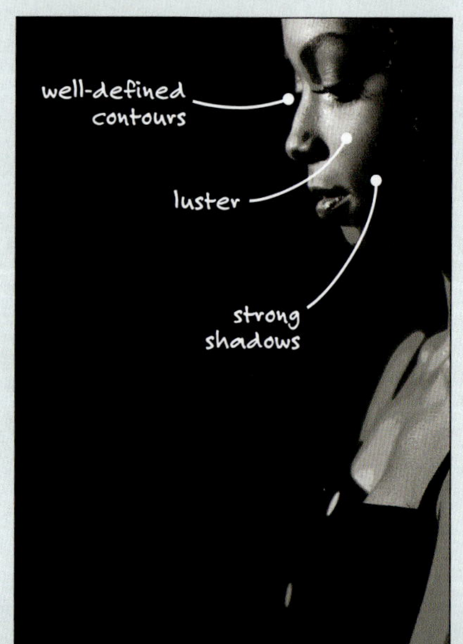

THE SETUP

1. Place the standard reflector **(1)** about 3 feet to the left of your subject around head height. Position it to produce a clear neck shadow and so that the bridge of her nose is just illuminated.

2. Position your subject about 5 feet from the yellow background.

"Make sure that enough spill light reaches the background to prevent it from appearing completely black. This is especially important when your subject is wearing dark clothes."

Lines Within the Frame

You can use clear visual lines within the frame to aid composition. Such lines can be real, such as the edges of buildings, a street, or perspective lines; or they can be imaginary, such as the direction of your subject's gaze or a line that connects to a point that lies outside the frame. Use lines to steer your viewer's gaze toward the subject, and always make sure that you leave plenty of space when your subject looks toward the edge of the frame.

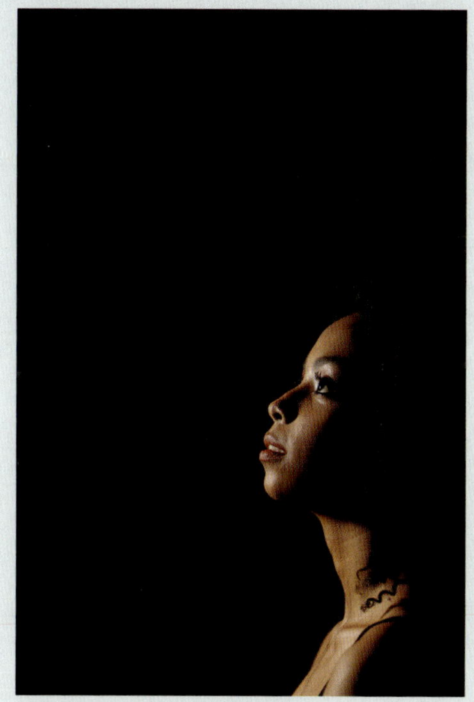

Getting your subject to look up is another way to use empty space as part of your composition.

Happy Character Portrait

Character portraits don't have to be composed in dark tones and don't always portray people with serious expressions. If you set up a colored background and strike up a cheerful mood in the studio, upbeat portraits will result virtually automatically. All you need are two flash heads and a reflector, and the fun can start! In this shot, the yellow background adds to the feel-good atmosphere.

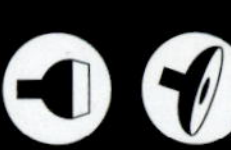
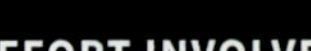

EFFORT INVOLVED

Medium

SUITABLE FOR

Close-up to three-quarter-length portraits

THE LOOK

Classic high-key portrait

Soft shadows

Accented face

Brown-toned smokey eyes and nude lips

Hair tied back with a black ribbon

EQUIPMENT

1 × 24" softbox

1 × 20" beauty dish

1 × 43" circular silver reflector

188

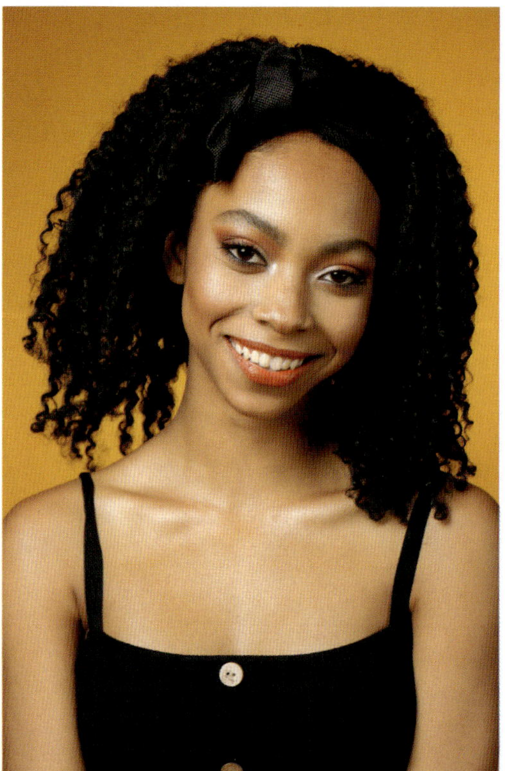

85mm | f6.3 | 1/125 sec. | ISO 100 | Model: Melissa

HOW IT WORKS

The slightly overhead, diagonal position of the softbox produces soft neck and cheek shadows. The line of the subject's cheek on the shadow side is well defined. The shadow to the side of the nose accents the line between the nose and the eyebrow. The light side of the face is brightly but softly lit, and thus contributes to the gentle, airy feel of the image, and the shadows lightened by the reflector do the same. The beauty dish keeps the background light subdued and keeps the viewer's attention focused on the subject's face.

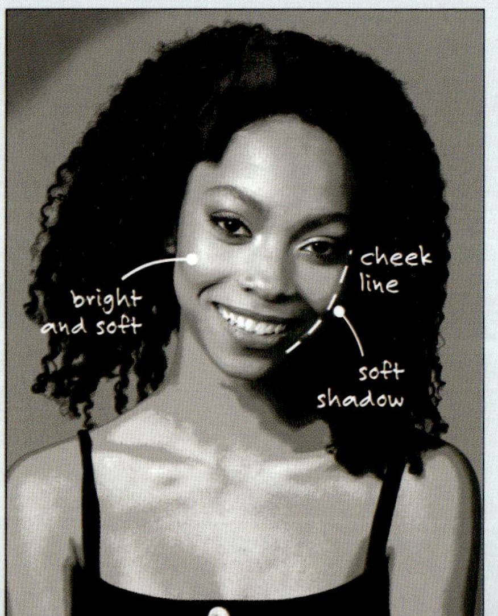

THE SETUP

1. Place the softbox **(1)** about 3 feet to the left of your subject in a raised position and at an angle of about 45 degrees. Set it up to form a clear neck shadow and a nose shadow that points diagonally toward her cheek.

2. Now place the reflector **(2)** about 3 feet to the right of your subject with its center at about head height. Position it to moderately lighten the shadow on the unlit side of her face.

3. To brighten the background and produce the vignette effect, place the beauty dish **(3)** above your subject about 18 inches to the right. Position it to brighten the area behind your subject's shoulders.

4. Position your subject about 5 feet from the yellow background.

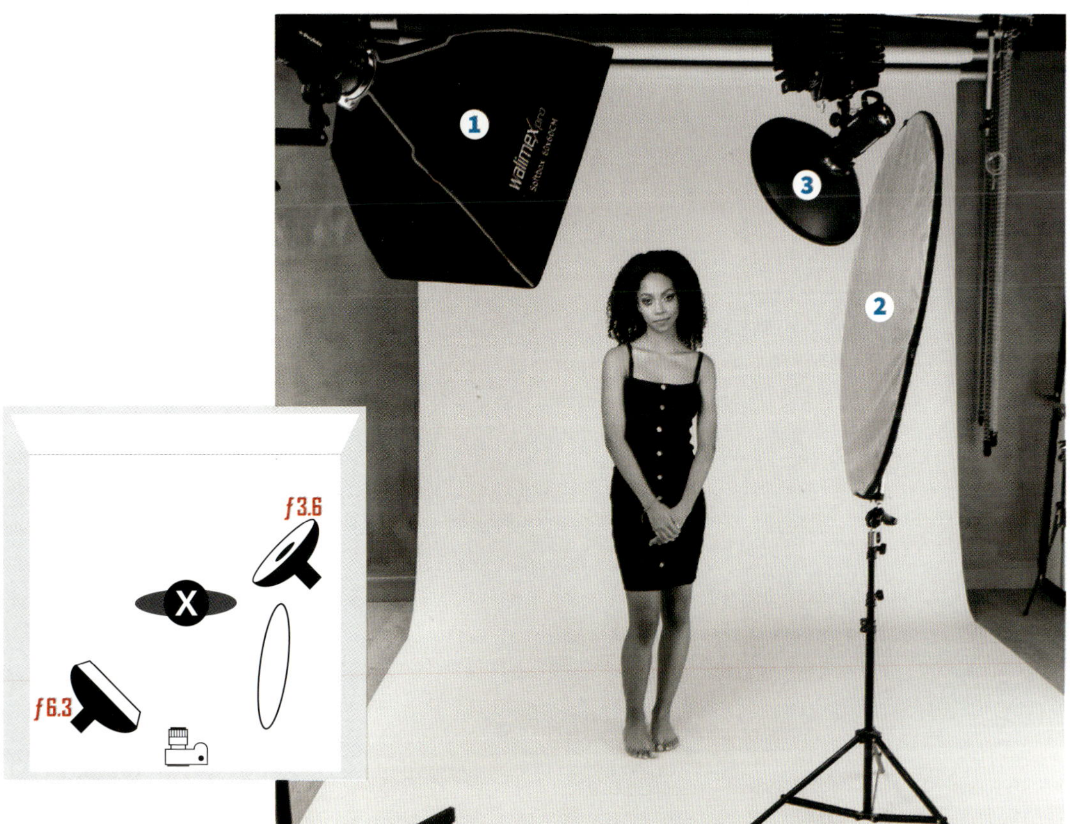

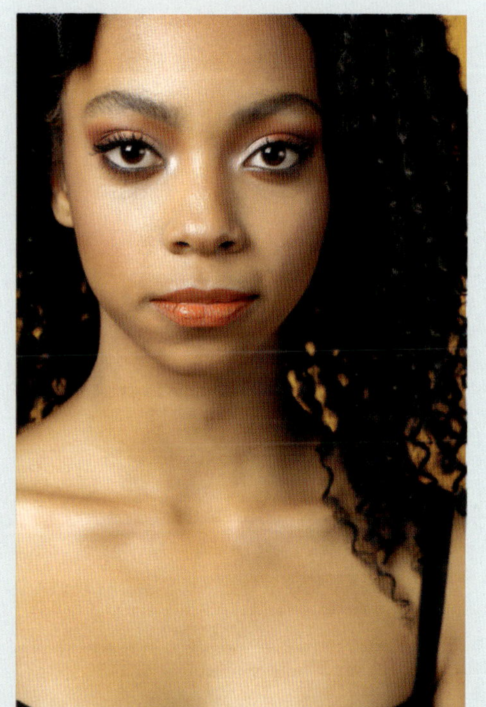

"A hairband gives a hairdo more volume and prevents loose hair from obscuring your subject's face."

Close-Ups

This setup is great for close-ups too, giving you plenty of additional options for portraying your subject. The colored background is no longer as visible in this version of the shot, but the bright lighting keeps it open and friendly looking.

189

Accenting One Side of Your Subject's Face

Character portraits are particularly effective if you use the classic Rembrandt setup to light them. The triangular accent this produces creates a classic but nevertheless highly appealing look. Shooting from a slightly higher position than normal makes your subject's eyes appear larger.

EFFORT INVOLVED

Low

SUITABLE FOR

Close-up to three-quarter-length portraits

THE LOOK

High-contrast character portrait with plenty of shadow play
Natural-looking hair and makeup, strapless top

EQUIPMENT

1× 31.5" octabox

190

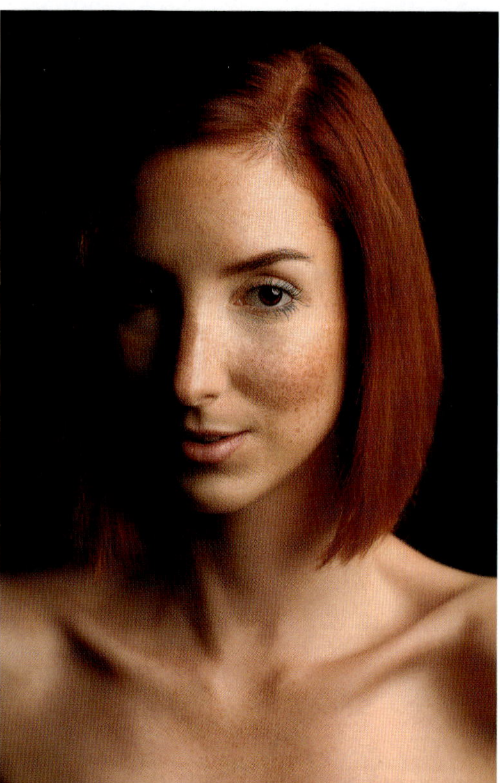

85mm | f6.3 | 1/160 sec. | ISO 100 | Model: Kristina

HOW IT WORKS

The high position of the octabox to the side of the subject produces strong shadows and plenty of definition. The light side of the face is strongly highlighted, with clear contours. The clear shadows beneath both lips accent the mouth and the shape of the lips. The raised shooting position makes the eyes look bigger and intensifies the subject's gaze. The subtle background light provides just enough contrast to separate the subject from the background and make the outline just visible. The shadow side of the face with its typical triangular Rembrandt accent also shows enough detail to keep it interesting.

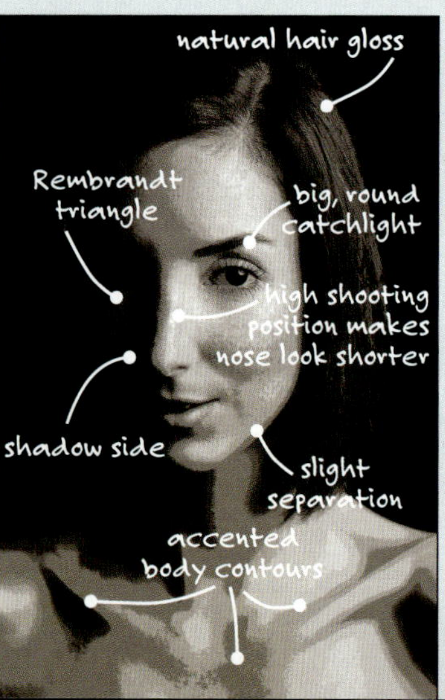

THE SETUP

1. Get your subject to stand about 8 feet in front of the black background.

2. Place the octabox **(1)** about 5 feet to the front right in a strongly raised position and at an angle of about 45 degrees. Your subject should get into position and remain still while you position the light. Set up the octabox to produce a Rembrandt triangle on the shadow side of your subject's face. The nose shadow should point diagonally downward and blend in with the cheek shadow. For more details on Rembrandt lighting, see the Quick and Easy setup on page 62.

3. Make sure that some spill light reaches the background to keep it from looking completely black.

Vary the distance between the octabox and your subject to produce different looks.

4. If you are taller than your model, it may be sufficient for you to stand on tiptoes to obtain a raised shooting position. If this doesn't provide the desired effect, you will need to stand on a stool or a low step-ladder.

"Make sure you capture a catchlight in both eyes to keep your image vivid."

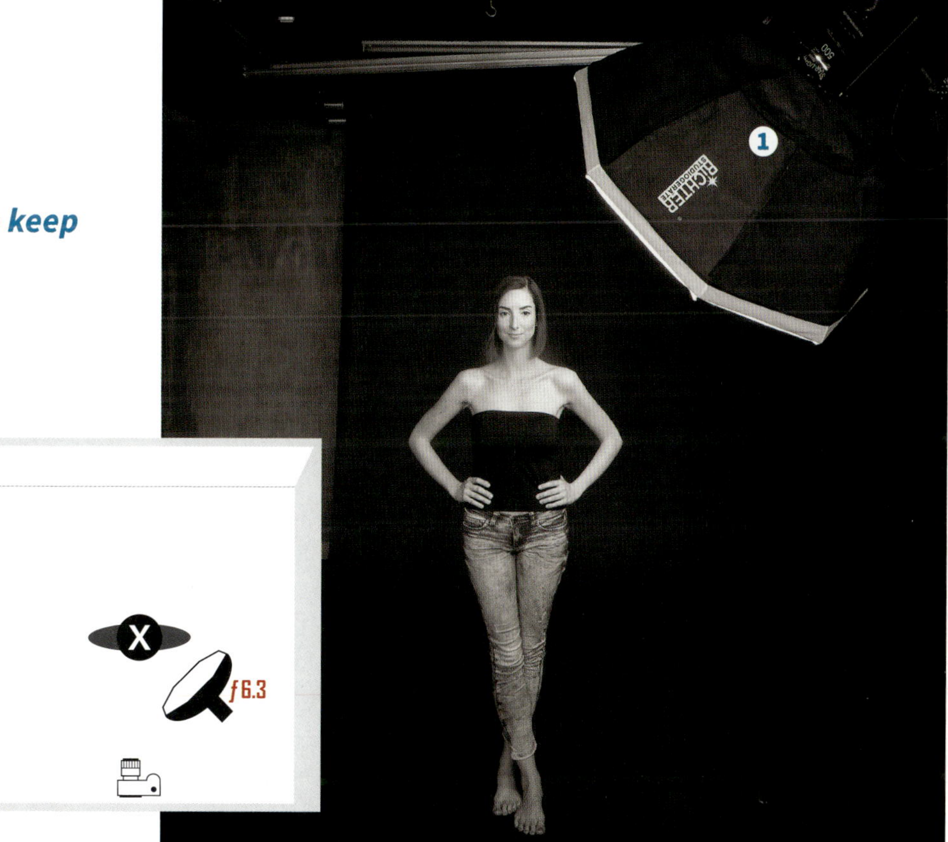

A Sassy Expression Shot from Above

This setup is based on the classic Rembrandt lighting, too. However, to tone down the mood and to underscore the subject's sassy expression, I added a reflector that lightens the shadows.

EFFORT INVOLVED

Low

SUITABLE FOR

Close-up to three-quarter-length portraits

THE LOOK

Character portrait in toned-down Rembrandt light
Natural-looking hair and makeup, strapless top

EQUIPMENT

1× 31.5" octabox
1× 30"×40" silver reflector

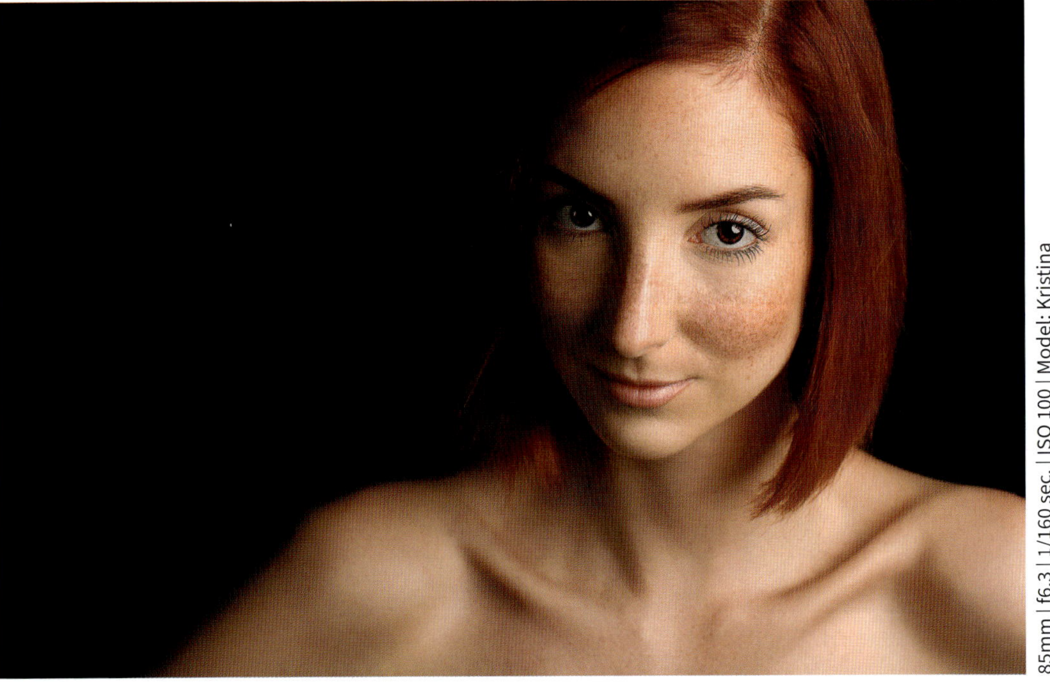

85mm | f6.3 | 1/160 sec. | ISO 100 | Model: Kristina

HOW IT WORKS

The raised, lateral position of the octabox provides plenty of definition and produces clear shadows and shoulder/collarbone contours. The light side of the face is accented, while the reflector brightens the shadow side and ensures that both eyes are clearly visible. The strong shadows beneath both lips accent the shape of the mouth. The raised shooting position makes the eyes look bigger and intensifies the subject's gaze, while the subtle background light provides just enough contrast to separate the subject from the background and keep the outline of the hairdo just visible.

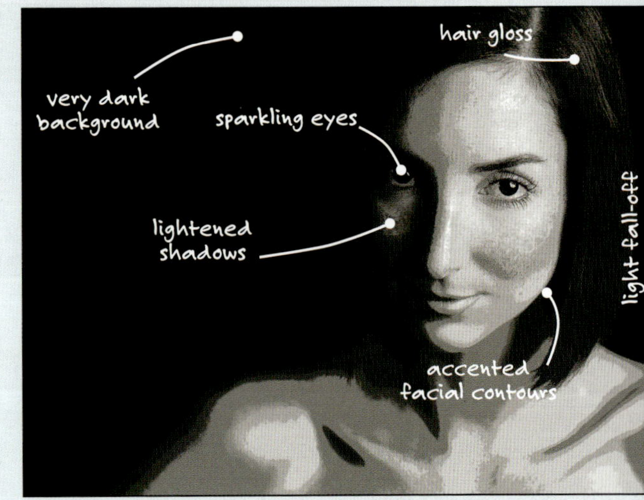

THE SETUP

1. Place the octabox **(1)** about 5 feet to the right of your subject in a raised position and at an angle of about 45 degrees. Your subject should get into position and stay still while you position the light. Position the octabox so that the nose shadow is still visible beneath the tip of her nose and to produce a Rembrandt triangle on the shadow side of her face. The nose shadow should point diagonally downward and blend in with the cheek shadow.

2. Mount the reflector **(2)** on a stand about 5 feet to the left of your subject in a slightly raised position, and set it up to brighten the shadow side of her face.

3. Position your subject about 8 feet from the black background.

Some spill light from the octabox should reach the background to prevent it from looking completely black. To achieve this, you may have to alter the distance between your subject and the main light.

To achieve the raised shooting position for this shot, I stood on a low step-ladder.

Variation: Narrow Lighting

If your subject turns her face slightly toward the main light, the classic Rembrandt look turns into a pleasing narrow-lighting look. Both eyes are well lit and more pronounced than in the standard setup, and automatically grab the viewer's attention. The overall effect also makes her face look slightly narrower.

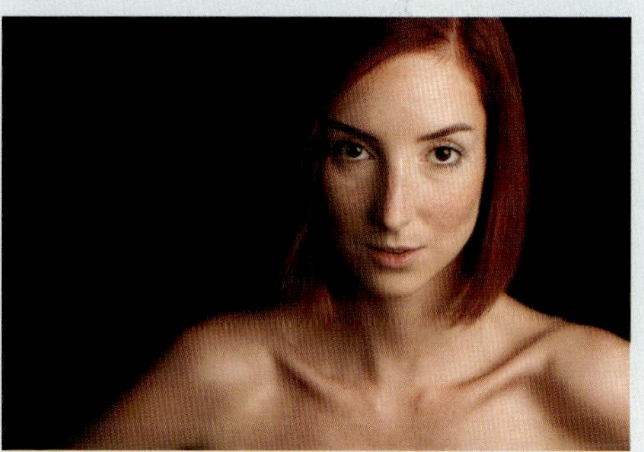

Character portrait shot from above in narrow light.

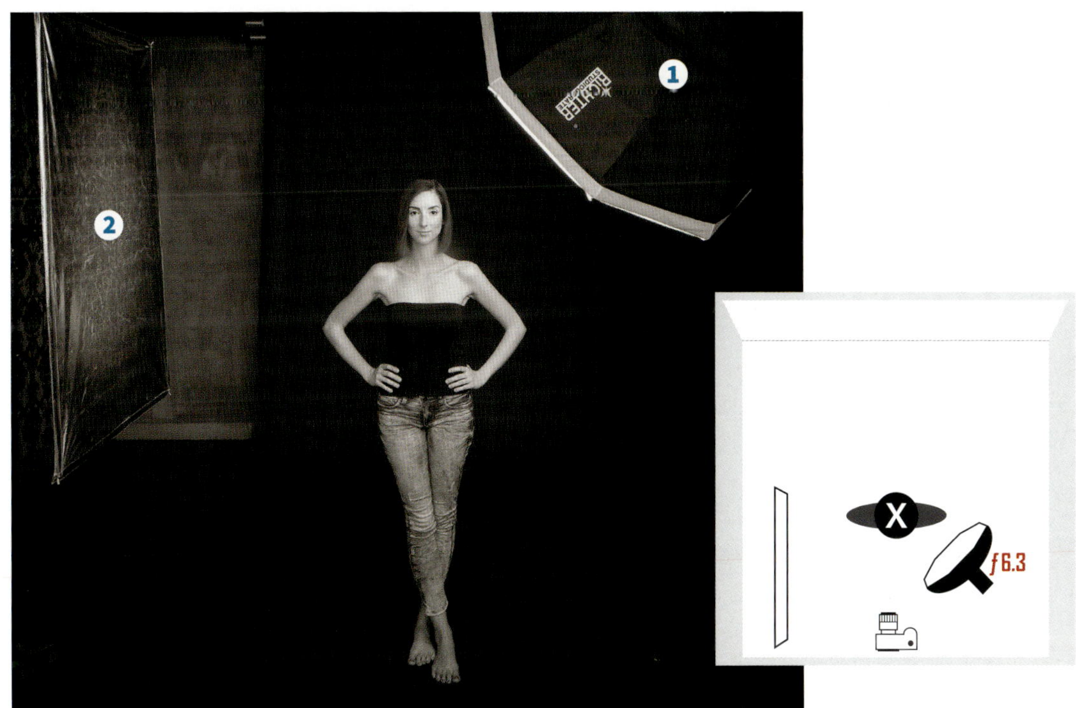

"Keep a careful eye on your subject's posture. Moving her shoulders just a tiny bit forward adds a lovely accent to her collarbones."

Background Accent Light

Character portraits live from the subject lighting, but you can add verve by using a distinctive background accent. In this shot, I used barndoors to replace the typical circular background light with an eye-catching diagonal strip of light.

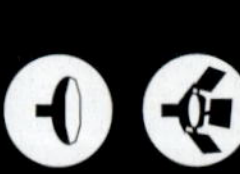

EFFORT INVOLVED

Medium

SUITABLE FOR

Close-up to three-quarter-length portraits

THE LOOK

Character portrait with a distinctive background accent

Natural-looking hair and makeup, strapless top

EQUIPMENT

1× 31.5" octabox

1× standard reflector with barndoors

1× 30"×40" silver reflector

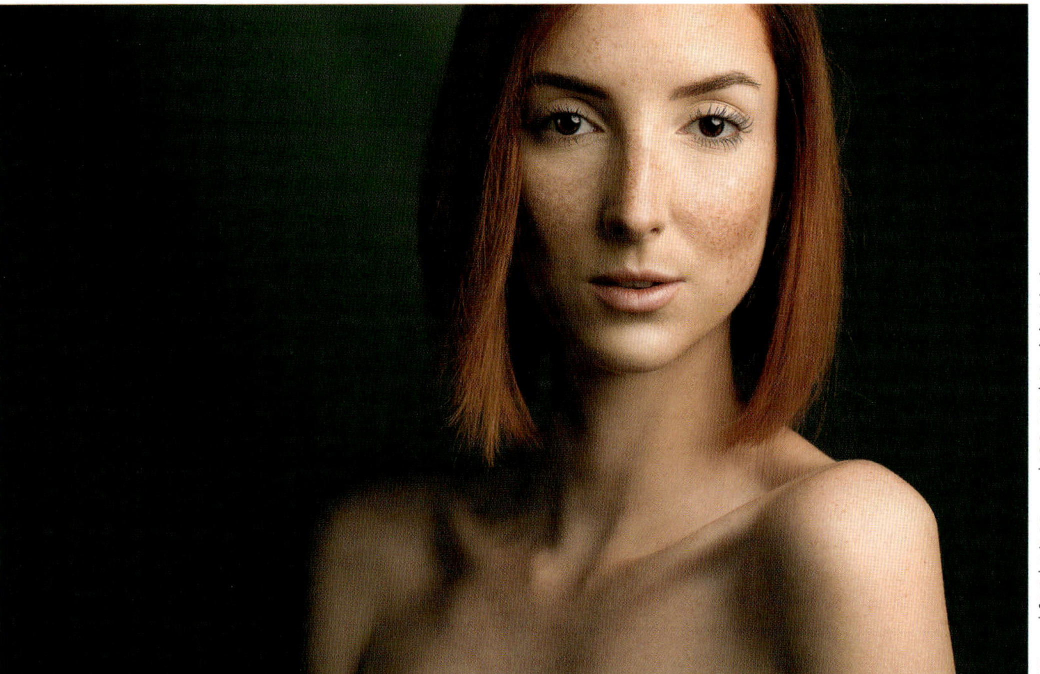

85mm | f6.3 | 1/160 sec. | ISO 100 | Model: Kristina

HOW IT WORKS

The raised diagonal position of the octabox produces soft neck and cheek shadows. The line of the cheekbone on the shadow side of the face is well defined and gives the face a pleasing shape. The nose shadow underscores the line between the nose and the eyebrow. The close proximity of the main light to the subject produces strong light fall-off from front to rear, and makes the right shoulder much darker. The light side of the face is bathed in soft, bright light that gives the subject a gentle-looking presence. The background light draws attention to the subject's face.

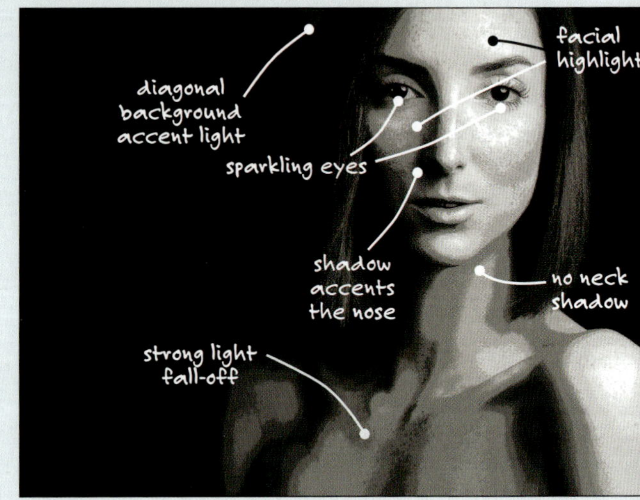

THE SETUP

1. Place the octabox **(1)** at front right about 30 inches from your subject at an angle of about 45 degrees. Position it above head height so that the nose shadow points diagonally downward.

2. Place the reflector **(2)** about 5 feet to the left of your subject to slightly lighten the shadows. Make sure it is almost vertical so that the light coming from diagonally above is reflected downward.

3. Position your subject about 8 feet from the black background, which will then appear dark gray.

4. To produce the background accent, place the standard reflector/barndoors **(3)** to the left about 3 feet behind your subject. Adjust the leaves of the barndoors to create a narrow strip of light that runs from top left to bottom right in the area between your subject's head and waist.

Keep an eye on the background and adjust your shooting position to keep the accent light visible to the left of your subject.

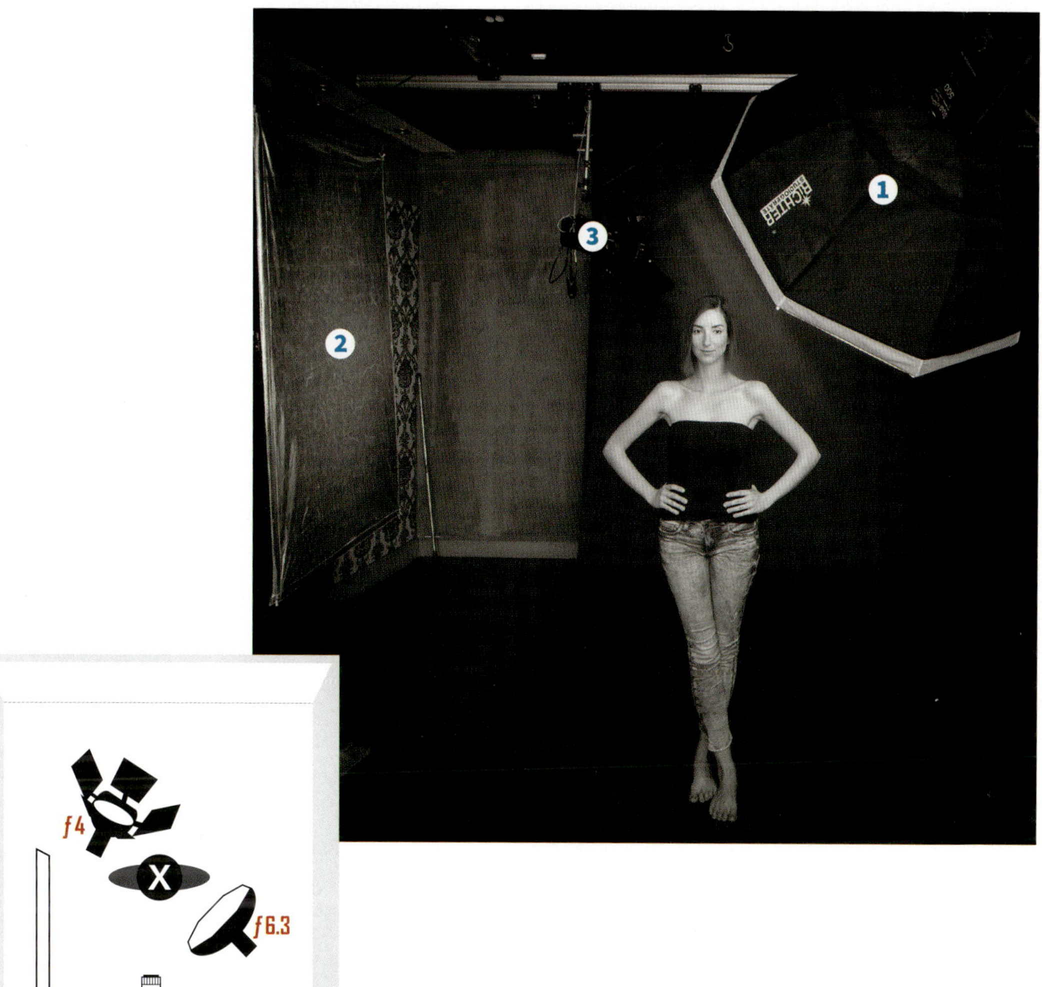

"You can change the shape of the background accent by adjusting the barndoors. Try out different configurations and choose the one that best suits your subject and your overall concept."

Off-Center Background Light

Lateral main light always produces contrasting light and shadow sides in a subject's face. This shot plays with this contrast and uses an off-center background light to separate the subject from the background.

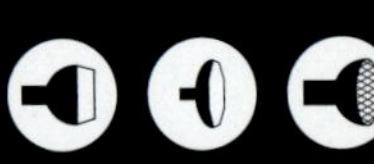

EFFORT INVOLVED

Medium

SUITABLE FOR

Close-up to three-quarter-length portraits

THE LOOK

Character portrait with strong accents and a well-defined facial expression

Natural-looking hair and makeup, strapless top

EQUIPMENT

1× 24" softbox

1× 31.5" octabox

1× standard reflector with a honeycomb grid

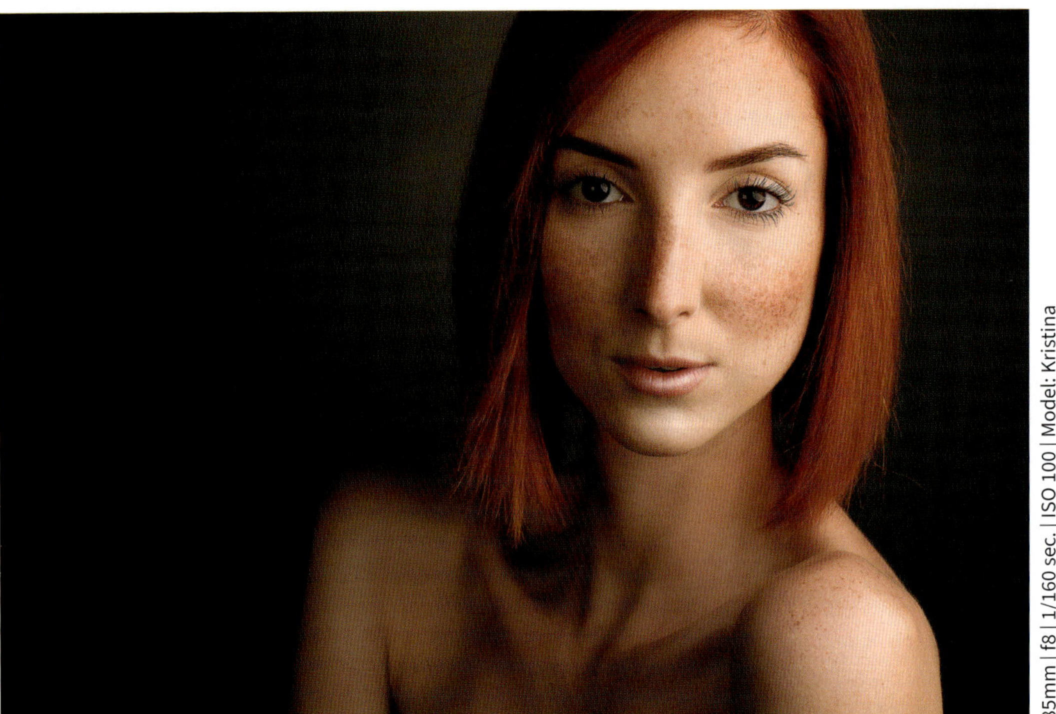

85mm | f8 | 1/160 sec. | ISO 100 | Model: Kristina

HOW IT WORKS

The diagonally positioned main light illuminates the subject's face from one side. This effect is intensified if the subject then rotates their upper body to the shadow side. The fill light sculpts the body contours on the shadow side, and the overall effect is a well-defined image with clearly contrasting light and shade. The dark background on the right provides a nice contrast with the red glow of the subject's hair, while the off-center background spot provides a counterpoint on the shadow side. The subject's entire outline is clearly visible but visual focus is still on the face.

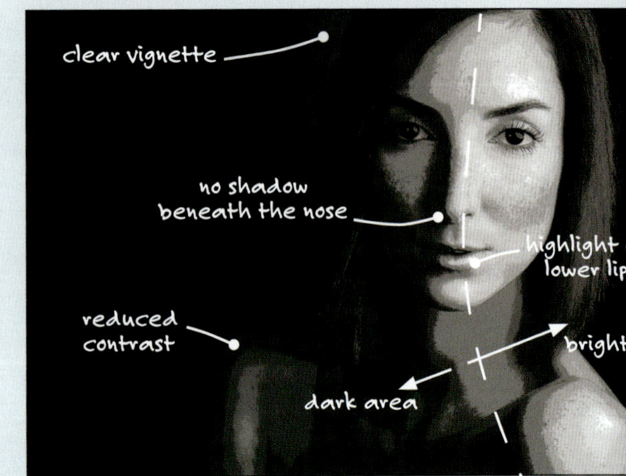

THE SETUP

1. Place the octabox main light **(1)** about 2 feet to the front right of your subject in a slightly raised position and at an angle of about 30 degrees. Position it to produce a clear nose shadow and a triangle of light on the shadow-side cheek.

2. Now place the softbox **(2)** at front right about 5 feet from your subject at an angle of about 45 degrees. Position it pointing slightly downward with its center at head height.

Place the gridded background spot **(3)** to the left rear of your subject at a height of about 6 feet. Set it up to produce a pool of light about the same size as your subject's head with its center behind her right eye.

The photo below shows the background spot with barndoors rather than the honeycomb grid listed in the description. In this case, the result was the same. Barndoors almost completely eliminate spill light, so you can position a light with barndoors closer to your subject than one with a grid.

3. Position your subject about 6 feet in front of the black background to ensure a clear vignette effect toward the edges of the frame.

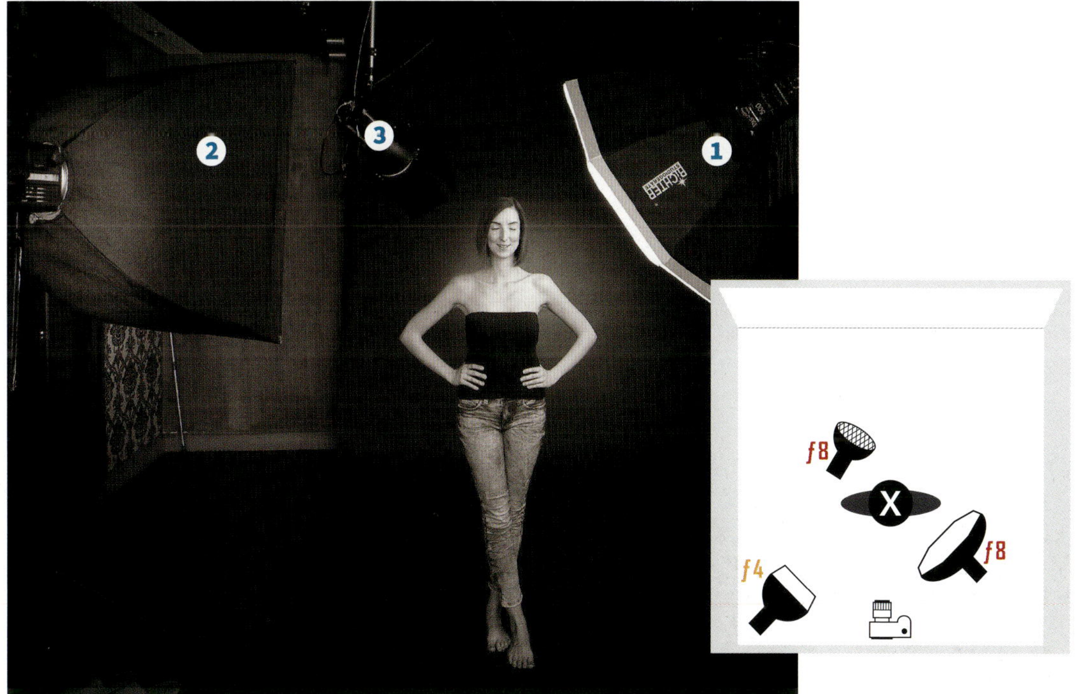

"When using a tight crop, make sure that it is really tight. If just a small part of your subject's head is missing, it can easily look like a mistake."

Variation

Getting your subject to turn toward the main light produces an interesting variation on the standard setup. This illuminates her torso more strongly and adds it to the viewer's field of focus while reducing the visual significance of the face. This type of pose is useful if you want to portray more than just the subject's face, or if the body posture plays a role in the overall look of the image.

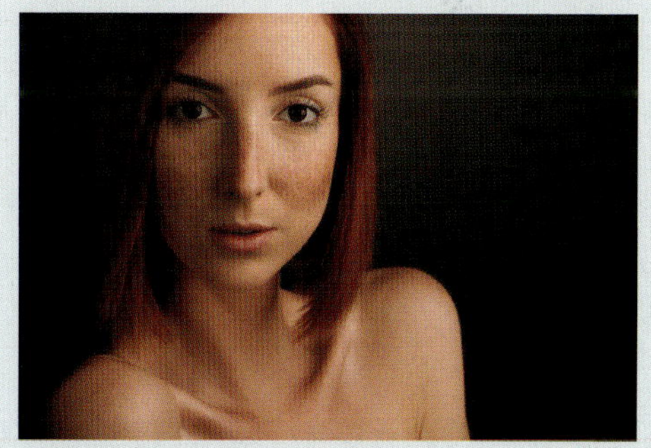

Variant with the subject's upper body turned toward the main light.

Rembrandt Light Revisited

Rembrandt light is a classic setup that still enjoys widespread use in studio photography. This setup uses a narrow version of the setup to keep the subject looking slim. The typical Rembrandt triangle is clearly visible on the subject's cheek and the overall emphasis is on her face. This is a versatile one-light setup that works well for women and men, but you need to give your subject precise directions to make it work (for more tips and tricks, see the Quick & Easy setup on page 62).

EFFORT INVOLVED

Low

SUITABLE FOR

Close-up to three-quarter-length portraits

THE LOOK

Classic portrait with clear shadows

Emphasis on the face

Smokey eyes, subtle lips, accented hair curls

EQUIPMENT

1 × 24" softbox

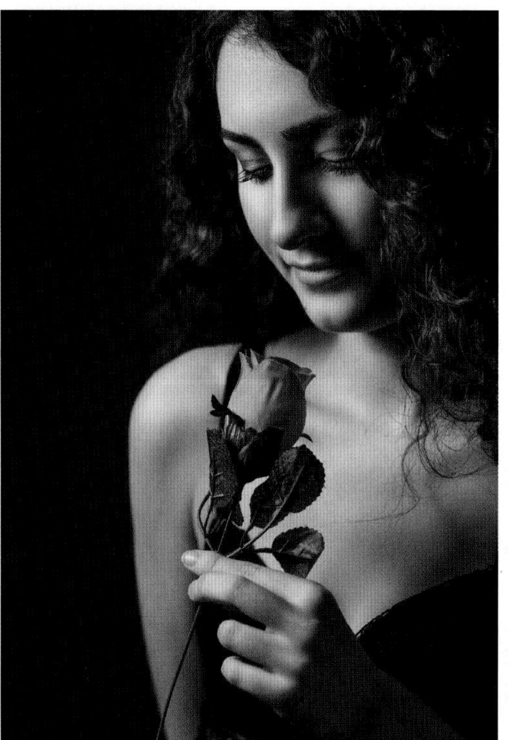

HOW IT WORKS

This setup provides a unique effect with almost palpable intimacy. The diagonally positioned main light produces the typical Rembrandt triangle on the subject's cheek. Both eyes are well lit, the shape of the nose is unmistakable, and even the dimple in her chin has its own accent. The hair curls have a soft, glossy feel, and the image invites you to take a good, long look at every square inch. The viewer's gaze wanders around the frame and keeps coming back to the rose, while the line of the stem inevitably takes you back to the face. The conversion to fine-toned black and white underscores the classic feel of the final image.

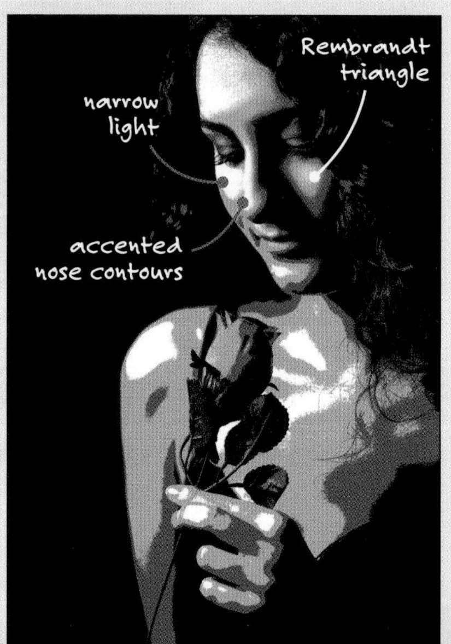

THE SETUP

1. Place the softbox **(1)** about 3 feet to the left of your subject in a slightly raised position and at an angle of about 30 degrees.

2. Get your subject to stand about 5 feet in front of a dark background and position the light to produce a clear neck shadow and a nose shadow that points diagonally toward her cheek. Take great care positioning the Rembrandt triangle, as this is influenced by both your subject's pose and the position of your light (see the Quick & Easy setup on page 62 for more details).

Beauty Dish or Softbox?

A beauty dish produces a clear central shadow and is highly directional, and is therefore the light shaper of choice for high-contrast shots. The light a beauty dish provides is clearly defined and doesn't produce too much spill light. In contrast, a softbox produces softer, more diffuse light with smoother shadows and more background spill. You can decide whether to take the harder beauty dish route or the softer softbox approach depending on the concept you are working on and the overall effect you are aiming for.

"In this setup, fine-tuning is the key to a perfect Rembrandt effect. The interplay between the pose and the lighting are crucial to the final result."

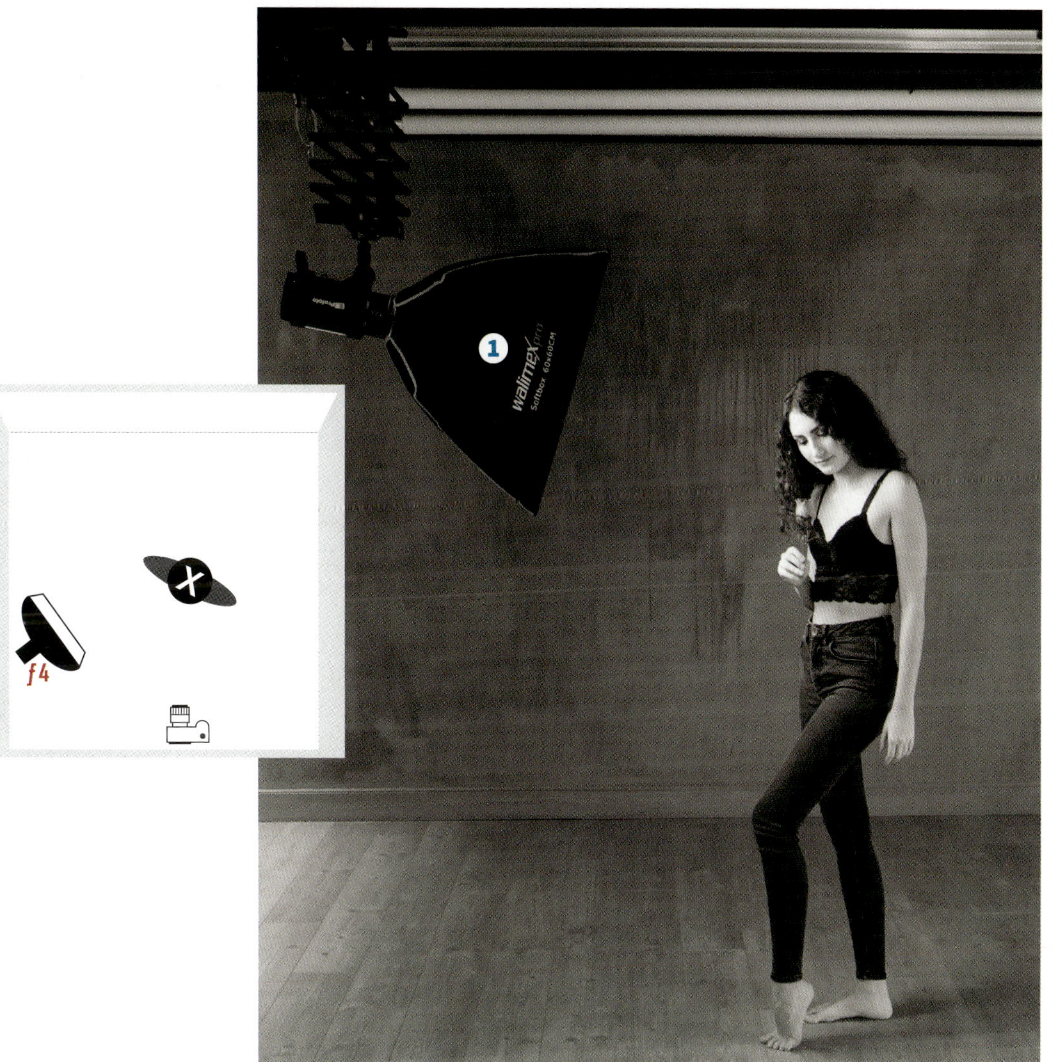

Capturing the Mood of the Moment

If you want to capture your subject's emotions and facial expressions, high-contrast lighting with well-defined shadows is often the way to go. This approach gives your subject plenty of scope for different poses and varied body language, so you can concentrate fully on your flow and capturing the mood.

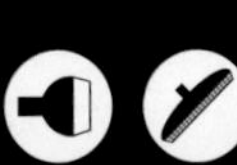

EFFORT INVOLVED

Low

SUITABLE FOR

All kinds of portraits

THE LOOK

Character portrait with plenty of room for maneuvering

Natural-looking makeup and a light-colored shirt

EQUIPMENT

1× 24" softbox

1× 47" strip box with a honeycmb grid

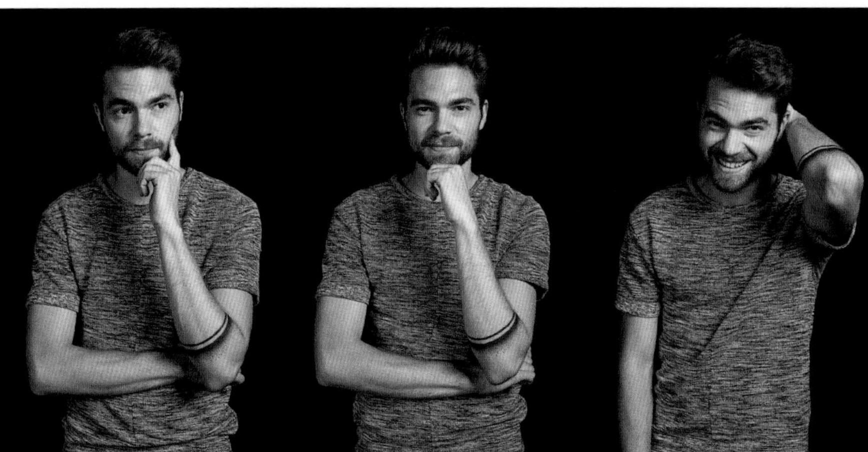

HOW IT WORKS

The softbox produces soft main light with diagonal shadows that accent the subject's facial expression. The lateral position of the main light creates clear shadows in the face and body, and thus plenty of definition. The octabox provides plenty of light for the eyes and makes the emotions they convey clearly visible. The eyes are also framed by the shadows beneath the upper eyelids and the catchlights. The strip box fill light provides the necessary lightening in the shadows without producing any spill light in the background. The distance between the subject and the background makes the background appear almost black and enhances the contrast between it and the subject.

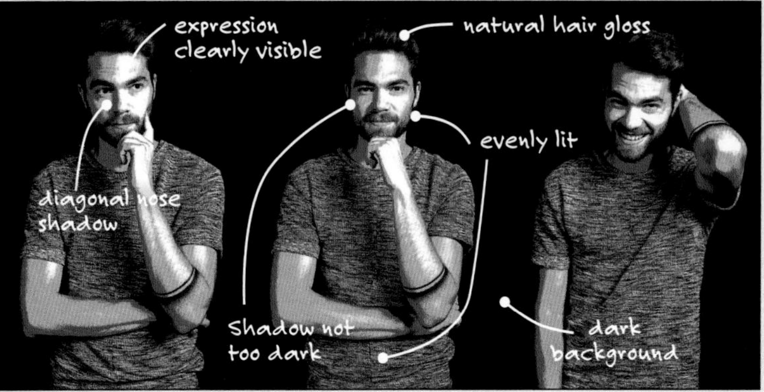

1. Place the softbox **(1)** about 6 feet to the right of your subject in a raised position and at an angle of about 45 degrees. Position it so that the nose shadow points diagonally downward but doesn't reach the cheek shadow.

2. Mount the gridded strip box **(2)** about 6 feet to the left of your subject at about head height and set it up to lighten the shadows.

3. Position your subject about 10 feet from the black background.

"Make sure the background remains dark and, if necessary, use flags to suppress any unwanted spill light."

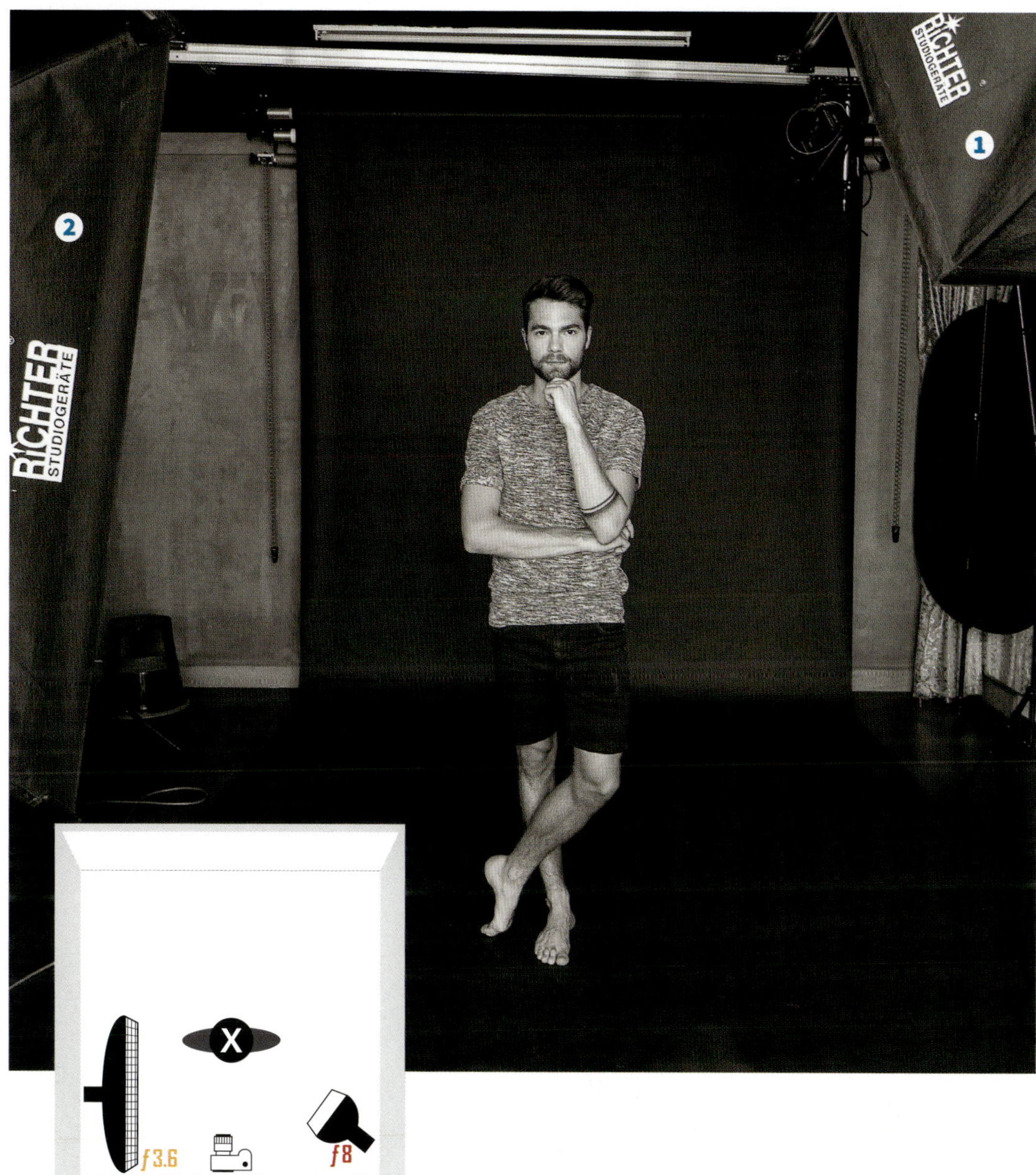

Gritty Character Portrait

This setup creates a dark mood with very hard shadows, and is ideal for portraits with a serious and/or masculine tone. Depending on your subject's facial expression, you can use it to convey a spooky or even a sinister atmosphere.

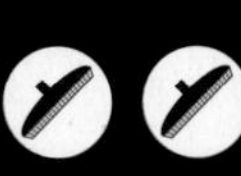

EFFORT INVOLVED

Medium

SUITABLE FOR

Close-up to head-and-shoulders portraits

THE LOOK

Dark mood with heavy shadows
Natural-looking makeup, dark-colored shirt

EQUIPMENT

2× 47" strip boxes with honeycomb grids
1× 30"×40" silver reflector

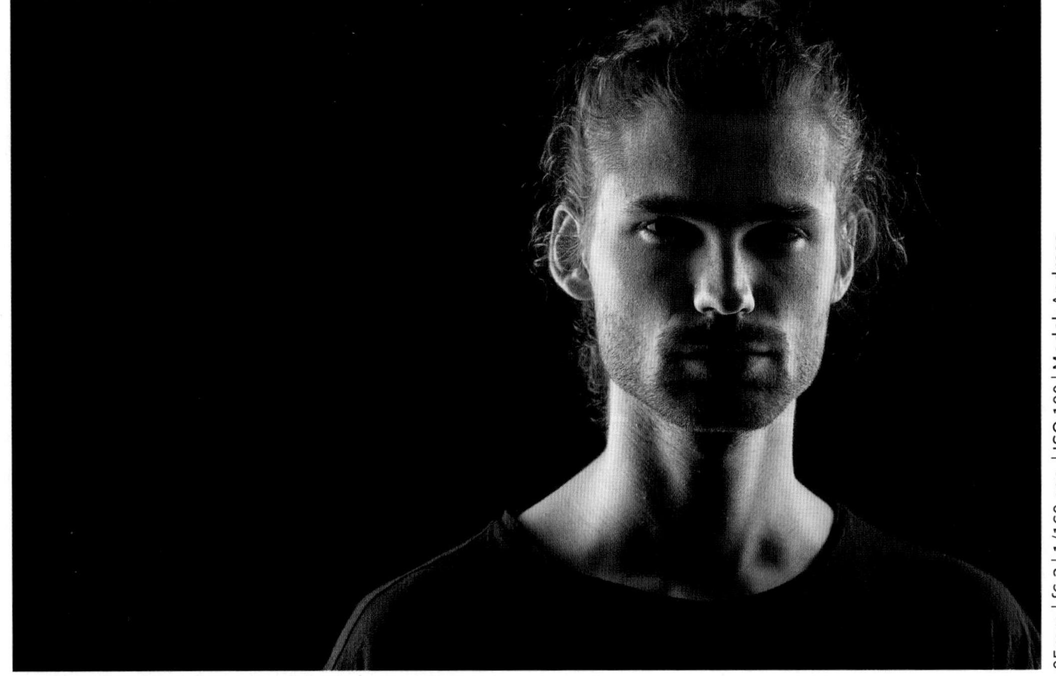

85mm | f6.3 | 1/160 sec. | ISO 100 | Model: Andreas

HOW IT WORKS

The straight, symmetrical head posture is the key to this image. The composition is dominated by the dark shadows in the center of the subject's face, and the reflector lightens them just enough to make the details of the eyes, nose, and mouth visible. The lack of catchlights in the eyes makes them appear implacable and almost sinister. The clear accents on both sides of the face provide contrast with the dark background and produce a clear outline. The lighting in this setup is not at all natural and, together with the subject's expression, contributes to the slightly eerie look.

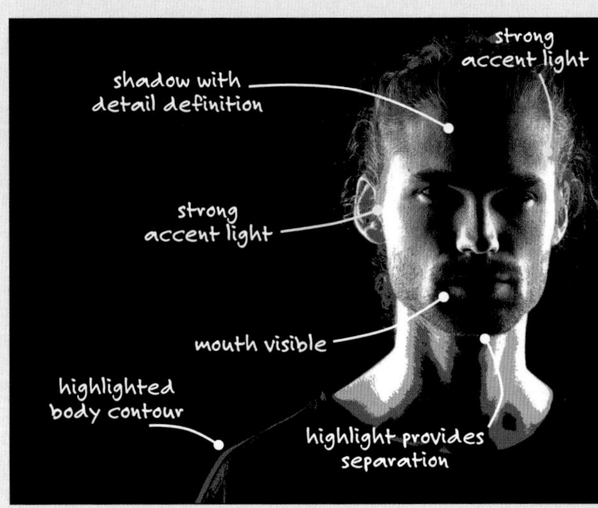

THE SETUP

1. Place one of the strip boxes **(1)** about 2 feet to the left rear of your subject at head height and at an angle of about 45 degrees. Set it up so that it produces clear accents on his cheek and shoulder.

2. Mirror this setup with the second strip box **(2)** and position it to produce the same accents on your subject's face and shoulder on the right-hand side.

3. Mount the silver reflector **(3)** centrally above head height about 3 feet in front of your subject and pointing downward at an angle of about 30 degrees. Fine-tune its position to lighten the shadow in the center of your subject's face.

4. Position your subject about 5 feet form the gray background. A black background works for this setup too.

"Make sure the twin strip boxes are set up equidistant from your subject and that they provide even lighting from both sides."

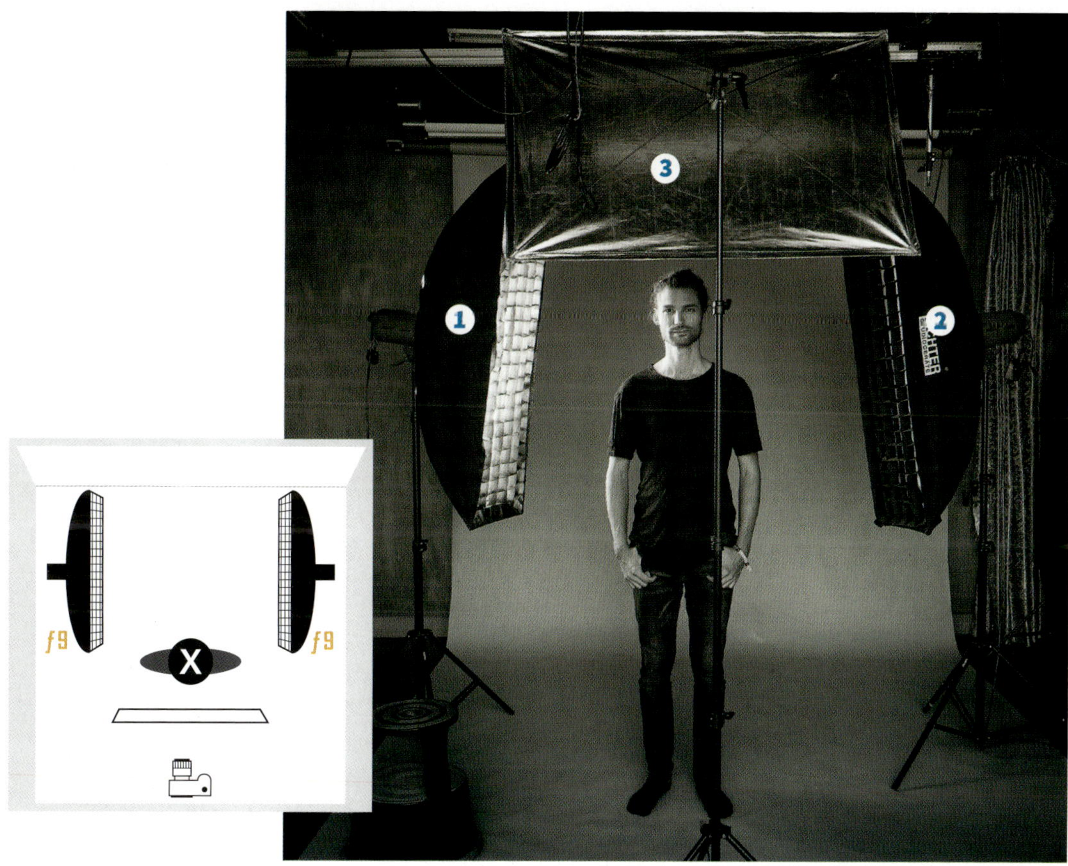

Character Portrait in Lateral Light

You often only need to light one side of a person's face to capture their mood. This setup provides a striking but minimalistic look that is particularly effective for portraying the mood of male subjects.

EFFORT INVOLVED

Low

SUITABLE FOR

Close-up and head-and-shoulders portraits

THE LOOK

Minimalistic but striking character portrait with partial lighting

Natural-looking makeup and light-colored shirt

EQUIPMENT

1× beauty dish

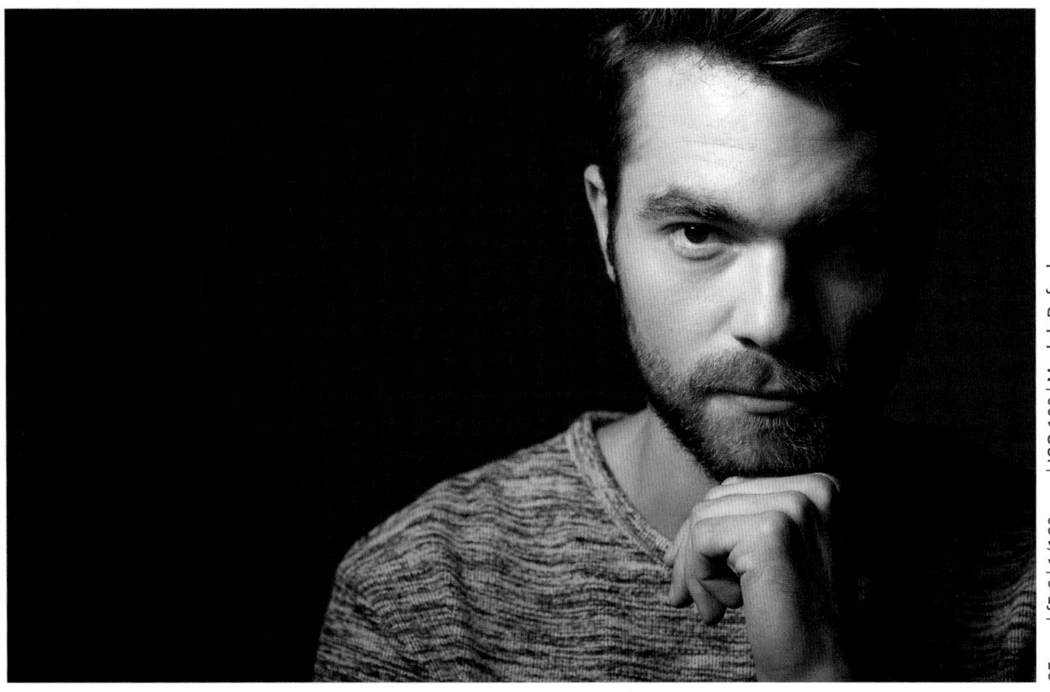

85mm | f5.6 | 1/160 sec. | ISO 100 | Model: Rafael

HOW IT WORKS

The raised, lateral position of the beauty dish produces strong shadows and great definition. The light side of the face is strongly accented with clear facial contours. The dark background on the left contrasts nicely with the light side of the face and is an important element in the overall composition. The subject is nicely separated from the subtly lit background. The shadow side of the face shows only a small Rembrandt triangle and a minimum of perceptible detail, thus creating a slightly mysterious look that is underscored by the way the subject's left eye disappears into shadow. The black-and-white conversion turns this shot into a timeless character portrait.

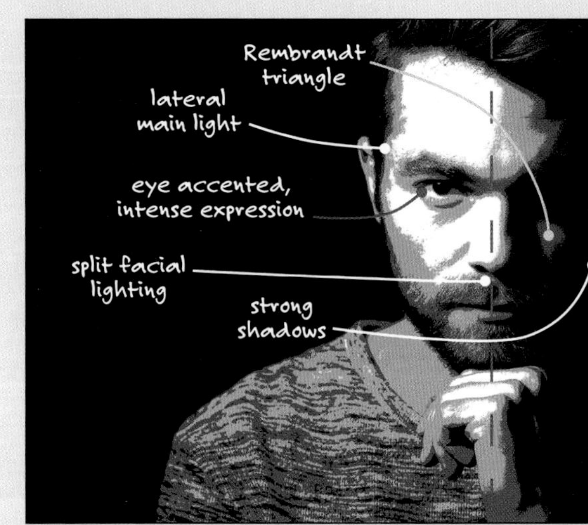

1. Get your subject to sit or stand about 5 feet from the black background.

2. Place the beauty dish **(1)** high up about 3 feet to the front left of your subject and point it downward at an angle of about 15 degrees. Your subject should get into pose and sit still while you fine-tune your lighting. Set the light up to form an unobtrusive triangle of light on the shadow-side cheek that is much smaller than a typical Rembrandt light (see page 62 for more details on the standard Rembrandt setup).

"Make sure the atmosphere in the studio is relaxed, and don't forget to provide your subject with something to sit on."

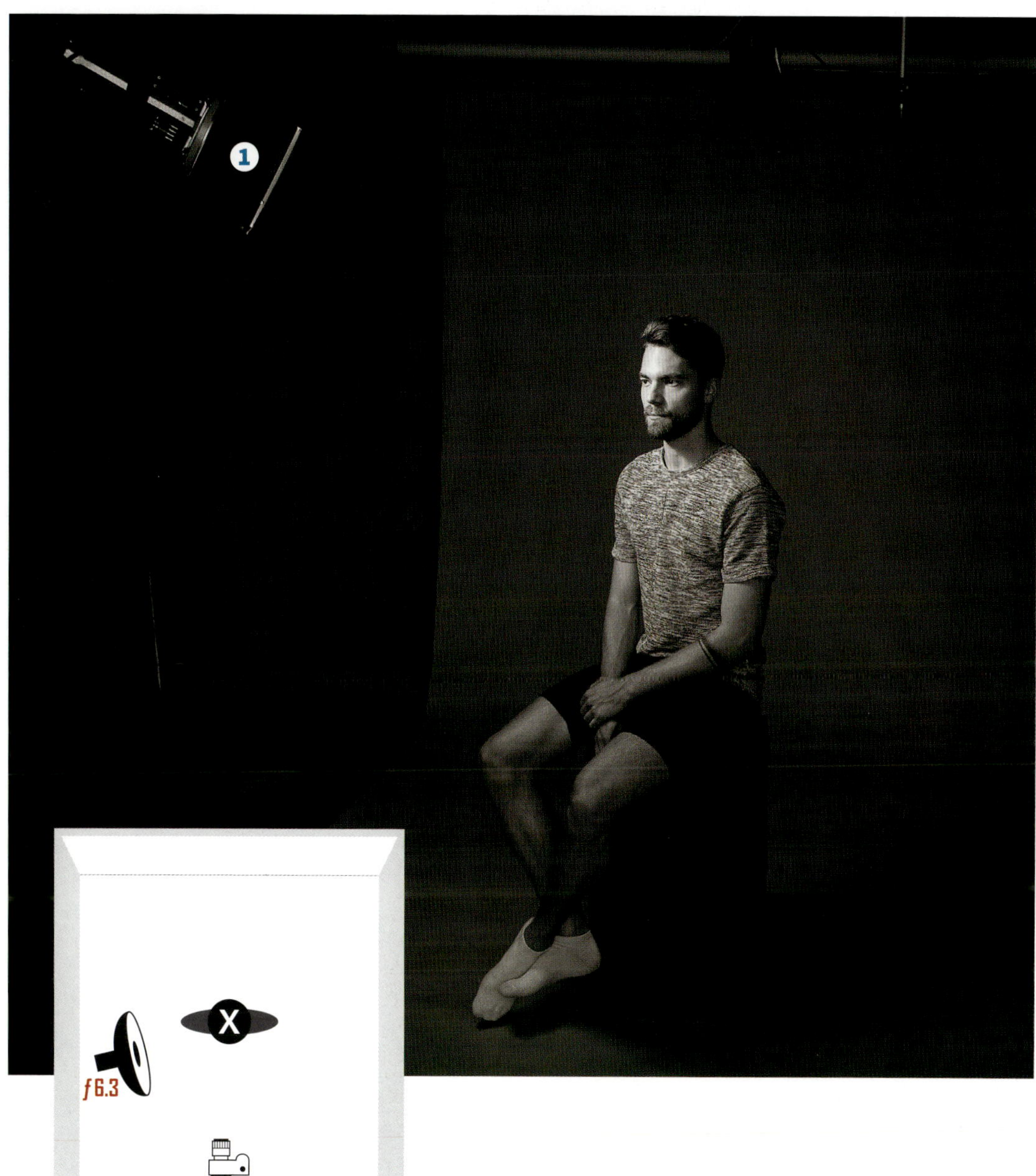

A Setup
for Sitting Poses

A sitting pose is a good way to incorporate a subject's body language in a character portrait. In this laterally lit shot, I used an additional background light to keep the viewer's focus on the subject's face.

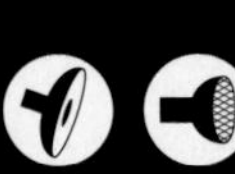
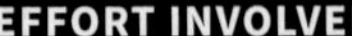

EFFORT INVOLVED

Medium

SUITABLE FOR

All kinds of portraits

THE LOOK

High-contrast lighting for large crops
Natural-looking makeup and light-colored clothing

EQUIPMENT

1× beauty dish
1× standard reflector with a honeycomb grid
1× 30"×40" silver reflector

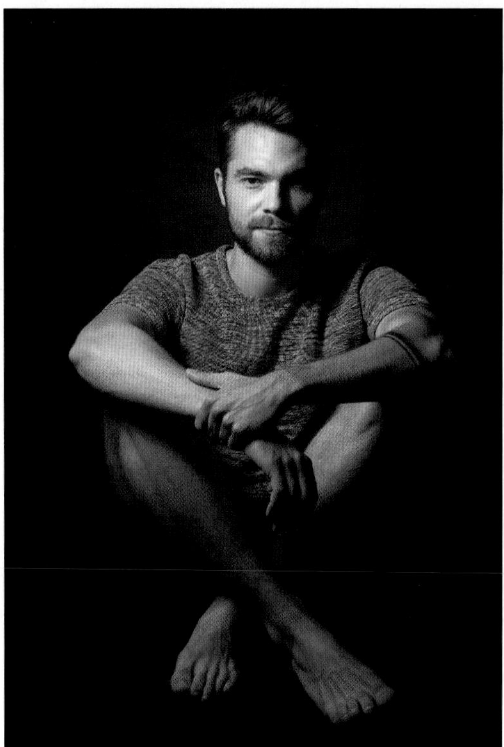

85mm | f8 | 1/160 sec. | ISO 100 | Model: Rafael

HOW IT WORKS

The limited size of the light beam produced by the beauty dish produces a clearly defined area of brightness in the subject's face and upper body. The raised, lateral position of the main light once again produces a typical Rembrandt-style effect. The diagonal shadows provide good definition, especially on the light side of the face. The left eye, mouth, and nose are all nicely accented and help to underscore the subject's facial expression. The fall-off from the main light makes the lower parts of the subject's body less distracting. The background spot steers the viewer's attention toward the face and lightens the background enough to make the outline of the head clearly visible.

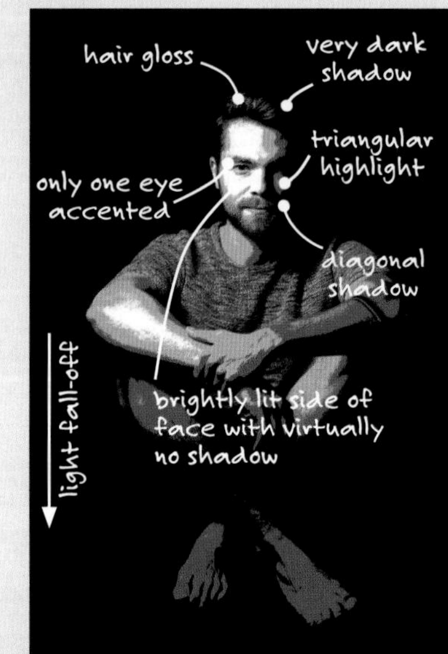

THE SETUP

1. Position your model about 5 feet from the black background.

2. Place the beauty dish **(1)** at front left in a high overhead position about 3 feet away from your subject and at an angle of about 15 degrees. Make sure your subject doesn't alter his pose while you fine-tune your lighting. Position the main light to produce a small triangle of light on the shadow-side cheek. The nose shadow should point diagonally downward and blend in with the cheek shadow.

3. Now position the silver reflector **(2)** about 3 feet away from your subject above and to the right. Set it up to reflect the light coming from above downward to brighten the shadow side of your subject. Vary the brightness of the reflected light by altering the distance between reflector and subject.

4. Mount the gridded background spot **(3)** centrally on a ceiling rail or a boom stand above your subject at a height of about 8 feet. Position it to create a pool of light with its center behind your subject's head that is large enough to extend beyond the top of his head in the final image.

Variations with Tighter Crops

Vary your framing while you shoot and don't be afraid to try out some really tight crops. Different framing can be the key to portraying your subject's true character.

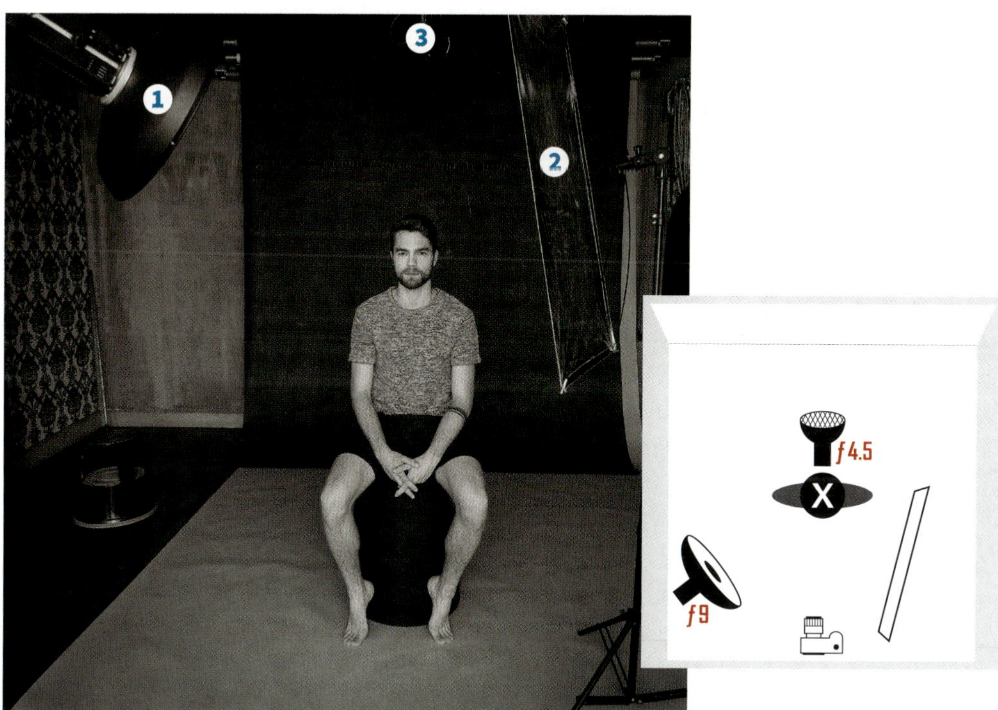

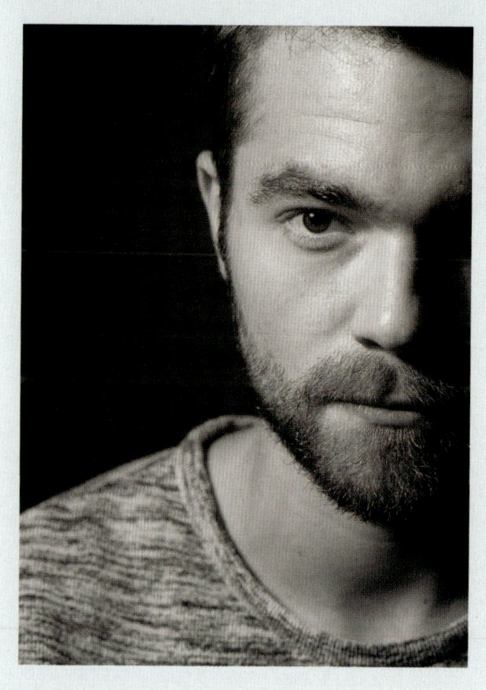

A Futuristic Lighting Mood

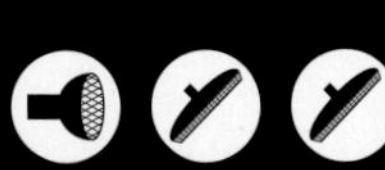

EFFORT INVOLVED

Medium

SUITABLE FOR

All kinds of portraits

THE LOOK

Highly three-dimensional character portrait with pronounced shadows and highlights

Brown-toned, natural-looking makeup, hair tightly tied back, strapless top

EQUIPMENT

1× standard reflector with a honeycomb grid

2× 47" strip boxes with honeycmb grids

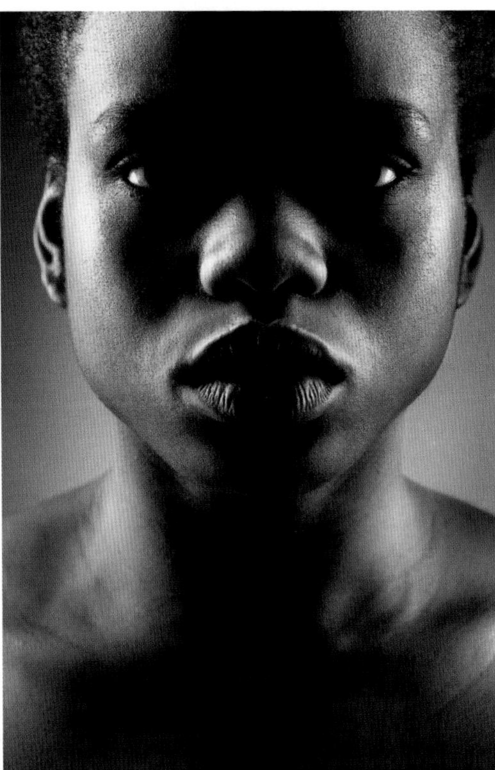

100mm | f7.1 | 1/160 sec. | ISO 100 | Model: Deborah

HOW IT WORKS

The straight, symmetrical pose is the key to this image. The center of the frame is dominated by a strong shadow that is, in turn, interrupted by the highlights on the nose and mouth. These highlights contribute to the way the subject's face appears to jut out of the frame, while the lack of catchlights gives the eyes a slightly empty look. The clear accents on the left and right contrast with the background, and the strong vignette toward the edges of the frame contributes to the three-dimensional look. This lighting doesn't look natural and produces an image that is anything but relaxing to look at.

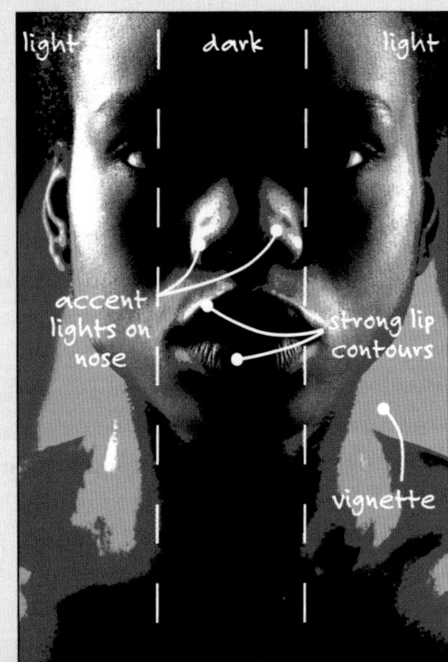

THE SETUP

1. Place one of the strip boxes **(1)** about 2 feet to the left rear of your subject at head height and point it downward at an angle of about 15 degrees. Position it to produce clear highlights on your subject's cheek, nose, and shoulder.

2. Use the second strip box **(2)** to mirror the setup of the first one and to produce similar highlights on the opposite side.

3. Mount the gridded background spot **(3)** centrally on a ceiling rail or a boom stand slightly behind your subject at a height of about 8 feet. Set it up to focus behind your subject's neck and to cast a pool of light that reaches about eye level.

4. Position your subject about 6 feet in front of the gray background.

"You can adjust the width of the shadows by altering the angles of your accent lights."

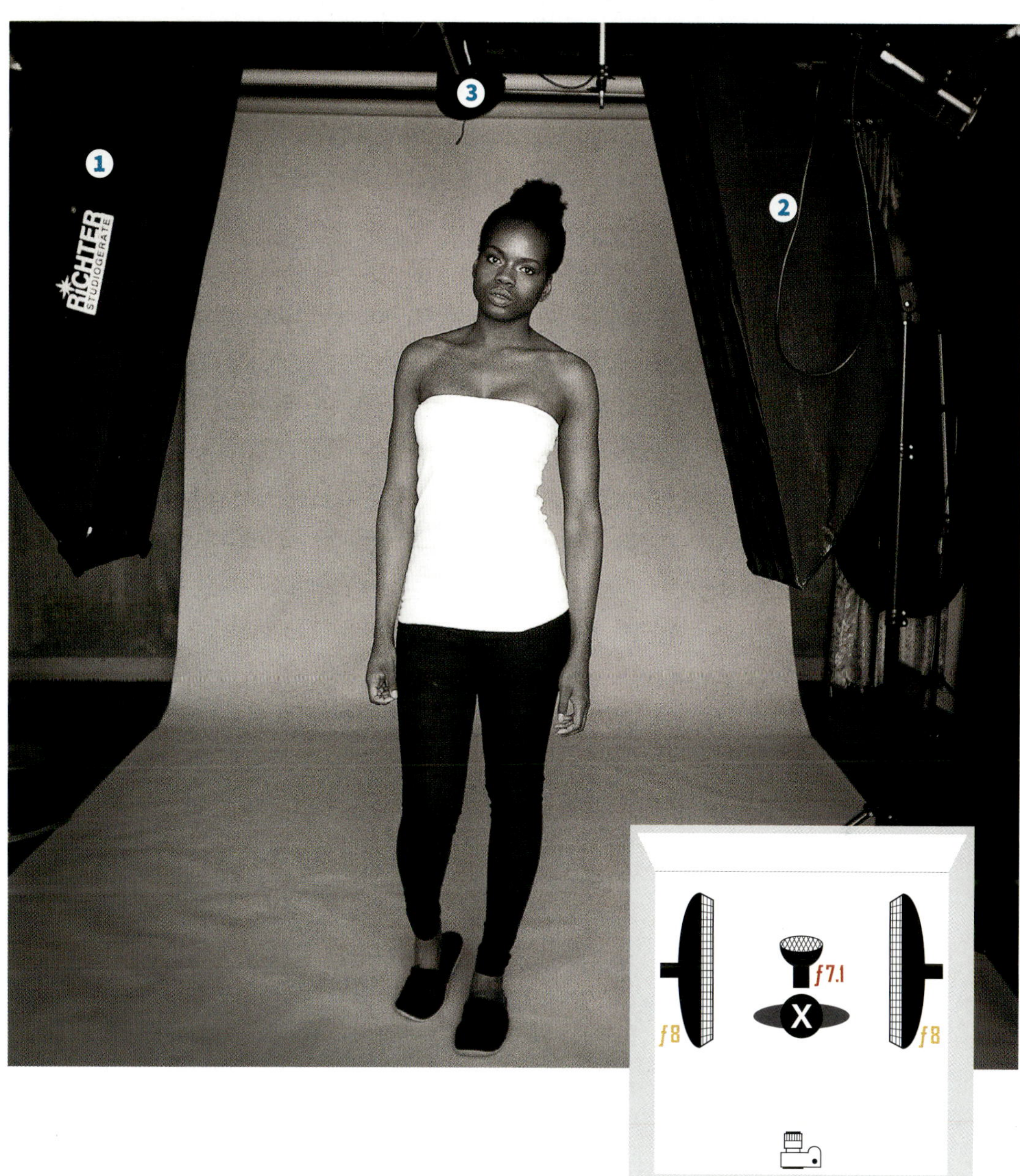

Flashlight Portrait

The setups we have looked at so far in this chapter all use studio flash units. This setup shows that you can actually produce professional-looking photos using just a pocket flashlight as a light source! The great thing about a handheld flashlight is that you can precisely control your lighting in real time while you shoot.

EFFORT INVOLVED
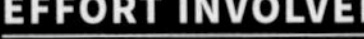

Low

SUITABLE FOR

Close-up to three-quarter-length portraits

THE LOOK

Character portrait with a stage-style spotlight
Natural-looking makeup, simple hairdo

EQUIPMENT

1× 1000-lumen (20W) LED flashlight

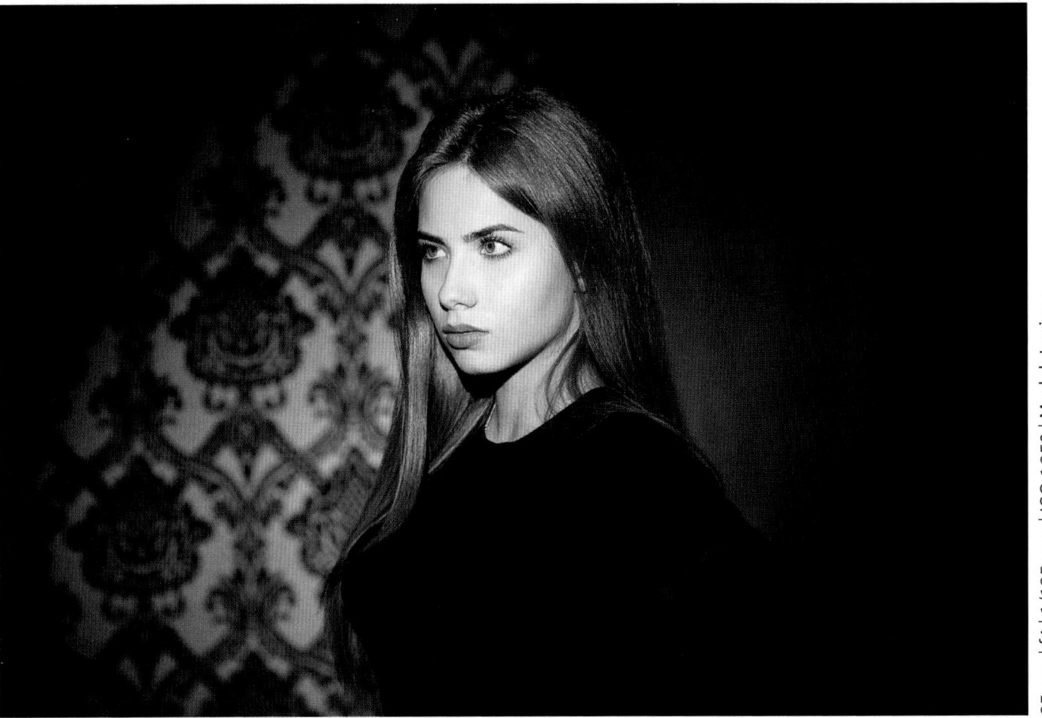

85mm | f4 | 1/125 sec. | ISO 1250 | Model: Larissa

HOW IT WORKS

The flashlight illuminates only a small part of the frame and produces very strong contrast. The strong vignette effect and the shallow depth of field steer the viewer's attention toward the subject's face. I positioned the flashlight above the camera to the left (see the "making of" photo opposite). This means that the shadows point downward and to the right. The subject's gaze and expression are clearly visible. The look this setup creates is reminiscent of a stage spotlight and works with all kinds of moods, from friendly through serious to properly dramatic.

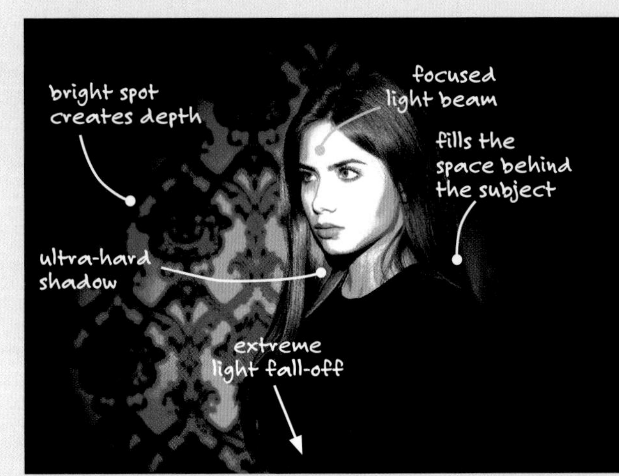

THE SETUP

1. Position your subject about 10 feet away from any interesting backdrop. For this shot, I used a corner of my studio that is decorated with patterned wallpaper. You can, of course, use a conventional studio background, a wall, or anything else that you may have at hand. The relatively large distance between subject and background ensures that the background itself will be out of focus and separated from the subject.

2. Get into position about 6 feet from your subject and hold the flashlight **(1)** up high in one hand while you shoot using the other. Make sure your subject's face is well lit. This maneuver can quickly become tiring, especially if you use a heavy camera. You can, of course, mount your flashlight on a stand using a clamp, tape, or whatever.

3. You will need to adjust your shooting parameters to suit the continuous light source. Set the exposure time to 1/125 sec. to avoid camera shake and use the largest aperture you can to keep the background blurred (I used f4 for this shot). You can then set an appropriate ISO value to complement your other settings (for this shot, I selected ISO 1250).

"The color temperature of LED flashlights is usually pretty cool, so it is often a good idea to convert your results to black and white."

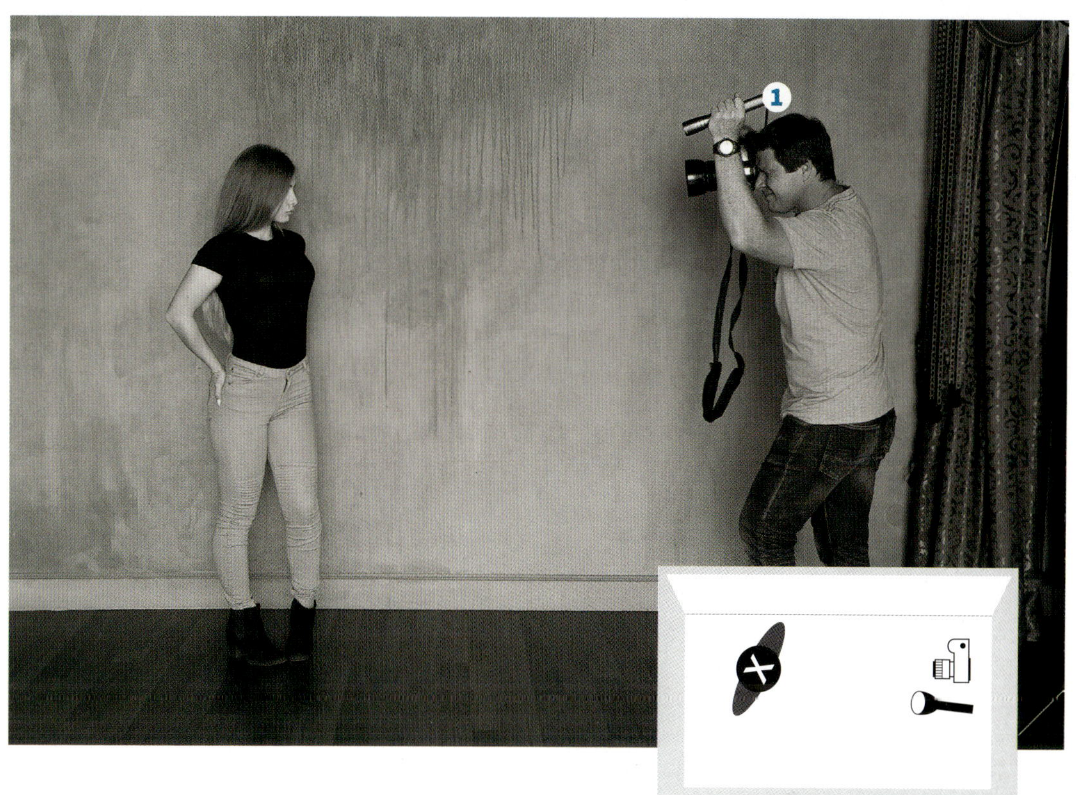

Variations

My LED flashlight is focusable and, at its zoomed-in setting, produces a pattern like a window frame that makes a great improvised alternative to a straight spot.

For more details on how to produce your own custom shadow effects, see Playing with Light and Shadow on page 114.

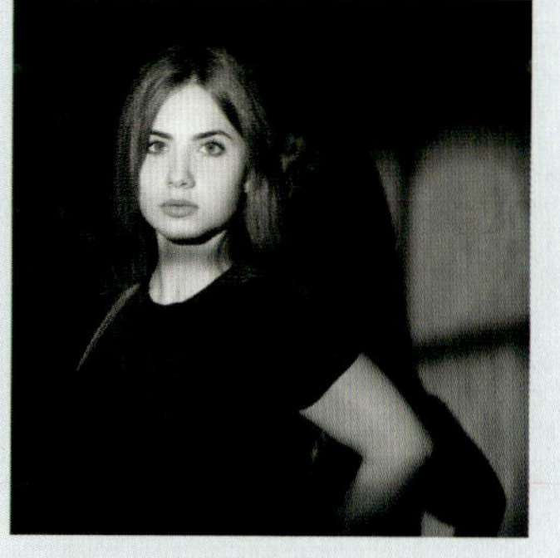

Portrait Through a Gap

For this setup, I used two flags to create a unique lighting effect with just a thin slice of light. Effects like this give the subject a mysterious look and put the viewer in a kind of "spectator" mode. You are free to choose how your subject poses and how broad you want your light to be. If you are aiming for a particularly high-contrast look, you can simply leave out the fill light and stick to a two-light setup.

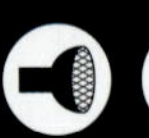 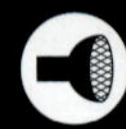 optional 

EFFORT INVOLVED

Medium

SUITABLE FOR

Close-up to three-quarter-length portraits

THE LOOK

Experimental portrait style

Bold shadows

Accent on a selected portion of the face

Brown-toned smokey eyes, dramatic dark red lipstick

EQUIPMENT

2 × standard reflectors with honeycomb grids

2 × flags or similar as partitions

Optional: 1 × 31.5" octabox and 1 × 43" circular silver reflector

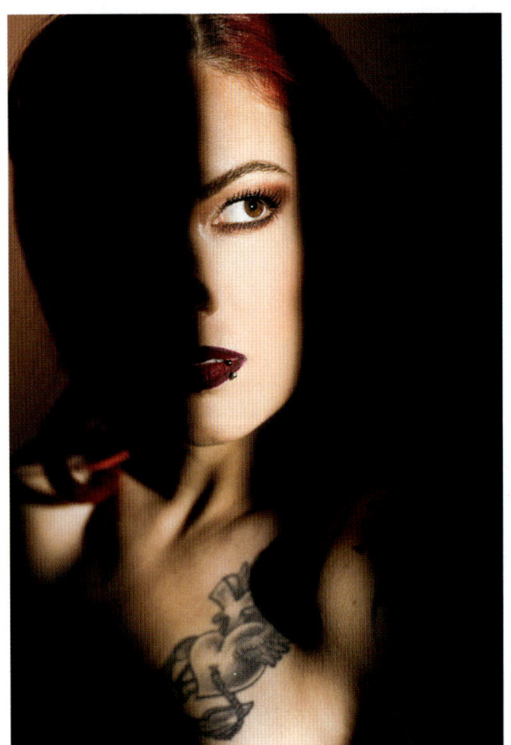

85mm | f4 | 1/125 sec. | ISO 100 | Model: Bianca

HOW IT WORKS

This image is dominated by strong shadows and the clear division into bright and dark areas. The viewer's gaze heads automatically toward the single brightly lit eye that is unmistakably accented by the frontal lighting. The nose is nevertheless discernible and the semi-illuminated mouth implies the shape of the unseen rest of the face. The light fall-off toward the bottom of the frame turns the tattoo into an additional eye-catcher (without it, this area of the image would be far less interesting). The tiny catchlight accents the eye and the background lighting ensures that the outline of the subject's head remains just visible.

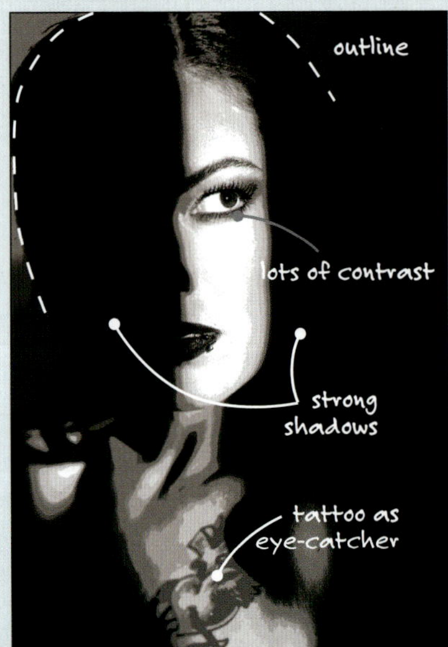

THE SETUP

1. Position the two flags **(1)** to create a narrow gap that you can fire your flash through. Place the standard reflector **(2)** about 6 feet from the gap.

2. Place the gridded standard reflector **(3)** slightly above head height about 20 inches to the right of your subject and position it to brighten the background behind her head.

3. For the variation shown below you need the octabox **(4)** and the reflector **(5)**. Place the octabox in a slightly raised position about 6 feet to the left of your subject to lighten the shadows, and place the reflector on the left to create the accent shown in the photo.

4. Position your subject about 3 feet in front of the brown background.

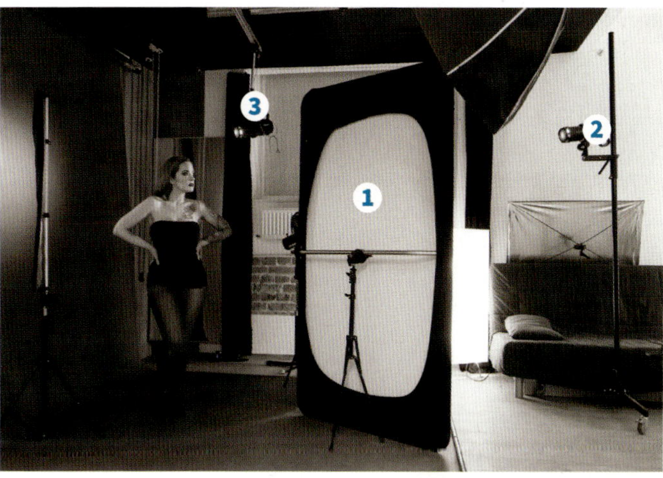

"You can vary the hardness of the shadows by altering the distance between the main light and the flags."

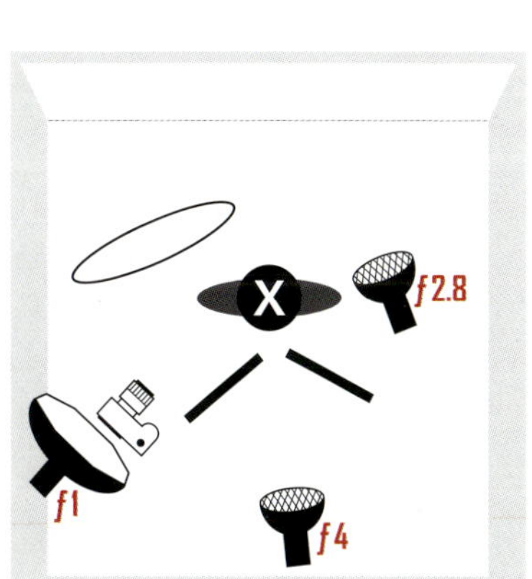

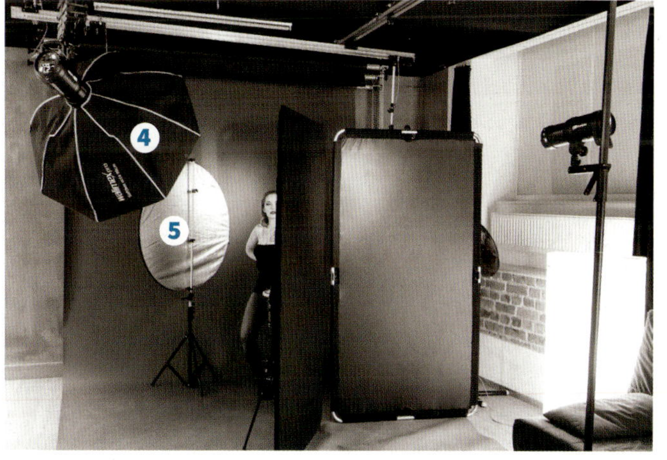

Variations with Accent Lights

If you want to add an accent light, you can use the close proximity of the subject to the background to bounce light off a reflector and light your subject from behind.

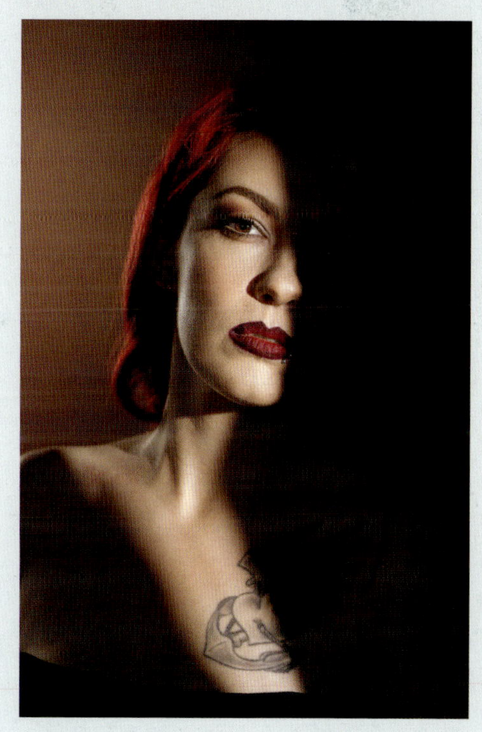

Elegant Full-Length Portrait

A pretty, lacy dress and a luxury chair cry out for a refined portrait treatment. Elisa likes to dress elegantly and likes to put on a slightly haughty look. Two flashes and a reflector are all you need to perfectly capture this kind of mood.

EFFORT INVOLVED

Medium

SUITABLE FOR

All kinds of portraits

THE LOOK

Elegant character portrait with plenty of contrast
Pink-toned, natural-looking makeup

EQUIPMENT

1× 47" strip box with a honeycomb grid
1× standard reflector with a honeycomb grid
1× 30"×40" silver reflector

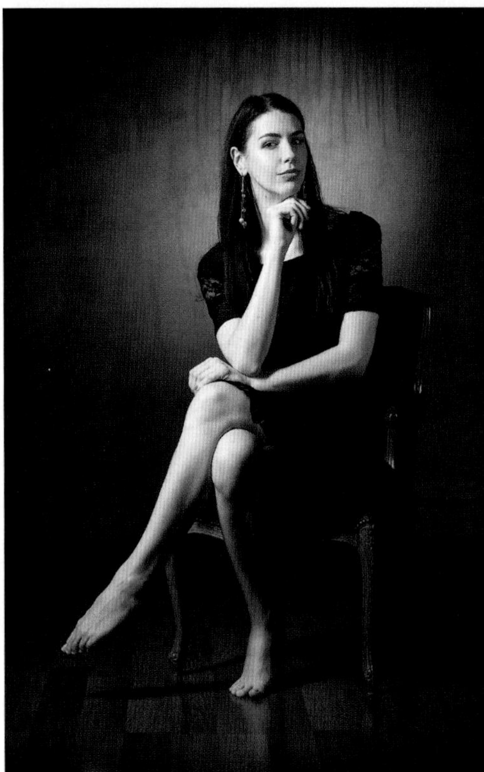

100mm | f8 | 1/160 sec. | ISO 100 | Model: Elisa

HOW IT WORKS

The gridded strip box produces a clearly defined stripe of light across the subject and virtually no background spill. This highly directional light is reflected by the polished wood of the chair, producing several subtle highlights. The head posture creates clear light and shadow sides in the face and underscores the subject's slightly arrogant expression. The reflector lightens the shadow side and ensures that the shaded eye is still clearly visible. The balanced lighting accents the subject's slightly dismissive body language. The background spot helps to focus attention on the face.

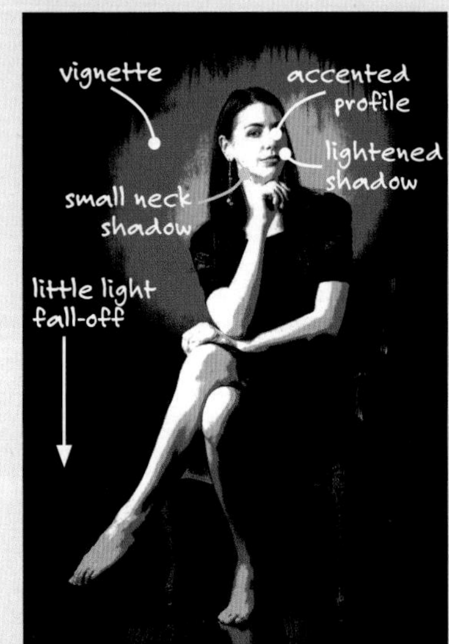

THE SETUP

1. Place the gridded strip box **(1)** in a raised position 8 to 10 feet to the left of your subject at an angle of about 45 degrees. Position it so that the shadows point diagonally downward.

2. Mount the reflector **(2)** on a stand and place it about 20 inches to the right of your subject. Position it to lighten all of the shadows.

3. Place the gridded background spot **(3)** about 3 feet to the right of your subject and slightly above head height. Position it to focus at around neck height and light an area that extends to slightly above the top of your subject's head.

4. In this shot, my subject sat about 6 feet in front of an unevenly painted partition screen. A plain dark gray backdrop would work equally well.

"Shooting from a low position underscores a subject's assertive attitude."

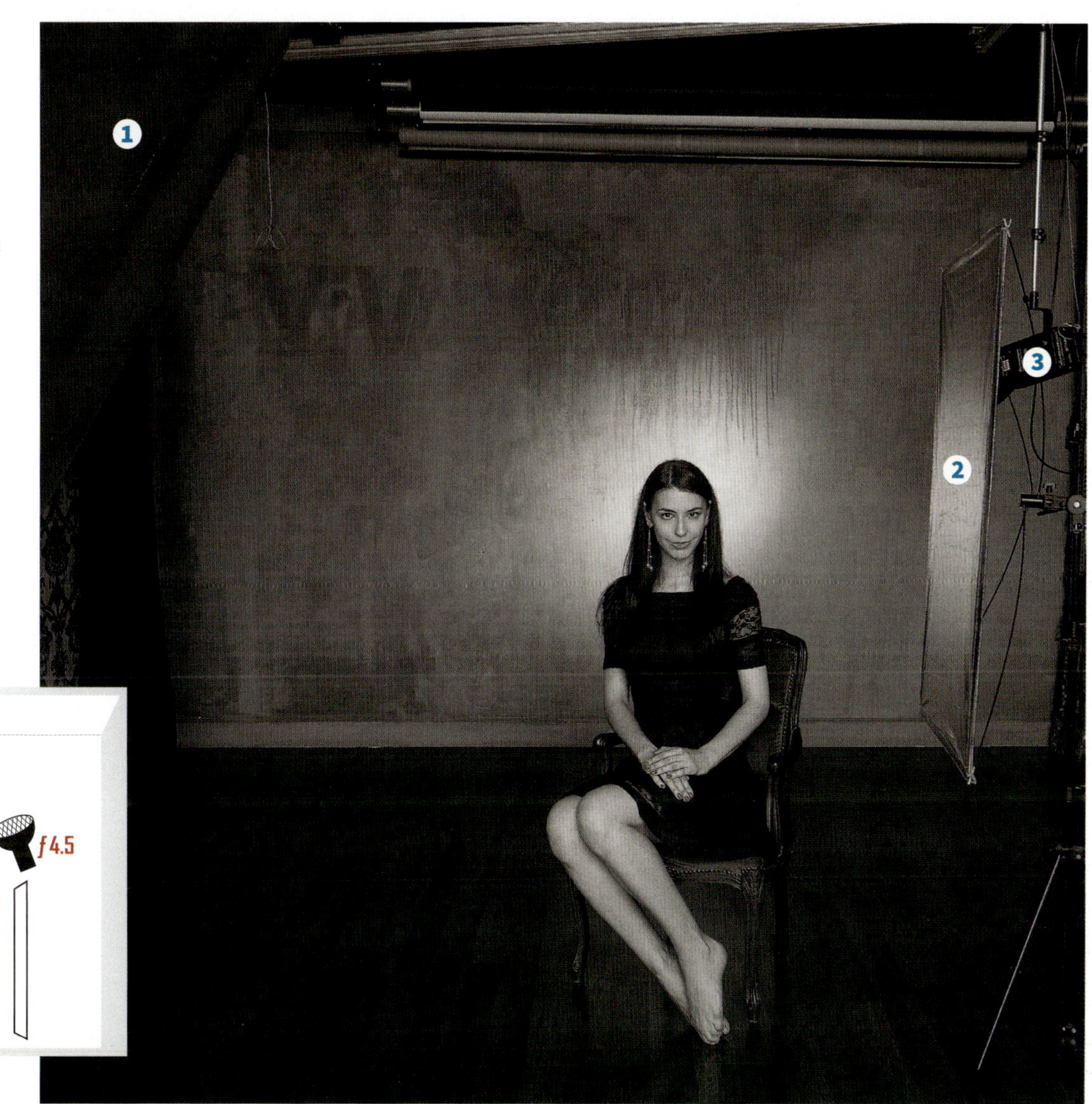

Couples
and Groups

Couples and Groups

If you want to capture two or more people in a single photo, you need to follow a few basic rules. This chapter introduces the most important standard setups, and shows you how to use them creatively to successfully capture everything from loving couples to photos of a rock band.

Lighting Design

As soon as you put multiple subjects in the frame, you have to adjust your lighting setup so that they are all adequately and effectively lit. This usually requires the use of large light shapers and/or greater distances between the subjects and the light source. This isn't so much of a problem for shots of couples, as they usually pose close to one another. You nevertheless have to be make sure that one partner doesn't mask the other and that neither casts unwanted shadows on their counterpart.

Depth of Field

Take care when using a wide aperture to shoot couples and group photos, as it is all too easy for one or more of the subjects to slip outside the field of focus. In order to keep everyone in sharp focus, and depending on the

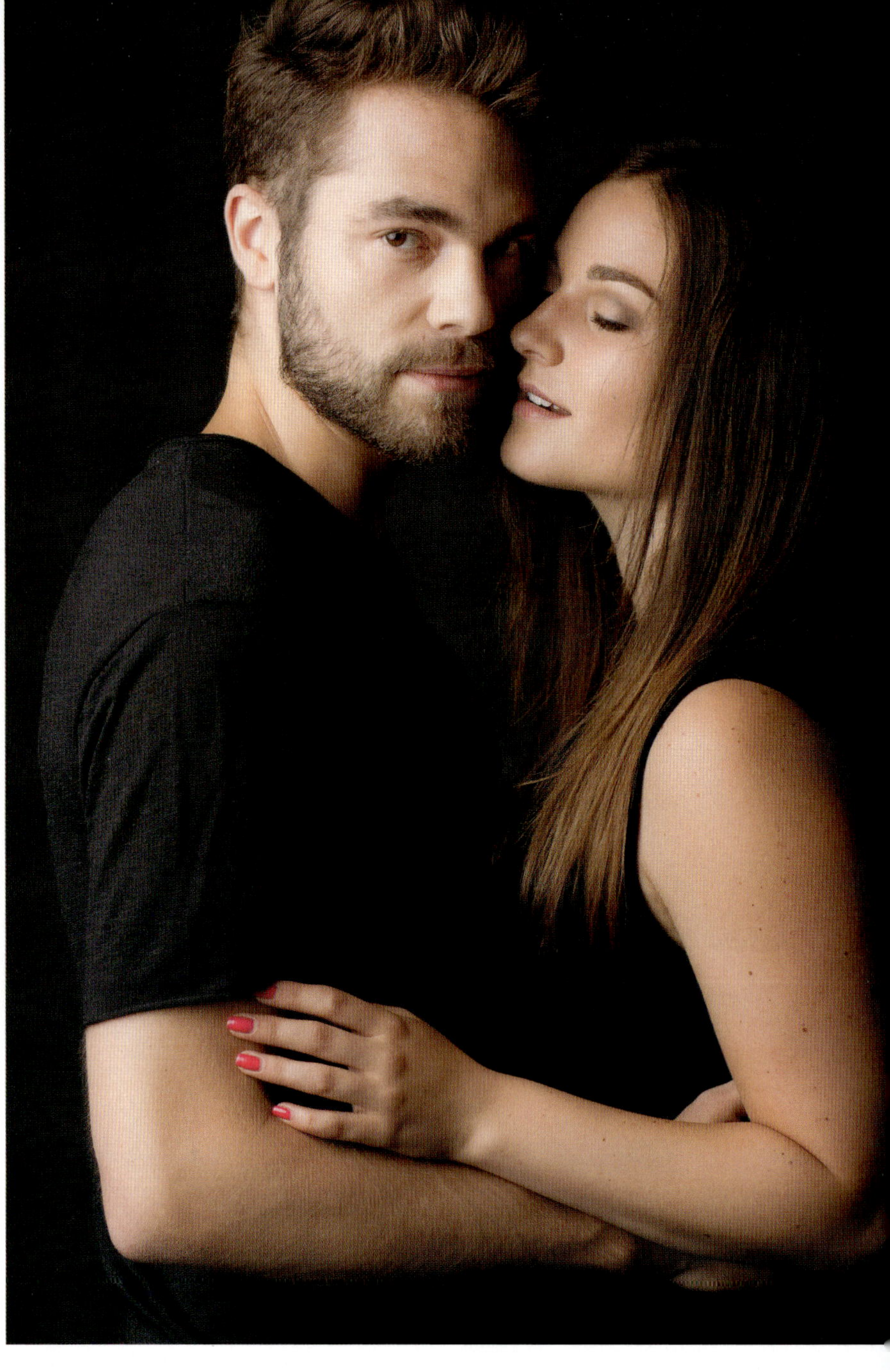

Portrait of a couple captured using a single octabox.
85mm | f8 | 1/160 sec. | ISO 100 | Models: Manon and Rafael

pose and the distances between the subjects, you will usually need to set an aperture between f8 and f22. An exception to this rule is when you use depth of field to deliberately place focus on a specific person. In such situations, you can use a wider aperture to defocus the rest of the group.

Space Issues

Another issue that plagues group shoots is the potentially limited width of the available background. Most rental studios use standard 9-foot backdrop rolls.

If you position a group of people 6 feet or more in front of this kind of background, you will notice that this is simply too narrow. The simplest solution is either to get your subjects to stand closer to the background or to use a wider backdrop (12 feet is the next largest standard-width backdrop). If this still doesn't suit your purposes, you will most likely have to use a wall for your background.

Open Eyes and Suitable Expressions

On a single-subject shoot, it is not usually an issue if the subject blinks or momentarily looks away from the camera—all you have to do is wait a moment and take another shot. The challenge is greater when you are shooting a group scenario, and the simplest route to success is to wait for the right moment and immediately capture a sequence of shots. Take care to wait for your flash units to recycle though—otherwise, some of the shots in the sequence will be incorrectly lit.

So now you know what to look out for, you can dive right in and begin shooting your own couple and group scenarios. And don't forget: make sure there's a good atmosphere on set and have fun while you work!

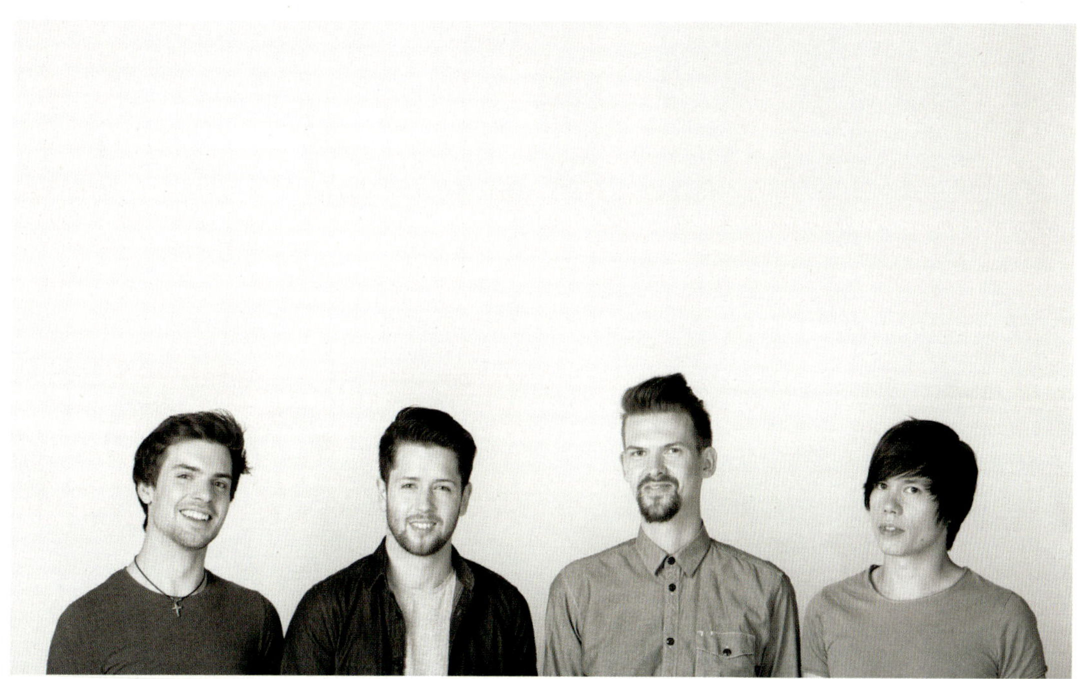

A simple setup with two octaboxes is fine for this shot of a four-man band. Because they are all standing at the same distance from the camera, an aperture of f8 is small enough to keep them all in focus.

100mm | f8 | 1/160 sec. | ISO 100 | Models: nature band

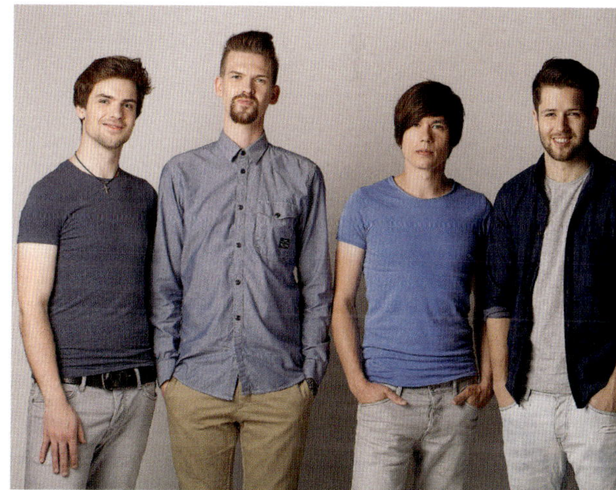

For this shot, I used a single octabox mounted low and to the left. This produced clear light fall-off toward the right-hand end of the frame. As a result, the guy on the far right shows much darker shadows than the others.

100mm | f9 | 1/160 sec. | ISO 100 | Models: nature band

A Simple Setup for Most Situations

One light is great, but two are better, especially when it comes to even lighting for a group subject. This set-up gives you plenty of flexibility regarding the number of subjects and the poses they use, and produces well-defined results with a minimum of effort.

EFFORT INOLVED

Low

SUITABLE FOR

All kinds of portraits

THE LOOK

Evenly lit group portrait

Natural-looking makeup, color-coordinated outfits

EQUIPMENT

1 × 31.5" octabox

1 × 47" octabox

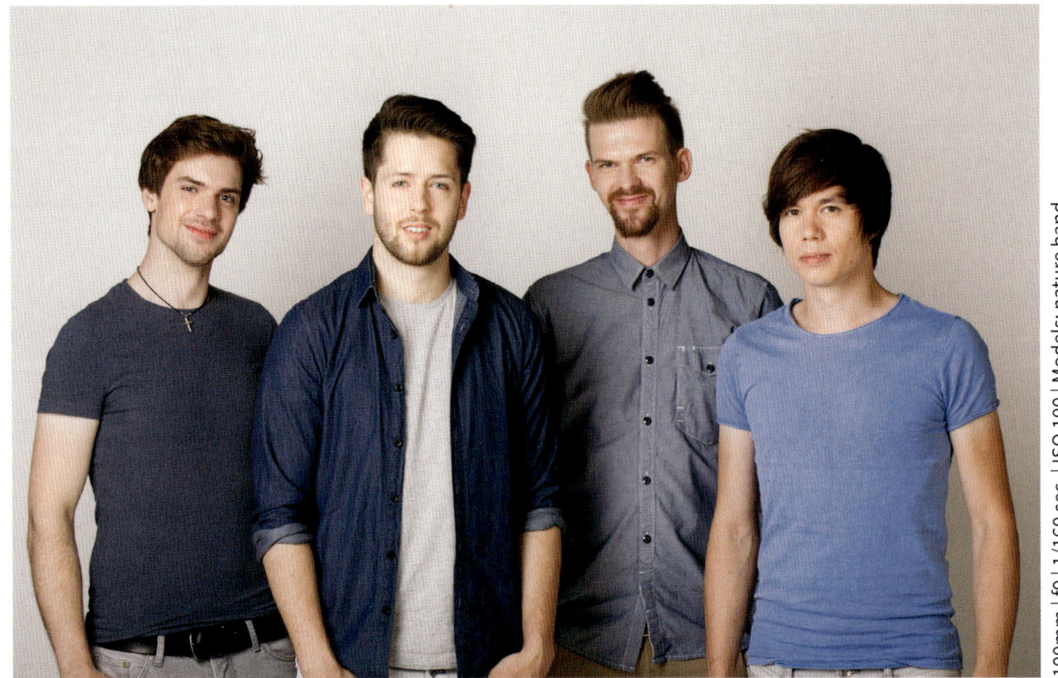

HOW IT WORKS

The size of the left-hand octabox and its distance from the subjects provide even lighting across the entire frame. Its slightly raised, lateral position produces pleasing shadows in the faces and upper bodies, giving the image a feeling of depth. The fill light on the right significantly lightens the shadows and provides an additional source of brightness. The distance between the subjects and the background ensures that the background, too, is evenly lit, and that the subjects don't cast any direct shadows on the backdrop.

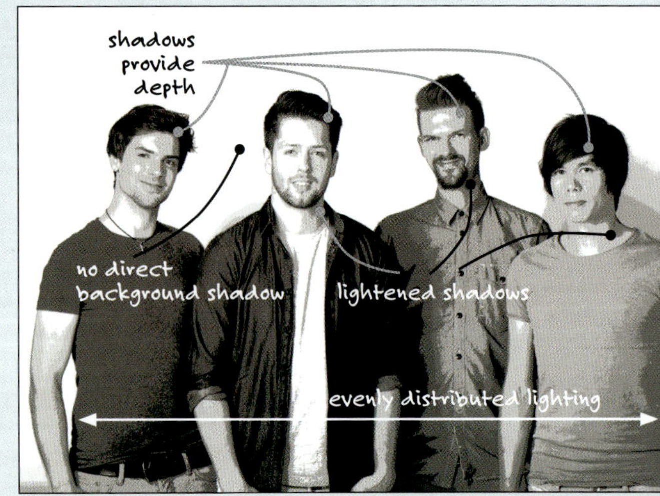

THE SETUP

1. Place the larger octabox **(1)** in a raised position about 10 feet to the left of your models at an angle of about 45 degrees. Position it to produce shadows that point diagonally downward. The larger the area you are lighting and the more even you want your lighting to be, the farther away you need to place your light from your models.

2. Mount the smaller fill octabox **(2)** on a low stand about 8 feet to the right of your models and at an angle of about 45 degrees. Position it so that the shadows from the main light are noticeably lighter. You can alter the distance between your models and the fill light too, depending on the effect you want to achieve.

3. Position your models about 3 feet from the white background.

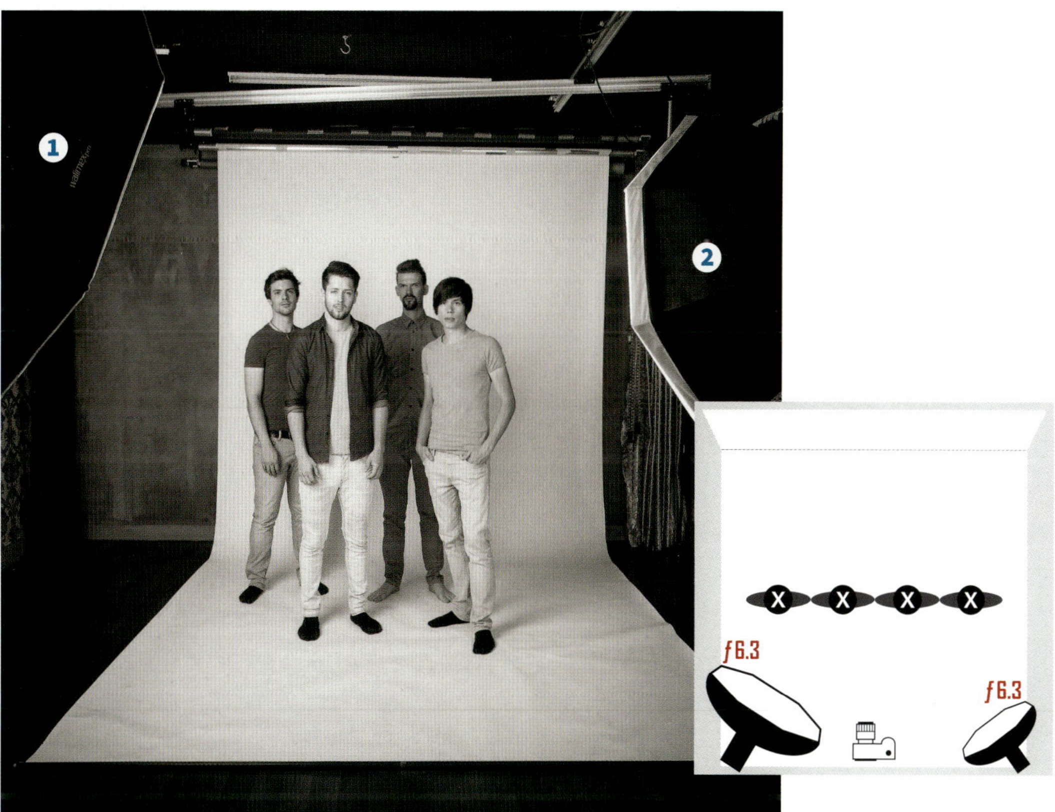

Posing Groups of People

When posing groups of people, always try to get them to form the shape of a triangle standing on its long side. In other words, place the taller people in the middle and the others to the sides. For example, if you are photographing a family, you can get one of the parents to pick up their child and thus form the tip of the imagined triangle. This shape subconsciously conveys a feeling of stability and gives a group a balanced feel.

You can also get your subject to stand closer to one another in a kind of "nested" pattern. If you take this approach, make sure that your subjects' shoulders overlap and that anyone who stands alone is in the back row but close to those in front. This approach ensures that your subjects' faces get closer together, too.

"Pay attention to each individual's position and the lighting in each person's face."

Natural-Looking Couple

Soft, natural light from a single octabox is ideal for capturing intimate, emotional shots of couples. The light is flattering and produces soft shadows that emphasize the subjects' togetherness.

EFFORT INOLVED

Low

SUITABLE FOR

Close-up to three-quarter-length portraits

THE LOOK

Softly lit, natural-looking couple portrait

For her: natural-looking makeup, brown-toned eyeshadow

For him: natural-looking makeup

EQUIPMENT

1 × 47" octabox

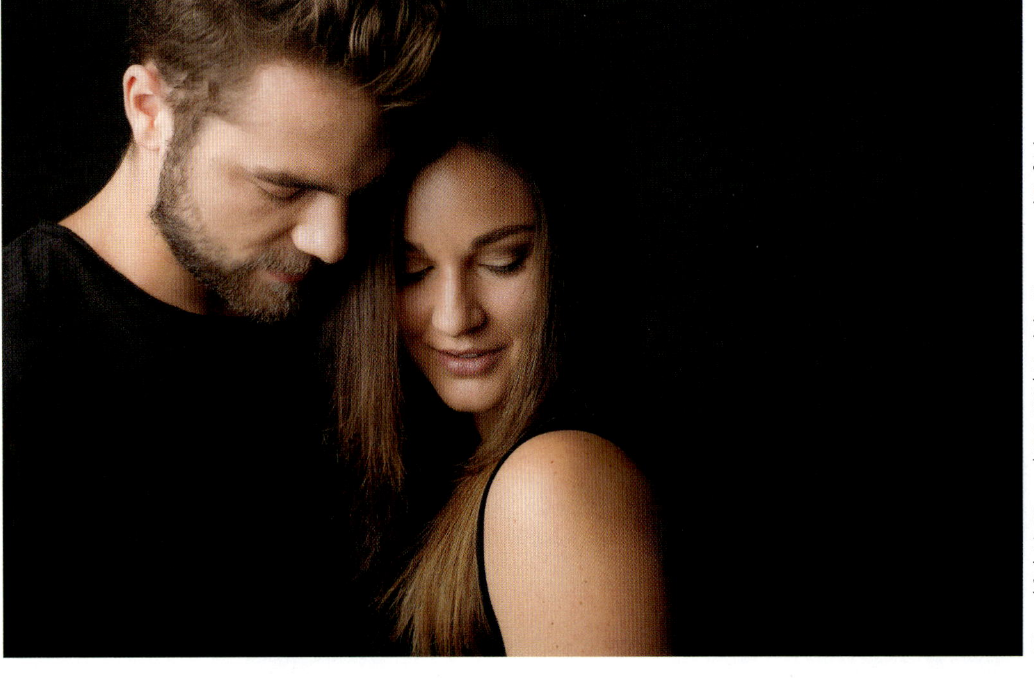

HOW IT WORKS

The large octabox positioned close to but slightly above the subjects produces very soft light with fluid shadows that underscore the natural look of the image. The soft shadows accent the facial contours and the slight spill ensures that the subjects' shadow-side outlines are discernible against the softly lit background. The negative space on the right is only dimly lit by the main light and helps to focus attention on the subjects. The lightening effect in the facial shadows works particularly well, with the light reflected directly off the subjects' skin.

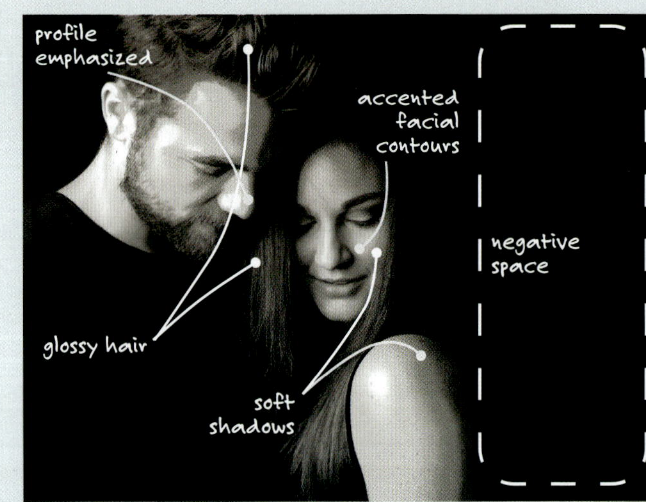

THE SETUP

1. Place the octabox **(1)** in a raised position about 3 feet to the left of your subjects and at an angle of about 45 degrees.

2. Your models should stand about 6 feet from the black background.

3. Adjust the height of the octabox so that her nose shadow is just visible beneath the tip of her nose.

4. Pay attention to the background light and adjust it if necessary by rotating the flash head toward or away from the background. If you do make adjustments, check for any knock-on effects these may have on the main light illuminating your models.

"Get your models to face the light if you don't want the shadows to turn out too dark."

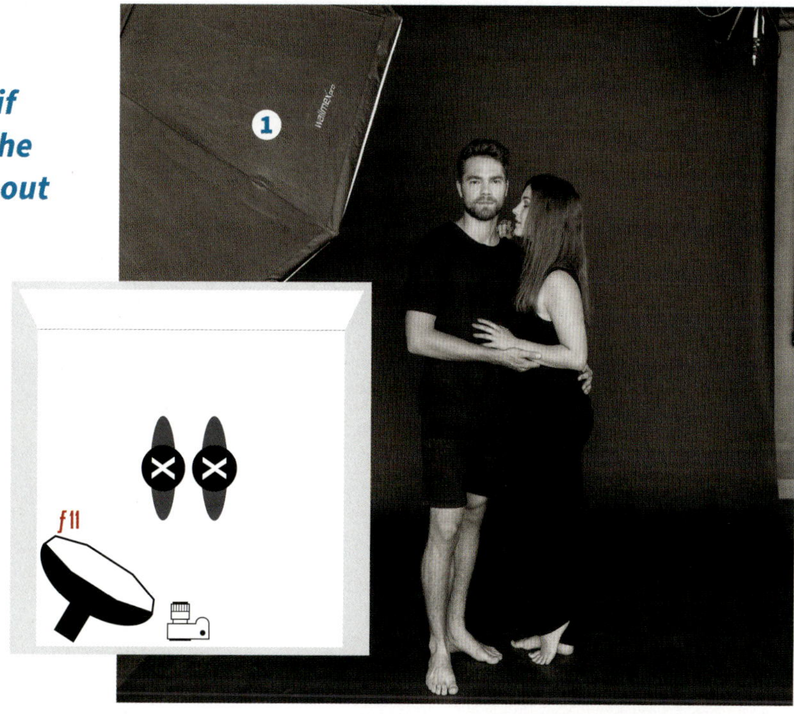

The Feel-Good Factor

A friendly atmosphere on set is essential. If you show genuine interest in your subjects, this will help to build up trust. Ask how they met, or about their hobbies and interests, and try to let them find their own poses. Real emotions have to be present on set if you want to capture them in your images, and this works best if your subjects feel good about the situation and don't think about what's actually going on. Couples should feel free to look each other in the eyes or embrace, and you need to be ready to capture naturally beautiful moments when they occur.

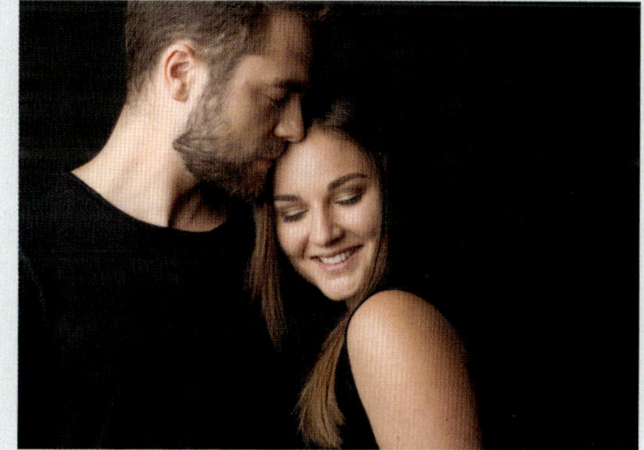

You won't miss a tender scene or a sweet smile if you concentrate on shooting and give your models plenty of space to be themselves.

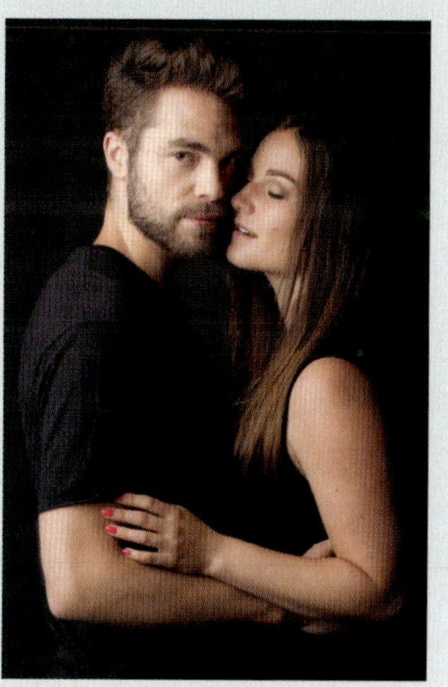

This setup, with its large octabox, is great for portrait-format shots, too.

A Reflector for More Versatility

You can add versatility to the simple setup shown on the previous page simply by adding a reflector. This keeps things natural-looking but gives your subjects more posing flexibility, especially for their shadow sides.

EFFORT INOLVED

Low

SUITABLE FOR

Close-up to three-quarter-length portraits

THE LOOK

Natural-looking portrait with lightened shadows
For her: natural-looking makeup, brown-toned eyeshadow
For him: natural-looking makeup

EQUIPMENT

1× 47" octabox
1× 30"×40" silver reflector

224

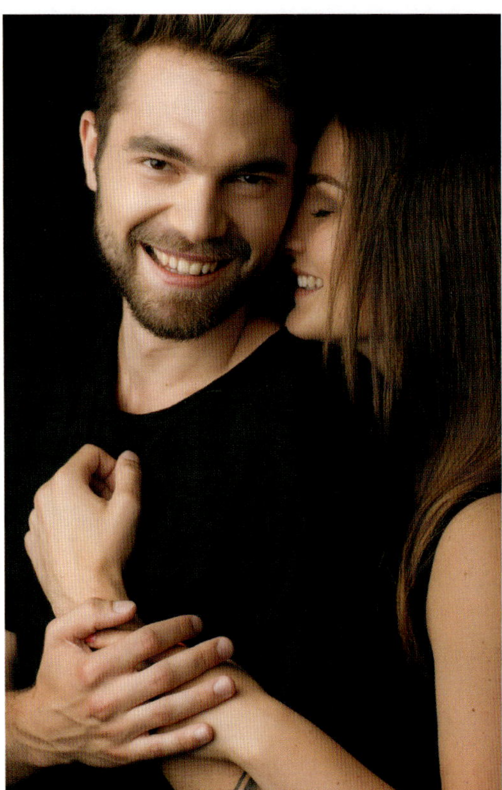

HOW IT WORKS

The large octabox positioned close to but slightly above the subjects produces very soft light with fluid shadows that underscore the natural look of the image. The diagonal shadows accent the facial contours and provide plenty of depth. The soft background light provides enough contrast to separate the black t-shirt and the subjects' dark hair from the background and keep their outlines visible. The shadow sides of the faces benefit from the effect produced by the reflector, and emphasize both of his eyes and her radiant expression.

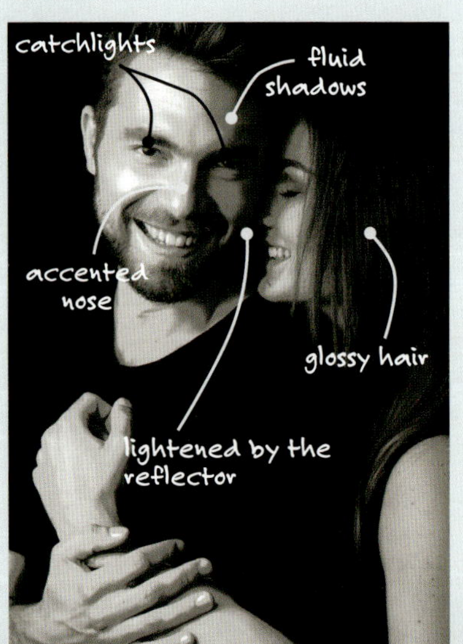

THE SETUP

1. Place the octabox **(1)** in a raised position about 20 inches to the left of your subjects and at an angle of about 45 degrees.

2. Position your subjects about 6 feet in front of the black background.

3. Position the octabox so that the nose shadows are still visible beneath the tips of your subjects' noses.

4. Pay attention to the background light and adjust it if necessary by rotating the flash head toward or away from the background. If you do make adjustments, check for any knock-on effects these may have on the main light illuminating your models.

5. Place the reflector **(2)** in a raised position about 3 feet from your subjects and position it to lighten the shadows and reflect the light from the main light downward.

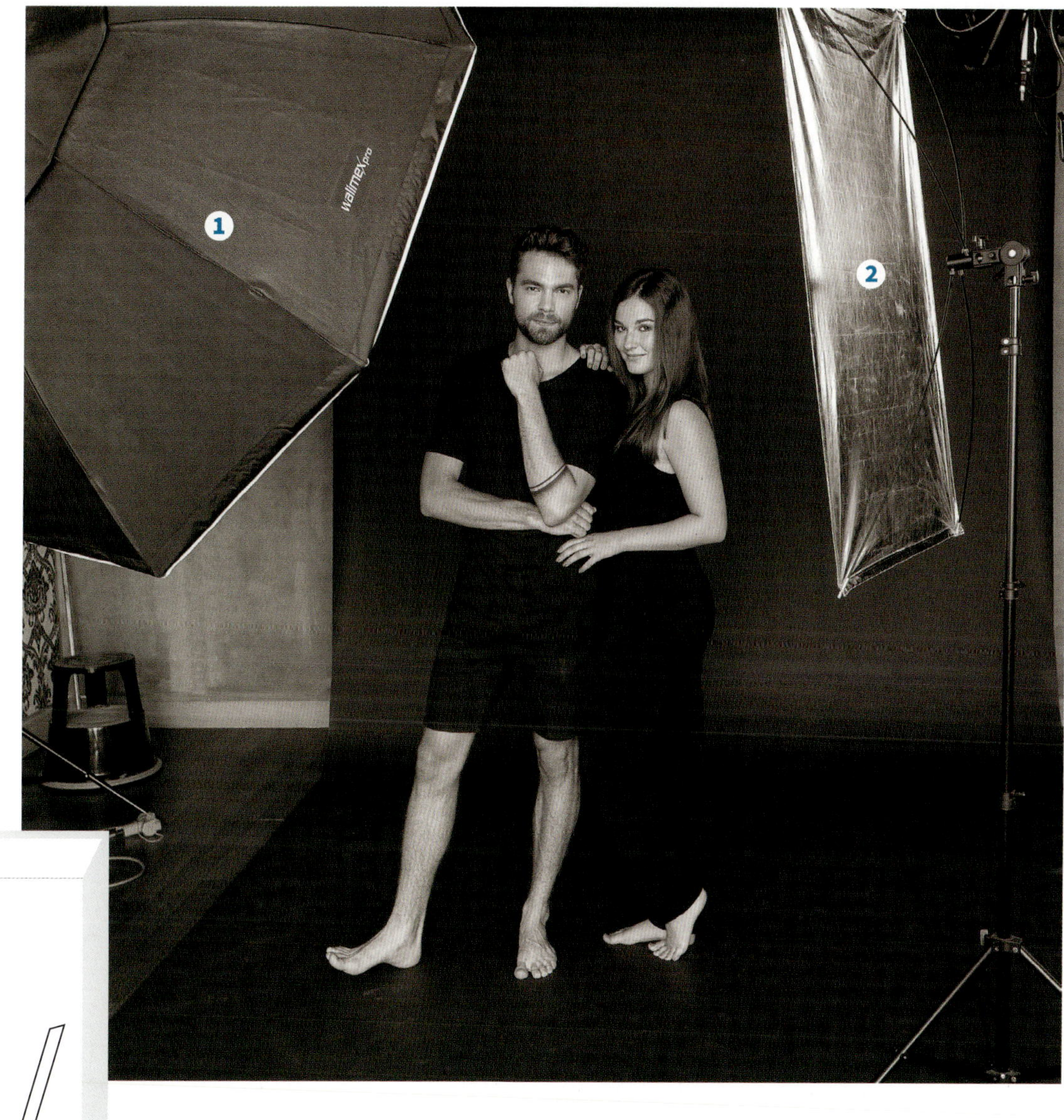

"Select your ideal framing while you shoot, not later during post-processing."

Accenting Faces

A background spot at head height is a great tool for focusing attention on your subjects' faces. In this setup, the large octabox main light ensures that the overall lighting remains soft and natural looking.

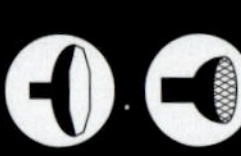

EFFORT INOLVED

Medium

SUITABLE FOR

Close-up to three-quarter-length portraits

THE LOOK

Soft and natural-looking portrait with a background light that accents the faces

For her: natural-looking makeup, brown-toned eyeshadow

For him: natural-looking makeup

EQUIPMENT

1× 47" octabox

1× standard reflector with a honeycomb grid

1× 30"×40" silver reflector

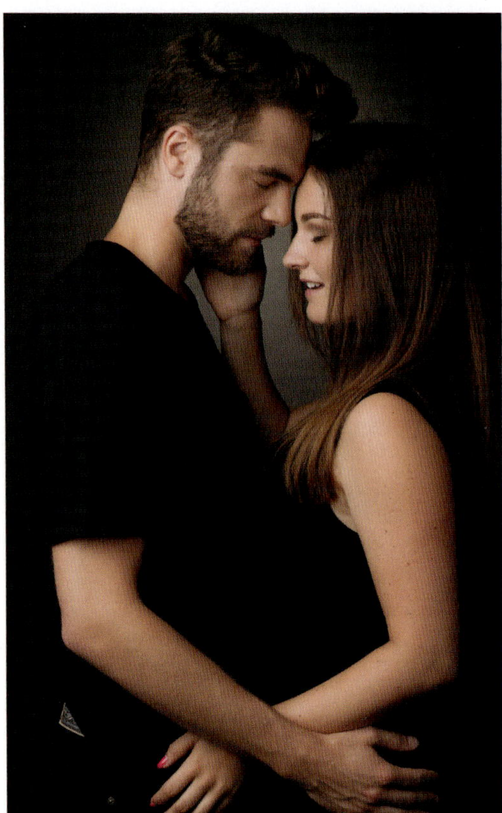

85mm | f8 | 1/160 sec. | ISO 100 | Models: Manon and Rafael

HOW IT WORKS

The large octabox positioned diagonally and slightly above the subjects produces very soft light with fluid shadows that accent the facial contours and produce natural-looking glossy hair. The reflector subtly lightens the shadow areas and underscores the soft overall look. The dark gray background provides enough contrast to keep the outlines of the dark clothing visible. The bright background spot focuses attention on the subjects' faces and intensifies their outlines.

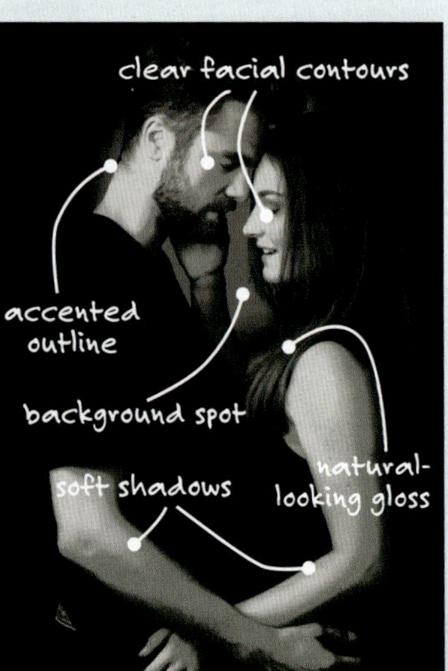

1. Place the octabox **(1)** in a raised position about 5 feet to the left of your subjects at an angle of about 45 degrees. Position it so that its light hits your subjects diagonally and illuminates the entire area between head and knee height.

2. Mount the reflector **(2)** on a stand about 5 feet to the right with its center at head height and pointing slightly downward. Use it to brighten your left-hand subject's face.

3. Mount the gridded background reflector **(3)** on a ceiling rail or a boom stand centrally behind your subjects at a height of about 8 feet.

4. Position your subjects about 6 feet from the black background.

"For shots with an affectionate undertone, instead of giving your subjects precise instructions, let them find their own poses."

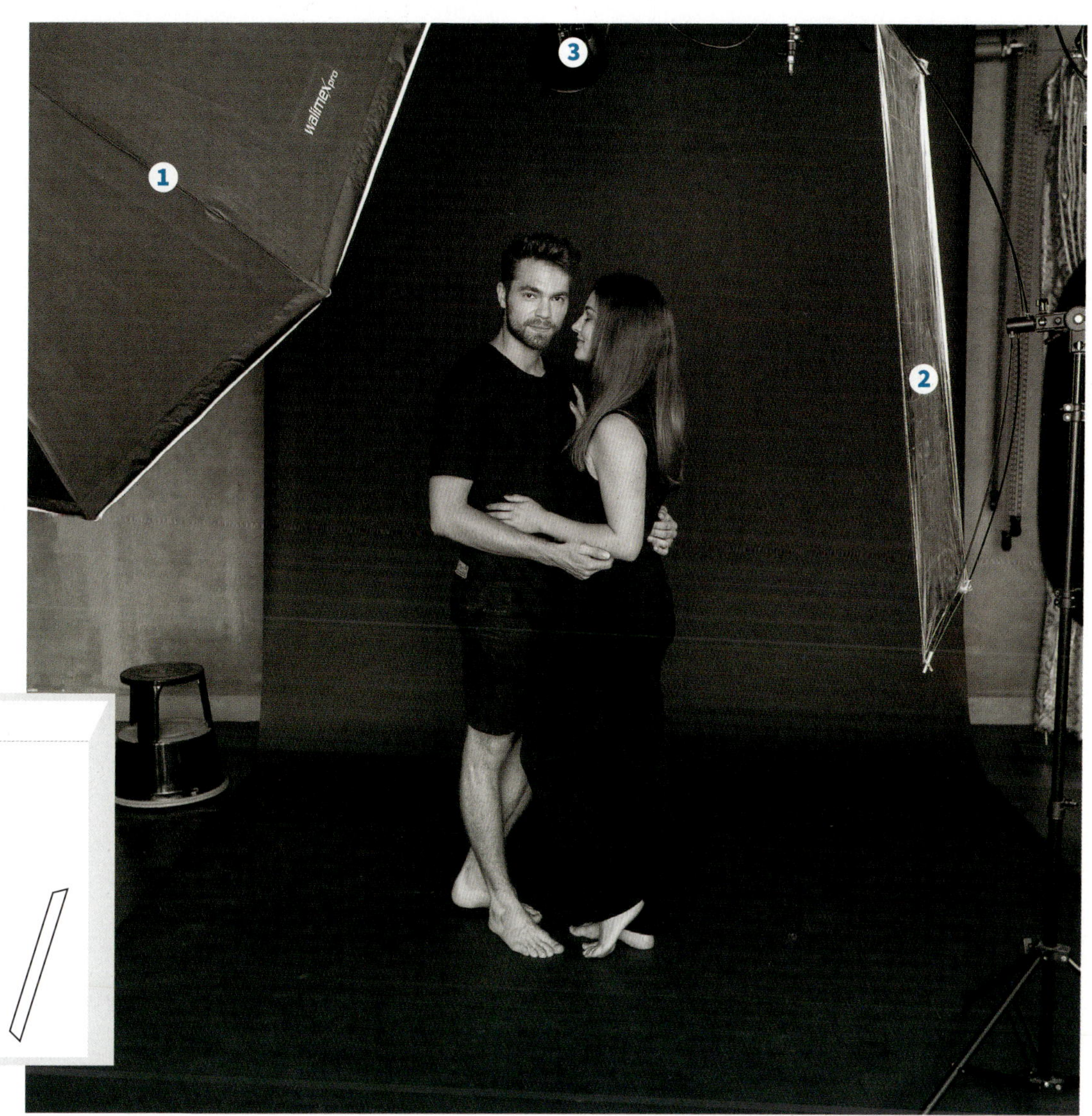

Bold and Simple

Portraits of couples captured for advertising purposes typically require a more intense look. This setup uses three flashes and a reflector to produce an appropriate look and feel, while the accent light adds emphasis to the subjects' faces.

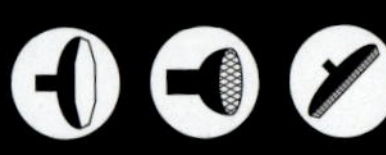

EFFORT INOLVED

High

SUITABLE FOR

Close-up to three-quarter-length portraits

THE LOOK

Bold composition with multiple accents

For her: natural-looking makeup, brown-toned eyeshadow

For him: natural-looking makeup

EQUIPMENT

1× 47" octabox

1× standard reflector with a honeycomb grid

1× 47" strip box with a honeycomb grid

1× 30"×40" silver reflector

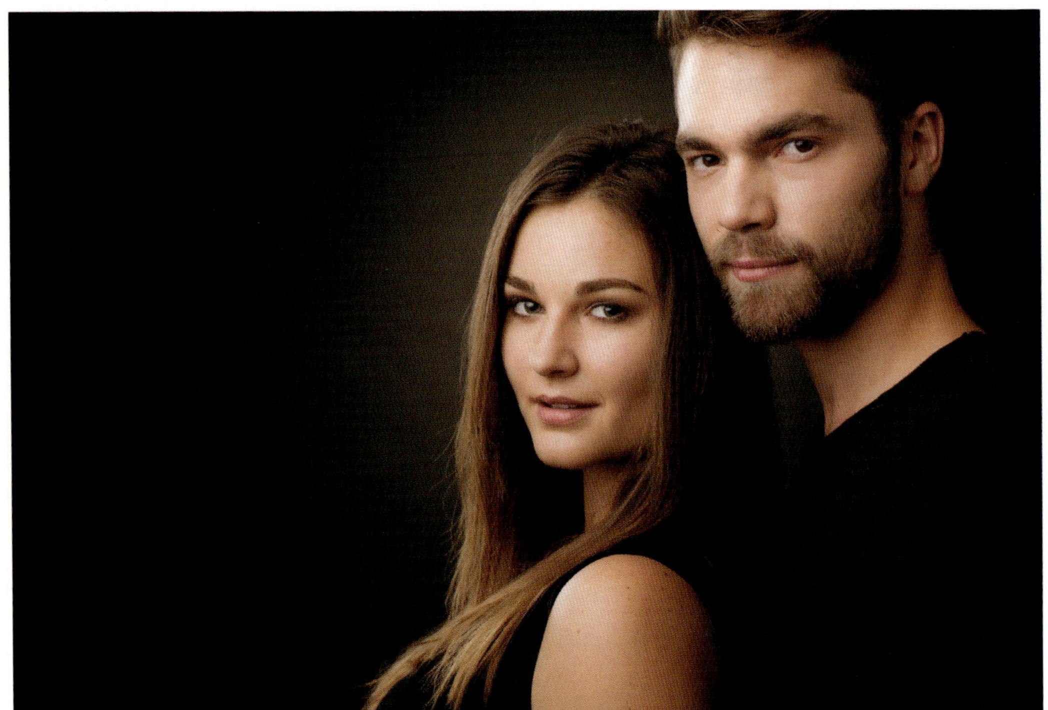

85mm | f8 | 1/160 sec. | ISO 100 | Models: Manon and Rafael

HOW IT WORKS

The diagonal, slightly raised position of the large octabox produces soft shadows that are further attenuated by the reflector. The result is highly natural-looking lighting that highlights the facial features and reveals plenty of detail in the shadow areas. The accent light from the left adds presence to the faces and, together with the diagonal shadows from the main light, gives this image its three-dimensional look. The main light provides sufficient brightness to separate the dark clothing from the background.

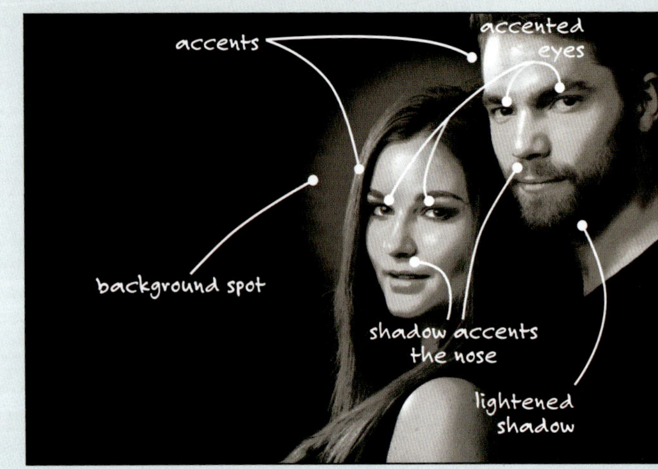

THE SETUP

1. Place the octabox **(1)** about 5 feet to the left in a raised position and at an angle of about 45 degrees. Set it up so that its light hits your subjects diagonally and illuminates the entire area between head and knee height.

2. Mount the reflector **(2)** in a slightly raised position about 5 feet to the right and position it to lighten your left-hand subject's face.

3. Place the accent strip box **(3)** to the left rear about 5 feet from your subjects and at an angle of about 45 degrees. Position It with its center at head height so that it produces nice accents on the left.

4. Mount the background light **(4)** centrally on a ceiling rail or a boom stand slightly behind your subjects at a height of about 8 feet.

5. Get your subjects to stand about 6 feet away from the black background.

Variations

Because the main light comes from their right, your subjects have plenty of space to try out different head postures. In this example, Rafael turns his head completely toward Manon to reveal his profile. This gesture produces a strong feel of togetherness in the resulting image.

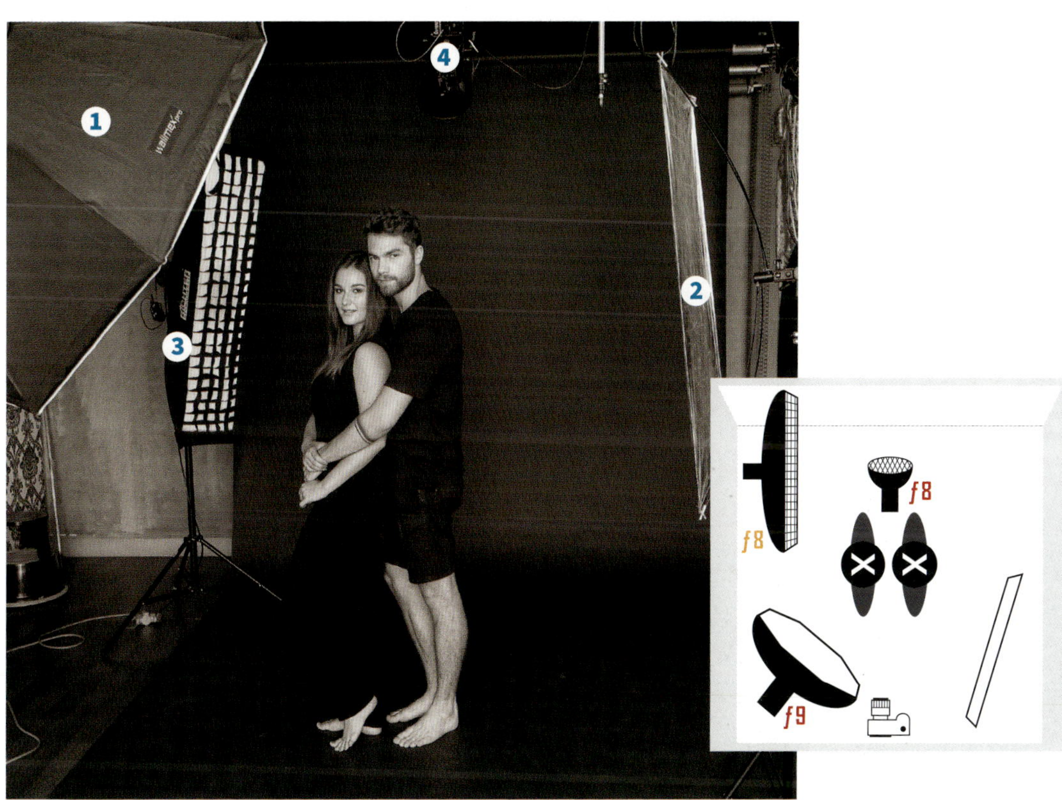

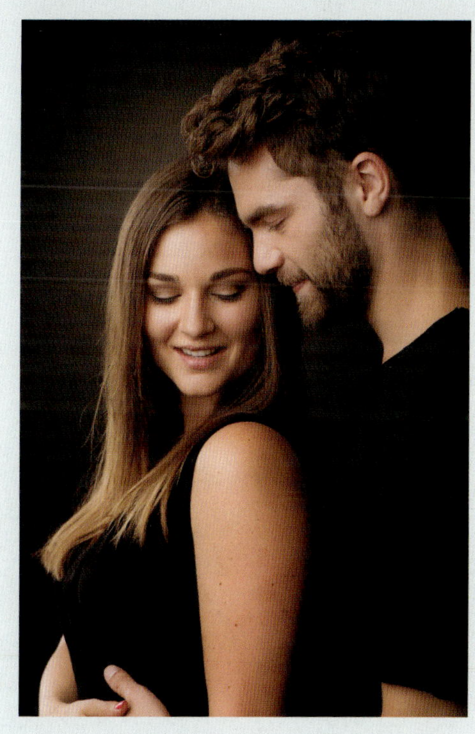

Natural Look from a Construction Site Lamp

Even a simple construction site lamp can produce beautifully soft light that is ideal for capturing silky smooth portraits of couples. The result looks like it was shot near a window.

EFFORT INOLVED

Low

SUITABLE FOR

Close-up to three-quarter-length portraits

THE LOOK

Portrait with a natural, daylight look

For her: natural-looking makeup, brown-toned eyeshadow

For him: natural-looking makeup

EQUIPMENT

1× 500W LED construction site lamp

1× 30" ×40" silver reflector

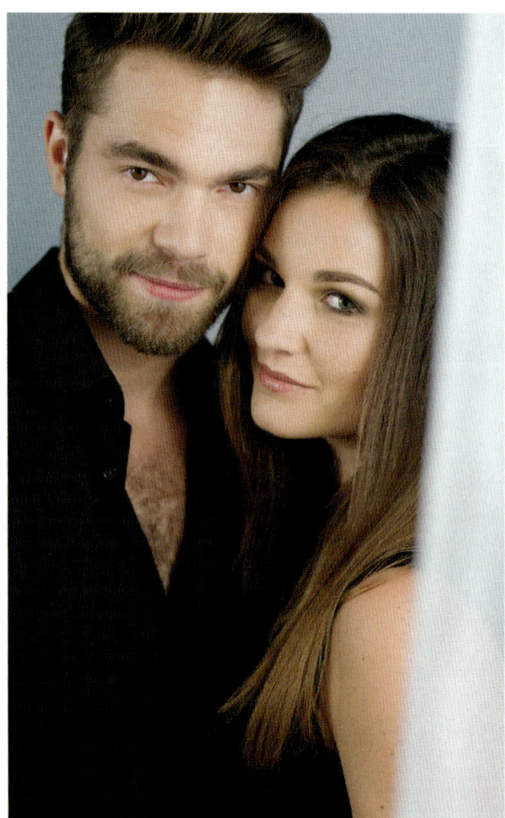

85mm | f2.8 | 1/160 sec. | ISO 800 | Models: Manon and Rafael

HOW IT WORKS

In this setup, the light from the construction light lamp is significantly softened by shining it through a curtain. It produces virtually no shadows on the light side. The shadow side is only slightly darker thanks to the raised reflector that helps to produce clear facial contours. The curtain material produces highly diffuse light and virtually no fall-off (a very natural look). This setup accents the eyes while reducing the nose shadows and the contours they would otherwise produce. This is a great setup for capturing intense but natural-looking portraits.

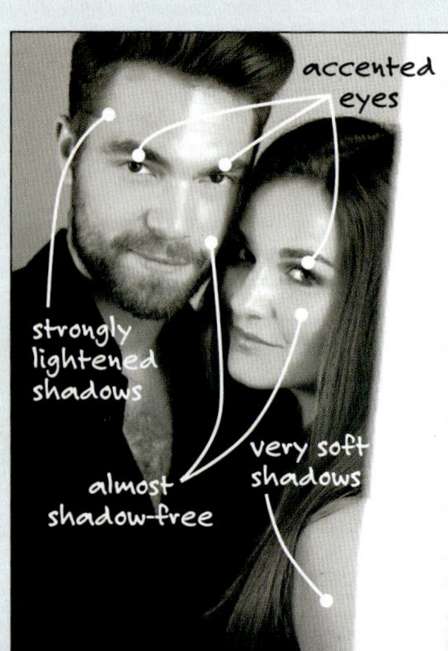

THE SETUP

1. Mount a regular LED construction site lamp **(1)** on a 6-foot stand about 5 feet to the front right of your subjects and at an angle of about 45 degrees. Make sure it points directly toward their faces.

2. Hang a double layer of translucent curtain material **(2)** from a boom stand or a mobile background holder in front of the lamp and about 18 inches from your subjects.

3. Position your subjects about 5 feet in front of the white background.

4. Position the reflector **(3)** vertically to the front left about 3 feet from your subjects and at an angle of about 45 degrees.

5. You will need to adjust your camera settings to suit the weaker light from the construction lamp. For this shot, I used an aperture setting of f2.8 and increased my ISO setting to 800.

If you want, you can use the curtain material as a compositional element too. If you allow it to appear hazily in the foreground it turns the viewer into a spectator and enhances the feeling of intimacy in the photo. Leaving the foreground prop out of focus also adds depth to the result.

Variations

I shot this variant in landscape format and cropped the top of Rafael's head to emphasize the proximity of the camera to the subjects. This makes Manon the central point of focus and moves both of their heads toward the top of the frame, thus enabling their shoulders to form a stable visual basis for the composition.

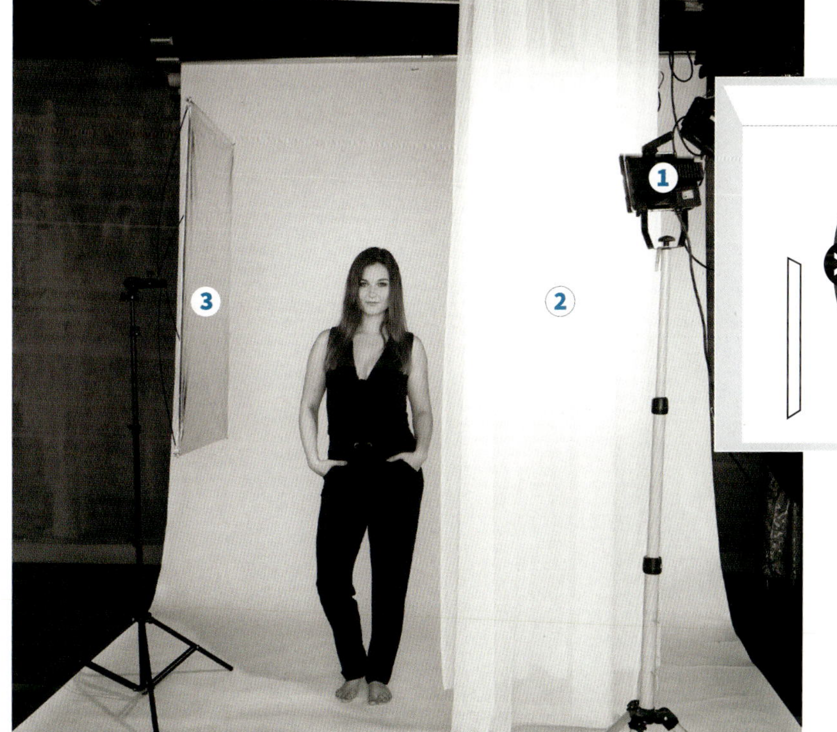

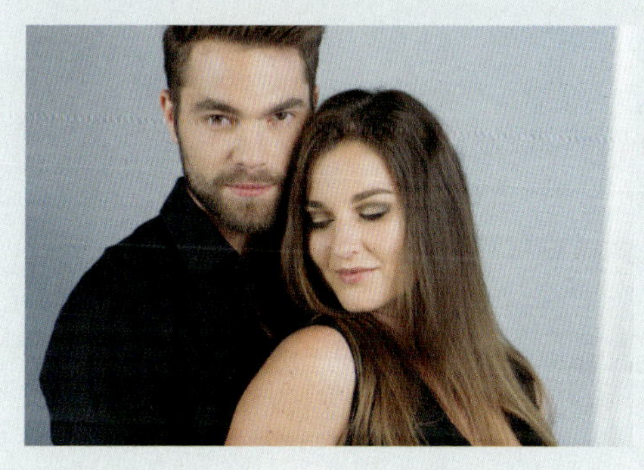

"To avoid potential loss of sharpness due to the wide aperture, make sure that both your subjects' eyes are the same distance from the camera."

Backlit Rock Band

This eye-catching silhouetted "paper cut-out" look is great for stylized portraits of couples, groups, or even a rock band. This simple setup enables you to produce images in which the subjects appear to "walk out of the light" toward the viewer.

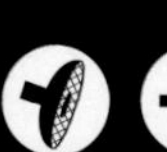
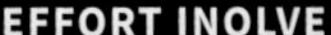

EFFORT INOLVED

Low

SUITABLE FOR

All kinds of portraits

THE LOOK

Backlit, silhouette-style composition

Natural-looking makeup

Casual clothing and musical instruments

EQUIPMENT

1× beauty dish with a honeycomb grid

1× standard reflector with barndoors

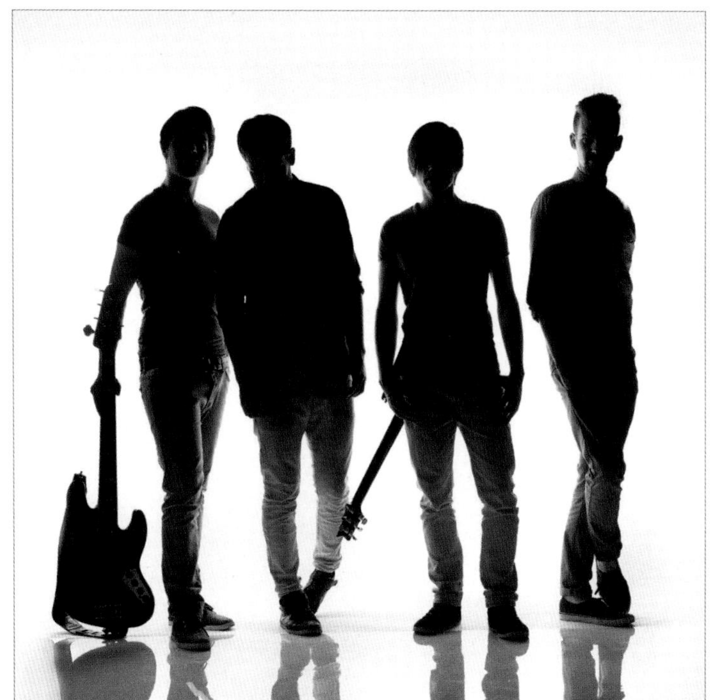

HOW IT WORKS

This silhouette-style portrait uses backlight. The gridded beauty dish on the left and the standard reflector with its barndoors produce a very bright backlight and reflections from the background that in turn produce accents on both sides of the subjects' faces. Together with spill light from the main light, these make some vague details in the faces and the clothing just visible. This gives the image a slightly less anonymous feel and invites the viewer to take a closer look. The shiny reflection on the floor is an additional visual highlight.

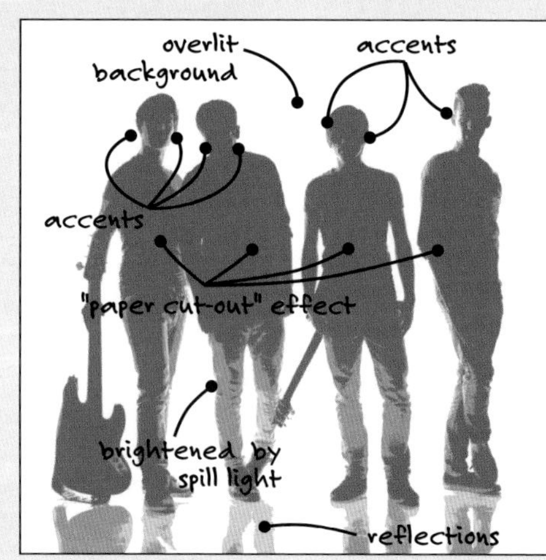

1. Mount the gridded beauty dish **(1)** on a stand at head height about 18 inches to the left of the leftmost subject. The light shaper needs to be positioned slightly behind the subject and positioned to hit the background slightly left of center. In a four-person shot like this, that is somewhere between the two guys on the left.

2. Mount the standard reflector with its barndoors **(2)** about 18 inches to the right of the rightmost subject at head height. Position this light slightly behind your subject too. Position this light to hit the background slightly right of center (i.e., between the two guys on the right).

Instead of using two different main lights, you can use two gridded beauty dishes or two standard reflectors with barndoors for this setup.

To create the reflection on the floor, use either a sheet of mirrored laminate or plexiglass (usually available in 10 × 5–foot sheets from a woodwork shop or a hardware store). Make sure that any reflective surface you use is clean and free from dirt and other marks. Place it directly beneath (or slightly in front of) your subjects and pointing toward the camera (see the photo below). If your reflective surface is narrower than your backdrop, make sure they both have the same color. This makes it easier to remove any unwanted edges during post-processing.

"Light-colored clothes produce better detail definition in this kind of setup."

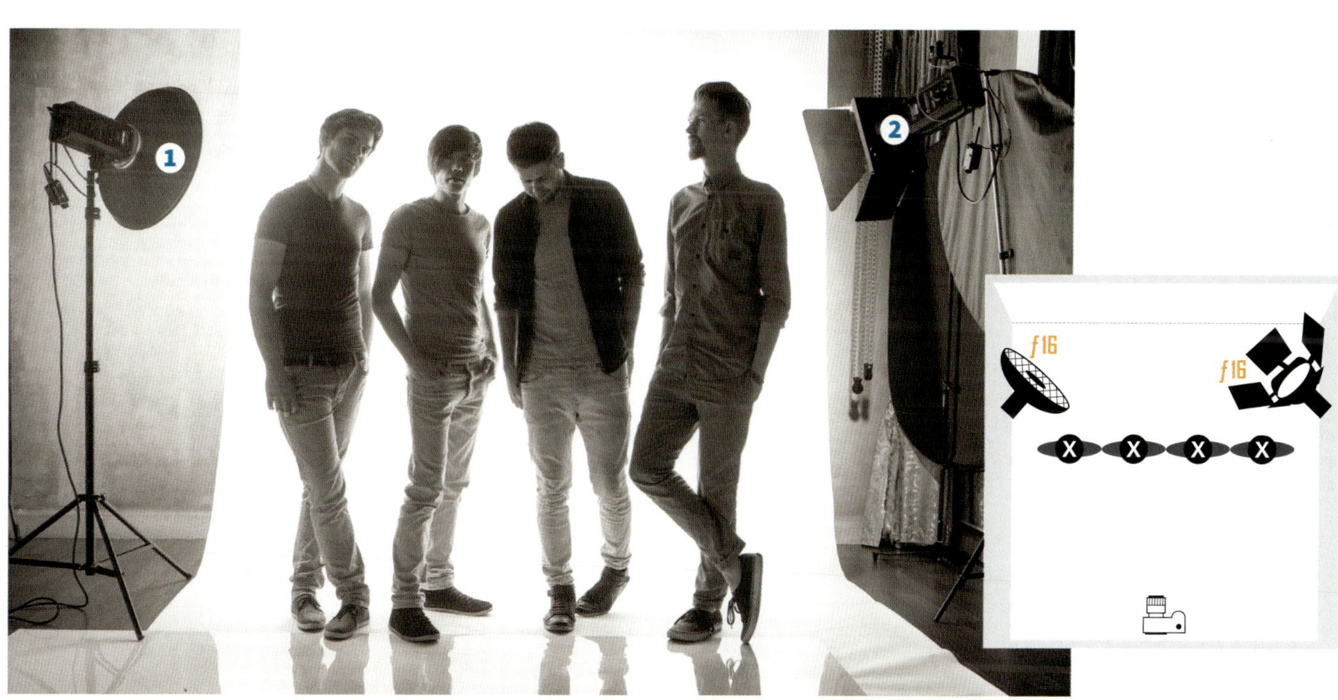

Group Portrait with Additional Highlights

Accent lights are great for producing additional high-lights that emphasize contours and grab the viewer's attention. The shadows reflected in the floor provide an additional eye-catcher that contrasts nicely with the accent lights.

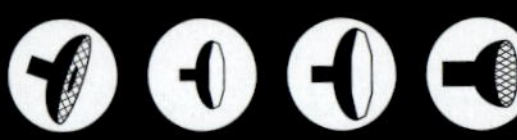

EFFORT INOLVED

High

SUITABLE FOR

All kinds of portraits

THE LOOK

Group portrait with interesting reflections and accents

Natural-looking makeup

Color-coordinated outfits

EQUIPMENT

1× beauty dish with a honeycomb grid

1× 31.5" octabox

1× 47" octabox

1× standard reflector with a honeycomb grid

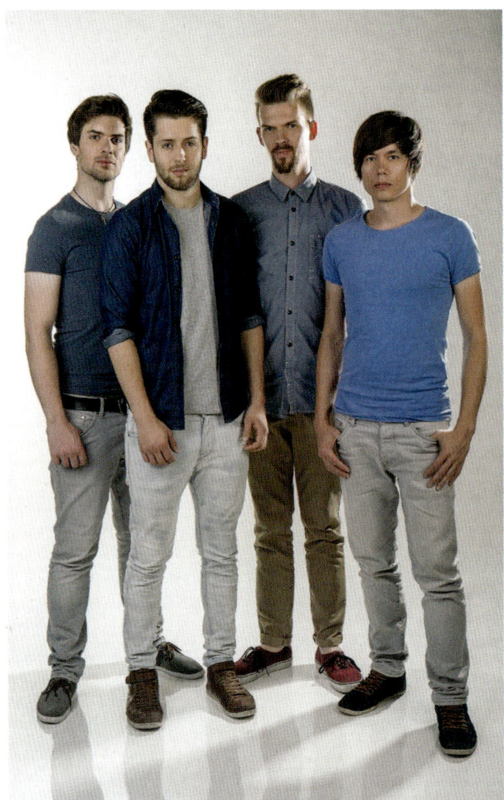

54mm | f8 | 1/160 sec. | ISO 100 | Models: nature band

HOW IT WORKS

This style of portrait features reflections and highlights for added interest. The twin octaboxes illuminate all four subjects evenly from both sides, thus reducing the strength of the shadows and reducing overall definition. The even lighting accents each subject individually and provides plenty of detail. The strong accent light on the right produces highlights that counteract the slightly flat main light. The background gradient darkens from left to right and provides a nice contrasting counterpoint to the accent light.

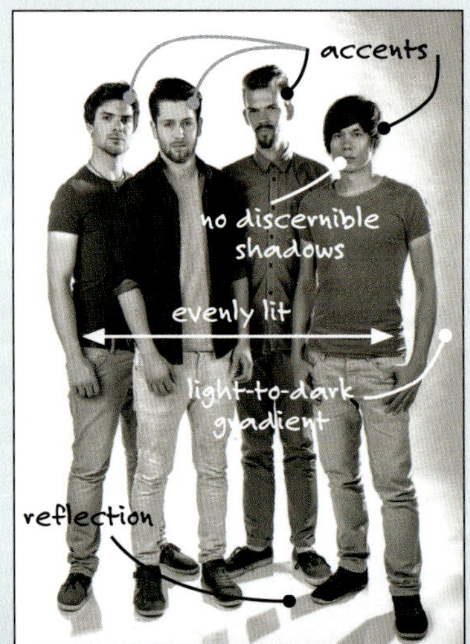

THE SETUP

1. Place the smaller octabox **(1)** in a raised position about 6 feet to the right of your subjects and at an angle of about 45 degrees. Set the flash output to produce clear shadows beneath the tips of your subjects' noses.

2. Mirror the position of the smaller octabox with the larger one **(2)** on the left and set its flash output to significantly lighten the shadows.

3. Place the standard reflector **(3)** about 5 feet behind your subjects to the right at head height and at an angle of about 30 degrees. Set it up to produce accents on your subjects' faces, hair, and shoulders.

4. Place the beauty dish **(4)** on the left about 5 feet behind your subjects and at an angle of about 30 degrees. Use it to brighten the left-hand end of the backdrop.

5. Your subjects should be standing about 6 feet in front of the white background.

Make sure that your framing leaves space within the frame for the reflections on the floor and don't crop too tightly. You can vary the reflections depending on the size of your reflective sheet and the shooting position you choose.

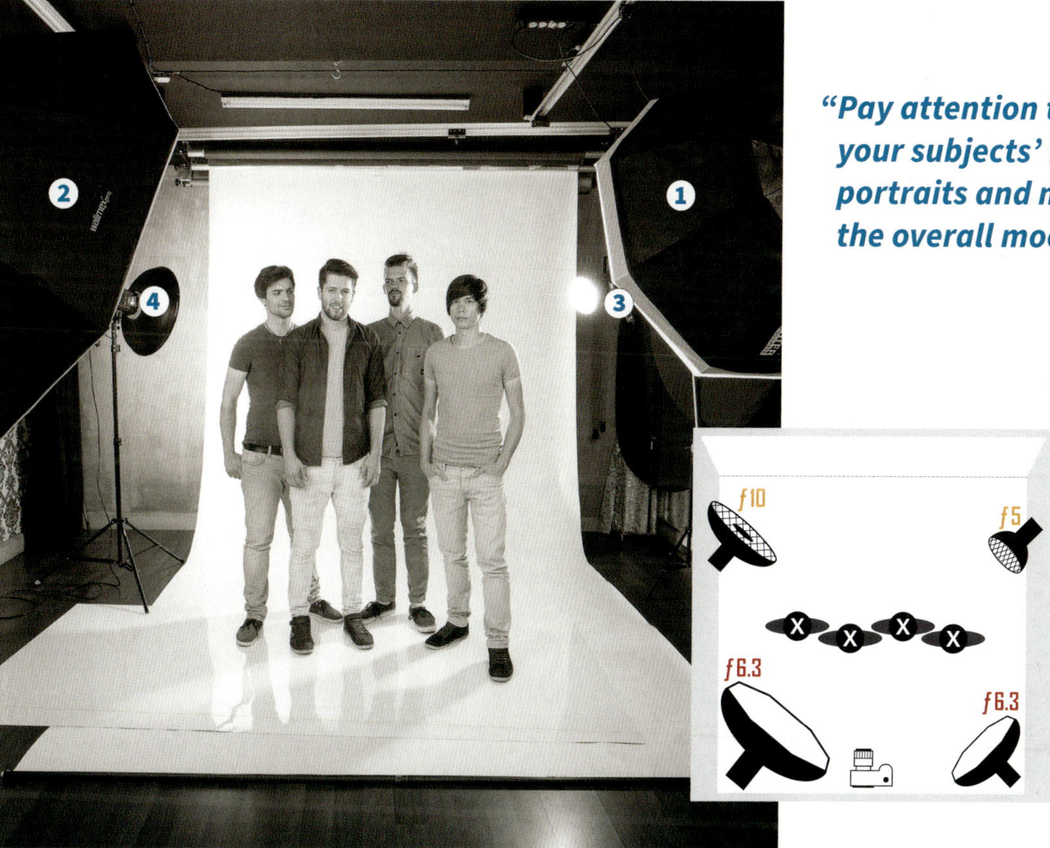

All That Is Good Comes from on High

This unusual setup uses a single large octabox positioned directly above the subject(s). Thanks to the close, diffuse light it provides, the effect is similar to that of midday sun, but with softer shadows and nicer hair gloss.

EFFORT INOLVED

Low

SUITABLE FOR

All kinds of portraits

THE LOOK

Group portrait with unusual overhead lighting

Natural-looking makeup

Coordinated outfits

EQUIPMENT

1 × 47" octabox

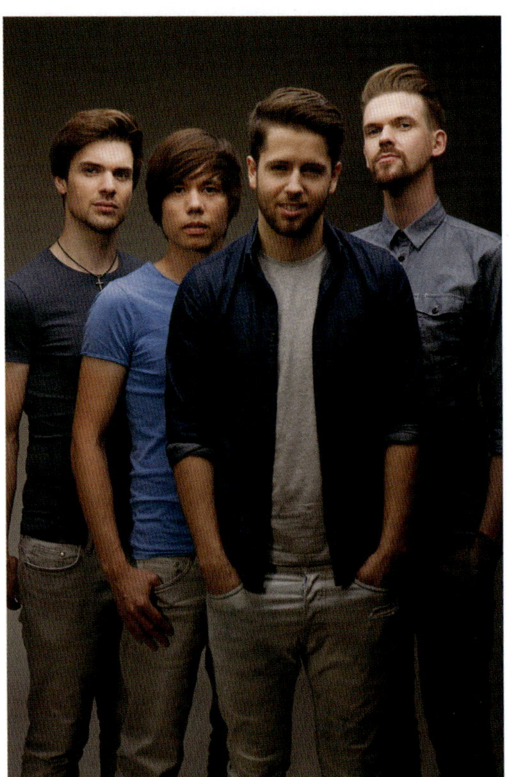

70mm | f9 | 1/160 sec. | ISO 100 | Models: nature band

HOW IT WORKS

The direct overhead light and its close proximity to the subjects produces clear light fall-off from top to bottom of the frame and automatically focuses attention on the subjects' faces. In contrast, the spill light from the main light produces a background gradient that is darker at the top than it is at the bottom. The facial shadows are unusually long but remain soft thanks to the large octabox. This setup accents the facial contours without making them appear too hard. A particular highlight in this setup is the intense but natural-looking luster in the subjects' hair.

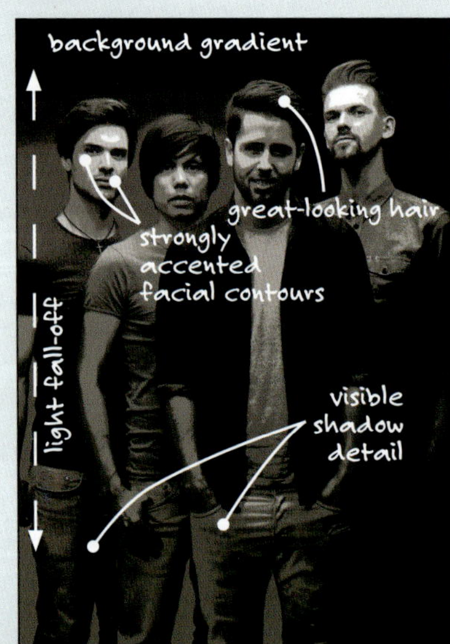

THE SETUP

1. Mount the large octabox **(1)** on a ceiling rail or a boom stand 8–10 inches above your subjects' heads.

2. Position your subjects about 10 feet in front of the white background.

Keep an eye on the brightness gradient in the background and move your setup back or forward to adjust its effect.

Take care not to shoot above eye level to prevent the edge of the octabox encroaching on the frame.

"Vary the positions of your subjects beneath the octabox to produce more or less facial shadow from front to back of the group."

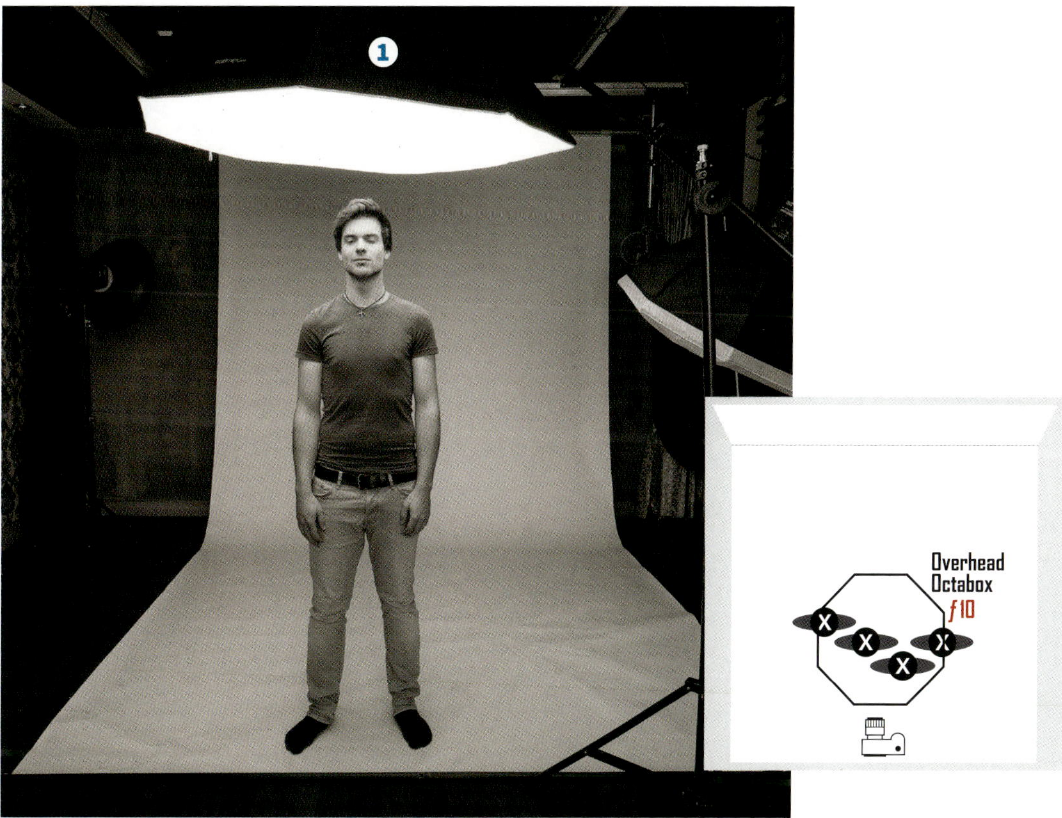

Lighting a Casual Scenario

Using a couch as a prop you can quickly turn a strictly posed portrait into a casual scenario. All you need to light a scene like this are octabox main and fill lights and a background spot.

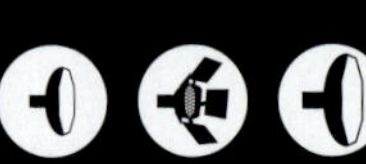

EFFORT INOLVED

Medium

SUITABLE FOR

All kinds of portraits

THE LOOK

Casual group portrait on a couch

High-contrast lighting with the focus on the center of the frame

Natural-looking makeup, coordinated outfits

EQUIPMENT

1× 31.5" octabox

1× 47" octabox

1× standard reflector with a honeycomb grid and barndoors

238

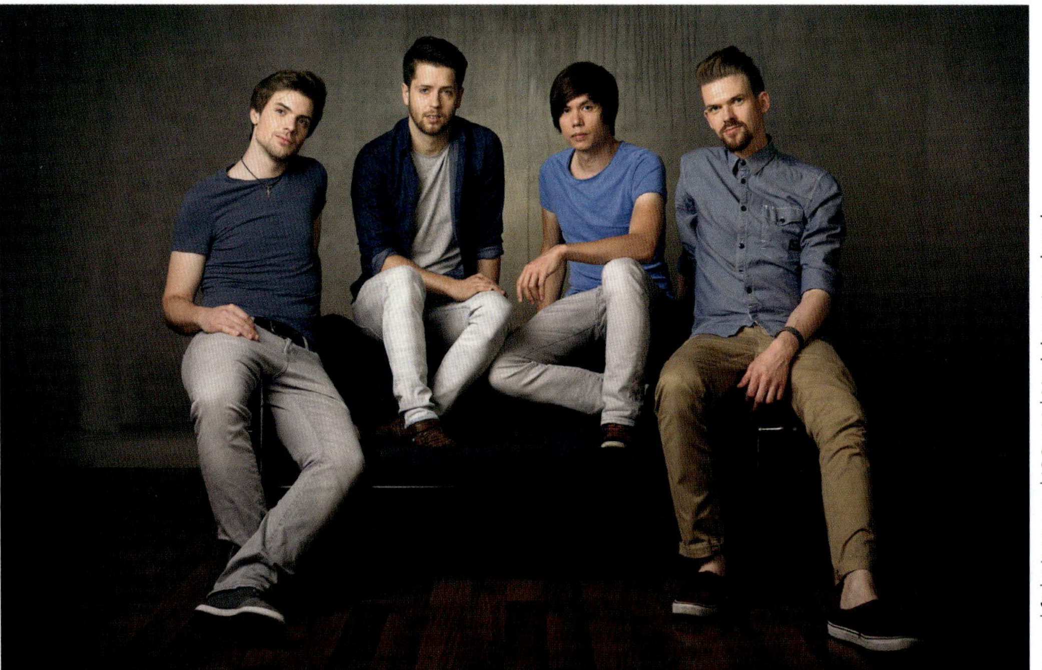

HOW IT WORKS

The large octabox main light produces broad, soft light and creates a scene with plenty of depth and enough emphasis on each of the individuals. The octabox fill light ensures that the shadows aren't too dark and that finer details remain visible. Spill light from both octaboxes subtly lightens the background and provides an extra portion of light toward the edges of the frame. The background spot provides additional contrast in the center of the frame and focuses attention on the group.

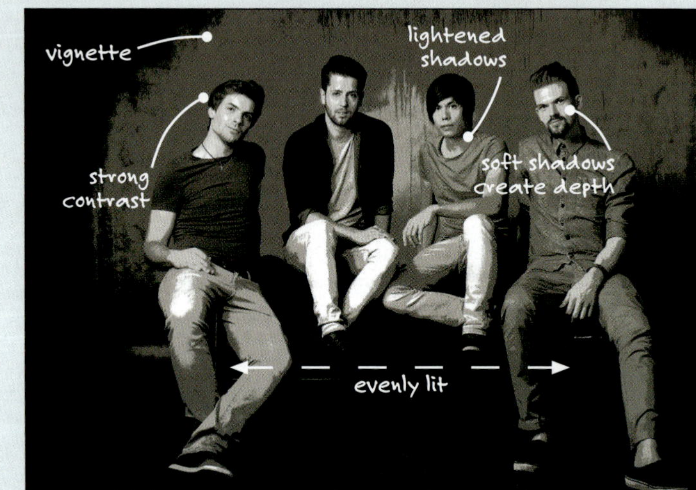

THE SETUP

1. Place the large octabox **(1)** about 8 feet to the left of your subjects in a raised position and at an angle of about 45 degrees. Set it up so that the facial shadows point diagonally downward. The larger the area you want to illuminate and/or the greater the depth of the area you are lighting, the further away from your subjects the octabox needs to be.

2. Mount the fill octabox **(2)** on a stand about 6 feet to the right of your subjects in a slightly raised position and at an angle of about 45 degrees, and set it up to lighten the shadows. As with the main light, you can adjust the fill light's effect by altering the distance between it and your subjects.

3. Place the standard reflector **(3)** close to your scene on the right at a height of about 8 feet. Position it to create a bright spot on the background directly behind the group. Use the barndoors to prevent any unwanted spill light from reaching the main subject.

4. Position your subjects and the couch about 6 feet from the backdrop.

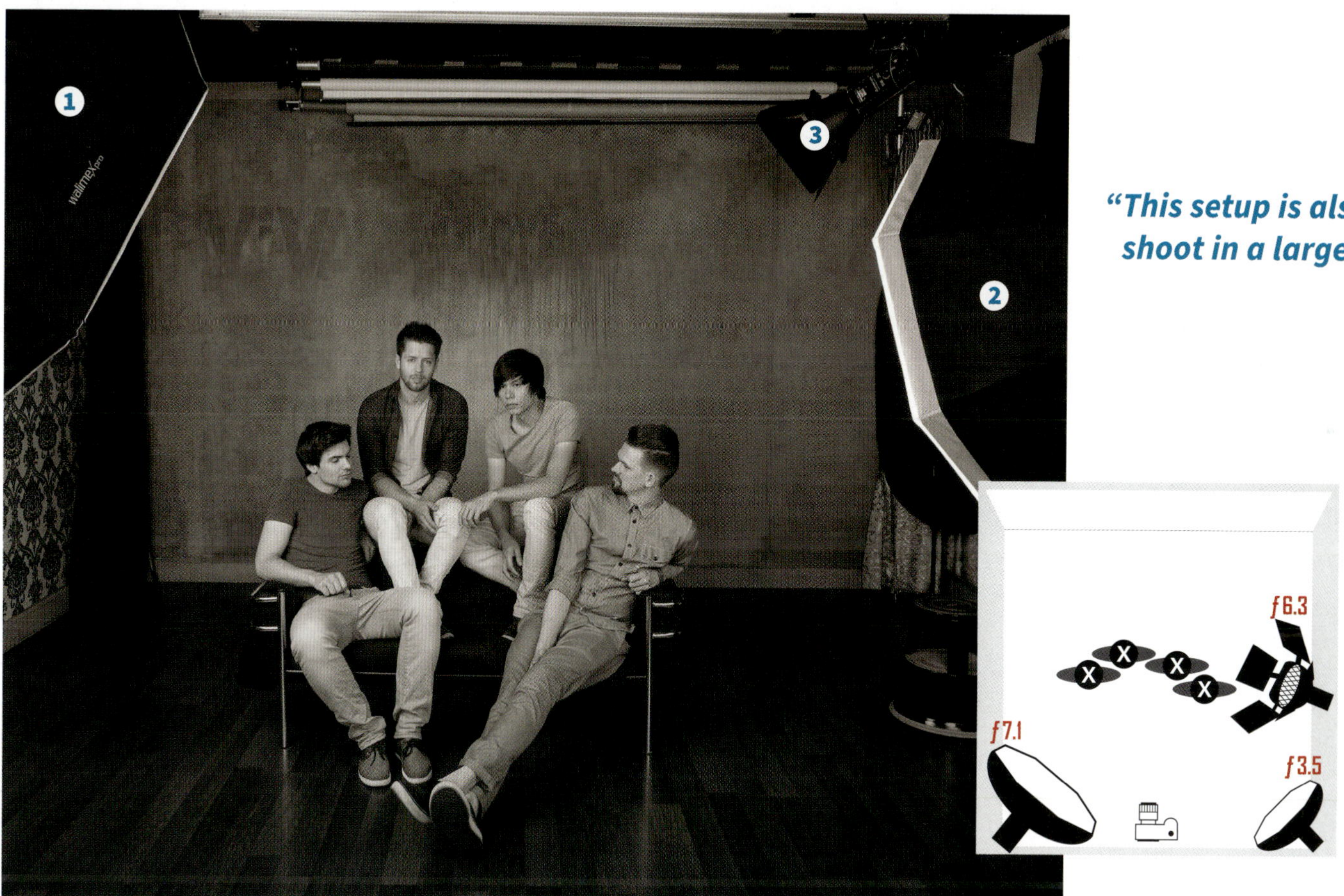

"This setup is also suitable for a shoot in a large living room."

Accenting an Individual Within a Group

Most bands have a frontperson, and you can use targeted focus as a compositional tool to place emphasis on this individual. If you add an unusual pose and crafty lighting, the result is an eye-catching group photo.

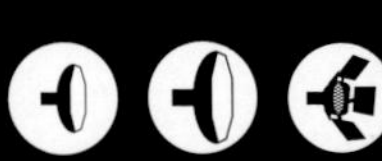

EFFORT INOLVED

Medium

SUITABLE FOR

All kinds of portraits

THE LOOK

Group portrait with emphasis on one individual
Natural-looking makeup
Coordinated outfits

EQUIPMENT

1 × 31.5" octabox
1 × 47" octabox
1 × standard reflector with a honeycomb grid and barndoors

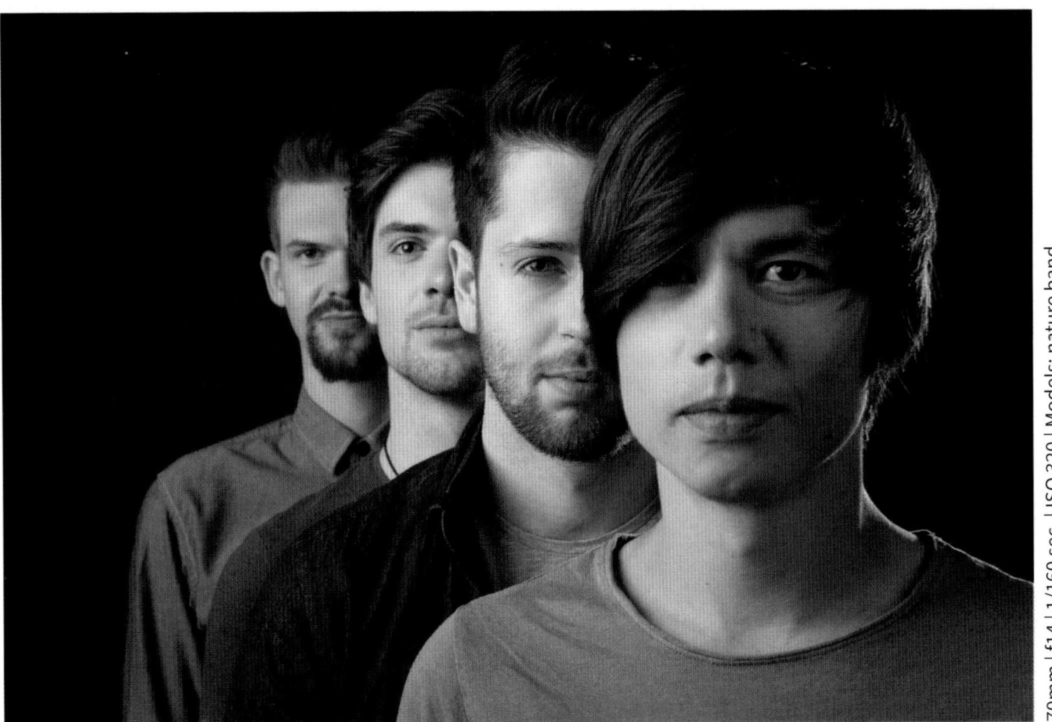

HOW IT WORKS

The tension in this setup is created by the lateral main light coming from the large octabox on the left. This is set up to light the entire group but has its focus on the second guy from the front. The emphasis on this individual is intensified by focusing deliberately on him while keeping the other members of the group very slightly out of focus. The fill light on the right also produces nice rim accents on the outlines of the front guy's head, thus keeping the shadow side of the image visually separated from the black background.

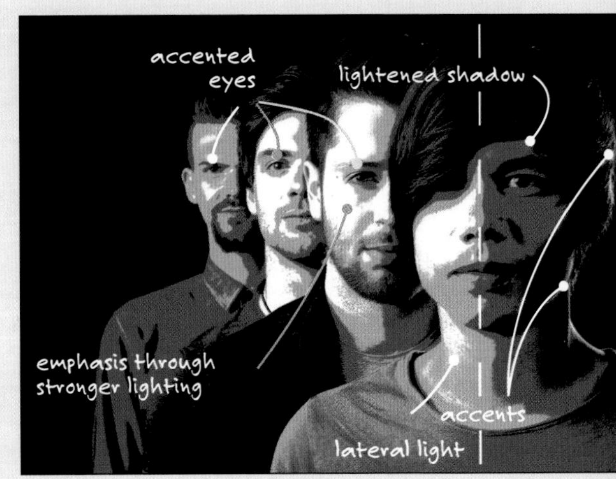

1. Place the large octabox **(1)** in a raised position about 5 feet to the left of your subjects at an angle of about 30 degrees. Set it up to illuminate the foremost subject with strong, lateral light.

2. Mirror the position of the main light with the smaller octabox **(2)** on the right, and set it up to lighten the shadows from the main light on the right of the frame.

3. Place the gridded standard reflector with the barn-doors **(3)** at head height about 5 feet behind your subjects to the right and pointing at an angle of about 45 degrees. Position it to produce clear accents on the foremost subject's hair and shoulder.

4. The back of the group should be about 6 feet in front of the black background.

"The person of interest should be second in line to prevent the guy at the back from looking too blurred."

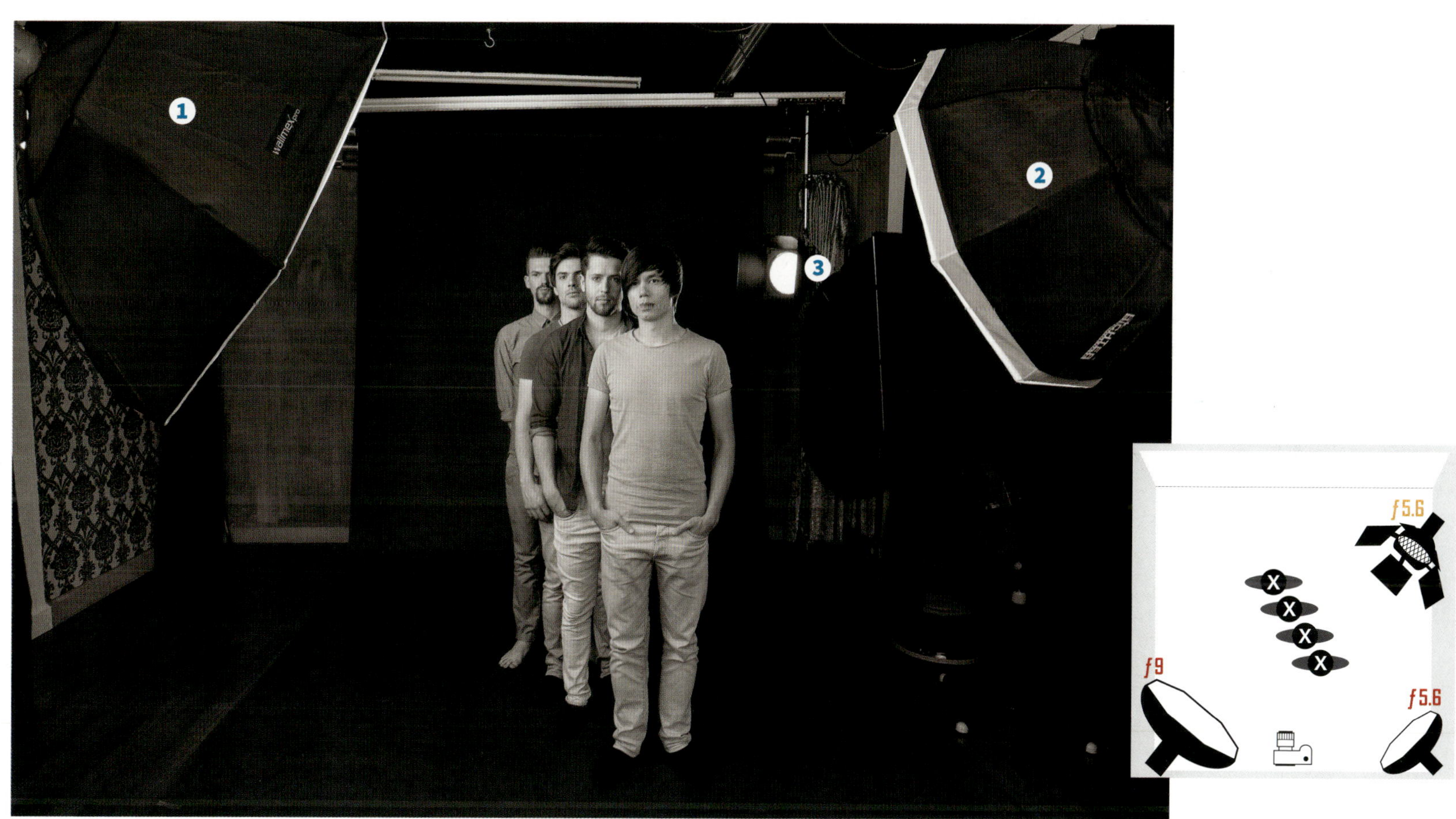

Bird's-Eye Group Portrait

How about a change of perspective? Shooting from above enables you to use the floor as your background and create interesting and unusual group photos.

EFFORT INOLVED

Low

SUITABLE FOR

All kinds of portraits

THE LOOK

Group portrait with soft contours and accented hair

Floor used as background/prop

Natural-looking makeup, coordinated outfits

EQUIPMENT

1× 31.5" octabox

1× 47" octabox

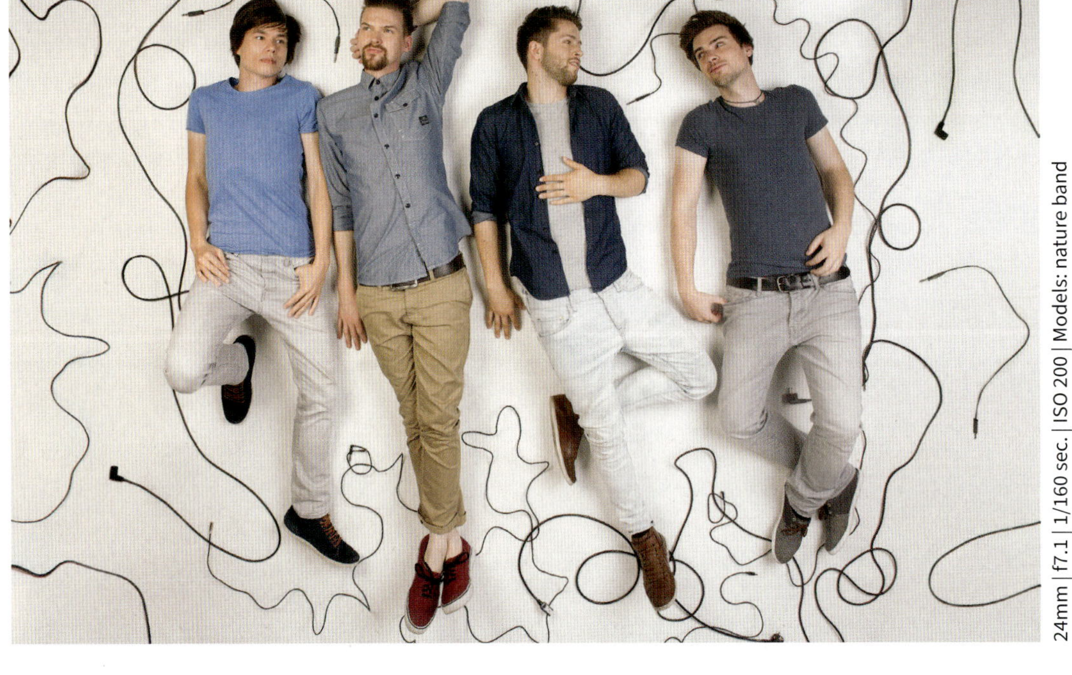

24mm | f7.1 | 1/160 sec. | ISO 200 | Models: nature band

HOW IT WORKS

The large octabox provides even lighting from the right, soft shadows on the left, and good definition across the frame. The position of the light slightly above the subjects' heads also helps to define their facial contours and produce narrow neck shadows. There is some light fall-off toward both sides of the frame, although the second, smaller octabox acts as a fill light on the right. On the left, the smaller octabox acts as the main light, while the larger one provides fill light. As a result, most of the shadows point toward the center of the frame.

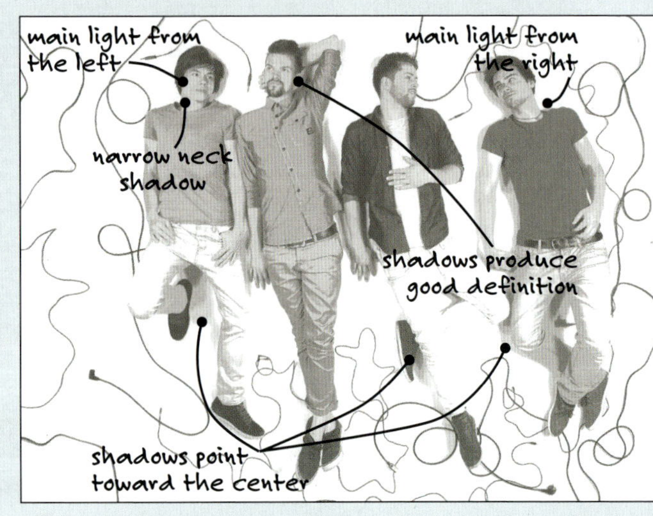

THE SETUP

Note that I captured this image with the subjects' heads pointing toward the bottom of the frame and rotated it through 180 degrees during post-processing to get the 'correct' result.

1. Mount the large octabox **(1)** on a ceiling rail or a boom stand and place it about 18 inches to the left of the leftmost subject. Point it downward so that your subjects are well lit from head to toe. The brightest point should be on the second guy from the left. Mount your light as high as possible to obtain even overall lighting.

2. Mount the smaller octabox **(2)** on the right and mirror the position of the larger octabox so that its focus is on the second guy from the right. Here too, you need to mount your light as high as possible to keep your lighting even.

3. Now get your subjects to lie down and pose.

When shooting from a ladder, it is essential that it is stable if you want to avoid camera shake. In order to best accent the subjects' faces, I captured this shot 'upside-down' and rotated it later during post-processing.

If your backdrop isn't wide enough to accommodate four reclining models, you can always get them to lie down from front to back and shoot at 90 degrees to their body length. The width of the backdrop will then dictate the height of the frame during your shoot.

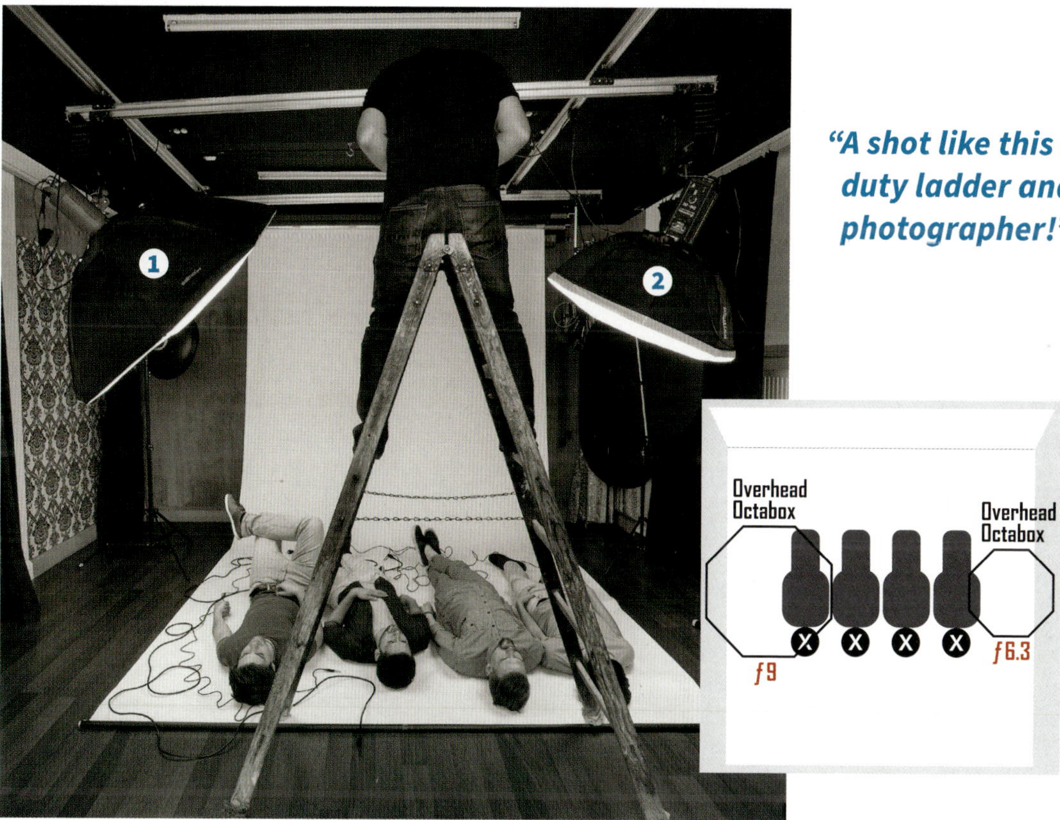

"A shot like this requires a heavy-duty ladder and a sure-footed photographer!"

Kids and Families

Kids and Families

Kids move around a lot and quickly get bored, so you need to take a practical, hands-on approach when you work with young "supermodels" aged between 2 and 12.

Waiting Is Boring!

Most kids aren't very patient, so you need to work quickly if you want to keep them interested during a photo shoot. You need to find ways to make a shoot fun, and to distract your subjects or make them laugh. As soon as a youthful subject gets bored and you can no longer hold their interest, you will simply have to give up and end the shoot.

Functional Setups

The setups introduced in this chapter are highly functional and have little to do with technical finesse. Photos of kids work best with a simple main light/fill light setup or with a single, centrally positioned main light. These kinds of setups give your models plenty of freedom of movement. To keep things really simple, you can use a universal setup with both lights set to similar outputs and with large light shapers positioned as far possible from your subject(s). This produces relatively flat-looking lighting but gives you a great basis for shooting and the maximum possible space for active kids to move around.

The Importance of Preparation

A visit to a photo studio is exciting for most kids but, if they have to wait for any length of time before the shoot actually begins (and that isn't very long in a kid's mind), you may find yourself quickly confronted with youthful mood swings.

The secret to a smooth shoot is to prepare well in advance. Plan the shots you want to capture and make sure you have all the necessary props and accessories close at hand. Build your initial setup before your subjects arrive and make sure you have any additional light shapers and other gear close by. Make sure that your camera is all set up and ready to go, too.

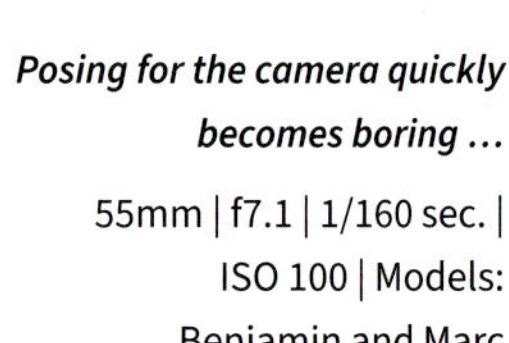

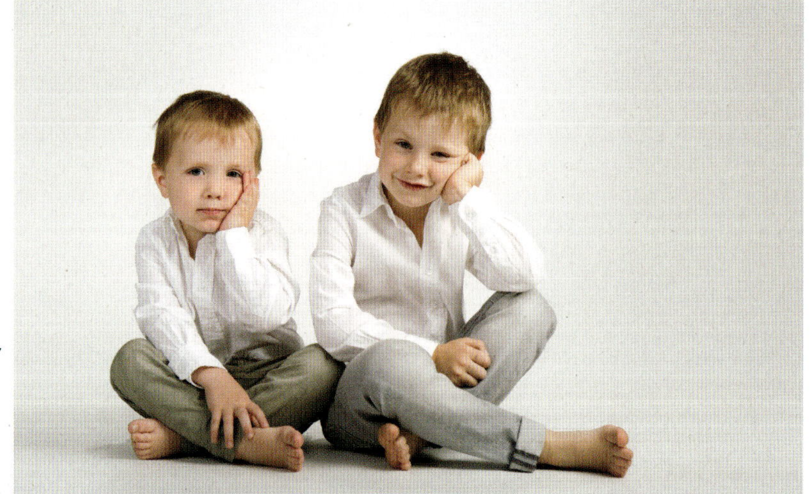

Posing for the camera quickly becomes boring …
55mm | f7.1 | 1/160 sec. | ISO 100 | Models: Benjamin and Marc

Setting the Mood

Remember to be friendly and open with your models and their parents. As soon as you meet them, you will usually know right away how the shoot will progress. Some kids are open-minded and genuinely interested in what's going on, and you can usually begin shooting right away. In contrast, some kids are shy and reserved, and take a while to warm up before they will cooperate. It often helps to explain what you are doing and to show your subjects your camera and other gear. Kids need encouragement, and you will need to work hard to keep the atmosphere relaxed. Keep some toys close at hand to grab their attention or to use as props during your shoot. Don't be afraid to experiment with different ways to keep kids interested. If you show you are interested in them, they will reward you with happy, natural-looking photos!

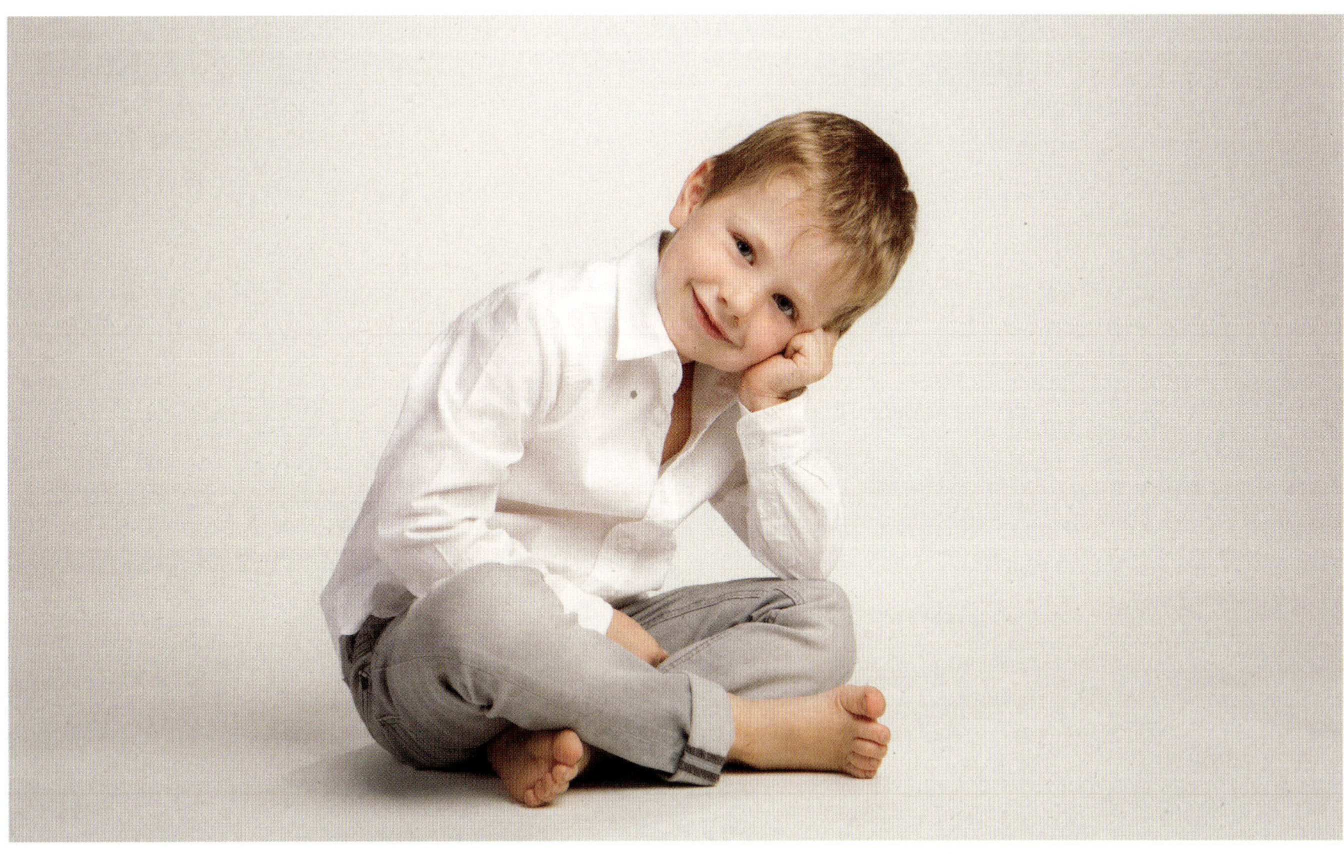

Small superstars: Capturing a balanced, natural-looking portrait of a child isn't as easy as you might think. Building a simple, functional setup in advance with main, fill, and background lights enables you to work quickly when the moment arrives.

59mm | f7.1 | 1/160 sec. | ISO 100 | Model: Benjamin

Standard Setup for Photos of Kids

Two large, frontally placed light shapers give you plenty of compositional freedom, and you can always adjust the softness of the shadows by altering the output of your fill light. You can use this setup for all sorts of variations, from strong shadows to completely flat lighting.

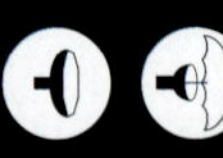

EFFORT INVOLVED

Low

SUITABLE FOR

All kinds of portraits

THE LOOK

Portrait setup with soft contours and variable shadows

Color-coordinated clothing

EQUIPMENT

1 × 31.5" octabox

1 × 36" translucent umbrella

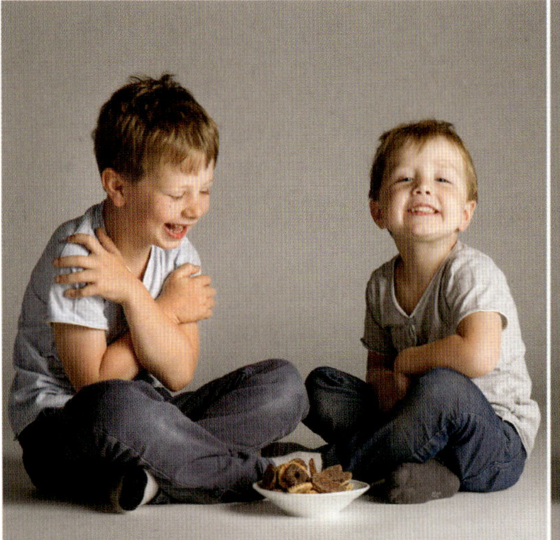
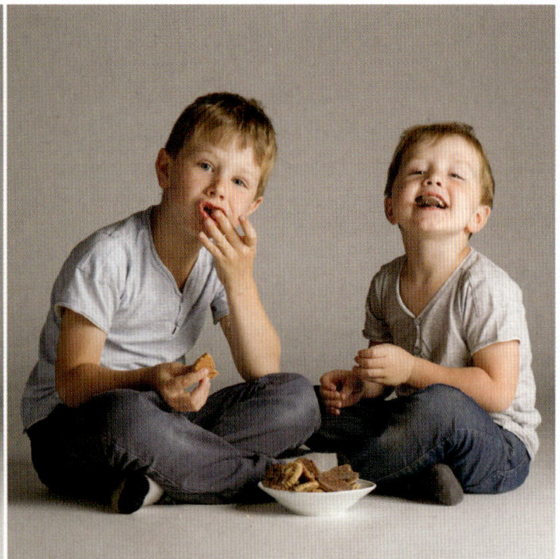

70mm | f6.3 | 1/160 sec. | ISO 100

Models: Benjamin and Marc

HOW IT WORKS

The octabox provides a clear main light with strong shadows. Its high, lateral position creates broad shadows that provide plenty of definition in the body contours and facial expressions. The relatively large distance between the light and the subjects produces pleasing, even lighting. The translucent umbrella fill light softens the shadows to keep all the relevant details visible. Spill light from the octabox and the umbrella makes the background appear gray and helps to focus attention on the subjects.

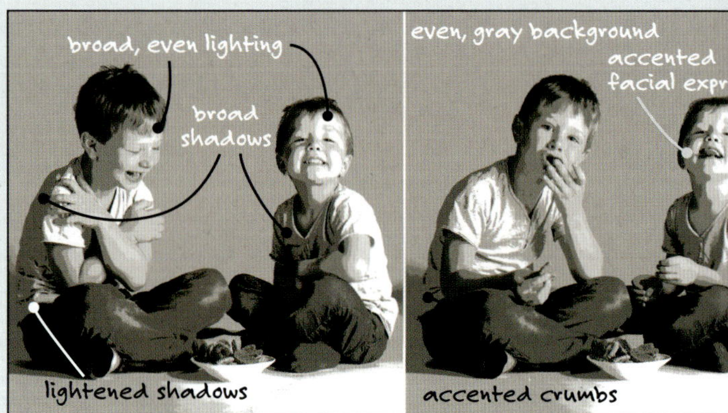

THE SETUP

1. Place the octabox **(1)** about 5 feet to the front right of your models in a slightly raised position and at an angle of about 30 degrees. Position it to produce visible nose shadows and mild chin shadows.

2. Now place the fill light **(2)** with its translucent umbrella about 5 feet to the left in a slightly raised position and at an angle of about 45 degrees.

3. The V-shaped lighting setup is clearly visible in the photo below. Your models should sit/stand about 6 feet in front of the white background. The translucent umbrella produces very soft, broad-based light and plenty of spill that illuminates the background in an even mid-gray tone.

4. If you want to further soften the shadows, simply increase the output of your fill flash.

If your models' parents are OK with it, you can also try bribing them with biscuits or cookies. This trick worked perfectly on this shoot, and the bowl of snacks ended up being an integral part of the finished image.

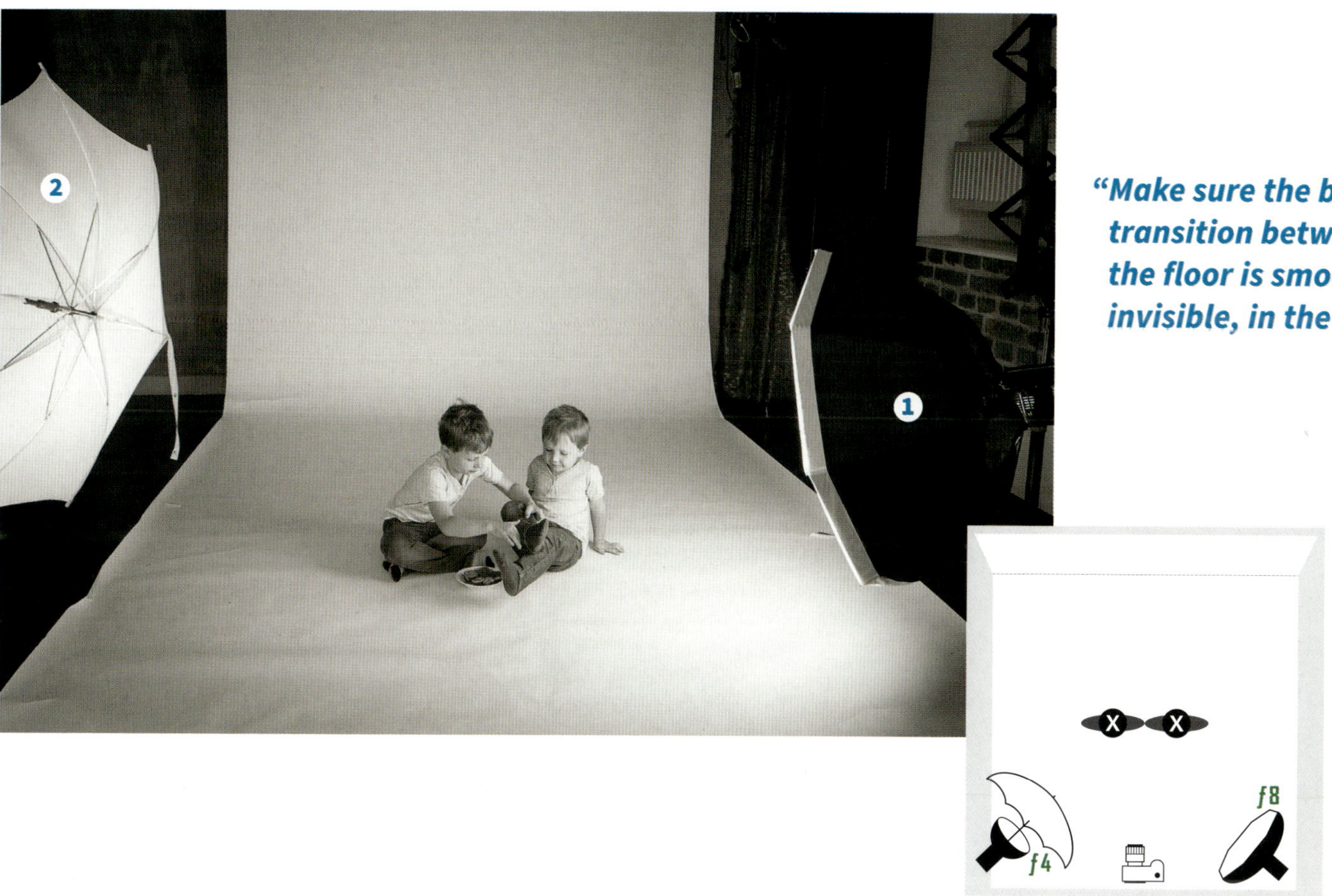

"Make sure the background transition between the wall and the floor is smooth, and therefore invisible, in the final image."

Happy Families

A setup with twin main lights is ideal for making sure that no family member eclipses any other. It also gives you maximum posing flexibility and no irritating shadows in the bright background.

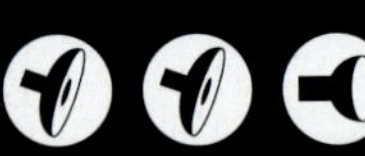

EFFORT INVOLVED

Medium

SUITABLE FOR

All kinds of portraits

THE LOOK

Evenly lit family portrait with no obvious shadows
For Larissa: natural-looking makeup
Color-coordinated clothing

EQUIPMENT

2× beauty dishes
1× standard reflector

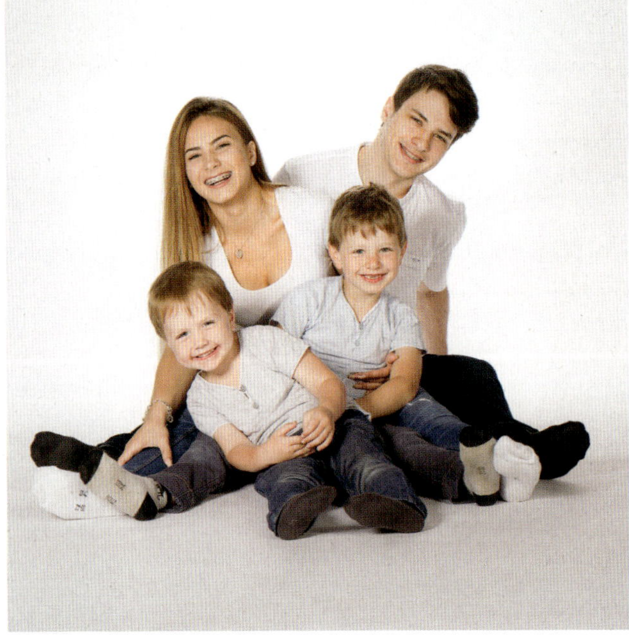

85mm | f13 | 1/160 sec. | ISO 100 |
Models: Larissa, Rafael, Benjamin, and Marc

HOW IT WORKS

The twin beauty dishes produce very even lighting from both sides. The left-hand (main) beauty dish has a slightly higher output setting and produces slight shadows that ensure that the subjects don't appear entirely contour-free. The raised positions of both lights produce slight neck shadows that separate the faces from the subjects' bodies. The head postures ensure that all four faces are evenly lit from both sides. Any background shadows are negated by the bright background light, thus producing a light, airy atmosphere that underscores the positive mood of the image.

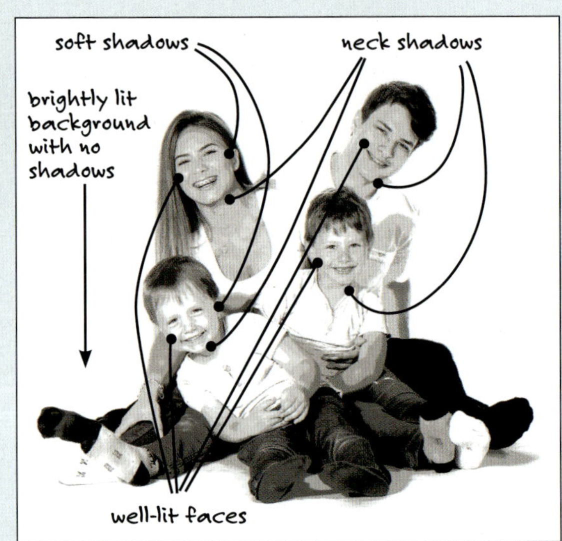

THE SETUP

1. Place the main beauty dish **(1)** about 12 feet to the left of your models in a slightly raised position and at an angle of about 30 degrees. Position it so that the nose shadows are still just visible beneath the tips of your subjects' noses.

2. Mirror the position of the first beauty dish with the second one on the right **(2)** and position it to slightly lighten the nose shadows.

3. Mount the standard reflector **(3)** on a ceiling rail or a boom stand at a height of about 6 feet directly above your models. Point it down to the rear so that it brightly lights the space behind your models, and adjust its height so that the background is evenly lit over the entire width of the frame. The backs of the parents' heads should be slightly illuminated too.

4. Position your models about 6 feet in front of the white background.

"Select a shooting position somewhere between the tallest and the smallest member of the family."

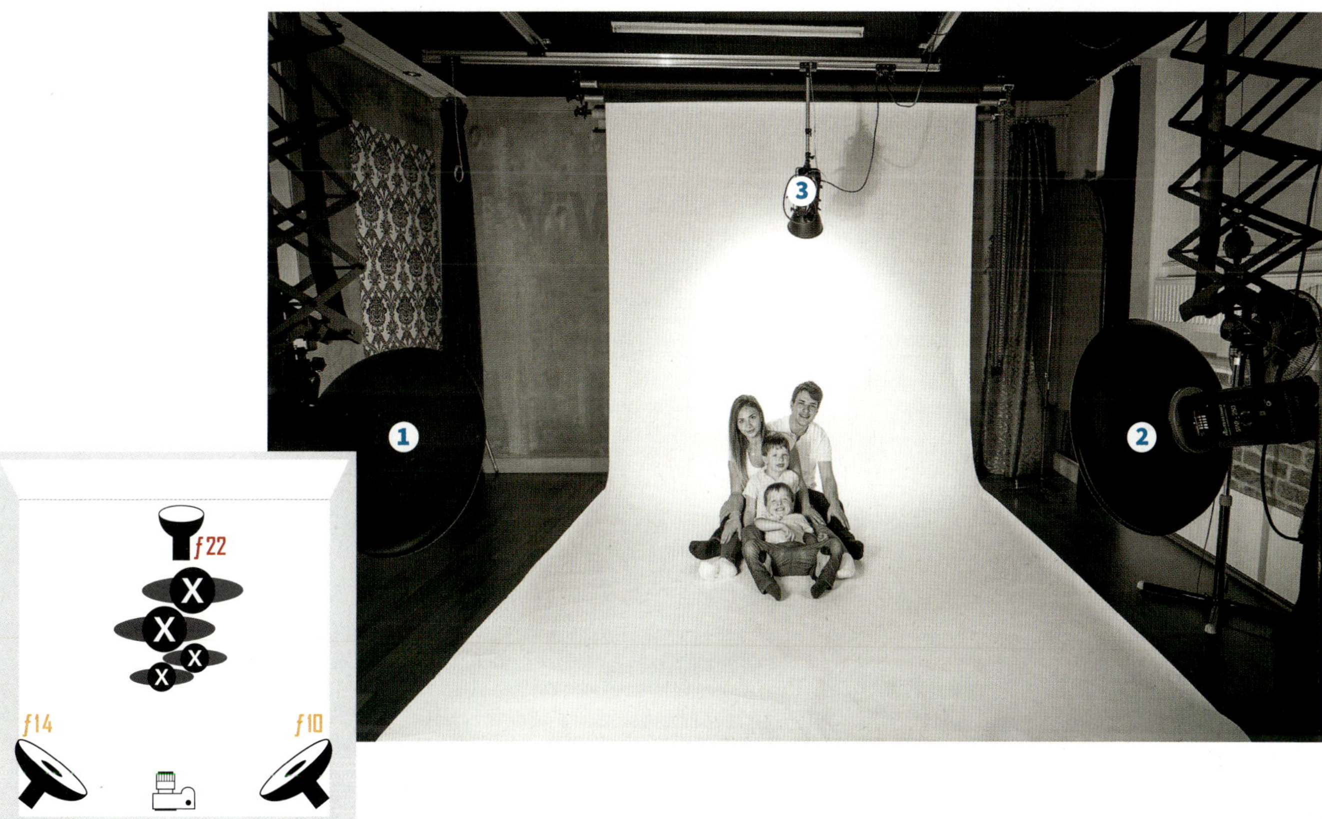

L.O.V.E.

This fun shot gets the four members of the family to form the word LOVE with their arms and legs. This a great eye-catcher for the family album or for sending to friends. The lighting is quick to set up but your subjects need to bring a little coordination and patience to the game. The result is a creative and fun family portrait.

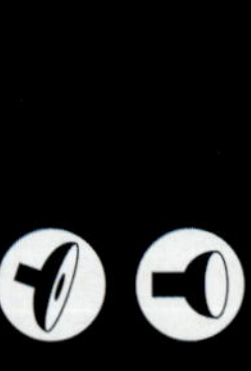

EFFORT INVOLVED

Low

SUITABLE FOR

Full-length portraits

THE LOOK

Creative family portrait

For Larissa: natural-looking makeup

Color-coordinated clothing

EQUIPMENT

1× beauty dish

1× standard reflector

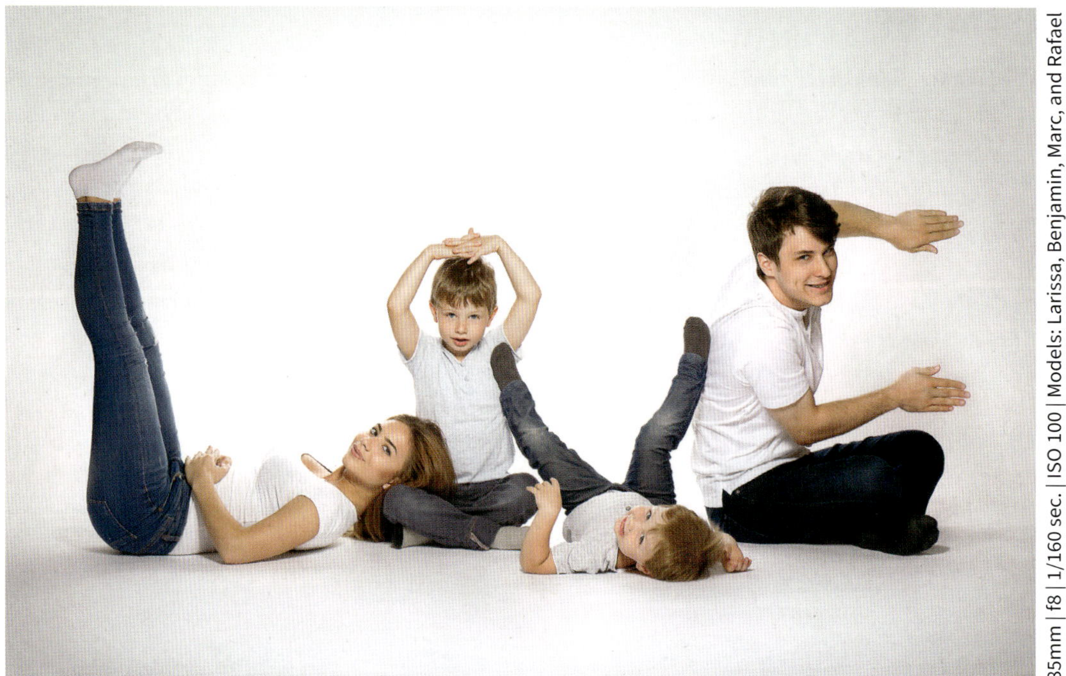

HOW IT WORKS

The centrally placed beauty dish produces theater-style lighting, and the shadows it provides accent the subjects' faces and body contours. The raised position of the main light produces clear neck shadows and its distance from the subjects ensures that the entire scene is well lit. The background light produces a very bright area behind the subjects and a slight vignette effect toward the edges of the frame, thus emphasizing the lettering created by the pose. The background light also subdues any background shadows and helps to focus attention on the LOVE motif.

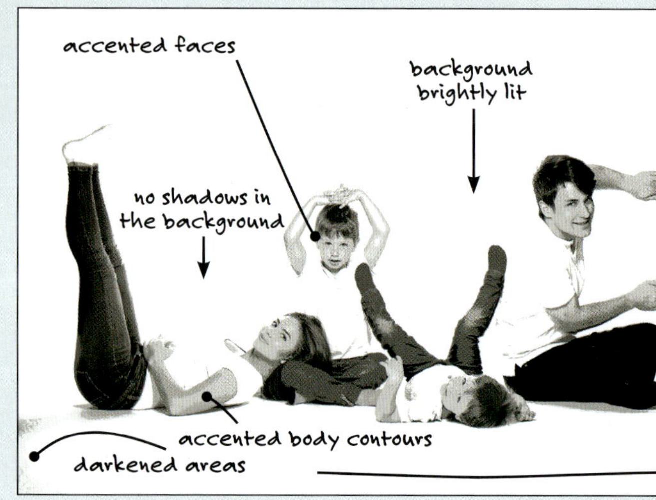

THE SETUP

1. Mount the beauty dish **(1)** on a ceiling rail or a boom stand in a central position at a height of about 5 feet. Place it about 6 feet from your models and set it up so that it focuses on the center of your group.

2. Now mount the standard reflector **(2)** slightly behind your models on a ceiling rail or a boom stand.

3. Point the standard reflector downward so that it illuminates the area directly behind your models.

4. Adjust the distance between the standard reflector and the background to produce a mild vignette effect toward the edges of the frame.

5. Place your models about 3 feet from the white background.

6. Instruct your models to get into position to form the word LOVE. You can show them the photo opposite to help them imagine the result and memorize the positions they need to get into. If necessary, you can step in and help them get into position.

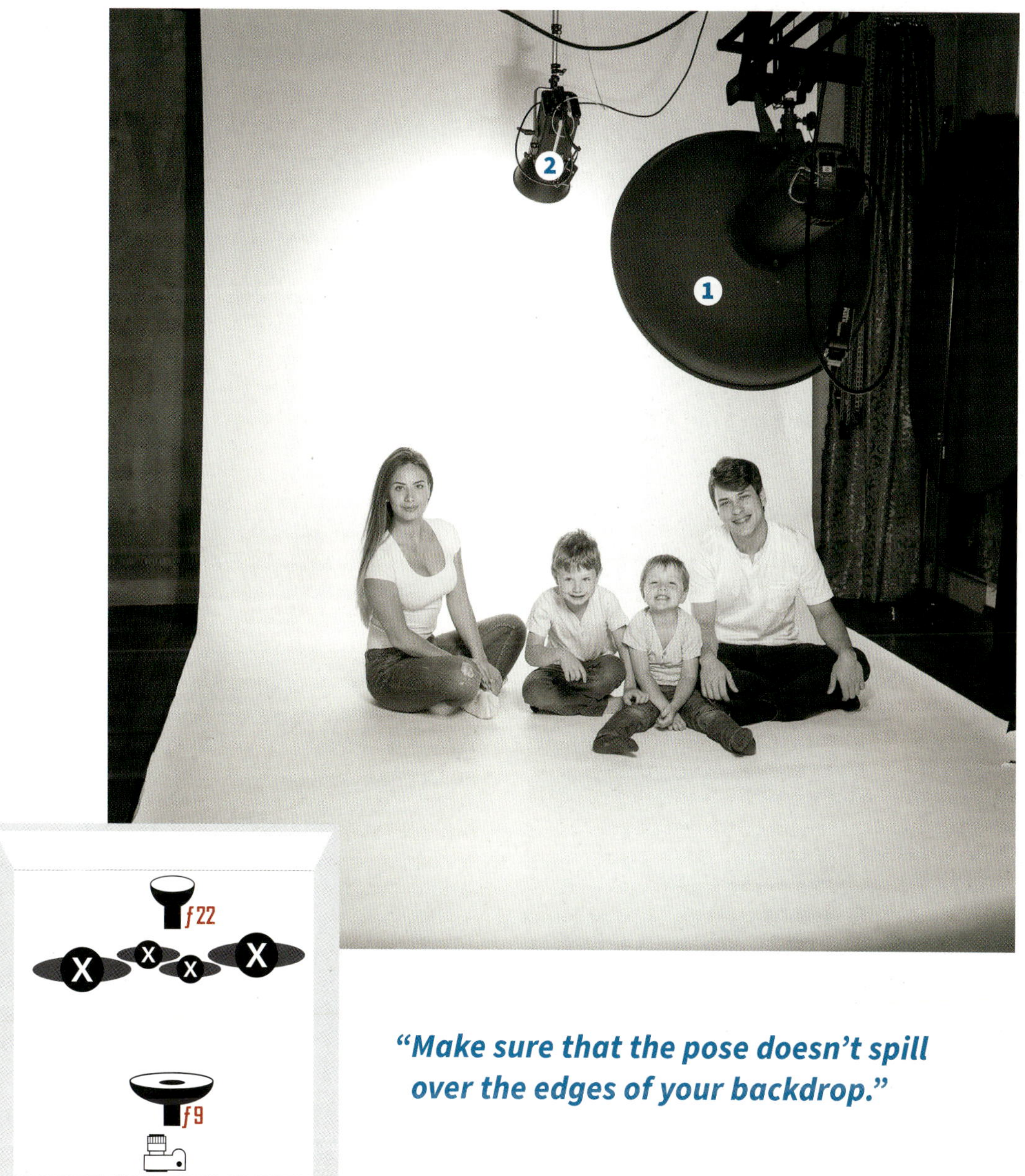

Vignetted Baby Portrait

This is a simple standard setup that works well for a wide variety of portraits of babies and young kids. All you need is an octabox, a gridded standard reflector, and a standard reflector with a translucent umbrella to lighten the shadows. I created the vignette in this variation using an additional background spot.

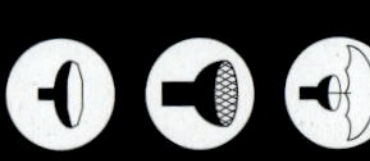

EFFORT INVOLVED

Medium

SUITABLE FOR

All kinds of portraits

THE LOOK

Simple setup for photos of babies and kids with an optional vignette

Appropriate accessories include baskets, blankets, and the like

Color-coordinated clothing

EQUIPMENT

1× 31.5" octabox

1× standard reflector with a honeycomb grid

1× standard reflector with a translucent umbrella

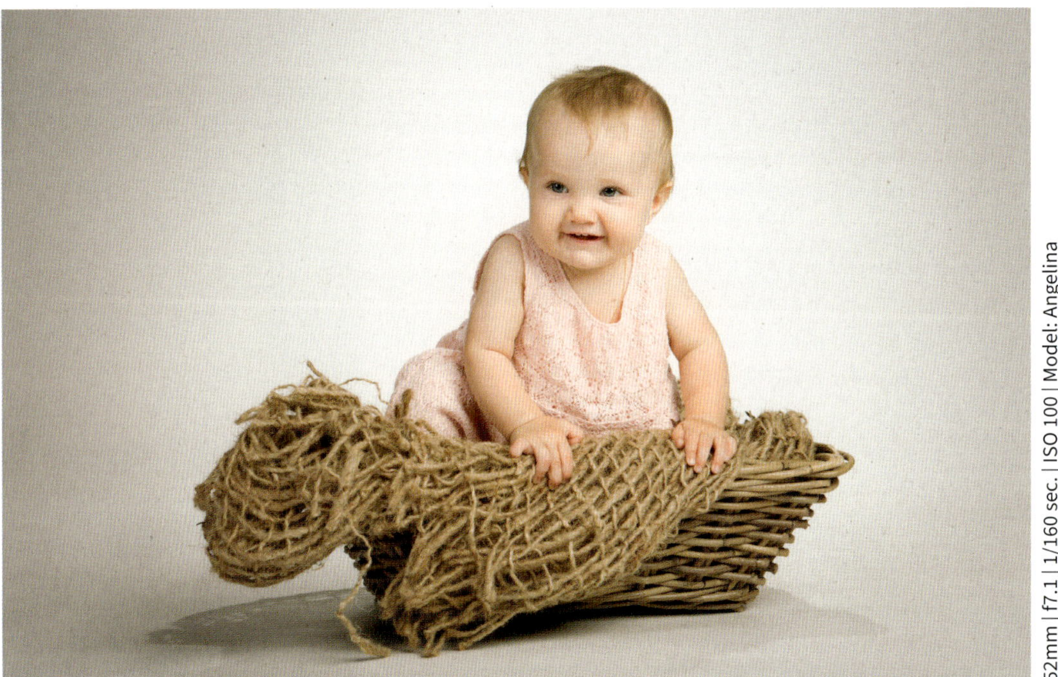

52mm | f7.1 | 1/160 sec. | ISO 100 | Model: Angelina

HOW IT WORKS

The octabox produces soft main light with mild shadows that nevertheless give the subject good definition. The soft shadows point diagonally downward and accent the nose, the facial contours, and the neck shadow. The translucent umbrella significantly lightens the shadows to produce a gentle overall effect. The only dark shadows are formed in the areas that no light reaches (beneath the basket, for example). The background spot and the vignette it creates ensures that the viewer's attention focuses on the real subject of the image.

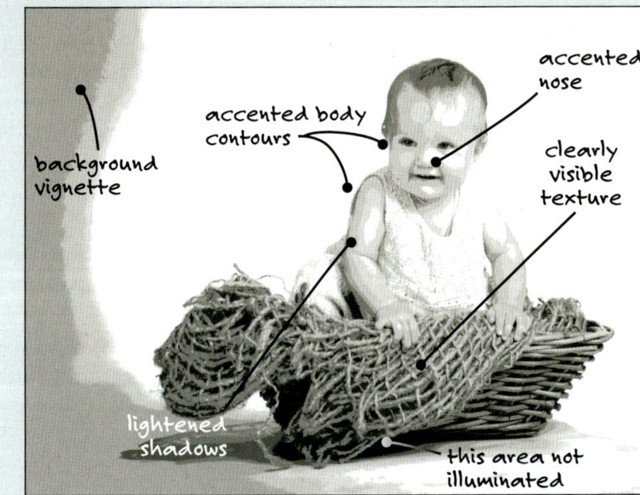

THE SETUP

1. Place the octabox **(1)** about 6 feet to the right in a slightly raised position and at an angle of about 45 degrees. Position it so that its center is at (your model's) head height.

2. Mount the translucent umbrella **(2)** about 6 feet to the left and in front of your model in a slightly raised position. Position it to lighten the shadows from the main light.

3. Mount the background spot **(3)** at a height of 5 to 6 feet and position it to brighten the area behind your model and to produce a vignette effect toward the edges of the frame. To do this, you may have to point it so far downward that its light hits the floor too.

4. Place your model about 6 feet in front of the white background.

Set up your lights well before you actually start shooting. As the photo below shows, you can use a prop to help you set things up before your young model arrives on the scene.

And a quick tip to finish up: If you use a prop like the basket shown here, placing a barbell in it prevents it from tipping when you position your model. You can always pad out a basket or whatever prop you use with blankets and cushions too.

"This universal setup enables you to fully concentrate on your work."

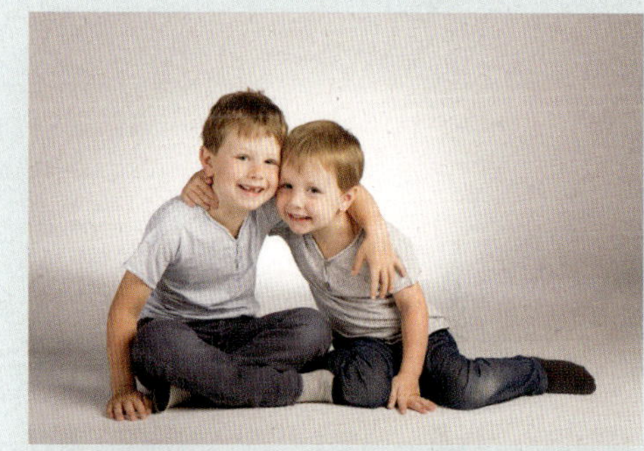

Variations

This simple setup is great for photographing older kids too.

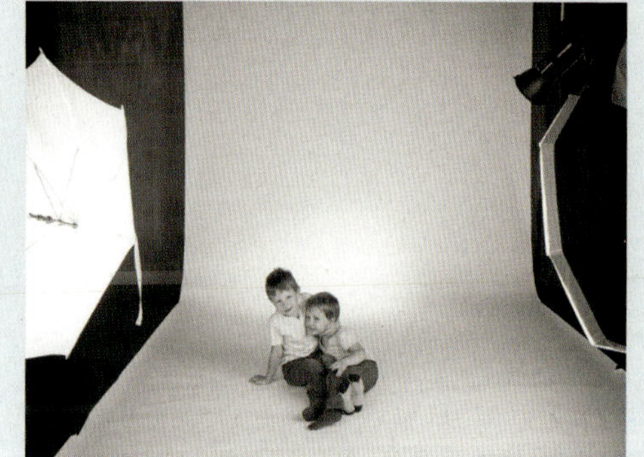

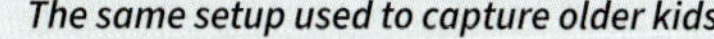

The same setup used to capture older kids.

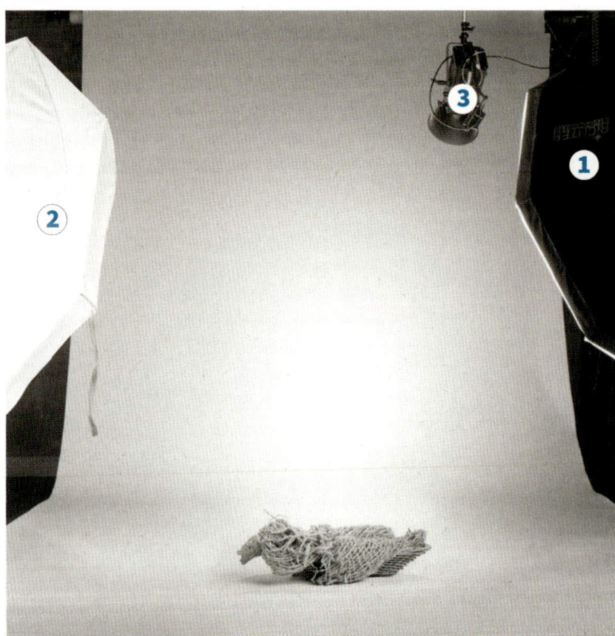

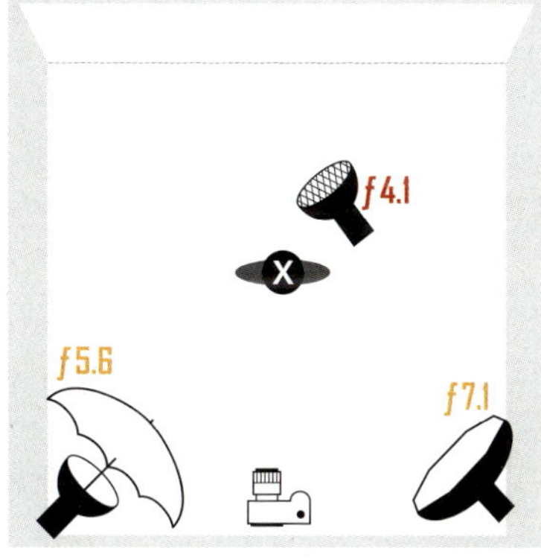

Bird's-Eye Family Photo

This setup is a great way to place all members of a family on a single focal plane. The lying-down pose is great for helping kids to relax, and makes it easier to work with them while you shoot. All you need for the lighting is two octaboxes.

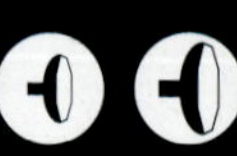

EFFORT INVOLVED

Low

SUITABLE FOR

Close-up to three-quarter-length portraits

THE LOOK

Family portrait from an unusual viewpoint

For Larissa: natural-looking makeup

Coordinated outfits

EQUIPMENT

1× 31.5" octabox

1× 47" octabox

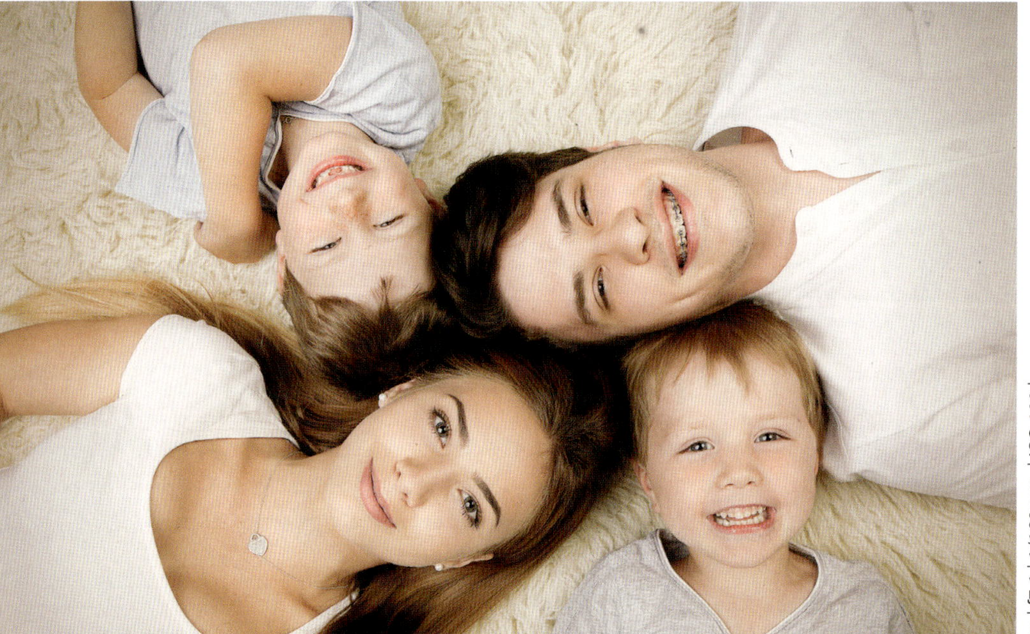

32mm | f7.1 | 1/160 sec. | ISO 100 |
Models: Larissa, Benjamin, Rafael, and Marc

HOW IT WORKS

The V-shaped setup provides relatively flat lighting that evenly illuminates all four faces. The broad light produces soft shadows and a natural-looking image. The shadows are similar throughout the frame and mildly accent all four subjects' features. The strong catchlights accent everyone's eyes and the delicate neck shadows help to accent the faces too. The camera position produces a diagonal line from bottom left to top right and ensures that all four faces are centrally placed. The soft overall lighting and the balanced composition produce a friendly family portrait.

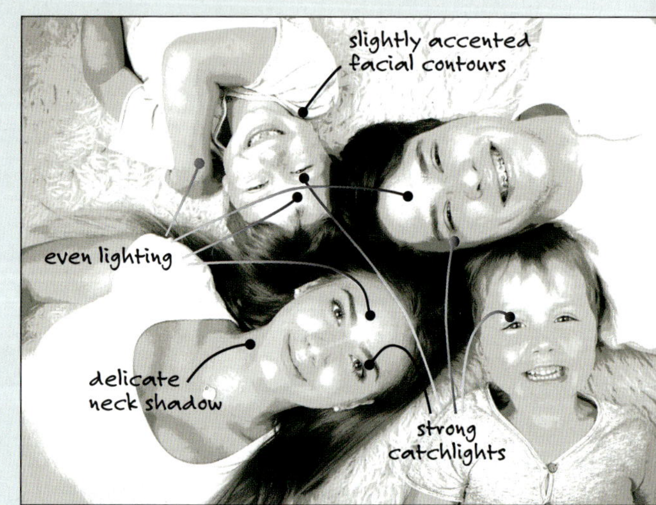

THE SETUP

1. Place the large octabox **(1)** about 5 feet above your models to the left and tip it to evenly light everyone.

2. Place the second octabox **(2)** about 5 feet above your models on the right and perform the same tipping action to provide even lighting from this side too.

3. The distance between the top edges of the two light shapers should be about 18 inches.

4. Position your models so the tops of their heads touch their neighbor's cheek. If you are photographing just two models, they can lie cheek to cheek with their feet pointed in opposite directions.

5. Stand right up close to your models and lean over them as far as you can to shoot.

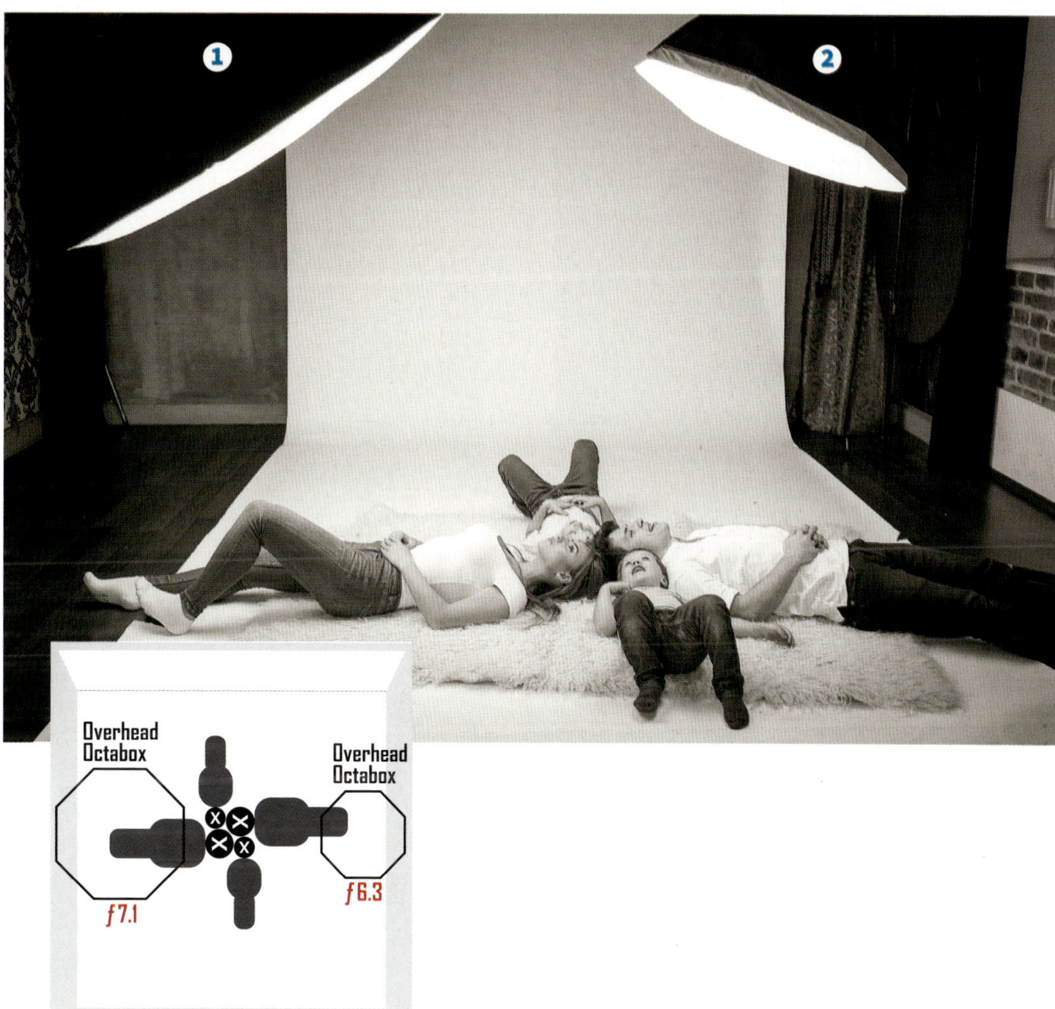

Piggyback

Family photos are often a lot of fun to shoot, and fun poses are part of the deal. When lighting these kinds of shots, you need a setup that is practical and versatile, and that works for subjects who are sitting or lying on the floor. The more felxible the lighting, the more fun everyone can have while you shoot!

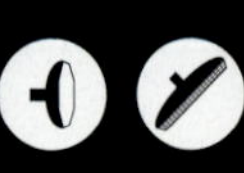

EFFORT INVOLVED

Low

SUITABLE FOR

All kinds of portraits

THE LOOK

Functional setup for floor-level poses

Soft light with accents from the fill light

Coordinated clothing

EQUIPMENT

1× 31.5" octabox

1× 47" strip box with a honeycomb grid

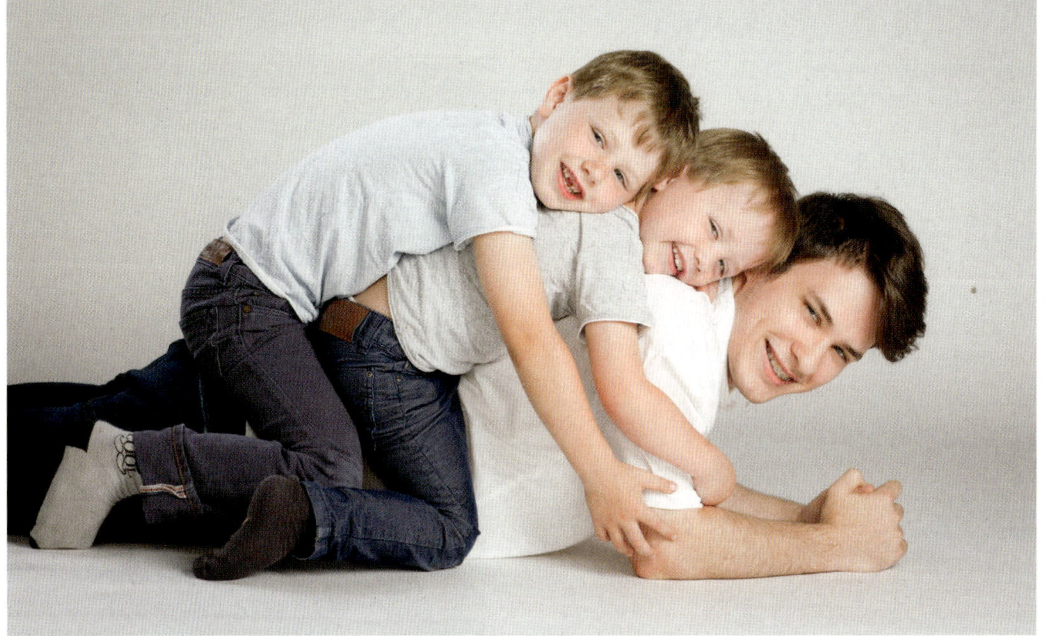

85mm | f6.3 | 1/160 sec. | ISO 100 | Models: Benjamin, Marc, and Rafael

HOW IT WORKS

The octabox placed diagonally above and to the front produces soft light and clear shadows that contribute definition to the image. The slight light fall-off toward the left also helps to accent the facial contours of the subjects. The compactness of the pose lends itself to a landscape format shot and forms a pleasing standing triangle shape that also symbolizes the family bond. The fill light on the left creates accents on the back and cheek of the child on top. The light from the octabox creates a subtle vignette in the background that also helps to focus attention on the subjects.

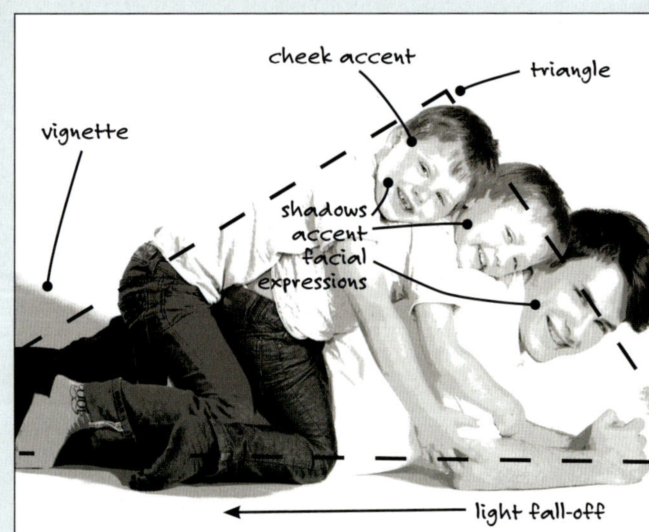

THE SETUP

1. Mount an octabox **(1)** on a stand about 5 feet from your models and at an angle of about 45 degrees. The octabox needs to be raised slightly above your posing models and should produce clear but soft nose shadows.

2. Set up the strip box **(2)** on the left slightly to the rear and about 3 feet from the child on the top of the heap. Position it to create clear accents on his back and hair. You can alter the strength of these accents by altering the angle of tilt in the strip box.

3. Your models should pose about 3 feet in front of the white background.

If you get your models to sit rather than lie on the floor, you will need to raise both lights accordingly.

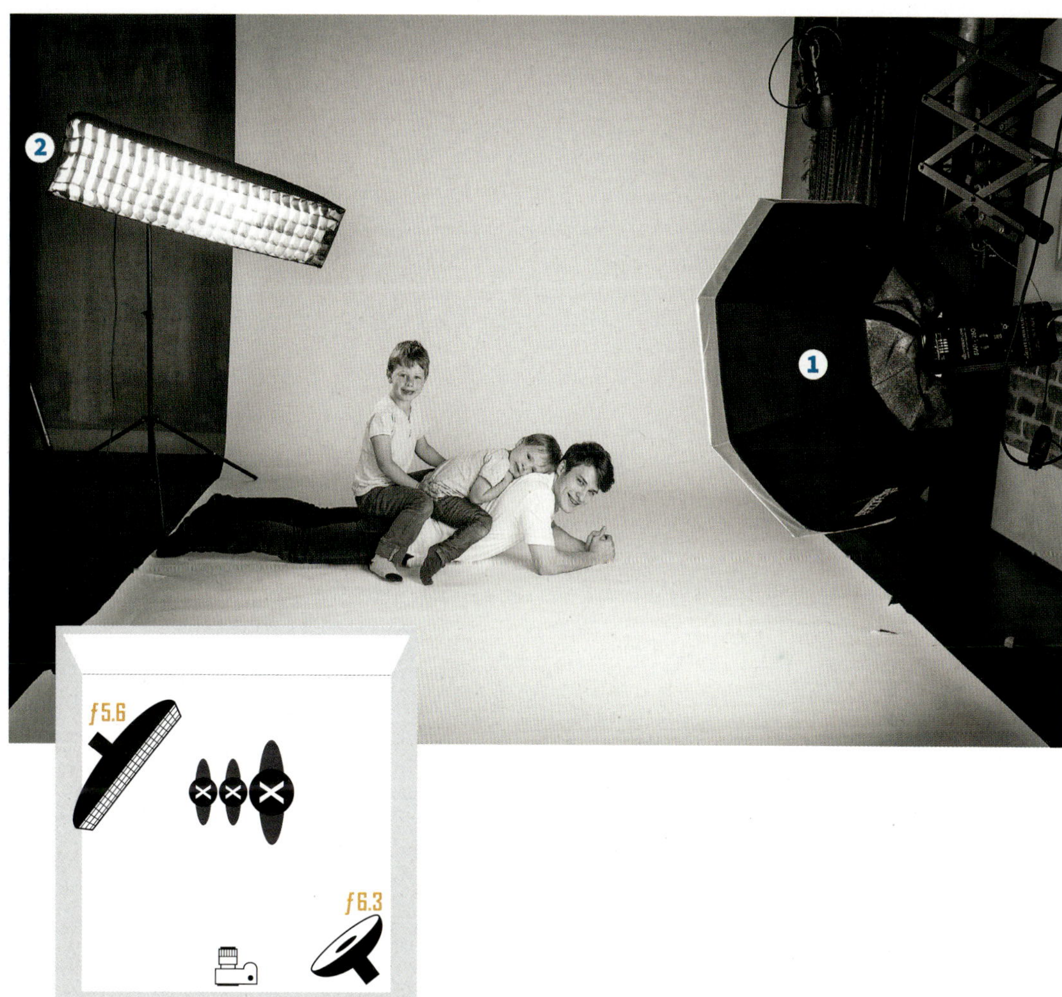

"The head postures of the models need to be staggered so that the line they form and the line of their backs create an implied triangle within the frame."

Movement and Action

Movement and Action

When it comes to "freezing" movement and capturing it pin sharp in a studio-based environment, there are two basic flash techniques that allow you to use the very short exposure times this requires.

Short Flash Duration vs. High Speed Sync

You can either use flash heads with very short flash durations or ones that support so-called High-Speed Sync (HSS).

Flash Duration

Exposure times are an important factor in capturing movement photographically. In a studio, the exposure times you can use are strongly influenced by the duration of the flashes produced by your flash heads. Because flash duration can be quite a lot shorter than the exposure time set in the camera, you can capture

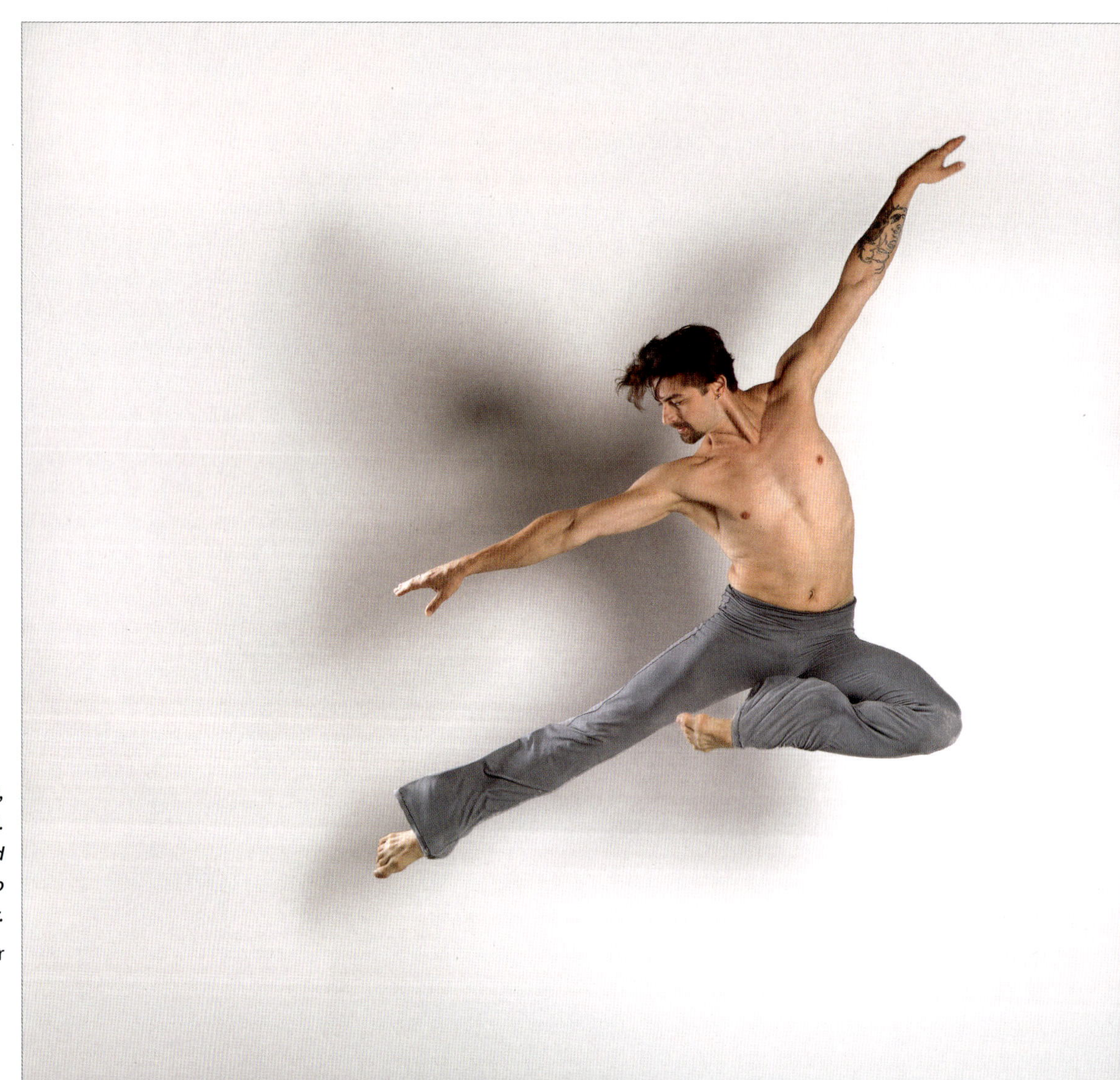

With a soloist from the Vienna State Opera as a subject, fantastic images of wonderful balletic leaps are achieved. For shots like this, the interplay between photographer and subject is particularly important, especially when it comes to finding precisely the right moment to release the shutter.

54mm | f9 | 1/160 sec. | ISO 200 | Model: Vladimir

fast movements using relatively long exposure times. The actual flash duration varies from flash head to flash head, and you will need to refer to the user manual to find the precise specifications of the particular flash you are using. When we talk about flash duration, there are two important values that you need to know about:

- **Total flash duration t0.1:** This is the time it takes your flash to reach full output and then drop to 10% output.
- **Effective flash duration t0.5:** This is the time it takes your flash to reach full output and then drop to 50% output.

In order to avoid capturing motion blur in your images, you need to compare the t0.1 value for your flash with your exposure time. This is because the t0.5 value only accounts for the brightest phase of the flash burst but not its entire duration.

Unfortunately, to make their gear appear more capable, many manufacturers only state the t0.5 value in their documentation and, if it is not otherwise specified, you can be pretty sure that this is the value quoted. In order to calculate the all-important t0.1 value, you can generally multiply the t0.5 value by 4. You may have heard that you can use a factor of 3 to calculate the t0.1 value too, but my experience has shown that this is often not sufficient, especially when shooting with cheaper flash heads. I recommend that you always use the factor 4 to give yourself a good margin of safety.

Let's take a look at an example:

For a specified flash duration of 1/200 sec., the t0.1 value will be around 1/300 sec. For slow movements or shots in which you are prepared to accept a little motion blur, you can use flash heads with a long flash duration (i.e., t0.1 > 1/300 sec.). For faster movements like the dance shots shown here, you should use a flash head with a t0.1 value of less than 1/1000 sec.

HSS Flash

Flash sync times for studio flash are usually somewhere between 1/160 and 1/250 sec. This is the length of the phase during which the shutter is fully open and the subject is illuminated by the flash. However, this is much too slow for fast-moving subjects and produces motion blur in the resulting images. Instead of emitting a single burst of light, High-Speed Sync (HSS) flash units emit light in a series of very short stroboscopic pulses during the entire time the shutter curtains open and close across the frame. This technique works for exposure times as short as 1/8000 sec. but, due to the large number of individual flashes, the flash unit can no longer work at full output—i.e., the effective flash output is reduced.

Ceiling Height

The available space in a studio is extremely important when it comes to capturing vertical movements. While ceiling heights of 8 to 10 feet are fine for stationary subjects, this is not usually enough for a subject such as a dancer. If your space is limited, you can compensate a little by moving your model closer to the background and using a longer lens and/or a relatively high shooting

position. If you are lucky enough to have access to a studio with a ceiling height of 12 feet or more, you and your model will enjoy much more freedom of movement during the shoot.

When to Release the Shutter

When shooting action photos in a studio, photographer and model need to work closely together to capture precisely the right moment. As a photographer, you need to know all about the movements your subject makes in order to anticipate the right moment, and you also need to develop a feel for the shutter lag in your particular camera and the recycle times of your flash heads. This all takes practice, but you will soon develop a reliable flow.

Flash duration and the flash output curve.

Capturing Moments of Stillness

Many dance moves follow intense movement with a moment of stillness. You don't need a lot of gear to capture moments like this, just the skill to anticipate precisely the right moment to release the shutter.

EFFORT INVOLVED

Low

SUITABLE FOR

All kinds of portraits

THE LOOK

Spatial portrait for capturing still dance poses
Sports pants, natural-looking makeup

EQUIPMENT

1 × 31.5" octabox

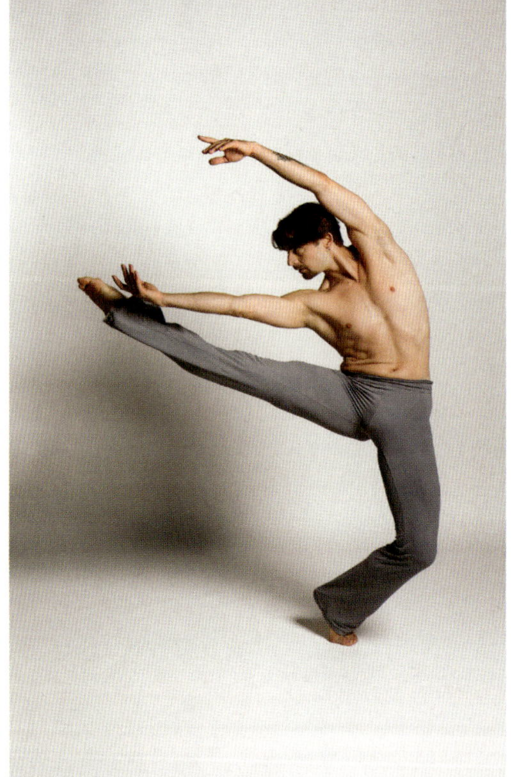

55mm | f9 | 1/160 sec. | ISO 200 | Model: Vladimir

HOW IT WORKS

This single-light setup produces natural-looking light. The raised position of the octabox produces soft shadows on the subject's body, and the light reflected from the white floor and background softens these shadows. This accents the muscles and emphasizes the wonderful curves in the pose. The shadow play creates pleasing definition, and the shadows on the floor and in the background provide spatial orientation while giving the image additional depth. These shadows also provide detail to fill the otherwise empty space in the lower left portion of the frame.

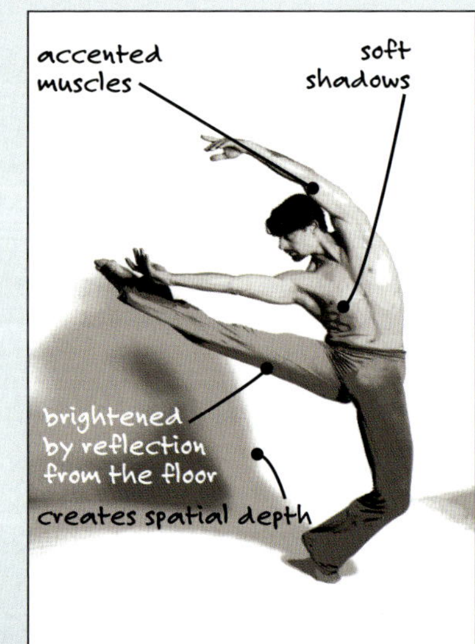

1. Place the octabox **(1)** about 10 to 12 feet to the right of your model at an angle of about 30 degrees. Position it above head height so that the shadows point diagonally down toward the floor and don't reach above belly height.

2. To keep the background bright, position your model about 18 inches in front of the white backdrop.

"Rehearse your model's movements well so that you know precisely when to release the shutter."

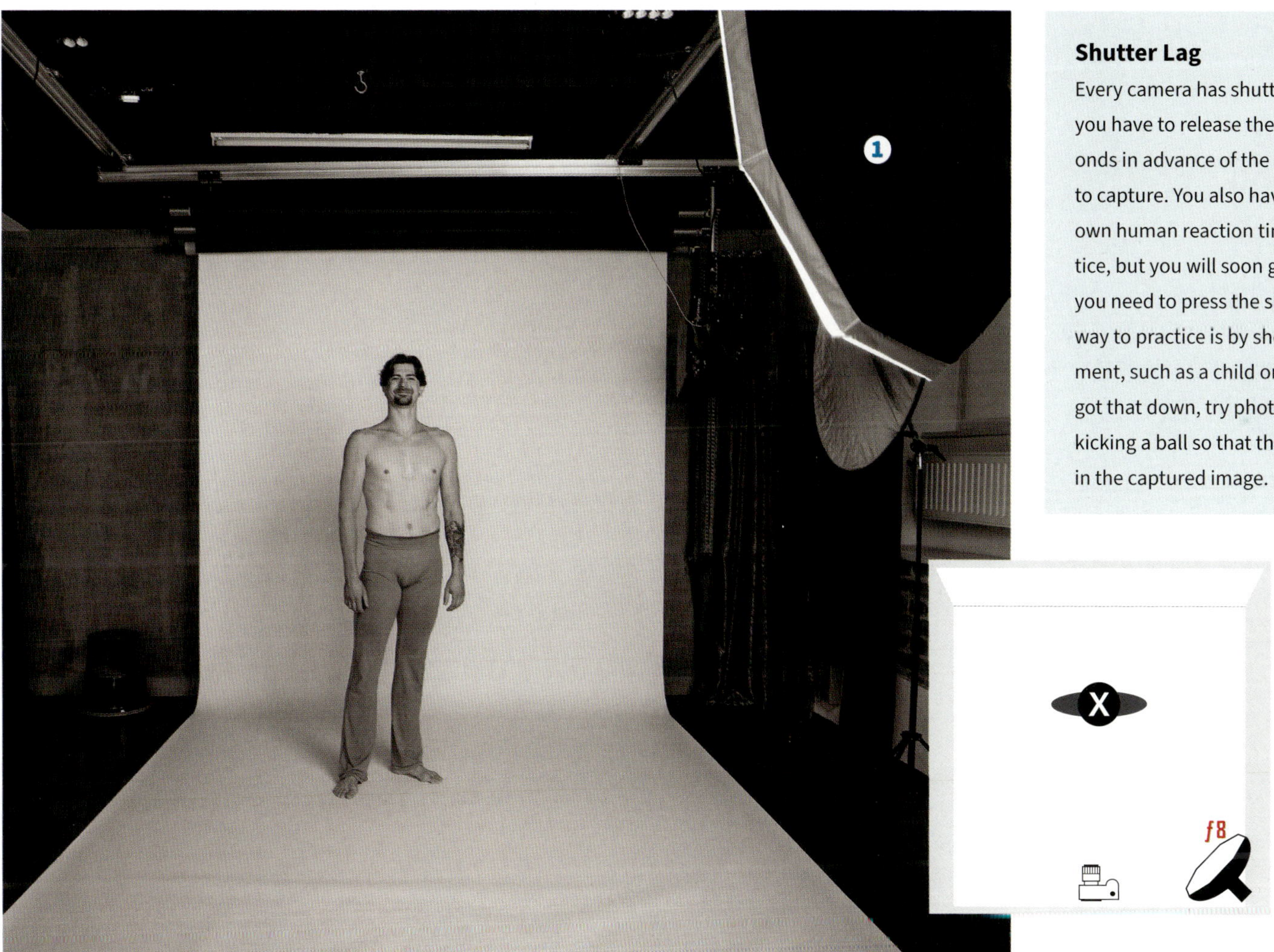

Shutter Lag

Every camera has shutter lag. This means that you have to release the shutter a few milliseconds in advance of the actual moment you want to capture. You also have to compensate for your own human reaction time. It takes a little practice, but you will soon get a feel for exactly when you need to press the shutter button. The best way to practice is by shooting a repeated movement, such as a child on a swing. Once you've got that down, try photographing a soccer player kicking a ball so that the ball is still in the frame in the captured image.

Balletic Leap with Motion Blur

As discussed in the introduction to this chapter, completely freezing fast movements relies on using the right technology. However, in this shot I wanted to include a little motion blur, so I used standard (i.e., non-HSS) flash heads to capture it. The slight blur nicely accents the movement of the subject's rear foot and his flying hair.

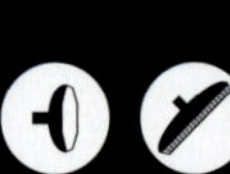

EFFORT INVOLVED

Low

SUITABLE FOR

All kinds of portraits

THE LOOK

Action portrait with slight motion blur
Sports pants, natural-looking makeup

EQUIPMENT

1× 31.5" octabox
1× 47" strip box with a honeycomb grid

266

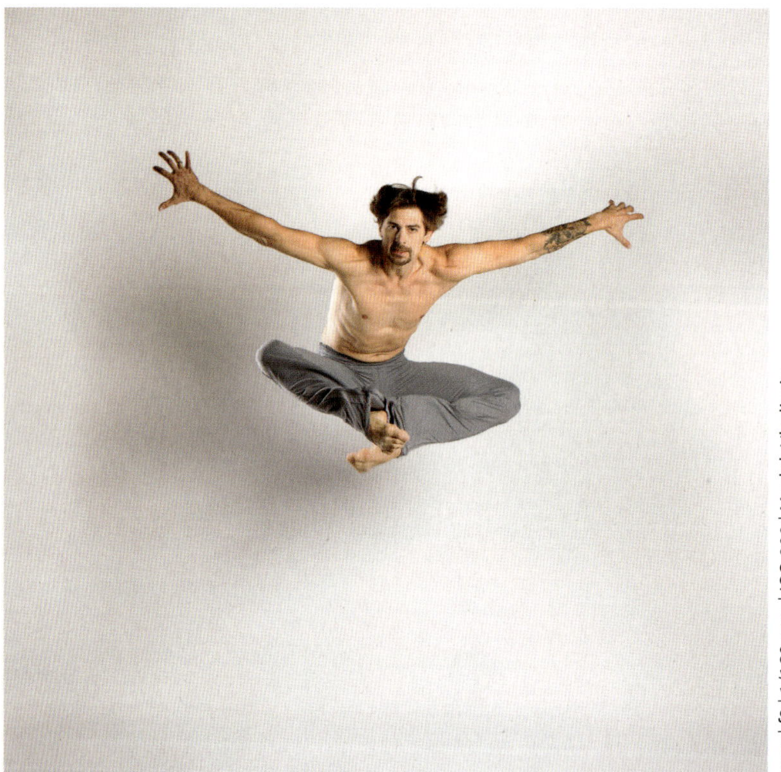

50mm | f9 | 1/160 sec. | ISO 200 | Model: Vladimir

HOW IT WORKS

This classic setup with a raised, diagonally positioned main light provides great definition in the face and body that make the subject appear to leap out of the page. The accent light on the subject's back provides a nice highlight and adds contrast. The muscles are nicely accented and the folds in the subject's pants add to the feeling of momentum. The slight shadow in the transition between wall and floor enables the viewer to estimate the height of the leap, while the shadow in the background adds depth and spatial location.

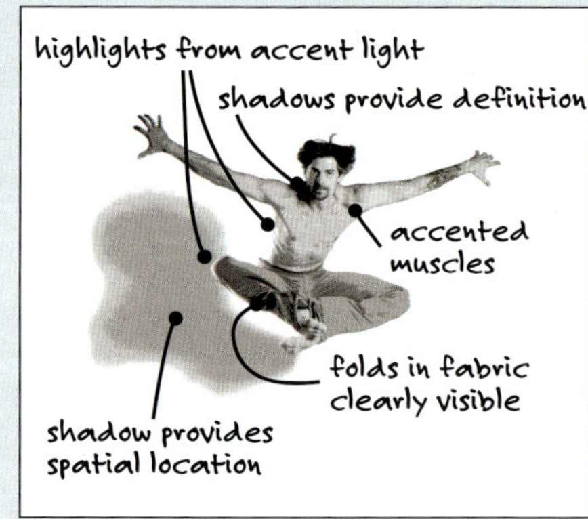

THE SETUP

1. Place the octabox **(1)** about 10 to 12 feet to the right of your model in a raised position and at an angle of about 30 degrees. Position it so that your model's shadow points diagonally toward the background.

2. Now place the gridded strip box **(2)** at left rear very close to the backdrop and about 5 feet from your model. The center of the strip box should be at about head height. The accent light should produce highlights on your model's cheek, neck/hair, and upper arm.

3. Place your model about 18 inches in front of the white background.

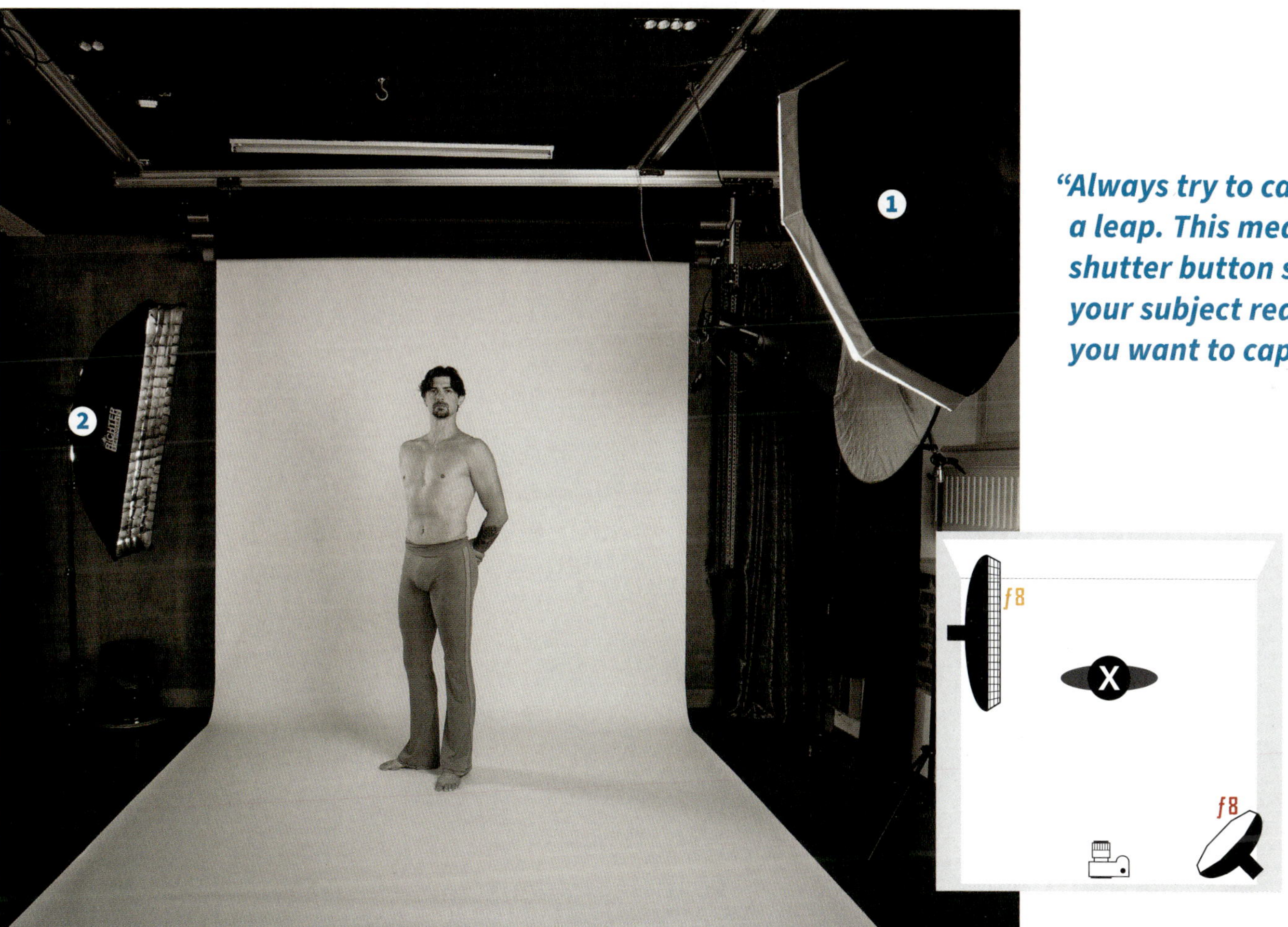

"Always try to capture the apex of a leap. This means pressing the shutter button slightly before your subject reaches the position you want to capture."

Dramatic Lighting

Hard light and a dark background are the main ingredients for this simple but dramatic theater-style lighting setup. The strong shadows and powerful pose complete the picture.

EFFORT INVOLVED

Low

SUITABLE FOR

All kinds of portraits

THE LOOK

High-contrast portrait with dramatic theater-style lighting

Sports pants and open shirt

Natural-looking makeup

EQUIPMENT

1× beauty dish with a honeycomb grid

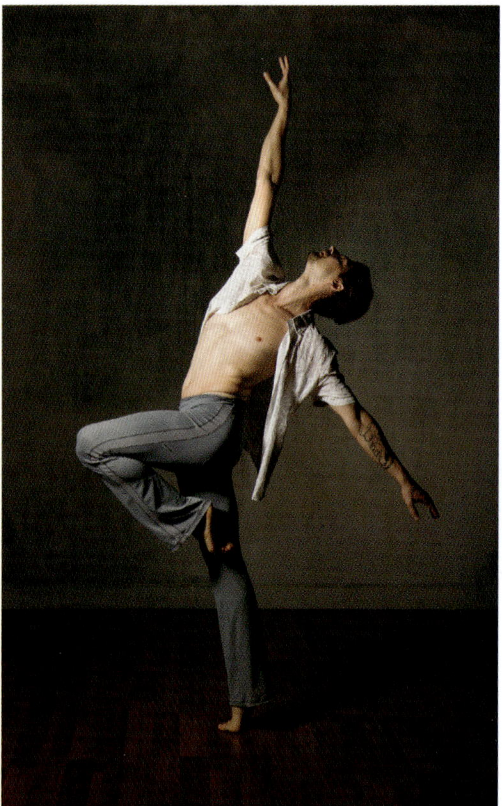

59mm | f11 | 1/160 sec. | ISO 100 | Model: Vladimir

HOW IT WORKS

This image clearly demonstrates the benefits of the classic raised, diagonally placed main light. The subject's torso is brightly lit and the shadows create well-defined body contours. The subject's muscles are clearly visible and the shirt provides a nice accent in the shadow area. The dark background provides plenty of contrast and steers visual focus toward the subject. The one-sided lighting produces a dramatic look-and-feel that is emphasized by the subject's striking pose.

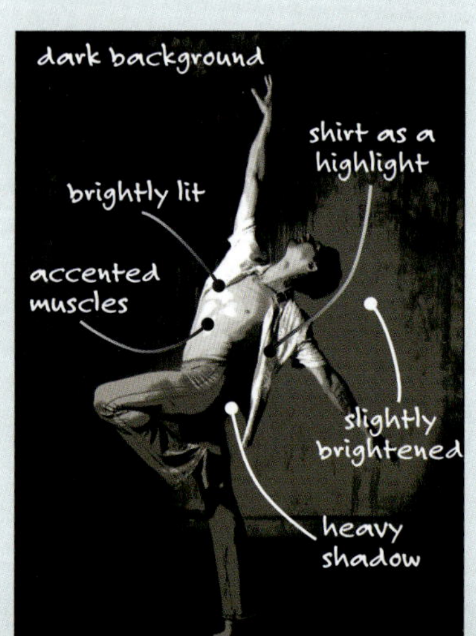

1. Place the gridded beauty dish **(1)** in a slightly raised position about 10 feet to the left of your model and at an angle of about 45 degrees. Position it well above head height to create obvious light fall-off around the level of your model's thighs.

2. Place your model about 18 inches in front of the dark background. For this shot I used the dark laminated studio floor and a dark painted wall for my background. A black paper background would serve just as well.

"Moving the light farther to the side increases the feeling of drama in this image."

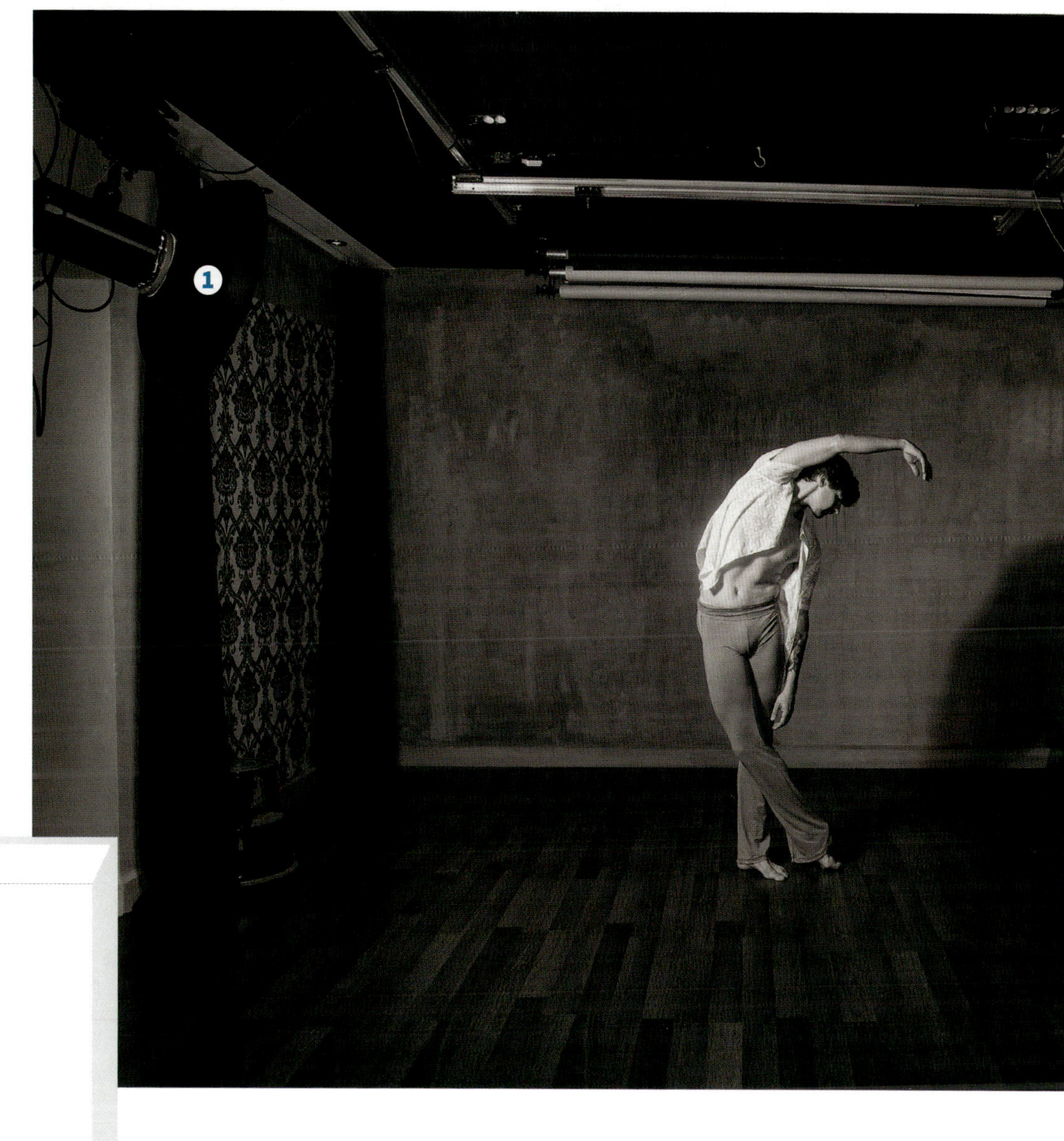

Movement and High Contrast

A brightly lit body in front of a dark background creates strong contrast in this image, and the slight motion blur produced by the standard studio flash heads adds to the dynamic feel. Using the studio wall instead of a paper background gave my subject more space for his impressive jeté.

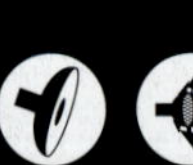

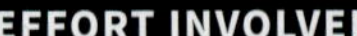

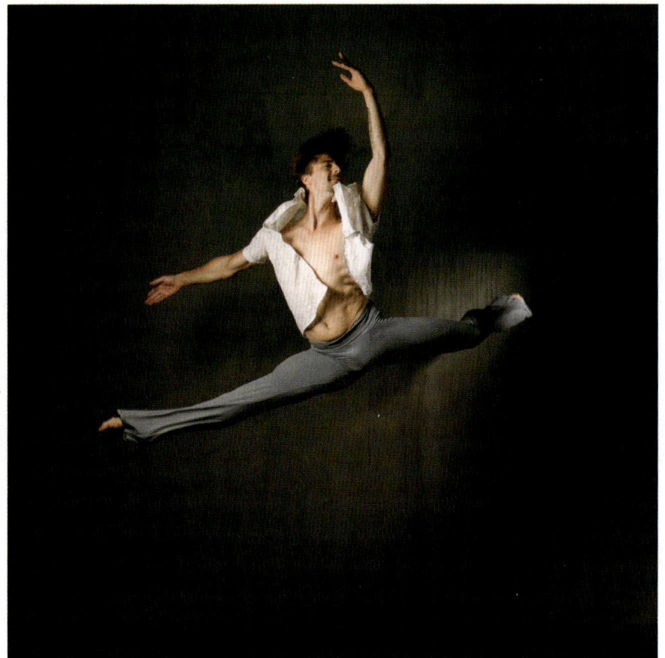

EFFORT INVOLVED

Medium

SUITABLE FOR

All kinds of portraits

THE LOOK

High-contrast action portrait

Sports pants, loose shirt

Natural-looking makeup

EQUIPMENT

1× beauty dish

1× standard reflector with a honeycomb grid and barndoors

1× 30" ×40" silver reflector

HOW IT WORKS

The beauty dish main light produces focused light from head to toe. Vertical lines are accented and the strong shadows provide good definition. The flowing hair and the movement in the fabric of the subject's shirt add to the dynamic feel, as does the slight motion blur in the feet. The background highlight provides contrast for the leg shadows and helps to accent the body contours. The rear foot is lit by the fill light instead of simply disappearing into the shadows. The slightly lightened shadows provide added detail.

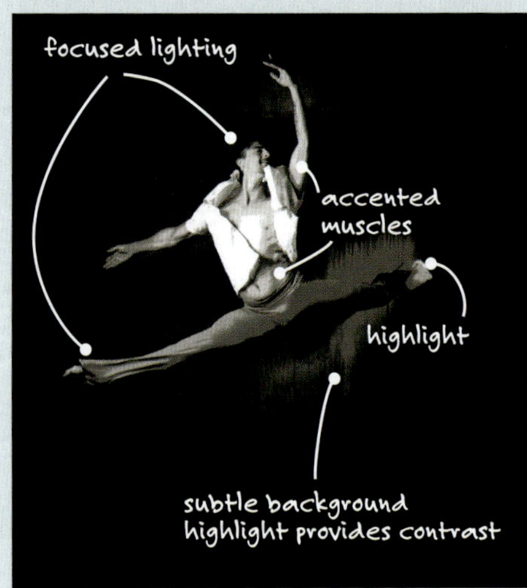

THE SETUP

1. Place the beauty dish **(1)** about 6 feet to the left of your model in a raised position and at an angle of about 15 degrees. Position it to produce lateral light with shadows that point slightly downward.

2. Mount the reflector **(2)** in a raised position about 6 feet from your model and set it up to slightly lighten the shadows from the main light.

3. Place the gridded standard reflector with barndoors **(3)** about 6 feet to the right of your model at about head height. Position it so that your model's leg is lit when he jumps. Close the barndoors right down so that just a narrow strip of light hits the background.

4. Position your model about 18 inches in front of the dark background.

"To get the background highlight right, you will need to discuss your model's movements before you set up your lights."

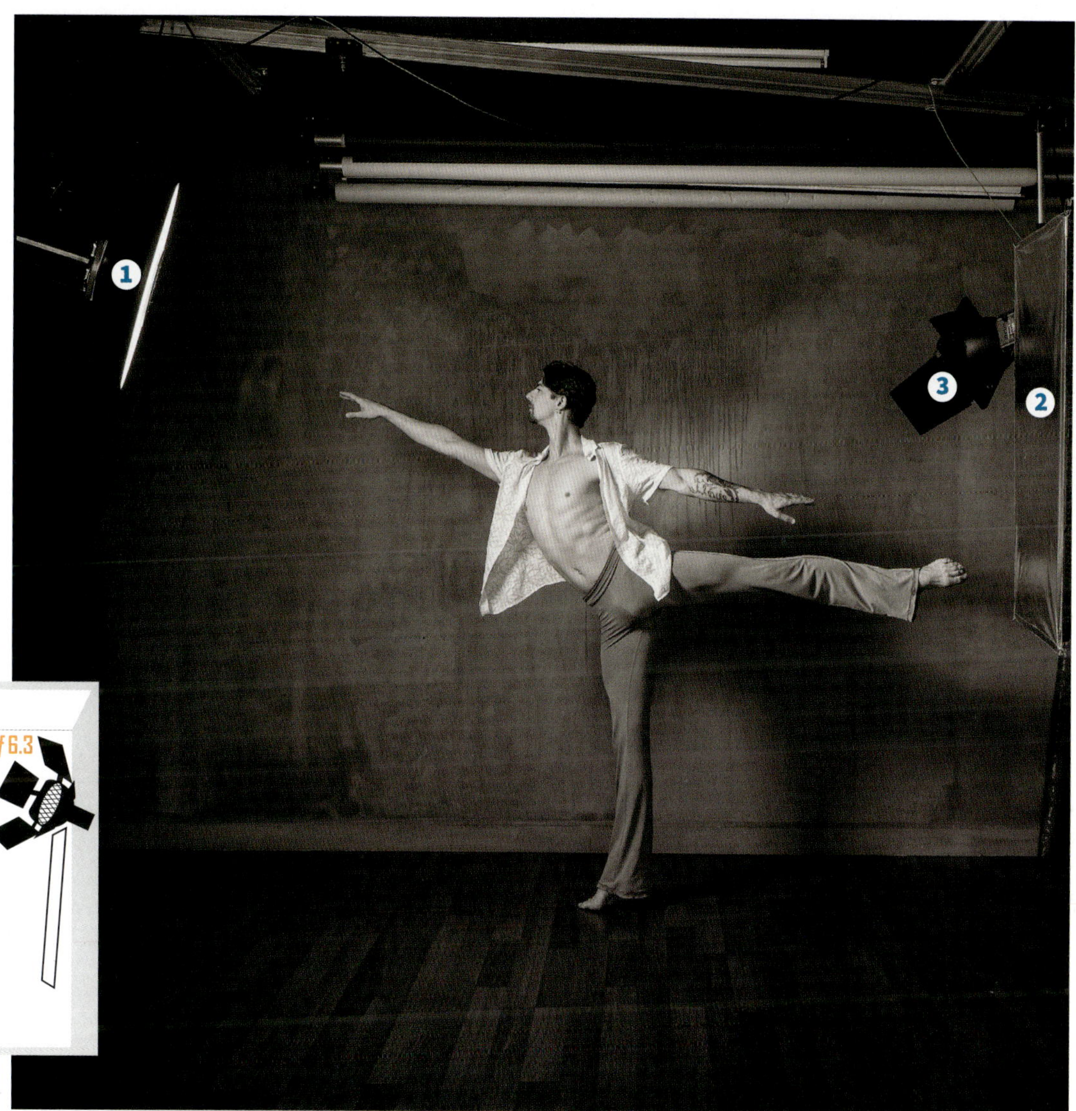

Freezing a Pirouette

The basic idea for this setup was to freeze a ballet dancer's pirouette. Soft shadows and light/dark gradients on the floor and in the background add vividness, while the glossy white floor produces a nice reflection to round out the composition.

EFFORT INVOLVED

Low

SUITABLE FOR

Three-quarter length or full-length portraits

THE LOOK

Vivid portrait with light/dark gradients

Natural-looking makeup, glossy lips

Tied-back hair, ballet dancer's dress

EQUIPMENT

2 × 47" strip boxes with honeycomb grids

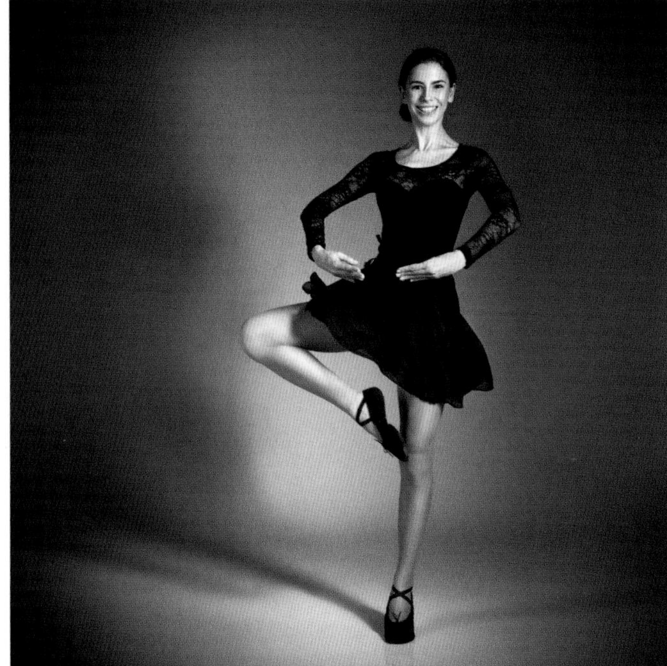

54mm | f8 | 1/160 sec. | ISO 100 | Model: Elisa

HOW IT WORKS

The raised main light accents the subject's body contours, while the facial shadows provide plenty of definition and underscore the radiant expression. The position of the light also underscores the folds in the dress and thus helps to emphasize the light, airy feel to the pirouette. The fill light lightens the shadows on the subject and in the background to prevent the image from looking too dark, and to separate the dark-haired subject and the black dress from the background.

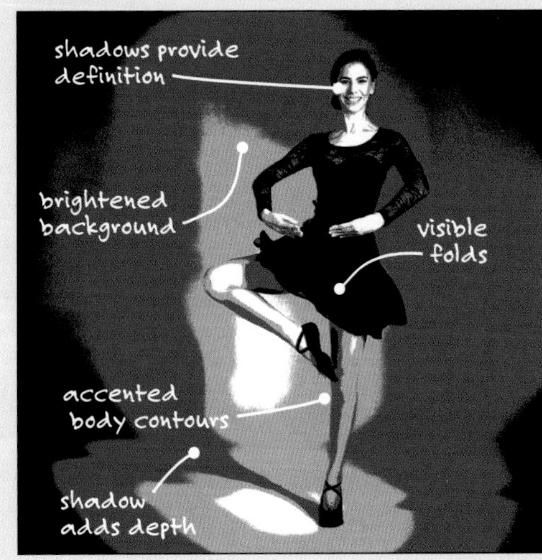

1. Place one of the gridded strip boxes **(1)** in a raised position about 8 feet from your model at an angle of about 45 degrees. Position it so that the nose shadow points diagonally downward but doesn't quite reach your model's upper lip. Make sure that her collarbones produce visible shadows and that her legs are sufficiently brightly lit.

2. Place the second gridded strip box **(2)** about 8 feet to the left of your model at around chest height and at an angle of about 45 degrees. Use it to lighten the shadows formed by the main light. See the image below to get an idea of the relative positions of the model and the lights.

3. Position your model about 6 feet in front of the white background. The similar distances between the model and the flashes, and between the model and the background, make the background appear mid-gray.

For this shot, I placed a sheet of glossy white laminate on the floor to help my model perform her pirouette (a paper background is too grippy). I retouched the hard edge between the relatively small sheet of laminate and the matte background during post-processing.

> ### *"Styling that suits the overall concept helps to emphasize the message transported by an image."*

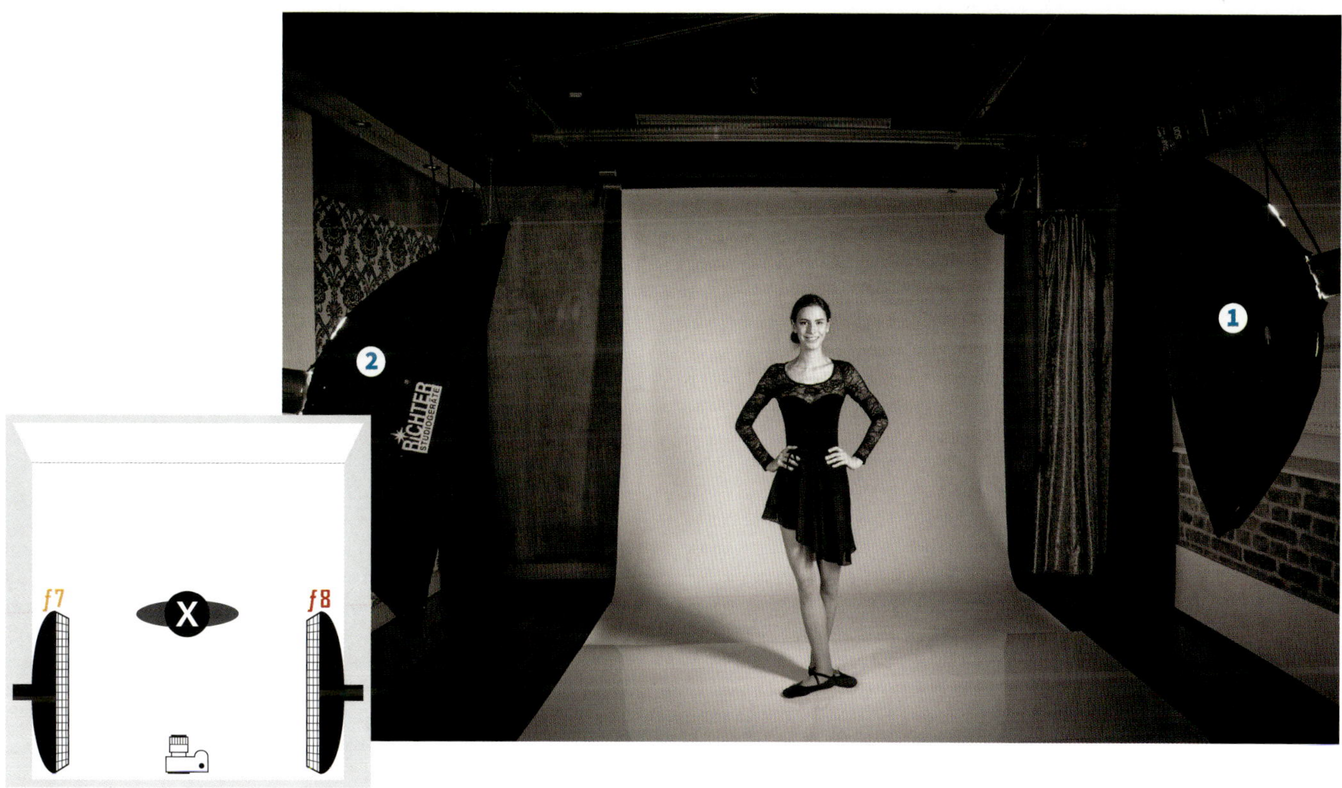

Flyaway Hair with HSS

A cheap wind machine is all you need to get a cool flyaway hair effect for models with short haircuts. For models with big hair, you can achieve a similar effect with a resolute shake of the head and the help of centrifugal force. To freeze this movement in pin-sharp focus, I used HSS-capable flash.

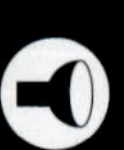

EFFORT INVOLVED

Low

SUITABLE FOR

Close-up to three-quarter-length portraits

THE LOOK

Softly lit portrait

Accents on individual strands of hair

Pink-toned makeup with punchy eyeliner

EQUIPMENT

1× HSS standard reflector

1× 30" ×40" silver reflector

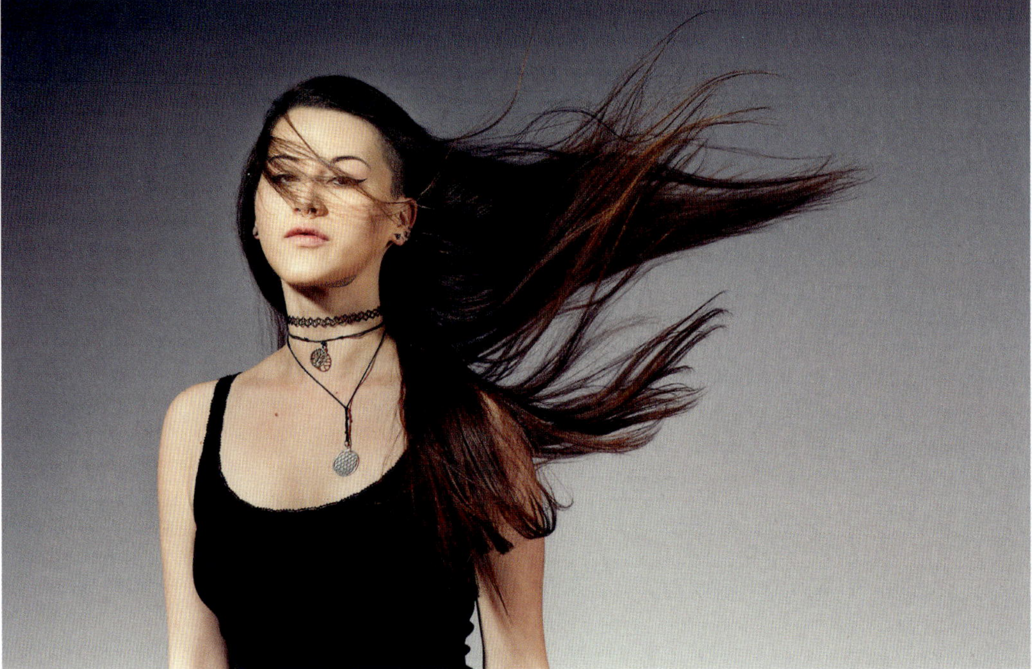

HOW IT WORKS

Once again I used just a single light to produce a well-lit image with a super-soft background gradient. The diagonally placed flash and the way the subject faces into the light produces an almost frontal lighting effect in the face, with clearly accented eyes and lips. The bold eyeliner underscores this effect. The close proximity of the reflector makes the shadows significantly lighter, making even fine details in the subject's dark hair clearly visible. The swing in the hair produces a nice, natural-looking gloss, and the soft background gradient ensures that the subject remains the focus of the viewer's attention.

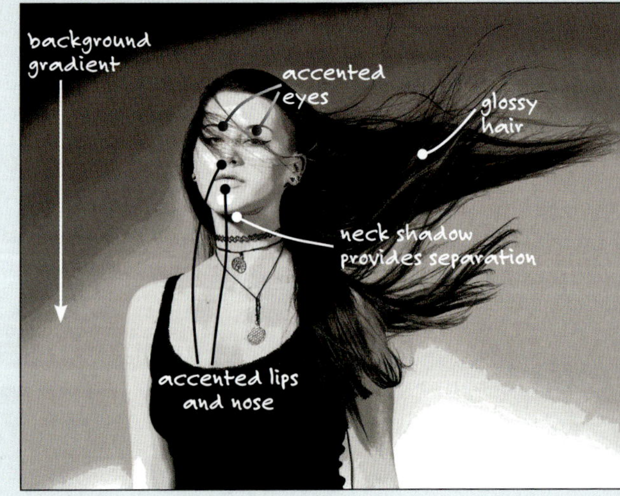

THE SETUP

1. Place the standard reflector **(1)** about 6 feet to the left of your model in a raised position and at an angle of about 45 degrees. Position it to produce a clear nose shadow.

2. Mount the silver reflector **(2)** on a stand about 3 feet to the right of your model with its center at about head height. Set it up to brighten the shadows from the main light.

3. Your model should stand about 10 feet in front of the white background. If you don't have enough space and your model has to stand closer to the background, you will need to use a mid-gray backdrop instead to produce a similar level of brightness.

4. To get her hair to "fly," Sonja turned her head sharply and stopped the movement as soon as she was facing the camera. Once again, capturing the right moment requires perfect timing on the part of the model and the photographer.

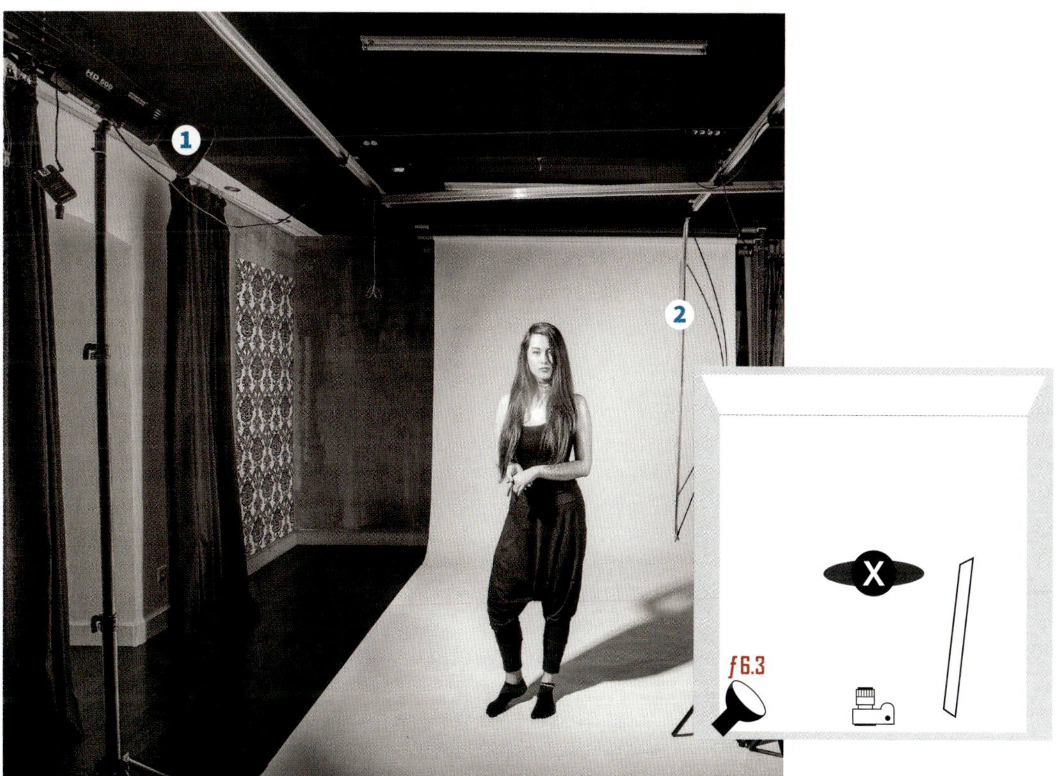

High-Speed Flash for Ultra-Sharp Details

Because I captured this image using an exposure time of 1/800 sec. there is no motion blur. To make the most of this kind of effect you need to use an HSS-capable flash head—for this shot I used a Photon Europe HD-600.

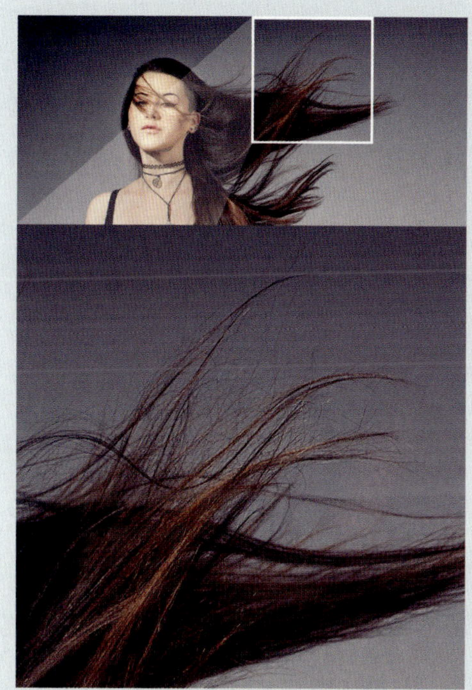

This 100% crop detail shows that there is no motion blur in the flyaway hair located on the focal plane.

"Freshly washed hair 'flies' better."

Everything Is Spinning

To freeze fast-moving subjects you need to use flash heads with a short flash duration or ones with HSS capability. This tandem lighting setup uses the spill light from the fill flash twice.

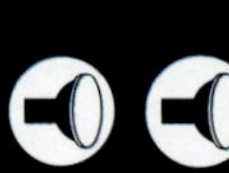

EFFORT INVOLVED

Low

SUITABLE FOR

All kinds of portraits

THE LOOK

Freezing fast-moving subjects

Pink-toned, natural-looking makeup

Light dress and flowing scarves

EQUIPMENT

2× HSS-capable standard reflectors with diffusers

276

HOW IT WORKS

The raised standard reflector main light provides focused light from head to toe and plenty of spill light too. This produces nice shadows that are nevertheless lightened by the spill. The flowing scarves produce multiple tiny highlights and the hair has its own silky gloss. The second flash is positioned almost next to the subject, producing subsidiary lateral light and simultaneously brightening the background too, giving the image a light, airy feel. The shadows on the floor and in the background enable the viewer to locate the subject in space and provide an anchor for this beautifully light-footed image.

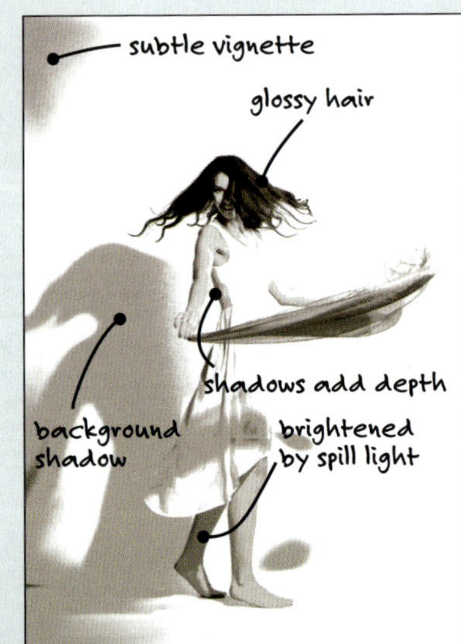

THE SETUP

1. Place the standard reflector with its diffuser **(1)** at front right in a raised position and at an angle of about 45 degrees. Place it about 8 feet from your model and position it to produce a small, diagonal shadow beneath your model's nose.

2. Place the second standard reflector **(2)** next to your model at a distance of about 5 feet and above head height. Position it to illuminate the background and to provide extra spill light on your model.

3. Position your model about 3 feet from the white background.

The two light shapers that make up this setup are positioned in tandem in a single line, producing an image with clearly differentiated light and shadow sides.

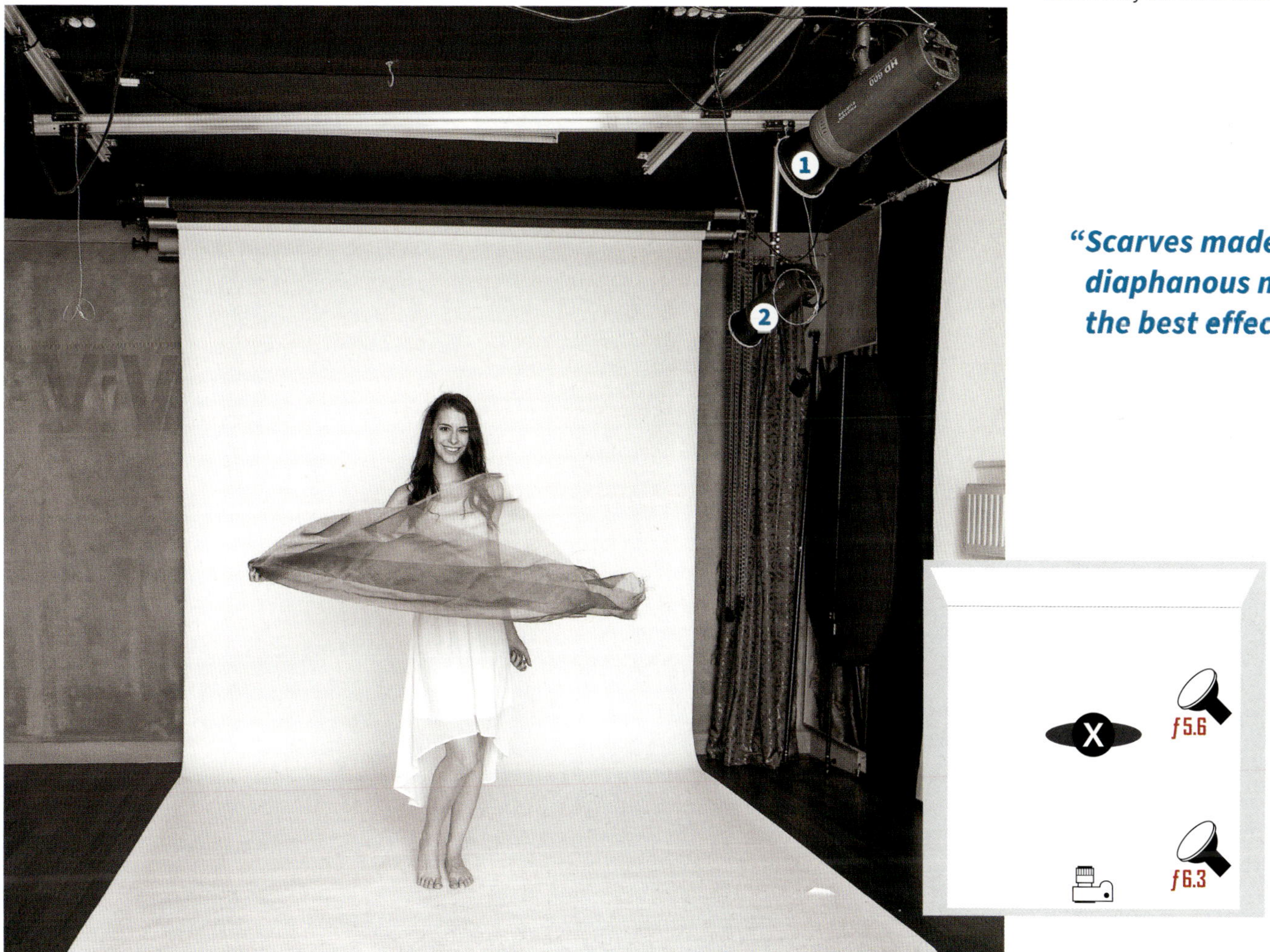

Stage Jump Using HSS

This kind of shot is often used in advertising—either for sports clothing or to symbolize someone jumping for joy. The main elements here are a short exposure time and a simple but flexible two-light setup.

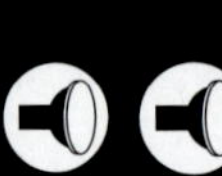

EFFORT INVOLVED

Low

SUITABLE FOR

All kinds of portraits

THE LOOK

Jump shot with strong contrast
Natural-looking makeup, hair in ponytail
Sporty outfit

EQUIPMENT

2× HSS-capable standard reflectors with diffusers

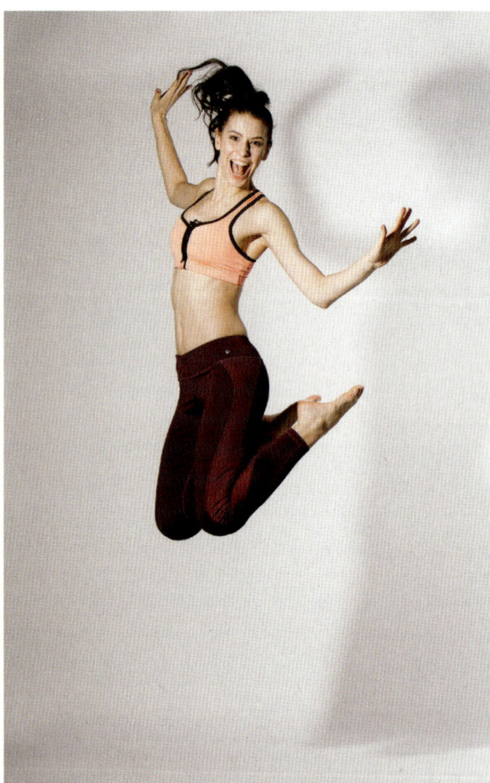

75mm | f6.3 | 1/1000 sec. | ISO 800 | Model: Elisa

HOW IT WORKS

In the middle of the jump the subject's head is at around the same level as the main light (see the shadow in the background for proof!). This produces a vertical facial shadow that nicely accents the subject's expression. The raised position of the light also accents the body contours, the stomach muscles, and the ribs. The strong shadows on the subject provide plenty of definition, while the shadows in the background and the transition between wall and floor show just how high the jump is, and emphasize the dynamic feel. The fill flash lightens the background shadows to keep the mood upbeat.

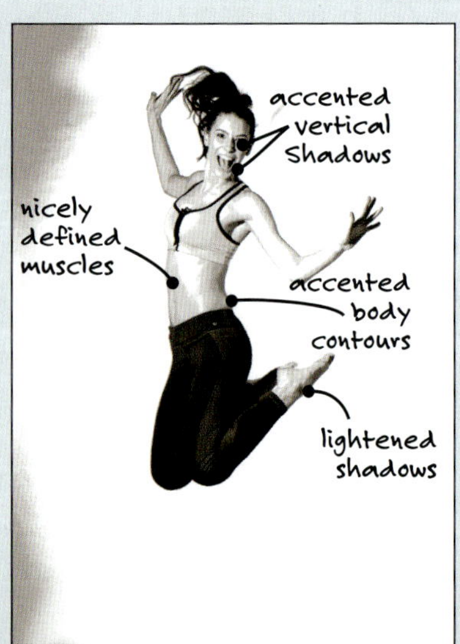

THE SETUP

1. Place the standard reflector with its diffuser **(1)** in a raised position about 8 feet to the left of your model and at an angle of about 45 degrees. Position it so that the nose shadow is still visible beneath the tip of your model's nose.

2. Mount the second standard reflector/diffuser **(2)** on a ceiling rail or a boom stand in a raised position about 5 feet from your model and about 3 feet form the background. Point it at the center of the backdrop.

3. Your model should stand about 5 feet in front of the white background.

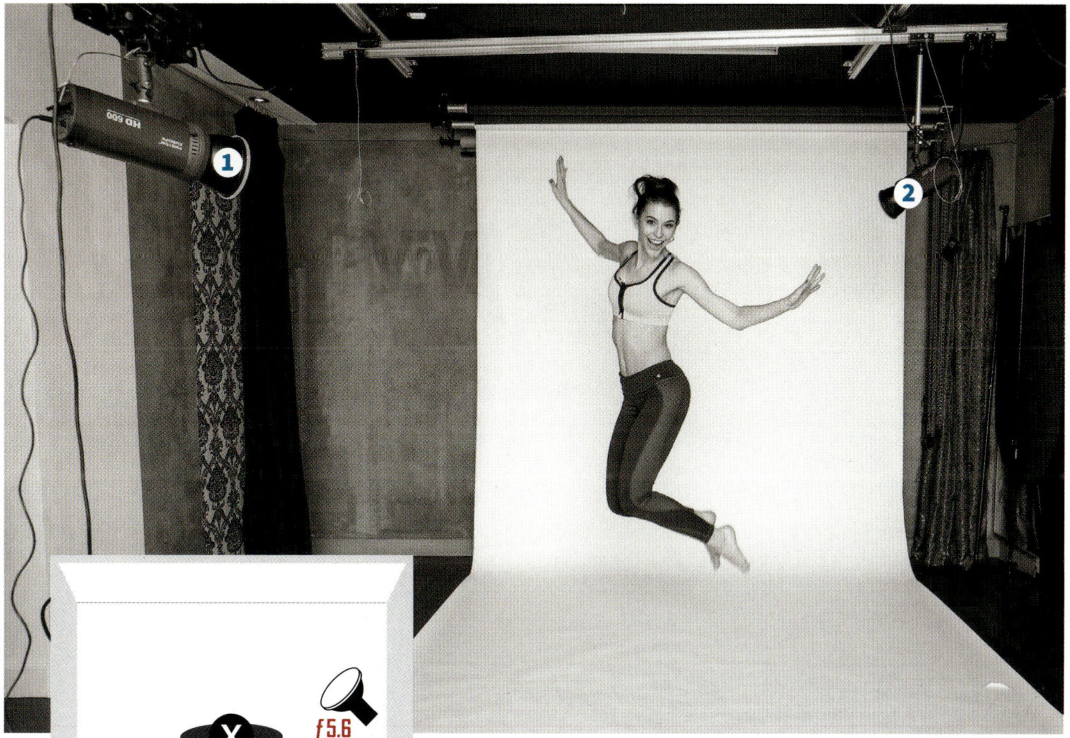

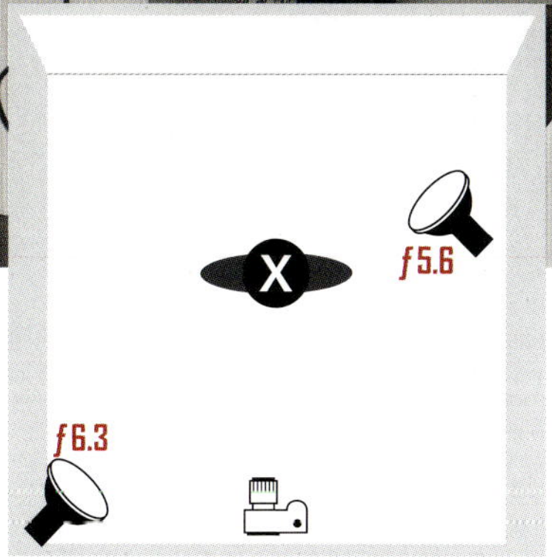

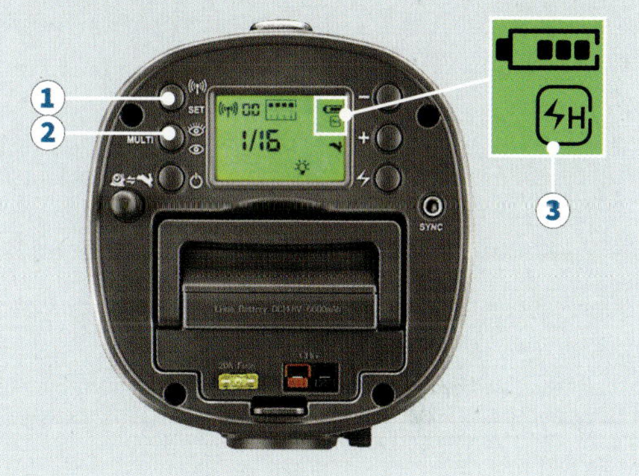

HSS Mode Settings

To activate HSS mode on a Photon HD-600 flash head, you have to simultaneously press the Set/Transmit button **(1)** and the Modeling Light button **(2)**. The display then shows the H flash icon **(3)** at top right.

Refer to the user manual for instructions on how to set up HSS mode for your particular flash head.

"Select an aperture setting and a shooting position to suit the available space and the height of your model's jump."

Dancer in Rim Light

The silhouette of the performer's body contrasted against the background is an important element in dance photography. In any dance shot, you also have to decide whether to illustrate the movements being made or— as in this example—to freeze the moment. This simple setup enables you to create images with strong accents and clear separation between the subject and the background. The frozen movement produces a dream-like silhouette and is equally suitable for sports, magazine, or advertising shoots.

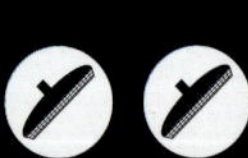

EFFORT INVOLVED

Medium

SUITABLE FOR

Full-length portraits

THE LOOK

Full-length portrait with strong rim light
Accented body shape
Smokey eyes, subtle lipstick, accented hair curls
Dancer's clothing

EQUIPMENT

2 × 47" strip boxes with honeycomb grids
1 × 43" circular silver reflector

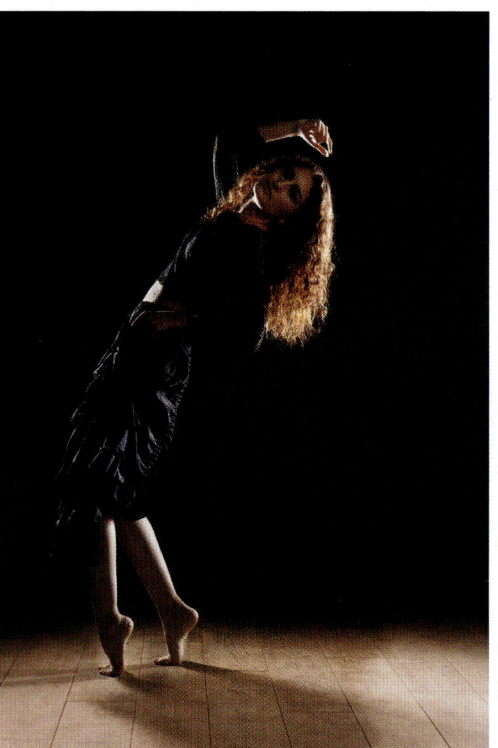

65 mm | f5.6 | 1/125 sec. | ISO 100 | Model: Anika

HOW IT WORKS

The effect of this image is based on the clear, glowing rim lights on both sides of the subject. These accent the outline of the subject's body and provide clear separation from the background in spite of the dark clothing. The light flooding the subject's hair provides an additional eye-catcher. The lighting on the floor provides contrast to the generally dark atmosphere and anchors the subject within the frame. The folds in the skirt are full of tiny highlights that contrast with the dark overall feel. The subject's face is discernible but isn't the focal point. The subject in this shot is the entire body, attractively framed by the rim lights.

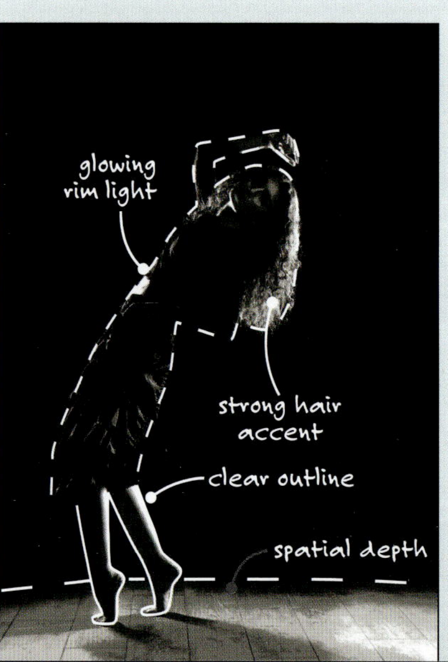

1. Begin by placing the two strip boxes **(1)** and **(2)** behind your model in slightly raised positions and each at an angle of about 45 degrees. Tip both strip boxes downward to light your model from head to toe.

2. Now place the reflector **(3)** about 6 feet to front right of your model with its center at head height. Make sure that it slightly brightens your model's face when she is moving and not just when she is standing still.

3. Position your model about 5 feet in front of the dark background.

"Timing is key when photographing dancers. Giving your model clear instructions will help you to release the shutter at exactly the right moment."

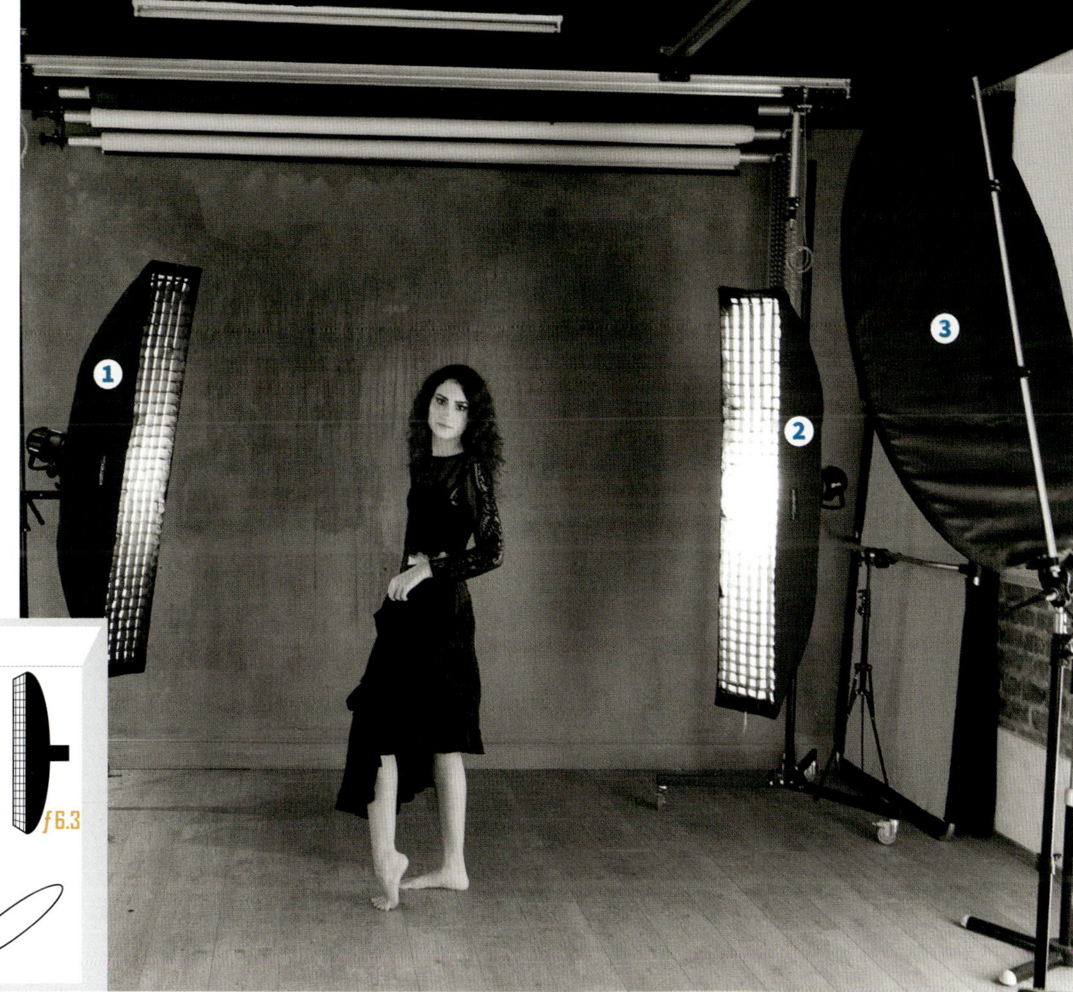

Sporty Portrait

A shot of a person using a jump rope requires frontal lighting to ensure that both arms and the rope are adequately lit. Once again, this shot uses HSS flashes to capture the fast-moving rope and freeze the subject in mid-jump.

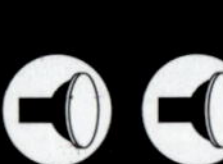

EFFORT INVOLVED

Low

SUITABLE FOR

All kinds of portraits

THE LOOK

Flat lighting for good overall illumination
Natural-looking makeup, hair in ponytail
Sporty outfit, jump rope

EQUIPMENT

2 × HSS-capable standard reflectors with diffusers

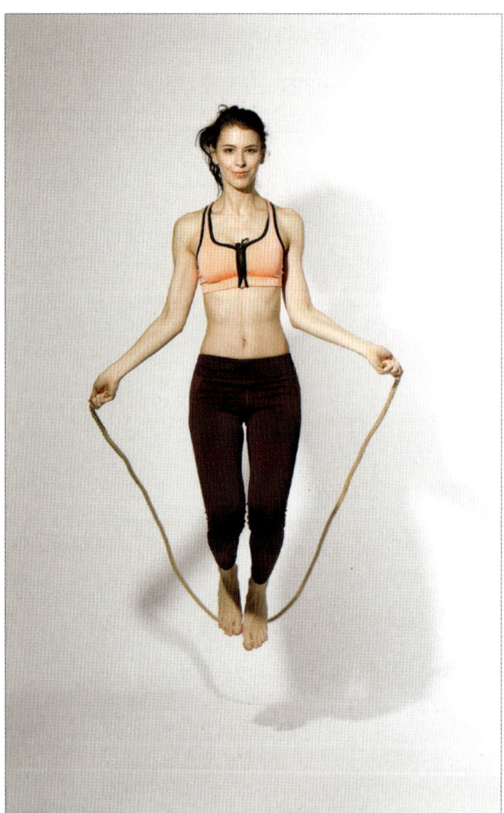

70mm | f6.3 | 1/1000 sec. | ISO 800 | Model: Elisa

HOW IT WORKS

Because the subject doesn't jump too high, the slightly raised main light produces natural-looking shadows that accent the eyes, nose, and mouth, and the broader facial contours. The main light also accents the subject's ribs and stomach muscles. The strong shadows also accent the subject's body contours, and the shadows in the background and the transition from wall to floor help the viewer to estimate the magnitude of the jump. The fill light reduces the strength of the background shadow to give the image a breezy feel.

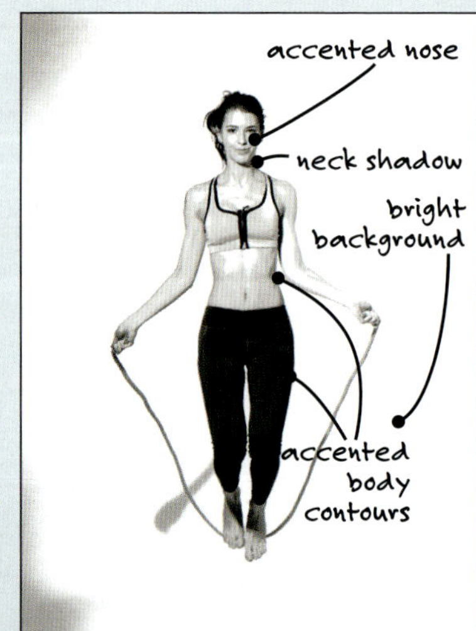

THE SETUP

1. Place the standard reflector with its diffuser **(1)** about 8 feet in front and slightly to the side of the camera in a raised position. Position it so that the shadow beneath the tip of your model's nose is still visible.

2. Mount the background reflector **(2)** on a ceiling rail or a boom stand in a raised position about 5 feet from your model and 3 feet from the background. Point it at the center of the backdrop.

3. Your model should stand about 5 feet from the white background.

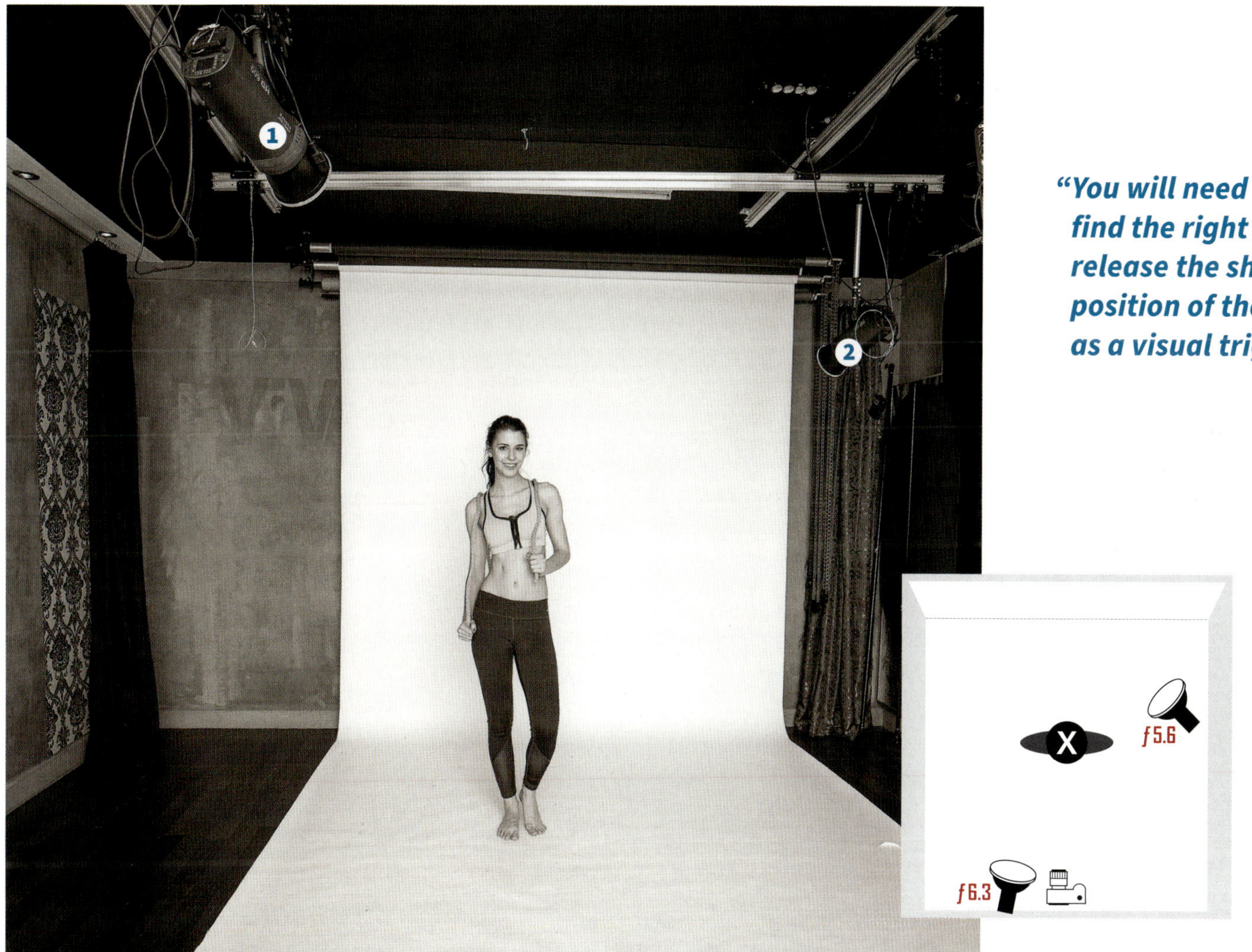

"You will need to practice to find the right moment to release the shutter. Use the position of the circling rope as a visual trigger."

Gentle Movements

The flash duration of regular studio flash heads is ideal for capturing slow, gentle movements. The slight motion blur that this creates underscores the gentle nature of the movement portrayed in the image.

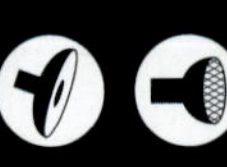

EFFORT INVOLVED

Low

SUITABLE FOR

All kinds of portraits

THE LOOK

Airy portrait with slight motion blur

Natural-looking makeup

Suitably colored flowing scarf

EQUIPMENT

1× beauty dish

1× standard reflector with a honeycomb grid

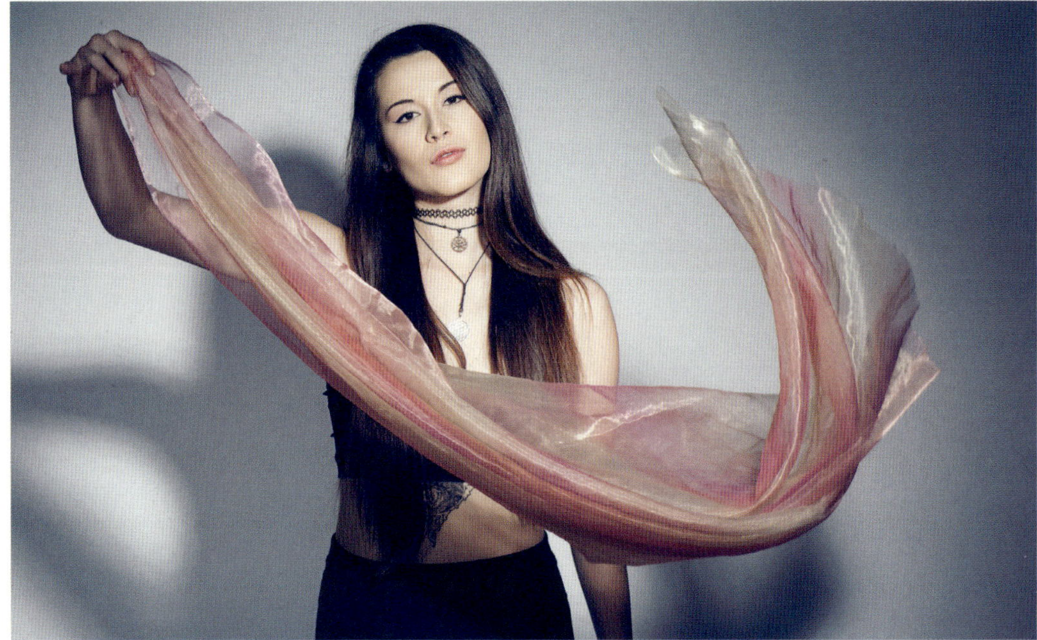

85mm | f7.1 | 1/160 sec. | ISO 100 | Model: Sonja

HOW IT WORKS

The gridded standard reflector produces highly controlled light with an obvious center that automatically focuses attention on the subject. The hard shadows contrast well with the flowing movement of the scarf, which shows slight motion blur due to the relatively long exposure time. The slightly raised position of the main light produces good overall lighting with soft definition. The focused light nevertheless produces a nice glow in the subject's hair and in the highlights on the scarf, as well as a clearly visible shadow in the background. The light from the beauty dish slightly brightens the left-hand side of the frame.

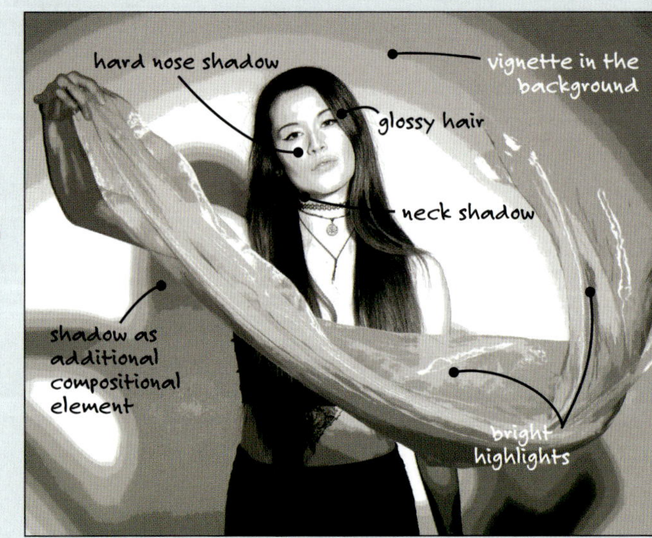

THE SETUP

1. Place the gridded standard reflector **(1)** on the right about 12 feet from your model in a raised position and at an angle of about 30 degrees. Position it to produce a slight shadow beneath the tip of your model's nose.

2. Now place the beauty dish fill light **(2)** at a similar distance, height, and angle on the left.

3. The V-shaped "clamshell" lighting setup is clearly visible in the photo on the right. The model is standing about 12 inches from the white background.

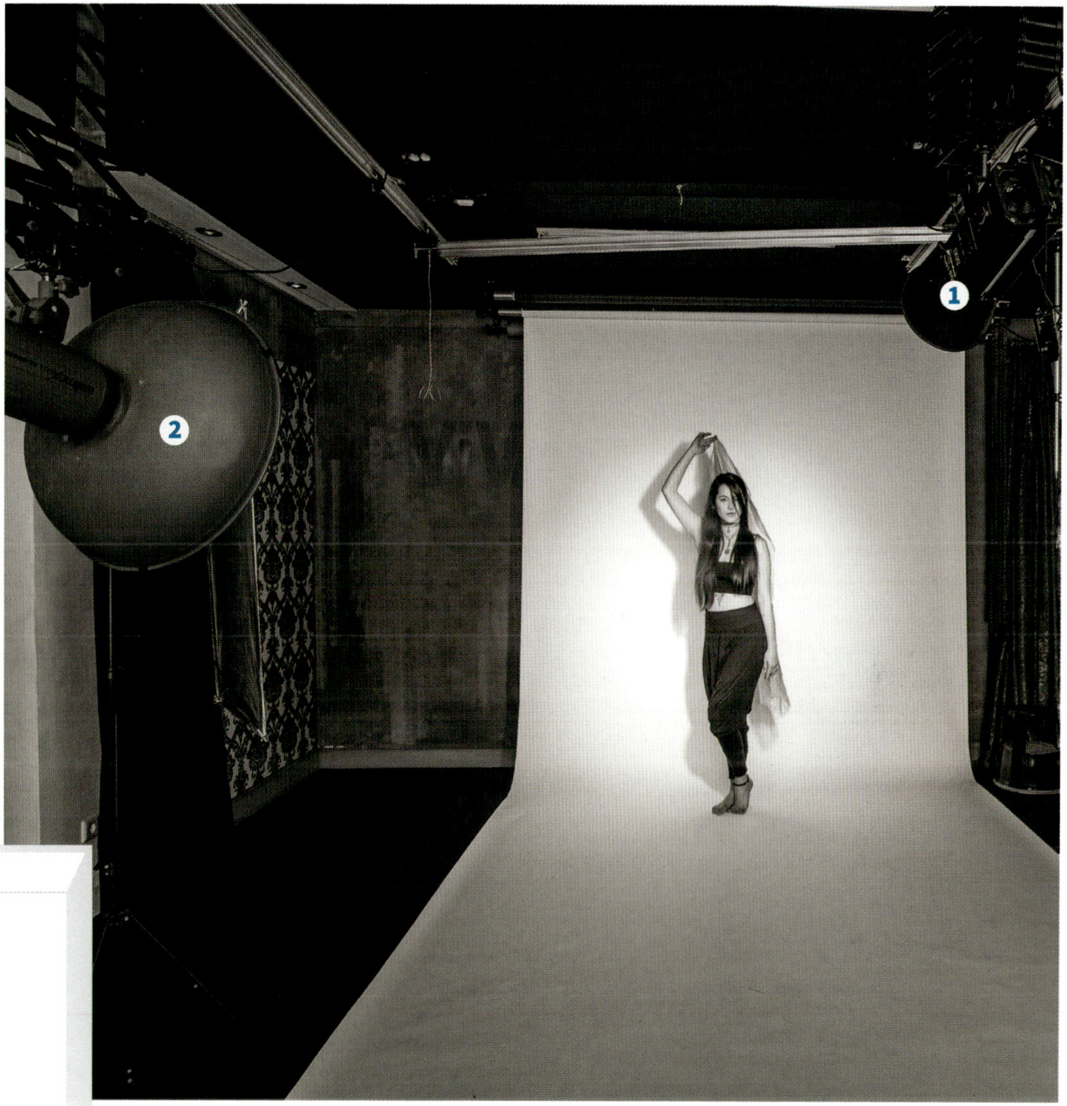

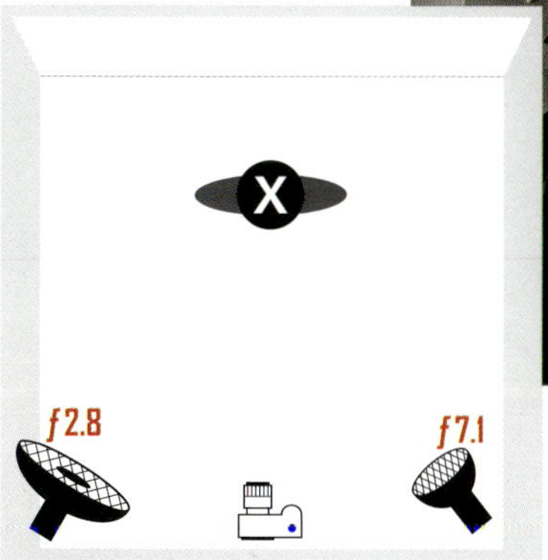

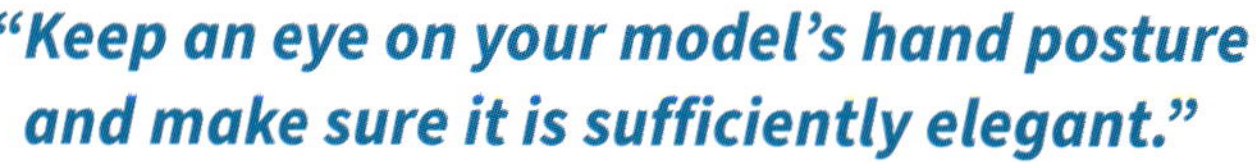

Modeling Light Magic

Creating special effects in the camera is fun to do and is something of a specialty, even for experienced photographers. The effect demonstrated here is guaranteed to fascinate your models and your friends. It is simple to create, and all you need is a flash with a built-in modeling light. The result is unusual enough to use as a flagship photo in your portfolio, for an art exhibition, or simply as a fun eye-catcher.

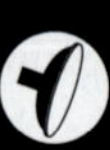

EFFORT INVOLVED

Medium

SUITABLE FOR

All kinds of portraits

THE LOOK

Experimental portrait
Intense colors
Accents on face and clothing

EQUIPMENT

1 × 20" beauty dish with a diffuser
1 × 30" ×40" silver reflector

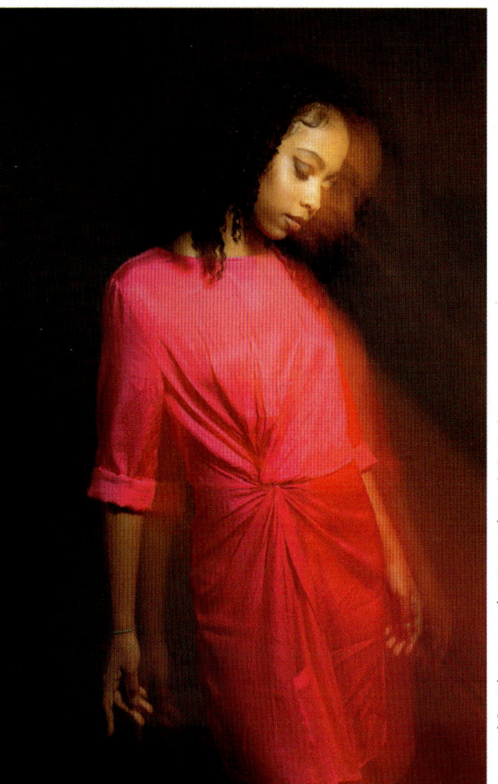

85 mm | f7.1 | 0.5 sec. | ISO 100 | Model: Melissa

HOW IT WORKS

The beauty dish provides classic lighting from diagonally in front of the subject, and its raised position produces clear light fall-off toward the bottom of the frame, that in turn focuses attention on the subject's face and upper body. The clearly lit face is framed by the obvious neck shadow and the subject's dark hair. However, the real stars of this image are the light trails produced by the long exposure time and the movements illuminated by the available light (or the modeling light on the flash) after the shutter has been opened.

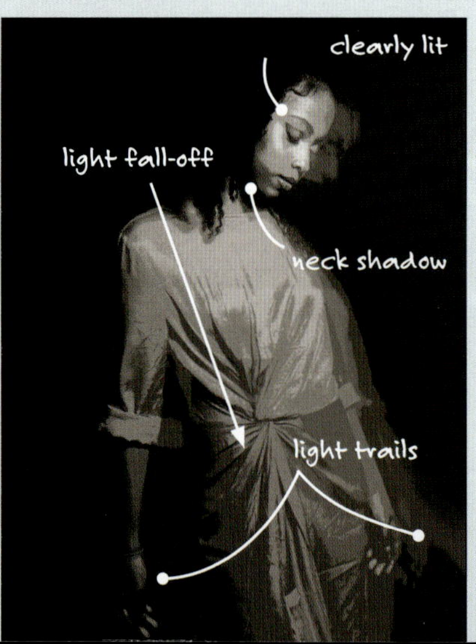

THE SETUP

1. Place the beauty dish **(1)** in a raised position about 3 to 5 feet to the front right of your model at an angle of about 45 degrees. Position it to produce a clear neck shadow and a nose shadow that points diagonally toward her cheek. To produce the necessary ambient light for the special effect, set the modeling light on this flash to 100% output.

2. Now place the reflector **(2)** about 5 feet to the left of your model with its center at head height, and position it to lighten the shadows on the darker side of your model.

3. Place your model about 5 feet in front of the dark background.

4. Set the exposure time in your camera to between 0.5 and 1 sec. and then follow the instructions in the box on the right.

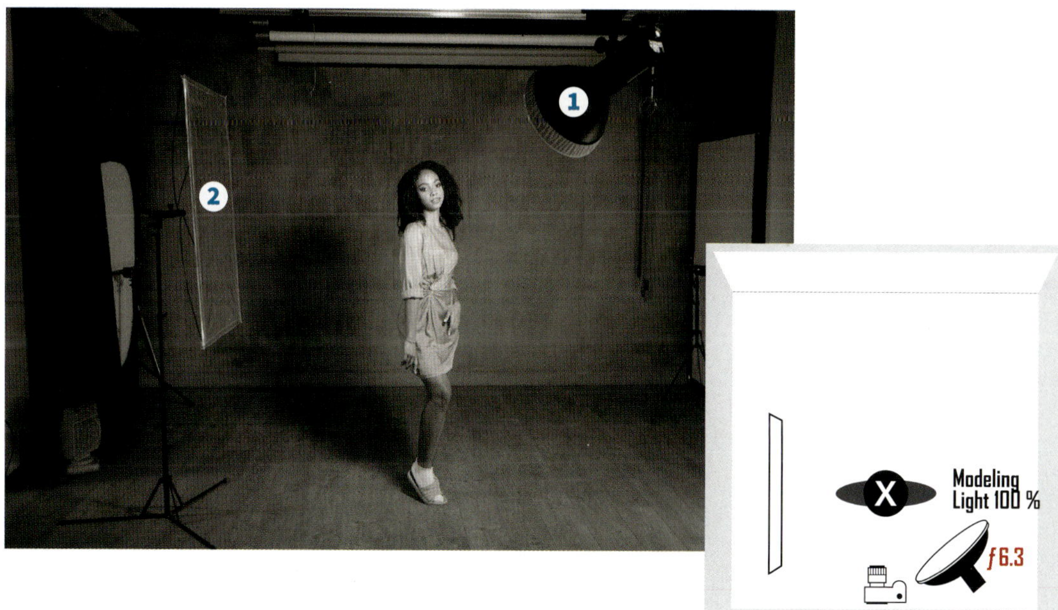

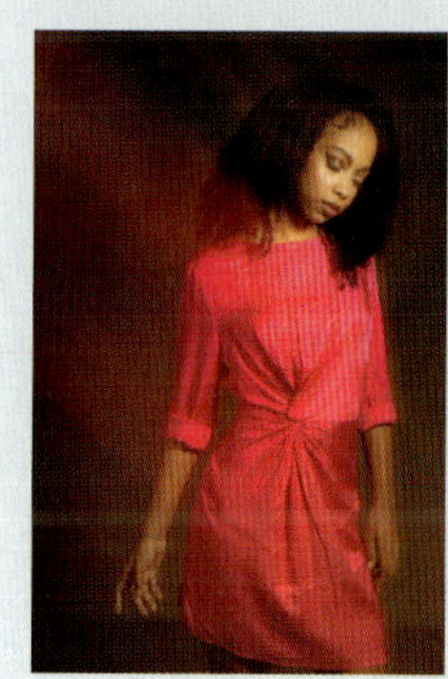

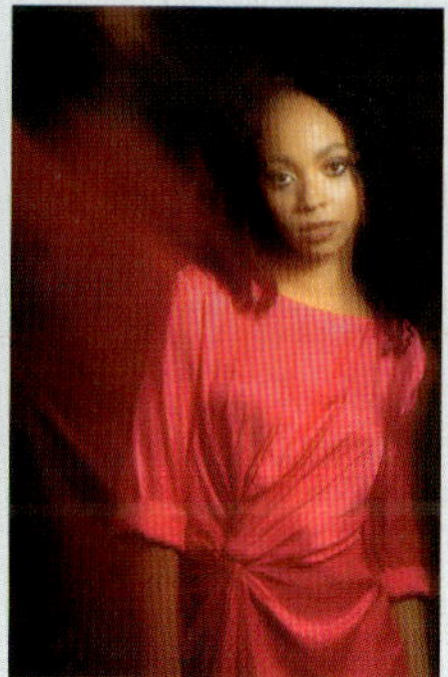

Creating the Special Effect

The results of applying this technique vary from shot to shot and also depend on the type of movements your model makes. Begin by setting an exposure time between 0.5 and 1 sec. in your camera, then focus on your model. You then need to pan and/or tilt the camera slightly the moment you press the shutter button—for example, tilting it toward the lower left corner of the frame will create light trails in the upper right-hand corner. It takes some practice to get the timing and the movements right. If the effect isn't clear or bold enough, you can try brightening the ambient light and/or panning and tilting your camera in different directions.

To make the most of this effect It is important that your model's clothing contrasts strongly with the background. In other words, she needs to wear light-colored clothing if you use a dark background or darker clothing for a light-colored background.

"You can alter the brightness gradient by changing the position of the beauty dish. The closer to your model you place the light source, the more intense the light fall-off toward her torso will be."

Index

Lights, Camera, Action!

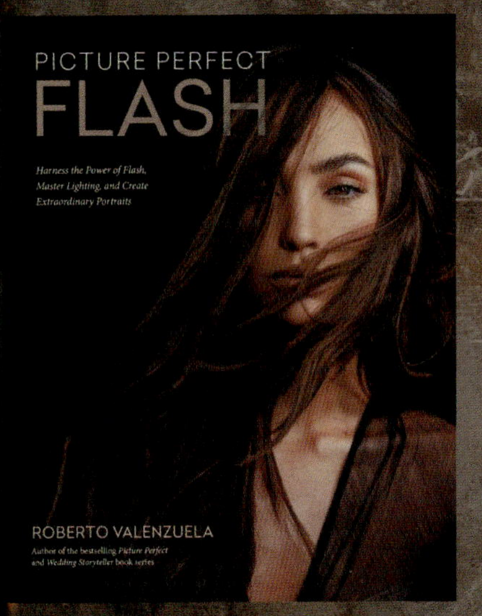

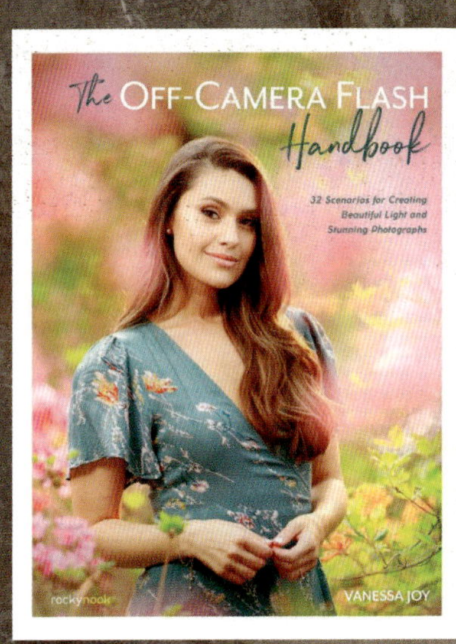

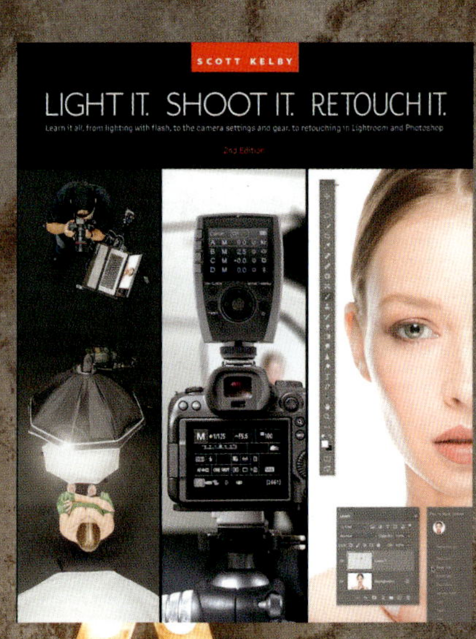

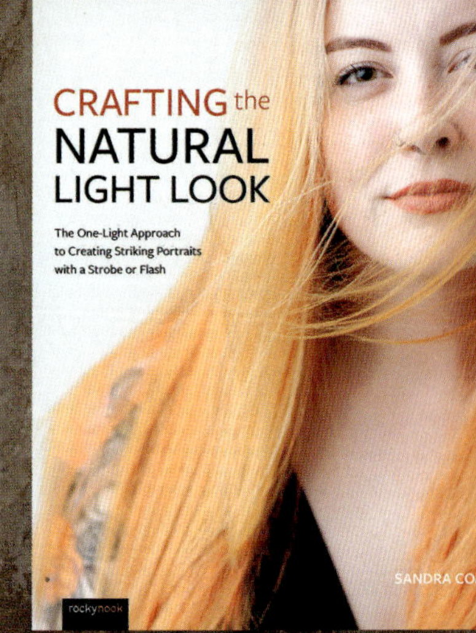

WWW.ROCKYNOOK.COM/LIGHTING